D1548502

THE REJECTION OF PASCAL'S WAGER

A Skeptic's Guide to the Bible and the Historical Jesus

by
Paul Tobin

with foreword by
Gerd Lüdemann

Visit us online at www.authorsonline.co.uk

An Authors OnLine Book

ISBN 978-07552-0461-8

Authors OnLine Ltd
19 The Cinques
Gamlingay, Sandy
Bedfordshire SG19 3NU
England

This book is also available in e-book format, details of which are available at
www.authorsonline.co.uk

To my family:

my wife, Jackie,
my mother, Julia,
my father, Tom,
my sister, Alice,
my brother, Tom
and
my children, Pat, Sean, Liam and Lizzie.

Who are always in my thoughts.

CONTENTS

FOREWORD

Paul Tobin's book, the result of a long spiritual and intellectual journey, holds up to examination what from his childhood he had been taught to believe. As he put away childish things, he became increasingly convinced that one must follow where the evidence leads, and in this volume he scrutinizes the historical foundations of Christianity portrayed in the Bible, making a special attempt to shed light on the life of Jesus. His extensive and detailed studies drove him to the conclusion that the accounts on which Christianity was based have no historical validity. Intellectual honesty therefore compels the recognition that we can no longer be Christians even if we wish to.

While the historical insight of Paul Tobin's book is increasingly shared by many of today's laity, clergy, and liberal theologians, most of them refrain from leaving Christianity and instead resort to analogical or other non-historical interpretations of the Bible. While I do not doubt the honesty of such efforts, I wonder whether they pay serious enough attention to the fact that most of the biblical authors were convinced of and indeed emphasize the historical veracity of their writings. Does this not make such liberal rendering duplicitous? Worse yet, the growing legions of fundamentalism as well as large numbers within the mainline churches cling still desperately to outmoded beliefs founded on texts they fondly imagine to be historically reliable.

For **these reasons** the historical approach to the Bible remains important – not only in the classroom but also in the public forum. Moreover, this discourse must be carried on in language so clear that any interested layperson can follow it. Not the least merit of Paul Tobin's book is that it fully meets that requirement. In fact, Tobin seems to be the ideal explicator: here is a non-scholar who has for almost two decades immersed himself in the intricacies of biblical scholarship. Fortunately equipped with knowledge of the biblical languages, he is able to draw examples from both the Old and New Testaments, and proves himself amply informed on current critical scholarship. Indeed, it is not too much to say that his historical judgment on almost any given biblical passage or subject has the solid backing of the majority of objective modern scholars. Unlike them, though, he has ventured to write a single volume dealing with the historical validity of the entire Bible.

To anyone who wishes to know how far he or she can trust the Bible historically, I recommend this book with the utmost enthusiasm. It is a unique and exceptionally intelligent work that brings a strong and welcome burst of fresh air into the often-turgid atmosphere of theological and church-oriented scholarship. It will warm the hearts of the present generation of seekers and skeptics alike.

Dr. Gerd Lüdemann
Professor of the History and Literature of Early Christianity
Georg-August University, Göttingen

PROLOGUE: THE REJECTION OF PASCAL'S WAGER

In the 17th century the French mathematician and theologian, Blaise Pascal (1623-1663) put forward a wager in his *Pensees* (*Thoughts*):

> If there is a God, He is infinitely incomprehensible, since, having, neither parts nor limits, He has no affinity to us. We are then incapable of knowing either what He is or if He is ... you must wager. It is not optional. You are embarked. Which will you choose then? Let us weigh the gain and the loss in wagering that God is. Let us estimate these two chances. If you gain, you gain all; if you lose, you lose nothing. Wager then without hesitation that he is.[1]

Pascal's wager sounds deceptively simple. Many a religious person finds such a call attractive; one only needs to *believe* without considering the evidence and one would immediately be in a better position than that of the non-believer. After all, they say, if I believe and it turns out to be true I get to enjoy heavenly bliss; but if my belief turns out to be false, and there is no God, then when I die, I lose nothing. An atheist, the religious person may continue, if he turns out to be wrong will suffer an eternity of torment. If the atheist turns out to be right, then it is only equal to the believer's "worst case." Obviously then, the believer will say, you must wager on the side of belief.

But the argument is seriously flawed. The religious environment that Pascal lived in was simple. Belief and disbelief only boiled down to two choices: Roman Catholicism and atheism. With finite choices, his argument would be sound. But on Pascal's own premise that God is infinitely incomprehensible, then, in theory, there would be an *infinite number of possible theologies* about God, all of which are equally probable.

First, let us look at the more obvious possibilities we know of today - possibilities that were either unknown to, or ignored by, Pascal. In the Calvinistic theological doctrine of *predestination*, it makes no difference what one chooses to believe since, in the final analysis, who actually gets rewarded is an arbitrary choice of God. Furthermore, we know of many more gods of many different religions, all of which have different schemes of rewards and punishments. Given that there are more than 2,500 gods known to humankind,[2] and given Pascal's own assumptions that one cannot comprehend God (or gods), then it follows that, even the *best case* scenario (i.e. that God exists *and* that one of the *known* gods and theologies happen to be the correct one) the chances of making a successful choice is less than one in 2,500 or 0.04%.

Second, Pascal's negative theology does not exclude the possibility that the true God and true theology is not one that is currently known to the world. For instance, it is possible to think of a God who rewards, say, only those who purposely step on sidewalk cracks. This sounds absurd, but given the premise that we cannot *understand*

---

[1]   Popkin, *Pascal*: p257-258
[2]   Krueger, *What is Atheism?*: p 161

God, this possible theology cannot be dismissed. In such a case, the choice of what God to believe in would be irrelevant as one would be rewarded on a premise that does not involve one's beliefs. Furthermore, as many atheist philosophers have pointed out, it is also possible to conceive of a deity who rewards *intellectual honesty*: a God who rewards *atheists* with eternal bliss simply because they dared to follow where the evidence leads - that given the available evidence, no God exists! Finally, we should also note that given Pascal's premise, it is possible to conceive of a God who is evil and who punishes good and rewards evil.[3]

Pascal's call for us *not* to consider the evidence but to *simply believe* on prudential grounds fails. As the philosopher, J.L. Mackie wrote:

> Once the full range of such possibilities is taken into account, Pascal's argument from comparative expectations falls to the ground. The cultivation of non-rational belief is not even practically reasonable.[4]

Apart from all these difficulties, there is another, more serious, problem with the wager. Pascal's fundamental assumption - that we cannot know the truth of Christianity and are therefore forced to wager - no longer holds true today. Modern science and historiography now have the tools to critically evaluate the central claims of Christianity. It is the aim of this book to show the results of these modern critical analyses of these claims.

If the central claims of a religion can be shown to be false, there is no longer any need to place a bet. The only rational course available is *the rejection of Pascal's wager*.

---

[3]   Gale, *On the Nature and Existence of God*: p345-354
Mackie, *The Miracle of Theism*: p200-203
Martin, *Atheism: A Philosophical Justification*: p228-238
[4]   Mackie, *The Miracle of Theism*: p203

INTRODUCTION

There are today 2.1 billion people in the world who call themselves Christian.[5] Divided into more than 20,000 denominations, these Christian churches have widely diverse theologies and practices. Within this label we find staid masses that the Roman Catholic Church dishes out to its 1 billion followers each week (many of whom do not attend!) and the lively, and sometimes scary, *glossolalia* sessions in the Pentecostal Churches (now more than 100 million strong – many of whom attend church faithfully).[6]

Yet within this sometimes bewildering diversity there are broadly similar core beliefs. They all believe that the Bible is somehow "special" and that Jesus was the "Son of God." Exactly how the Bible is special and how Jesus is the Son of God are points of contention among believers, with views lying within a more or less continuous spectrum. At one end of the continuum we have the Fundamentalists. To these Christians every statement in the Bible, where there is clearly no allegorical intent, is literally true. In other words, they believe that Jesus was actually born of a virgin, that he actually walked on water and that he was physically raised from the dead. On the other end, we have the liberals. The liberals adopt a more cautious attitude; to them biblical "truths" are not as clear-cut as what the fundamentalists make them out to be. To them, even some passages that clearly do not contain any allegorical intent can be reinterpreted symbolically. Many liberals do not accept the story of the virgin birth, the miracles and the resurrection of Jesus as true in a literal-historical sense. They see these stories as true in the sense they convey moral and spiritual truths.

This book is a rationalistic critique of these central beliefs of Christianity. It is the result of a journey that began long ago when I was still a young man. When I decided to take it upon myself to see whether what I had been taught since childhood, what I had *believed* since as long as I can remember, is true. At this moment of my journey, I can say safely that I no longer consider myself a Christian or even a theist. I am a skeptic, a humanist and an atheist. I am a happier, more fulfilled and more moral person as a result of this journey I have taken. This book is written in the hope that others who may be thinking of embarking on, or who are already on, such a journey may find in it useful information to lead them along the way.

It is important to point out that I am not out to "debunk the Bible." The Bible, like the *Iliad*, the *Upanishads* and the *Dhammapada*, is a great work of ancient literature. It represents attempts by an ancient tribe to understand the problems of human existence through the telling of myths, legends and poetry. When it is read as such, no harm is done. The problem is when such works are treated as the word of God and its teachings – some of which are archaic and barbaric – are accepted without question. This critique of the Bible in this book is to be looked at in this light.

---

5   Barret, *World Christian Encyclopedia*: p792
6   The estimates on number of adherents given here are based on three principle sources:
    i)   Barret, *The World Christian Encyclopaedia:* p792-793
    ii) Hoffman, *The World's Almanac* : p724-725
    iii) http://www.adherents.com/Religions_By_Adherents.html, accessed on April 4, 2006

Finally, I would like to say a few words of thanks. A heartfelt "thank you" to Professor Dr. Gerd Lüdemann for graciously agreeing to write the foreword to this book and for his kind words of encouragement on the manuscript. To my wife, Jackie, I owe a great debt for helping with the manuscript in various ways and in providing emotional support throughout the writing of this book. Finally, a million thanks to the many readers of my website, *The Rejection of Pascal's Wager*, who encouraged me to push ahead with this book.

QUOTATIONS FROM PRIMARY SOURCES

In the evaluation of any historical claims, it is always important to be able to check the primary sources for oneself. To this end, primary sources are extensively quoted throughout this book. To avoid copyright problems, I have generally used quotes from translations of sources that are now in public domain and freely available on the internet. I have used the World English Bible (WEB) as the "default" Bible to quote from. The WEB is a modern English version of the ASV. Although it is not the most accurate of translations and has a clear conservative/fundamentalist slant, it is in public domain and is in more understandable English than the KJV or the ASV. In cases where its accuracy is lacking I have generally quoted from the RSV or NRSV.

For other primary sources, as far as possible I have used translations that are in public domain and are available online. I have used the translations of Philip Schaff (*Early Church Fathers*), William Whiston (*The Works of Flavius Josephus*) and Charles Yonge (*The Works of Philo Judaeus*)

BIBLICAL QUOTATIONS

Given below are the various versions of the Bible used in this book:

ASV: American Standard Version (1901) – public domain

KJV: King James Version (1611) – public domain

GNB The Good News Bible (Old and New Testament), copyright 1976, American Bible Society. Used by permission. All rights reserved.

NIV: New International Version Copyright © 1973, 1978, 1984 by International Bible Society. Used by permission of Zondervan Publishing House. All rights reserved.

NRSV: New Revised Standard Version Bible, copyright 1989, Division of Christian Education of the National Council of the Churches of Christ in the United States of America. Used by permission. All rights reserved

RSV: Revised Standard Version of the Bible, copyright 1952 [2nd edition, 1971] by the Division of Christian Education of the National Council of the Churches of Christ in the United States of America. Used by permission. All rights reserved

WEB: World English Bible (WEB) – public domain

(full text is available from http://www.ebible.org/bible/web/)

OTHER PRIMARY SOURCES

Unless otherwise noted, all quotations from the Church Fathers are taken from Philip Schaff, Alexander Roberts (eds) "The Early Church Fathers" - public domain (full text - http://www.bible.ca/history/fathers/)

Unless otherwise noted, all quotations from Josephus' works are taken from William Whiston (trans) "The Works of Flavius Josephus" – public domain (full text - http://www.earlychristianwritings.com/text/josephus/josephus.htm)

Unless otherwise noted, all quotations from Philo's works are taken from Charles Duke Yonge's (trans) "The Works of Philo Judaeus" – public domain (full text - http://www.earlychristianwritings.com/yonge/index.html)

Unless otherwise noted, all quotations from the Gospel of Thomas and Gospel of Peter are taken from Wilhelm. Schneemelcher, ed, *New Testament Apocrypha Volume I: Gospels and Related Writings*, English translation by R. McL. Wilson, James Clarke & Co. Ltd.; Westminster/John Knox Press, Cambridge; Louisville, 1991

Unless otherwise noted, all quotations from the Apocryphon of James are taken from Ron Cameron, *The Other Gospels* Westminster Press, Philadelphia, 1982

Part One
THE BIBLE

We find collected in this book [The Bible] *the superstitious beliefs of the ancient inhabitants of Palestine, with indistinct echoes of Indian and Persian fables, mistaken imitation of Egyptian theories and customs, historical chronicles as dry as they are unreliable and miscellaneous poems, amatory, human and Jewish-national, which is rarely distinguished by beauties of the highest order but frequently by superfluity of expression, coarseness, bad taste, and genuine Oriental sensuality.*

Max Nordau (1849-1923)

The dogma of the infallibility of the Bible is no more self-evident than is that of the infallibility of the popes.

Thomas Henry Huxley (1825-1895)

Chapter One
THE BIBLE AS IT IS

THE BIBLE IN CHRISTIAN BELIEF

To Christians, the Bible is the word of God. All accept the authority of the Bible in one way or another. Baptists, Presbyterians, Pentecostals and Methodists accept the Bible as the sole religious authority. All the solutions to problems of theology, morals and even day to day living are to be found in the Bible. Anglicans, too, accept the sole authority of the Bible. However, its interpretation is subject to the traditional Anglican statements of faith. The position of the Lutheran Churches is similar to the Anglican one: the Bible is the sole authority but subject to the interpretation based on traditional Lutheran statements of faith. The Roman Catholic and Eastern Orthodox Churches recognize the traditional church councils as authoritative alongside the Bible. Catholics, in addition, treat certain pronouncements of the pope as equally binding.[1]

Fundamentalist and liberals view this "authority" very differently. The strict fundamentalist says that the Bible is literally true and is without any error whatsoever. Where allegory is intended, the context is made clear. Where there is no allegory, the statements are accepted a literally true. For example, if the Bible makes certain pronouncements on astronomy, these are accepted without equivocation as true. For reason cannot contradict revelation.[2] As the television evangelist Jerry Falwell (1933-2007) confidently asserted:

> The entire Bible, from Genesis to Revelation, is the inerrant word of God and totally accurate in all respects.[3]

A different stance is that taken by the liberals. They, too, assert that the Bible is true, but that the truth of the Bible is not scientific or historical and should not be analyzed as such. The Bible, say the liberals, speaks of *spiritual truth*. Hence when it speaks of the 6 day creation of the universe, one must not take it literally but allegorically.

In subsequent chapters we will critically examine these views on the Bible. In this chapter we will provide an introduction to the Bible and its contents. Despite the importance placed on the Bible by all Christians, many – if not most – are only vaguely familiar with its contents.

THE BOOKS OF THE BIBLE

One of the way documents were made in ancient times was to write them down on rolls of *papyrus*. The material to make these rolls comes from the inner bark of a reed plant that grows only in swampy places. The plant was called *byblos*. This name is derived from the Canaanite seaport in Phoenicia (modern Lebanon) called Byblos.

---

[1]   Hoffman, *The World's Almanac*: p596
[2]   In subsequent chapters we will examine this assertion in depth.
[3]   Haiven, *Faith Hope No Charity*: p 52

Hence, the Greek word for the roll of papyrus is *biblion* which is translated into English as "book." The plural of *biblion* is *biblia*. It is from this word, *biblia*, that the word Bible is derived.[4]

The Greek name for the Bible, *Ta Biblia* (the books), is apt. For it is really a collection of many books. The modern Bible, not including the group of books known as the Apocrypha, comprises 66 books. The lengths of these books vary from Isaiah, which comes close in length to a modern short novel, to the Third Epistle of John, which has only 294 words.

The books in the Bible are divided into two main sections; known respectively as The Old Testament and The New Testament. Christians view the Old Testament as an account of the old covenant between God and the Hebrews. The Old Testament is also supposed to contain references and prophecies to the coming of Jesus Christ. The New Testament presents, through Jesus, a new covenant, this time between God and all mankind.

In some Bible there exists a third section, known as the Apocrypha. These books are those which have their canonicity disputed in various churches. The Roman Catholic Church accepts some of these books as canonical and places them together with the books of the Old Testament.

THE OLD TESTAMENT

The early Christians adopted the Hebrew Scriptures as their own. What the Jews called the *Tanakh*,[5] the Christians labeled the Old Testament. While the contents of these are the same, the arrangements of the books are different. The Hebrew Tanakh comprises 24 books divided into 3 sections while the Christian Old Testament consists of 39 books grouped into 4 separate sections. Below we give a tabular comparison of the two.

The arrangement and division of books of the Old Testament came from the Greek translation of the Hebrew Scriptures known as the *Septuagint*. Most of the early Christians were Greek-speaking Gentiles. Not being able to read Hebrew, they turned to the Greek translation. It was this version that was *the* Bible for the early Christians.[6]

---

[4]   Bruce, *The Books and the Parchments*: p11

[5]   The term *Tanakh* comes from the 3 sections of the Hebrew Bible: The *T*orah [The Law], *N*ebiim [The Prophets] and the *K*etubim [The Writings]

[6]   Bruce, *The Books and the Parchments*: p89-91

Hebrew Tanakh (24 books)	Christian Old Testament (39 Books)
Torah (5 books) Genesis, Exodus, Leviticus, Numbers, Deuteronomy	**Pentateuch (5 books)** Genesis, Exodus, Leviticus, Numbers, Deuteronomy
Nebiim [The Prophets] (8 Books) *i. The Former Prophets* Joshua, Judges, Samuel, Kings *ii. The Latter Prophets* Isaiah, Jeremiah, Ezekiel, and the 12 Minor Prophets [12 Minor Prophets = Hosea, Joel, Amos, Obadiah, Jonah, Micah, Nahum, Habakkuk, Zephaniah, Haggai, Zechariah, Malachi]	**The Historical Books (12 books)** Joshua, Judges, Ruth, I & II Samuel, I & II Kings, I & II Chronicles, Ezra, Nehemiah, Esther **Books of Poetry and Ethics (5 books)** Job, Psalms, Proverbs, Ecclesiastes, Song of Solomon
Ketubim [The Writings] (11 books) Psalm, Proverb, Job, Song of Solomon, Ruth, Lamentations, Ecclesiastes, Esther, Daniel, Ezra-Nehemiah, Chronicles	**Books of the Prophets (17 books)** Isaiah, Jeremiah, Lamentations, Ezekiel, Daniel, Hosea, Joel, Amos, Obadiah, Jonah, Micah, Nahum, Habakkuk, Zephaniah, Haggai, Zechariah, Malachi

Table 1.1: Books of the Tanakh and Old Testament

PENTATEUCH

The first five books of the Old Testament - *Genesis, Exodus, Leviticus, Numbers* and *Deuteronomy* – also known collectively as the Pentateuch, were traditionally believed to be the work of Moses.

Genesis narrates the mythical creation of the world in six days and the creation of the first humans: Adam and Eve. The story of Adam and Eve is central to the Christian doctrine of the atonement. The first human couple was originally created to live forever in the paradise called the Garden of Eden. They were given only one command: not to eat the fruit of the tree of knowledge of good and evil, the original forbidden fruit. However, tempted by the serpent, Eve partook of the fruit and induced her partner to do likewise. In punishing their disobedience, God expelled the couple from the garden, imposed hard labor on Adam, promised pain in childbirth for Eve and took away their immortality. Christian theologians call this event The Fall, the loss of man's primal innocence. From thence on every generation would inherit this *Original Sin* of Adam and Eve.

The next notable event in Genesis is the story of the Deluge. God, dismayed at mankind's wickedness, decided to destroy the whole world with a cataclysmic flood. He called on the one human worth saving, Noah, and commanded him to build an ark big enough to house his family and specimens of every kind of animals in the world. When the flood finally came, Noah, his family and the menagerie of animals were preserved by the ark which floated on the waters. When the waters subsided, God made a covenant with Noah, symbolized by a rainbow, promising never again to "curse the ground any more for man's sake."

Ten generations after Noah, another major figure arose, Abraham, the father of all the Semitic races. Born in Ur in Chaldea (see figure 1.1 below), he traveled many lands, through Haran and Canaan, searching for a land he could call his own. He fathered two sons, Ishmael and Isaac. One day God called on Abraham to sacrifice his son Isaac. With a heavy heart, he took Isaac to the mountain to do as God had commanded him. Seeing the obedience of his subject, God commanded that a ram be substituted for Isaac, sparing the boy's life. God then made a covenant with Abraham, promising him that his descendents will be as numerous as the stars and that they would inherit the land of Canaan. Christian theology considers Abraham's willingness to sacrifice his son as a precursor to God's sacrifice of his own Son to save the world.[7]

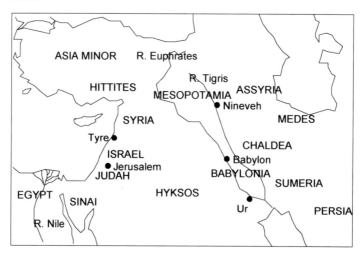

Figure 1.1: The Middle East in Old Testament times

Isaac begat two twin sons, Esau and Jacob. Esau was the first born and the "hairier one." Just before Isaac's death, he sent for Esau. Esau, being the first born, was the rightful recipient of his father's final blessings. Rebekah, the mother of Esau and Jacob, overheard this and loving Jacob more, sent for Jacob instead. Isaac was nearly blind and to make the trick work, Rebekah had her favorite son wear sheep's skin on his hands and neck to simulate the hairiness of his brother. When Isaac asked "Esau" to come near, the sheep's skin fooled him and he gave the younger son his final blessing, making him the head of the family. Fearing that Esau would kill Jacob, Rebekah sent the latter to Haran.[8]

In Haran, Jacob married his cousins, Leah and Rachel, the daughters of Laban. After working with Laban for twenty years, Jacob left Haran. In his return to his home country, Jacob stopped at Gilead and there met with a mysterious stranger who wrestled him throughout the night until daybreak. Jacob held on to the person and would not release him until he received his blessing. The stranger agreed and said that

---

7   Livingstone, *Dictionary of the Christian Church*: p3
8   Comay & Brownrigg, *Who's Who in the Bible*: p158-161

from then on he shall be called "Israel" which means "he who prevails with God." In other words, *Jacob had wrestled with God and won!* [9]

Jacob's twelve sons eventually had the twelve tribes of Israel named after them: Reuben, Simeon, Levi, Judah, Zebulun, Issachar, Dan, Gad, Asher, Naphtali, Joseph and Benjamin. Joseph, as the exception, was the ancestor of *two* tribes, Ephraim and Mennasseh. [10]

The narratives now center on Joseph. He was the favorite of Jacob. Jealous of their father's love for Joseph, his brothers conspired to kill him. One of them could not go through with the plan and Joseph was sold to the Ishmaelites instead. The Ishmaelites in turn sold him to an Egyptian official. Joseph turned out to have a knack for the interpretation of dreams. Eventually this talent became known to the Pharaoh. Joseph's prognostication helped Egypt through seven years of famine and made him a favorite of Pharaoh. Joseph met his brothers again when they came to Egypt to buy grain. He sent them back for his father and his other brother Benjamin. His whole family eventually moved to Egypt on his invitation. This was the biblical account of how the nation of Israel came to settle in Egypt.[11]

The term *patriarch* is normally applied to Abraham, Isaac, Jacob and Jacob's twelve sons.[12] The term *patriarchal narratives* refers to the story from Abraham to the settlement in Egypt mentioned above.

Exodus deals with the deliverance of the Israelites under the leadership of Moses from bondage in Egypt. Moses was hidden by his mother for three months from the Pharaoh who instructed all Israelite male babies to be killed. No longer able to hide him after that, his mother made a basket out of bulrushes, placed the baby Moses in it and let it float away on the river. The baby was found and raised by the Pharaoh's daughter. In adulthood Moses was commanded by God to lead his people out from bondage in Egypt via the Sinai Peninsula to the Promised Land. It was while leading the Israelites to Canaan that Moses received the Ten Commandments on Mount Sinai. Due to an earlier transgression, Moses was forbidden to enter the land of Canaan but before he died he was given a glimpse of the Promised Land from the top of Mount Nebo. This deliverance from bondage is regarded throughout Jewish history as the outstanding instance of God's favor for his chosen people, the Israelites.[13]

Leviticus consists almost wholly of religious legislation. Written in the form of a sermon of Moses, the book contains a variety of laws on such things as the eating of meat, religious duties, marriage, the priesthood, festivals, real estates and slaves. *Numbers* presents a narration of the experiences of the Israelites under Moses during their exodus from Egypt. *Deuteronomy* lays downs Moses' instructions on Israel's religious law. It also contains an account of his death.[14]

---

[9]   Comay & Brownrigg, *Who's Who in the Bible*: p175-177

[10]   Note that there are actually *thirteen* names for the *twelve* tribes of Israel. However, the tribe of Levi was mainly a priestly caste and was not given any parcel of land. [Asimov, *Guide to the Bible*: p115]

[11]   Comay & Brownrigg, *Who's Who in the Bible*: p219-224

[12]   Livingstone, *Dictionary of the Christian Church*: p384

[13]   Riedel et.al., *The Book of the Bible*: p 71-74
       Livingstone, *Dictionary of the Christian Church*: p186

[14]   Livingstone, *Dictionary of the Christian Church*: p150, 363

THE HISTORICAL BOOKS

Joshua tells of the story of the Israelites after the death of Moses. Led by Joshua, they crossed the river Jordan into the promised land of Canaan and conquered it. The land acquired was divided among the twelve tribes of Israel.

Judges traces the history of Israel from Joshua's death through the period just before a monarchy was established over Israel. During this time Israel was more or less informally ruled by leaders known as "Judges" without any central administration.

Ruth is set in the latter days of Judges and revolves around a Moabite woman of that name who married a Jew. Upon the death of her husband, Ruth was taken under the protection of Boaz, a kinsman of her husband, who eventually married her. Ruth, being a foreigner, was shown as a gentle person and as an ancestor of David. By showing that a foreigner could be the ancestor of the greatest king of Israel, the book can be seen as an early argument for inter-racial tolerance.

I & II Samuel relate the story of the first two monarchs of Israel, Saul and David, and their relationship with the prophet Samuel. Saul led the Israelites through many victorious wars against foreigners. But Saul disobeyed Samuel and the prophet promptly anointed David, then only a child, as the new King of all Israel. David did not immediately ascend the throne but became king only when he was 30 years old, after Saul was killed in a battle with the Philistines. In between the time of his anointment and his actual ascension to the throne, David roamed the countryside with an armed band. It was during this period that David slew the Philistine giant, Goliath, with his slingshot. Under the leadership of David, Israel grew due to his conquest of neighboring lands and became the dominant power in the Middle East. It was David who made Jerusalem the capital of all Israel.

I and *II Kings* cover the history of Israel from the death of David until the fall of Jerusalem in 586 BCE. After the death of David, his son Solomon, from an illicit relationship with Bathsheba, became King of Israel. Solomon substantially enriched Israel both culturally and economically by developing profitable trade routes. It was Solomon who, with the help of craftsmen and engineers from Phoenicia, built the Temple of Jerusalem. This temple was to remain the center of Jewish worship until the fall of Jerusalem. After Solomon's death Israel was divided into two separate kingdoms: Israel in North and Judah in the South. Divided, Israel and Judah lost all the power of Solomon's kingdom. Israel fell to the Assyrians in 722 BCE, while Judah in turn was conquered by the Babylonians in 586 BCE.[15] With the fall of Judah, Jerusalem was obliterated and the Temple was destroyed. Like the people of the northern kingdom, the people of Judah were either deported to the land of their conquerors as slaves or fled to the neighboring countries in the Mediterranean. This dispersion of the Jews became known as the *Diaspora*.

Parmelee, *A Guidebook to the Bible*: p35, 45-46

[15] Strictly speaking there was no "Babylonian people". Babylonian is a designation given to which ever nation that happened to hold sway in Babylon, a city with a long history of coups and conquests. Among the nations that ruled the city were the Sumerians, Akkadians, Amorites, Assyrians, Chaldeans and Persians.

A considerable amount of overlap exists between *I and II Chronicles* on one hand and *II Samuel* and the two books of Kings on the other. In fact most scholars are of the opinion that the chronicler used II Samuel and the books of Kings as his main sources. The books of Chronicles end with the return of the Jews from exile in 536BCE.

Ezra records the return of the exiles from Babylon and their attempts to rebuild the temple at Jerusalem. The book also chronicles the mission and work of the Jewish priest and scribe, Ezra. *Nehemiah* records the plans of the Jewish leader of that name for the restoration of Jerusalem. In his zeal to keep Israel racially pure he excluded from the city people not of Jewish blood and strongly forbade inter-racial marriage. *Nehemiah* is probably one of the earliest records of a racist.

The last book in this section, the book of *Esther,* relates how a Jewish girl of that name became Queen of Persia and risked her life to save her people (the Israelites). Its inclusion into the Old Testament is probably due to the book's introduction of a patriotic holiday, the Feast of Purim.[16]

THE BOOKS OF POETRY AND ETHICS

The book of *Job* relates how Job, a wealthy and upright man, had his faith tested by God. The test came about through a *bet* between God and Satan as to whether Job could remain faithful if all his earthly blessings were to be taken away. Job was deprived of all his wealth, lost his whole family in a freak accident and became afflicted with a terrible disease. His friends, Eliphaz, Bildad and Zophar, came to console him. They asked him to seek forgiveness from God for whatever wrong he may have committed that had caused this calamity to befall him. Job protested his innocence and within this lays the message of the whole book: that the innocent sometimes suffer for no apparent reason while the wicked prosper. Job refused to curse God amidst his suffering and reiterated his faith in God by saying, "I know that my redeemer lives." (Job 19:25) Having passed this test, Job's wealth was restored and his suffering ended. The book did not offer any solution to the problem of the suffering of the innocent. All it did was to assert the superior wisdom of God in all things by making the creator ask Job rhetorically: "Where were you when I laid the foundation of the earth?" (Job 38:4).

The book of *Psalms*, traditionally attributed to David, is an anthology of Hebrew religious poetry. These 150 psalms are normally interpreted as covering the whole range of relationship between God and man. Some of the psalms are beautiful, even after translation into English, as is the one below:

Psalms 8:3-4[17]
When I consider your heavens, the work of your fingers,
the moon and the stars, which you have ordained;

---

[16] Livingstone, *Dictionary of the Christian Church*: p107, 108, 280, 282, 289, 457
Parmalee, *Guidebook to the Bible*: p57, 78
Riedel et.al., *The Book of the Bible*: p10-16, 268-270, 454, 520
[17] When Biblical verses are not referenced to any particular version they are normally taken from the World English Bible (WEB).

what is man, that you think of him?
What is the son of man, that you care for him?

Yet amidst this beauty there lies a schizophrenic ugliness that is evidenced in the passages below

Psalms 58:6
Break their teeth, God, in their mouth.

Psalms 109:9-10
Let his children be fatherless, and his wife a widow
Let his children be wandering beggars.
Let them be sought from their ruins.

Psalms 137:8-9
O daughters of Babylon...
Happy shall he be,
who takes and dashes your little ones against the rock.

Proverbs is a collection of traditional Hebrew wisdom literature. The book is divided into eight clearly defined sections of which three are attributed to Solomon. Unlike the book of Job, the emphasis of the teachings contained here is that virtues such as honesty, chastity and regard for others will be rewarded by God with long life, happiness and prosperity.

The book of *Ecclesiastes* has a cynical message; human life is meaningless and futile. The author sees blind chance ruling the world:

Ecclesiastes 9:11
I returned, and saw under the sun, that the race is not to the swift, nor the battle to the strong, neither yet bread to the wise, nor yet riches to men of understanding, nor yet favor to men of skill; but time and chance happen to them all.

Indeed, when one compares Ecclesiastes and Proverbs, the two books carry almost diametrically opposite views of life, something hard to reconcile with the belief that they share a single (supernatural) source! Some examples of this:

1. On Wisdom and Understanding
In Proverbs we find a general appreciation of knowledge and wisdom. In Ecclesiastes wisdom is disparaged.

Proverbs 10:1 & 17:27
A wise son makes a glad father; but a foolish son brings grief to his mother...
He who spares his words has knowledge. He who is even tempered is a man of understanding.

Ecclesiastes 1:18
For in much wisdom is much grief; and he who increases knowledge increases sorrow.

2. On the Poor and Poverty

In Proverbs one is called to help the poor. In Ecclesiastes one is simply told "not to be amazed" at poverty as it is a natural state of things.

Proverbs 14:31	Ecclesiastes 5:8
He who oppresses the poor shows contempt for his Maker, but he who is kind to the needy honors him.	If you see the oppression of the poor, and the violent taking away of justice and righteousness in a district, don't marvel at the matter;

3. General Outlook

In general, we find a positive outlook in life in Proverb, while in Ecclesiastes one is confronted with the view that life is futile and meaningless with "time and chance happening" to everyone.

Proverbs 3:21-26	Ecclesiastes 1:2 & 9:11
My son, let them not depart from your eyes. Keep sound wisdom and discretion: so they will be life to your soul, and grace for your neck. Then you shall walk in your way securely. Your foot won't stumble. When you lie down, you will not be afraid. Yes, you will lie down, and your sleep will be sweet. Don't be afraid of sudden fear, neither of the desolation of the wicked, when it comes: for Yahweh will be your confidence, and will keep your foot from being taken.	"Vanity of vanities," says the Preacher; "Vanity of vanities, all is vanity."… the race is not to the swift, nor the battle to the strong, neither yet bread to the wise, nor yet riches to men of understanding, nor yet favor to men of skill; but time and chance happen to them all.

The last book in this section is the *Song of Solomon*. It is actually a collection of love songs and religion has no place in it. The book is a dialogue between two very human lovers and the theme is overtly sexual, as the passages below will testify:

Song of Solomon 1:2
Let him kiss me with the kisses of his mouth

Song of Solomon 3:1
By night on my bed,
I sought him whom my soul loves.

Song of Solomon 4:3,5
Your lips are like scarlet thread...
Your two breasts are like two fawns.

Indeed, there seems to be a rather overt suggestion of *fellatio* in one verse:

Song of Solomon 2:3 (RSV)
As an apple tree among the trees of the wood, so is my beloved among young men.
With great delight I sat in his shadow, and his fruit was sweet to my taste.

Probably the only reason why this book was included in the Old Testament was the traditional ascription of its authorship to Solomon. Both Jewish and Christian theologians, left with little choice, interpret the book allegorically as an oblique reference of God's relationship with his people. It shows that, when push comes to shove, the fundamentalists can allegorize any passage in the Bible as thoroughly as any liberal![18]

THE BOOKS OF THE PROPHETS

The first four books in this section were ascribed to the three "major prophets": Isaiah, Jeremiah and Ezekiel. The book of Daniel follows. The rest of the books are attributed to the twelve "minor prophets": Hosea, Joel, Amos, Obadiah, Jonah, Micah, Nahum, Habakkuk, Zephaniah, Haggai, Zechariah and Malachi.

The Book of *Isaiah* is mainly concerned with the political situation in Judah under the threat from Syria in 740-700 BCE. Isaiah criticized Judah for religious hypocrisy, cruel injustice, pride, greed and idolatry. Some parts of Isaiah are interpreted by Christians to be prophecies regarding Jesus Christ.

Jeremiah spoke out against the moral degradation of the unfaithful and extols God's divine justice who condemns his people as a result. He predicted the fall of Jerusalem and the deportation of the Jews to Babylon. Jeremiah was writing just before Jerusalem fell to the Babylonians. It was a time of great social stress. It was therefore natural for the prophet to predict calamities to befall Judah and to attribute this to the wrong doings of the Jewish people which has turned God away from them.

Lamentations is a collection of mournful songs that lament the fall of Jerusalem. Its authorship has been traditionally ascribed to Jeremiah. Christians had reinterpreted the mournful songs as a reference of Christ's passion.

Ezekiel was the last of the "major prophets" and the successor of Isaiah and Jeremiah. The book prophesies the destruction of Jerusalem but also the redemption of the Jewish people. Ezekiel reported many startling visions, one of which was that of God transporting him to Temple in Jerusalem by grabbing him by the hair.

The first six chapters of *Daniel* relate the story of a Jewish hero, Daniel, who successfully resisted the older tyranny of Persia, and withstood every test of his faith. The rest of the book consists of a series of visions which reveal the future of the Jewish people.

The last twelve books in the Old Testament are those ascribed to the twelve "minor prophets." *Hosea* interpreted his experience with his unfaithful wife, Gomer, as a parable of God's relationship with the unfaithful Israel. Just as Hosea was finally reconciled with his wife, God, in his enduring love will be reconciled with Israel. *Joel* called on the people to repent and make offerings to the Lord after a plague of locusts had befallen Israel. *Amos* denounced the impiety of Judah and Israel, which at a time of prosperity and accumulation of wealth, the poor was oppressed and unjustly treated. *Obadiah* had a vision in which God denounced the Edomites and gave his reasons for their destruction and for the salvation of the Israelites. *Jonah* relates how the prophet of that name was swallowed up by "a great fish" and stayed in the belly of

---

[18]   Livingstone, *Dictionary of the Christian Church*: p166, 274, 421, 480
       Parmalee, *Guidebook to the Bible*: p32, 65-70

the fish for 3 days as a result of his refusal to prophecy against Nineveh. Jonah was spewed up from the fish and called again to prophesy, which he did. His work was successful as those he prophesied to finally repented. *Micah* denounced the greedy, dishonest merchants, hypocrites, the rich and all inhabitants of the cities. He believed these people are all responsible for the oppression of the rural poor. Unlike the other prophets, *Nahum*, lashed out at a foreign city, Nineveh, the capital of the Assyrian Empire and described the battle that would destroy the city. *Habakkuk* complained of oppression and lawlessness and asked why the righteous suffer more than the wicked. *Zephaniah* condemned idolatry, astrology, and other cult practices in Jerusalem. *Haggai* called on the Israelites to rebuild the Temple in Jerusalem after their return from the Babylonian exile. *Zechariah*, too, called for the rebuilding of the Jerusalem Temple. Zechariah also prophesied of the future glory of Judah where the Gentiles will be converted. *Malachi* criticized the priests for their "sub-standard" offerings to God, such as offering crippled animals. He also lashed out at the Jewish people for neglecting to pay for their religious dues, for inter-racial marriage and for doubting the profit in fulfilling the will of God.[19]

THE NEW TESTAMENT

The New Testament consists of 27 seven books written by first and second century Christians. The books can be grouped into three different categories as shown in Table 1.2 below.

THE NEW TESTAMENT
Narrative Books (5 books)
The 4 Gospels (Matthew, Mark, Luke, Matthew)
The Acts of the Apostles
The Epistles (21 books)
The 13 Epistles of Paul (Romans, I & II
Corinthians, Galatians, Ephesians, Philippians,
Colossians, I & II Thessalonians, I & II Timothy,
Titus, Philemon)
The Epistle to the Hebrews
James
I & II Peter
I, II & III John
Jude
The Apocalypse (1 book)
Revelation

Table 1.2: The books of the New Testament

---

[19] Livingstone, *Dictionary of the Christian Church*: p142, 186-187, 265, 294
Parmalee, *Guidebook to the Bible*: p32
Riedel et.al., *The Book of the Bible*: p489-492

The first four books of the New Testament are called gospels.[20] These books, known as The Gospels According to *Matthew*, *Mark*, *Luke* and *John* relate the birth, ministry, suffering, death and resurrection of Jesus Christ. According to the gospels, Jesus was born in the Judean town of Bethlehem but grew up in the Galilean town of Nazareth. At about 30 years of age he started his preaching, initially in the towns of Galilee and finally in Jerusalem. There he was betrayed by one of his twelve apostles, Judas Iscariot, and handed over to the Jewish court. He was tried, found guilty of blasphemy and handed over to the Roman court on a trumped up charge of sedition. Under Pontius Pilate he was sentenced to death by crucifixion. Three days after his death on the cross he appeared to his disciples who finally understood his teachings.

The *Acts of the Apostles* is a continuation of the Gospel of Luke. It relates the story of the apostles of Jesus after his ascension into heaven. The first part of Acts relates the beginning of the nascent community in Jerusalem. A new apostle is also introduced here, Saul (or Paul) of Tarsus. Saul initially persecuted the followers of Jesus but the experience of an overpowering vision while he was on the road to Damascus converted him. Saul changed his name to Paul upon conversion. The midpoint of Acts relates the Jerusalem council which allows uncircumcised Gentiles into the nascent group with minimal requirements. From this point onwards the focus of the narrative is entirely on Paul and his missionary journeys. The book ends with Paul being arrested and placed under house arrest in Rome.

The next thirteen books are epistles (letters), traditionally believed to have been penned by Paul, and sent to various churches and persons. It is within these epistles that we find the kernels of subsequent Christian theology. The epistles of Paul are not arranged chronologically. They are arranged by length; placing the longest epistles first and shortest ones last. The epistle to the *Romans* is the longest and the most systematic of all the Pauline epistles. In it, Paul argued that sin is so universal that no act of man can redeem himself in God's eyes. Man can only be saved by the grace of Jesus' propitiatory sacrifice. The two epistles to the *Corinthians* deal with a variety of subjects. In the first epistle, Paul discusses the Eucharist, love and the resurrection. In the second epistle, Paul was defending his status as an apostle to his followers in Corinth. The epistle to the *Galatians* had Paul again trying to defend his status as an apostle and his theology. Apparently some of Jesus' original apostles had told the Christians in Galatia that they had to keep all the commandments of the Jewish Law. To Paul this was an erroneous teaching and his epistle clearly shows his self assurance in the correctness of his theology. The epistles to the *Ephesians* and *Colossians* have much the same message; to recall the people to faith in Jesus Christ. The epistle to the *Philippians* contains the usual Pauline warning against the Judaizing party within the new religion. In this epistle he also recounted the successes of his missionary work. The epistles to the *Thessalonians* contain Paul's teachings regarding the second coming of Christ. The next three epistles, the epistles to *Timothy* and *Titus* are normally called the "pastoral epistles" since their chief concern was the appointment and duties of church elders – i.e. their "pastoral" responsibilities. The last epistle is the one to *Philemon*. The epistle is addressed to a Christian master whose slave, Onesimus, had escaped and sought refuge with Paul. The letter was a plea for Philemon to forgive Onesimus and to take him back.

---

[20] The word gospel came from an old English word *godspel* which means "glad tidings".

The epistle to the *Hebrews* asserts the finality of the Christian faith and its superiority to the old covenant. The tone is definitely Pauline (i.e. from the same theology as Paul) but its original author is unknown. The epistle of *James*, attributed to the brother of Jesus, is entirely moral in content, emphasizing the importance of good works. *I Peter*, attributed to the apostle, was written to Christian communities in Asia Minor to give them strength for the persecution they were going through. *II Peter* is a warning against false and ungodly teachers. The next three epistles were traditionally attributed to John the apostle and author of the fourth gospel. *I John* was written to oppose false doctrines on the person of Christ. *II John* talked about the need to avoid people who teach false doctrines. *III John* encouraged hospitality to Christian brothers who travel spreading the good news. The epistle of *Jude* was written to counter the spread of false doctrines.

The last book of the New Testament is the book of *Revelation*. The book, like the second part of Daniel in the Old Testament, consists of a series of visions of the author, John the Divine. The *Revelation* is called an apocalypse, in the sense that it tells things to come without extolling the right living, as in prophecies. John had visions of angels, beasts, the throne of God, the Lamb who turns into the conqueror on the white horse, dragons and many other things. These visions are hard to make sense of and Christians throughout history have interpreted these to events, countries and people in their own time. The book of Revelation closes with a promise of the imminent return of Jesus.[21]

THE APOCRYPHA

The Apocrypha[22] consist of 14 different books: *I & II Esdras, Tobit, Judith,* Additions to the book of Esther, *Wisdom of Solomon, I & II Maccabees, Baruch, Song of the Three Children, Susanna, Bel and the Dragon* and the *Prayer of Manasses*. With the exception of I & II Esdras and the Prayer of Manasses, the Roman Catholic Church accepts these books as canonical. Chronologically these books were written in the last period of Hebrew literature, from about 300 BCE to 100 CE.

The apocryphal books actually come from the same literary family as the canonical books. The books of *Tobit, Judith* and *Susanna* can rightly be called romances. Much in the same mould as the book of Ruth and Esther, *I Esdras* is a rewriting of history based mainly on II Chronicles, Ezra and Nehemiah. In this sense, I Esdras is very similar to the books of Chronicles. *II Esdras* is a collection of apocalypses, not unlike the book of Revelation. The books of *Maccabees* recount the history of the Maccabean revolt of the second century BCE which won religious freedom for the Jews. *Sirach* (also called *Ecclesiasticus*) and the *Wisdom of Solomon* are typical wisdom literature, much in the same mould as Proverbs. *Baruch* is a book of prophecy. *Bel and the Dragon*, like the story of Jonah and the giant fish, is pure myth. *The Prayer of Manasses* consists of a penitential prayer put into the mouth of Manasseh, King of Judah.[23]

---

21 Livingstone, *Dictionary of the Christian Church*: p119, 130, 131, 204, 205, 233, 274, 282, 394, 398, 399, 438, 444, 510
22 *Apocrypha* is Greek for "hidden"
23 Parmalee, *Guidebook to the Bible*: p80

*****

Our brief overview of the book of the Bible has shown us that it is a collection of many different types of books. Not all the books carry the same message. For instance, Nehemiah, calls for the preservation of racial purity by the prohibition of inter-racial marriages, while Ruth has for its heroine a Moabite woman who married a Jew. As another example, the book of Proverbs extols living the good life which it says is God's reward for righteous living while Ecclesiastes says life is meaningless and prosperity is accidental.

The New Testament, although deriving much of its theology from the Old, stands in uneasy contrast with it. It is no longer a story about God's relationship with Israel. The focus is now on a man, called the "Son of God," who lived, died and was resurrected in first century Palestine.

Chapter Two
BIBLICAL INERRANCY

THE FUNDAMENTALIST ATTITUDE

As God's word to man, the Bible had in the past been viewed by Christian theologians as an inerrant work. This is only reasonable, for the one guarantee that the Bible is God's word must be that it cannot contain any errors whatsoever. With the development of human knowledge, especially in the sciences, fewer and fewer theologians are holding on to this view of biblical inerrancy. However, there is still a substantial group of theologians, the fundamentalists, who accept, or shall I say, assert, the strict inerrancy of the Bible.

The Roman Catholic Church has started to distance itself from the doctrine of strict verbal inerrancy but it is not clear just how far it will go along this line. Until recently, the position of the Catholic Church can be summed up by the 1893 encyclical *Providentissimus Deus* of Pope Leo XIII (1810-1903):

> All of the books, and the whole of each, which the Church receives as sacred and canonical were written down at the dictation of the Holy Spirit; and in fact, so far from there being possibly any error present in divine inspiration, this latter of itself not only excludes but rejects it with the same necessity that God himself, who is the Supreme Truth, cannot be the author of any error whatsoever...For the Holy Spirit himself with supernatural power so stirred and moved them to write, and so assisted as they wrote, that they both conceived correctly in mind, and wished to write down faithfully, and expressed aptly with infallible truth, all and each of these things which he bades, otherwise he himself would not be the author of the entire scripture.[1]

The Protestants of the 19th century held essentially the same views. Given below is a typical statement - made in 1872 by Charles Hodge (1797-1878), the Presbyterian theologian from the Princeton Theological Seminary:

> The Bible is the word of God. If granted, then it follows that what the Bible says, God says. That ends the matter.[2]

Such a view is typical of fundamentalism - the belief that the Bible is inerrant comes first - and provides the framework which is then used to evaluate the external world. Everything else – ethics, science and history - is judged based on the standard of the Bible.

This attitude has hardly changed at all to this day among fundamentalists. Below is a statement made 100 years after the one above (by John Montgomery, then Professor of Melodyland School of Theology, Anaheim, California):

---

[1]   Miller, *God and Reason*: p13-14
[2]   Wilken, *The Myth of Christian Beginnings*: p133-134

I believe that the Bible is completely, entirely and verbally the word of God. I refuse to stand above and criticize it; I insist rather, on standing below it and letting it criticize me.[3]

A POINT ON LOGIC

The dogma of the inerrant Bible is not that only *some* parts of the Bible are true. It asserts that the Bible is completely and absolutely without any error. Such an assertion is testable and can be shown to be mistaken. How do we go about showing that it is wrong? Do we need to show that the Bible is completely and absolutely false? No, we do not. To show that the fundamentalist position is mistaken all we need to do is to show that *some* things in the Bible are not true. To understand the logic of this we need to know the difference between *contrary* and *contradictory* statements. An example will make this clear. Let the statement below be the main proposition, which we shall label *A*.

All Chinese today live in China   *A*

A statement that is the *contrary* to the above is A' below

No Chinese today live in China   *A'*

Contrary statements are statements which cannot both be true at the same time. However it is possible for contrary statements to be simultaneously false, as is evident from the statements *A* and *A'* above. It would be logically fallacious to claim that the only way to prove statement *A* false is to prove statement *A'* to be true, since it is possible for both statements to be false at the same time. This would be akin to a fundamentalist saying that as long as one cannot prove everything in the Bible to be false, he would continue in his belief in biblical inerrancy.

What we need to prove statement *A* wrong is to write a statement that is *contradictory* to it. We will label the contradictory statement to *A* as *-A*. The relationship between contradictory statements is such that they are mutually exclusive. In other words, *-A*, and *A* cannot both be wrong or right at the same time; if *-A* is wrong, then *A* must be right and if *-A* is right, then *A* must be wrong. In our example, the statement that is contradictory to A is given below:

Some Chinese today do not live in China   *-A*

Hence all we need to do to show that the statement "All Chinese live in China" is false, is simply to show that *some* Chinese today do not live in China.

Applying this logic to our present discussion, the fundamentalist position is obviously:

Everything in the Bible is true.

---

[3]   Montgomery, *Damned Through the Church*: p26

All we need to show to prove this statement false is to find supporting facts for the statement below:

> *Some* things in the Bible are not true.

In this chapter we will show that the Bible cannot possibly be inerrant. We will show that it contains internal contradictions, numerical contradictions, mathematical errors and scientific blunders. We will also look at typical apologetic defenses to these and expose their inadequacy. In other words, this chapter shows that *some* things in the Bible are not true.

INTERNAL CONTRADICTIONS

There are many verses in the Bible that contradict one another. We will be taking a look at a few below.

WAS MAN CREATED BEFORE OR AFTER PLANTS AND ANIMALS?

In chapter one of Genesis, God is said to have created plants on the third day, with animals being created on the fifth and sixth day. Man was made after all these, on the sixth day. Given below are the relevant verses:

Genesis 1:11-13; 20-27; 31

God said, "Let the earth put forth grass, herbs yielding seed, and fruit trees bearing fruit after their kind, with its seed in it, on the earth;" and it was so. *The earth brought forth grass, herbs yielding seed after their kind, and trees bearing fruit, with its seed in it, after their kind*; and God saw that it was good. There was evening and there was morning, a **third day**....

God said, "Let the waters swarm with swarms of living creatures, and let birds fly above the earth in the open expanse of sky." *God created the large sea creatures, and every living creature that moves, with which the waters swarmed, after their kind, and every winged bird after its kind.* God saw that it was good. God blessed them, saying, "Be fruitful, and multiply, and fill the waters in the seas, and let birds multiply on the earth." There was evening and there was morning, a **fifth day**.

God said, "Let the earth bring forth living creatures after their kind, livestock, creeping things, and animals of the earth after their kind;" and it was so. *God made the animals of the earth after their kind, and the livestock after their kind, and everything that creeps on the ground after its kind.* God saw that it was good.

God said, "Let us make man in our image, after our likeness: and let them have dominion over the fish of the sea, and over the birds of the sky, and over the livestock, and over all the earth, and over every creeping thing that creeps on the earth." *God created man in his own image. In God's image he created him; male and female he created them...*

There was evening and there was morning, a **sixth day**.

However, in the very next chapter, the Bible contradicts itself by explicitly noting that man was created *before* the plants and animals.

Genesis 2:4-9, 18-19

[I]n the day that Yahweh God made the earth and the heavens. *No plant of the field was yet in the earth, and no herb of the field had yet sprung up*; for Yahweh God had not caused it to rain on the earth. There was not a man to till the ground, but a mist went up from the earth, and watered the whole surface of the ground. Yahweh God formed man from the dust of the ground, and breathed into his nostrils the breath of life; and man became a living soul...

Yahweh God planted a garden eastward, in Eden, and there he put the man whom he had formed. Out of the ground Yahweh God made every tree to grow that is pleasant to the sight, and good for food; the tree of life also in the middle of the garden, and the tree of the knowledge of good and evil....

Yahweh God said, "It is not good that the man should be alone; I will make him a helper suitable for him." Out of the ground Yahweh God formed every animal of the field, and every bird of the sky, and brought them to the man to see what he would call them.

The difference between the above two accounts cannot be more explicit.

- In Genesis 1:12 it was noted that the land had already produced vegetation on the third day, three days before the creation of man. Yet in Genesis 2:5, no shrub or plant had even grown when man was created.

- Furthermore, in Genesis 1:20-25, we are told that the animals were created on the fifth and sixth day of creation, all before man; yet in Genesis 2:18-19, they were created explicitly to find man a companion![4]

HOW MANY PAIRS OF EACH ANIMAL DID NOAH BRING INTO THE ARK?

In the story of the Great Flood, we are first told that God commanded Noah to bring a single pair of every animal into the ark:

Genesis 6:19-20

Of every living thing of all flesh, you shall bring *two of every kind* into the ship, to keep them alive with you. They shall be male and female. Of the *birds after their kind*, of the livestock after their kind, of every creeping thing of the ground after its kind, *two of every kind* shall come to you, to keep them alive.

---

[4] The New International Version (NIV), an evangelical translation of the Bible, tried to erase this contradiction by translating Genesis 2:19 as "Now the Lord God *had formed* out of the ground all the beasts of field and the birds of the air." By translating thus, the verse could be taken to mean that the animals had already been formed *before* Adam – thus removing the contradiction with Genesis 1. However, as Hector Avalos, professor of Biblical Studies at Iowa State University, pointed out, the original Hebrew text does not allow for such a translation – the verse is more accurately rendered as a simple past as above. [Avalos, *The End of Biblical Studies*: p46-47] For more examples of such "evangelical friendly" translations – see Excursus B: Not All Versions are Created Equal.

The wording here is very specific that each and every kind of animals was sent to the ark in pairs. However, a few verses later, a different commandment from God was recorded:

> Genesis 7:2-3
> You shall take *seven pairs of every clean animal* with you, the male and his female. *Of the animals that are not clean, take two*, the male and his female. Also of the *birds of the sky, seven and seven, male and female*, to keep seed alive on the surface of all the earth.

Again, we have another obvious contradiction staring at us.[5] Genesis 6:19-20 says there are to be *two* of every kind of birds and no separation is made between clean and unclean animals, the word every before the kind of animal excludes the possibility, yet Genesis 7:2-3 says that there are to be *seven* of every kind of birds and seven pairs of every kinds of clean animals.[6]

WHO CONQUERED HEBRON: JOSHUA OR CALEB?

In chapter ten of the book of Joshua, the successor of Moses was described as conquering Hebron himself, yet five chapters later it was Caleb who supposedly did the job.[7]

> Joshua 10:36-37
> Joshua went up from Eglon, and all Israel with him, to Hebron; and they fought against it. They took it, and struck it with the edge of the sword, with its king and all its cities, and all the souls who were in it. He left none remaining, according to all that he had done to Eglon; but he utterly destroyed it, and all the souls who were in it.

> Joshua 15:13-14 (RSV)
> According to the commandment of the LORD to Joshua, he gave to Caleb the son of Jephun'neh a portion among the people of Judah, Kir'iath-ar'ba, that is, Hebron (Arba was the father of Anak). And Caleb drove out from there the three sons of Anak, She'shai and Ahi'man and Talmai, the descendants of Anak....

WHO SLEW GOLIATH: DAVID OR ELHANAN?

Any child with an exposure to Christian education would have heard of the story of David and Goliath. David was the Hebrew hero who slew the Philistine giant Goliath. This story comes from I Samuel.

---

[5]   Even a cursory reading of Genesis is sufficient to convince anyone that the book is a haphazard compilation of a few different traditions. In fact modern critical historical scholars have accepted the hypothesis that Genesis is an amalgam of four different documents and traditions namely the "J" (Jahwehist) document, the "E" (Elohim) document, the "D" (Deuteronomic) document and the "P" (Priestly) tradition. See chapter 5 ("Authorship of the Pentateuch") for a short explanation of these documents.

[6]   Howell-Smith, *In Search of the Real Bible*: p20

[7]   Andersen, *A Critical Introduction to the Old Testament*: p59

I Samuel 17:23-50
As he talked with them, behold, there came up the champion, *the Philistine of Gath, Goliath by name*, out of the ranks of the Philistines, and spoke according to the same words: and David heard them... *So David prevailed over the Philistine with a sling and with a stone, and struck the Philistine, and killed him.*

But things are not that simple. In II Samuel we have an entirely different account of the slaying of Goliath.

II Samuel 21:19 (RSV)
And there was again war with the Philistines at Gob; and *Elha'nan the son of Ja'areor'egim, the Bethlehemite, slew Goliath the Gittite*, the shaft of whose spear was like a weaver's beam.

Gittite means "man of Gath". So it is the same Goliath that was described as being slain in both I and II Samuel. In the former, David was the giant killer, in the latter it was Elhanan. So at least one of these verses must be false. Who slew Goliath: David or Elhanan?

This inconsistency was so obvious to the translators for the King James Bible (or "The Authorized Version") that, in an act of dishonest piety, they actually rewrote the verse in II Samuel 21:19 to read as

II Samuel 21:19 (KJV also ASV & WEB)
Elhanan, the son of Joareoregim, the Bethlehemite, slew *the brother of* Goliath the Gittite

The words "the brother of" are not found in the ancient manuscripts and have been supplied by the translators from a similar verse in the Bible (I Chronicles 20:5).[8] The fact remains that there exist two contradictory accounts of the slaying of Goliath in the Bible.

WHY WAS DAVID INTRODUCED TO SAUL *TWICE*?

In I Samuel, David was introduced to Saul twice![9] In the first incident, Saul called for Jesse to send his son, David to enter into the King's service as an armor bearer:

I Samuel 16:19-23
... Jesse took a donkey loaded with bread, and a bottle of wine, and a young goat, and sent them by David his son to Saul. David came to Saul, and stood before him. He loved him greatly; and he became his armor bearer. Saul sent to Jesse, saying, "Please let David stand before me; for he has found favor in my sight." It happened,

---

[8]   For those who want to conclude that the passage from Chronicles may be the correct original reading I would like them to consider this point: the book of Chronicles was written centuries later than Samuel and in no way forms an independent confirmation of this. This addition of "the brother of" could also well be an indication of *its* author's misguided piety.

[9]   Howell-Smith, *In Search of the Real Bible*: p20
       Asimov, *Asimov's Guide to the Bible*: p288

when the *evil* spirit from God was on Saul, that David took the harp, and played with his hand: so Saul was refreshed, and was well, and the evil spirit departed from him.

The above passage clearly shows that David, as his armor bearer and entertainer, was known to Saul. Yet a little later, after David's fight with Goliath, Saul is made to inquire from his chief captain as to the identity of the giant slayer (I Samuel 17:56). And he is again made to inquire from David who he is, when he should have known this all along:

I Samuel 17:57-58
As David returned from the slaughter of the Philistine, Abner took him, and brought him before Saul with the head of the Philistine in his hand. Saul said to him, "Whose son are you, you young man?" David answered, "I am the son of your servant Jesse the Bethlehemite."

DID MICHAL DIE CHILDLESS OR WAS SHE A FECUND MOTHER OF FIVE SONS?

Our last example from Samuel is regarding Michal, the daughter of Saul. We are told in the passage below, that she never did bear any children:

II Samuel 6:23
Michal the daughter of Saul had no child to the day of her death.

But we are told just 15 chapters later that Michal had children: she had, at least, five sons![10]

II Samuel 21:8
But the king took … *the five sons of Michal the daughter of Saul*, whom she bore to Adriel the son of Barzillai the Meholathite.

Here, just as in the case of Elhanan's slaying of Goliath, the pious translators of the Authorized Version tried to hide this contradiction by some vague wording. Let us see how the verse is translated in the King James Version:

II Samuel 21:8 (KJV)
But the king took … the five sons of Michal the daughter of Saul, *whom she brought up* for Adriel the son of Barzillai the Meholathite:

They translated the word "bore" as "brought up," keeping the actual maternity relationship vague. Most modern translations translate it correctly as "bore" or "borne."

---

[10]   Lofmark, *What is the Bible?*: p43

WAS SHELAH THE SON OR *GRAND*SON OF ARPHAXAD?

Luke, in his genealogical tree of Jesus mentioned that Shelah was the *grandson* of Arphaxad:

> Luke 3:35,36
> ... Shelah, the son of Cainan, the son of Arphaxad...

But this is explicitly contradicted by Genesis who noted that Shelah was his *son*:[11]

> Genesis 11:12
> Arpachshad lived thirty-five years and became the father of Shelah.

WAS JOSEPH'S FATHER HELI OR JACOB?

Matthew and Luke also contradicted each other fabulously in their respective genealogies of Jesus; both supposedly derived from Joseph's side. They could not even agree who was Joseph's father!

> Matthew 1:16 (RSV)
> .. and *Jacob the father of Joseph* the husband of Mary, of whom Jesus was born, who is called Christ...

> Luke 3:23
> Jesus himself, when he began to teach, was about thirty years old, being the son (as was supposed) of *Joseph, the son of Heli*...

Now, pray tell, who was Joseph's father, Jacob or Heli?

Many apologists have tried their hand at explaining away this "difficulty". It has been suggested that the genealogy given in Luke was traced from Mary's side and that given in Matthew was traced from Joseph's side. Yet it is clear from both verses from Matthew and Luke that the genealogies are being traced from Joseph's side: in Matthew, Jacob was the father of Joseph (not Mary!) and in Luke, Joseph (not Mary!) was the son of Heli.

Others have accepted both genealogies but tried to use the levirate[12] to help explain the contradiction. According to this explanation, one of the genealogies traces Joseph's legal ancestry while the other traces his biological ancestry. This explanation is absurd for there are only two similar names in both genealogies from David to Jesus. This would mean that almost every legal father in the long list of genealogies died before fathering a child! Needless to say there is no evidence at all in support of this explanation.

Still others have tried yet another explanation. In this one Jacob (Joseph's father as given in Matthew) and Heli (Joseph's father as given in Luke) were brothers. When

---

11   Lofmark, *What is the Bible?*: p43
12   The levirate was the law that decreed that if a man died without leaving any offspring, it is the duty of the deceased man's brother to impregnate his brother's wife to give him offspring to perpetuate the family line.

Heli died childless, Jacob impregnated his sister-in-law, and presto (!), both Heli and Jacob are Joseph's fathers: Heli being the legal father while Jacob is the biological father via the levirate. The obvious question then is this: why do these two brothers have different fathers: Heli's father is Matthat and Jacob's father is Matthan. The solution here is typical apologetic nonsense: he claimed that Jacob and Heli were half brothers! They shared the same mother who after the death of her first husband, Matthan, remarried this time to Matthat!

No evidence, textual or historical, has ever been supplied for any of these attempts at harmonizing the two gospels. The only reason why they were thought up (note, in passing, that each of the explanation contradicts the others!) was to save the doctrine of Bible inerrancy.[13]

WHY DID MATTHEW ATTRIBUTE TO JEREMIAH WHAT WAS ACTUALLY WRITTEN IN ZECHARIAH?

One of the most glaring mistakes in the New Testament is this one by the author of the first gospel:

Matthew 27:9-10
Then that which was spoken through *Jeremiah* the prophet was fulfilled, saying, "They took the thirty pieces of silver, the price of him upon whom a price had been set, whom some of the children of Israel priced, and they gave them for the potter's field, as the Lord commanded me."

The problem with this passage is that the prophecy is nowhere to be found in Jeremiah. We find it instead in the book of *Zechariah*!

Zechariah 11:12-13
I said to them, "If you think it best, give me my wages; and if not, keep them." So they weighed for my wages thirty pieces of silver. Yahweh said to me, "Throw it to the potter, the handsome price that I was valued at by them!" I took the thirty pieces of silver, and threw them to the potter, in the house of Yahweh.

WHAT DID JUDAS DO WITH HIS THIRTY SILVER COINS AND HOW DID HE DIE?

There was also another point Matthew and Luke (writing in *Acts*) couldn't agree on: the manner of Judas' death.

Matthew 27:3-5
Then Judas, who betrayed him, when he saw that Jesus was condemned, felt remorse, and brought back the thirty pieces of silver to the chief priests and elders, saying, "I have sinned in that I betrayed innocent blood." But they said, "What is that to us? You see to it." *He threw down the pieces of silver in the sanctuary, and departed. He went away and hanged himself.* The chief priests took the pieces of silver, and said, "It's not lawful to put them into the treasury, since it is the price of

---

[13]   We shall review the genealogies of Jesus in more detail in Chapter 11.

blood." *They took counsel, and bought the potter's field with them, to bury strangers in.*

Acts 1:18-19
Now this man [i.e. Judas] obtained a field with the reward for his wickedness, and *falling headlong, his body burst open, and all his intestines gushed out.* It became known to everyone who lived in Jerusalem that in their language that field was called 'Akeldama,' that is, 'The field of blood.'

Note that the two stories above are incompatible in a couple of major details.

- In Matthew, Judas returned the money to the chief priests. The chief priests then used the money to buy the potter's field. In Acts it was Judas himself who bought the field.

- Matthew said that Judas committed suicide by hanging himself while Luke said Judas fell off a precipice.[14]

NUMERICAL CONTRADICTIONS

II Kings tells us that Jehoiachin became king when he was eighteen while II Chronicles alleged that he became King at age eight: [15]

II Kings 24:8
Jehoiachin was *eighteen years old* when he began to reign; and he reigned in Jerusalem three months.

II Chronicles 36:9
Jehoiachin was *eight years old* when he began to reign; and he reigned three months and ten days in Jerusalem.

The same problem exists with the age Ahaziah ascended the throne.

II Kings 8:26
Twenty-two years old was Ahaziah when he began to reign; and he reigned one year in Jerusalem.

II Chronicles 22:2
Forty-two years old was Ahaziah when he began to reign; and he reigned one year in Jerusalem.

Not only does II Chronicles contradict the information in II Kings, it even contradicts itself. For the author mentioned that Ahaziah took over from his father, Jehoram, who had just passed away at the age of forty! (II Chronicles 21:20) According to II Chronicles, Ahaziah was two years *older* than his own father![16]

---

14   We shall review the story of Judas' betrayal in more detail in chapter 14.
15   Howell-Smith, *In Search of the Real Bible*: p21
16   Lofmark, *What is the Bible?*: p43

This is a glaring contradiction. How does the fundamentalist apologist explain away such an occurrence? It turns out that they have a "catch all" explanation for contradictions: "copyist error"! An example of such an explanation on the above two contradictions can be found in Gleason Archer's apologetic *Encyclopedia of Biblical Difficulties*:

> It is beyond the capability of anyone to avoid any and every slip of the pen in copying page after page from any book-sacred or secular. *Yet we may be sure that the original manuscript of each book of the Bible, being directly inspired by God, was free from all error.*[17]

What Archer is trying to suggest is that the Bible, as it stands today, contains contradictions such as that given above-however, these have crept in due to scribal error. In other words, the *original* manuscript - when it left the hand of the author - was error free. There are a few problems with this explanation:

Firstly, the original manuscript no longer exists! This explanation is based on the *assumption* that the Bible is without error. We already see the beginnings of a circular argument here: The Bible is without error, if any error exists it must have crept in at a later date, since the Bible could not possibly contain any error! However, the current editions of the Bible are based on the best scholarly attempt to get to the original manuscript - and the best still says that the contradiction exists. Far from proving that the Bible is without error, modern attempts to get at the original rendition (an academic endeavor known as "lower" or "textual criticism") show that such errors exist within the biblical text.[18]

Secondly, if one assumes that the mistakes are the result of copyist error, one can with equal validity, assume that the errors arose at the very first writing down of Chronicles. Since we know that the writer of Chronicles used much of II Kings as his source, it is equally likely the Chronicler himself, while copying from II Kings, got the numbers wrong! So here is a case where "copyist" error does not exclude the Bible from being inerrant.[19]

We give few more Chronicler-Kings numerical contradiction below:[20]

- The number of foremen Solomon used in building the temple: I Kings 5:16 he is said to have used 3,300 of them, while in II Chronicles 2:18 he was supposed to have used 3,600.

- The number of stalls Solomon had for his chariot horses: I Kings 4:26 said there were 40,000 stalls while II Chronicles 9:25 said there were only 4,000.

---

[17]   Archer, *Encyclopedia of Bible Difficulties*: p206

[18]   McKinsey, *Encyclopedia of Biblical Errancy*: p490

[19]   Some evangelical Bible versions (translations) have tried to "resolve" these problems by simply "translating away" the contradictions without any textual support. See *Excursus A: Not All Versions Are Created Equal* later in this book.

[20]   McKinsey, *Encyclopedia of Biblical Errancy*: p72-73

- The actual capacity of the tank built by Solomon. I Kings 7:26 said that its capacity was 2,000 baths while II Chronicles 4:5 contradicts this by mentioning that its capacity was 3,000 baths!

Now how does the apologists account for these discrepancies? The usual "copyist's error" explanation is used - with the same difficulty we have mentioned above. Perhaps aware that using the same unproved assumption could be hazardous to their ecclesiastical paychecks - some apologists have thought up other *ad hoc* explanations. The funny thing is that they often provide these explanations side by side with the "copyist's error" one. In other words, what they are saying, in effect, is "well, this may be an explanation but if you don't like this one, try another!" This is not a rational method. An explanation has to be *probable* - just because an explanation is *possible* does not mean that the contradiction has been accounted for.

The Encyclopedia of Biblical Errancy quotes a typical fundamentalist attempt (William Arndt, *Does the Bible Contradict Itself?)* at solving the "difficulty" of Solomon's stalls (I Kings 7:26 and II Chronicles 9:25):

> [T]he First Kings deals with the affairs of Solomon and the beginning of his reign, while that in Second Chronicles belongs to the closing verses of the section describing the life and deeds of the wise king [at the end of his reign].

The explanation is *ad hoc*, since in no way do the verses lead one to conclude what Arndt had suggested. It is introduced purely as an attempt to get out of the obvious contradiction. One senses that even he was not too happy with such a defense when he later says:

> If anyone feels that the difficulty is not fully removed by this method, he may assume that a copyist's error has crept into the text, a scribe writing 40,000 instead of 4,000.

Amazing! Notice that it does not matter which explanation is true, so long as it can be used! It is obvious that apologists are not looking for the truth but merely for ways to keep to their faith.

Here's another lame explanation, this time regarding the contradiction of the capacity of the tank built by Solomon (Carl Johnson, *So the Bible is Full of Contradictions?)*:

> There are at least two possible solutions to this. It could be a copyist's error, or it could be that the molten sea ordinarily contained 2,000 baths, but that when filled to capacity it received and held 3,000 baths. Either way there is no real contradiction here.

Note again the ad hoc explanation. There is no hint in any of the passages that I Kings gave the "ordinary" capacity while the Chronicler gave the "maximum" capacity. It was introduced purely to resolve the problem. And, if that is not good enough, try "copyist's error!"

There are also many numerical contradictions between II Samuel and I Chronicles:[21]

In II Samuel 8:4, David was said to have captured 1700 of the King of Zobah's charioteers. Yet I Chronicles 18:4 said that David actually captured 7,000.

Now for an example of two contradictions in one verse:

II Samuel 24:9
Joab gave up the sum of the numbering of the people to the king: and there were in Israel *eight hundred thousand valiant men* who drew the sword; and the men of Judah were *five hundred thousand men.*

I Chronicles 21:5
Joab gave up the sum of the numbering of the people to David. All those of Israel were *one million one hundred thousand men* who drew sword: and in Judah were *four hundred seventy thousand men* who drew sword.

The verse in Samuel said that there were 800,000 fighting men in Israel while the Chronicler gave this figure as 1.1 million - a total discrepancy of 300,000. Furthermore, Samuel said that there were 500,000 men in Judah, while the Chronicler gives this as 470,000. The numbers are so different here that even the "copyist's error" excuse does not work. Apologists have tried other ad hoc explanations: one is that the numbers of one verse are simple "rounded off" versions of the other. It is hard to see how 1.1 million could be a "rounded off" figure of 800,000!

Here is another example of one verse with two contradictions:

II Samuel 10:18
The Syrians fled before Israel; and David killed of the Syrians the men of *seven hundred chariots,* and forty thousand *horsemen...*

I Chronicles 19:18
The Syrians fled before Israel; and David killed of the Syrians the men of *seven thousand chariots,* and forty thousand *footmen...*

So which is which, did David slay the men of 700 or 7,000 chariots? And were there 40,000 *foot soldiers* or 40,000 *horsemen*?

MATHEMATICS

Mathematics is obviously not the *forte* of the biblical authors. In the Bible we find a grossly inaccurate value for π, mistakes in sums and even a marked inability to count in some of its authors. These mistakes form another piece of the evidence that the Bible is not inerrant.

---

[21]   McKinsey, *Encyclopedia of Biblical Errancy*: p73-74

THE VALUE OF π

π (pronounced as "Pie") is the ratio of the circumference of a circle to its diameter. It is an irrational number whose value is represented by an infinite sequence of numbers of which the first six numbers are 3.14159. What does the Bible say about the value of π?

> I Kings 7:23-26 (II Chronicles 4:2-5) (NRSV)
> [23]*Then he made the molten sea; it was round, ten cubits from brim to brim, and five cubits high. A line of thirty cubits would encircle it completely.* [24]Under its brim were panels all around it, each of ten cubits, surrounding the sea; there were two rows of panels, cast when it was cast. [25]It stood on twelve oxen, three facing north, three facing west, three facing south, and three facing east; the sea was set on them. The hindquarters of each were towards the inside. [26]It's thickness was a handbreadth; its brim was made like the brim of a cup, like the flower of a lily; it held two thousand baths.

Nobody knows what the molten sea was for. It could be a container for water used in various rituals.[22] It is quite obvious that the passage above (verse 23) is talking about the dimensions on the top of the molten sea. Since the diameter is 10 cubits ("10 cubits from brim to brim") and its circumference is 30 cubits ("A line of thirty cubits would encircle it completely"), the value of π as defined by the passage above is 30/10 or exactly 3! 3.0 is gravely inaccurate when compared to 3.14159. Here is another nail in the coffin of biblical inerrancy - it got one of the most basic ratios of mathematics (and nature) wrong.

Fundamentalist apologists have attempted many explanations to explain away this very obvious error. These defenses can be grouped as follows:

1.   The value of π given in I Kings 7:23-26 is a good enough approximation.

2.   The value of π given in I Kings 7:23-26 is a "rounded off" number.

3.   The measurements given for the circumference and diameter are not for the *same* circle.

4.   There is a hidden correction factor within the Hebrew Bible, which provides a value of π that is very close to the modern estimate.

Let us have a look at each of these apologetic attempts.

1.   The value of π given in I Kings 7:23-26 is a good enough approximation

Strictly speaking, since π is *irrational*[23], we can never have a completely accurate representation of it. So one may argue that although 3.14159 is certainly a better approximation of π that 3.0, it is still "in error". But there are good approximations

---

22   Asimov, *Guide to the Bible*: p328

23   An irrational number is any number which cannot be formed from the division of two integers. In decimal form an irrational number has infinite number of decimals that are non-repeating.

and there are poor ones. 3.0 is certainly much worse as an approximation than the modern number. This should be enough for fundamentalists to pause: for their *omniscient God* was unable to provide his people with a value more accurate than what modern *humans* have been able to achieve.

Another line of defense would be that since we are talking about something that was written approximately two and a half millennia ago, it would be unfair to judge it by modern standards. An example of such a defense is from the fundamentalist Robert Mounce. In his book *Answers to Questions about the Bible* he wrote:

> The rough measurements of antiquity do not have to conform to space age requirements. In the culture of that day the measurements were not only adequate *but also inerrant*. In our determination of what constitutes an error we must judge the accuracy of the scripture according to the prevailing standards of the time.[24] [Emphasis added-PT]

Note the audacity here. Mounce admits that the figure of π is less than accurate by modern day standards but still *insists that the measurement is inerrant* because it was "inerrant" for its day. He wants to be able to continue calling the Bible inerrant despite this inaccuracy because it was "inerrant" given the knowledge of the cultures of its day. Here is a case of having your cake and eating it too!

Mounce wrote that we should "judge the accuracy of scripture according to the *prevailing standards of the time*". However, even when we judge the ratio with the "prevailing standards of the time", we find that the value comes up short. For we know of cultures that were contemporaneous with the Hebrews that were able to come up with values for π *far superior* to the one given in I Kings.

Date	Culture & Source	Value of π	% Error Compared to Modern Value
1650 BCE	Egyptian: Ahmes Papyrus	3.16049	0.6%
1600 BCE	Babylonian: Susa Tablet	3.125	0.5%
800-500 BCE	Indian: Sulbasutras	3.09	1.6%
550 BCE	Hebrew: I Kings 7:23-26	3.0	4.5%
250 BCE	Greek: Archimedes	3.14163	0.001%

Table 2.1: The value of π[25]

Table 2.1 above clearly shows just how far off the mark the biblical figure is compared to the other cultures. Comparing the percentages of error, the ratio in I Kings is three times less accurate than the Indian, eight times less accurate than the Egyptian, nine times less accurate than Babylonian and more than *three thousand times* less accurate than the Greek figures! So when Mounce insisted that we judge

---

24   quoted in McKinsey, *Encyclopedia of Biblical Errancy*: p211
25   Beckmann, *A History of π*: p15, 21, 24, 196
      Joseph, *The Crest of the Peacock*: p190

the accuracy of the biblical ratio by the "standards of the time", our judgment is obvious - it is hopelessly inaccurate!

Another variation of this defense is for the apologist to simply shrug his shoulders and to assert that 3.0 is a "good enough" approximation for π. This is what the fundamentalist apologist, Gleason Archer, tried to do in his *Encyclopedia of Bible Difficulties*:

> While it is true that the more exact calculation of pi is essential for scientific purposes...the use of approximate proportions or total is a familiar practice of normal speech, even today...The Hebrew author here is obviously speaking in the approximate way that is normal practice even today.[26]

Archer had taken to simply asserting that even if it is inaccurate, it is still okay because "everyone else is doing it".

This defense is hollow for a couple of reasons. Firstly, it seems that the best defense of this apologist has is that this supposedly inerrant work contains a gross inaccuracy (which is what it is). Secondly, it is by no means true that anyone who speaks in an "approximate way today" would use 3.0 as an approximate value for π. Indeed, anyone who is familiar with the concept of π would use 22/7 or 3.14 as approximations rather than 3.0.

A reasonable person looking at this passage will simply conclude that it is not a big deal. The Hebrew culture was a pre-scientific one and, as such, for them to estimate a value of 3.0 for π, while grossly inaccurate, is to be expected. We have no reason to expect the Hebrew authors of the Bible to be mathematically literate. Of course, it also means that the Bible is a *human document* with all its inherent flaws.

2. The value of π given in I Kings 7:23-26 is a "rounded-off" number

According to the fundamentalist website *Answers in Genesis*[27] the numbers given in I Kings are rounded off numbers. The dimensions are supposedly "cubitized", i.e. those less than half a cubit are rounded down to the nearest cubit while those more than half a cubit would be rounded up. They suggest, as examples, a circumference of 30.32 cubits and diameter of 9.65 cubits. This would have been rounded up to 30 and 10 cubits respectively, just as in the biblical passage. However, when we take the actual figures and divide them we get, *viola!*, a ratio of 3.142, or π!

This argument carries no weight for two very simple reasons. Firstly, the idea that the lengths are "cubitized" (measured in quantums of whole cubits) in the Bible is pure nonsense. In fact we have seen other places in the Bible where more detailed measurements ("non-cubitized") are given. As an example, the passage below is part of the instructions for the construction of the Ark of the Covenant:

> Exodus 25:17
> You shall make a mercy seat of pure gold. *Two and a half cubits* shall be its length, and a cubit and a half its breadth.

---

[26] Archer, *Encyclopedia of Bible Difficulties*: p198-199
[27] http://www.answersingenesis.org/creation/v17/i2/pi.asp, accessed on Apr 8, 2006

If we use the "exact" numbers suggested above and round them up to half cubits (which is certainly possible), the circumference would be 30.5 cubits and the diameter would have been 9.5 cubits. This would give a value of π of 3.211 or about 2.2% off the value of π. The actual value given, 3.0 (or 30/10), is about 4.5% off the mark. Even allowing for the coarseness of the measuring unit available (½ a cubit), the writers of I Kings *still* did not get the most accurate available result.

Secondly, where did they get the numbers (30.32 and 9.65) from? A magician's hat! It was merely *guessed* that these could be the numbers. But guesses prove nothing. If one is allowed to simply come up with any numbers in place of the supposedly "rounded off" ones then why couldn't it have, say, a circumference of 29.65 cubits and the diameter to be 10.45 cubits? These numbers could also be rounded up to 30 and 10 cubits respectively. However, the ratio of these comes up to 2.837. This is even more inaccurate than 3.0 as an approximation of π, showing that the biblical authors were even more mathematically inept than once thought.

3. The measurements given for the circumference and diameter are not for the same circle

In the same posting in *Answers in Genesis* (given as a second alternate explanation) it is "explained" that the molten sea is shaped more like a cup where the top portion, the rim, expands out like a lily. The 10-cubit diameter measurement is taken from the brim while the 30-cubit circumference was measured off the body of the molten sea *below* the brim. The diameter of the body below the rim is smaller than the rim itself. As an example, they guessed that the diameter may have been 9.55 cubits. Then the ratio of these two numbers (30/9.55) becomes 3.142! There are a couple of problems with this explanation.

Firstly, note that the number 9.55 cubits *came from nowhere* in the passage! It is merely used as the number, when used as the denominator with 30 as the numerator, it gives 3.142! In other words, the apologist has worked backwards, just to get the result as π.

Secondly, note that a natural unforced reading of the passage tells us that the dimensions given for diameter and circumference refer to the same circle (at the brim). Let us look at the passage. It is first mentioned that the molten sea was five cubits high (to the brim), 10 cubits wide (brim to brim) and 30 cubits in circumference (I Kings 7:23). Only after these dimensions were given did the passage begin to speak about other parts of the molten sea; for it then starts with (I Kings 7:24) "*Under* its brim..." If it was already talking about the measurement of the circumference under its brim as the website suggested, the beginning of verse 24 makes no sense. We can dismiss this attempt as a failed one.

Yet another version of the "different circles" apologetic is this: the measurements for both the diameter and circumference were taken from the brim but while the measurement of 10 cubits is taken from the *outer* diameter of the brim, the measurement of 30 cubits is taken from the *inner* circumference of the same brim. The inner diameter of the brim would be 10 cubits less double the width of the brim, which is supposedly given in I Kings 27:26 as "a handbreadth thick". He then goes on to give a cubit as 20 inches and a handbreadth as 4.5 inches. The inner diameter is now [(10 x 20) - (2 x 4.5)] 191 inches. With the circumference as 600 inches (20 x 30), the value of the circumference over the diameter is now 600 divided by 191, which gives 3.14136. [28]

There are a couple of problems with this explanation that is fatal to accepting it as correct.

Firstly, it made an unwarranted assumption that the *width of the brim* is equal to the *thickness of the wall* of the molten sea. Note that verse 26 is talking about the *thickness of wall* of the molten sea not the *width of the brim*. One cannot simply assume that these two are identical.

Secondly, this too is a forced reading of the passage. The last part of I Kings 7:23 goes: "A line of thirty cubits would *encircle* it completely." This clearly indicates it is the *external* dimension that is being described. How would an inner circumference "encircle" the molten sea completely? An inner circumference would be the one that is encircled by the molten sea![29]

The argument fails for these reasons. The identity of the *width* of the brim, with the *thickness* of the molten sea is not warranted. The verse clearly implies a dimension (in this case the circumference) *external* to, or on the outside of, the molten sea.

4. There is a hidden correction factor within the Hebrew Bible

To understand this apologetic argument we must acquaint ourselves with one particular practice of the Jewish scribes who copied and preserved the Masoretic[30] text. The rabbis held a high regard for the integrity of the text of their Bible. So even when they noted something amiss or unclear in the main text, they would leave it unchanged but would add notes on the margins to explain what they thought may be the correct reading, spelling or pronunciation for it. The word in the main text is called *kethiv*, which is Aramaic for "(that which is) written", while the alternate word, spelling or pronunciation given in the margin is called *qere*, which means "(that which is) read." This *kethiv / qere* apparatus was the means by which the scribes "corrected" or explained the text without actually changing it.

The *kethiv / qere* apparatus is used by Christian apologists to claim that the value of π derived from I Kings 7:23 is actually *very* accurate. The argument goes something like this. First it is noted that the word translated as "line" in I Kings 7:23 is spelled as *kavh* in the Hebrew Bible. Written in Hebrew alphabet, *kavh* would be:[31]

---

[28]   http://home.teleport.com/~salad/4god/pi.htm accessed on April 8, 2006

[29]   The *Biblia Hebraica Stuttgartensia* (the Leningrad Codex of the OT used by most Bible translation as "the" Hebrew Bible) gives the word here as *saviv*. This is given in Holladay's *A Concise Hebrew and Aramaic Lexicon of the Old Testament* as "all around", "from all sides" or the "surrounding environs" or "neighborhood."

[30]   The Masoretic Text refers to the text of the Hebrew Bible. See chapter 5 for a fuller explanation of what the Masoretic Text is.

[31]   Hebrew is read from right to left so the spelling of the alphabet is given in reverse direction to the Hebrew letters.

Hebrew	ה	ו	ק
Alphabet	he	vav	qof
Transliteration	H	V	Q
Spelling	kavh or qavh		

However, the Hebrew word for "line" is normally not spelt this way. The usual spelling is *kav;* without the final "h" or ה (he).

Hebrew	ו	ק
Alphabet	vav	qof
Transliteration	V	Q
Spelling	kav or qav	

Since the spelling in the main text (*kethiv*) is *qof-vav-he* is not the normal one for the word, the rabbis gave, in the *qere*, the standard spelling of *qof-vav*. Now it is claimed that the presence of this *kethiv / qere* apparatus "hints" of a deeper meaning. This "deeper meaning" is that the alternate words for "line" should be treated as a *mathematical ratio* for correcting the value of π derived from the passage.

Then it is noted that the Hebrew letters, depending on their position in the alphabet table, have numerical values attached to them: *qof* represents 100, *vav* represents 6 while *he* represents 5. *Qof-vav,* the normal way the word "line" is written, gives a total value of 106 (100 + 6). While *qof-vav-he,* the word written in the main text, gives a total value of 111 (100 + 6 + 5). The ratio of these two numbers, 111/106, is the hidden correction factor for the measurement of the circumference. This gives a value of π of 3.141509 [(111/106) x (30/10)] which is *very* close to the modern value of 3.141592.[32]

The argument is unconvincing. Given enough ingenuity and with no strict rules to abide by, any kind of numerical co-incidences or numerical value can be "discovered". For instance, why must the value of "line" be considered a correction factor? And why is it 111/106? Why not 106/111, 111+106 or 111-106 or even 111 x 106? The answer is simple; these wouldn't give the desired result! The derivation is merely driven by the need to get the value to come close to 3.14159. This is just another failed, *ad hoc,* defense of biblical inerrancy.[33]

---

[32]   http://www.ldolphin.org/pi/, accessed on April 8, 2006

[33]   As an example of how easy it is to show numerological significance with a little ingenuity let me give you an example I thought of myself.

Suppose, that a naive believer claim that the whole focus on the value of π is misguided and that God "wants us to go back and focus on Jesus". I can use the very same word (and its numerical value) to argue such a case.

The word line can be represented by two numbers, 111 and 106 - as we have seen above. Now add this two numbers you get 217. If we divide the first two numbers ("21") by the last number ("7") and vice versa [why not?] we get 3 (=21/7) and 2-1/3 (=7/(2+1)). Put together, this is 32-1/3. Now remember that Jesus was born in December (I did say this is a *naive* believer!) and died in April. Between the end of December and the following April is approximately 1/3 of a year. We know from Luke (3:23) that Jesus was about 30

That is not the only thing wrong with the defense. It must be remembered that numbers are *invariably* spelled out in full in the main text of the Hebrew Bible. For instance, the word "thirty" (for the circumference) is written here as *sheloshim*. Why is it not written as lamed or kaf-yod (Either of which would be the alphabetical representation of the number 30.)[34]? The answer is simple, the practice of using Hebrew alphabets to represent numbers only started in the Maccabean period,[35] around the mid second century BCE.[36] The Book of Kings reached its final form around the middle of the 6th century BCE, *a full four centuries before the Maccabean period!*[37] Applying the alphabets-as-numerals concept would be grossly anachronistic. In addition, the *kethiv/qere* apparatus is found only in the Masoretic Text which itself dates from the medieval period. The *qere,* or marginal note, is not part of the original manuscript.

Furthermore, while the Bible does attach significance to numbers (for instance 7 means perfection, 40 is normally taken to mean a long period of time), it does not contain numerological speculation one finds in the works of the Pythagoreans or in the later Jewish Qabbalah.[38] To apply such numerological explanations actually goes against the grain of the whole Hebrew Bible.

---

when he started his preaching. According to John, there were three Passover festivals that happened during Jesus' ministry (John 2:13, 6:4, 11:55). Thus Jesus died when he was 32-1/3 years of age. Exactly the number predicted above! Thus "Jesus died for your sins, stop haggling about the value of π!"

All this is nonsense, of course. But I think as an example of how easy it is to come up with numerologically significant numbers when there are no hard rules to abide by, it should suffice.

[34] In some Hebrew numerical systems, the alphabet lamed is used to represent 30. But in the masorah of the *Biblia Hebraica Stuttgartensia*, the lamed with a diacritical mark (the "dot" on top) is used to represent the *Hapax Legomena*, meaning that the word occurs only in one specific context but not found elsewhere, thus kaf-yod is used to represent 30 instead.

[35] Harrison, *Biblical Hebrew*: p108

[36] The oldest archaeological evidence for the use of Hebrew alphabets as numbers is a clay seal now in the Jerusalem Archaeological Museum. The seal has the inscription "Jonathan, High Priest, Jerusalem, M". The letter "M" (*mem*) is really quite mysterious but some archaeologists think it could mean the number "40"; for the fortieth year of the reign of Simon Maccabeus. Since Simon Maccabeus became the leader of the Jews in 143 BCE, it would date the seal to around 103 BCE. Thus the earliest archaeological evidence for the use of Hebrew alphabets as numbers is 103 BCE, no earlier. Yet even after this, evidence seems to indicate its use did not become widespread before the beginning of the Common Era. For instance a brass cylinder scroll found in the caves at Qumran (part of the Dead Sea Scrolls) dated to the first century BCE, used totally different number signs from the Hebrew alphabetic numerals. Evidence for use can be found after the beginning of the Common Era. Coins from the first and second Jewish revolts (66-73 CE & 132-134 CE respectively) have Hebrew alphabetic numerals on them. Archaeological evidence from the pre-Maccabean period showed conclusively that a different numbering system was used by the Jews before this. [Ref: Ifrah, *The Universal History of Numbers*: p232-237]

[37] Anderson, *A Critical Introduction to the Old Testament*: p90

[38] Metzger & Coogan, *The Oxford Companion to the Bible*: p562-563

Finally, the idea that the presence of a marginal note in the Masoretic Text, substituting a *kethiv* with a *qere*, implies a "hidden" meaning is pure nonsense. As the *Oxford Companion to the Bible* explains, *kethiv* is simply an Aramaic term meaning "(that which is) written" and *qere* "(that which is) to be read". Textual scholars only recognize three uses for the *kethiv/qere* apparatus:[39]

- Due to the scribal respect for the Hebrew consonantal text, errors in the main text are not changed (i.e. left as the *kethiv*), instead a note at the margins of the Bible is added giving either the correct spelling or correct vowels (the *qere*).

- Sometimes words such as the name of God (yod-he-vav-he or YHWH), which are not uttered, are left in the main text. The *qere* provides another reading, which can be pronounced, such as *Adonai*.

- Finally, some scholars think that the *kethiv/qere* method is also used to preserve variant readings when the text of the Hebrew Bible was standardized during the first century CE.[40]

Nothing "hidden" is implied by the *kethiv/qere* apparatus. The whole idea that a mathematic formula is being hinted at by the presence of the *qere* is pure nonsense. The numerological/mystical argument of a hidden factor fails.

The Biblical Value of π: A Summary

We have seen how fundamentalist apologists have tripped all over themselves trying to "save" their inerrant Bible from an obvious error. They tried to say it was "good enough" and when that didn't work they say "it's accurate", but that the measurement should be taken at a different place (unfortunately they couldn't decide among themselves just exactly *where* the measurements should be taken). Finally, when all this was beginning to look silly, they borrowed a page from the Qaballah and started using a mystical interpretation.

It is also important to note that these "explanations" are mutually exclusive. At best only one could be true. (But, as we have seen, there is no logical reason why they can't *all* be false.) Some of these are given side by side in the same apologetic work for the believer to pick and choose whichever "explanation" they prefer. It is obvious that to these apologists the truth of the matter is irrelevant and is subordinated to saving the faith of the believer.

Why this proliferation of mutually exclusive explanations? The answer is simple, because the *natural, unforced* reading of the passage gives π as 3.0. And 3.0 is not only grossly inadequate by our modern standards but also in comparison with the contemporaneous cultures of Egypt, Babylon, India and Greece.

There is not a hint anywhere in the passage that either the numbers refer to somewhere else on the molten sea or that the numbers were approximate. The apologists are *left to their own devices* and simply choose the first *ad hoc* explanation

---

[39]   Metzger & Coogan, *The Oxford Companion to the Bible*: p407
[40]   See chapter 5 for information on the textual history of the Hebrew Bible.

that come to their minds. All the while the natural reading stares upon their faces from I Kings 7:23.

The defenses are unconvincing and the error still stands in I Kings 7:23, the Bible says π is equal to 3.0!

MISTAKES IN SUMS

From the value of π we now move one notch down the level of mathematical sophistication. We realize that some authors of the Bible can't even do simple sums. Here is one taken from the book of Numbers. Here the male members more than one month old of the three clans of Levi, namely Gershon, Kohath and Merari were counted. This is how the figures came out:

Verse	Description	Number of members
Numbers 3: 21	The clan of Gershon	7,500
Numbers 3: 27-28	The clan of Kohath	8,600
Numbers 3: 33-34	The clan of Merari	6,200
	Total	22,300

This is how the author of Numbers did the sums:

> Numbers 3:39
> All who were numbered of the Levites, whom Moses and Aaron numbered at the commandment of Yahweh, by their families, all the males from a month old and upward, were *twenty-two thousand.*

So instead of 22,300 we have the nice, round, and wrong, figure of 22,000! It is pointless to explain away this discrepancy of 300 by suggesting that the author was simply "rounding off" the total. Why then, did he not round up the original numbers? It is more likely that the author of Numbers simply got his sums wrong!

There is another summation error, this time big enough to give even the "round off" apologetic explanation a "headache" (in trying to come up with an explanation!). The passage Ezra 1:7-11 concerns the articles from the Temple that were returned to the Jews. It was mentioned, in Ezra 7:8, that the chief royal treasury made an inventory and that these are the items returned:

Verse	Description	Number of items
Ezra 1:9-10	gold basins	30
	silver basins	1,000
	silver pans	29
	small gold bowls	30
	small silver bowls	410
	other vessels	1,000
	Total	2,499

The total number of articles returned was 2,499. Yet at the very next verse the total is given as:

Ezra 1:11
All the vessels of gold and of silver were five thousand and four hundred...

Note that Ezra 1:10 does not allow other unlisted items to be assumed since the last portion already mentioned "other vessels" or other articles. There is a discrepancy of 2,901 between the given total of 5,400 and the actual calculated total of 2,499.

Another mistake in arithmetic that, as far as I can tell, was first pointed out by the American patriot, Thomas Paine (1737-1809), in his book *The Age of Reason*,[41] comes from the books of Ezra and Nehemiah. In the second chapter of Ezra and the seventh chapter of Nehemiah, the authors gave a list of tribes and families, and the numbers of people of each, that were returning from the Babylonian exile. Table 2.2 below gives a breakdown of the list of the number of people given by Ezra and Nehemiah.

There are many problems with these two lists. They contradict one another in the total headcounts for sixteen different families. The biggest contradiction is the number for the sons of Azgad: Ezra gave this figure as 1,222 while Nehemiah had 2,322 – a difference in head count of 1,100. Other major differences in headcount include those for the sons of Arah (Ezra: 775, Nehemiah: 652), sons of Zattu (Ezra: 945, Nehemiah: 845), sons of Adin (Ezra: 454, Nehemiah 655), sons of Hashum (Ezra: 223, Nehemiah: 328) and the sons of Senaah (Ezra: 3630, Nehemiah: 3930).

There is also a problem with the total headcount of the returnees. Both books gave the same total - 42,360 - for the number of people returning:

Ezra 2:64 (Nehemiah 7:66)
The whole assembly together was forty-two thousand three hundred sixty...

However, if you add up the headcount of the families in these two lists, you get different numbers. Ezra's total was 29,818 and Nehemiah's was 31,089. Not only do these again contradict each other, they also do not add up to the total number given in the verse above. Ezra missed the final total by 12,542 while Nehemiah missed it by 11,271. Both the authors can't do simple sums!

---

[41]   Paine, *The Age of Reason*: p149
         Andersen, *A Critical Introduction to the Old Testament*: p210

EZRA		Total	NEHEMIAH		Total
2: 3	sons of Parosh	2172	7: 8	sons of Parosh	2172
2: 4	sons of Shephatiah	372	7: 9	sons of Shephatiah	372
2: 5	sons of Arah	775	7:10	sons of Arah	652
2: 6	sons of Jeshua & Joab	2812	7:11	sons of Jeshua & Joab	2818
2: 7	sons of Elam	1254	7:12	sons of Elam	1254
2: 8	sons of Zattu	945	7:13	sons of Zattu	845
2: 9	sons of Zaccai	760	7:14	sons of Zaccai	760
2:10	sons of Bani	642	7:15	sons of Binnui	648
2:11	sons of Bebai	623	7:16	sons of Bebai	628
2:12	sons of Azgad	1222	7:17	sons of Azgad	2322
2:13	sons of Adonikam	666	7:18	sons of Adonikam	667
2:14	sons of Bigvai	2056	7:19	sons of Bigvai	2067
2:15	sons of Adin	454	7:20	sons of Adin	655
2:16	sons of Ater	98	7:21	sons of Ater	98
2:19	sons of Hashum	223	7:22	sons of Hashum	328
2:17	sons of Bezai	323	7:23	sons of Bezai	324
2:18	sons of Jorah	112	7:24	sons of Hariph	112
2:20	sons of Gibbar	95	7:25	sons of Gibbeon	95
2:21	sons of Behtlehem	123	7:26	men of Behtlehem	
2:22	sons of Netophah	56		& Netophah	188
2:23	men of Anathoth	128	7:27	men of Anathoth	128
2:24	sons of Azmaveth	42	7:28	men of Bethazmaveth	42
2:25	sons of Kiriatharim...	743	7:29	Men of Kiriathjearim...	743
2:26	sons of Ramah & Geba	621	7:30	Men of Ramah & Geba	621
2:27	men of Michmas	122	7:31	Men of Michmas	122
2:28	men of Behtel & Ai	223	7:32	Men of Behtel & Ai	123
2:29	sons of Nebo	52	7:33	Men of other Nebo	52
2:30	sons of Magbish	156			
2:31	sons of other Elam	1254	7:34	Sons of other Elam	1254
2:32	sons of Harim	320	7:35	Sons of Harim	320
2:33	sons of Lod, Hadid & Ono	725	7:37	Sons of Lod, Hadid & Ono	721
2:34	sons of Jericho	345	7:36	Sons of Jericho	345
2:35	sons of Senaah	3630	7:38	Sons of Senaah	3930
2:36	sons of Jedaiah	973	7:39	Sons of Jedaiah	973
2:37	sons of Immer	1052	7:40	Sons of Immer	1052
2:38	sons of Pashhur	1247	7:41	Sons of Pashhur	1247
2:39	sons of Harim	1017	7:42	Sons of Harim	1017
2:40	sons of Hadaviah	74	7:43	Sons of Hodevah	74
2:41	sons of Asaph	128	7:44	sons of Asaph	148
2:42	sons of gatekeeper	139	7:45	Gatekeepers	138
2:58	servants of temple...	392	7:46	servants of temple...	392
2:60	sons of Delaiah, Tobiah & Nekoda	652	7:47	sons of Delaiah, Tobiah & Nekoda	642
	Total Number of People	**29,818**		**Total number of People**	**31,089**

Table 2.2: The lists of Ezra and Nehemiah

MISTAKES IN COUNTING

We now move on to the lowest notch of arithmetic ability: that of counting. We will see that even on this modest benchmark, the Bible is not error-free.[42] Let us begin with I Chronicles:

---

[42]   McKinsey *Encyclopedia of Biblical Errancy* p211-213

I Chronicles 3:22
The sons of Shemaiah: Hattush, and Igal, and Bariah, and Neariah, and Shaphat, six.

Note that there were five sons listed, yet the Chronicler counted six![43] We find a similar error in I Chronicles 25:3, where five names were also given and again the chronicler counted six.

I Chronicles 25:3
Of Jeduthun; the sons of Jeduthun: Gedaliah, and Zeri, and Jeshaiah, Hashabiah, and Mattithiah, six

The mathematically challenged Chronicler is not the only author in the Bible who cannot count; we see the same problem in the book of Joshua:

Joshua 15:33-36 (RSV)
And in the lowland, Eshta'ol, Zorah, Ashnah, Zano'ah, En-gan'nim, Tap'puah, Enam, Jarmuth, Adullam, Socoh, Aze'kah, Shaara'im, Aditha'im, Gede'rah, Gederotha'im: fourteen cities with their villages.

Anyone who can count will see that there are fifteen cities listed above, not fourteen.[44] Again, in Joshua 15:21-32 there were 36 cities actually listed but the author only counted 29! Also in Joshua 19:2-6 we have fourteen cities listed but the author said there was only thirteen.

So we have seen that some of the authors of the Bible didn't know the value of π, some didn't know how to do simple sums and some couldn't even count correctly! How are we to define a book as inerrant when its authors lack even these simple skills!

THE PHYSICAL SCIENCES

From mathematics and numbers we now turn to science. One sometimes hears fundamentalists harping about the fact that the Bible provides accurate scientific facts about the world that was simply unknown to the people of ancient times. In the remaining sections of this chapter we will review these so-called "scientific" allusions in the Bible to see if such claims hold any water.

---

[43] The NIV – a fundamentalist version of the Bible - translates the passage thus:

I Chronicles 3:22-24 (NIV)
3:22 ...Shemaiah *and his sons*: Huttush, Igal, Bariah, Neriah, and Shaphat - six in all.

This translation is illegitimate and is without any textual support. It made purely to "wish-away" the discrepancy. See Excursus B later in this book

[44] Some versions (such as the WEB) try to cover up the discrepancy in Joshua 15:33-36 by equating Gederah with Gederothaim. In other words, presenting the latter as just another name for the former. This is not a reading supported by the original texts.

THE FLAT EARTH

We know today that the earth has the shape of a slightly flattened sphere. The proofs of a spherical earth are known to every school child,[45] and will not be elaborated here. But the Bible contains passages that almost certainly show that its authors believed the world to be flat. Take, for instance, the following verses from the book of Daniel:

> Daniel 4:10-11
> Thus were the visions of my head on my bed: I saw, and behold, a tree in the midst of the earth; and its height was great. The tree grew, and was strong, and its height reached to the sky, and its sight to the end of all the earth.

A question naturally arises, where is the "end of all the earth"? This phrase only makes literal sense if the author believed the world to be flat. Even if we assume this to be meant allegorically as "all over the world", the passage still presents the world as flat. For if this if so, then Daniel 4:11 can only mean that the tree can be seen all over the world. On a sphere, there can be no object that can be seen everywhere from its surface: how many people in the southern hemisphere can see the North Star? A tree, even of infinite length, cannot be seen from everywhere in the world. The author of the book of Daniel is a flat-earther.

There is another passage that gives further support to the fact that the original authors of the Bible were flat-earthers. This one is from the book of Isaiah:

> Isaiah 40:22
> It is he who sits above the *circle* of the earth, and its inhabitants are like grasshoppers; who stretches out the heavens like a curtain, and spreads them out like a tent to dwell in;

The presence of the word *circle* here has led some over-enthusiastic Christians to present this passage as proof that the Bible tells of a spherical earth. This, however, is not the case. True, a circle and a sphere are both "round", but the shapes are not interchangeable. A coin is an example of a circular object, flat but circular. A tennis ball is an example of a spherical object. The shapes are different.

Attempts to go back to the original language do not help the believer's cause. The Hebrew word which is translated as "circle" in this verse is *khug*. That it means *circle* and not *sphere* is indisputable. *Strong's Concordance* (no. 2328 & 2329), *Holladay's A Concise Hebrew and Aramaic Lexicon of the Old Testament* (p97) and *Brown Driver-Briggs Hebrew and English Lexicon* (p295) give the verbal form of the word as "to draw a circle". The noun is translated as either "circle" or "vault" - a vault being a semi-circular arch. Other instances of the occurrence of the word *khug* include:

---

[45] Among the proofs include: the view of faraway ships disappearing from the horizon, hull first; not all stars and constellations can be seen from one location on earth; the shadow of the earth on the moon during a lunar eclipse; and finally the actual seeing of a spherical earth by satellites and spaceships with astronauts.

Job 26:10 (RSV)
He has described a *circle* (Hebrew *khug*) upon the face of the waters...

Proverbs 8:27 (RSV)
When he established the heavens, I was there, when he drew a *circle* (Hebrew *khug*)
on the face of the deep

The translations of *khug* as "circle" in the above instances are correct, for the passages are talking about drawing something on a surface: i.e. a *two dimensional* representation.

Furthermore, there *is* a word in Hebrew that means sphere: *dur*. If the author of Isaiah 40 had had this in mind he would surely had used this word instead of *khug*. Earlier on in Isaiah we see this word being used to describe a ball:

Isaiah 22:17-18
He will seize firm hold on you, and whirl you round and round, and throw you like
a *ball* (Hebrew *dur*) into a wide land; there you shall die

It comes as no surprise then that all the major, non-paraphrased, Bible translations - the NRSV, RSV, NASB, ASB, KJV, NKJV, and even the evangelical NIV - give the translation of *khug* in Isaiah 40:22 as "circle".

Note further the use of the word *tent* to describe the sky. A tent is something you put on a *flat* surface. Figure 2.3 below shows what the author of Isaiah actually meant:[46]

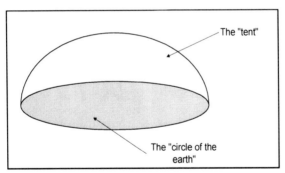

Figure 2.3 The circle of the earth: a *flat* object.

In passing, it should come as no surprise that the last bulwark of flat-earthism is a fundamentalist biblical sect. The movement had its beginning in 1895 when Scottish faith healer John Alexander Dowie founded the Christian Catholic Apostolic Church in Zion, Illinois. In 1905, the leadership of the church was taken over by Wilbur Glenn Voliva. Voliva made no bones about his beliefs: "We are the fundamentalists, we are the only true fundamentalists." Voliva was a convinced flat-earther and declared that he wants to "...strain the gnat of evolution and swallow the camel of

---

[46]   Asimov, *X Stands for Unknown*: p244-248

modern astronomy." Voliva died in 1942 but the flat earth movement is still alive and is presently headquartered in Lancaster, California.[47]

THE IMMOVABLE EARTH

Modern astronomy has proven, with a series of observations,[48] that it is the earth that circles round the sun and not vice versa as the ancients believed. The authors of the Bible clearly belonged to the group of the ancients as they state in plain Hebrew that the earth was immovable:

> I Chronicles 16:30 (RSV)
> Yea, the world stands firm never to be moved.

> Psalms 93:1 & Psalms 96:10 (RSV)
> Yea, the world is established, it shall never be moved.

> Psalms 104:5
> He laid the foundations of the earth, that it should not be moved forever.

Another passage that clearly shows that the biblical view of the solar system is geocentric (i.e. with the earth at its center) is from the book of Joshua:

> Joshua 10:12-13
> Then Joshua spoke to Yahweh in the day when Yahweh delivered up the Amorites before the children of Israel; and he said in the sight of Israel, *"Sun, stand still on Gibeon!* You, moon, stop in the valley of Aijalon!" *The sun stood still,* and the moon stayed, until the nation had avenged themselves of their enemies. Isn't this written in the book of Jashar? *The sun stayed in the midst of the sky, and didn't hurry to go down about a whole day.*

For Joshua to command the sun to stop, it must have been moving in the first place. Whoever wrote these passages evidently thought that it was the sun that orbited round the earth. Some Christians had tried to defend this by saying that the story should be taken to mean that Joshua commanded the earth to stop rotating about its axis for about a day.[49] But this solution is even more difficult. As the space scientist Charles Pellegrino explains:

---

[47]   Schadewald, Robert, "The Evolution of Bible Science", Godfrey (ed), *Scientists Confront Creationism*: p292
Gardner, *Fads and Fallacies in the Name of Science*: p16-19

[48]   These observations include: Mercury and Venus, observed from the earth cannot be separated by more than 27° and 47° from the sun; the retrograde motion of Mars; and the parallax shift of nearby stars.

[49]   There is an urban legend circulating in evangelical circles relating to engineers and scientists at NASA somehow finding Joshua's "missing day" through mistakes in their calculations. The legend is without foundation and so easily proven false, and thus a source of embarrassment, that even fundamentalists have distanced themselves from it. (A couple of examples of such rebuttals from fundamentalist Christians themselves are given below:
    http://www.reasons.org/resources/apologetics/joshualongday.shtml

Under this "slamming of the brakes", as it were, inertia would have taken over, piling billions of tons of the Earth's atmosphere into mighty shockfronts, and producing wind speeds twice the velocity of sound in the Jordan Valley. Joshua's army would have had enough time for a very short scream.[50]

A verse normally paraded by fundamentalist as proving that the Bible had scientific foreknowledge is this one from the book of Job:

Job 26:1,7
Then Job answered: "... He stretches out the north over empty space, and *hangs the earth on nothing...*"

This verse supposedly proves that the verse understood the earth to be not balanced on anything but is held by the gravitational pull of the sun. But remember it was Job, *not God*, who was saying this in Job 26:7. This is how God replied to Job's "scientific foreknowledge":

Job 38:1-4
Then Yahweh answered Job out of the whirlwind, *"Who is this who darkens counsel by words without knowledge*? Brace yourself like a man, for I will question you, then you answer me! *"Where were you[51] when I laid the foundations of the earth*?

In effect, after the long speeches by Job (and that of his friends), Yahweh declared Job to be "without knowledge" and affirmed that the earth had foundations!

THE PROXIMITY OF THE STARS

Today we know that stars are simply suns that are very far away. The authors of the Bible do not have the benefit of this modern scientific discovery and made assumptions about the stars any primitive pre-scientific tribe would make. Take this passage below from the book of Revelation:

Revelation 6:12-14
I saw when he opened the sixth seal, and there was a great earthquake. The sun became black as sackcloth made of hair, and the whole moon became as blood. The stars of the sky fell to the earth, like a fig tree dropping its unripe figs when it is shaken by a great wind. The sky was removed like a scroll when it is rolled up.

---

http://answersingenesis.org/docs/1117.asp -
both sites accessed on April 11, 2007) A similar rebuttal can be found in the article by Samuel Larson "Nasa's Discover's Bible's 'Missing Day'...Not", *Skeptic*, Vol. 8, No.4 2001.

[50]   Pellegrino, *Return to Sodom & Gomorrah*, p261
[51]   "Where were you" is given in the original Hebrew as *Ifoh hayita*. The second word, *hayita* is the second person masculine *singular* form of *hayah*, which means "to become" or "to exist." Thus the word *"you"* is *singular* and is targeted at Job, not at his companions, since it was Job God was answering; as Job 38:1 clearly states.

In his understanding of cosmology, stars could be shaken by an earthquake and fall to the earth, just like the fruits of the fig tree when shaken by the wind! This passage clearly shows that the author of Revelation had no understanding whatsoever as to what the stars really were. He looked at the stars and assumed they were little balls of light that, if the heavens were shaken hard enough, would plunge into the earth.[52]

Modern astronomy tells us that the earth is a sphere, that it rotates round its axis once every twenty four hours, that it circles round the sun once a year and that the stars are very large objects that are very far away from the earth.

The Bible, on the other hand, tells us that the earth is flat, that it is the sun that rotates round the earth and that stars are very small objects that can drop down to earth should there be a powerful earthquake. Where is the truth in these biblical utterances?

THE HYDROLOGIC CYCLE

The hydrologic (or water) cycle is the name given to the circuitous route taken by water starting from evaporation (caused by solar energy) of bodies of water (e.g. lakes, rivers and the sea), condensation (in the form of clouds), precipitation (as rain or snowfall) and its final runoff back into the bodies of water.

It is quite obvious that the authors of the various biblical books have no idea about this cycle. The author of the book of Job, for instance, thinks that snow and hail are kept in *warehouses* (in heaven?) before they are sent down to earth!

> Job 38:22 (RSV)
> Have you entered the *storehouses* of the snow, or have you seen the *storehouses* of the hail?

The author(s) of Genesis believed that rain water came from what had been initially placed above the sky (firmament) by God. Rain fell when this firmament is opened.

> Genesis 1: 6-7 (KJV)
> And God said, "Let there be a firmament in the midst of the waters, and let it separate the waters from the waters." And God made the firmament and separated the waters which were under the firmament from the waters which were above the firmament. And it was so. And God called the firmament Heaven.

> Genesis 7:11-12 (KJV)
> [O]n that day all the fountains of the great deep burst forth, and the windows of the heavens were opened. And rain fell upon the earth forty days and forty nights.

The author of Ecclesiastes guessed that the water in the ocean somehow gets circulated back into the rivers. It is obvious he has no knowledge of how it actually gets circulated back. No mention of evaporation or precipitation as rain!

> Ecclesiastes 1:7
> All the rivers run into the sea, yet the sea is not full. To the place where the rivers flow, there they flow again.

---

[52] Asimov, *X Stands for Unknown*: p252

This is what the Bible teaches about the hydrologic cycle: snow and hail are kept in storehouses, rain is kept in the sky ("firmament") which is then "opened" when heavy rain is required. Not particularly confidence-inspiring examples!

It therefore comes as a surprise that some fundamentalists *still* claim that the Bible shows scientific foreknowledge in its understanding of the hydrologic cycle. They simply ignore all the verses above and made reference to this verse from chapter 36 of Job.

> Job 36:27-28 (RSV)
> For he draws up the drops of water, he distils his mist in rain which the skies pour down, and drop upon man abundantly.

We should remind ourselves that this verse was written by the same person who believed that snow is kept in warehouses before being used! The verse seems to imply a familiarity with evaporation and precipitation as rain. Yet this is merely an artifact of translation. In its original Hebrew, the word translated as "draw *up*" (which gives the implication of *evaporation*) is *gara*. *Strong's Concordance* gives the meaning of *gara* as "to diminish, to restrain or to withdraw". Within the context of this verse, it obviously means "to withdraw". *Brown Driver-Briggs Hebrew and English Lexicon* (p175) indicates that "withdraw" in this case could also mean draw *up* or to draw *down*. It is by no means clear in the original Hebrew that the passage implies something that is drawn *upwards*. It could easily also mean something which is drawn *down* - perhaps from the "firmament" above [see Genesis 1:6-7 and 7:11-12!] or something that is withdrawn from the inventory of rain (like the snow in the heavenly warehouse!).

Furthermore, "*he* distils" is actually a mistranslation. The original Hebrew gives "they distil". It is unclear if this distillation refers to God or to the clouds of rain. Indeed, the KJV translation gives a totally different picture:

> Job 36:27-28 KJV
> For he maketh small the drops of water: they pour down rain according to the vapor thereof: Which the clouds do drop and distil upon man abundantly.

The only "fact" that can be unambiguously ascertained from this passage is that *rain pours down from the clouds as drops of water abundantly upon people*. Hardly something unknown to anyone living during the pre-scientific age!

The balance of evidence shows that there is no reason to believe that the author of Job knew any more about the water cycle than any of his contemporaries.

OCEAN CURRENTS

While we are on the subject of water, it is important to examine a verse normally claimed by fundamentalists to show evidence of scientific foreknowledge in the Bible:

> Psalm 8:8
> The birds of the sky, the fish of the sea, and whatever passes through the *paths of the seas*.

The words "paths of the sea" is claimed by fundamentalists to be a reference to ocean *currents*; and since ocean currents were unknown during that time, this then is another evidence for the divine origin of the Bible. Yet to equate "path" (Hebrew *orach*) with "sea current" is surely jumping the gun a little. *Strong's Concordance* gives the meaning of this word as *a well-trodden road*. We find such meanings within the Old Testament itself:

> Judges 5:6 KJV
> In the days of Shamgar the son of Anath, in the days of Jael, the *highways* [Hebrew *orach*] were unoccupied, and the travelers walked through byways.
>
> Isaiah 41:3 RSV
> He pursues them and passes on safely, by *paths* [Hebrew *orach*] his feet have not trod.

Some versions translate *orach* in Judges 5:6 as "caravans" and in Isaiah 41:3 as "the way". But the point is clear. The word, when used in its literal sense and as pointed out by *Strong's*, is used to denote a "well trodden road".

Furthermore, note that in Psalm 8:8, the passage first talks about birds *in the air* and then fishes *of the sea*. One is *above* the surface and the other is *below* the surface of the sea. Whatever comes after this is more naturally interpreted as something *between* the air and the sea: namely, the *surface* of the ocean - i.e. something *on* the sea between the birds and the fish. A more natural, and simpler,[53] interpretation of the passage is that it refers to *seafaring routes*, the "paths" in the oceans taken by ships. There is no need to invoke a supernatural interpretation of that phrase.

THE BIOLOGICAL SCIENCES

The various authors of the Bible also betray their poor knowledge of the biological sciences; typical of a pre-scientific race. In this section we will look at some of the biological errors in the Bible.

BIOLOGY OF MAMMALS

It seems that the maker of the universe sometimes forgets the detailed biology of the things He has created:

> Leviticus 11: 1-6 (RSV)
> And the Lord said to Moses and Aaron, "Say to the people of Israel, there are living things which you may eat among all the beasts that are on the earth. Whatever parts the hoof and is cloven footed and chews the cud, among the animals you can eat. Nevertheless among those that chew the cud or part the hoof, you shall not eat these: The camel because it chews the cud but does not part the hoof, is unclean to you. And the rock badger, because it chews the cud but does not part the hoof, is unclean to you. And the hare, because it chews the cud but does not part the hoof, is unclean to you.

---

[53] To understand why simpler explanations are normally preferred in scientific discourse see our discussion of Ockham's Razor in chapter 7.

There are two *major* mistakes here:

- "Parting the hoof" refers to the foot of the animals being divided into two parts. The feet of cows and sheep are of this kind. The problem with the biblical passage above is that the camel too is a cloven-footed animal. Like, the cow and the sheep, the camel has only two bones connecting the upper bones of the foot to the anklebones. These connecting bones, called metacarpals in the forefoot and metatarsals in the hind foot, are actually fused for most of its length but remain unfused towards the end - giving the "cloven" look to the feet. The camel is certainly an animal that "parts the hoof". Therefore, by the standards set in the Leviticus passage, it should actually be a clean animal!

- "Chewing the cud" is an expression that means ruminating. It involves rechewing the food that has been eaten earlier and passed on to the stomach. To do this, some mammals have evolved four-chambered stomachs; these mammals include deer, giraffes, sheep, goats, antelopes and oxen. Some animals, such as the camel, ruminate inefficiently as they do not have the four-chambered stomach. The main point in the paragraph in Leviticus is that the rock badger (or rock hyrax) and the rabbit do not ruminate their food. The constant chewing action of these animals may have misled the author of Leviticus.

ANATOMY OF INSECTS

In the same chapter of Leviticus as the one we have seen above, we find that the author does not even know that insects have *six* legs.

We are told that insects such as the locust, grasshopper and the cricket have *four* legs.[54]

Leviticus 11:20-23
All flying insects that walk on all fours are an abomination to you. Yet you may eat these: of all winged creeping things that go on all fours, which have legs above their feet, with which to hop on the earth. Even of these you may eat: any kind of locust, any kind of katydid, any kind of cricket, and any kind of grasshopper. *But all winged creeping things which have four feet, are an abomination to you.*

It is indeed strange, if one considers the Bible to be the directly inspired word of God, that He should have forgotten the anatomies of the insects he created!

---

[54] Clements, *Science vs. Religion*: p201-202
Lofmark, *What is the Bible?*: p44
Schwartz, *The Red Ape*: p98-100

BOTANY OF THE MUSTARD PLANT

There is a claim attributed to Jesus about the botany of the mustard plant in the thirteenth chapter of Matthew that goes like this:

Matthew 13:31-32 (NRSV)
He [Jesus] put before them another parable: "The kingdom of heaven is like a *mustard seed* that someone took and sowed in the field; *it is the smallest of all seeds.*[55]

Here was Jesus, supposedly God himself, reported in the Bible, the supposed inerrant word of God, as claiming something which is manifestly false. The mustard seed is *not* the smallest of *all* seeds. For while it is true that mustard seeds are small, they are not the smallest. According to the *Guinness Book of World Records*, the smallest seeds are those of the epiphytic orchids. Each seed weighs in at approximately 0.0000008 grams!

This one passage proves that neither the Bible, *nor Jesus*, can be considered *the word of God* in the fundamentalist sense.

GENETICS

The Bible's knowledge of genetics is dismal.

Genesis 30:37-39 (RSV)
Then Jacob took fresh rods of poplar and almond and plane, and peeled white streaks in them, exposing the white of the rods. He set the rods which he had peeled in front of the flocks in the runnels, that is, the watering troughs, where the flocks came to drink. *And since they bred when they came to drink, the flocks bred in front of the rods and so the flocks brought forth striped, speckled, and spotted.*

This passage tells us that cattle can give birth to striped, speckled and spotted cattle merely by *looking* at striped rods. Modern genetics have discovered many of the causes of chromosomal abnormalities and genetic mutations, but *staring at striped rods* is not one of them![56]

FAILED PROPHECIES

Prophecies are writings or utterances about the future by prophets. It is important to say a few words here about some prophecies in the Bible that seemed have been fulfilled. Some prophecies were accurate because, quite simply, they were written

---

[55]   In desperation, fundamentalist translations of the Bible, such as the NIV, have resorted to adding words that are not present in the original Greek into the verse here. Thus if you turn to the NIV you will find that the verse is now given as "Though it is the smallest of all *your* seeds". The "your" is not found in any extant Greek manuscripts and was added there merely at the whim of the translators of the NIV.

[56]   Clements, *Science vs. Religion*: p204
McKinsey, *The Encyclopedia of Biblical Errancy*: p214

after the event they purports to have foreseen. The Book of Daniel is a good example of this. It pretends to have been written during the time of the exile (around the 6th century BCE). Today, it is has been shown that Daniel was actually written in the second century BCE. Still other supposed prophecies occur in the same book; in other words, the reports of the prophecies and of the events that "fulfill" them are conveyed to us by the same author. One such example is I Kings 13:2 where it is prophesied that a descendent of David named Josiah will burn the bones of the pagan priests on the altar at Bethel. This prophecy is fulfilled in II Kings 13:32. However, since this prophecy and its fulfillment are written by the same author we have no way of knowing whether the story of the prophecy was "made up" to make the whole story more impressive.[57] Other prophecies were not prophecies at all, but have readings forced into them by believers into them. The "virgin birth" prophecy of Jesus found in Isaiah 7:14 is one such case.[58] Still other prophecies "fulfilled" events that never occurred! Many of the events surrounding the trial, crucifixion and resurrection of Jesus are examples of these.[59] Apart from these, there were many occasions where the Biblical prophets simply got their prophecies wrong! Prophecies that can fail are further evidence that the Bible is by no means an error free book.

ISAIAH'S FAILED PROPHECIES

The prophet Isaiah, for instance, foretold the drying up of all the waters of Egypt, and the destruction of all land used for plantation due to this drying up of the River Nile.

> Isaiah 19:5-7
> The waters will fail from the sea, and the river will be wasted and become dry. The rivers will become foul. The streams of Egypt will be diminished and dried up. The reeds and flags will wither away. The meadows by the Nile, by the brink of the Nile, and all the sown fields of the Nile, will become dry, be driven away, and be no more.

This part of Isaiah, widely accepted by scholars to be written around the 8th century BCE, is about 2,750 years old. And in all this period of two and three quarters millennia, this prophecy has yet to be fulfilled! Moreover, it is clear from the context that Isaiah prophecy was meant for the Egypt of his time. For it was with that Egypt that Isaiah and his people had a grievance against and the prophecy was a warning to them. This is a clear example of an unfulfilled prophecy.[60]

In a similar vein, Isaiah predicted the complete and utter destruction of Damascus.

> Isaiah 17:1-2 (NRSV)
> An oracle concerning Damascus. See, Damascus *will cease to be a city*, and will become a heap of ruins. Her towns *will be deserted forever*...

---

57   Callahan, *Bible Prophecy*: p47
58   For more discussion on this see the chapter on the Nativity.
59   See Excursus C later in this book.
60   Howell-Smith, *In Search of the Real Bible*: p40

As we noted above, it is now almost three millennia since that prophecy and Damascus remains a vibrant city. While Damascus have been overrun many times in its past, it is still standing. Clearly, the prophecy that says Damascus will cease to be a city *forever* is false.[61]

Isaiah also spoke of a prophecy God made to Ahaz, the King of Judah that he would not be harmed by his enemies:

> Isaiah 7:1-7
> It happened in the days of Ahaz ...king of Judah, that Rezin the king of Syria, and Pekah the son of Remaliah, king of Israel, went up to Jerusalem to war against it, but could not prevail against it...Then Yahweh said to Isaiah, "Go out now to meet Ahaz, you, and ...[t]ell him, 'Be careful, and keep calm. Don't be afraid, neither let your heart be faint ... for the fierce anger of Rezin and Syria, and of the son of Remaliah. Because Syria, Ephraim, and the son of Remaliah, have plotted evil against you, saying, "Let's go up against Judah, and tear it apart, and let's divide it among ourselves, and set up a king in its midst, even the son of Tabeel." This is what the Lord Yahweh says: *"It shall not stand, neither shall it happen."*

Yet according to II Chronicles, Syria and Pekah did conquer Judah!

> II Chronicles 28:1, 5-6
> Ahaz was twenty years old when he began to reign; ...*Yahweh his God delivered him into the hand of the king of Syria*; and they struck him, and carried away of his a great multitude of captives, and brought them to Damascus. He was also delivered into the hand of the king of Israel, who struck him with a great slaughter. For Pekah the son of Remaliah killed in Judah one hundred twenty thousand in one day...

EZEKIEL'S FAILED PROPHECIES

Ezekiel made a prophecy that, at the time he wrote, seemed most likely to be fulfilled. The prophet was writing, in 587 BCE, at the time when Nebuchadnezzar was laying siege on Tyre. With such a powerful army like Nebuchadnezzar's, it was not surprising that Ezekiel prophesied the fall of Tyre to the Babylonian king.

> Ezekiel 26:7-14 (RSV)
> For thus says the Lord: "Behold I will bring upon Tyre from the north Nebuchadnezzar of Babylon, king of kings, with horses and chariots, and with horsemen and a hosts of many soldiers. He will slay with the sword your daughters on the mainland; he will set up a siege wall against you. He will direct the shock of his battering rams against your walls, and with his axes he will break down your towers...With the hoofs of his horses he will trample all your streets; he will slay your people with the sword and your mighty pillar will fall to the ground...they will break down your walls and destroy your pleasant houses... I will make you a bare rock...you shall never be rebuilt, for I have spoken," says the Lord God.

The whole passage clearly prophesied the sack and complete destruction of Tyre by Nebuchadnezzar. However, the vivid description of the sack and fall of Tyre never

---

[61]   Callahan, *Bible Prophecy*: p60

happened. After a siege of thirteen years, in 573 BCE, Nebuchadnezzar lifted his siege on Tyre and had to arrive at a compromised agreement.[62] Contrary to the prophecy, Nebuchadnezzar did not destroy Tyre. Tyre was instead destroyed by Alexander the Great 240 years later. And furthermore, despite the prophet, the city of Tyre was eventually rebuilt.[63]

It's amazing that despite this disconfirming evidence some apologists try to salvage that prophecy by claiming it was actually fulfilled. One example is Josh McDowell in his *Evidence that Demand a Verdict*.[64] We will look at two of his specific arguments regarding the prophecy.[65] First this is what McDowell writes about the "destruction of Tyre":

> When Nebuchadnezzar broke the gates down he found the city almost empty. The majority of the people had moved by ship to an island about one half mile off the coast and fortified the city there. The mainland city was destroyed in 573, but the city of Tyre on the island remained a powerful city for several hundred years.

The implication of this paragraph is clear: that Nebuchadnezzar destroyed a major portion of Tyre. However McDowell got it wrong! Tyre's main city was always on the island. The part of the city on the mainland is nothing more than a suburb. In other words, Nebuchadnezzar could achieve no more than take over a relatively minor part of the city. Furthermore, it is obvious from the passage in Ezekiel that the complete destruction of Tyre by Nebuchadnezzar was prophesized. McDowell tried to argue that the complete destruction by Alexander the Great was the one actually prophesized here. This is a forced reading on the passage - nowhere in the passage was anyone else except Nebuchadnezzar mentioned.

However, the most powerful argument against McDowell's apologetics is that Ezekiel himself admitted that this prophecy was a mistake!

> Ezekiel 29:17-20 (RSV)
> ...the Lord God came to me: "Son of man, Nebuchadnezzar king of Babylon made his army labor hard against Tyre; every head was made bald and every shoulder was rubbed bare; *yet neither he nor his army got anything from Tyre to pay for the labor that he had performed against it...*"

Second, McDowell tried to twist history to show that Tyre has never been rebuilt. His argument is that the modern city of Tyre is not the old city of Tyre since the former was not on the exact location of the latter. Suffice to say that no one agrees with such a twisted method to fulfill prophecy. Furthermore, the prophecy says that Tyre shall never be rebuilt after the destruction by Nebuchadnezzar - which never happened. Even after the destruction by Alexander the Great, the city was still rebuilt. In fact

---

[62] Asimov, *Guide to the Bible:* p587-588

[63] Howell-Smith, *In Search of the Real Bible*: p40-41

[64] McDowell, *Evidence that Demands a Verdict*, p274 to 280

[65] A full critique of McDowell book is available on the internet at www.infidel.org. The argument here is taken from there but was first raised by Bernard Katz in *American Rationalist* 1982.

the city of Tyre was even referred to, by that name, in the New Testament (Mark 7:24, Acts 12:20). The city exists to this day.

Having failed in one prophecy did not make Ezekiel shy about making more:

Ezekiel 29:8-12
Therefore thus says the Lord Yahweh: "Behold, I will bring a sword on you, and will cut off man and animal from you. The land of Egypt shall be a desolation and a waste [1]; and they shall know that I am Yahweh...No foot of man shall pass through it [2], nor foot of animal shall pass through it, neither shall it be inhabited forty years [3]. I will make the land of Egypt a desolation in the midst of the countries that are desolate [4]; and her cities among the cities that are laid waste shall be a desolation forty years [5]; and I will scatter the Egyptians among the nations, and will disperse them through the countries [6]."

This passage must take the cake for the most prophecies proven wrong!

1. Egypt has never been desolate and laid waste.

2. Men and people have always walked through it.

3. There has never been a single moment (let alone forty years) when Egypt was uninhabited.

4. Egypt has never been a desolated country surrounded by more desolated countries.

5. Its cities have never been desolated for any period of time.

6. There was no Egyptian diaspora.[66]

Ezekiel tried his luck with another prophecy regarding the Babylonian king, Nebuchadnezzar:

Ezekiel 29:19-20
Therefore thus says the Lord Yahweh: Behold, I will give the land of Egypt to Nebuchadnezzar king of Babylon; and he shall carry off her multitude, and take her spoil, and take her prey; and it shall be the wages for his army. I have given him the land of Egypt as his recompense for which he served, because they worked for me, says the Lord Yahweh.

Unfortunately, here too he failed! For Nebuchadnezzar never conquered Egypt.

---

66   McKinsey, *Encyclopedia of Biblical Errancy*, p304

JEREMIAH'S FAILED PROPHECY

The last prophecy we will look at is that by the prophet Jeremiah. He prophesied that Jehoiakim will have no successor:

> Jeremiah 36:30
> Therefore thus says Yahweh concerning Jehoiakim king of Judah: He shall have none to sit on the throne of David.

Unfortunately his prophecy is proven false by another passage in the Bible:

> II Kings 24:6
> So Jehoiakim slept with his fathers; and Jehoiachin his son reigned in his place.

* * * * *

With such glaring examples of internal contradictions, historical inaccuracies, scientific blunders and failed prophecies, it should be clear to all that the doctrine of biblical inerrancy is false.

Chapter Three
MYTHS AND LEGENDS

THE HISTORICITY OF THE BIBLE

The first eleven chapters of Genesis have all the elements required for a Hollywood blockbuster. We have the accounts of the creation of the universe, the expulsion of the first humans from paradise, a worldwide cataclysmic flood and an account of how the various languages were created by God to confound humanity. The stories are dramatic, captivating and memorable. It is almost anti-climactic for one to assert that wonderful and entertaining these stories are, they are nevertheless, myths with no grounding in history. They are folklores of a pre-scientific Middle Eastern tribe. In this sense these stories are no different from, and indeed in some cases were *copied from*, the myths and folklore of other ancient tribes such as the Babylonians, the Egyptians, the Persians and the Greeks. In this chapter we will see for ourselves why these stories are not historical.

THE CREATION MYTHS I:
INTERNAL DIFFICULTIES

There are actually *two* separate and different stories of creation contained in Genesis. The first is given in Genesis 1: 1-2:4 while the second is given in Genesis 2: 4-24.

According to the first creation story the whole universe was made in six days, while on the seventh day, God rested. The table below gives the order of creation as described in those verses:

Day	Relevant Verses	Things Created
One	Genesis 1:1-5	Light
Two	Genesis 1:6-8	"Firmament" (the sky)
Three	Genesis 1:9-13	Dry Land, Seas, Plants
Four	Genesis 1:14-19	Sun, Moon and "the stars also"
Five	Genesis 1: 20-23	Fish, "sea monsters", winged bird.
Six	Genesis 1:24-31	Cattle, "creeping things", beasts and finally man.

Table 3:1 Order of creation in Genesis 1

Given below is the second story.

> Genesis 2:4-9, 18-19
> [I]n the day that Yahweh God made the earth and the heavens. *No plant of the field was yet in the earth, and no herb of the field had yet sprung up;* for Yahweh God had not caused it to rain on the earth. There was not a man to till the ground, but a mist went up from the earth, and watered the whole surface of the ground. Yahweh God formed man from the dust of the ground, and breathed into his nostrils the breath of life; and man became a living soul...
>
> Yahweh God planted a garden eastward, in Eden, and there he put the man whom he had formed. Out of the ground Yahweh God made every tree to grow that is pleasant to the sight, and good for food; the tree of life also in the middle of the garden, and the tree of the knowledge of good and evil....
>
> Yahweh God said, "It is not good that the man should be alone; I will make him a helper suitable for him." Out of the ground Yahweh God formed every animal of the field, and every bird of the sky, and brought them to the man to see what he would call them.

The two stories contradict each other in many areas:

- *The order of creation*: The reader will notice that the order of creation is completely different from the first story in Genesis 1. Note the wording italicized. Man, according to Genesis chapter two, was made *before* any plants and animals were created. There is no ambiguity with the wording. It is clearly stated that there were no plants of any kind when man was first created. It was also clearly stated that animals were created after man as helpers for him! According to Genesis chapter one, plants created in day three and animals in day five and six with man being the last item of creation on the sixth day.
- *The creation of man and woman.* According to Genesis 1:27 man and woman were created simultaneously.

> Genesis 1:27
> God created man in his own image. In God's image he created him; male and female he created them.

Yet the story in Genesis 2 was that woman was created as an afterthought; only after God was unable to find a suitable helper for Adam among the animals:

Genesis 2:20-22

The man gave names to all livestock, and to the birds of the sky, and to every animal of the field; but for man there was not found a helper suitable for him. Yahweh God caused a deep sleep to fall on the man, and he slept; and he took one of his ribs, and closed up the flesh in its place. He made the rib, which Yahweh God had taken from the man, into a woman, and brought her to the man.

- *Other contradictions.* There are other contradictions[1] between the two stories which we will simply list down here:

  o In the first account, water first covered the earth and dry land was not made until the third day (Genesis 1:9-13). In the second account, the earth was dry land before a mist came up from the earth and watered the whole earth (Genesis 2:5-6)

  o The first story tells of the creation of the universe in seven days. Yet the second story implies that all was created in a single day (Genesis 2:4 *In the day that the Lord God made the earth and the heavens…*)

  o In the first story, the man and woman were allowed to eat any fruit (Genesis 1:29 *and every tree with seed in its fruit; you shall have them for food*), yet in the second story there is a prohibition from eating the fruit from the tree of the knowledge of good and evil (Genesis 2:17 & 3:3).

  o The reference to God in the first account was simply *Elohim* (normally translated as God) while in the second account the creator is always referred to as *Yahweh Elohim* (usually translated as Lord God). [2]

It is quite obvious that we are looking at two contrary accounts of the creation of the universe. There are further problems with the story of creation in Genesis 1:[3]

- We know today that the phenomenon of night and day is caused by the rotation of the earth moving different parts of the earth away from or towards the sun. Yet, we are told that there was evening and morning from the first day - but that the sun was only created on the fourth day!

- Why does God need to "separate the light from the darkness" (Genesis 1:18) on the fourth day when there was already "evening and morning" on the first day? (Genesis 1:5)

The second account also has its own internal problems:

- Firstly, we are confronted with a *talking serpent*. (Genesis 3:1-5) This, *prima facie*, is a mythical element.

---

[1] McKinsey, *Encyclopedia of Biblical Errancy*, p354-356
[2] Graves & Patai, *Hebrew Myths*: p24-25
[3] McKinsey, *Encyclopedia of Biblical Errancy*, p356-357

- Next, we are introduced to a fruit from a tree that can convey knowledge. (Genesis 2:16 & 3:1-7). While it can be argued that eating fruits form part of a proper nutritional diet required for a healthy mental development, it surely is stretching credulity a bit far when one asserts the existence of a fruit which actually *imparts* knowledge. We have here another *prima facie* mythical element.

- Finally, we are presented with the situation where it was the serpent that spoke the truth instead of God. Given below is God's warning:

> Genesis 2:16-17
> Yahweh God commanded the man, saying, "Of every tree of the garden you may freely eat; but of the tree of the knowledge of good and evil, you shall not eat of it; *for in the day that you eat of it you will surely die.*"

Now the serpent contradicted this and told Eve that they (she and Adam) will not die (Genesis 3:5). And since Adam lived to a ripe old age of 930 (Genesis 5:5), God was obviously telling a little fib in Genesis 2:16-17.

The creation accounts in Genesis are filled with contradictions, mythical and pre-scientific elements. We will now turn our attention to the "predictions" that flow from these accounts: the age of the universe and the separate creation of species.

THE CREATION MYTHS II:
THE AGE OF THE EARTH AND THE UNIVERSE

Many theologians had tried in the past to fix the date of creation of the universe according to the Bible; the most well known of these was the Anglican Archbishop James Ussher (1581-1656). In 1654 he published his book *Annales Veteris Nove Testamenti* where he argued that based on the chronology given in the Bible the date of creation was 4004 BCE. In the old editions of King James Bible we still find, as a footnote to the Genesis story, the date of creation calculated by the Ussher.[4] Fundamentalists generally do not subscribe to the exact date given by Ussher, but they do believe that, at the very least, Ussher's date is "within the ballpark." Given a literal understanding of the Bible, Ussher's date is not very far off. Table 3.2 below shows how such a creation date, which differs from Ussher's calculation by only around 160 years, can be derived.

---

[4]   Asimov, *Guide to the Bible*: p36

Passages	Years	YSC[5]
Genesis 5:3 When Adam had lived 130 years, he became the father of a son...Seth	130	130
Genesis 5:6 When Seth had lived 105 years, he became the father of Enosh	105	235
Genesis 5:9 When Enosh had lived 90 years, he became the father of Kenan	90	325
Genesis 5:12 When Kenan had lived 70 years, he became the father of Mahalalel	70	395
Genesis 5:15 When Mahalalel had lived 65 years, he became the father of Jared	65	460
Genesis 5:18 When Jared had lived 162 years, he became the father of Enoch	162	622
Genesis 5:21 When Enoch had lived 65 years, he became the father of Methuselah	65	687
Genesis 5:25 When Metheselah had lived 187 years, he became the father of Lamech	187	874
Genesis 5:28 When Lamech had lived 182 years, he became the father of ... Noah	182	1056
Genesis 5:32 After Noah was 500 years old, Noah became the father of Shem	500	1556
Genesis 7:11 In the 600th year of Noah's life...the rain fell...40 days and 40 nights	100	1656
Genesis 8:13-14 In the 601st year...the earth was dry	1	1657
Genesis 11:10 Shem became the father of Arpachshad two years after the flood	2	1659
Genesis 11:12 When Arpachshad had lived 35 years, he became the father of Shelah	35	1694
Genesis 11:14 When Shelah had lived 30 years, he became the father of Eber	30	1724
Genesis 11:16 When Eber had lived 34 years, he became the father of Peleg	34	1758
Genesis 11:18 When Peleg had lived 30 years, he became the father of Reu	30	1788
Genesis 11:20 When Reu had lived 32 years, he became the father of Serug	32	1820
Genesis 11:22 When Serug had lived 30 years, he became the father of Nahar	30	1850
Genesis 11:24 When Nahar had lived 29 years, he became the father of Terah	29	1879
Genesis 11:26 When Terah had lived 70 years, he became the father of Abram	70	1949
Genesis 21:5 Abram was 100 years old when his son Isaac was born to him	100	2049
Genesis 25:24-26 When (Isaac's wife)...delivered...Jacob. Isaac was 60 years old	60	2109
Genesis 47:9,11 And Jacob said to the Pharaoh, "The days of my sojourning are 130 years"... Then Joseph (Jacob's son) settled his father and his brothers...in...Egypt	130	2239
Exodus 12:40-41 The time that the people of Israel dwelt in Egypt was 430 years...	430	2669
I Kings 6:1 In the 480th year after the people...came out of...Egypt, in the 4th year of Solomon's reign	480	3149
I Kings 11:42 The time that Solomon reigned in Jerusalem over all Israel was 40 years. Solomon [died]...and Rehoboam his son reigned in his place.	36	3185
I Kings 14:21 Rehoboam...reigned 17 years in Jerusalem	17	3202
I Kings 14:13-15:12 And Rehoboam, [died]...Abijam his son reigned...3 years	3	3205
I Kings 15:8-10 And Abijiam [died]...Asa his son reigned...41 years	41	3246
I Kings 22:41-42 Jehoshapat, the son of Asa...reigned 25 years	25	3271
II Kings 8:16-17 Jehoram the son of Jehoshapat...reigned 8 years	8	3279
II Kings 8:25-26 Ahaziah the son of Jehoram...reigned 1 year	1	3280
II Kings 11:1-3 Athaliah, the mother of Ahaziah, saw that her son was dead, she arose... Jehosheba...took Joash, the son of Ahaziah...she hid him from Athaliah... he remained with her for 6 years...while Athaliah reigned	6	3286
II Kings11:21-12:1 Joash was 7 when he began to reign...he reigned 40 years	40	3326
II Kings 14:1-2 Amaziah, the son of Joash...reigned 29 years	29	3355
II Kings 15:1-2 Azariah, the son of Amaziah...reigned 52 years	52	3407
II Kings 15:32-33 Jotham the son of Uzziah (=Azariah)...reigned 16 years	16	3423
II Kings 16:1-2 Ahaz, the son of Jotham...reigned 16 years	16	3439
II Kings 18:1-2 Hezekiah, the son of Ahaz...reigned 29 years	29	3468
II Kings 20:21-21:1 Hezekiah [died]... and Manasseh his son...reigned 55 years	55	3523
II Kings 21:18-19 Manasseh [died]..., and Amon his son...reigned 2 years	2	3525
II Kings 21:23-24, 22:1 The servants of Amon...killed the king...and ...made Josiah his son king. Josiah...reigned 31 years	31	3556
II Kings 23:30-31 Jehoahaz the son of Josiah...reigned 3 months	¼	3556¼
II Kings 23:34, 36 Pharoah Neco made Eliakim the son of Josiah king and changed his name to Jehoiakim... Jehoiakim...reigned 11 years in Jerusalem	11	3567¼
II Kings 24:6-8 Jehoiakim [died], and Jehoiachin his son...reigned 3 months...	¼	3567½
II Kings 24:17-18 Jehoiachin's uncle... Zedekiah... reigned 11 years	11	3578½

Table 3.2: The age of the universe according to biblical chronology[6]

---

[5]   YSC = Years since creation

[6]   Bradlaugh & Besant, *The Freethinker's Textbook*: p4-9

The books in the Old Testament gave an unbroken succession of events and genealogies from the creation of Adam to the conquest of Jerusalem by the Babylonians. The fall of Jerusalem is an historical event that has been dated by historians to either 586 or 587 BCE.[7] King Zedekiah was the last king of Judah. The account of the fall of Jerusalem is given in II Kings 25:1-19 (also II Chronicles 36:13-21)

Table 3.2 above shows the biblical chronology from the moment of creation to the fall of Jerusalem. The table shows that from the time of creation of the Adam, when the world and the universe was only six days old, to the fall of Jerusalem, the time elapsed was 3578 ½ years. If this is added to the year of Jerusalem's fall (587 BCE), the date of creation can be set at 4165 ½ BCE or approximately 6,200 years ago. According to the Bible, the universe and the earth is only about 6,000 to 8,000 years old.[8]

Let us look at how modern science determines the age of the earth and the universe and compare these results with what the Bible says.

Our knowledge of the age of the earth comes from the science of nuclear physics, from the phenomenon known as *radioactivity*. Many atoms are unstable and will spontaneously decay into other kinds of atoms. While the moment of decay of each individual atom is completely random, in a large sample the rate of decay has been shown to be constant. The rate of decay of the radioactive atoms is specific to that particular element. This rate of decay is normally given in terms of half-life, which is the time it takes for half the original amount of atoms (the "parent" atom) to decay to another type of atom (the "daughter" atom). The decay rates of the various elements have been determined experimentally.

There are many naturally occurring radioactive elements, with known "half-lives", embedded within rocks. This scientific fact is used by geologist to measure the age of rocks. By comparing the relative amount of "parent" and "daughter" atoms in a rock sample, the scientist can determine the age of that particular sample. Since there is normally more than one type of radioactive element with different decay rates found in these samples, they can be used, when found together, to cross check the dating given by each other. One example of a radioactive element that is used for the dating of rocks is the element Potassium-40. Potassium 40 decays to Argon-40 with a half-life of 1.25 billion years. Other examples include Rubidium-87, which decays into Strontium-87 with a half-life of 4.88 billion years, and Uranium-238, which decays eventually into lead-206 with a half-life of 4.47 billion years.[9] By using these

---

[7]   Roberts, *The Pelican History of the World*: p129

[8]   The calculations here is based on the *Masoretic* or Hebrew text, this is the version most modern translations of the bible are based on. It should be mentioned that some Greek texts give differing time spans for some of the characters in the Bible, but these, at most can stretch the chronology another 1,500 years. Thus the maximum age for the universe a fundamentalist can claim is less than 8,000 years.

[9]   The reader may ask: how does one know the half-life of an element when it is measured in billions of years? The answer to this is that we can. Physicists have shown that the governing equations for all natural radioactive decay is

$$N_t = N_0 e^{-Lt}$$

radioactive clocks the oldest rock yet found in the earth (from western Greenland) is dated at 3.9 billion years. Some moon rock samples, brought back to earth by the astronauts have been dated at 4.5 billion years. Analysis of these and other geologic and astronomical evidence led scientists to conclude that the solar system was formed about 4.6 billion years ago. Let us compare the two numbers side by side; the Bible says the earth is approximately 6,000 years old while scientific evidence points compellingly to an age around 4,600,000,000! These numbers differ by a factor of a *million*.

Unlike the Bible which states that the universe and the earth was all created within a few days of each other, scientists have discovered that the universe is much older than the earth or our solar system. To understand how they make this determination, we must first understand a physical phenomenon known as the *Doppler Effect*. The classic illustration of this effect would be that of an old fashioned train. If an observer is standing at a railway station, waiting for an approaching train, the horn of the train will sound higher pitched when it is approaching the station, and lower pitched when it is moving away from the station (and the observer). The explanation is simple. Sound is made up of pressure waves, and all waves have what are called wavelengths, the distance between two peaks or troughs on the wave. The pitch of a sound is determined by how fast each wavelength reaches the observer (in technical jargon - the *frequency* of the wave). The faster the wave propagation, the higher the pitch and vice versa. When the train is moving towards the observer, the source of the waves get successively closer and closer to the observer, this means that each wave gets compressed and reaches the observer at a faster rate than it would if the source was stationary. When the source is moving away, the reverse happens. Figure 3.1 gives an illustration of this.

If we know the pitch of the horn when the train is stationary, we can, by measuring the apparent pitch, calculate the speed of the moving train. This is the same principle used by the Doppler Gun – the equipment that comes to you courtesy of the traffic police and a speeding ticket.

Light consists of electromagnetic waves. Our eyes perceive the different wavelengths as different colors. Blue light has higher frequency (hence a shorter wavelength) than red light.[10] Doppler Effect can also be seen with electromagnetic waves.

---

where N_t is the number of radioactive atoms left at time "t", N_0 is the original number of radioactive atoms, e is the base of natural logarithm (2.718), t is the time elapsed and L is the decay constant.

The mathematically inclined will immediately notice that the equation above gives an exponentially decaying curve. In fact, physicists have shown that all natural radioactive decay follows an exponentially decaying curve. They have also discovered that the rate of decay for each particular radioactive element is constant. This rate of decay cannot be changed (slowed down or speeded up) by any physical means such as temperature or pressure. The decay constant, L, which can be measured from experiments, is inversely proportional to the half-life. Thus by knowing the decay constant, physicists can determine accurately the half life of any particular radioactive isotopes.

[10] Actually visible light makes up only a very small portion of the electromagnetic spectrum of waves. There are electromagnetic waves with a higher frequency than blue (the ones

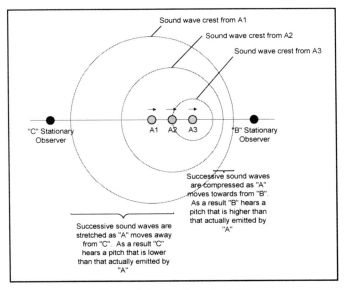

Figure 3.1: The Doppler Effect

In the late 1920s and early 1930s, the American astronomer, Edwin Hubble (1889-1953), found that the light from distant galaxies "shifts" towards the red end of the spectrum.[11] Many explanations were tried, but the only explanation that was finally consistent with all the available facts is that the light waves are being stretched. And this stretching comes from the fact that the galaxies are moving away from us. This can be understood clearly from figure 3.1. The earth is equivalent to stationary observer "C" while the galaxies are the moving source "A". Hubble also showed that the recession of the galaxies is directly proportional to their distance from the earth. This discovery is now known as Hubble's Law and is generally interpreted to mean that the universe is expanding.

An expanding universe is also the only type of universe that is consistent with Einstein's general theory of relativity. If the universe is expanding now, it was not unreasonable to suppose that there was a time when the universe was very much smaller than it is today. So in the 1940s and 1950s theoretical cosmologists worked out the implications of this hypothesis. Using the best known laws of physics, they discovered that in the early stages of the universe when all its mass are huddled together in a very small space, the universe must be very dense and very bright. Their calculations showed them that in this dense, hot universe, approximately 25% of all the mass would be fused into helium, the rest remaining as hydrogen. Moreover, their calculations further predicted that as the universe expanded, a background radiation would flow freely through space. And that due to the expansion, these waves will be

---

immediately higher than blue are called *ultra-violet*) and with lower frequency than red (the ones immediately lower are called *infra-red*).

[11] Note that this *does not* mean that the lights from these galaxies appear redder. What it means is that the stellar spectra with the characteristic absorption lines appear shifted towards the red end of the spectrum.

so stretched that it will be shifted from visible light to radio waves (radio waves have much longer wave lengths than visible light). All possible observations today have confirmed the predictions of these calculations. About ¾ of all matter in the universe is Hydrogen, the remaining, close to ¼ being Helium with a very small percentage of other elements such as carbon, oxygen etc which make up the basic constituents of the planets. More importantly in 1965, two physicists, Arno Penzias and Robert Wilson, discovered the background radiation predicted by the cosmologists. The evidence is extremely strong that the universe evolved from a hot and dense state. The evolution commenced with a primordial explosion known as the *Big Bang*. The rate of expansion of the universe can be calculated from Hubble's Law. With this, the calculations can be used to find out the time when the universe was in its initial dense and hot state. This calculation showed the universe to be around 15 billion years old. [12] This is more than *two million* times the estimate given by the Bible.

The findings of science show that when it comes to the ages of the earth and the universe the Bible is not just inaccurate it is very very wrong: inaccurate by factors measured in *millions*.

The fundamentalist Christian responses range from accepting the age of the earth as revealed by science to stubbornly insisting the Genesis account is the correct one. Both explanations involve some "massaging" of the facts.

Some defenders of the biblical chronology, wishing to reconcile it to the scientific findings mentioned above, suggested that the "days" in Genesis should not be taken in the literal 24-hour sense. Each day in Genesis chapter 1, they argued, represents an indefinite period of time. Hence a single day mentioned there could mean millions or even billions of years. This explanation is lame. What does "there was morning and there was evening", repeated for every day of creation in Genesis, mean if "days" are "an indefinite period of time"? Genesis 2:2 also said that God rested on the seventh day and made it holy, which was the biblical origin and explanation of the Hebrew Sabbath. Are the Jews then, supposed to rest for millions or billions of years at a time, instead of one day a week? Reading through the creation account in Genesis will show that the narrative is presented in a matter of fact way. No allegorical rendering of "days" was ever intended by the author. It is impossible to read the "day" in Genesis as meaning anything else, except the literal 24-hour day.

The other end of the spectrum comes from a group of fundamentalists who call themselves "young earth creationists". Their methods include quoting scientists out of context and invoking miracles whenever their rationalization fails to explain away the difficulty. As an example, let us take the fact that using Hubble's Law scientists can measure the distance of galaxies that are billions of light years away. This means that the light that is now seen by astronomers, left those galaxies billions of years ago. How do the young earth creationists account for this? They merely asserted that the light was created already on its way to the earth! That is, they admit that the stars may be billions of light years away, but the light we see today never really left the star. God created it, in the midst of its travel to earth! The problem with this explanation is simple: it squares away with all *possible* observations – in other words,

---

[12]   Abell, G., "The Ages of the Earth and the Universe", Godfrey (ed) *Scientists Confront Creationism*: p35-45

it is meaningless! The world showing evidence of being "old," to these biblical literalists, is simply God making it *look* old. This is no different from a hypothesis, which states that the world was created only two minutes ago (or three hours ago or 4,000 years ago – take your pick) but with all the characteristics (including our memories!) made to look as though it has been here a long time. Such explanations are beyond the realm of reason.

THE CREATION MYTHS III:
THE ORIGIN OF SPECIES

The two stories of creation in Genesis both say that every species of living things was created separately. How does this square with what we know from modern science?

Modern science has accumulated a vast amount of compelling evidence that this account in Genesis is simply false. Science has also discovered the main mechanism of how the present diversity of life came to be – natural selection. Before we go any further, let us look at the evidence and how it is incompatible with the myth of separate creation.

The first evidence comes from the study of geographical distribution of plants and animals, called *Biogeography*. Some anomalies with regards to the distribution of animals and plants simply cannot be coherently explained by postulating a creator apart from the typical cop-out phrase: *It is not for us to understand the workings of the Lord*. We see for instance that places with very similar environments but very far apart or with large natural barriers (deserts, oceans or mountain ranges) do not have the same native creatures. Central Africa for instance, has the same climate and other environmental conditions as Brazil, but both places do not share the same native animals. Central Africa has elephants, gorillas, chimpanzees, lions and antelopes. Brazil has none of these, but instead has prehensile tailed monkeys, sloths and tapirs.[13] And why does Australia have such a peculiar group of mammals called marsupials? Seven of the nine families of Marsupials are exclusive to Australia. Outside Australia only South America and the island of New Guinea have a few species of marsupials. North America has only one species (the Virginia Opossum). The varieties and numbers of these marsupials outside Australia are small. In Australia we have the marsupial equivalent of the antelope, the mouse, the wolf, the mole the cat and the anteater.[14] Why this strange distribution of placental analog in the marsupial? Was the creator playing a cosmic joke on mankind? The most the creationist can say about the geographical distribution of animals and plants is to simply say "God made it that way".

The second evidence is from the science of classification of all living things, *taxonomy*. In the 18th century, the Swedish naturalist, Carolus Linnaeus (1707-1778), himself a believer in the creation myth of Genesis, developed a system of classification of living things. This system, with some modification, is still in use today. Recognizing that certain species of animals resemble one another very closely, Linnaeus grouped them together in a category called genus. For example, wolves

---

13   Villee, *Biology*,: p777

14   Biscare et. al. (ed), *The Marshall Cavendish Illustrated Encyclopedia of Plants and Animals*: p232-234

(*Canis lupus* - of which the dog [*canis lupus familiaris*] – is now recognized as a subspecies), share such obvious similarities with jackals (e.g. *Canis mesomelas*) and coyotes (e.g. *Canis latrans*) that they are all grouped under the same genus, *Canis*. That these animals resemble each other more closely than they would, say, an elephant, shows that there is a natural system of classification. This level of classification is not all there is to it. Groups of genera can be clustered into larger assemblages that share more fundamental and more general characteristics.

For instance the genus *Canis* shares similar characteristics with the genera *Vulpus* (foxes) and *Lycaon* (wild dogs). These are grouped under the Family of Canidae. What this classification tells us is that wolves and jackals resemble each other closer than they do a fox. But wolves, jackals and foxes resemble each other closer than an animal not in the family of *Canidae*, such as the elephant. Nature not only seems to allow for a system of classification but also favors one that is hierarchical; that each group can be further grouped together on the basis of more general similarities. To continue our example, the family of *Canidae* is group together with other families such as *Ursidae* (the bear family), *Mustelidae* (which includes weasels, polecats and badgers) and *Felidae* (the cat family which includes the lion, tiger, leopard and the domestic cat). These families share similarities which include the fact that they are all flesh eating mammals, have strong jaws and large sharp teeth for tearing and cutting flesh. These families are grouped under the order of *Carnivora*. Carnivora is further grouped with some other orders under the class of *mammalia*. Some other orders of mammals include *Marsupialia*, the *Primates* (which includes monkeys, apes and human beings) and *Proboscidea* (which includes, finally, our friend the elephant). All mammals share the characteristic of being warm blooded, hairy, vertebrates (having backbones), giving birth to live young who are nourished with its mother's breasts. The class of mammals has a total of about 4,500 species. Mammals can be further grouped with other animals under the phylum *Chordata*. The members of this phylum have, at least sometime during their life, an elongated skeletal rod, or notochord, which stiffens the body, with a single hollow nerve chord located at the back side of the body. Other classes of animals included in this phylum include *Pisces* (the bony fishes), *Amphibia* (amphibians e.g. frogs, toads and salamanders), *Reptilia* (the reptiles e.g. snakes, lizards and crocodiles) and *Aves* (the birds). The phylum *Chordata* can again be group with other phyla into the kingdom of *Animalia* or of animals.[15]

The grouping we have seen above is certainly hierarchical. We can group living things into bigger and bigger groups sharing more generalized similarities. Linnaues tried in vain to develop different system of classification such as map like diagrams that would always group similar organisms together and separate dissimilar groups. Many other early taxonomists tried other ingenious systems of classification, all of which proved unsatisfactory. The fact remains that the only satisfactory way of classifying living things is with a hierarchical system.[16] Why would living things illustrate this natural tendency of groups in such a system? The idea of separate creation simply cannot even begin to explain this.

---

[15] McWhirter, *Guinness Illustrated Encyclopaedia of Facts*: p415-433
Biscare, *Encyclopedia of Plants and Animals*: p310-318
[16] Stanfield, *The Science of Evolution*: p98-101

The third evidence comes from the study of *comparative anatomy*. Figure 3.2 shows the fore limbs of four different animals: man, the dog, the whale and the bird.

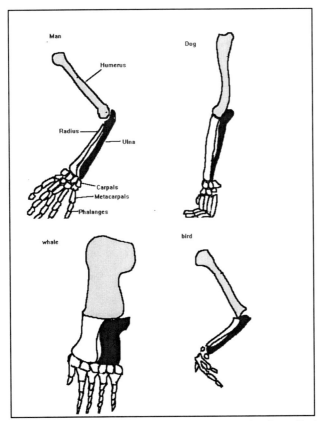

Figure 3.2: Comparative Anatomy between the front limbs of a man, a dog, a whale and a bird.

All these fore limbs have different uses in each of the animals: for the man it is used as a hand for manipulating things; for the dog, it is for walking; for the whale, it is for swimming; and for the bird, it is for flying. Yet remarkably, we see that the basic bone structures of these limbs are similar. We can also see that all the bones from the fingers (phalanges) have the same basic design: the phalanges are joined to the metacarpals and then to the carpals, to the two long bones, radius and ulna, and finally, to the humerus bone. We can see how the five phalanges (the fingers) are used by man for grasping but what is the use of the same phalanges in the whale, the dog and the bird? An engineer starting from scratch would surely have done away with these phalanges for the other three animals.[17] In fact, our hypothetical engineer would almost certainly have designed different basic bone structures for all of them. From a creation-design point of view, these homologies are almost like the work of a craftsman or craftsmen who, left with little choice, modified a basic structure that was

---

[17]   Hall, *Biology*: p255

available to suit the varied applications. Modification, surely an ugly word for an all-powerful and all wise creator!

The fourth evidence comes from the existence of vestigial organs, which have no use in some animals but are useful in other animals. For instance, snakes have small bones, which are rudimentary hind limbs, while whale have a rudimentary pelvic girdle. These structures used primarily in land locomotion, is of little or no use in the snake and the whale. These organs are called *vestigial organs*. The human being has more than 100 such organs, of which the most well known are the fused tail (the coccyx) and the appendix.[18] Human beings have no tail, yet we see in the human bone structure an obvious tailbone called the coccyx. This tailbone has been shortened to the point where it is completely covered by the muscles of the buttocks. The appendix is a blind sac at the juncture between the small and large intestines. It has no use in modern humans and can sometimes be an outright nuisance, as some people who have had appendicitis will tell you. However, this very organ has an important function in other mammals. In mammals such as the guinea pig and the horse, this organ, called the *caecum*, is the location of the bacterial digestion of food.[19] Why would an all powerful creator put similar organs in different animals, some of which have no use for them at all[20]?

The next evidence we will look at is from *Paleontology*. Paleontology is the study of living things that have long since died but left their remains mainly in the form of skeletal imprints found in rocks. These imprints are called fossils. Fossils can also be of shells, or petrified remains (of plants and animals) or even trails and footprints of animals. Paleontologists have long since known that not all classes of animals and plants are found in all the rock strata. The older the strata, the less "modern" the types of animals, or plants, one would find. For example, in formations older than 400 million years, fossil fishes are the only representative among the vertebrates. Amphibians and reptiles appear only in rock strata younger than 350 million years. Birds and mammals can only be found in formations younger than 180 million years. All these do not make sense, given a six-day creation.

Another example from paleontology is the seeming modifications different animals go through in time. Paleontologists have a very complete collection of fossils of animals that resemble closely the modern horse, *Equus*. Working our way backwards we can find fossils, some of them dating all the way back to the Eocene

---

[18] Other examples of human vestigial organs include the nictating membrane, muscles that move the ear, the pointed canine, the third molar or wisdom tooth, the male nipple, the body hair, segmented abdominal muscles and the pyramidalis muscle.

[19] Stanfield, *The Science of Evolution*: p121-123

[20] Some creationists are fond of arguing that some of these vestigial organs may yet have some functional use still undiscovered. Sure it is difficult to prove something in the negative. But criticisms such as this miss the whole point. For even if we do discover that some organs thought to be vestigial are still functional it merely proves evolution from the angle of homology. One such example is the pelvic girdle of the whale mentioned above. The fossil whale Basilosaurus had pelvic bones that may have been used for copulating. These bones in modern whales *may* play a role similar to this. However, this merely strengthens the evidence for homologous organs. For an organ originally used for locomotion has been modified (i.e. evolved) for another function; namely for copulation. (Ref: Ridley, *Evolution*: p60)

epoch (about 60 million years ago), which resembled the horse. These early fossils are small – about the size of a beagle - and have full complements of phalanges (toes) and metatarsals (the bones that join to the toes). While these fossils resemble a tangled ticket of various forms of proto-horses, through time, there is a discernable increase in size and also a loss of most of its phalanges and metatarsal bones in the fossils that precede the modern horse.[21]

This is not all. The modern sciences of biochemistry and molecular biology have added further evidence to the reality of evolution.

Modern biochemistry has enabled detailed comparison of the amino-acid sequences of similar proteins in different species of animals. One such study compared five different proteins (α-hemoglobin, β-hemoglobin, Fibrinopeptide A, Fibrinopeptide B and Cytochrome C) in 11 different species of mammals (gorilla, cow, dog, horse, human, kangaroo, mouse, rabbit, pig, rhesus monkey and sheep). The study showed that humans and gorillas (both "great apes") have the closest amino-acid sequence for all five proteins studied. These two species are also most closely related (in the trees generated) to rhesus monkeys (all primates). All three are closer in their sequences to the mouse (a placental mammal like the primates) than to the kangaroo (a marsupial). Trees of relationship were drawn based on the similarity of the amino-acid sequences for each type of protein between the 11 different species. All five groups of trees[22] (for the five different proteins) are similar to each other and to those drawn from other disciplines such as paleontology, anatomy and taxonomy.

If these animals were separately created, there is no reason why the relationship trees for all five proteins should be similar to each other. For instance, one can imagine the kangaroo having some protein amino-acid sequences more similar to humans than the same protein for humans and gorillas. Indeed, there are more than 34 *million* possible trees that could be drawn. We certainly would not expect these to be similar to the general phylogenetic trees based on the other evidence for evolution (e.g. paleontology, anatomy and taxonomy). Why then do we get these restrictive types of trees? Why aren't these trees all over the place? This tree of relatedness cannot be explained by the idea of separate creation except "God chose to do it that way"! [23]

The discovery that the genetic code is the same for *all* living species is monumental. The coding of a protein is now understood in fine detail. The genetic code is stored in giant molecules known as Deoxyribonucleic acid (DNA). The amino acid sequences are stored in the sequence of the bases of the DNA – the bases are normally referred to with the alphabets A, T, G, and C. Three of these bases are required to make the code for a single amino acid. The DNA is stored in the nucleus

---

[21]   Prothero, *Evolution*: p300-305

[22]   The trees were generated based on the minimal steps of changes required to accomplish the differences in amino-acid sequences between the different species. For four of the five proteins, there was more than one tree that could be constructed based on this minimal step requirement. Fibrinopeptide B has the most trees – eight, while Fibrinopeptide A has only one tree that best fit the minimal step requirement. The total number of trees constructed, 27, is much smaller than the 34 million possible trees that could be drawn if there is no relationship at all between the 11 species.

[23]   Ridley, *Evolution*: p61-63

of the cell, while protein is manufactured outside the nucleus in the cytoplasm (in structures known as ribosomes). The code of the DNA is read by another similar molecule known as mRNA (messenger-ribonucleic acid). The RNA has the same bases as DNA except the T is replaced by U. The mRNA leaves the nucleus and heads for the ribosomes. In the cytoplasm, different amino acids are held up by another class of similar molecule known as tRNA (transfer-RNA). These molecules will recognize only specific codes of the mRNA in the ribosome, thereby allowing the amino acids of the protein to be strung together. For examples, the codes (or "codons") for the amino acid Phenylalanine are UUU and UUC and for Lysine are AAA and AAG. The same codes are used by all living things to make the same amino-acids. Yet there is no reason why UUU should code for Phenylalanine or AAA for Lysine. In other words, these relationships are contingent and not borne out of chemical or physical laws. Hence there is no reason why these codes should be the same across all living things if they are separately created.[24]

All this evidence is irreconcilable with the myth of separate creation and provides a compelling case for the reality of organic evolution. But, as I said earlier, science has used these evidences to discover the actual underlying process of the origin of species: this process is known as *evolution*.

In the evidence from biogeography, taxonomy, comparative anatomy and paleontology quoted above were first collected and presented by Charles Darwin (1809-1882) in his book *The Origin of Species* which was published in 1859 to support his idea of "descent with modification" or evolution. Darwin suggested that all living things descended from a few or even one primitive form. The primitive forms, through successive generations, underwent gradual changes, modifications and diversifications to become the modern animals and plants that we know today. All living things today are descended from living things that had lived before, though the descendants may look almost completely different if we trace the ancestry far enough back. Since the publication of the *Origin*, further scientific discoveries in molecular biology and biochemistry have led all scientists competent to assess the evidence to assert that evolution is a scientific fact.

Let us see how evolution can explain all the evidences we have stated above. The reason why we see different animals in widely separated geographic locations with similar climates is simple: the original animals that were in these locations followed different paths of evolution. We have very good geological evidence to explain why the marsupials are concentrated in Australia. During the Mesozoic era, Australia became isolated from the rest of the world; its primitive mammals did not have to compete with the better-adapted placental mammals. The marsupials started to occupy every available niche in the continent by evolution. In other places, such as South America, the marsupials were eliminated by competition with the placental mammals.

The hierarchical structure of classification that forces itself on the early taxonomists is even easier to explain with evolution. Genus is collection of species that share a common ancestor not too long ago. Hence many of the similarities are still shared. The higher the division, the more remote the common ancestors are.

---

[24] Ridley, *Evolution*: p57

As for comparative anatomy, the man, the dog, the whale and the bird all evolved from an ancestor that has the stated forelimb configuration. As they evolved separately to fill different environments and surroundings, these structures were modified accordingly, always retaining the basic configuration.

It is the same with vestigial organs. Snakes evolved from reptiles that had functioning limbs, but as it evolved to fill a niche where the limbs were not needed these organs degenerated into vestigial organs. The whale evolved from a four-legged mammal and the pelvic girdle is a vestige of this ancestor. Human beings, at a remote period back in time, share the same ancestors as horses and pigs which have the precursor to the appendix.

The fossil record from paleontology gives the most direct evidence of evolution. The fossils show that more complicated animals appeared on the earth later than the simpler ones. Bird and mammals appear in the fossil record later than reptiles. Reptiles, in turn, appear in the fossil record later than the amphibians. If we go back even further, only the simplest unicellular organisms can be found, showing that all living things must have evolved from these.[25] The fossil record also shows *how* more modern animals evolve from earlier ones. Perhaps the most well known example is *Archaeopteryx*. The fossil, first found in 1861 in Bavaria, is about the size of a crow, had both reptilian and avian features as we would expect from a pioneer species. It has reptilian like teeth and tail, yet it has wings that are covered with feathers and the wishbone, a feature found only in birds today.[26] Similarly, the fossil record of the horse shows evolution occurring right before our eyes. The hind leg of the horse evolved through the millions of years to fit into its environment.

The reason why the protein sequences of the animals show only a certain type of relatedness is obvious given that evolution occurred. We know that proteins (or their codes) do mutate over time. Animals that are more closely related to each other share a common ancestor in more recent times, so there is less time for mutation to accumulate. This explains why gorillas share closer protein sequences with humans than both do with rhesus monkeys and all three are closer to each other than to the mouse. All these share more similarities in their protein sequences than they do with kangaroos.

The case of the genetic code is the strongest evidence we have that all living things evolve eventually from the same ancestor. As we have noted above, there is no physical or chemical constraint that would tie in any particular codon to any particular amino acid. The only explanation for this arbitrary correlation is that the code evolved early during the history of the earth. And since it was crucial that replication of proteins is as accurate as possible, this code was preserved throughout the history of life in this planet.[27]

Fossil records of forms ancestral to modern humans have also been found and extensively studied by paleoanthropologists. Recent discoveries in human evolution have shown that the human evolutionary tree is just like any other species – a thick tangled bush. From this bush we can discern the path of human evolution from 4

---

[25] The oldest fossils yet found are threadlike microbes in Northwestern Australia dated to approximately 3.5 billion years ago. [Schopf, *Cradle of Life*: p71-100]

[26] Ruse, *Darwinism Defended*: p208, 312

[27] Ridley, *Evolution*: p59

million years. The ancestral human form had the brain the size of a chimpanzee's (about 400 cc) but walked on two legs. This form is known as *Australopithecus afarensis*. The evolution continued through *Australopithecus africanus*, *Homo habilis*, *Homo ergaster*, *Homo heidelbergensis* and, finally, *Homo sapiens*.[28]

The verdict is clear: evolution is the explanation for the present diversity of living things. The biblical story of creation is an ancient myth and is to be read as such.[29]

THE CREATION MYTHS IV:
ORIGINS

Traditionally, Christians had always believed that the creation stories in Genesis were historical depictions of what actually happened and were not simply stories copied from still older myths. This all changed in the 19th century when British archaeologists unearthed seven tablets containing the Babylonian myth of creation known as *Enuma Elish*. Like the famous *Epic of Gilgamesh* (see the next section below), the archaeologists assigned the date of composition of this work to around 2000 BCE. Although the story differs in specifics from that told in Genesis, the similarities in general tone have convinced archaeologists that the Genesis accounts was derived from the Babylonian one. Some of the similarities include:

1. *The reference to the initial state as being a disordered chaos of water.* Genesis 1:1 refers to the "darkness" upon the face of the deep. In the Babylonian myth, in the beginning there was only Apsu, the sweet water ocean and Tiamat, the salt-water ocean. In fact, archaeologists have generally acknowledged that the Hebrew word for the chaos of the waters or "the deep", *tehom*, is actually derived from the Akkadian *Tiamat*.

2. *The creation of a firmament to separate the waters above from the waters below.* In Genesis 1:6-8 God is said to have created the firmament on the second day of creation. In the Babylonian myth, Marduk, son of the Ea the god of wisdom, killed Tiamat and split her into two. The upper half of Tiamat was fixed onto the sky to keep the waters above in place.

3. *The sequence of successive acts of creation.* In the Babylonian myth, after Tiamat was killed, the firmament was created by Marduk to separate the waters above from below. Then he created the sun, the moon, the planets and the stars. Finally, man was created. This order is very closely

---

28 Brace, C.L. "Humans in Time and Space" in Godfrey (ed) *Scientists Confront Creationism*: p247-277
    Tettersall & Schwartz, *Extinct Humans*: p244

29 For those who are interested in a detailed critique of creationists – in the guises of "scientific creationism" or "intelligent design" - the best websites to consult respectively are:
    -    Talk-Origins (http://www.talkorigins.org/)
    -    Talk-Design (http://www.talkdesign.org/)

paralleled in Genesis I where the firmament was created on the second day, the sun, moon and stars on the third day and man on the sixth day.[30]

It simply cannot be denied that the creation myth from Genesis must have been derived from the Babylonian one. To quote the late Professor S.H. Hooke (1874-1968) an expert on Old Testament Studies:

> [I]n spite of the complete transformation of the Babylonian material effected by the priestly writer[31] , it is difficult to avoid the conclusion that the original form of the creation story upon which he is depending is ultimately of Babylonian origin.[32]

The Garden of Eden and the story of Adam and Eve were also derived from older Sumerian and Akkadian myths.[33] It is important to recall the story of Adam and Eve from the second and third chapters of Genesis in order to compare this with the Sumerian version:

Genesis	Sumerian Myths[34]
1. The setting - a garden in paradise	
In Genesis 2 we are told of a garden called Eden where God "made every tree to grow that is pleasant to the sight, and good for food" (Genesis 2:9) and where there is no death	The Sumerian paradise is called Dilmun. (It should be noted, that Eden (*edinu*) was also originally a Sumerian word, meaning 'plain' or "steppe'.) Dilmun was a divine garden where sickness and death do not exist.
2. The watering of the gardens with water from the earth.	
In Genesis 2:5-6 we are told that God has yet to cause it to rain and that "a mist went up from the earth, and watered the whole surface of the ground."	The only thing Dilmun lacked was fresh water; the god Enki (or Ea) ordered Utu, the sun god, to bring up fresh water from the earth to water the garden.
3. The consumption of forbidden fruits and the curse associated with consuming them.	
In Genesis 2:17, God forbade Adam to eat from the tree of the knowledge of good and evil "for in the day that you eat of it you will surely die."	Ninhursag, the mother-goddess caused eight plants to grown in the garden of the gods. Enki ate from these plants. In her anger, Ninhursag cursed Enki to die.

---

30   Graves & Patai, *Hebrew Myths*: p21-23
      Hooke, *Middle Eastern Mythology*: p41-45, 119-120
31   The "editor" of the Genesis account.
32   Hooke, *Middle Eastern Mythology*: p120
33   The Sumerian civilization is the oldest in the world. The Sumerians developed the first system of handwriting and (probably) the first cuneiform script.   The Sumerian civilization lasted for approximately 1,000 years until they were finally conquered by the Akkadians.
34   Hooke, *Middle Eastern Mythology*: p114-115

4. Relationship of a female to the rib of the male	
In Genesis 2:21-22, God created Eve from one of Adam's *rib*.	As Enki lay dying, Ninhursag was induced to help. She created eight goddesses of healing who proceeded to heal each of the diseased parts of Enki's body. One of these parts was the god's *rib*, and the goddess who was created to deal with the rib was named *Ninti*, which means "lady of the rib".
5. The name of the female related to the rib	
In Genesis 3:20 we are told the name of Adam's wife is Eve, which in its original Semitic form, *Hawah*, means "life".	The word *ti* from the name *Ninti* has a double meaning; it could mean either 'rib' or 'life'. Thus Ninti can be rendered as "lady of the rib" or "lady of life".

Table 3.3 Comparison between the Hebrew myth of Adam and Eve and the Sumerian myth of Enki and Ninti

That is not all, the Babylonian myth, the *Epic of Gilgamesh,* contains an episode that doubtless also influenced the writers of Genesis. In it, Gilgamesh, in his quest for immortality, was told by Utnapishtim (the Babylonian "Noah" –see below) that there exists a plant at the bottom of the sea that has the property of making the old young again. Gilgamesh dived into the sea and brought up the plant. However, the plant was stolen while he was taking bath. The thief who stole the plant of everlasting youth away from him was a serpent.[35] In Genesis 3, it was a serpent that influenced Eve to partake of the fruit which deprived both Adam and Eve of immortality!

That Babylonian myths should influence the stories in the Bible is really not surprising. The Babylonian empires were influential throughout the whole Middle Eastern region for over 3,000 years. The history of Jews was also very closely tied to Babylon. For it was there that the Jews were taken into exile in the year 587 BCE.

THE FLOOD MYTH I:
A SCIENTIFIC AND HISTORICAL IMPOSSIBILITY

Genesis chapters 6 to 9 give an account of a cataclysmic deluge that once swept the whole earth. It relates the story of Noah and his ark.[36]

This deluge, had it really happened, would have left behind unmistakable evidence of its occurrence. While geological records show that there had been epochs when some of the earth's surface now covered by land was covered by water and vice versa. This flooding and drying happened repeatedly in many places at different times. However, there is no evidence whatsoever of a worldwide flood as recorded in the book of Genesis.[37]

In fact some of the evidence *against* the actual occurrence of a worldwide flood was already known more than a century ago. The man who bought forward one such

---

[35] Hooke, *Middle Eastern Mythology*: p54-55
[36] See chapter 2 for a summary of this story.
[37] Ward, *A Dictionary of Common Fallacies I*: p96

evidence was the one considered to be the father of modern geology, Charles Lyell (1797-1897). In his 1863 book, *The Geological Evidences for the Antiquity of Man*, he noted that the extinct volcanoes of France in the Auvergne district were composed of loose ashes. The volcanoes had been extinct for a long time, certainly longer than the purported time of the biblical flood. He continued:

> "Had the waters once risen, even for a day, so high as to reach the level of the base of one of these cones-had there been a single flood fifty or sixty feet in height since the last eruption occurred- a great part of the volcanoes must have inevitably been swept away"[38]

Today the geological (and historical) evidence for the non-occurrence of a worldwide flood is simply overwhelming. Ian Plimer, Professor of Geology at the University of Melbourne, gave a thorough listing of these in his book *Telling Lies for God: Reason versus Creationism*. We will give two of the evidence cited by Professor Plimer:[39]

The first concerns the sequence of the sedimentary deposits. There are two kinds of sediments: high energy and low energy sediment. Based on simple laboratory tests and field observations of actual floods, it can be shown that high-energy sediments, such as gravel, are deposited during the height of floods. Low energy sediments, such as siltstone, mudstone and claystone, are deposited during the waning of the floods. If there was once a worldwide flood, we would expect a uniform worldwide sedimentary formation with the high-energy sediments (ancient gravel, sands) at the bottom and the low energy sediments at the top. Yet, this is not seen on anything close to a global scale. As Professor Plimer pointed out, if this is to be seen on a global scale, oilfield geologists would have an easy job since all sedimentary formation would invariably have sandstone at the bottom and siltstones, mudstones and claystones at the top!

The second concerns the evidence of the environment of the sediments during its time of deposition. Chemical and fossil evidence show that some sedimentary rocks were formed in freshwater environments while others were formed in a saline (salty-seawater) environment. Clearly the water that was sent by God during the deluge was either fresh or saline; it couldn't be both!

Actually the story of Genesis is, even at first glance, absurd. First let us look at the ark built by Noah. Genesis 6:15 gives its measurements as 300 cubits long, 50 cubits wide and 30 cubits high. The length of the cubit is based on the length of the human forearm and varies among the various ancient cultures. For instance, the Babylonian cubit was approximately 0.53 meters, the Roman cubit was about 0.44 meters while the Hebrew cubit was about 0.56 meters. Using the Hebrew cubit, the ark would have measured 168 meters long, 28 meters wide and 17 meters high. There are two problems with this ark as described: it is both too big *and* too small at the same time.

- ***It is too big***, because before the invention of steel, the wooden ark of Noah simply could not have been structurally sound and would have been

---

[38]   Howell-Smith, *In Search of the Real Bible*: p47

[39]   Plimer, *Telling Lies for God*: p75

unseaworthy. The *Wyoming*, a six-masted schooner, was the longest historically documented wooden ship ever built. Built in 1909, this vessel, was, at 110 meters long, a full 50% shorter than the purported length of Noah's ark. The Wyoming was so unstable that it could only be used for short coastal hauls to avoid rough conditions further out in the sea. The huge structural stresses that developed in the ship distorted its structure, causing it to leak. Water had to be pumped out continuously to prevent the ship from sinking. In 1924, it finally sank in rough sea conditions. Here we have Noah's ark, built with wood, twice as long as the Wyoming, before the invention of steel and hydraulic pumps, undergoing the turbulent conditions of the flood unscathed. It is simply an engineering impossibility.

- ***It is too small***, because there is simply not enough room for all the animals. There are today over 4,500 species of mammals, 6,000 species of reptiles, 8,600 species of birds and 3,000 species of amphibians. Many of these species are big animals: elephants, camels, rhinoceros, hippopotamuses, giraffes, horses, donkeys, zebras, cattle, bison, tapirs, pigs, tigers, lions, jaguars, panthers, sea lions, walruses, crocodiles, alligators, giant turtles, Komodo dragon, snakes, ostriches, emus, falcons and giant salamanders. There are 23,000 species of fishes, many of which will not be able to survive the flood if not taken up into the ark. Each kilogram of fish requires about a cubic meter of water to survive - this is simply to provide enough oxygen and provide space for swimming while sleeping and feeding. The volume of water required for the fishes alone would be larger than the ark.

And then there are the little creatures; there are about a million species of insects and 60,000 species of arachnids. How were these species stored in the ark?

Gathering all these animals would be a problem. Genesis 7:11-15 makes it clear that the gathering of all the animals took only one 24 hour day. Each pair of animals has less than 1/10th of a second to get into the ark! The question of pairs also raises the issue of organisms that simply don't survive or reproduce in pairs: insects such as bees and flies.

Noah was also supposed to store food for these animals (Genesis 6:21). This presents another problem in terms of storage space and the actual variety required. A pair of elephants would require about 300 kilograms of bulky greenery per day. Enough meat must be stored for the various carnivores such as tigers, lions, jaguars and panthers. The 10,000 species of termites would have to be fed to ensure that they do not consume the ship itself! The giant panda would have to be fed only bamboo shoots. The koala must be fed only *fresh* eucalyptus leaves. Animals such as snakes, penguins and bats need to be fed with living food; so Noah would need additional storage space for rats, fishes and insects for these creatures. Removing the wastes and excrements of the animals in the ark would provide a logistical nightmare. How could pairs of all these be taken up the ark and looked after by only eight people (Noah, his wife, his three sons and their wives)? [40]

And what about terrestrial plants and vegetation? The immense weight of the floodwater would have destroyed them all. What kept the plant alive through the flood? It is naive and pointless to say that God kept these alive by miraculous means; for what is the reason then for Noah building the ark? If God could keep the plants and the fresh water fishes alive without Noah taking them into the ark, He surely could have kept all the rest alive without needing the ark. [41]

There are still more difficulties with the story. It fails to explain the distribution of animals after the flood; how did the animals get to their respective habitat after the flood? What an amazing coincidence that almost all marsupials end up in Australia. Why did the penguins head for the South Pole and not the North? Where did all the water go after the flood? What did the carnivores eat before the first pairs of their food had a chance to reproduce? What did the herbivores eat, since all the plants would have died during the flood?

It is obvious that the story of the deluge is simply a tale told by a pre-scientific tribe who had no idea of the totally impossible situation that would have developed had the story been true:

- *Impossible engineering*: The ship would have been structurally unsound.

- *Insurmountable space constraints*: There was no way more than one million pairs of animals could have fitted into the ark.

- *Unrealizable logistics*: It was impossible for the animals to have been transported into the ark, cleaned and fed by eight people or even by 800 people.

- *Unsound biology*: The current worldwide distribution of animals simply could not be explained by the flood.

- *Unsound physics*: Where did all the floodwaters go?

THE FLOOD MYTH II:
ORIGINS

The story of Noah is not even an original one. In the middle of the 19th century, archaeologists unearthed twelve ancient clay tablets in an excavation on the banks of the River Tigris. The tablets, written in an ancient Babylonian language, Akkadian, tell of the story of Gilgamesh – a Sumerian King who lived around the middle of the third millennium BCE.

What interests us here is the story told on the eleventh tablet. We are told that Gilgamesh, in his quest for immortality set out on a long journey to look for his ancestor, Utnapishtim. Utnapishtim was already bestowed with eternal life by the

---

[40] Plimer, *Telling Lies for God*: p108, 111-112, 121-123
      See also http://en.wikipedia.org/wiki/Wyoming_(schooner) (accessed on April 24, 2009)
[41] Howell-Smith, *In Search of the Real Bible*: p46

gods. Upon reaching the island of Utnapishtim's abode, Gilgamesh was told a story by his ancestor of a great flood that once swept the world. The similarities between this story and that of Genesis are astounding. We give a comparison below: [42]

- The behavior of mankind led the gods to destroy the world through a worldwide flood.

    The Epic of Gilgamesh
    In those days the world teemed, the people multiplied, the world bellowed like a wild bull, and the great god was aroused by the clamor. Enlil[43] heard the clamor and he said to the gods in the council "The uproar of mankind is intolerable and sleep is no longer possible by reason of the babble." So the gods agreed to exterminate mankind...

    Genesis 6:11-13
    The earth was corrupt before God, and the earth was filled with violence. God saw the earth, and saw that it was corrupt, for all flesh had corrupted their way on the earth. God said to Noah, "The end of all flesh has come before me, for the earth is filled with violence through them. Behold, I will destroy them with the earth."

- There was a single person singled out by the gods to be saved who was commanded to build a massive ark.

    The Epic of Gilgamesh
    Ea[44], because of his oath, warned me [i.e. Utnapishtim] in a dream "...O man of Shurrupak, son of Ubara-Tutu, tear down your house and built a ship; abandon wealth seek after life; scorn possessions save your life"

    Genesis 6:14a
    [God said to Noah,] "Make a ship of gopher wood."

- The dimensions, design and sealing material of the ark were described in some detail.

    The Epic of Gilgamesh
    "Let its dimensions be well measured."
    (In accordance with the command of the god Ea, Utnapishtim builds the ship and says):
    "On the fifth day, I laid the framework. One whole acre was her floor space. Ten dozen cubits the height of each of her walls. Ten dozen cubits each edge of the square deck. I laid out the outside shape and joined her together, I provided her with six decks, dividing her thus into

---

[42]   The excerpt from the Epic of Gilgamesh above are taken (depending on which reading is clearer) from three sources:
Keller, *The Bible As History*: p52-59; Sanders, *The Epic of Gilgamesh*: p108-113 & Gray, *Near Eastern Mythology*: p47-50
The full text of the Epic of Gilgamesh is also available in the internet: http://www.ancienttexts.org/library/mesopotamian/gilgamesh/

[43]   *Enlil* was the chief god of the Sumerian pantheon

[44]   Ea was another god in the Babylonian pantheon and is the half- brother of the chief god, Enlil

seven parts. Her floor plan I divided into nine parts...Six sar-measure of *pitch* I poured into the furnace."

Genesis 6:15-16
"This is how you shall make it. The length of the ship will be three hundred cubits, its breadth fifty cubits, and its height thirty cubits. You shall make a roof in the ship, and you shall finish it to a cubit upward. You shall set the door of the ship in its side. You shall make it with lower, second, and third levels."

Genesis 6:14b
"...You shall make rooms in the ship, and shall seal it inside and outside with *pitch.*"

- The main protagonist is commanded to bring samples of all living things onto the ark

  The Epic of Gilgamesh
  (The god Ea telling Utnapishtim)
  "Bring up the seed of all kinds of living things into the ship; the ship which you shall built."

  Genesis 6:19
  (Yahweh telling Noah)
  Of every living thing of all flesh, you shall bring two of every sort into the ship, to keep them alive with you.

- The ark is to house him, his kinfolk and all kinds of beasts.

  The Epic of Gilgamesh
  (Utnapishtim continues...)
  "All that I had I loaded, of the seed of all living things. I brought into the ship my whole family and kinsfolk. The cattle of the field, the beasts of the field, all craftsmen-I made them go up into it. I went into the ship and closed my door."

  Genesis 7:13-16
  In the same day Noah, and Shem, Ham, and Japheth, the sons of Noah, and Noah's wife, and the three wives of his sons with them, entered into the ship; they, and every animal after its kind, all the livestock after their kind, every creeping thing that creeps on the earth after its kind, and every bird after its kind, every bird of every sort. They went to Noah into the ship, by pairs of all flesh with the breath of life in them. Those who went in, went in male and female of all flesh, as God commanded him; and Yahweh shut him in.

- In the Akkadian version, the flood lasted seven days while in the Hebrew version the flood started seven days after Noah and his contingent got into the Ark.

  The Epic of Gilgamesh
  "Six days and six nights raged the wind, the flood, the cyclone devastated the land.

When the seventh day came, the cyclone, the flood, the battle was over...the sea became calm and the cyclone died away, the flood ceased."

Genesis 7:10-12
It happened after the seven days, that the waters of the flood came on the earth. ...The rain was on the earth forty days and forty nights.

Genesis 8:1-3
God made a wind to pass over the earth. The waters subsided. The deep's fountains and the sky's windows were also stopped, and the rain from the sky was restrained. The waters receded from the earth continually. After the end of one hundred fifty days the waters decreased.

- Both arks have windows that were opened after the rain had subsided.

> The Epic of Gilgamesh
> "I opened a window and light fell on my face..."

> Genesis 8:6
> It happened at the end of forty days, that Noah opened the window of the ship which he had made

- After the flood receded, both arks came to rest on a mountain.

> The Epic of Gilgamesh
> "...fourteen leagues distant there appeared a mountain, and there the ship grounded; on the mountain of Nisir the ship held fast, she held fast and did not budge."

> Genesis 8:4
> The ship rested in the seventh month, on the seventeenth day of the month, on Ararat's mountains.

- Both myths describe birds being released from the ark. The birds were released *a few times* from the ark once it came to rest on the mountain. Only in the last one are we told the bird never returned.

> The Epic of Gilgamesh
> "When the seventh day dawned I loosed a dove and let her go. She flew away but finding no resting place she returned. Then I loosed a swallow, and she flew away but finding no resting place she returned. I loosed a raven, she saw that the waters had retreated, she ate, she flew around, she cawed and she did not come back."

> Genesis 8:6-12
> It happened at the end of forty days, that Noah ... sent forth a raven. It went back and forth, until the waters were dried up from the earth. He sent forth a dove from him, to see if the waters were abated from the surface of the ground, but the dove found no place to rest her foot, and she returned to him into the ship...He stayed yet another seven days; and again he sent forth the dove out of the ship. The dove came back to him at evening, and, behold, in her mouth was an olive leaf plucked off. So Noah knew that the waters were abated from the earth. He stayed

yet another seven days, and sent forth the dove; and she didn't return to him anymore.

The obvious similarities could not have been, not by any stretch of imagination, due to coincidence. One of the accounts is clearly dependent on the other. So the question is this, which is the original and which is the copy? There are many reasons to believe that the Babylonian version is the original:

- The first is antiquity. The writing of the epic of Gilgamesh has been dated by archaeologists to around 2,000 BCE. It predates the Genesis account by at least a few centuries.[45]

- The second is the presence of loan words. The Akkadian word for pitch (or bitumen): *kofer*. This is precisely the word used in the Genesis story (Genesis 6:14b). Nowhere else in the Bible does the word *kofer* appear except in the story of the flood.[46]

- The third is the general flow of influence. We would expect the greater civilization to have a greater cultural influence on a lesser one. Compared to Babylonia, Israel was, as Cyrus Gordon said, a "backwater of sorts".

- The fourth reason is from the original source of the myth. Floods are common in the Mesopotamian plains; it is unusual in usually arid Israel. It is easy to see how the flood myth could have originated from some stories told in Babylonia, it is not so easy to see how anyone from Israel could have thought of that myth originally.

- Finally, the location of the story gives a clue to its origins. The geography of the ark story points towards its Mesopotamian origin. Noah's ark landed on Mount Ararat, which is at the headwaters of the Tigris and Euphrates.[47]

It is therefore conclusive that the story in Genesis was a direct descendent of the Babylonian story.[48]

The Akkadian tablet, like the story in Genesis, is a myth. There was, however, a brief period of respectability in the first half of the 20th century, given to the notion of

---

[45] The story of the twelve tablets was written around 2000 BCE. Even assuming "best case" biblical chronology, i.e. that Genesis was written by Moses himself, this brings the writing of Genesis to only about 1400 BCE. Thus the Akkadian tablet is earlier than the Genesis story. According to critical theologians, the earliest form of the Hebrew flood story was written only around 900 BCE. But the version as we have it in the Bible was not complete until the period of the exile c. 6th century BCE.

[46] Riedel et.al., *The Book of the Bible*: p29

[47] Gordon, *The Bible and the Ancient Near East*, p50

[48] Since then archaeologists have discovered two even earlier versions of the flood myths – the Sumerian Epic of Ziusudra, (c 2600 BCE) and the Akkadian Epic of Atrahasis (c 1900 BCE). Together with the Epic of Gilgamesh – the myths involve the gods causing a worldwide flood and a hero who built an ark saving himself, his family and some animals. The Epics of Ziusudra and Atrahasis do not survive in their complete forms and are today extant only in fragments. [see Cline, *From Eden to Exile*: p20-24; Hooke, *Middle Eastern Mythology*: p30-32]

the occurrence of an actual catastrophic flood. An archaeological expedition in 1929 led by Sir Charles Leonard Wooley (1880-1960) found at the site of the ancient city of Ur, a stratum of clean clay about eight feet thick. Wooley originally estimated the layer of silt to be about 400 miles long and about 100 miles wide. The layer was dated at around 4000 BCE. Had this been true, a flood of such a magnitude would certainly has qualified as "world-wide" to the ancient Babylonians, for the area estimated by Wooley represented the whole of the known world to them. However, subsequent expeditions have shown that the thick layer of silt is localized and was nowhere as widespread as Wooley first thought it to be.[49]

Biblical literalists continue to try and look for non-existent evidence of an obvious myth. One of the most sought after "evidence" is the remnants of Noah's Ark. These modern day Indiana Joneses travel to Turkey and Iran hoping to find remnants of the ancient mythical ship. Yet unlike the movie character, these men are religious fundamentalists with no training in the relevant fields of archaeology and geology. Needless to say their quests are characterized by wild exaggerated claims that are invariably shown to be wrong. We list here the claims of some modern "arkeologists":[50]

- In 1955, a Frenchman named Fernand Navarra claimed to have found a five-foot piece of wood on Mount Ararat which was initially dated by a Spanish laboratory to 3000 BCE. However, subsequent carbon-14 tests dated the wood to around 260-790 CE, much too late to be coming from a piece of Noah's ark.

- In a period spanning fourteen years, from 1977-1991, a nurse-anesthetist, Ron Wyatt, made multiple trips to Turkey looking for Noah's ark. In his study of a "boat shaped object" near Dogubayazit in Turkey – Wyatt claimed to have found the "horizontal deck support timbers" and even a rivet head with a washer around it! His claims have been shown to be manifestly false. Upon examining rock samples and photos from the site, Lorence Collins, a geologist from the California State University Northridge, showed that the formation has a natural origin.[51]

- In 2006, a former police officer, Bob Cornuke, believing that the actual Mount Ararat is Mount Suleiman in Iran, launched an expedition there. Like Wyatt, he claimed to have discovered a boat-like structure on the rock. He also claimed to be able to discern plant cell structures from thin sections of the rock! His claims have been dismissed by two English geologists, Kevin Pickering from University College London and Robert Spicer from the Open University. Upon examining the photos of the site, Pickering noted that the formation is made of "iron stained sedimentary rocks...laid down in a marine environment a long time ago." Similarly,

---

[49] Ward, *A Dictionary of Common Fallacies I*: p96-97
[50] Cline, *From Eden to Exile*, p30-31
[51] Collins, L. D. and Fasold, D. (1996). "Bogus 'Noah's Ark' from Turkey Exposed as a Common Geologic Structure" *Journal of Geoscience Education* **44**, 439-444 [URL: http://www.csun.edu/~vcgeo005/bogus.html - accessed on September 14, 2007]

Spicer called the "evidence" presented by Cornuke and his team "most unconvincing."

Was Noah actually an historical person? Again, archaeological evidence supplies the answer. In 1933 clay tablets were discovered in Mari, an ancient city in the Mesopotamian plain. In these tablets (there were about 20,000 discovered), the name Noah appeared many times; *as the name of a god.* In fact Noah's name is actually a musculanisation of the *goddess of rain*, Nuah.[52]

OTHER MYTHS IN GENESIS

There are two remaining myths in the first 11 chapters of Genesis; the story of Cain and Abel and the Tower of Babel.

The story of Cain and Abel, the first two offspring of Adam and Eve, is told in chapter 4 of Genesis. The problem with the story begins after Cain, the elder son, slew Abel out of jealousy (Genesis 4: 3-8).

Genesis 4:13-15
Cain said to Yahweh, "My punishment is greater than I can bear. Behold, you have driven me out this day from the surface of the ground. I will be hidden from your face, and I will be a fugitive and a wanderer in the earth. It will happen that whoever finds me will kill me." Yahweh said to him, "Therefore whoever slays Cain, vengeance will be taken on him sevenfold." Yahweh appointed a sign for Cain, lest any finding him should strike him.

The "mark of Cain" was placed by God to warn anyone against striking Cain. But we are told a little later (in Genesis 4:25) that Seth was only the third offspring of Adam and Eve:

Genesis 4:25
Adam knew his wife again. She gave birth to a son, and named him Seth, "for God has appointed me *another child* instead of Abel, for Cain killed him."

Note Seth was born to *replace* Abel. This means that in the whole world then there were only four people: Adam, Eve, Cain and Seth. So who was it the "mark of Cain" supposed to be a warning to?

A similar problem is raised for the verse below:

Genesis 4:16-17
Cain went out from Yahweh's presence, and lived in the land of Nod, east of Eden. Cain knew his wife. She conceived, and gave birth to Enoch....

Now where did Cain's wife come from? There is no mention till then that Adam and Eve had borne any other children apart from Cain and Abel. Driven to the wall,

---

[52]   Riedel et.al., *The Book of the Bible*: p30
        Harwood, *Mythology's Last Gods: Yahweh and Jesus*, p 132

fundamentalist apologists have had to come up with quite perverse *ad hoc* explanations. Firstly, they say, although it is not stated in Genesis at that point, Adam and Eve already had more children. Secondly, they say, Cain probably married his own sister (or niece!) - in short, driven to the wall, they suggest *incest* as the solution![53]

The solution to the Cain problem is simple: it is a myth. The science of evolution (living things always evolve in a population not in pairs) tells us that there was no Adam and Eve[54] and hence no Cain and Abel.

The myth about the Tower of Babel is told in Genesis 11:1-9. There the story is told of the descendants of Noah who settled in the land of Shinar (Babylonia) and decided to build a tower that was to "reach unto Heaven" (Genesis 11:4). God defeated their purpose by confounding their languages and scattering them over the face of the earth.

First, let us point out a contradiction here. Genesis 11:1 mentioned that there is only one language.

Genesis 11:1
The whole earth was of one language and of one speech.

Yet, only one chapter earlier we find the following verses:

Genesis 10:5
Of these were the islands of the nations divided in their lands, *everyone after his language*, after their families, in their nations.

Genesis 10:20
These are the sons of Ham, after their families, *after their languages*, in their lands, in their nations.

Genesis 10:31

---

[53] Archer, *Encyclopedia of Bible Difficulties*: p77
Torrey, *Difficulties in the Bible*: p44-48

[54] Some Christians might object here and say that science has *indeed* found Adam and Eve. What they are referring to is the so-called "mitochondrial Eve" and the "Y-chromosome Adam", actual ancestors derived from genetic comparison of various races of humans all over the world. However, this "Eve" is merely a woman whose mitochondrial DNA happens to be the one that survives in all of us – she was not the first human being. There were other women in her time that simply, through the vagaries of luck ("genetic drift"), did not have their mitochondrial DNA survive in any modern human. Similarly "Adam" is merely one living male among many whose non-recombining part of his Y-chromosome happens to be the ones that we all inherited. Estimates as to how many of these individual ancestors that supplied the unique parts of our modern genome varies between 2,000-10,000 (Oppenheimer, *Out of Eden*: p46) and 86,000 (Olsen, *Mapping Human History*: p27) Furthermore, "mitochondrial Eve" lived around 150,000 to 190,000 years ago while the earliest estimates for "Y-chromosome Adam" is 140,000 years (actual estimates for the "African Adam" range between 40,000 to 140,000 years ago). In short, the Adam and Eve discovered by science never met each other! (Ref: Wells, *Journey of Man*: p54-55, Oppenheimer, *Out of Eden*: p39-40)

These are the sons of Shem, after their families, *after their languages*, in their lands, after their nations.

The world, according to Genesis 10:5, already had multiple languages before Babel.

Second, the story is pre-scientific in the extreme. Note that the people wanted to build a tower that actually reached "unto heaven" (Genesis 11:4). Also note that God came down to look at the tower (Genesis 11:5). It is obvious that the reason why God confounded their language and scattered them was that he was afraid these people might actually reach heaven! As William Harwood notes:

> A modern god, knowing the distance even to the nearest star would laugh at such an enterprise, but the Yahweh of 920 BCE could hardly be blamed for being as ignorant as his biographer.[55]

The story probably originated from the experience of the original Hebrews upon seeing the mighty buildings in the cities of Babylon:

> The myth...reflects the attitude of nomads entering the fertile plains of the Delta, beholding with wonder and dread the soaring towers of Babylonian cities, and despising the multitudes speaking the various tongues of the ancient Near East.[56]

* * * * *

Our analysis in this chapter has shown us one undeniable fact: that the first eleven chapters of Genesis is pure mythology.

---

[55]   Harwood, *Mythology's Last Gods: Yahweh and Jesus*: p 135
[56]   Hooke, *Middle Eastern Mythology*: p138

Chapter Four
ARCHAEOLOGY

THE DEMISE OF "BIBLICAL ARCHAEOLOGY"

Many fundamentalists and evangelicals[1] are fond of claiming that the Bible has been "proven by archaeology" or that archaeology has never proven the Bible wrong. While there are *some* historical facts in the Bible (e.g. the account of the fall of Jerusalem in 587 BCE) it represents a gross misrepresentation of the current state of the science of archaeology to say that it has "never" contradicted the Bible. Indeed, there is now so much contrary evidence against the historical accuracy of the Bible that the term "biblical archaeology" has been discarded in professional archeology! [*Syro-Palestinian archaeology*[2] is becoming accepted as the more appropriate term.] The whole paradigm of archaeology in the Near East has shifted away from thinking of the Bible as a reliable archaeological field guide to that of a collection of ancient fairy tales and legends.

The BBC journalist Matthew Sturgis summarizes the current situation nicely in his book *It Ain't Necessarily So* (2001):

> A new generation of archaeologists has emerged...they are challenging the intellectual assumptions of their predecessors...During the years since World War II it has become harder and harder to escape this sense of doubt. The expected discoveries of specific biblical artifacts and buildings were simply not being made...Discrepancies between the biblical account and the ever increasing archaeological record become more noticeable and harder to ignore...Rather than using the Old Testament as a field guide, the current crop of archaeologists is increasingly putting the Bible aside...The very term biblical archaeology has become tainted, and is now rejected by many academics...The old quest to confirm the historical truths of the events in the Bible has been replaced by a new agenda: to build a full and detailed picture of life in the ancient Near East. If the Bible is consulted at all, it is approached with varying degrees of skepticism. The onus of proof has shifted: the text [of the Bible] is now considered historically unreliable until proven otherwise.[3]

---

[1] A little note on nomenclature here. *Fundamentalists* are those who believe that the Bible is without any error whatsoever. Evangelicals, strictly defined, are born again Christians whose views on the Bible range from strict fundamentalism to pure liberalism. However, the term "evangelical" has been used more and more by fundamentalists with PhD's to disassociate themselves from the negative connotation of the former term. The term "evangelical scholarship" is more or less synonymous with "fundamentalist apologetics." As Robert M. Price deliciously remarked in his book *The Reason Driven Life* (Prometheus Books, 2006: p45): "An evangelical is a fundamentalist who'll let you go to the movies." We will use the terms rather interchangeably in this book.

[2] Davis, *Shifting Sands*: p145
Moorey, *A Century of Biblical Archaeology*, p173-175

[3] Sturgis, *It Ain't Necessarily So*: p36-39

Over the last decade, quite a number of books have been published outlining this state of affairs.[4] Basically the main thesis of these books can be summarized as follows: much of what passed as history - such as Abraham and the "patriarchal narratives," Moses and the Exodus and the conquest of Canaan - is now considered, based on the mass of available archaeological evidence, to be largely mythical.[5]

One of the reasons why these stories in the Pentateuch are unreliable is that they were written many centuries after the events they describe. The verse quoted below reveals the lateness of Genesis:

Genesis 36:31
These are the kings who reigned in the land of Edom, before any king reigned over the children of Israel.

It is obvious from the verse above, the author was writing at a time when the Israelites already had, at least, one king. The first king of the Israelites was David who became king around 1000 BCE.[6] This means that the earliest possible date for the composition of the Pentateuch, or parts of it, would be the 10th century BCE. Scholars vary in their estimate on exactly when the oldest portion (called the "J" document) of the source document for these books was written. Some estimate the document to be written as early as the 10th century BCE (during the reign of Solomon, David's son), while others estimate it to have been written as late as the 6th century (during the time of the Babylonian exile). These estimates are not relevant to our current analysis. The only point worth noting is that the verse above, have set an upper limit on the date of composition of the Pentateuch.[7]

Now calculating from our table of biblical chronology (see Table 3.2), Abraham lived around the 23rd century BCE, while Moses lived around the 15th century BCE. (As a mark of the historical uncertainty surrounding these two, there exist many different estimates for these dates. Abraham has been estimated to live in the 25th, 21st, and the 16th century BCE; i.e. the estimates fall within a span of 1,000 years!

---

[4] Some examples:

H. Avalos, "Chapter 3: History and Archaeology: Fields Full of Holes," *The End of Biblical Studies*, Prometheus 2007

T.W. Davis, *Shifting Sands: The Rise and Fall of Biblical Archaeology*, Oxford 2004

A.D. Marcus, *The View from Nebo*, Little, Brown & Co 2000

M. Sturgis, *It Ain't Necessarily So*, Headline 2001

[5] Some of the more important books treating this subject are:

I. Finkelstein & N. A. Silberman *The Bible Unearthed*, Free Press 2001

N.P. Lemche, *The Israelites in History and Tradition*, Westminster John Knox, 1998

N.P. Lemche, *Prelude to Israel's Past*, Hendrickson, 1998

T.L. Thompson, *The Mythic Past*, Basic Books 1999

T.L. Thompson, *The Historicity of the Patriarchal Narratives*, Trinity 1973/2002

J. Van Seters, *Abraham in History and Tradition*, Yale UP, 1975

[6] This verse is taken from the portion of Genesis believed to have formed part of the original "J" document. The "J" document is generally believed to be the oldest source documents for the Pentateuch.

[7] Anderson, *A Critical Introduction to the Old Testament*: p34

Fox, *The Unauthorized Version*: p58

Livingston, *Dictionary of the Christian Church*: p143

Moses has been estimated to live either in the 15th or 13th century BCE.[8]) Taking the latest estimated dates for these patriarchs and the earliest estimated date for the composition of the "J" document - in other words, the "best case" scenario for believers - we still have a gap of 600 years between the "historical" Abraham and his story in Genesis and 300 years between "historical" Moses and his story in Genesis! The historian, Robin Lane Fox, has this to say about the effect of this time gap on the historicity of the Pentateuch:

> Its chances of being historically true are minimal because none of these sources [the source documents for the Pentateuch] was written from primary evidence or within centuries, perhaps a millennium, of what they tried to describe. How could an oral tradition have preserved true details across such a gap? At most, it might remember a great event or new departure: like... the Israelites Exodus from Egypt...As for...the exploits of Jacob or Abraham, there is no good reason to believe any of them.[9]

Save for very rough social memories of major events or turning points in the history of these people, all the rest are folklore accreted through centuries of oral transmission. Note that we are not simply dismissing the rest as myths without any evidence. In many cases where references were made in the Bible to events or things that could be verified historically, we find the stories to be false or anachronistic. Let us look at a few such examples.

THE PATRIARCHAL NARRATIVES

We will start by looking at the *patriarchal narratives*: the stories in Genesis about Abraham, Isaac, Jacob and Joseph. These characters used to be accepted as historical primarily because the narratives refer to elements that *seemed* historical.[10] These elements include references to actual place names such as the cities of Ur and Gerar, to real peoples such as the Philistines, the Hittites and the Arameans, to specific details about nomadic lifestyles such as domesticated camels and to customs which set them apart from other peoples, such as circumcision.

"Historical" elements such as these, according to the biblical archaeologists of yesteryear, separate the stories in the patriarchal narratives from the myths of many other religions in the region. However, modern archaeology no longer regards such arguments as convincing evidence for historicity. Let us see the reasons why.

---

[8]   Barthel, *What the Bible Really Says*: p78-79
       Stiebing, *Out of the Desert*: p33
[9]   Fox, *The Unauthorized Version*: p176
[10]   Lemche, *Prelude to Israel's Past*: p27

PLACES AND PEOPLES

The first thing we are told about Abraham is that he came from "Ur of the Chaldees":

> Genesis 11:26-28
> Terah lived seventy years, and became the father of Abram, Nahor, and Haran...Haran died before his father Terah in the land of his birth, in Ur of the Chaldees.

As we have seen above, estimates for Abraham's lifetime vary between the 25th and 16th century BCE. Now archaeologists do have evidence that Ur was already a major city even before 2,800 BCE – well before the time of Abraham. This is not the problem. The issue lies with the designation "of the Chaldees." The Chaldeans as a people *simply did not exist* until long after the time of Abraham; around the eighth to seventh century BCE.[11]

At the very least, this anachronism suggests that the final form of the story we find in Genesis must have been written later than the 8th or 7th century BCE.

Next we discuss an incident from the story of Isaac, son of Abraham:

> Genesis 26:1
> There was a famine in the land, besides the first famine that was in the days of Abraham. Isaac went to Abimelech king of the Philistines, to Gerar.

Isaac was born when Abraham was 100 years old (Genesis 21:5). The events narrated above would have happened (if it did happen) somewhere between 24th and 15th century BCE, depending on where Abraham is located in time. (The Biblical chronology points to 24th century BCE.)

Archaeological evidence shows that the Philistines did not have any settlements in the coastal plain of Canaan until after 13th century BCE. Archeological excavation at Gerar (now identified as Tel Haror northwest of Beersheba) shows that it was no more than a "small, quite insignificant" village during the initial settlement of the Philistines during the Iron Age I (1150-900 BCE). Gerar only became a significant city in the 7th century BCE.[12]

The archaeological finds tell us that there were *no city of Gerar* and *no king of the Philistines* to meet with Isaac during the historical period in which he would have lived!

There are many such anachronisms and mistakes regarding people and places in the patriarchal narratives – betraying its late composition. Genesis 31:20 refers to Isaac's brother-in-law as "Laban the Aramean." Yet the region became Aramean territory only towards the end of the second millennium BCE, at least 500 years too late for the story. Genesis chapter 23 relates the story of Abraham purchasing a land in Hebron as a burial place from "Ephron the Hittite." It also mentioned that the Hittites were "the people of the land" (Genesis 23:7). Yet Hebron, which is in

---

[11]   Cline, From Eden to Exile: p56-57
       Lemche, *Prelude to Israel's Past*: p39, 62
[12]   Finkelstein & Silberman, *The Bible Unearthed*: p37

Palestine, was never part of the Hittite empire. That empire did not extend south of the Beirut-Damascus line.[13]

DOMESTICATED CAMELS

There are two references to domesticated camels in the story of Abraham:

Genesis 12:14-16
It happened that when Abram had come into Egypt, the Egyptians saw that the woman was very beautiful. The princes of Pharaoh saw her, and praised her to Pharaoh; and the woman was taken into Pharaoh's house. He dealt well with Abram for her sake. He had sheep, cattle, male donkeys, male servants, female servants, female donkeys, and camels.

Genesis 24:10-11
The servant took ten *camels*, of his *master's* camels, and departed, having a variety of good things of his master's with him. He arose, and went to Mesopotamia, to the city of Nahor. *He made the camels kneel down outside the city* by the well of water at the time of evening, the time that women go out to draw water...

As noted earlier, Abraham's lifetime has been estimated anywhere between the 25th century BCE and the 16th century BCE. The above passage implies that camels were already domesticated and in use during that time in the regions where Abraham lived. However, based on every other available evidence we have, tame camels were simply unknown during Abraham's time. Egyptian texts of that era mentioned nothing of them. Even in Mari; the kingdom that is situated next to the Arabian deserts; which would have had the greatest use for camels; and of which archaeologists have a large collection of documents; not a single mention is made of camels in contemporaneous text. In fact, it was only in the 11th century BCE that references to camels started to appear in cuneiform texts and reliefs. After the 11th century, references to camels become more and more frequent.[14]

We find a similar anachronism in the story of Joseph – the great grandson of Abraham. Genesis 37 relates how Joseph's brothers, jealous of him being a favorite of their father, planned to sell him off to slavery. The brothers initially threw Joseph into a pit (Genesis 37:22-23). They then left the pit for a while and following that:

Genesis 37:25-28
They [Joseph's brothers] sat down to eat bread, and they lifted up their eyes and looked, and saw *a caravan of Ishmaelites* was coming from Gilead, *with their camels bearing spices and balm and myrrh*, going to carry it down to Egypt. Judah said to his brothers, "What profit is it if we kill our brother and conceal his blood? Come, and let's sell him to the Ishmaelites, and not let our hand be on him; for he is our brother, our flesh." His brothers listened to him. Midianites who were

---

13   Lemche, *Prelude to Israel's Past*: p64

14   Barthel, *What the Bible Really Says*: p79
    Finkelstein & Silberman, *The Bible Unearthed*: p37
    Keller, *The Bible As History*: p168
    Lemche, *Prelude to Israel's Past*: p64

merchants passed by, and they drew and lifted up Joseph out of the pit, and sold Joseph to the Ishmaelites for twenty pieces of silver. They brought Joseph into Egypt.

As we have shown above, camels were not yet domesticated during that time. Excavations in the southern coastal plain of Israel found that camel bones increased dramatically only in the *7th century BCE*. More importantly these bones were of *adult* camels, as one would expect of beast of burden used in traveling to different places. If they were bred there one would expect to find a scattering of young camel bones as well.

This is further supported by Assyrian sources that mentioned camels being used as beast of burden in caravans during that time. The items being traded, gum, balm and resin [written as "spices and balm and myrrh" in the translation above] were Arabian exports that were traded commonly only from the 8th and 7th century BCE under the control of the Assyrian empire.

According to the biblical chronology, this event (Joseph being sold to the Ishmaelites) happened 268 years after the birth of Abraham.[15] Assuming the latest possible date for Abraham (around 15th century BCE), this brings us only to the mid 12th century BCE. This is more than a century before the domestication of the camel and it would be another *500 years* before Arabic (*Ishmaelites* is the Bible's name for Arabs) camel caravan trade in gum, balm and resin, could be referred to in an "incidental manner" as above.[16]

This mention of the Arab camel caravan trade and the Arab traders buying Joseph in Genesis 37 cannot be historical as it stands due to this salient anachronism.

Fundamentalists continue to challenge these findings, claiming that camel domestication could have happened earlier in the ancient near east. This flies against the evidence and against the general consensus among archaeologists and historians. This consensus can be summed up by two quotes.

The first quote about the domestication of camels is from, Lawrence Stager, Dorot Professor of the Archaeology of Israel and Director of the Semitic Museum at Harvard University, who had excavated in Israel, Tunisia and Cyprus, in his article in the recent book *Oxford History of the Biblical World* (1998):

> W.F. Albright's Assessment, based on contemporary texts and limited faunal remains, that dromedary camels became important to the caravan trade only towards the final centuries of the second millennium BCE is still valid.[17]

---

[15] Genesis 37:2 says Joseph was 17 years old when he was sold off to the Ishmaelites. We are told later on that his father, Jacob, was 130 when he met the Pharaoh (Genesis 47:9). This was nine years (Genesis 41:53, 45:6) after a 30 year old Joseph found favor with the same Pharaoh (Genesis 41:46). This means that Joseph was born when Jacob was 91 years old. Jacob, in turn, was born when his father Isaac was 60 years old (Genesis 25:24-26) And Isaac was delivered when his father Abraham was 100 years old. (Genesis 21:5). Adding all these numbers give us 268 (=100+60+91+17).

[16] Finkelstein & Silberman, *The Bible Unearthed*: p37

[17] Coogan (ed), *Oxford History of the Biblical World* : p109

The second is from another archaeologist, Wayne T. Pitard of the University of Illinois, has this to say about camels and their uses:

> Scholars have also observed a number of anachronisms in the stories, another characteristic of oral literature...Camel caravans are mentioned in Genesis 26 and 37, but camels were probably not used before the beginning of the iron age (1200 BCE) when Israel was already emerging as a nation.[18]

CIRCUMCISION

Finally, we will look at the story in the patriarchal narratives relating to the institution of circumcision.

> Genesis 17: 9-11
> God said to Abraham, "As for you, you will keep my covenant, you and your seed after you throughout their generations. This is my covenant, which you shall keep, between me and you and your seed after you. Every male among you shall be circumcised. You shall be circumcised in the flesh of your foreskin. It will be a token of the covenant between me and you."

We know that circumcision was widely practiced in ancient times in the Fertile Crescent. In particular, the Egyptians and the Canaanites, the people Abraham would have had most contact with, practiced the rite. How could the act of circumcision be "a sign of the covenant" between God and Abraham when everyone else was doing it? It was only during the time of the Babylonian captivity, during the 6th century, that this custom could have set the Jews apart. For the Babylonians of that time did not practice circumcision.[19] The story of circumcision being a sign of covenant between God and Abraham is another late addition to the legend.

CONCLUSION ON THE PATRIARCHAL NARRATIVES

What can we conclude from the above? Firstly, *at the very least*, we can conclude that many elements in the patriarchal narratives are unhistorical. The story of Isaac meeting the Philistine king in Gerar for instance *could not have happened* because there was simply no Philistine settlement in Canaan during that time and Gerar has not yet existed. The story of how Joseph got shipped to Egypt is in the same boat (pardon the pun). There were simply no Arabic camel caravan trade groups during the time of Joseph.

Secondly, there is a more disturbing (for believers) conclusion. Thomas Thompson, Professor of Old Testament at the University of Copenhagen, noted that *if* the specific references in the patriarchal narratives have been shown to be anachronistic, *then* they add nothing to the story; *but* these very references were the *historical anchors* that supposedly rooted the narratives into history in the first place.

---

[18]   Coogan (ed), *Oxford History of the Biblical World* : p28

[19]   Asimov, *Asimov's Guide to the Bible*: p80
Barthel, *What the Bible Really Says*: p77-78
Riedel et.al., *The Book of the Bible*: p205-206

Without them how are we to distinguish the narratives from other completely mythical folk tales?[20]

The above examples show what we would generally expect from a document written many centuries after the events with only an oral tradition to support it: myths born of later generations become incorporated into the original core story until the historical truth is crushed beyond recognition beneath the weight of mythological falsehoods.

MOSES AND THE EXODUS

Modern archaeology, in line with critical historical scholarship, no longer accepts the major events described in the Pentateuch about Moses' life as historical. We will look first at the origins of Moses' birth story and the Mosaic laws before providing the current *status quaestionis* in archaeology on the historicity of the Exodus.

THE STORY OF MOSES' BIRTH

The story of Moses' birth is given in Exodus chapter 2:

> Exodus 2:2-6,10
> The woman conceived, and bore a son. When she saw that he was a fine child, she hid him three months. When she could no longer hide him, she took a papyrus basket for him, and coated it with tar and with pitch. She put the child in it, and laid it in the reeds by the river's bank. His sister stood far off, to see what would be done to him. Pharaoh's daughter came down to bathe at the river. Her maidens walked along by the riverside. She saw the basket among the reeds, and sent her handmaid to get it. She opened it, and saw the child, and behold, the baby cried. She had compassion on him, and said, "This is one of the Hebrews' children."

There is a legend of the founder of the Semitic dynasty of Akkad, King Sargon, which dates to the third millennium BCE and is certainly earlier than the story in Exodus. This legend was found on Neo-Babylonian cuneiform tablets dated to the 1st millennium BCE. This is how the tablets sound like, in English:

> Sargon, mighty King of Akkad, am I. My mother was of mixed blood; I never knew my father...My city is Azupiranu, on the banks of the Euphrates. My mother conceived and she secretly bore me. She put me into a basket of rushes, and sealed its lid with tar. She cast me into the river which did not drown me. The river swept me to Akiki, the drawer of water. Akiki, the drawer of water scooped me up in his pitcher. Akiki, the drawer of water raised me as his son.[21]

Here, like the stories of the flood, creation and paradise, the parallels are amazing:

- The mother had a baby in secret.

- Due to dire circumstances, the baby had to be cast away.

---

20   Finkelstein & Silberman, *The Bible Unearthed*: p38
21   Riedel et.al., *The Book of the Bible*: p27-28

- This was done by making a basket out of bulrushes and sealing it with tar.
- The baby was put into the basket and left adrift on the river.
- The baby was discovered by the person who became his foster parent.

Given the similarities above, it is obvious that the story of Moses' birth is based on the legend of Sargon. There can be no historical truth in stories which are used, repeatedly on different persons, by ancient cultures to glorify their heroes. As Werner Keller, the author of *The Bible as History*, admits:

> The basket story is an old Semitic folk-tale. It was handed down by word of mouth for many centuries...It is nothing more than the frills with which posterity has always loved to adorn the lives of great men.[22]

THE BABYLONIAN SOURCE OF THE MOSAIC LAWS

Everyone is familiar with Moses receiving the Ten Commandments in two stone tablets from God in Mount Sinai. Not everyone knows that this story is originally Babylonian. One of the most well known ancient code of law was the *Code of Hammurabi*, so named after the Amorite king Hammurabi who lived around 1700 BCE. On the great Babylonian stone monument, known as the stele of Hammurabi, a drawing inscribed on it shows the great Amorite King receiving the *tablets of the law* from the sun god, Shamash. The similarity does not end here. On the stele too is inscribed the laws that made up the Code of Hammurabi. The general similarity between the code and The "Book of the Covenant" (Exodus chapters 21 to 23) and the legal codes of the books of Leviticus and Deuteronomy cannot be denied. In some cases, even the words used are uncannily close to one another. For example take this one from the Babylonian code on the principle of an-eye-for-an-eye:

> If a citizen shall put out the eye of another, then let his own eye be put out.
> If a citizen shall knock out the teeth of another who is higher in rank, then let his own teeth be knocked out.[23]

This closely parallels one of the Lord's commands in Exodus:

> Exodus 21:23-24
> But if any harm follows, then you must take life for life, eye for eye, tooth for tooth, hand for hand, foot for foot...

Here is another example, the code of Hammurabi gives the following principle:

> If a citizen steals the son of another citizen, he shall be put to death.[24]

---

[22]   Keller, *The Bible As History*: p122-123
[23]   Barthel, *What the Bible Really Says*: p119
       Riedel et.al., *The Book of the Bible*: p34
[24]   Riedel et.al., *The Book of the Bible*: p31-32

The principle and wording is closely followed in Deuteronomy:

Deuteronomy 24:7
If a man be found stealing any of his brothers of the children of Israel...then that thief shall die.

The Mosaic laws were clearly written under the influence of the Babylonian code.[25]

THE EXODUS

Exodus chapters 1 through 12 tell the story of the miraculous escape of the Israelites under the leadership of Moses from Egypt. It is this story that provides the main anchor for Israelite identity as a people and as a religion. What do the textual and archaeological data tell us about the event described in Exodus?

Until recently, most biblical scholars and biblical archaeologists took it for granted that, however much the story may have been overlaid by myths, there was an historical core to it. Until the late 1980's even skeptical scholars accepted the idea that there may have been an "historical kernel" to the story of the Exodus. However, since the last decade of the 20th century, new archeological evidence has led most mainstream archaeologists to doubt the historicity of any type of mass Exodus of the Israelites from Egypt.[26]

Before presenting the archaeological evidence on the historicity of the Exodus, we should point out that even a casual reading of the account in the Pentateuch would raise doubts as to its general historical veracity.

By the time the different strands of tradition were put in writing, many of the details had already been lost or corrupted. How else would we explain the following discrepancies?

- The name of Moses' father-in-law is no longer known for we have two different names for him:

    Exodus 3:1 (also 18:1)
    Now Moses was keeping the flock of *Jethro*, his father-in-law, the priest of Midian...

    Numbers 10:29 (also Judges 4:11)
    Moses said to *Hobab*, the son of Reuel the Midianite, Moses' father-in-law...

- There are two different accounts of the burial of Moses' brother-in-law, Aaron:

---

[25]   Barthel, *What the Bible Really Says*: p118-119
       Hooke, *Middle Eastern Mythology: p147*
       Riedel et.al., *The Book of the Bible*: p31
[26]   Fox, *The Unauthorized Version*: p176
       Laughlin, *Archaeology and the Bible*: p86-87
       Stiebing, *Out of the Desert*, p197

THE REJECTION OF PASCAL'S WAGER

Numbers 33: 38 (Also Numbers 20:22-29)
Aaron the priest went up into *Mount Hor* at the commandment of Yahweh,
and *died there...*

Deuteronomy 10:6
The children of Israel traveled from Beeroth Bene Jaakan to *Moserah. There
Aaron died*, and there he was buried...

That Moserah and Mount Hor are not the same place can be seen from the fact that
Numbers 33:30-37 placed the former *six stages before* Mount Hor.[27]

THE EXODUS – ARCHAEOLOGICAL EVIDENCE

The Bible apparently gives a very exact date for the Exodus:

I Kings 6:1
It happened in the four hundred and eightieth year after the children of Israel were
come out of the land of Egypt, in the fourth year of Solomon's reign over Israel, in
the month Ziv, which is the second month, that he began to build the house of
Yahweh.

Correlating this with the other dates in the Bible (see the Biblical Chronology given in
table 3.2 in the previous chapter) gives this as 1495 BCE. Correlation of the dates of
the Israelite Kings with external sources (Egyptian and Assyrian) using I Kings 6:1
gives a date for the exodus half a century later: 1440 BCE.[28] However, the Bible also
says that the Israelites were forced by the Egyptians to build the city of Ramses:

I Exodus 8:11
Now there arose a new king over Egypt, who didn't know Joseph. He said to his
people, "Behold, the people of the children of Israel are more and mightier than we.
Come, let us deal wisely with them, lest they multiply, and it happen that when any
war breaks out, they also join themselves to our enemies, and fight against us, and
escape out of the land." Therefore they set taskmasters over them to afflict them
with their burdens. They built storage cities for Pharaoh: Pithom and Raamses.

Now the first Egyptian Pharoah named Ramses came to power only in 1320 BCE. It
would be impossible to build a city of that name before that time.[29] However, there is

---

Stiebing, *Out of the Desert*: p20
28 Finkelstein & Silberman, *The Bible Unearthed*: p56
29 These two reasons are also why attempts to point to equate the Hyksos - a line of Semitic
Kings who ruled Egypt from the mid 17th to the mid 16th centuries BCE - with the
Israelites fail. Firstly, the Hyksos were expelled from Egypt into Canaan around 1570 by
Pharoah Amose. This is too early for any of the biblical chronology to work – even
taking the oldest gets one to only 1495 BCE. Secondly, the specific detail about building
the city of Ramses as we have seen could not have been undertaken before there was any
"Ramses"! It is possible, of course, that the violent expulsion of the Hyksos became
embedded in the folktales of the Canaanites people and its broad outlines of entry into
Egypt and violent expulsion forms the basis for the oral tales that eventually became the
Exodus narrative. But the details of the Exodus: Moses, the forty-year trek in Sinai and

evidence from Egyptian sources that a city called Pi-Ramses was built under Ramses II who was Pharoah from 1279-1213 BCE. The story of the use of Israelites as forced labor to build the city could only happen during this time.

Furthermore, there is the testimony of a 7-½ foot stela made of black granite found in Merneptah's Temple in Thebes in 1896. Dated to around 1208 BCE, the stela, erected to commemorate the military victory of Pharoah Merneptah, son and successor of Ramses II, tells of a violent Egyptian conquest of Canaan. This is the relevant part for our purposes:

> The Canaan has been plundered with every sort of evil;
> Ashkelon has been overcome;
> Gezer has been captured;
> Yanoam is made non-existent;
> *Israel is laid waste and his seed is not;*

The stela says nothing about an Israelite escape from Egypt but merely that they were in Canaan before 1208 BCE. Bracketed by the dates of the Pi-Ramses and the Merneptah Stela, the Exodus, if it happened at all, had to happen around the end of the 13th century BCE.[30]

However, the moment we start looking for sources outside the Bible for this event, we come up empty handed. Now according to Exodus 12:40, the Israelites lived in Egypt for 430 years. Yet for all this time, there is simply no literary and archaeological evidence outside the Hebrew Scriptures that records the sojourn of the Israelites in Egypt. As the archaeologists Israel Finkelstein and Neil Silberman noted:

> [W]e have no clue, not even a single word, about the early Israelites *in* Egypt: neither in monumental inscriptions on the walls of temples, nor in tomb inscriptions, nor in papyri. Israel is absent – as a possible foe of Egypt, as a friend, or as an enslaved nation.[31]

It is amazing that *four centuries* of settlement did not leave a single trace of evidence. When we come to the actual Exodus, things are even worse. According to the Pentateuch, more than a million people were involved in the Exodus:

> Exodus 12:37 (Also Numbers 1:45-46)
> The children of Israel traveled from Rameses to Succoth, about six hundred thousand on foot who were men, besides children.

With 600,000 men, besides children and presumably women, we are talking about an Exodus of more than *one million people*. We are also told (Joshua 5:6) that this one

---

the locations the Israelites went through, are all pieces of historical fiction. [Finkelstein & Silberman, *The Bible Unearthed*: p54-57]

[30] Finkelstein & Silberman, *The Bible Unearthed*: p56-57
Marcus, *The View from Nebo*: p56
Laughlin, *Archaeology and the Bible*: p87,90
Sturgis, *It Ain't Necessarily So*: p104

[31] Finkelstein & Silberman, *The Bible Unearthed*: p60

million plus wandered for forty years in the wilderness in Sinai Surely more than a million people wandering around for forty years would have left some traces for archaeologists to find. Yet, not a single piece of archeological evidence has been found. This is not for want of trying. Between 1967, when Israel captured the Sinai Peninsula from Egypt, and 1982, when it was returned in the peace treaty, Israeli archaeologists made dozens of expeditions throughout the peninsula. Yet, not a single shred of evidence for an ancient Israelite presence was found.[32]

The case is not helped by arguing that the numbers stated in Exodus may have been exaggerated and that these people were mainly *wandering* in the desert without any permanent station.

Firstly, modern archaeological techniques, as archaeologists Finkelstein and Silberman point out, are capable of detecting even the smallest remains of hunter-gatherers and pastoral nomads all over the world. Secondly, in this case, even a relatively small group of escaped slaves, would not have escaped detection by the Egyptians. Archaeologists have discovered a letter dated to 13th century BCE from an Egyptian border guard who reported the escape of two slaves from the city of Rameses into the desert. Thirdly, although the Pentateuch do describe wanderings in the desert, 38 out of the 40 years was supposedly spent in one location: Kadesh-Barnea (Numbers 13:26, 20:1, 20:14; Deuteronomy 1:46.). The location of Kadesh-Barnea has been safely identified. Despite many expeditions and digs over the entire area, no evidence of occupation earlier than the 10th century BCE – 300 years after the supposed Exodus – has surfaced. Ezion-Geber, which the ancient Israelites supposedly encamped (Numbers 33:35), is another site that has been identified by archaeologists. Yet here too no artifacts dating to the time of the Exodus can be found.[33] Finally, despite numerous digs on Mount Sinai, on the southern tip of Sinai Peninsula, no evidence has been found of any ancient Israelite presence there.[34]

It is not that the archaeologists found nothing in Sinai dating to the 13th century. In fact much evidence about the situation in Sinai was discovered. What they found is further evidence that the Exodus story is myth. Elizier Oren, an Israeli archaeologist, led expeditions over a period of ten years and studied more than 1300 sites on northern coast of Sinai. He found ancient campsites, forts, cities, cemeteries and granaries for the Egyptian army. This infrastructure allowed the Egyptian army to cross the Sinai Peninsula quickly and with ease. Contemporary Egyptian texts tell us that the Egyptian troops could reach Gaza from the eastern delta (some 250 kilometers) in only ten days. Excavations in Canaan also found Egyptian strongholds dating to the time of the Exodus and conquest. In short, the evidence shows us that in the 13th century Egypt was at the height of its powers and had complete control over not only Egypt but also Canaan. Throughout the period of the New Kingdom (c1569-

---

[32]   Marcus, *The View from Nebo*: p75
       Laughlin, *Archaeology and the Bible*: p91
       Sturgis, *It Ain't Necessarily So*: p72

[33]   Finkelstein & Silberman, *The Bible Unearthed*: p61-63
       Marcus, *The View from Nebo*: p56
       Laughlin, *Archaeology and the Bible*: p90-92
       Sturgis, *It Ain't Necessarily So*: p71-72

[34]   Finkelstein and Silberman, *The Bible Unearthed*, Appendix B: p326-328

1076 BCE), Egyptian armies have been known to march through Canaan as far north as the Euphrates in Syria. From the 15th to the 11th century BCE, Canaan was a province of Egypt!

It is important here to pause and let this evidence sink in and see how it relates to the story of the Exodus and the Conquest of Canaan (see below). If Canaan was under complete control of the Egyptians throughout this period, then the Israelites could not have escaped from Egyptian rule. They would be merely leaving one region and entering another – all under the administrative control of the empire of Ramses II![35]

William Dever, an archaeologist normally associated with the more conservative end of Syro-Palestinian archaeology, has labeled the question of historicity of Exodus "dead."[36] Israeli archaeologist Ze'ev Herzog, provides the current consensus view on the historicity of the Exodus:

> The Israelites never were in Egypt. They never came from abroad. This whole chain is broken. It is not a historical one. It is a later legendary reconstruction – made in the seventh century [BCE] – of a history that never happened.[37]

Since the whole story of the Exodus itself is unhistorical, we can safely dismiss the stories of the miracles [the parting of the Red Sea (Exodus 14:21), the manna from heaven (Exodus 16:15-35) and the supply of water from the Rock in Horeb (Exodus 17:7) as mythical additions to an already fictitious account.

From the previous chapter and this one, we can see that *all* of the Pentateuch is virtually devoid of real history, as Niels Peter Lemche, Professor of Old Testament Studies at the University of Copenhagen, concluded:

> [T]he Old Testament is a poor source for constructing the history of Palestine and Syria during the Bronze Age. The historian has virtually nothing with which to work. Thus, it is useless to mine the Old Testament narratives for material to reconstruct that period. Instead, historians should look for other sources. The narratives in the Pentateuch will not and cannot pretend to be historical documents pertaining to Israel's past.[38]

JOSHUA AND THE CONQUEST OF CANAAN

The Book of Joshua, as we know, narrates the story of Moses' successor, Joshua and his conquest of Canaan. According to the biblical chronology, Joshua's conquest would be placed around 1450 BCE.[39] Estimates for its actual date vary between 1450

---

[35] Finkelstein & Silberman, *The Bible Unearthed*: p60-61
Marcus, *The View from Nebo*: p76
Sturgis, *It Ain't Necessarily So*: p69-70
[36] Quoted in Laughlin, *Archaeology and the Bible*: p92
[37] Quoted in Sturgis, *It Ain't Necessarily So*: p74
[38] Lemche, *Prelude to Israel's Past*: p65
[39] The traditional dating for the conquest of Canaan is derived thus: now from the fourth year of Solomon's reign to the fall of Jerusalem, which can be precisely dated to 587 BCE, to Nebuchadnezzar is 430 years. From Solomon's fourth year to the Exodus is

and 1200 BCE[40] . The author of Joshua, as we shall see in the next chapter, is unknown. We can, however, fix an earliest possible date for its writing; or, at least, the writing of some of the source documents that were used in the writing of Joshua. One clue is found in the Joshua 10:12. Here a reference is made to a document called the "Book of Jashar". Whatever else this book may contain, we do know, from II Samuel 1:18 that the Book of Jashar contains the poetic lamentations of David. Therefore, the Book of Jashar must have been compiled *after* the time of David, i.e. after the 10th century BCE. Therefore, the Book of Joshua, or one of its source documents, was written at least three centuries after the events it purports to describe. Modern scholarship dates the final form of Joshua to around 550 BCE.[41] So, we have every reason to be skeptical of the chronicles in this book: we do not know the identity of the author(s) and the time gap between the events and their actual documentation is too long for firsthand accounts to survive.

The incidents related in Joshua are those that could conceivably be verified by archaeology. We are told, for instance, in the book of Joshua chapter 6 that he made the walls of Jericho tumble, by having his men circle the city seven times and blowing their trumpets:

Joshua 6:1-5,15-21
Now Jericho was tightly shut up because of the children of Israel. No one went out, and no one came in. Yahweh said to Joshua, "Behold, I have given Jericho into your hand, with its king and the mighty men of valor. All your men of war shall march around the city, going around the city once. You shall do this six days. Seven priests shall bear seven trumpets of rams' horns before the ark. On the seventh day, you shall march around the city seven times, and the priests shall blow the trumpets. It shall be that when they make a long blast with the ram's horn, and when you hear the sound of the trumpet, all the people shall shout with a great shout; and the wall of the city shall fall down flat, and the people shall go up every man straight before him."

It happened on the seventh day, that they rose early at the dawning of the day, and marched around the city in the same way seven times. Only on this day they marched around the city seven times. It happened at the seventh time, when the

---

given in I Kings 6:1 as 480 years. This makes 910 years from the fall of Jerusalem to the Exodus. If we minus 40 years for the wanderings of the Israelites before the start of the conquest (Joshua 5:6), this gives 870 years. Thus the date of the start of the conquest would be (587 + 870 years) 1457 BCE.

[40] The earlier date was suggested for the conquest by scholars after it was realized that a 15th century or early 14th century "conquest" does not coincide well with historical and archaeological evidence of Palestine. For it was during the 15th to the 13th century that Egyptian control of the Palestine was at its peak. (see Steibing p53). The chaotic situation that prevailed from circa 1200 to 1050 BCE seems to allow for conquest, settlement and the period of the "judges". The later portion of this period would be too close period of the united monarchy under Saul, David and Solomon (between 1050-920BCE) and would leave no room for the period of the "Judges." Thus, conservative scholars have chosen 1200 BCE as the "best compromise" although it does not agree with the time frame given by I Kings 6:1.

[41] Anderson, *A Critical Introduction to the Old Testament*; p58
Parmalee, *A Guidebook to the Bible*: p38

priests blew the trumpets, Joshua said to the people, "Shout, for Yahweh has given you the city! The city shall be devoted, even it and all that is in it, to Yahweh...."

So the people shouted, and the priests blew the trumpets. It happened, when the people heard the sound of the trumpet, that the people shouted with a great shout, and the wall fell down flat, so that the people went up into the city, every man straight before him, and they took the city. They utterly destroyed all that was in the city, both man and woman, both young and old, and ox, and sheep, and donkey, with the edge of the sword.

There was a flurry of excitement when, in 1930, a British archaeological expedition led by John Gerstang on the ancient site of Jericho found a collapsed defensive wall and a destroyed city at the site. Based on some vessels broken pieces of pottery found in a few houses built over the fortifications and in tombs, Gerstang dated the destruction to around 1400 BCE, just right at the point where biblical chronology had predicted. This discovery was hailed by some as proving that "the Bible was right after all".[42]

However, in the 1950s another British expedition to the site, led by Kathleen Kenyon, showed that Gerstang's interpretation of the pottery evidence had been wrong. She showed conclusively that the walls and the city were destroyed almost 1,000 years earlier, in 2300 BCE! Kenyon's interpretation of the pottery evidence is today accepted by all archaeologists as the correct one. The site excavated by Gerstang could not have been contemporaneous with Joshua.[43] For the period between 1400 and 1300 BCE, Kenyon's team found only one little building (dated to 1,320 BCE) and a few reused old tombs. After 1300 BCE, Jericho was not even settled at all. She concluded that Jericho was almost a "ghost town" in the period between 1550 to 1200 BCE. Joshua's men would have found either a few small huts or nothing at all in Jericho. They would certainly not have found a walled and fortified city. Therefore, one of the most dramatic events in the Joshua narrative, the fall of the wall of Jericho, is a piece of historical fiction.[44]

---

[42] The German journalist, Werner Keller, for instance included Kenyon's discovery in his book *The Bible as History* (1956). The book has a presumptuous subtitle: *Archaeology Confirms the Book of Books*! The impression one gets from reading Keller's book is that archaeology is continuously discovering things that show the biblical depiction to be true. However, as we have seen earlier on the "discovery" or an ancient Mesopotamian flood by Leonard Wooley and now on the walls of Jericho, more often than not these findings and especially their interpretations supporting the biblical narrative have been shown to be wrong.

[43] Kenyon did find that the wall was destroyed a second time around 1550-1500 BCE. However, even this date is at least 100 years too early for the traditional date (c1400 BCE) or the more modern date (c 1250 BCE) of the conquest. The second destruction has been shown to be part of the Egyptian campaign of expelling the "Hyksos" around the mid sixteenth century BCE. [Dever, *Who Were the Early Israelites*: p45-46; Sturgis, *It Ain't Necessarily So*: p58-59]

[44] Davidson & Leaney, *Biblical Criticism*: p46
Dever, *Who Were the Early Israelites*: p45-46
Fox, *The Unauthorized Version*: p226-227
Stiebing, *Out of the Desert*: p46-47
Sturgis, *It Ain't Necessarily So*: p58-59

Current archaeological digs at Jericho by a joint Italian-Palestinian team only served to confirm the dates and conclusions derived by Kenyon.[45] The comment by archaeologist William Dever on the non-existence of Jericho during the supposed time of the conquest is delicious:

> I always reassure those who need it that here we have a stupendous "miracle": Joshua destroyed a site that was not even there.[46]

The same "fate" is being suffered by many of the cities supposedly conquered by Joshua. The city of Ai was another city which was supposedly burnt by Joshua and made into a heap of ruin, after he had its 12,000 inhabitants killed (Joshua 8:21-29). The various excavations that took place there from the 1930s to the 1970s showed that while there is evidence that Ai was a city with strong defensive walls that was destroyed in the 2300 BCE, there is not a single shred of evidence to show that Ai was settled beyond that time. In other words, *Ai simply did not exist during the time of the conquest.*[47]

Gibeon was described in Joshua 10:2 as a "great city...greater than Ai". Here too, excavations done in the 1950s and 1960s found no settlement in that place during the 1400 and 1200 BCE period.[48] Indeed according to archaeologists Bill Dever and Lawrence Stager, almost all of the roughly thirty cities Joshua was supposed to have conquered were either uninhabited during the time of conquest or destroyed by other means or were undestroyed.[49]

Attempts have been made by believers to discredit the archaeological findings by suggesting that the excavations sites or the dating methods were wrong, or that more digging was needed. Given the well-controlled and scientific methods of excavating, classifying specimens and dating, these explanations are highly unlikely to succeed. More so, when we take into account that more than one site showed the same result: that there was simply no city of any great size for Joshua to conquer between 1400 to 1200 BCE.[50]

As we have pointed out in the previous section, the archaeological evidence tells us that Canaan at the time of the supposed conquest was under the administrative governance of Egypt. There is no way Joshua could have "conquered" Canaan when it remained under the control of Egypt until the 12th century BCE.[51]

Based on the above evidence, this is what the historian Robin Lane Fox had to say:

---

[45] Sturgis, *It Ain't Necessarily So*: p63

[46] Dever, *Who Were the Early Israelites*: p46-47
(see also Sturgis, *It Ain't Necessarily So*: p61)

[47] Indeed the very name "Ai" means "ruin". This suggests that the Israelites know the place only as the ruins of an old settlement. (Sturgis, It Ain't Necessarily So: p65)

[48] Fox, *The Unauthorized Version*: p226-228
Stiebing, *Out of the Desert*: p84-87

[49] Sturgis, *It Ain't Necessarily So*: p66

[50] Fox, *The Unauthorized Version*: p228-229

[51] Sturgis, *It Ain't Necessarily So*: p69-70

The book of Joshua tells a powerful tale of conquest, supported by a God who showed no respect for most of the Holy Land's existing inhabitants. Even now the tale has not lost its power, but it is not history and it never was.[52]

FROM JUDGES TO KINGS

The books of Judges, I & II Samuel and I & II Kings are normally considered to be the most historically reliable. Judges, for instance, contains the account of the Canaan conquest that is at variance with the one told in Joshua.[53] Here, in contrast to the swift and total conquest under the unified command of Joshua narrated in the previous book, the conquest was more gradual, not always successful and affected by the various tribes separately. Many scholars thus believe that the accounts in Judges is more historically reliable here than in Joshua.[54]

Certainly no one doubt that, although overlaid with theological "spin", much of I and II Kings is historical; the fall of Israel (II Kings 17), the fall of Judah and the deportation of the Jews into exile in Babylon (II Kings 25) are all events which are well attested historically.

The exact dates of composition of these books are unknown.[55] Although there are varying scholarly opinions as to the actual number of editions the books went through, the consensus is that, for the "final edition" (the books as we know them in the Old Testament), the language and outlook seems to point to a post exilic period (after 586 BCE) of composition.[56]

Saying that these books may contain some historical facts should in no way be confused with the claim that these books are accurate, or true, in *all* aspects. In the next four sections we will be looking at the contradictions and anachronisms in these books and to the archeological evidence for the historicity of the biblical accounts of the united monarchy under David and Solomon.

CONTRADICTIONS BETWEEN JUDGES AND I KINGS

The Book of Judges, for instance, contains chronologies that contradict I Kings, another book considered to be historically reliable. The relevant verse from the latter is given below:

---

[52] Fox, *The Unauthorized Version*: p229

[53] A natural question to ask is this: If the Israelites did not come from Egypt, where did they come from? Archaeological discoveries since the mid-1980s have pointed to the inescapable conclusion that, ironically, the "Israelites" were originally Canaanites. A discussion of this is beyond the scope of this book, however, the interested reader may refer to the following works: Finkelstein & Silberman, *The Bible Unearthed*, p97-122; Laughlin, *Archaeology and the Bible*: p111-118.

[54] Asimov, *Asimov's Guide to the Bible*: p226
Anderson, *A Critical Introduction to the Old Testament*: p63
Sturgis, *It Ain't Necessarily So*: p103

[55] For a good account of how scholars discover the textual layers behind the historical books and the Pentateuch, see *Who Wrote the Bible?* By Richard E. Friedman, Harper 1989

[56] Stiebing, *Out of the Desert*: p20

I Kings 6:1

It happened in the four hundred and eightieth year after the children of Israel were come out of the land of Egypt, in the fourth year of Solomon's reign over Israel, in the month Ziv, which is the second month, that he began to build the house of Yahweh...

Now, after the Exodus, there was the wandering in the wilderness, the conquest of Canaan and division of the land by Joshua. The period of the Judges started after the death of Joshua. After the Judges there were two "latter Judges", Eli and Samuel. Samuel appointed Saul king and after Saul's death, David became king. David's son, Solomon ascended the throne after that. Table 4.1 below gives the relevant verses that cover the period from the Exodus until the building of the temple.

Explanation	Verses	Years
Wanderings in the Wilderness	Joshua 5:6	40
Conquest of Canaan to the death of Joshua		(25)?
Subjection under Cushanrishathaim of Mesopotamia	Judges 3:7	8
The rule of the judge Othniel	Judges 3:9-11	40
Subjection under Eglon of Moab	Judges 3:12-14	18
The rule of the judges Ehud and Shamgar	Judges 3:30-31	80
Subjection under Jabin of Hazor	Judges 4:1-3	20
The rule of the judge Deborah	Judges 5:31	40
Subjection under Midian	Judges 6:1	7
The rule of the judge Gideon	Judges 8:28	40
The rule of the judge Abimelech	Judges 9:22	3
The rule of the judge Tola	Judges 10:1-2	23
The rule of the Judge Tair	Judges 10:3	22
Subjection under the Philistines & Ammonites	Judges 10:8	18
The rule of the judge Jepthnath	Judges 12:7	6
The rule of the judge Ibzan	Judges 12:9	7
The rule of the judge Elon	Judges 12:11	10
The rule of the judge Abdon	Judges 12:13	8
Subjection under the Philistines	Judges 13:1	40
The rule of the judge Samson	Judges 16:31	20
The rule of the judge Eli	I Samuel 4:18	40
Ark taken from the Israelites	I Samuel 7:2	20
The rule of the judge Samuel		(12)?
The kingship of Saul	I Samuel 13:1	(42)?
The kingship of David	I Kings 2:11	40
Four years of Solomon's reign	II Samuel 5:4	4
Total Elapsed Time		**633**

Table 4.1: The chronology of Judges

From the table we can calculate the total elapsed time between the Exodus and the building of the Temple: 633 years. This clearly does not square with the 480 years given in I Kings 6:1. The numbers in brackets (for the reign of Joshua and the judgeship of Samuel) are guesstimates since there is no exact number given in the respective books. However, even if we take out these two numbers (as though Joshua and Samuel never existed!) we still have 596 years. The period of Saul's reign is not given in the Hebrew version of I Samuel (although Acts 13:21 refers to a reign of forty years), if we were to minus the number there, 42, we would still be left with 554 years. We have, at the very minimum, a discrepancy of more than 70 years between the chronology of Judges and Kings.

The constant repetition of the number 40 or its multiples or divisor, in the reigns of the Judges, reveal the artificial nature of the chronology.[57] Forty is a commonly used number for designating a long period of time. In the account of the flood it rained for 40 days and 40 nights, the Israelites wandered in the wilderness for 40 years after the Exodus and Jesus fasted for 40 days.

The number in the book of Kings is also suspect. Note, for example, that both David & Solomon (and probably Saul see Acts 13:21) reigned for 40 years. 480 is actually a multiple of 40 and 12. Twelve, as we may recall, is also a significant number; there being 12 tribes of Israel. In fact, one will note that 480 years also separate the construction of the first temple from that of the second temple. If we calculate the biblical chronology from the building of the first temple to the destruction of Jerusalem in 587 BCE, we find that 430 years have passed. Furthermore, we find from the book of Ezra that the second temple was begun two years after the Jews were released from exile (Ezra 3:8-10). According to the same book, they were release in the first year of "Cyrus, King of Persia" (Ezra 1:1-4). Now Cyrus became king in 538 BCE, or on the 50th year of the exile. These 50 years added to the 430 years give - 480 years! According to these calculations, the time that separates the exile from the building of the first temple and that separating the building of the second temple from the first is exactly equal - 480 years. This is too incredible to be a coincidence - somebody has manipulated the numbers along the way to make the two numbers the same. As the historian Robin Lane Fox remarked "grand number patterns have no place in good history: they make a point about the past, while fudging the truth of it."[58]

ANACHRONISMS IN THE BOOKS OF SAMUEL AND KINGS

As for I & II Samuel, the discrepancies we pointed out in chapter two should be enough to convince anyone that the history here is by no means impeccable. In fact it is worth looking more closely at the David and Goliath story again to illustrate the point. As we have seen in chapter 2, there are two stories within the books of Samuel about the slaying of Goliath; II Samuel 21:19 credits the slaying of Goliath to Elhanan while I Samuel 17:50 assigns the feat to David. We have good reason to believe that the David account is fictitious. Our proof lies in the passage below, set immediately after David killed the giant from Gath:

---

[57]   Anderson, *A Critical Introduction to the Old Testament*; p67-68

[58]   Fox, *The Unauthorized Version*: p194

I Samuel 17:51-58

Then David ran, and stood over the Philistine, and took his sword, and drew it out of its sheath, and killed him, and cut off his head therewith...David took the head of the Philistine, and brought it to *Jerusalem*; but he put his armor in his tent. When Saul saw David go forth against the Philistine, he said to Abner, the captain of the army, "Abner, whose son is this youth?" Abner said, "As your soul lives, O king, I can't tell." The king said, "Inquire whose son the young man is!" As David returned from the slaughter of the Philistine, Abner took him, and brought him before Saul with the head of the Philistine in his hand. Saul said to him, "Whose son are you, you young man?" David answered, "I am the son of your servant Jesse the Bethlehemite."

The passage above contains a glaring anachronism. At the time the event was taking place, Saul's capital was Gibeah, in Judah (I Samuel 10:56; 11:4; 15:34). Jerusalem did not even form part of Saul's kingdom. It was David himself who conquered Jerusalem, seven years after Saul's death (II Samuel 5:-5-9). The whole episode is cast into doubt due to this anachronism. Further, we can understand the reason why the author of Samuel, or one of the original source document, wanted to credit David with the slaying of Goliath, for David by then must have been a semi-mythical superhero; someone who can do anything![59] Thus, it is more probable that Elhanan was the slayer of Goliath.

We also know that some of the speeches attributed to Solomon in I Kings are much later inventions and cannot be authentic. Solomon's prayer and blessing in I Kings 8: 14-61 contains two explicit references to the exile and to the destruction of the temple (which was supposedly still another four centuries away):[60]

I Kings 8:46

If they sin against you (for there is no man who doesn't sin), and you are angry with them, and deliver them to the enemy, *so that they carry them away captive to the land of the enemy,* far off or near;

I Kings 9:6-8

But if you turn away from following me, you or your children, and not keep my commandments and my statutes which I have set before you, but shall go and serve other gods, and worship them; *then will I cut off Israel out of the land which I have given them; and this house, which I have made holy for my name, will I cast out of my sight*; and Israel shall be a proverb and a byword among all peoples. Though this house is so high, yet shall everyone who passes by it be astonished, and shall hiss; and they shall say, 'Why has Yahweh done thus to this land, and to this house?'

To again quote Robin Fox: "It would be naive in the extreme to take the narrative of Kings as a true or comprehensive history."[61]

---

[59] Barthel, *What the Bible Really Says*: p159-162

[60] Anderson, *A Critical Introduction to the Old Testament*; p83

[61] Fox, *The Unauthorized Version*: p195

DAVID

Apart from Abraham and Moses, King David is the other main character in the Old Testament. In I & II Samuel and I Kings 2, we are told of a king whose conquests united Israel and Judah into one kingdom and whose empire included Syria and Hamath to the north, Moab, Ammon to the east, Philistine to the west and Edom to the south. (II Samuel 8: 3-13; 10). Surely such a vast empire would have left immense archaeological evidence of its existence.

The date normally ascribed to King David's reign is 1005-970 BCE. Although no one doubts the *existence* of King David[62], there is no archaeological evidence for his kingdom beyond his existence. As archaeologist John Laughlin noted:

> [T]here is little in the overall archaeological picture of the tenth century BC that can be connected with David.[63]

Whatever evidence there is points to the fact that the story about the grandeur of David's empire is a myth of a fictional golden age created by later writers. Earlier discoveries which were touted as evidence of David's feats have been discredited. Perhaps the most well known, as described in the rose tinted "biblical archaeology" book, *The Bible as History*, was the "discovery" in 1867 by British explorer Charles Warren of the water shaft that runs into the city from the Gihon spring, the one that was supposedly used by David in his attack on Jerusalem. (II Samuel 5:8)[64] However, according to archaeologist Ronny Reich of the Israel Antiquities Authority, who led the extensive digs in Jerusalem in the late 1990s, the "Warren Shaft" as it is now called, is a natural fissure in the rock that has nothing to do with the Jerusalem water system or with David's surprise attack. There is nothing there dating from the time of David. There are only potteries dating to the 18th century BCE (Canaanite) and 8th century BCE (Israelite). The "Warren Spring" is just one example of an archaeological dead end.[65] After 150 years of archaeological digs there is not a single piece of evidence of the Davidic capital.[66]

What of David's *vast* empire? *It never existed.* One would expect to find such a vast empire to be described by the neighboring kingdoms. Yet there is no description of any kind about any vast empire in Palestine during that time in the texts of the Egyptians, Babylonians and Assyrians. The extensive conquests narrated of David would have required enormous infrastructure and manpower. Yet extensive

---

[62] The discovery of the "Tel Dan Stela" in 1993, a 9th century BCE inscription seems to clinch this. The inscriptions tell of the invasion of Israel by Hazael, King of Damascus around 835 BCE. In the inscription is written how this king slew the king who was of "The House of David". (See Finkelstein & Silberman, *The Bible Unearthed*, p128-129; Laughlin, *Archaeology and the Bible*, p122 and Sturgis, *It Ain't Necessarily So*, p.162-164; For a skeptical evaluation of the Tel Dan Stela and its use as evidence for David's historicity , the reader can refer to Hector Avalos' excellent book *The End of Biblical Studies*: p.127-130)

[63] Laughlin, *Archaeology and the Bible*: p124

[64] Keller, *The Bible as History*: p190-191

[65] Sturgis, *It Ain't Necessarily So*: p143-144

[66] Finkelstein & Silberman, *The Bible Unearthed*, p132-134
Sturgis, *It Ain't Necessarily So*: p145

archaeological studies concentrating on Judah – David's base - have shown that the Judah of the 10th century BCE was sparsely populated – only 5,000 inhabitants *including* Jerusalem - with no major urban centers. It consisted of Jerusalem which was "no more than a typical highland village", Hebron and about twenty small villages.[67]

The above findings explain why there is no archaeological evidence for the 10th century empire of David. Judah was still remote and underdeveloped. If David was indeed king, he never ruled over the vast regions described in the Bible.[68]

SOLOMON

According to the Bible, Solomon, David's son and successor, who was king around 970-931 BCE, ruled over an even larger empire than his father's. His vast kingdom spans from the Euphrates to the border of Egypt (I Kings 4:21). Solomon's fame and influence spread far and wide. (I Kings 10:1) His diplomatic skills are proven by his securing alliances with other nations such as Egypt (I Kings 3:1) and Tyre (I Kings 5). He was also known for his massive architectural projects including the Temple in Jerusalem (I Kings 6) and the royal palace on Ophel (I Kings 7). He also improved on the fortifications of Jerusalem, Hazor, Megiddo and Gezer (I Kings 9:15). He also built 40,000 stalls of horses for his 14,000 chariots and 12,000 horseman (I Kings 4:26).

As in the case with his father, David, modern archaeology simply has no evidence for this empire or for any of his supposed architectural undertakings. Solomon's Temple is described in details in I Kings 6 yet despite the extensive archaeological digs in the city, in the words of archaeologist John Laughlin, "not a single piece of this building has been found."[69] There is also no sign of any of the other grand architectural works that he supposedly built; his palace, or the fortifications at Jerusalem, Hazor, Megiddo and Gezer.[70]

Discoveries in the earlier part of the 20th century that supposedly showed the extensive building network of Solomon has been discredited by modern digs.

In the 1920s and 1930s an expedition to Megiddo was made by the Oriental Institute of the University of Chicago. On the lowest level of the excavation, they found two sets of buildings. Each of these buildings has long chambers connected to one another. Inside each chamber are two low partition walls made up of pillars and troughs (like mechanical gears spread out horizontally). This was identified by one of the leaders of the expedition, P.L.O. Guy, as the famed stables of King Solomon. He based his interpretation on passages in I Kings which mentioned Solomon's building techniques, his activity at Megiddo and his cities for chariots and horseman (I Kings 7:2, 9:15, 9:19, 10:26). He even counted the stalls for horses (450) and shed for chariots (150).[71]

---

[67]   Finkelstein & Silberman, *The Bible Unearthed*: p132, 142-143
      Marcus, *The View from Nebo*: p125
[68]   Finkelstein & Silberman, *The Bible Unearthed*: p132, 142-143
[69]   Laughlin, *Archaeology and the Bible*: p127
[70]   Finkelstein & Silberman, *The Bible Unearthed*: p131-135
[71]   Finkelstein & Silberman, *The Bible Unearthed*: p135-137

However, things got a little more complicated soon after. In the 1960s further excavations were done at Megiddo. Below the layer of the "stables" were found buildings with architecture which parallels a distinctive (and common) Syrian palace architectural style known as *bit hilani*. This architecture was similar to the one discovered in Hazor in the 1950s which was attributed also to Solomon. This means that the "stables" being on a higher stratum could not have been from the time of Solomon. Since then, even the building at Hazor has been proven to be of a later date than Solomon. Furthermore, *bit hilani* palaces first appeared (in Syria) only in the early 9th century BCE, *after* the time of Solomon. How could a copy precede the original? Improved dating methods with architectural styles, pottery and carbon-14 have also supported the conclusion that the buildings discovered at Hazor and Megiddo date to the early 9th century BCE. Long after the death of Solomon![72]

We are also told that Solomon was a skilled diplomat and that his influence was felt outside his empire as well. This is not corroborated by any extra-biblical source. In no ancient Near Eastern text do we hear even a whisper about Solomon's great kingdom. He was supposed to have married the Pharaoh's daughter and secured an alliance with Egypt (I Kings 3:1), yet we find no reference to this in contemporaneous Egyptian records. This silence is deafening. It speaks volumes against the historicity of the description of the extent of Solomon's empire and influence.[73]

The archeological evidence on the population, settlement patterns and economic resources of Judah mentioned in the section on David extends to the time of Solomon also. As the archaeologists Finkelstein and Silberman succinctly put it:

> As far as we can see on the basis of archaeological surveys, Judah remained relatively empty of permanent population, quite isolated and very marginal right up to and past the presumed time of David and Solomon, with no major urban centers and with no pronounced hierarchy of hamlets, villages and towns.[74]

The archaeological evidence shows that Jerusalem rose in prominence only in the 9th century BCE when the united monarchy had split back into two parts. Jerusalem was, at best, only a small town during the time of David and Solomon. It may have been the capital of Judah but it was never the capital of Israel.[75]

Like the story of his father, David, the story of Solomon told in the Bible is a piece of historical fiction.

"THE SPLENDID LIAR": THE CHRONICLER

The next set of books we will look at are widely considered to have been written or edited by the same person. These books, I & II Chronicles, Ezra and Nehemiah are normally referred to having been written by "the chronicler." While Nehemiah and probably Ezra were derived from primary documents (i.e. to eyewitness accounts) the

---

Keller, *The Bible as History*: p205-207

[72] Finkelstein & Silberman, *The Bible Unearthed*: p137-142

[73] Sturgis, *It Ain't Necessarily So*: p181

[74] Finkelstein & Silberman, *The Bible Unearthed*: p132

[75] Sturgis, *It Ain't Necessarily So*: p146

evidence in the text showed that the chronicler had rewritten the narratives quite considerably. The chronicler has no qualms about rewriting history. He transformed the image of David (from the lifelike one in Samuel) into an ideal figure. He did not mention any courtroom intrigue before David was crowned as the King of the united monarchy of Israel and Judah nor about David's wrong doings which was mentioned in Samuel: for instance II Samuel 11:2-17 narrates how David committed adultery with Bathsheba, and then plotted, successfully, to have her husband, Uriah, murdered in the battlefield. Yet, David's acts which he considers important are narrated in detail, such as his bringing the Ark of the Covenant to Jerusalem and his failed attempt to build the temple.[76]

The chronicler had no qualms about falsifying ancient works that were before him. One example here is the following verse from the second book of Samuel:[77]

> II Samuel 24:1
> Again the anger of *Yahweh* was kindled against Israel, and *he* moved David against them, saying, "Go, number Israel and Judah."

Probably he couldn't stomach the idea of God inciting an evil act in David, he changed it to:

> I Chronicles 21:1
> *Satan* stood up against Israel, and moved David to number Israel.

The chronicler had freely changed an action which God did into one which Satan performed instead!

Robin Fox calls the chronicler a "splendid liar". Alice Parmalee in her book *Guidebook to the Bible* has this to say about the books of Chronicles:

> On every page we find anachronisms. The account of music and worship in David's reign is really a picture of the Jewish Church of the Chronicler's day, nearly seven hundred years after David. He magnifies the function of the Levites and singers to such an extent that at one point they overcome two armies merely by singing hymns (II Chronicles 20:21-31)! Indeed, there is so much singing in the Chronicler's books that we wonder at times whether this is history or opera.[78]

PURE FICTION IN THE BIBLE

We will now look at four narrative books generally regarded as fictitious works: Ruth, Esther, Job, and Jonah.

Many factors point to the fact that the book of Ruth is a work of fiction. We note that it makes no pretence that it is writing close in time to the events it purports to describe. For instance, the author felt compelled to explain to his readers a custom prevalent during the period his character was set which was no longer current then:

Ruth 4:7

---

[76] Asimov, *Asimov's Guide to the Bible*: p407-408

[77] Asimov, *Asimov's Guide to the Bible*: p408-409

[78] Parmalee, *A Guidebook to the Bible*: p76

> Now this was *the custom* in former time in Israel concerning redeeming and concerning exchanging, to confirm all things: a man took off his shoe, and gave it to his neighbor; and this was the *way of* attestation in Israel.

The book is unusually detailed in its description of the events of Ruth's life. Now if it was not written close to the time of the event, how could such detail have been preserved? Even more so, Ruth was no more than a commoner (her being the great grandmother of David [Ruth 4:17] – even if this was true – it could not have been known at that time) how could such detail be kept in ancestral memory without being written down?

Some of the details can be easily shown to be made up. Take for example this passage describing some details in Naomi's (Ruth's mother in law) life:

> Ruth 1:4-5
> They took them wives of the women of Moab; the name of the one was Orpah, and the name of the other Ruth: and they lived there about ten years. Mahlon and Chilion both died, and the woman was bereaved of her two children and of her husband.

This is a very detailed description. Note however, that "Mahlon" means "sickness" while "Chilion" means "wasting". These are strange names to give to one's children. It is even stranger that these sons of Naomi - who died relatively young - had such appropriate names! Appropriate names are a characteristic of fiction and myths not history.

These considerations show that book of Ruth should be classified as an "historical novel."[79]

Like the book of Ruth, the Book of Esther is fiction. Esther narrates the exploits of a Jewish woman who became queen of Persia. There is absolutely no historical evidence that there ever was a Jewish Queen of Persia.[80] There are also other historical problems with the story as it stands. We will discuss the most obvious here. The book mentions very clearly that Esther was the cousin of one Mordecai, who was among those taken into captivity by Nebuchadnezzar:

> Esther 2:5-7
> There was a certain Jew in the citadel of Susa, whose name was Mordecai, the son of Jair, the son of Shimei, the son of Kish, a Benjamite, who had been carried away from Jerusalem with the captives who had been carried away with Jeconiah king of Judah, whom Nebuchadnezzar the king of Babylon had carried away. He brought up Hadassah, that is, Esther, *his uncle's daughter*; for she had neither father nor mother. The maiden was fair and beautiful; and when her father and mother were dead, Mordecai took her for his own daughter.

Then in Esther 2:15-23 we are told that Esther became queen in the seventh year of King Xerxes' (or Ahaseurus) reign and that Mordecai became an administrator in the

---

[79]   Asimov, *Asimov's Guide to the Bible*: p261-264
       Barthel, *What the Bible Really Says*: p155-158
[80]   Parmalee, *A Guidebook to the Bible*: p78

king's court. Here is the problem: Jehoiachin's (and Mordecai's) exile was a historical event that took place in the year 597 BCE. Xerxes became king in 486 BCE when his father, Darius, died. This means that the seventh year of Xerxes' reign is 479 BCE. Now, let us charitably assume that Mordecai was a newborn when he was taken into exile. This would mean that at that time of Esther's marriage to the king, Mordecai was already 118 years old! Esther could not have been much younger since she was only the *cousin* of Mordecai. Are we asked to belief that a *centenarian* woman had the capability to charm the mighty king of Persia? All this shows that the author must have been writing a long time after the purported events and got his historical dates terribly wrong.

There are many elements within the story that lead one to conclude that the origin of the story was not from history but from an ancient Persian folktale. The very name Esther is a derivative of the Babylonian goddess Ishtar. In fact, the Aramaic version of the goddess' name was Esther. Even her original Hebrew name, Hadassah (Esther 2:7), is closely related to the Babylonian word for "bride". The name Mordecai itself is not Hebrew and seems like a derivative of Marduk, the chief god of the Babylonians. In Babylonian mythology, Marduk and Ishtar are cousins, just like Mordecai and Esther in the story. The name of King Xerxes' original wife Vashti, mentioned in the book (Esther 1:11-2:1) was not a historical figure. The real wife of Xerxes during the earlier years of his reign, according to the Greek historian Herodotus, was Amestris, the daughter of a Persian general. The name Vashti also came from Babylonian mythology. Vashti was the name of an Elamite goddess. Even the name of the chief villain of the story, Haman, the prime minister in Xerxes' court (Esther 3:1), is fictional. There is no historical reference to any ministers in Xerxes' court with such a name. Furthermore, the name of the chief male Elamite god is Hamman. So apart from King Xerxes, the names of all the other major characters from the book of Esther can be shown to be derived from Babylonian mythology.

Isaac Asimov in his *Guide to the Bible* suggested an interesting way in which the story could have started. In the book of Esther, The Queen Vashti was replaced by Esther, while the Prime Minister Haman was replaced by Mordecai. This, in a sense, was what actually happened to these mythological figures. When the Babylonian culture replaced the Elamite one in the city of Susa during the final decades of the Assyrian Empire, the chief Babylonian god, Marduk (Mordecai) replaced the chief Elamite god, Hamman (Haman), while the chief Babylonian goddess Ishtar (Esther) replaced the chief Elamite goddess, Vashti (Queen Vashti).[81]

The book of Job is also a piece of fiction. It is enough to point to the conversations between God and Satan which supposedly took place in heaven (Job 1:6-12; 2:1-6). Who was a witness to that?

Next we have the book of Jonah. The storyline itself sounds absurd. Given below is a summary of the story by Alice Parmalee:

> A man called to be a prophet runs away. A missionary preaches repentance to a city, hoping all the while that the people will not repent and that Yahweh will destroy them! A successful missionary, with a whole repentant city to his credit,

---

[81]   Asimov, *Asimov's Guide to the Bible*: p466-470
Barthel, *What the Bible Really Says*: p238
Harwood, *Mythology's Last Gods*: p229-230

simply sits down in the shade of his vine and sulks! Our credulity is strained on every page...It seems incredible that anyone ever thought the story was actual history.[82]

It is probable, in any case, that the author of Jonah wanted his story to believed as the truth, for he chose, as his main character a man whose name should be known to readers of the Jewish scriptures:

> Jonah 1:1-2
> Now the word of Yahweh came to *Jonah the son of Amittai*, saying, "Arise, go to Nineveh, that great city, and preach against it, for their wickedness has come up before me."

The reference to Jonah is found in the book of Kings:

> II Kings 14:25
> He restored the border of Israel from the entrance of Hamath to the sea of the Arabah, according to the word of Yahweh, the God of Israel, which he spoke by his servant *Jonah the son of Amittai*, the prophet, who was of Gath Hepher.

According to II Kings, Jonah lived during the reign of Jeroboam II and was active during the early part of that reign, or sometime around 780 BCE. Now Nineveh, a city by the northern part of the river Tigris, was a "great city" once, for it was the capital of the Assyrian empire. However, by the time of Jonah, Assyria was no longer the power it was, and Nineveh was little more than a small provincial town. Now the whole story of Jonah centers around this city- a city that simply *did not exist* during the supposed main character's lifetime!

This is not all. According to chapter 3 of Jonah, the whole city of Nineveh repented when they heard the prophet's warning. The people of Nineveh all put on sackcloth and fasted as a sign of repentance. Such a conversion, a truly miraculous victory for the Jewish God, is neither recorded in Kings nor in any extra-biblical or secular documents. This lack of corresponding documentation of such an unusual event in other sources (including biblical ones) showed that the supposed event never happened.[83] Without even needing to consider the absurd case of Jonah surviving for three days in the belly of a "great fish", it is obvious that the book of Jonah is fiction, not fact.

---

[82] Parmalee, *A Guidebook to the Bible*: p58-59
[83] Asimov, *Asimov's Guide to the Bible*: p642-647

DANIEL: PROPHESYING THE PAST

The book of Daniel consists of twelve chapters of which only the first half, the narrative portion, concerns us here. Like the book of Jonah, its pretence at being an historical work is foiled by the author's poor knowledge of history.

The book of Daniel is so filled with historical errors and inaccuracies that most mainstream biblical scholars now conclude that Daniel was written very much later than the period it pretends to be (6th century BCE). Let us look at some of these mistakes:

Mistake # 1

Daniel 1:1-2
In the third year of the reign of *Jehoiakim* king of Judah came *Nebuchadnezzar king of Babylon* to Jerusalem, and besieged it. The Lord gave Jehoiakim king of Judah into his hand, with part of the vessels of the house of God; and he carried them into the land of *Shinar* to the house of his god: and he brought the vessels into the treasure house of his god.

The passage is filled with historical errors and anachronisms.[84]

- The name of the reigning king of Judah during the siege is wrong. II Kings 24: 8-13 showed that it was during the reign of Jehoiachin, Jehoiakim's son, that Nebuchadnezzar laid siege on Jerusalem.

- The third year of Jehoiakim's reign would be 606 BCE. Nebuchadnezzar was not yet king of Babylon at that time! Nebuchadnezzar only become king in 605 BCE, the *fourth* year of Jehoaikim's reign.

- The use of the term Shinar is an anachronism. The name was used to refer to Sumeria during the time of Abraham. During the exilic period, around the time the book of Daniel was supposed to have been written, the correct term was Chaldea, not Shinar.

- The correct spelling for the neo-Babylonian king was Nebuchadrezzar. We noticed that books that were actually written during the exilic period such as Jeremiah (25:9) and Ezekial (26:7) got this spelling right at least some of the time. Daniel *always* incorrectly spells the name with an "n" rather than "r".[85]

---

[84] Asimov, *Asimov's Guide to the Bible*: p599
      Helms, *Who Wrote the Gospels*: p20
      Roux, *Ancient Iraq*: p349

[85] Due to Daniel's error, the use of Nebuchadnezzar is now more common than the correct term Nebuchadrezzar. Thus the former is now more commonly used. We are following this convention. However, note that the latter is actually the correct form.

Mistake # 2

Daniel 5:1-2
Belshazzar the king made a great feast to a thousand of his lords, and drank wine before the thousand. Belshazzar, while he tasted the wine, commanded to bring the golden and silver vessels which *Nebuchadnezzar his father* had taken out of the temple which was in Jerusalem; that the king and his lords, his wives and his concubines, might drink from them.

This innocent looking passage is simply loaded with historical errors.[86]

- Belshazzar, or more correctly Bel-shar-utsur ("Bel, Protect the King") was never a king. He was a crown prince but never became king of Chaldea, for the kingdom collapsed during the reign of his father.

- Nebuchadnezzar was *not* the father of Belshazzar. In fact there is no family relation at all between the two. Nebuchadnezzar died in 562 BCE leaving the kingdom to his son Amel-Marduk. Amel-Marduk, in turn was murdered by his brother-in-law Nergal-ashur-usur two years later. Nergal-ashur-usur reigned for only four years. After his death in 560 BCE, his son, Nebuchadnezzar's grandson, Labashi-Marduk became king. There was a revolt, and Labashi Marduk was dethroned. The new king was Nabu-naido ("Nabu is glorious"), or in its Greek form, Nabudonius. Nabudonius was not related at all to Nebuchadnezzar. He was the last king of the Chaldean Empire, and Belshazzar was *his* son.

Mistake # 3

Daniel 5:30-31
In that night Belshazzar the Chaldean King was slain. *Darius the Mede* received the kingdom, being about sixty-two years old.

Again, another statement that is historically false.[87]

- In the first place the Chaldean Kingdom, fell not to the *Medes* but to the *Persians* (in 538 BCE). The King who conquered Chaldea was Cyrus the Persian.

- There was no historical Darius the Mede who conquered Chaldea! However, there was a *Persian* named Darius who became king in 521 BCE, seventeen years after the fall of Babylon. Darius was a renowned

---

[86] Asimov, *Asimov's Guide to the Bible*: p605-606
      Andersen, *A Critical Introduction to the Old Testament*: p210
      Roberts, *The Pelican History of the World*: p129
[87] Asimov, *Asimov's Guide to the Bible*: p608
      Andersen, *A Critical Introduction to the Old Testament*: p210
      Roberts, *The Pelican History of the World*: p129

king in antiquity and it is obvious that the author of Daniel erroneously thought he was the conqueror of the Chaldean Empire.

Mistake # 4

Daniel 9:1
In the first year of *Darius the son of Ahasuerus*, of the seed of the Medes, who was made king over the realm of the Chaldeans

Now, if he is referring to the historical Darius (the Persian) this is another false statement. The father of Darius was Hystaspes. Ahasuerus, based on Ezra 4:5-6, can be correctly identified with Xerxes I. But Xerxes I was the *son* of Darius, not his father![88]

Mistake # 5

Daniel 6:28
So this Daniel prospered in the reign of Darius, and in the reign of Cyrus the Persian.

This verse forms a fitting "tribute" to the author of Daniel's monumental ignorance of history. The passage above clearly shows that he believed that the Chaldean empire fell first to the Median Empire and this, in turn, fell to the Persian. This is clearly unhistorical. History tells us that the Chaldean and the Median empires existed together and *both* fell to the Persians.[89]

DATING THE BOOK OF DANIEL

We mentioned above that scholars now know that the book of Daniel was written much later than the time it pretends to be. Indeed, the date of its composition can be quite certainly placed between 167 and 164 BCE. How do we know this? Let us sum up the evidence:[90]

- First, as we have shown above, the book could not have been written in the 6th century BCE because it made errors that anyone living during that time would know to be false.

- Second, is this revealing statement from Daniel 9:2:

  I was studying the *sacred books* and thinking about the seventy years that Jerusalem would be in ruins, according to what the Lord had told the prophet Jeremiah.

---

[88]   Asimov, *Guide to the Bible*: p609
[89]   Asimov, *Guide to the Bible*: p609
[90]   Helms, *Who Wrote the Gospels*, p29-34

The prophet Jeremiah lived during the fall of Jerusalem to Nebuchadnezzar in 587 BCE. He was, therefore, a very near contemporary of Daniel. The time of the supposed Daniel was simply too soon for the book of Jeremiah to be considered scripture (which is another word for "sacred books"). In fact we know that the book of Jeremiah was only canonized, i.e. widely considered as "scripture", around 200 BCE. Daniel could not have been written earlier than that.

- Daniel was *very accurate* in "predicting" events leading to and including the desecration of the Jerusalem temple by Antiochus in December 167 BCE.[91]

- After this Daniel starts to go wrong again. Daniel 11:45 predicted that Antiochus IV would die "between the sea and the mountain on which the temple stands", i.e. between Jerusalem and the Mediterranean Sea. Yet Antiochus IV died in *Persia* in 164 BCE.

To summarize, he made errors regarding events in the distant past (6th century BCE), was remarkably accurate in describing details of the events leading to the desecration of the temple in 167 BCE and then made errors about events after that. It is obvious that Daniel must have been written at a time *after* the temple desecration but *before* the death of Antiochus IV; in short between 167 and 164 BCE.

These discrepancies in the book of Daniel have been pointed out by skeptics almost 2,000 years ago. Around the end of the third century CE a pagan critic named Porphyry called attention to the fact that Daniel's prophecy stopped being accurate for

---

[91] Some examples:
- Daniel 11:1-5 "predicted" that a Greek warrior king will conquer Persia, rule a vast kingdom, will not pass on the empire to his descendent, and that his kingdom will be divided into the "four winds of heaven". We know that Alexander the Great, a "Greek warrior" conquered the Persian Empire and upon his death 323 BCE had his empire divided among his four generals: Cassander, Lysimachus, Ptolemy and Seleucus.
- Daniel 11:5-6 "predicted" that "after some years", the daughter of "king of the south" shall marry the "king of the north" to make peace. We know that around 253 BCE, Antiochus II, the grandson of Seleucus 1 the king of Syria and Palestine ("north"), married Berenice, daughter of Ptolemy II, king of Egypt ("south").
- Daniel 11:6-7 "predicted" that she (together with her husband and children) will be killed by one from her "own branch". We know that Berenice and Antiochus were murdered circa 246 BCE by Berenice's brother Ptolemy III.
- These remarkably accurate and detailed predictions continued until Daniel 11:20 where he predicted the succession of a king who "shall send an extractor of tribute through the glory of the kingdom" who shall meet his death "neither in public nor in war". We know that Seleucus IV, the grandson of Seleucus II, tried to extract money from the temple funds ("extractor of tribute") in Jerusalem to pay a huge indemnity to Rome and was assassinated by Heliodorus ("died neither in public nor in war").
- Finally Daniel "predicted" the ascension of a "contemptible person" who will set up the "abominable thing that causes desolation". This is Antiochus IV, who succeeded his brother of Seleucus IV, desecrated the Jerusalem temple by placing an altar to Zeus (on which pigs were sacrificed) there. This happened in December 167 BCE.

events after the year 167 BCE. He rightly concluded that Daniel must have been written around that time. When Christianity became the dominant power in the Roman Empire, the "Christian thing" was done: Porphyry's books were burned. It was only around the 19th century that biblical scholars began to accept Porphyry's views as the correct one.

So Daniel is a book written late in 2nd century BCE that tries to "dress itself up" as a work written four centuries earlier. Why did it adopt this pretence? The book pretended to be written in the 6th century BCE for a simple reason; by the time it came to be read many of the so-called "prophecies" would have already been "fulfilled". This would lend credence to the book and add more weight behind the prophecies yet to be fulfilled. In a nutshell, the author of Daniel tried to fool his readers into believing that the book is of an ancient origin in order to have them believe his future prophecies.

The summary below on the book of Daniel, made by Robin Fox is apt:

> The book [of Daniel] has the familiar ingredients of a biblical success story: its hero probably never existed; he was credited with visions he never saw and actions he never did; ...while its dates and kings are incorrect and its setting is a fiction, posing as history.[92]

In short, the author of Daniel is a fraud.

* * * * *

Modern archaeology, far from continuing to confirm the biblical accounts, have found so much that is unhistorical in the Bible that professional archaeologists have stopped using the term "Biblical Archaeology" altogether! The patriarchal narratives cannot be considered history. The Exodus and the Conquest never happened. David and Solomon may have existed but their vast kingdom described in the books of Samuel and Kings never existed. We have books that are pure fiction: Esther, Ruth, Job, Jonah and Daniel are those of this genre. We have books that are falsified history, history changed and rewritten to suit a certain preconceived opinion: I and II Chronicles and large parts of Ezra and Nehemiah are such books.

In commenting on the state of archaeology vis-à-vis the historicity of the accounts in the Bible, Hector Avalos, associate professor of Religious Studies at Iowa State University, noted in his recent book *The End of Biblical Studies* that:

> Biblical archaeology has helped to bury the Bible, and archaeologists know it. Ronald Hendel was exactly right when he said "Archaeological research has – against the intentions of most of its practitioners – secured the non-historicity of much of the Bible before the era of kings." We can now expand Hendel's observation and affirm that there is not much history to be found in the era of Kings either...Instead of revealing biblical history, archaeology has provided a fundamental argument to move beyond the Bible itself.[93]

---

92 Fox, *The Unauthorized Version*: p331, 337
93 Avalos, *The End of Biblical Studies*: p163-164

Chapter Five
AUTHORSHIP

AUTHORSHIP AS TESTIMONY

The question of authorship is important because the Bible, unlike treatises on mathematic and logic, is a book of *testimony*. In works on mathematics or logic, the question on authorship is largely irrelevant with regards to the *truth* of the content. This is because the expert reader can follow for himself the mathematical derivation or the logical reasoning of the works and from this comes to a conclusion regarding their correctness. In testimonies, we are being told of *contingent* events, events that may or may not have happened. We cannot tell merely from reading the text whether what we are being told is true or not. Apart from trying to compare what is written with other documentary sources and archaeological evidence, we need to know if whoever wrote the text was in position to know, either first hand and via sources available to him, what he was writing about. The identity of the author and our knowledge of his intentions and *integrity* are important considerations in our final judgment on the historicity of the account being narrated.

It is therefore not surprising that Jewish tradition ascribed the authorship of the books in the Old Testament to well known Jewish kings and prophets. To Moses, certainly the most important figure in Judaism, was attributed the authorship of the first five books of the Bible: Genesis, Exodus, Leviticus, Numbers and Deuteronomy. In a similar trend, Joshua, Moses' successor, was supposed to have penned the book that carries his name. David and Solomon, the kings of a united Israel, also had books attributed to them.

There is a similar trend in the New Testament. Most books in the New Testament had their authorship attributed to the disciples of Jesus, or at least their immediate followers. For examples the two letters of Peter were supposed to have been written by the chief apostle himself, while the Gospel of Matthew was supposed to have been penned by the apostle of that name.

These attributions of authorship were accepted, almost without question, by Christians for close to two millennia. These attributions began to be questioned with the advent of critical historical research, or "higher criticism," in the 18th century. Scholars such as Jean Astruc (1684-1766) and Johann Eichhorn (1752-1827) showed that the books of the Pentateuch, attributed to Moses, were actually composed from different sources. Hermann Reimarus (1694-1798) was one of the first to apply critical historical thinking to the issue of the historical Jesus. Ferdinand Baur (1792-1860) questioned the authenticity of many of the Pauline epistles which were hitherto accepted without question as originating from the apostle himself. Critical historical research has reached a point today where almost all the books in the Bible are no longer held to be written by the people tradition thought them to be.

In this chapter we will provide a summary of the result of this critical examination on the question of authorship of the Bible.

THE AUTHORSHIP OF THE PENTATEUCH

Tradition attributes the authorship of the first five books of the Bible, the *Pentateuch*, to Moses. Even today all Christian (and Jewish) fundamentalists continue to assert Mosaic authorship for these works. The Roman Catholic Church issued a decree in the early 20th century, to be accepted without question by all Catholics, that Moses was the literal author of these books.[1]

Whether by blind faith or by decree, it can be shown that this attribution, like the myth of the inerrant Bible, *is false.*

Firstly, there is no such claim of Mosaic authorship in any of the five books. Although there are passages attributed to Moses (Deuteronomy 1:5, 4:45, 31:10) and passages that said that Moses made specific written records (Exodus 17:14, 24:4, 34:27, Numbers 33:2, Deuteronomy 31:9,24). But nowhere in any of these books is there any allusion to itself being written by the Jewish prophet. In fact, whenever we find references to Moses they are always in the third person (see for example Numbers 2:1, 5:1, 31:1, Deuteronomy 33:1). While it may be possible that Moses chose to write in that sort of a fashion, this supposition adds no weight whatsoever to the assertion of Mosaic authorship.[2]

Secondly, there are passages about Moses within the five books that simply could not have been written by the prophet himself. One example:

Numbers 12:3
Now the man Moses was very humble, above all the men who were on the surface of the earth.

As Richard Friedman, Professor of Hebrew and Comparative Literature at the University California, San Diego, mentioned in his book *Who Wrote the Bible?*:

[N]ormally one would not expect the humblest man on earth to point out that he is the humblest man on earth.[3]

We find references to Moses that spoke of him as though he was a long gone prophet. Some examples:

Exodus 11:3
Moreover the man Moses was very great in the land of Egypt, in the sight of Pharaoh's servants, and in the sight of the people.

Deuteronomy 34:10
There has not arisen a prophet since in Israel like Moses, whom Yahweh knew face to face, in all the signs and the wonders, which Yahweh sent him to do in the land of Egypt, to Pharaoh, and to all his servants, and to all his land...

---

[1]   Baigent & Leigh, *The Dead Sea Scrolls Deception*: p120
[2]   Anderson, *A Critical Introduction to the Old Testament*: p22
       Paine, *The Age of Reason*: p106
[3]   Friedman, *Who Wrote the Bible?*: p18

When we take into consideration Moses' reputed humility, such passages could only have been written by another who held Moses in high regard.

Thirdly, the presence of anachronisms, i.e. allusions to names or things in the wrong historical setting, adds further weight against Mosaic authorship. This idea needs a little explaining. A good illustration of this can be found in Thomas Paine's book *The Age of Reason* (1796). The city of New York, before 1664 was called New Amsterdam. Should we discover an undated document that discussed events of, let us say, mid 17th century New England, which referred to the city as *New York*, we can immediately conclude that it must have been written *after* 1664. For no one could have known *before* 1664 that New Amsterdam would be called New York after that year.

Now, the city in the Bible that went through a similar kind of name change was the city of Dan. The old name for this city was Laish, and the account of its conquest and change of names is given in the book of Judges.

> Judges 18:27-29
> They took that which Micah had made, and the priest whom he had, and came to Laish, to a people quiet and secure, and struck them with the edge of the sword; and they burnt the city with fire. There was no deliverer, because it was far from Sidon, and they had no dealings with any man; and it was in the valley that lies by Beth Rehob. They built the city, and lived therein. *They called the name of the city Dan, after the name of Dan their father, who was born to Israel: however, the name of the city was Laish at the first.*

This account of the conquest of Laish and the changing of its name to Dan is placed in the Bible, immediately after the death of Samson. Now Samson was the twelfth, and last, Judge. The Judges were the rulers of Israel after the death of Joshua. According to the chronology given in the book of Judges (see Table 4.1 in the previous chapter), Moses died *around 400 years* before Samson. Even if we were to take the best modern estimates, the time span between Moses and Samson would still be around 200 years.[4] Thus, the name of the city of Laish was changed to Dan at least two centuries *after* the death of Moses. Keep this in mind as you read this passage from Genesis below:

> Genesis 14:14
> When Abram heard that his relative was taken captive, he led forth his trained men, born in his house, three hundred and eighteen, and pursued as far as *Dan*.

As we have reasoned earlier, this allusion to Dan, is an anachronism, and could not have been written by Moses. The passage could only have been written by someone who lived after the period of the Judges, when Laish had become Dan, more than 200 years after the death of Moses.[5]

---

[4]   As we have seen in chapter 4, the Exodus, if it happened at all, probably happened towards the end of 13th century BCE. The period after the death of Samson was in the 11th century BCE as David was King around 1005 BCE. This gives a time span of around 200 years.

[5]   Anderson, *A Critical Introduction to the Old Testament*: p22

We find a similar type of anachronism in Genesis 23:2 which provided an explanatory note that Kirjath-arba, the town where Rachel died, is Hebron. The city of Kirjath-arba was not called Hebron until the time of the conquest when Joshua gave it to Caleb (Joshua 14:13-15).

Another passage which shows that the books – or at least some portions of it - were written after the time of Solomon:

Genesis 36:31
These are the kings who reigned in the land of Edom, before any king reigned over the children of Israel.

Now how could Moses have known that there would be kings that reigned over the Israelites? This passage must therefore have been written, at the very earliest, after the first Jewish King, Saul, began to rule over the Israelites, which was at least two centuries *after* the death of Moses.

Fourthly there is the account of Moses' death and burial in Deuteronomy.

Deuteronomy 34:5-8
So Moses the servant of Yahweh died there in the land of Moab, according to the word of Yahweh. He buried him in the valley in the land of Moab over against Beth Peor: but no man knows of his tomb *to this day*. Moses was one hundred twenty years old when he died: his eye was not dim, nor his natural force abated. The children of Israel wept for Moses in the plains of Moab thirty days: so the days of weeping in the mourning for Moses were ended.

It should be obvious, even to the most hardheaded fundamentalist, that *no one could write an account of his own death, burial and mourning.* Furthermore, the presence of the phrase *to this day* implies that a long time has elapsed between the death of Moses and the writing of the passage.[6]

Incidentally, the above passage has a built in absurdity that a skeptical reader can easily pick up. In the context of the passage, the "he" that buried Moses can refer to no one else except God himself. Now if God buried Moses, how did the writer come to know of it? Since the writer himself claimed that *no one knows* where Moses was buried, he obviously did not see it himself. Phrases like these betray the *fictional* nature of the narrative.

So we have shown that the Pentateuch could not have been written by Moses and was in fact written a long time after his death. Biblical scholars had even taken the evidence one step further. They found that the five books could not have been written by any one person. This is shown by the presence of "doublets": the same story told twice which sometimes contradict each other in details. For example, there were two accounts of creation (Genesis 1:1-2:4a; Genesis 2:4b-25), two accounts of the flood (in one only one pair of each kind of animal is to be taken into the ark, while in the other seven pairs of clean animals are required; Genesis 6:19f, 7:2f) and two accounts of how Hagar was driven out from Abraham's household (Genesis 16:4-14;

Paine, *The Age of Reason*: p112-113
Asimov, *Guide to the Bible*: p253
[6] Paine, *The Age of Reason*: p110

21:8,21). These examples could be multiplied but our purpose is simply to show that the best explanation for the doublets is that the books of Moses are really of composite work revealing the handiwork of more than one author. As Richard Friedman concludes:

> At present...there is hardly a biblical scholar in the world actively working on the problem who claims that the five book of Moses were written by Moses-or by any one person.[7]

Internal evidence tells us that the Pentateuch as we know it today was composed out of four separate documents written in different times by different authors.[8] These source documents are called the J (because the author refers to God by the name Yahweh), the E (the author refers to God generically as Elohim – i.e. "god"), the P (priestly), and the D (Deuteronomic) documents. Internal evidence shows that "J" originated from the southern kingdom of Judah and was the earliest to be documented around 848-722BCE (after Edom's independence from Judah in 848 but before the fall of the northern kingdom); "E" was written in the northern kingdom of Israel somewhere between 922-722 BCE (i.e. from the time the united monarchy separated into 2 kingdoms until the fall of Israel to the Assyrians). The "P" document was written between 722-609 (after the fall of the northern kingdom but before the death of King Josiah in 609). The first edition of the "D" document is dated to before 609 BCE (during the reign of King Josiah) with a final second edition dated to 587 BCE (after the fall of Judah). The documents were then combined into one by a "redactor" who combined it during the days of the Second Temple (around 516 BCE).[9] Although there may be disagreement in details, no critical historical scholar[10] doubts the broad outlines of this hypothesis. As Richard Friedman noted:

> [The Documentary Hypothesis] continues to be the starting point for research, no serious student of the Bible can fail to study it, and no other explanation of the evidence has come close to challenging it.[11]

---

[7]   Friedman, *Who Wrote the Bible*: p28, 261

[8]   We will not be presenting evidence for this here as it digresses from our immediate aim; which is simply to show that Moses could not have been the author of the Pentateuch. For those who are interested in such evidence I recommend Richard Friedman's *Who Wrote the Bible?* (HarperCollins 1987).

[9]   Andersen, *A Critical Introduction to the Old Testament*: p 22-49
     Friedman, *Who Wrote the Bible*: p87, 146, 210, 223

[10]   Obviously wary of fundamentalist theologians claiming to be Biblical scholars that still insist of Mosaic authorship, Professor Friedman add the following interesting footnote to the above quote:

> "There are many persons who claim to be biblical scholars. I refer to scholars who have the necessary training in languages, biblical archaeology, and literary and historical skills to work on the problem and who meet, discuss and debate their ideas and research with other scholars through scholarly journals, conferences, etc."

[11]   Friedman, *Who Wrote the Bible?* : p28

THE AUTHORSHIP OF THE JOSHUA

Joshua was the successor of Moses and the one who led the Israelites into the promised land of Canaan. The sixth book of the Bible, the book of *Joshua*, was supposed to have been written by him. Like the tradition of Mosaic authorship, this attribution does not stand up to critical scrutiny.

Firstly, references to Joshua are made in the third person. Secondly, we have some rather artless passages that betray a time of composition long after the events they were supposed to describe:

> Joshua 4:9
> Joshua set up twelve stones in the middle of the Jordan, in the place where the feet
> of the priests who bore the ark of the covenant stood; and they are there *to this day*.

We see the same phrase *to this day* in Joshua 5:9, 7:26, 15:63. A phrase such as *to this day* used in the context of the above passages can only mean that a long period has passed between the events described and the actual writing.

Thirdly, as in the case of Moses and the Pentateuch, we find the account of Joshua's death narrated in the book that was supposedly written by him.

> Joshua 24:29-30
> It happened after these things, that *Joshua the son of Nun, the servant of Yahweh,*
> *died, being one hundred and ten years old. They buried him* in the border of his
> inheritance in Timnathserah, which is in the hill country of Ephraim, on the north
> of the mountain of Gaash. *Israel served Yahweh all the days of Joshua, and all the*
> *days of the elders who outlived Joshua,* and had known all the work of Yahweh,
> that he had worked for Israel.

Now, how on earth could Joshua have written about his own death? And the last sentence in the passage quoted also mentioned that Israel lived right "*all the days* of the elders who *outlived* Joshua". This means that the passage above could not have been written until *all* of Joshua's contemporaries had died.

Another tradition has been proven wrong: Joshua did not write the book that was named after him.[12]

THE AUTHORSHIP OF THE BOOKS OF SAMUEL

Tradition attributes the writing of the book of Samuel to the prophet of that name. Let us look at the evidence why this traditional attribution is false.

We sometimes come across footnotes in history books where historians take great pains to explain meanings of certain words that had either fallen into disuse, had changed their meanings or had been replaced by other words. The evolution of words is something that does not happen overnight. The process can take from a few decades to many generations.

---

[12] Anderson, *A Critical Introduction to the Old Testament*: p58
Paine, *The Age of Reason*: p124-126

We come across one such footnote in I Samuel. The story relates how Saul who, having lost his asses, sought supernatural help to recover them.

> I Samuel 9:11, 18-19
> As they went up the ascent to the city, they found young maidens going out to draw water, and said to them, "Is the seer here?"... Then Saul drew near to Samuel in the gate, and said, "Please tell me where the seer's house is." Samuel answered Saul, and said, "I am the seer...."

The author of this passage was obviously trying to show the event as he thought it would have happened, for earlier he added the revealing footnote:

> I Samuel 9:9
> *In earlier times* in Israel, when a man went to inquire of God, thus he said, "Come, and let us go to the seer;" for he who is now called a prophet was before called a Seer.

This passage clearly shows that at the time I Samuel was written, the word "seer" was no longer in use and had been replaced by the word "prophet." The initial phrase "in earlier times" and the fact that the word "seer" had fallen into disuse to the point where it had been *forgotten* clearly indicate that a long time had passed from the events narrated to the time of writing. This piece of evidence shows that I Samuel must have been written at least a few generations after the prophet Samuel.

The final evidence is, again, the presence of the narration on Samuel's death:

> I Samuel 25:1
> Samuel died; and all Israel gathered themselves together, and lamented him, and buried him in his house at Ramah.

If I Samuel could not have been written by Samuel due to the presence of the above passage, II Samuel is even more certainly not penned by the prophet. II Samuel begins with the reign of King David and ends with his death. Now David ascended the throne a full four years *after* the death of Samuel and did not die until four decades later.[13]

In short the prophet Samuel did not write I and II Samuel. We do not know who the author(s) were. Another case of anonymous testimony stares at the believer.

THE AUTHORSHIP OF PSALMS

By now, the fact that tradition credits David as the author of the book of Psalms, should no longer have much weight for the skeptical reader. While it may be possible that David was responsible for *some* of the psalms in the book, it is obvious that he could not be the originator of *all* of them.

Some of the psalms centered on themes that were simply not present during the lifetime of David. An example of this is the 137th Psalm. This psalm was written in

---

[13]   Paine, *The Age of Reason*: p132-134

commemoration of the Jewish captivity in Babylon (from 586 to 536BC) an event which happened *four centuries after* the death of David.

> Psalm 137:1
> By the rivers of Babylon, there we sat down.
> Yes, we wept, when we remembered Zion.

It is interesting to note, that despite such clear-cut evidence against David's authorship of this psalm, the *Septuagint,* the Greek translation of the Bible, actually attributed the 137th Psalm to David by name.[14]

THE REST OF THE OLD TESTAMENT

Table 5.1 below and on the next page summarizes the results of critical research of the Bible. What does this critical scrutiny tell us? *All* the books that purport to narrate about the history of the Jewish nation and their relationship with God have unknown authors. It is precisely with this kind of books that the knowledge of the author's identity is needed to enable a forthright assessment of their reliability. The books attributed to David and Solomon were not written or compiled by them. It is only in the books of the prophets that there is some truth in the traditional attribution of authorship.

Old Testament Books	Traditional Authorship Attribution	Conclusion Based on Critical Research	Main Reasons Why Result of Critical Research Does not Agree with Tradition
1. Genesis 2. Exodus 3. Leviticus 4. Numbers 5. Deuteronomy	Moses	False	Amongst others, the presence of the account of Moses' death and burial in Deuteronomy
6. Joshua	Joshua	False	Amongst others, the presence of the account of Joshua's death and burial in Deuteronomy
7. Judges 8. Ruth 9. I Samuel 10. II Samuel	Samuel	False	Outlook, framework and language are post exilic (circa 550 BCE). The presence of the account of Samuel's death in I Samuel 25:1 and the narratives of events that occurred after the death of Samuel.
11. I Kings 12. II Kings 13. I Chronicles 14. II Chronicles 15. Ezra	No firm tradition regarding authorship	-	-

---

[14]   Anderson, *A Critical Introduction to the Old Testament*: p179
Asimov, *Guide to the Bible*: p488, 506
Paine, *The Age of Reason*: p156

16. Nehemiah 17. Esther 18. Job			
19. Psalms	David	False	The presence of post-exilic themes in some of the Psalms proves that David could not have written some of them.
20. Proverbs 21. Ecclesiastes 22. Song of Solomon	Solomon	False	Presence of word peculiar to post-exilic Hebrew vocabulary and syntax. Presence of Persian and Greek loan words disproves Solomon's authorship.
23. Isaiah	Isaiah	Partially false	Chapters 1-39 by Isaiah (circa 700 BCE), but chapter 40-66 is post exilic.
24. Jeremiah 25. Lamentations	Jeremiah	True False	The presence of many views in Lamentations that are in contradiction to those in Jeremiah suggests two different authors.
26. Ezekiel	Ezekiel	True	-
27. Daniel	Daniel	False	The presence of gross historical errors regarding supposedly contemporaneous events rules out the authorship of a 6th century BCE prophet.
28. Hosea	Hosea	True	-
29. Joel	Joel	True	-
30. Amos	Amos	True	-
31. Obadiah	Obadiah	**	Nothing is known about the author and Obadiah was a very common name.
32. Jonah	Jonah	False	Jonah was supposed to have lived in the 8th century BCE but the presence of gross historical errors and the language points to the 4th century BCE as the date of composition.
33. Micah	Micah	True	-
34. Nahum	Nahum	**	Nothing is known about the author.
35. Habakkuk	Habakkuk	True	-
36. Zephaniah	Zephaniah	True	-
37. Haggai	Haggai	True	-
38. Zechariah	Zechariah	Partially true	Chapters 1 to 8 generally accepted to have been written by Zechariah but differences in style from chapters 9 through 14 and presence of reference to Greece points to a later period.
39. Malachi	Malachi	True	-

Table 5.1: Comparison between the traditional attribution of authorship of Old Testament books and the result of critical research[15]

15   Anderson, *A Critical Introduction to the Old Testament*
      Asimov, *Guide to the Bible*
      Paine, *The Age of Reason*
      Riedel et.al., *The Book of the Bible*

THE AUTHORSHIP OF THE NEW TESTAMENT BOOKS

Forgery is defined by the *Webster's New World College Dictionary* as "the act...of imitating or counterfeiting documents... [in order] to deceive." A modern sensational example of a forgery is the so-called *Hitler Diaries*. Supposedly discovered in 1983 by a German journalist, it turned out to be the work of a well known forger of Hitler's work. Both the forger and the journalist were found guilty of fraud and sentenced to 42 months in prison.[16] The diaries contained nothing really "harmful" and consisted in the main of Hitler's speeches copied from elsewhere. Yet, the whole world was indignant at the revelation of the forgery. The main reason why we feel so viscerally repulsed by forgery is that it involves *an attempt to deceive*: it presents something as the work of one person when it was actually that of someone else's. It does not matter if such a work *may* have been written, in the sense of its content and style, by the one it is attributed to – the fact that it was not but presented as though it was is enough to make the whole enterprise unacceptable ethically.

We have seen that there are forgeries in the Old Testament; some examples include the book of Daniel, the later part of Isaiah and portions of the books of Psalms attributed to David that were manifestly post-exilic. Are there forgeries in the New Testament? Forgeries in exactly the same sense that the Hitler diaries are forgeries? The answer is *yes*. In this section we will show the evidence that many of the epistles[17] in the Christian scriptures fit this description.

The stance taken by liberal theologians, many of whom actually did the sterling work required to show these epistles to be fakes, is quite interesting. The first *side-step* is to avoid the very word *forgery* and replace it with more abstruse words *pseudepigraphy* (literally "false writing") and *pseudonymity* ("false name"). Next they claim that the ancients do not view forgeries the way we moderns do. When the ancients wrote in the name of famous persons, so we are told, they did it out of a sense of respect for that person's teaching. This statement, by the Catholic theologian Raymond Brown (1928-1998), on Pauline "pseudonymity", is a good example:

> Most often what is being suggested is that one of the Pauline "school" of disciples took it upon himself to write a letter in Paul's name because he wanted it to be believed authoritatively as what Paul would say to the situation addressed. Such a situation makes sense if one supposes Paul was dead and the disciple considers himself to be the authoritative interpreter of the apostle whose thought he endorsed. Attribution of the letter to Paul in those circumstances would not be using a false name or making a false claim that Paul wrote the letter. It would be treating Paul as the author in the sense of the authority behind a letter that was intended as an extension of his thought – an assumption of the great apostle's mantle to continue his work.[18]

This flies against the face of historical evidence. Of course, there were *some* examples where pseudepigraphy was genuinely meant to show the writers' humility and

---

[16]   Wikipedia Article on *Hitler Diaries* (http://en.wikipedia.org/wiki/Hitler_Diaries accessed on June 7, 2006)

[17]   We will be analyzing the gospels' authorship in chapters eight and nine.

[18]   Brown, *An Introduction to the New Testament*: p586

deference to their founder. The philosophers of the Pythagorean schools always attributed their writings to their founder because it was felt that all their thinking ultimately derived from him. But using this as *the* example of how ancients view forgeries is misleading. In most cases, the ancients were as indignant as we are when they discovered that a piece of writing was forged. Greek and Roman authors warned their audience about forgeries written in their names. The famous Greek doctor, Galen (129 – c200 CE) actually wrote a whole book telling his audience how to distinguish his work from forgeries.[19]

The early Christians treated forgeries more like the general Greco-Roman world than the Pythagoreans. One example involves an epistle attributed to Paul, known as III Corinthians. The epistle is not in the New Testament canon today but can be found in a number of ancient New Testament manuscripts. III Corinthians was even accepted as scripture by the early Syrian and Armenian churches. The epistle was written to support, among other things, the "proto-orthodox"[20] position that Jesus was truly human against the docetic teaching that Jesus only *appeared* to be human. This is certainly aligned with what Paul himself believed and could validly be considered "an extension of his thought." Now this fits exactly the definition of a "good" forgery given by Brown above. It was written by someone who believed he was writing what Paul himself would have written.

As it happened the work was discovered as a forgery by the ancient Christians themselves. The church father Tertullian (c160 – c225) told the story of how the forger, a Christian presbyter, was duly convicted by the ecclesiastical authority for this piece and other related work. The Presbyter's defense - that he did it "for the love of Paul" – exactly why Raymond Brown said such works were published – did not seem to find favor with the judges.[21]

As another example, we find the author of II Thessalonians (itself a forgery! – see below) warning his readers against letters that purports to be from Paul:[22]

II Thessalonians 2:1-3
Now, brothers, concerning the coming of our Lord Jesus Christ, and our gathering together to him, we ask you not to be quickly shaken in your mind, nor yet be troubled, either by spirit, or by word, or *by letter as from us*, saying that the day of Christ had come. *Let no one deceive you in any way.*

In other words, far from seeing such forgeries as benign, the ancients, in general, saw them the way we do - as intolerable acts of deception.

Since the majority of NT scholars still refuse to admit that many of the epistles found in the New Testament are forgeries in the fullest sense of the word, let us

---

[19]   Ehrman, *The New Testament*: p341-342
[20]   This label – *proto orthodox* - is the brainchild of the NT historian, Bart Ehrman. The label accurate since the adjective "proto" describes a movement that was evolving towards orthodoxy but was not quite there yet. You can take the term to mean the branch of Christianity that won the battle for dominance among the other early group of Christians and, subsequently, the right to call their teachings "orthodox."
[21]   Ehrman, *Lost Christianities*: p30-32, 210
       Ehrman, *The New Testament*: p341-344
[22]   Ehrman, *The New Testament*: p345

review the points we have raised above. Firstly, forgery has an ethical component; it involves an element of *deception*. This certainly was not the case with the Pythagoreans because we know that the disciples made no secret of writing under the founder's name; they *openly* tell people they do it. The case with Christian pseudepigrapha is different. Secondly, there is no recorded instance of *open acceptance* of documents that are pseudepigraphical – the example of Tertullian and the presbyter above proves this point clearly. As we shall see in the next chapter, books of the New Testament were accepted into the canon because they were believed to have been written by apostles. The doubts casted on some of the epistles as to their position in canon were precisely because the early Christians were unsure of their apostolic authorship. Thirdly, we have no documented statement by any of the so-called Pauline or Petrine "schools" that adumbrate a similar philosophy to the Pythagoreans. Indeed, the quote from II Thessalonians 2:1-3 above shows that they do not tolerate forgery perpetrated by others who do not share *their* interpretation of Pauline theology.

Uta Ranke-Heinemann, Professor of History of Religion at the University of Essen, hits the nail on the head when she wrote:

> When...such forged claims of authorship are conceded, they are nevertheless played down or justified. This, we are told, is a "legitimate, widespread custom" by the *Lexicon für Theology und Kirche* (VIII, 867). There is no denying that such forgeries were widespread in the early Church, but that does not make them legitimate. *It was and is religious counterfeiting.*[23] [emphasis added]

THE EPISTLES OF PETER

The epistles designated as I and II Peter clearly claim to have been written by the apostle Peter himself. If this is true, we have here the writings of one of the major eyewitnesses to the events in Jesus life. The discussions below will show that here, again, Christian tradition has lied to us. Peter could not have written those epistles attributed to him.

I Peter

The First Epistle of Peter claimed for itself Petrine authorship:

I Peter 1:1
Peter, an apostle of Jesus Christ, to the chosen ones who are living as foreigners in the Dispersion in Pontus, Galatia, Cappadocia, Asia, and Bithynia

The names mentioned above are provinces in Asia Minor.[24] I Peter was written when the Christians in these provinces were undergoing persecution.

---

[23] Ranke-Heinemann, *Putting Away Childish Things*: p226
[24] Today these provinces are all within the country of Turkey.

I Peter 1:6
Wherein you greatly rejoice, *though now for a little while, if need be, you have been put to grief in various trials...*

I Peter 4:12
Beloved, *don't be astonished at the fiery trial which has come upon you,* to test you, as though a strange thing happened to you.

Christian tradition asserts, in this case probably correctly, that Peter died in the Neronian persecution around 64-67 CE.[25] The persecution of Christians by Emperor Nero (37-68 CE) was the first specific persecution against the Christians. However, it was only confined to Rome, where Nero blamed the Christians for the great fire of Rome in 64 CE. Therein lies the problem: *There was no persecution of Christians in Asia Minor during the lifetime of Peter.*

The earliest evidence we have of any non-local persecution of Christians was that which happened towards the end of the reign of the emperor Domitian (51- 96 CE). Domitian propagated the cult of the worship of the Roman emperor especially in Greece and Asia Minor. If the epistle is not referring to a fictitious scenario, then the years 90-95 CE are the earliest time the communities addressed to could be experiencing such persecution.[26] This means that the persecution referred to in I Peter happened around two to three decades *after* the death of Peter!

---

[25] Writings from the end of the first century point to Peter dying the death of a martyr *probably* in Rome. John 21:18-19 (c 100 CE) hints that Peter will be put to death against his will when he is "old." The first epistle of Clement, written from Rome around the same time, also alludes to Peter's death as a martyr (I Clement 5:4). Ignatius in his epistle to the Romans (around 110 CE) ties Peter with Rome (Romans 4:3). I Peter 5:13 too connects Peter with Rome (=Babylon). The Acts of Peter (c 180-190 CE) describes Peter's martyrdom under Nero by being crucified upside down. Eusebius (History of the Church 2:25:8) quotes a letter from Dionysius of Corinth dated to c. 170 CE which stated that Peter and Paul died in Rome under Nero. [see Perkins, *Peter: Apostle for the Whole Church*: p131-147]

[26] Some apologists, in their efforts to keep to a Petrine authorship of the letter, have tried to argue that the persecution is not a systematic one but merely reflect the local tensions between pagans and Christians. But as many scholars have pointed out, such arguments ignore the evidence from within the epistle itself. As Udo Schnelle, Professor of New Testament at Halle, (Wittenberg, Germany) noted in his textbook *The History and Theology of The New Testament Writings* (p404-405):

> A few passages in I Peter cannot be explained merely as reflections of social tensions. According to I Pet. 4:15-16, Christians are brought before the courts merely because they are Christians just as is the case of murderers, thieves and other criminals. A fiery ordeal is taking place among them (I Peter 4:12); they are to resist the devil, and this suffering is being experienced by Christians throughout the world (I Peter 5:8-9). In these texts the persecution clearly has a different perspective and quality, being more than a matter of local harassment. This points to the later period of Domitian's administration, which propagated the Caesar cult especially in the provinces of Greece and Asia Minor. It is still not a matter of comprehensive measures directly organized by the state, but of actions supported by local authorities that lead to discrimination against and persecution of Christians.

Furthermore, we do not even have evidence that there were Christian communities in some of the provinces mentioned in Peter I 1:1 during Peter's lifetime. The earliest reference to Christians there come from Pliny the Younger (62-c.114 CE), the Roman Governor of Pontus-Bithynia who in 112 or 113 CE wrote to the Emperor Trajan (c.52-117 CE) asking for a ruling on how to deal with Christians in his provinces. In his letter he implied that there were Christians there as early as twenty years before. This however, only brings us back to around 90 CE.

Both lines of evidence, the systematic non-local persecution of Christians in Asia Minor and the presence of Christians in the areas addressed in I Peter, point to a period of about 25 years *after* the death of Peter. Clearly Peter could not have written something a quarter of a century after his own death![27]

The most telling argument against Petrine authorship of this epistle is based on a simple consideration. I Peter is the work of an author who reveals an extensive knowledge of Greek, of Greek philosophy and rhetoric and of the *Septuagint*. We know from the gospels (e.g. Mark 1:16) and *Acts* that Peter was a simple, uneducated Galilean fisherman whose mother tongue was Aramaic. (The Acts of the Apostles (4:13) called Peter and John, *unschooled and ordinary men*.) Based on this argument, it is even more improbable that I Peter could have been composed by the apostle of that name.[28]

Some more conservative scholars have tried to defend the Greek of I Peter by proposing that since Capernaum was a trading route, Peter could have picked up Greek in his business. Yet picking up conversational or colloquial Greek by way of doing business in no way explains the polished literary Greek pregnant with Hellenistic philosophy and rhetoric we find in I Peter.[29]

Still others have pointed to Silvanus who was mentioned in I Peter 5:12:

I Peter 5:12
Through Silvanus, our faithful brother, as I consider him, I have written to you briefly, exhorting, and testifying that this is the true grace of God in which you stand.

The word "through" Silvanus is taken by these apologists to mean that it was Silvanus who actually penned the letter - at the dictation of Peter. Perhaps this Silvanus, whom the apologists identify with a student of Paul called Silvanus/Silas (I Thessalonians 1:1, II Corinthians 1:9, Acts 15:22-32), was the one responsible for the polished Greek and the presence of Hellenistic philosophy and rhetoric in the epistle.[30]

Unfortunately there are many problems with this suggestion. Most importantly, as many scholars have pointed out, the Greek phrase - γραφειν δια τινος [*graphein dia*

---

[27]   Davidson & Leaney, *Biblical Criticism*: p316
       Riedel et.al., *The Book of the Bible*: p528
       Schenelle, *The New Testament Writings*: p404-405
[28]   Davidson & Leaney, *Biblical Criticism*: p316
       Ehrman, *The New Testament*: p400
       Koester, *Introduction to the New Testament: Volume 2*: p296
       Riedel et.al., *The Book of the Bible*: p528
[29]   Brown, *An Introduction to the New Testament*: p718n35
[30]   Ibid: p718

tinos - to write *through* someone] - usually refers to the *bearer* of the letter, *not* the author or scribe.[31] In other words, the evidence of the Greek tells us that more likely Silvanus is presented as the person who *carried* the letter to its destination, not the person who wrote it down.

Even if we accept for the sake of argument that the term "through Silvanus" could mean that Silvanus was the scribe, the suggestion still does not work. Firstly, it still does not explain the anachronism of persecutions of Christians in Asia Minor mentioned above which happened long after the death of Peter. Secondly, most of the detailed interpretations and arguments in the epistle are heavily dependent upon the Septuagint. This means that the arguments could not have been one which is *translated* from Hebrew or Aramaic. The ideas presented in I Peter had to start from someone who was already very familiar with the Septuagint - an unlikely scenario for an unschooled Aramaic speaking Galilean fisherman. Silvanus could not have been merely the scribe who wrote down Peter's ideas; he had to be the *originator* of the concepts and arguments himself. Thus, if Silvanus was the scribe, he was also the author! In this case, it does not make any sense to call Peter the *author* of the letter.[32]

To recap, the main reasons[33] why the majority of critical historical scholars do not consider I Peter to be an authentic letter from the apostle are:

- The presence of widespread non-local persecution against Christians in Asia-Minor did not happen during the lifetime of Peter.

- The Greek, Greek rhetoric and the reliance of its arguments from the *Septuagint* rule out Peter as the author or as someone who dictated the letter to an amanuensis.

Now that we know Peter did not write the first epistle attributed to him, we need to determine the date of composition of I Peter. For the various provinces to have undergone persecution at the same time, as the epistle clearly implies, the persecution

---

[31] Boring, *I Peter*: p179 quoted in Wells, *Can We Trust the New Testament?*: p118-119
Kümmel, *Introduction to the New Testament*: p424
Schenelle, *The New Testament Writings*: p401n70

[32] Ehrman, *The New Testament*: p400-401
Kümmel, *Introduction to the New Testament*: p423
Schenelle, *The New Testament Writings*: p401

[33] There are quite a few other reasons normally forwarded by scholars against Petrine argument, these include:
- The presence of Pauline (and post-Pauline!) theology in Peter points to a time after 70 CE.
- The church structure referred to in the epistle seems to have "settled" and is no longer the "fluid" ones we see in the authentic Pauline epistles. Such structures are only known to have been in place towards the end of the first century CE.
- The reference to Rome as "Babylon" is something attested to *only* in post 70 CE Jewish-Christian documents (e.g. Revelation, Sybilline Oracles, 4 Esdras etc). This makes sense since the destruction of the temple by Rome in 70 CE was equated to the destruction of the first temple by the Babylonians in 587 BCE. Calling Rome "Babylon" before 70 CE does not make much sense and is not attested to in other documents.

of Christians must have been a non-local and systematic exercise. As we have mentioned above, history tells us of such a systematic persecution during the first century CE. It was the persecution of the Jews, with which the Romans probably lumped the Christians together, under the Emperor Domitian around 95 CE. The earliest possible date we can assign to I Peter would be around 95 CE, three decades *after* the death of the apostle.[34]

II Peter

The second epistle of Peter is an even later document than I Peter. There are many proofs of this, all of which add to the compelling case both for its lateness and non-Petrine authorship.

The first line of evidence involves the fact that it is later than I Peter for it calls itself the *second epistle* (II Peter 3:1). So if we have dated I Peter correctly above to around 95 CE, II Peter must have been written later than this.

The second line of evidence is the close relation of the epistle, both in style and content, to the epistle of Jude. The latter is a very late work, definitely written during the second century CE (probably around 125). II Peter took over *almost the entire content* of Jude.[35] That it was the author of II Peter who copied from Jude and not vice versa is universally accepted by critical historical scholars. We will give one example of why scholars think so – a comparison between Jude 9 and II Peter 2:11:

> II Peter 2:11
> [W]hereas angels, though greater in might and power, don't bring a railing judgment against them before the Lord.

> Jude 9
> But Michael, the archangel, when contending with the devil and arguing about the body of Moses, dared not bring against him an abusive condemnation, but said, "May the Lord rebuke you!"

The verse in Peter looks strange and only makes sense when the specific example in Jude 9 - about Michael the Archangel arguing with the devil about the body of Moses - is provided. It is understandable why the author of II Peter omitted this, since the story was taken from a book outside the biblical canon – *The Assumption of Moses*. We can see how the process of copying worked. The author of II Peter understood the passage in Jude 9 and paraphrased it, but in removing the specific references to Archangel Michael, he made the passage hard to comprehend for his readers. The reverse – that the author of Jude could have hit upon a quote from outside the canon to clarify the passage of II Peter 2:11 - is extremely unlikely.

---

34   Parmalee, *Guidebook to the Bible*: p125
35   The similarities can be verified by the reader himself: Jude 2 = II Peter 1:2; Jude 4 = II Peter 2:1-3; Jude 5a = II Peter 1:12, Jude 6 = 2 Peter 2:4; Jude 7 = II Peter 2:6, 10a; Jude 8 = II Peter 2:10b, Jude 9 = II Peter 2:11; Jude 10 = II Peter 2:12, Jude 11 = II Peter 2:15; Jude 12 = II Peter 2:13; Jude 12f = II Peter 2:17; Jude 16 = II Peter 2:18; Jude 17 = II Peter 3:2; Jude 18 = II Peter 3:3 [Schenelle, *The New Testament Writings*: p428-429]

A further line of evidence against Petrine authorship (and for its late date) is that the epistle refers to Paul's epistles as though they were already collected together and seems to consider them as scriptures (i.e., sacred writings):

> II Peter 3:15-16
> Regard the patience of our Lord as salvation; even as our beloved brother Paul also, according to the wisdom given to him, wrote to you; as also in all of his letters, speaking in them of these things. In those, there are some things that are hard to understand, which the ignorant and unsettled twist, *as they also do to the other Scriptures*, to their own destruction.

Clearly the historical Peter could not have seen the collected letters of Paul and considered them in the same breath as *the other Scriptures*.

Another indication of the lateness of II Peter was the fact that some of the readers of his epistles have grown impatient waiting for the second coming that was endlessly delayed. The early Christians certainly expected the second coming of Jesus Christ to happen during their lifetime.[36] We find the author of this epistle twisting words out of their normal meanings to explain this delay:

> II Peter 3:8-9
> But don't forget this one thing, beloved, that one day is with the Lord as a thousand years, and a thousand years as one day. The Lord is not slow concerning his promise, as some count slowness.

Add to this, we note that Petrine authorship had its authenticity denied by many Christians up to the 4th century. The convergence of these considerations makes the case of non-Petrine authorship of II Peter compelling.

The dating of II Peter is pretty uncertain business. Some scholars date it as early as around the last decade of the first century. However, the balance of evidence seems to favor a later date. II Peter was written when Christians were beginning to accept a "New Testament" along with the Old which they considered to be sacred scriptures. As far as we know, this attitude started to take hold around 150 CE. II Peter, which accepts the Pauline epistles as scripture was very probably written around this date. The important thing to note is that all these dates, from the earliest (c. 95 CE) to the latest (c. 150 CE), exclude the idea of Petrine authorship for Peter died in around 64-67 CE.[37]

---

[36] See for instance Mark 13:24-30, Matthew 24:29-34, Luke 19:11,I Thessalonians 4:15, I Corinthians 7:29.

[37] Asimov, *Guide to the Bible*: p1165-1167
Barr, *New Testament Story*: p443-444
Davidson & Leaney, *Biblical Criticism*: p319-320
Howell-Smith, *In Search of the Real Bible*: p85
Kümmel, *Introduction to the New Testament*: p430-434
Parmalee, *Guidebook to the Bible*: p127
Schenelle, *The New Testament Writings*: p425-429

Clearly, the epistles of Peter could not have been written by the apostle himself. In other words, I and II Peter are *forgeries* or, as biblical scholars Robert Davidson and A.R.C. Leaney labeled them, "fictitious testaments".[38]

THE EPISTLES OF PAUL

There are thirteen letters or epistles in the New Testament today that are attributed to Paul. Another epistle, the epistle to the Hebrews used to be attributed to him as well but is no longer accepted today by most Christians as a Pauline work.[39] Four epistles, Romans, I and II Corinthians and Galatians, are generally accepted by all as authentic letters of Paul. The content, style and vocabulary of these four are normally used to evaluate the other nine epistles. Based on this, the best scholarship tells us that not all of the remaining nine epistles were actually written by him. Fundamentalists, who cannot accept an inerrant Bible filled with forgeries, assert that all the thirteen epistles attributed to him are genuinely his. Their argument has normally been along the lines of comparing the *similarity*, while ignoring the differences, of the other epistles to the basic four. This is a bad strategy for detecting fraud. For we would expect a forger to try for *verisimilitude*; in other words, they will try to imitate the historical situation of Paul's time as well as Paul's style and method. Thus, similarities with the authentic epistles do not settle the matter. It is in the *differences* - in content, vocabulary and style - that we discover whether something is genuine or fake. However good a forger is, sometimes he or she will falter and sometimes make stylistic and anachronistic mistakes.[40]

The Pastoral Epistles

The "pastoral epistles", I & II Timothy and Titus, are thus called because their chief aim was the establishment and maintenance of "pastoral" church offices. The three epistles are often placed together as a distinct group within the Pauline corpus because they share similarities in church structure, community, and theology. They also "share" the same enemies (i.e. "false teachers").[41]

Today a vast majority of critical scholars, around 80% to 90% according to Raymond Brown,[42] repudiates Pauline authorship for the pastorals. Indeed, the evidence is compelling for their lack of authenticity. We will present the evidence below.

1. External Attestation

   The earliest direct reference to the pastoral epistles was made by Irenaeus (c130-c200), Bishop of Hippo around 185 CE. Marcion (d. c160), [43] the

38	Davidson & Leaney, *Biblical Criticism*: p320
39	Davidson & Leaney, *Biblical Criticism*: p283
40	Ehrman, *The New Testament*: p342-344
41	Kümmel, *Introduction to the New Testament*: p367
	Schnelle, *The History and Theology of the New Testament Writings*: p326-327
42	Brown, *An Introduction to the New Testament*: p629, 654, 673
43	For more on Marcion see the next chapter.

"arch-Paulinist" branded by the early church as a heretic, was one of the earliest supporters of Pauline epistles as scripture, yet his collection of his letters, made around 140 CE, did not include the pastorals. The later church father, Tertullian (c160- c225) claimed that Marcion knew the pastorals but "rejected" them. However, we have no reason to believe that Tertullian, who was writing c. 210 CE, or more than 70 years after Marcion, was in any position to verify this assertion. When we contrast this to, say, I Corinthians, which was quoted as early as 95 CE by Clement (I Clement 47) we can see how late the attestation is for the pastorals.[44]

2. Internal Content

- Although the forger tries to add verisimilitude to the epistles – such as having the incarcerated Paul asking Timothy to bring him his belongings (I Timothy 4:13), the inconsistencies within the epistles point to the fictional nature of the writings. For instance, we are told that all of Paul's companions, except Luke, have abandoned him:

  II Timothy 4:10-11
  Be diligent to come to me soon, for Demas left me, having loved this present world, and went to Thessalonica; Crescens to Galatia, and Titus to Dalmatia. *Only Luke is with me.*

  Yet a few verses later the author forgot this fact and had Paul send greetings from all those with him, Eubulus, Pudens, Linus, Claudia and even all the brothers!

  II Timothy 4:21
  Be diligent to come before winter. Eubulus salutes you, as do Pudens, Linus, Claudia, and all the brothers.

  Paul would surely not have forgotten that only Luke was left with him![45]

- Timothy, the recipient of the epistle is presented as young and inexperienced (I Timothy 4:12, II Timothy 2:22), who must be told how to behave in church (I Timothy 3:15) and "urged" to fight heretics (I Timothy 1:3). Yet this flies against the evidence available from Paul's authentic epistle as well as from the Acts of the Apostles where we are told that Timothy has been Paul's co-workers for many years (I Corinthians 4:17, 16:10 II Corinthians 1:1, Acts 16:1, 18:5, 20:4). The setting of the pastorals, in the 60s CE,[46] would mean that by then Timothy would have been a "seasoned" evangelist and would have been thoroughly familiar with Paul's teachings and theology. The presentation of Timothy as a young and inexperienced follower, rather than as a co-worker, of Paul is a fictitious one. We find similar

[44] Barr, *New Testament Story*: p169
      Wells, *The Jesus Myth*: p79, p270 n32
[45] Schnelle, *The History and Theology of the New Testament Writings*: p329
[46] Kümmel, *Introduction to the New Testament*: p377

mistakes with the presentation of Titus.[47] In addition we find Paul's insistence that he is "not lying" in his apostolic claims (I Timothy 2:7) highly suspicious, since, as we have just pointed out, Timothy would have been his co-worker for quite some time by them.

- A revealing slip is when the author refers to the gospels as written documents:

  I Timothy 5:18
  For the Scripture says, "You shall not muzzle the ox when it treads out the grain." And, "*The laborer is worthy of his wages.*"

  The first half is a quote from Deuteronomy 25:4, while the second is from Luke!

  Luke 10:7
  Remain in that same house, eating and drinking the things they give, for *the laborer is worthy of his wages.*

  Referring to Luke as "scripture" – something *written* and in the same status as the Torah - is a mark of the lateness of the pastoral.[48] In the genuine epistles of Paul, he often refers to the Old Testament as written but treats the sayings and teachings of Jesus as a living tradition:[49]

  I Corinthians 9:9, 14
  For it is written in the law of Moses, "You shall not muzzle an ox while it treads out the grain." Is it for the oxen that God cares... Even so *the Lord ordained* that those who proclaim the Good News should live from the Good News

  I Corinthians 11:23-25
  For I received from the Lord that which also I delivered to you, that the Lord Jesus on the night in which he was betrayed took bread. When he had given thanks, he broke it, and said, "Take, eat. This is my body, which is broken for you. Do this in memory of me." In the same way he also took the cup, after supper, saying, "This cup is the new covenant in my blood. Do this, as often as you drink, in memory of me."

- Paul, in the authentic epistles, always refers to the Gentiles in the second person "you" (e.g. Romans 11:13 I Corinthians 12:2), but in Titus the first person plural "we" is used (Titus 3:3) when speaking about Gentiles. This inclusion of himself into the same group as Gentiles ("we" instead of "you") is not a characteristic of the historical Paul.[50]

---

47   Schnelle, *The History and Theology of the New Testament Writings*: p329
      Wells, *The Jesus Myth*: p80

48   The reader will see in chapter 10 that the evidence points to a date in the 90s for the composition of the gospel of Luke.

49   Barr, *New Testament Story*: p31-32, 171

50   Barr, *New Testament Story*: p171

3. Church Structure

During Paul's time, we see that the church structure is quite amorphous with no one really in command. In I Corinthians we see that there are many different types of members in the church – apostles, prophets, teachers, miracles workers and others (I Corinthian 12:28). Any of these may choose to speak freely during their worship service (I Corinthians 14:26-33). We can tell that no one was truly in charge when Paul had to ask these Christians to "wait for one another" (I Corinthians 11:33) to prevent a chaotic scramble during the common meal. In the pastorals, this is no longer the case. We find that there are bishops, presbyters and deacons who are formally appointed to their position (I Timothy 3:1-7, 4:14, Titus 1:5-9) and who have the right to get paid (I Timothy 5:27) by the congregation.[51]

4. Teachings and Theology

- In the authentic epistles of Paul, he expected the apocalyptic end of the world within his own lifetime, or at least the lifetime of most of his flock. (I Corinthians 7:29-21; I Thessalonians 4:15-17) In the pastorals, we find "Paul" making provisions for the death of *his* followers by commanding them to pass the teachings on. (II Timothy 2:1-14)[52]

- Due to his expectation of the imminent return of Christ, the historical Paul advised widows and the unmarried not to marry (I Corinthians 7:8 "But I say to the unmarried and to widows, it is good for them if they remain even as I am."). In the pastorals they are urged to do the exact opposite (I Timothy 5:14 "I desire therefore that the younger widows marry, bear children, rule the household...").[53]

- In the authentic Pauline epistles, his theology has always been salvation by grace through faith (e.g. Romans 3:28, Galatians 2:16) while in the pastorals salvation becomes the acceptance of religious dogma. (e.g. I Timothy 1:10, 4:6, II Timothy 1:13, Titus 1:9,13)[54]

5. Linguistic Features

- Of the 848 different words used in the Pastorals, 306 or 36% are not found anywhere else in the other ten letters of the Pauline corpus. Furthermore, of this unique vocabulary, 211 words are very commonly used by *second century* writers.[55]

---

[51] Barr, *New Testament Story*: p170
Schnelle, *The History and Theology of the New Testament Writings*: p170
[52] Kümmel, *Introduction to the New Testament*: p382
[53] Barr, *New Testament Story*: p170
[54] Ehrman, *The New Testament*: p360
Rhein, Understanding the New Testament: p283-284
[55] Barr, *New Testament Story*: p169
Ehrman, *The New Testament*: p357

- Even the words that are shared between the pastorals and genuine Pauline epistles have markedly different meanings. "Faith" for Paul meant a sense of trust one has in the redeeming feature of Jesus' death (e.g. Romans 1:16-17). However, in the Pastorals the word is used to mean the body of teachings of the church (e.g. Titus 1:13). As another example, "righteousness" meant for the historical Paul a sense of justification before God (Romans 3:21-28), while in the pastorals, the same term refers to being moral (I Timothy 1:9, Titus: 1:8).[56]

These arguments together provide a very strong case for rejecting the Pauline authorship for the pastoral epistles.

Now that we have shown the pastoral epistles to be non-Pauline it is time to re-examine the case for calling these *forgeries*. Recall that many liberal theologians refused to use that term to describe these epistles because they were supposedly written by disciples who were true to Paul's teachings. But, as we have shown above, the theology in the pastorals differs in quite a few instances from Paul. Even their understanding of certain key terms used by Paul (e.g. "faith", "righteousness") is faulty. It cannot be said that these epistles were faithful to the teachings of Paul.

Furthermore, we find in the Pastoral Epistles a very strong tendency to try and present themselves as though they were really written by Paul. The personal touch in having Paul ask Timothy to bring along his cloak and his books from Troas (II Timothy 4:6-8) is one example of this. This clearly shows the author wanted to *deceive* his readers into thinking them as authentic letters from Paul. As the critical historian Kurt Aland commented:

> The information about the sojourn of the various co-workers in the fourth chapter of 2 Timothy, the first trial of Paul, the instructions for the addressees, as well as the end of the epistle to Titus evince such a thorough knowledge, such a simulated perspective, and such a reconstruction of Paul's personal affairs, that we can hardly avoid assuming an *intended forgery*.[57] [italics added]

As an aside, it is ironic that the most often cited verse by fundamentalists supporting biblical inerrancy - II Timothy 3:16[58] - actually comes from a forgery!

The pastorals are dated by most scholars to around 100 CE. This is due to elements in the epistles which date to that time: the presence of a more developed church structure, an acceptance of the delay of the parousia and the presence of Gnostic opponents.[59]

---

[56] Barr, *New Testament Story*: p169
Ehrman, *The New Testament*: p358

[57] Kurt Aland "The Problem of Anonymity and Pseudonymity in Christian Literature in the First Two Centuries" *Journal of Theological Studies* 12 (1961) p 39-49 quoted in Wells, *The Jesus Myth*: p94

[58] "Every Scripture is God-breathed and profitable for teaching, for reproof, for correction, and for instruction in righteousness"

[59] Brown, *An Introduction to the New Testament*: p668
Ehrman, *The New Testament*: p362
Kümmel, *Introduction to the New Testament*: p387

II Thessalonians

A growing number of scholars, even among "moderates", are rejecting the Pauline authorship of II Thessalonians.[60] The main reason for this growing consensus is the fundamental difference in eschatology, in other word regarding the return of Jesus (the *parousia*), with the other authentic epistles of Paul. The real Paul expected the end of the world as we know it to come very soon:

I Corinthians 7:29-31 (RSV)
I mean, brothers, *the appointed time has grown very short*; from now on, let those who have wives live as though they had none, and those who mourn as though they were not mourning, and those who rejoice as though they were not rejoicing, and those who buy as though they had no goods, and those who deal with the world as though they had no dealings with it. *For the form of this world is passing away.*

I Thessalonians 4:15-17
For this we tell you by the word of the Lord, *that we who are alive, who are left to the coming of the Lord,* will in no way precede those who have fallen asleep. For the Lord himself will descend from heaven with a shout, with the voice of the archangel, and with God's trumpet. The dead in Christ will rise first, then we who are alive, who are left, will be caught up together with them in the clouds, to meet the Lord in the air. So we will be with the Lord forever.

Furthermore, Paul taught that the end will come suddenly. This is how he put it:

I Thessalonians 5:2-3
For you yourselves know well that *the day of the Lord comes like a thief in the night.* For when they are saying, "Peace and safety," then *sudden destruction will come on them,* like birth pains on a pregnant woman; and they will in no way escape.

The verses above show that the real Paul expected the *parousia* to happen very soon and without warning. This is not the case with the author of II Thessalonians:

II Thessalonians 2:1-4
Now, brothers, *concerning the coming of our Lord Jesus Christ, and our gathering together to him, we ask you not to be quickly shaken in your mind,* nor yet be troubled, either by spirit, or by word, or by letter as from us, saying that the day of Christ had come. Let no one deceive you in any way. *For it will not be, unless the departure comes first, and the man of sin is revealed, the son of destruction, he who opposes and exalts himself against all that is called God or that is worshiped; so that he sits as God in the temple of God, setting himself up as God.*

Note the difference here. This "Paul" is no longer expecting an immediate return of Jesus and warned his readers against others who may say so. Furthermore, it tells of signs such as the appearance of "the man of sin" or "son of destruction" who will

---

[60]   Schnelle, *The History and Theology of the New Testament Writings*: p333
Brown, *An Introduction to the New Testament:* p591

gather himself in the temple setting himself as God. The future appearance of the anti-Christ is mentioned only here in all the epistles attributed to Paul. Since those events have not happened yet, it is obvious that they will be used as benchmarks to predict the return of Jesus. This contradicts the real Paul who says that the end will come suddenly and without warning, "like a thief in the night." II Thessalonians linked the appearance of the "son of destruction" with the return of Jesus. Given the historical Paul's preoccupation with the *parousia*, it is indeed amazing, if we assume II Thessalonians to be authentic, that we do not find any mention of this "antichrist" in any other letter of the apostle.[61]

The author of II Thessalonians tries very hard to present itself as an authentic work of. However, there are occasions where this attempt fails. One example is taken from the end of the letter:

> II Thessalonians 3:17
> The greeting of me, Paul, with my own hand, which is the sign in *every letter*: this is how I write.

"Paul" here is claiming that he always ends by writing the greeting in his own hand. We know that while this is true of some of Paul's authentic letters (e.g. Galatians 6:11) but this is certainly not true with most of his authentic letters. This statement that he signed all his letters by hand, could not have been made by the real Paul. As the work of a forger, it makes perfect sense, because he is using this device to try to reassure his readers that the letter is genuine.[62]

Why was II Thessalonians written? It was written to reassure its readers that the end is not yet and to ask them to ignore other messages to the contrary. That it tries to imitate I Thessalonians is another clue. Compare the "section headings" of these two epistles:

Introduction	*Introduction*
I Thessalonians 1:1	II Thessalonians 1:1-2
Paul, Silvanus, and Timothy, to the assembly of the Thessalonians in God the Father and the Lord Jesus Christ: Grace to you and peace from God our Father and the Lord Jesus Christ.	Paul, Silvanus, and Timothy, to the assembly of the Thessalonians in God our Father, and the Lord Jesus Christ: Grace to you and peace from God our Father and the Lord Jesus Christ.
Beginning of Exhortative Material	*Beginning of Exhortative Material*
I Thessalonians 3:11	II Thessalonians 2:16
Now may our God and Father himself, and our Lord Jesus Christ...	Now our Lord Jesus Christ himself, and God our Father...

---

61 Ehrman, *The New Testament*: p345-346
    Schnelle, *The History and Theology of the New Testament Writings*: p316-317
62 Ehrman, *The New Testament*: p346

Ending	*Ending*
I Thessalonians 5:23,28	II Thessalonians 3:16, 18
May the God of peace himself sanctify you completely…	Now may the Lord of peace himself give you peace at all times in all ways…
The grace of our Lord Jesus Christ be with you. Amen.	The grace of our Lord Jesus Christ be with you all. Amen.

In II Thessalonians 2:2, the Thessalonians were warned against the deception of some who "by letter as from us" try to argue that the end is near. The writer was aware that there was an earlier letter to the Thessalonians proclaiming the imminence of the *parousia*. We have seen that the message of I Thessalonians is precisely that – the end *is* near (see I Thessalonians 4:15-17 above). Thus, the letter that II Thessalonians was referring to as being "deceptive" is none other than the *authentic* letter of Paul himself - I Thessalonians![63]

The forger is claiming that the real thing is a forgery! It is hard for any liberal theologian to argue that this "pseudepigrapha" was written "out of respect for Paul" or as a "development in Pauline thought" when II Thessalonians labels the original teachings of the historical Paul as *deceptive*, and probably heretical. The epistle was not written to further Pauline thought but to *replace* it.

Colossians

Modern scholarship is almost evenly divided on the authenticity of the epistle to the Colossians with about 60 percent favoring non-Pauline authorship.[64] There are a number of strong reasons for the rejection of Pauline authorship.

Firstly, there are differences in theological content. In the authentic letters, Paul's eschatological conviction had always been that while Christ's dying is emulated by the baptism of new converts, the resurrection of these Christians will come later, in some future date. In Colossians, believers had already been raised with Christ. Compare these two verses:

Romans 6:4	Colossians 2:12
We were buried therefore with him through baptism to death, that just like Christ was raised from the dead through the glory of the Father, *so we also might walk in newness of life.*	[H]aving been buried with him in baptism, in which *you were also raised* with him through faith in the working of God, who raised him from the dead.

Note that in Romans 6:4, the resurrection of the believers is still in the future, whereas for Colossians the believers had already been raised. This eschatology found in Romans is also found in I Corinthians 15. It is hard to imagine Paul changing his theology midstream during his career. The difference is better explained by the fact that whoever it was that wrote Colossians, it could not have been Paul.[65]

---

63   Lüdemann, *Heretics*: p110-115
64   Brown, *An Introduction to the New Testament*: p610
65   Ehrman, *The New Testament*: p348
      Schnelle, *The History and Theology of the New Testament Writings*: p285

Secondly, in the genuine epistles of Paul, very little emphasis is placed on social arrangements. This is understandable since he thought that the world as we know it would end anyway, so social arrangements are unnecessary (see I Corinthians 7:17-31). In Colossians 3:18-4:1 very elaborate advice is given on the relationship between husbands and wives, children and parents, and masters and slaves.[66]

Finally, the writing style of Colossians differs markedly from Paul's authentic letters. The real Paul tends to write in short and concise sentences. The "Paul" of Colossians is very fond of long convoluted ones. Colossians 1:3-8, for example, is a single sentence made up of approximately 100 Greek words![67]

We can conclude that Colossians is, very likely, another piece of early Christian forgery.

Ephesians

If there is some doubt in the scholarly community about the Colossians being a piece of "pseudepigraphy", there is very little of this with regards to Ephesians. Around 70% to 80% of scholars think Ephesians is non-Pauline.[68]

The author of Ephesians believes that Christians are already raised in Jesus.

Ephesians 2:5-6
[E]ven when we were dead through our trespasses, made us alive together with Christ (by grace you have been saved), *and raised us up with him, and made us to sit with him in the heavenly places in Christ Jesus*

This belief is also found in the epistle to the Colossians but not in the genuine Pauline writings. Compare this to Romans 6:4 above. It is highly unlikely that the same person would have such differing theological views.

The authors uses words that are common of Paul but with very different meanings. To the historical Paul, the word "church" refers to a particular congregation, some examples:

Romans 16:5 (RSV)
Greet also the church in their house.

I Corinthians 4:17 (RSV)
Therefore I sent to you Timothy, my beloved and faithful child in the Lord, to remind you of my ways in Christ, as I teach them everywhere in every church.

II Corinthians 8:18 (RSV)
With him we are sending the brother who is famous among all the churches for his preaching of the gospel.

Yet in all nine occurrences of the word "church" in Ephesians (1:22, 3:10, 3:21, 5:23, 5:24, 5:25, 5:27, 5:29 and 5:32) it always applies to the "universal" church and is

---

66   Ehrman, *The New Testament*: p349
67   Ehrman, *The New Testament*: p348
68   Brown, *An Introduction to the New Testament*: p629

always in singular rather than any individual congregation.[69] Below are a couple of examples:

> Ephesians 1:22
> [A]nd he has put all things under his feet and has made him the head over all things for *the church.*

> Ephesians 5:23-25
> For the husband is the head of the wife as Christ is the head of *the church,* his body, and is himself its Savior. As the church is subject to Christ, so let wives also be subject in everything to their husbands. Husbands, love your wives, as Christ loved *the church* and gave himself up for her…

Another starkly different use of terminology is in the word "works." In the genuine epistles "works" always refer to the "works of the law" – namely following the commandments of the Torah such as circumcision, dietary restrictions and the observations on holy days. A couple of examples should suffice:

> Galatians 2:16
> [Y]et knowing that a man is not justified by the works of the law but through faith in Jesus Christ, even we believed in Christ Jesus, that we might be justified by faith in Christ, and not by the works of the law, because no flesh will be justified by the works of the law.

> Romans 4:2
> For if Abraham was justified by works, he has something to boast about, but not toward God.

In Ephesians, the term "works" is taken to mean "good deeds":[70]

> Ephesians 2:8-10
> [F]or by grace you have been saved through faith, and that not of yourselves; it is the gift of God, not of works, that no one would boast. For we are his workmanship, created in Christ Jesus for good works, which God prepared before that we would walk in them.

A substantial number of old manuscripts actually lacked the words "in Ephesus". This gives good reason to believe that the whole document was originally not an epistle at all but a tract, written by an unknown early Christian author, to explain Pauline teachings.

All of the genuine Pauline documents contain discussions on eschatology. This is noticeably absent from Ephesians. The epistle's description of the Christian church as being "built on the foundation of the apostles" (Ephesians 2:20) is certainly incompatible with what we see in Galatians, where Paul spoke disparagingly about

---

[69]   Brown, *An Introduction to the New Testament*: p625
       Lüdemann, *Heretics*: p122
[70]   Ehrman, *The New Testament*: p353

"the Jerusalem pillars" (see Galatians chapters 1 & 2). The allusion to the existence of heretical sects (Ephesians 4:14) point to a period after the death of Paul. [71]

Ephesians is heavily dependent of Colossians. 73 out of its 155 verses have parallels in Colossians. Just like the forger of II Thessalonians copied I Thessalonians, the forger of Ephesians used Colossians as his template for concocting a Pauline epistle. A comparison of Colossians 3:18-4:1 and Ephesians 5:21-26; 6:1-should show this clearly. That the dependence is from Colossians to Ephesians and not vice versa can be shown by the fact that Ephesians "fills-out" or "expands" the former and toned down polemics in Ephesians into a more generalized form than one which is directed towards a specific heresy.[72]

The writing style is also another dead giveaway. Like Colossians, but unlike the genuine Pauline epistles, the author is fond of long sentences. In Colossians there are nine sentences with more than fifty words. This, out of 100 sentences, means that 9% of the sentences are long convoluted ones. When we compare this to the genuine epistles of Paul, the stark contrast stands out. Some examples: Philippians (102 sentences / 1 sentence over fifty words long or 0.9%), Galatians (181 / 1; 0.6%), Romans (581 / 3; 0.5%) and I Corinthians (621 / 1; 0.1%). In the authentic Pauline works, long sentences – those containing fifty words or more – form less than 1% of the whole body. Yet in Ephesians, long sentences make up almost 10% of the whole work.[73]

Together these provide a very strong case to reject the authenticity of Ephesians.

Authenticity of the Pauline Epistles

In general only seven of the thirteen epistles attributed to Paul are considered to have actually been written (or dictated) by him: Romans, I & II Corinthians, Galatians, I Thessalonians, Philippians and Philemon. Five are generally accepted as "pseudepigrahical" (i.e. "forgeries'): II Thessalonians, Ephesians, I & II Timothy and Titus. The last, Colossians, has its authenticity still disputed, although in the opinion of this author, it too is a forgery. Table 5.2 below summarizes the bulk of present scholarly opinion about the authorship of these epistles.

---

[71]   Davidson & Leaney, *Biblical Criticism*: p307-308
       Lüdemann, *Heretics*: p128
       Rhein, *Understanding the New Testament*: 266-268
[72]   Barr, *New Testament Story*: p161
[73]   Ehrman, *The New Testament*: p352-353

Epistles	Scholarly Consensus	Reasons for consensus
Romans **I &II Corinthians** **Galatians**	Genuine	
Ephesians	Forgery	1. No discussion of eschatology in the letter. 2. Presence of "household rules." 3. Style is sluggish and ponderous. 4. Anachronistic references to heretical sects. 5. Key technical phrases differ from the genuine Pauline epistles.
Philippians	Genuine	
Colossians	Very probably a forgery	The majority of scholars say that it is very probably not Pauline due to the difference in vocabulary, style and general slant.
I Thessalonians	Genuine	
II Thessalonians	Forgery	1. A contradiction between the two Thessalonians epistles about the manner of Christ's second coming (I Thessalonians 4:11-53 and II Thessalonians 2:1-12) 2. A large bulk of the second epistle seems to be a direct copy of the first.
I & II Timothy **Titus** **(The "pastoral" epistles)**	Forgery	All internal evidence points to a date of composition around 100 CE: 1. Late attestation (end of the 2nd century). 2. Presence of inconsistencies and incongruities in the content of the letter itself such as Paul's' relationship with Timothy and Titus, quoting from the Gospel of Luke and calling it "scripture", using "we" when speaking of Gentiles instead of "you. 3. The existence of a highly organized church which simply did not exist in Paul's time. 4. The expectation of an imminent return of Christ has been abated with provision now being made for continuation of the church and its teachings. 5. Significantly different theology from the genuine Pauline epistles.
Philemon	Genuine	

Table 5.2: Authorship of the Pauline Epistles

Dating of the Authentic Epistles of Paul

As we will be using the evidence from the authentic epistles of Paul in our analysis of Jesus' life later in this book, it is important for us to have an idea of when these letters were written. We can begin at setting the upper limit of their composition. There is a strong, and very likely authentic, tradition that Paul died in the Neronian persecution of Christians in 64 CE.[74] It is therefore reasonably certain that the genuine epistles must all be written before, or at the latest in, 64 CE.

If we assume the general reliability of the chronology of the Acts of the Apostles, we can set the lower limit. Based on internal evidence, the earliest Pauline epistle is the first epistle to the Thessalonians.

We can connect some statements found in this epistle with some events depicted in Acts. In chapter 17 of Acts we are told that Paul ran into trouble during his visit to Thessalonika. Paul and his followers had fled from there to Berea, another town in the province of Macedonia (See the map: figure 5.1). Again, trouble brewed in Berea and Paul left for Athens, leaving his followers, Timothy and Silas behind. We find Paul recalling this incident in the epistle:

> I Thessalonians 3:1-2
> So when we could stand it no longer, we thought it best to be left by ourselves in Athens. We sent Timothy, who is our brother and God's fellow worker in spreading the gospel of Christ, to strengthen and encourage you in your faith.

After leaving Athens, Paul went to Corinth (Acts 18:1). It was here that Silas and Timothy came from Macedonia[75] to join Paul:

> Acts 18:5
> When Silas and Timothy came from Macedonia, Paul devoted himself exclusively to preaching...

In the epistle, Silas and Timothy were already with Paul when he was writing it:

> I Thessalonians 1:1
> Paul, Silas and Timothy. To the Church of the Thessalonians who are in God the Father and the Lord Jesus Christ. Grace and peace to you.

According to Paul, Timothy had just joined him:

> I Thessalonians 3:6
> *But Timothy has just now came from us to you.*

We can therefore say with some certainty that this epistle was written while Paul was in Corinth.[76] Around this time, according to Acts 18;12, Gallio was proconsul of Archaia.

> Acts 18:12
> But when Gallio was proconsul of Achaia, the Jews with one accord rose up against Paul and brought him before the judgment seat...

---

[74] Davidson & Leaney, *Biblical Criticism*: p283
[75] Thessalonika is a town in the province of Macedonia.
[76] Asimov, *Guide to the Bible*: p1134-1135
      Livingstone, *Dictionary of the Christian Church*: p385

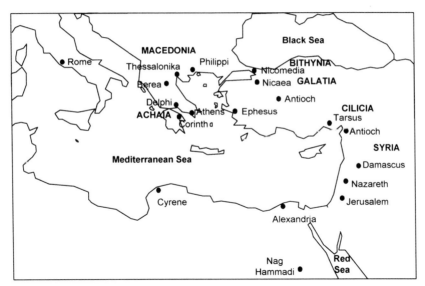

Figure 5.1:   The Mediterranean in New Testament Times

Based on an archaeological discovery (an inscription found in Delphi), Gallio's administration can be dated accurately to 51-52 CE.[77] The earliest extant Christian document, the epistle to the Thessalonians, was therefore written around 51 or 52 CE.

We can place the rest of his authentic epistles by looking for clues within these letters and the account in Acts. Paul left Corinth and moved to Ephesus around 52 CE (Acts 18:18-19). I Corinthians was written in Ephesus soon after his arrival there. (I Corinthians 16:8) This epistle is generally dated to around 53-55 CE.

The epistle to the Galatians is normally dated to around 52-53 CE. This is due to the fact that in I Corinthians 16:1-4, Paul mentioned that he had already given instructions to the Galatians regarding a collection for Jerusalem. Since such instructions can be found in this epistle, it is generally accepted that the letter to the Galatians was written before I Corinthians. However, some scholars have argued for a later date as the epistle deals with issues that are concurrent with II Corinthians. Since II Corinthians was written around 55-58 CE [see below], the alternate date of 55-57 CE is sometimes suggested for Galatians.

There are two epistles that were written while Paul was incarcerated: Philippians and Philemon. Both clearly allude to him being imprisoned:

Philippians 1:12-13
Now I desire to have you know, brothers, that the things which happened to me have turned out rather to the progress of the Good News; that it became evident to the whole palace guard, and to all the rest, that my bonds are in Christ

---

[77]   Davidson & Leaney, *Biblical Criticism*: p282
Wilson, *Jesus: The Evidence*: p115-116

Philemon 1:1, 12-13
Paul, a prisoner of Christ Jesus... Therefore receive him, that is, my own heart, whom I desired to keep with me, that on your behalf he might serve me in my chains for the Good News.

Scholars generally accept that Paul was placed in prison for extended periods in Ephesus (Asia) as well as Rome. The dating of these two epistles, therefore, depends on which of these two incarcerations they were written from. If it was the incarceration in Asia, then they were written around 55-56 CE. If it was Rome, then they were written around 61-62 CE.

II Corinthians looks back to Paul's incarceration in Asia:

II Corinthians 1:8-10
For we don't desire to have you uninformed, brothers, concerning our affliction which happened to us in Asia, that we were weighed down exceedingly, beyond our power, so much that we despaired even of life. Yes, we ourselves have had the sentence of death within ourselves, that we should not trust in ourselves, but in God who raises the dead, who delivered us out of so great a death, and does deliver; on whom we have set our hope that he will also still deliver us;

II Corinthians was[78] written before the letter to the Romans and before Paul's final visit to Jerusalem which is normally dated to around 57-58 CE.[79] Thus, the most likely dates for the composition of II Corinthians are generally accepted to be around 55-57/58 CE.

The epistle to the Romans was composed just before his final fateful trip to Jerusalem where he was arrested. His final trip to Jerusalem and arrest is narrated in Acts 21:27-40.

Romans 15:25
But now, I say, I am going to Jerusalem, serving the saints.

Most scholars date the epistle to around 58 CE.

Paul was sent to Rome around 60 CE and was under relatively loose house arrest for two years (Acts 28:30-31). Philippians and Philemon may have been written during this period (61-62 CE). As we noted above, he was probably condemned soon after that; around 64 CE. Given below is the summary of the dates:

---

[78] Many scholars consider II Corinthians to be a pastiche of two or more letters. However, even if we consider II Corinthians to be such a hodgepodge collection of different letters, the fragments all date to around 55-57/58 CE. For a summary of the various partition theories see White's, *From Jesus to Christianity*: p203-207.

[79] Gerd Lüdemann in his book *Paul, Apostle to the Gentiles: Studies in Chronology* attempts to date the activities of Paul purely from the genuine epistles alone (excluding Acts). He dates the final visit of Paul to Jerusalem as either 52 or 55 CE (depending on whether one dates the crucifixion of Jesus to 27 or 30 CE). [Lüdemann, *Paul*: p 263]

EPISTLES	DATE
Romans	58
I Corinthians	53-55
II Corinthians	55-57/58
Galatians	52-53 or 55-57
Philippians	55-56 or 61-62
I Thessalonians	51-52
Philemon	55-56 or 62

Table 5.3: Approximate Dates of the Pauline Epistles[80]

THE REST OF THE NEW TESTAMENT

Table 5.4 below summarizes the findings of critical scholarship on the authorship of New Testament books.

New Testament Books	Traditional Authorship Attribution	Conclusion Based on Critical Research	Main Reasons Why Result of Critical Research Does not Agree with Tradition
1. Matthew	Matthew	False	The obvious dependence of this gospel on the Gospel of Mark (who is a non eyewitness) means that it could not have been written by Matthew, who would have been an eyewitness to most of the events.
2. Mark	Mark	False	The John Mark referred to in Acts 12:12 could not have made the geographical mistakes committed by the gospel. (Mark 7:31, 5:1-13)
3. Luke	Luke	False	The internal evidence points towards a late date of composition, circa 100 CE. Certain historical errors in Luke-Acts made it unlikely that Luke was the author.
4. John	John the Son of Zebedee	False	Presence of Greek philosophy, mysticism and dogma that could not reasonably be expected of an unschooled Galilean peasant (Acts 4:13).
5. Acts of the Apostles	Luke	False	Same reason as Luke.
6. Romans 7. I Corinthians 8. II Corinthians	Paul	True	-

---

[80]   Armstrong, *The First Christian*: p182
Craveri, *The Life of Jesus*: p412-413
Schonfield, *The Original New Testament*: p271-411
White, *From Jesus to Christianity*: p171-214

9. Galatians			
10. Ephesians	Paul	False	Style is sluggish, unlike Paul's volatile one.
11. Philippians	Paul	True	-
12. Colossians	Paul	Doubtful	Difference in style and vocabulary.
13. I Thessalonians	Paul	True	-
14. II Thessalonians	Paul	Doubtful	Difference in style and vocabulary.
15. I Timothy 16. II Timothy 17. Titus	Paul	False	The existence of a highly organized church (I Tim 3:15), with definite creeds (I Tim 1:13, 4:6), and written gospels (I Timothy 3:16) seem presupposed in these three epistles.
18. Philemon	Paul	True	-
19. Hebrew	Paul	False	No internal evidence suggests Pauline authorship.
20. James	James the brother of Jesus	False	The cultured language of the epistle could not have been derived from a Palestinian with a humble background. It is unlikely that a Jew, whose mother tongue was Aramaic, could write the polished literary Greek of the epistle.
21. I Peter 22. II Peter	Peter	False	Author exhibits an extensive knowledge of Greek and Greek philosophical ideas. Highly improbable for an uneducated Galilean peasant. (Acts 4:13)
23. I John 24. II John 25. III John	John the son of Zebedee	False	Author introduces himself in II John and III John as John the Elder, a different person from John the son of Zebedee.
26. Jude	Jude the brother of Jesus	False	Based on literary style a mid 2nd century document.
27. Revelation	John the son of Zebedee	False	No internal claim that the author is John son of Zebedee. John was a very common Hebrew name.

Table 5.4: Comparison between the traditional attribution of authorship of New Testament books and the result of critical research[81]

Note how *dismal* the results of critical scholarship are with respect to the authorial authenticity of the New Testament.[82] Of the 27 books, only in seven (Romans, I & II Corinthians, Galatians, Philippians, I Thessalonians and Philemon - all epistles of

---

[81]   Davidson & Leaney, *Biblical Criticism*
        Schnell, *The History and Theology of the New Testament Writings*
        Kümmel, *Introduction to the New Testament*
        Ehrman, The New Testament: *A Historical Introduction to the Early Christian Writings*
[82]   Schnell, *The History and Theology of the New Testament Writings:* p276-277

Paul) do we know the identity of the author. In three (Revelation, II & III John) the author is identified in the text but we do not know *who* they are apart from their names; neither "John" in Revelation nor "John the Presbyter" in II & III John is to be identified with John the son of Zebedee. Seven were composed anonymously (Matthew, Mark, Luke, John, Acts, Hebrews and I John) where the names of the authors were added (i.e. *guessed*) by later tradition. The remaining ten (Ephesians, Colossians, II Thessalonians, I & II Timothy, Titus, I & II Peter, James and Jude) are *forgeries* – not written by the persons they purport to be.

* * * * *

We have examined the traditional claims of authorship to the Bible and found most of them to be false. It must be reiterated that the Bible consists of, in a large part, books of testimony and in testimonials knowing the identity of the author is of utmost importance. It is useless to say God wrote the books in the Bible when we didn't even know who they were whom God wrote through. Furthermore, the existence of outright forgeries in the Bible forces a question upon us: can we trust the writing of people who are willing to *deceive* to get their message across? With anonymous authors, authors of whom only their names are known and outright forgeries, the Bible cannot be said to be, *prima facie*, credible.

Chapter Six
CANONIZATION AND MANUSCRIPTS

THE CANONIZATION OF THE BIBLE

When Christians speak of the "canon of the Bible," they mean the list of books that are to be considered as sacred writings to the exclusion of all other books. There is no middle ground, no gray area. Either a book is inspired by God or it is not. There is no book that is "partially" inspired. The uninitiated would naturally expect these "inspired" books to be somehow so different from those rejected that it would be an easy matter to separate them. Surely a work written under the inspiration of the Holy Spirit would be clearly distinct from the works of mere mortals. The truth of the matter, as history shows, is very different.

THE HEBREW CANON

The *Tanakh* was originally the sole property of the Jewish people, who considered it as a collection of their sacred scriptures. However, the issue of which books to include as sacred texts was not settled until the first couple of centuries CE. This confusion carries on through the Christian Churches and partly explains why the Roman Catholic, Protestant and Orthodox Churches have differing lists of canonical books.

The *Torah*, the first five books of Moses, was considered sacred early on and its acceptance was universal among the various Judaisms before 70 CE. We know that as early as 400 BCE, this collection was already viewed as sacred for when the Samaritan sect broke away from more "mainstream" Judaisms around that time, they recognized only the Torah as sacred scripture.[1] By around 200 BCE, many of the books of the prophets (*Nebiim*) were accepted as canonical. In the book of Sirach (or Ecclesiasticus) written around 200-180 BCE, the author recognized as authoritative the prophetic books Joshua, Samuel, Kings, Isaiah, Jeremiah, Ezekial and the "Twelve [minor] prophets". The last part of the Hebrew canon, the writings (*Ketubim*), was the latest to be accepted as scripture. The complete canon was finalized only around the second or third century CE.[2]

So what were the criteria used for inclusion and exclusion from the canon? We get a glimpse of how the decisions were made by looking at what was discussed by

---

[1] Parmalee, *Guidebook to the Bible*: p63-64

[2] In the past it was thought that the last part of the Hebrew canon, the *writings* was closed around the "council" of Jamnia (Yavneh) around 90 CE. The growing consensus among scholars nowadays is that while certain books were discussed during that meeting there is no evidence that it was closed then and more probably the canon was finalized only somewhere around the second or third century CE.

the remnants of Pharisees[3] at Jamnia (Hebrew = *Yavneh*). The Jamnia "council" was formed around 90 CE by Rabbi Yochanan ben Zakkai in an effort to rebuild Judaism after the disaster of the Jewish revolt of 66-74 CE. Among the things discussed during this time was the canonicity of some of the books of the Bible: Song of Songs, Esther, Ecclesiasticus, Ecclesiastes, Daniel, Ezekiel and I Maccabees.

It seems that some of the decisions were based on political considerations as well as mistaken attribution of authorship! The Song of Solomon, an overtly sexual book, was accepted solely on the tradition that it was written by King Solomon. Jewish and Christians theologians have, ever since then been forced to interpret the book allegorically to give the book some semblance of religiousness. Daniel was accepted because it was believed to have been written before the closing of the prophetic period – which was accepted to be between the time of Moses and Ezra (around the mid 6th century BCE) Yet, as we have seen in chapter four, Daniel was a late work – written in the middle of the second century BCE! Books that were rejected were rejected for various reasons – none of them spiritual. Sirach was rejected because it was written after the prophetic period, yet it was actually written *earlier* than Daniel! I Maccabees was rejected due to political reasons. It described the revolt led by the Maccabean family against the Syrian king, Antiochus Ephiphanes (d.163 BCE) who attacked Jerusalem and pillaged the Temple in 167 BCE. The rabbis were in no mood to promote a book about revolt so soon after their own failed revolt against the Romans.[4]

The modern Hebrew canon developed from the Pharisees and their theological descendant, Rabbinic Judaism. In this sense it was an accidental development for we know that the canon of the Pharisees was not the only one current before the fall of Jerusalem in 70 CE. We have seen above that the Samaritans recognized only the Torah as scripture. We will look at three other canons that differ from the Pharisees.

The Septuagint

The Jews of the Diaspora, who fled Judah after the fall of Jerusalem 586 BCE, were widely distributed throughout the Mediterranean and the Middle East. A significant segment of these had chosen Alexandria in Egypt as their home. By the 4th century BCE the Jews there had largely lost much of their capability to communicate in or understand their original tongue, Hebrew. They adopted the language of the area, which was Greek. The need to understand their religious roots was strong and so the Hebrew Bible (then consisting only of the Torah) was translated into Greek.

---

[3]   The Pharisees were one of the four major Jewish sects before the first Jewish revolt of 70 CE intact. The other three were the Sadducees, the Essenes and the Zealots. See note 31 in chapter 7 for more information on these sects.

[4]   Allegro, *The Dead Sea Scrolls*: p59-60
Anderson, *A Critical Introduction to the Old Testament*:p192
Bruce, *The Books and the Parchments*: p97
Davidson & Leaney, *Biblical Criticism*: p215
Livingstone, *Dictionary of the Christian Church*: p327
McDonald, *The Formation of the Christian Biblical Canon*: p25-53
Soggin, *Introduction to the Old Testament*: p13-20

The story of how the Greek translation of the Bible came to be called the *Septuagint* can be found in *The Letter of Aristeas*. The epistle, presents itself as being written around 250 BCE by Aristeas, an official at the court of King Ptolemy Philadelphus (285-246 BCE). The letter was written to his brother, Philocrates, to explain how the Torah came to be translated in Greek. King Ptolemy was a great patron of literature and it was he who inaugurated the great Library of Alexandria, one of the world's cultural wonders. According to the letter, King Ptolemy wanted a translation of the Jewish Law and sent Aristeas to Jerusalem to meet the high priest, Eleazar. Having been lavished with fabulous gifts from the visiting delegation, the high priest chose as translators six elders from each of the twelve tribes of Israel. These 72 scholars were then sent to Alexandria where they labored for 72 days on the island of Pharos translating the Bible. At the end of 72 days, 72 voices shouted "Amen!" and 72 translations were completed. When they compared their translations with each other they found complete agreement among them, proving that the work was done under God's inspiration. From their number, came the word *Septuaginto*, which is Latin for seventy. The Septuagint is also sometimes referred to by the Roman numeral for seventy: LXX.[5]

The Letter of Aristeas reads like a myth and is a myth. It was not even written during the reign of King Ptolemy. Most scholars believe that it was written around 100 BCE by a Jewish apologist in Alexandria. Probably the only truth we can derive from the letter was that the Torah, the first five books of the Bible, was translated into Greek for the benefit of Greek speaking Jews during the reign of Ptolemy Philadelphus during the third century BCE.[6] For the rest of the Greek Old Testament, internal evidence suggests that it was the work of many different translators working in many different places at different times.[7] Most scholars believe that the whole of Hebrew Tanakh was not translated into Greek until the first century BCE.[8]

It is important to note that the Septuagint was *the* Bible to the early Christians and to the authors of the New Testament.[9] It was to the Septuagint that the gospel writers looked for prophecies and allusions to the coming of Jesus Christ, a fact that will become important in our discussions in the second part of this book.

As mentioned in chapter 1, the arrangement of the Christian Old Testament is taken from the Septuagint, which differs substantially from the Hebrew Bible. The arrangement of books led naturally to the questions of canonicity. The books today referred to as the Apocrypha[10] are included in the Septuagint but omitted from the Hebrew Bible. In the Greek Bible, these books are in no way differentiated from the

---

[5] Allegro, *The Dead Sea Scrolls*: p62
    Bruce, *The Books and the Parchments*: p146
    McDonald, *The Formation of the Christian Biblical Canon*: p85-86
    Parmalee, *Guidebook to the Bible*: p81-82
[6] Martin, *New Testament Foundations I*: p74
[7] McDonald, *The Formation of the Christian Biblical Canon*: p86-87
[8] Jobes and Silva, *Invitation to the Septuagint*: p34 n8
[9] Martin, *New Testament Foundations I*: p74
[10] See chapter one for a list of the apocryphal books. Note that all the books in the apocrypha were written within the period 300 BCE and 100 CE (as were some canonical books such as Daniel). They were all written before the definite separation of the Christian and Jewish religions.

rest of the "canonical" books, an obvious testament to the translators' and users' belief in their canonicity. The Septuagint gives evidence to a separate larger canon than the one accepted by the Pharisees.

The Essenes

Another different canon was found at Qumran, most probably that of the Essenes. In 1947 scrolls were discovered that came from caves associated with the ruined buildings belonging to a Jewish religious community that was destroyed by the Romans during the first century CE. The location of the find, Qumran, close to the Dead Sea, gave the findings its name: the Dead Sea Scrolls. The Dead Sea Scrolls include fragments representing every book in the Old Testament except the book of Esther. But other books, not included in the Pharisiac canon was also found at Qumran: *Sirach, Tobit, Jubilees, Enoch, the Testament of the Twelve Patriarchs* and *the Temple Scroll*. Indeed, some scholars have argued that The Temple Scroll was as holy as the Torah in the eyes of the Essenes.[11]

The Sadducees

Although we do not have extensive documentary evidence, we know from the writings of the Jewish historian, Josephus (37–c100 CE), that the Sadducees accepted only the Torah as authoritative:[12]

> Antiquities 18:1:3
> But the doctrine of the Sadducees is this: That souls die with the bodies; nor do they regard the observation of any thing besides what the [written] law [i.e. Torah] enjoins them…

> Antiquities 13:10:6
> What I would now explain is this, that the Pharisees have delivered to the people a great many observances by succession from their fathers, *which are not written in the laws of Moses; and for that reason it is that the Sadducees reject them*, and say that we are to esteem those observances to be obligatory which are in the written word, but are not to observe what are derived from the tradition of our forefathers.

We can see then that the historical development of the Hebrew canon was a haphazard, contingent one. Had the Pharisees not been the sect that survived the Jewish revolt, we would have had a different Hebrew canon.

THE MASORETIC TEXT

In the first century CE, there were many different renditions[13] of the Hebrew Scriptures around. After the Jewish revolt of 70 CE, one textual tradition eventually

---

11   McDonald, *The Formation of the Christian Biblical Canon*: p70-74
12   McDonald, *The Formation of the Christian Biblical Canon*: p67-69

became the dominant text. This standard text was not based on any scientific or critical study on the many extant manuscripts of the scriptures. It became the dominant text because it was the text favored by the Pharisees – the sect that eventually developed Rabbinic Judaism. This text eventually became known as the *Masoretic*[14] text.

Although the earliest extant manuscript of the Masoretic Text today is very late (916 CE), all the evidence we have, based on fragments that predate this oldest manuscript, point to the fact that the text remain practically unaltered since around the end of the first century CE.[15] Standard translations of the English Bible are still based on the Masoretic Text.[16]

The Septuagint and the Dead Sea Scrolls provide the evidence that textual tradition of the Masoretic Text was not the only extant one prior to the dominance of Rabbinic Judaism. The Dead Sea Scrolls (mentioned above) were the first pre-Masoretic Text in Hebrew ever discovered. Some readings in the scrolls were more closely related to the Septuagint version, others were closer to the Masoretic, while still others differ from both the Septuagint and the Masoretic. The obvious conclusion from this is that the text in today's Bible is just one of many variations that existed in the past.[17]

THE CHRISTIAN OLD TESTAMENT CANON

In the year 383 Eusebius Hieronymous (c340-420), better known as Saint Jerome, was commissioned by Pope Damasus (304-384) to prepare an authoritative translation of the Bible into Latin. As part of his preparation, Jerome went to Palestine and studied Hebrew under the Jewish scholars. The Jewish scholars showed him their canon and, not knowing much about the background of their selection, the church father was impressed with their arguments. It was Jerome who introduced the term *apocrypha* for the extra books in the Septuagint not included in the Hebrew canon. Jerome tried to persuade the Roman Church to reject the apocrypha but without any success. Jerome worked on the translation for fifteen years and produced the version

---

[13]   Normally referred to as a *textual tradition* as these differences are copied down faithfully by subsequent transcribers.

[14]   *Masorah* is Hebrew for *tradition*. The term refers to the method by which the medieval rabbis provided the received consonantal text with vowel points, accent markings and marginal notes. Their efforts ensured that stabilization of the Hebrew textual tradition (see Metzger and Coogan, *Oxford Companion to the Bible*: p500-501). The spelling of the word is sometimes rendered with two s's, i.e. *Massorah*. Different scholars seem to have difference preferences as to which spelling to use since the *samekh* (the Hebrew 's') is sometimes doubled in Hebrew. In this book, I prefer it with one 's' – easier to type!

[15]   Allegro, *The Dead Sea Scrolls*: p23, 59-60
Bruce, *The Books and the Parchments*: p115
Würthwein, *The Text of the Old Testament*: p13-14

[16]   Note that the *arrangement* of the books of the Christian Old Testament is based on the Septuagint but the actual *text* (words used for translation) is based on the Masoretic Text.

[17]   Allegro, *The Dead Sea Scrolls*: p59-67
Davidson & Leaney, *Biblical Criticism*: p105-106
Würthwein, *The Text of the Old Testament*: p13-14

known as the *Vulgate*.[18] The Vulgate included the books from the Apocrypha. The difference in opinion between the Roman Church and Jerome regarding what constitute canonicity was to be repeated throughout the history of Christendom.[19]

The earliest Christian list of Old Testament books was that of Melito, Bishop of Sardis, around 170-180. His list paralleled the Hebrew canon but lacked the books of Esther and Lamentations. From this time onwards the lists of the church fathers included the apocrypha. Origen (c185-245) seemed to include Esther, Judith, Tobit and Wisdom of Solomon in the canon. From some ancient Christian Greek manuscripts of the Bible we have today, we can see that up to the 4th century, there was still no agreement as to the complete list of canonical books. The *Codex Vaticanus*,[20] a 4th century manuscript, includes all the apocrypha except the books of Maccabees. The *Codex Sinaiticus*, another 4th century manuscript, adds Tobit, Judith and I & II Maccabees to the Hebrew canon. The *Codex Alexandrinus*, a 5th century manuscripts adds the apocrypha: the Wisdom of Solomon, the Psalms of Solomon, and III & IV Maccabees.[21]

During the Reformation, the Protestant leaders refused to accept the apocrypha as inspired works. Martin Luther (1483-1546) did, however, include the apocrypha in the appendix of his German translation of the Bible. The Anglican Church views the books of the apocrypha, not as inspired works, but as "example of life and instruction of manners, but not used to establish doctrine". The Roman Catholic Church in the Council of Trent (1548) accepted as inspired eleven of the fourteen books of the apocrypha. It excluded I & II Esdras and the Prayer of Manasses of the apocrypha from the list of canonical books. This decision was reiterated in the First Vatican Council in 1870. The Eastern Orthodox Churches accepted Tobit, Judith, Ecclesiasticus and the Wisdom of Solomon as canonical in the synod at Jerusalem in 1672.[22]

This problem is further compounded when we turn to references to the Old Testament by the New Testament authors. The epistle of Jude, for instance, quotes passages, as though they were authoritative, from a book that is today not even included in the apocrypha! The book Jude was quoting from the book of Enoch. This book was once regarded as proper scripture but was eventually lost to the Christian Church. Here is the passage from Jude:

Jude 14-15
About these also *Enoch, the seventh from Adam, prophesied*, saying, "Behold, the Lord came with ten thousands of his holy ones, to execute judgment on all, and to convict all the ungodly of all their works of ungodliness which they have done in

---

[18] *Vulgata* is Latin for *widespread*.
[19] Kelly, *Jerome*: p85-86
Livingstone, *Dictionary of the Christian Church*: p27-28
McDonald, *The Formation of the Christian Biblical Canon*: p113
Parmalee, *Guidebook to the Bible*: p83
[20] For an introduction to the various codices see the section *New Testament: Text and Transmission* below.
[21] Davidson & Leaney, *Biblical Criticism*: p216
McDonald, *The Formation of the Christian Biblical Canon*: p108-116
[22] Livingstone, *Dictionary of the Christian Church*: p27-28

an ungodly way, and of all the hard things which ungodly sinners have spoken against him."

This is a direct quotation from I Enoch 1:9! In Jude verse 9, we see another reference to a non-canonical book that is outside the apocrypha: The Assumption of Moses. In another New Testament book, the epistle to the Hebrews (11:37) quotes a passage from another book, The Martyrdom of Isaiah, that is outside the Christian canon. Paul (I Corinthians 2:9) quotes from The Ascension of Isaiah 11:34, as though it was scripture and makes use of the theological arguments from Wisdom of Solomon in his epistle to the Romans (Romans 1:24-32/Wisdom 14:22-31; Romans 5:12-21/Wisdom 2:23-24) [23]

To summarize, *there has never been a consensus within Christendom of what constitute the books of the Old Testament.* The obvious lack of agreement between the various Christian churches, and among the early Christians, as to which books were written under the inspiration of the Holy Spirit and are thus canonical, shows that there is no clear cut definition as to what constitutes sacred scripture.

NEW TESTAMENT: TEXT AND TRANSMISSION

Fundamentalists make many extravagant claims based on the extant New Testament manuscripts. The impression these claims leave the layman with is that somehow the *historical accuracy* of the New Testament has been proven. As a preliminary to examining these claims, we need to acquaint ourselves with some basic facts about New Testament manuscripts and textual tradition.

There are today more than 5500 extant manuscripts of the Greek New Testament. These manuscripts are normally divided into four basic groups: Papyri, Uncial, Minuscule and Lectionaries. The first three are called "continuous text" manuscripts in the sense that they have (or used to have, if what remains are merely fragments) the full continuous text of the scripture. Continuous text manuscripts number about 3,200.

Papyri refer to the material the text is written on, papyrus. These manuscripts are the earliest witnesses to the New Testament text. The 96 extant papyrus manuscripts range from the second century to the 8th century. These manuscripts are designated using the letter "P" followed by numerals in superscript (e.g. P^1, P^{52} etc).

The other two categories, rather inconsistently with the first, refer to the handwriting style of the manuscripts. *Uncials*, refers to the formal capital letters used in the writing of the text. Uncial manuscripts are normally written on parchments (animal hides). The dates of the extant uncial manuscripts, totaling 299, range from the turn of the third century to the 11th century. The modern designation for uncials is with an initial 0 followed by further numbers. However, for the first 45 manuscripts, the traditional designation of using capital letters is still used (thus א is 01, codex A is 02, codex B is 02 etc).

Minuscules refer to the small letters written with a running hand. Minuscules form the bulk of the extant manuscripts (approx 2800) but are also the latest and

---

[23]   Davidson & Leaney, *Biblical Criticism*: p174, 215-216
McDonald, *The Formation of the Christian Biblical Canon*: p100-103

furthest removed from the original autographs. The earliest minuscule manuscripts date from the 9th century. The latest dates to just before the advent of printing; in the 16th century. Minuscules are designated by simple numerals starting with 1.[24]

Numbering approximately 2300, *lectionaries* are "non-continuous text" manuscripts. These are essentially used for church worships where separate pericopes are arranged according to the requirements of the annual church ritual. These are not in the sequence of the canonical gospels. The earliest fragment extant is dated to the 4th century. However, the bulk dates from the 9th to the 16th century. Almost all of these lectionaries are not important for textual research and we will not be discussing them anymore below. Lectionaries are designated with the letter *l* followed by numerals (e.g. *l*1, *l*2 etc).[25]

Papyrus manuscripts, although being the earliest witness to the text, are almost always fragmentary. The earliest papyrus is P^{52}, a small fragment containing only six verses from the Gospel of John (John 18:31-34, 37-38). It is conventionally dated to 125 CE.[26] Most of these manuscripts date from the third and 4th centuries.

Two papyri finds that are of importance, as far as we are concerned, are the Chester Beatty Papyri and the Bodmer Papyri. The former, three manuscripts designated as P^{45}, P^{46} and P^{47}, were named after the American millionaire, Alfred Chester Beatty who bought the fragments in 1931 in an Egyptian black market. P^{46}, dated to the around 200 CE, contains the letters of Paul (but is missing some parts and is lacking completely in the pastorals, II Thessalonians and Philemon). P^{45} and P^{47} are both dated to the third century CE. The former consists of the gospels and Acts (beginning from Matthew 20:24 and ending at Acts 17:17 but with a lot of gaps) while the latter are fragments from the book of Revelation (Rev 9:10-17:2 with some gaps).

The Bodmer Papyri consist of three manuscript fragments, P^{66}, P^{72} and P^{75}. P^{66} dated to circa 200 CE, is a codex of the Gospel of John, with the first fourteen chapters complete and the remainder in fragmentary condition. P^{75}, a third century fragment, contains the gospels of Luke (from Luke 3:10 with some gaps) and John (John 1:1-15:8 with a few gaps). Finally, P^{72}, from around the turn of the third and 4th centuries, contains Jude and I & II Peter.[27]

Three other papyri manuscripts are of importance for they provide early evidence for the "Western" text rendition of the Acts of the Apostles (see below):

- P^{29} Consisting of Acts 26:7-8, 20 dating from the third century.

- P^{38} Consisting of Acts 18:27-19:6, 12-16 from circa 300 CE.

---

[24] Aland, K. & Aland B., *The Text of the New Testament*: p73-184
[25] Aland, K. & Aland B., *The Text of the New Testament*: p73, 163, 169
[26] Much nonsense has been spouted out by conservative theologians on the significance of this small fragment. The dating is based on paleography (i.e. style of writing). Thus the date could easily be as early as 110 CE or as late as 160 CE. (see Ehrman, B., "The Text as Window: New Testament Manuscripts and the Social History of Early Christianity", Chp 22 in Ehrman & Holmes, *The Text of the New Testament in Contemporary Research*: p371 n49)
[27] Aland, K. & Aland B., *The Text of the New Testament*: p57
Epp & Fee, *Studies in the Theory and Method of New Testament Textual Criticism*: p4

- P[48] Consisting of Acts 23:11-17; 4:31-5:13 from the third century.

Uncial manuscripts are, as a rule, more complete than the papyrus type. We will give a brief rundown of the earliest and most important manuscripts.

Perhaps the most famous uncial manuscript is the *Codex*[28] *Sinaiticus*, designated as ℵ 01, which was discovered by the German New Testament scholar, Constantine Tischendorf (1815-1874). He found the manuscript in 1844 in the monastery of St. Catherine in Mount Sinai. Tischendorf took the manuscript from the monks as a loan but gave it to the Czar of Russia as a present! In 1933 the Codex was bought from the Soviet government by the British museum. The manuscript has been dated from mid to late 4th century CE. The *Codex Sinaiticus* is the only extant complete copy of the Greek New Testament text in uncial script.[29]

The *Codex Vaticanus*, designated as B 03, is so named because it is now found in the Vatican Library. The codex has been in that place since 1481, although nobody knows how it got there in the first place! The *Vaticanus* is arguably the most important and probably the earliest (early 4th century) of all the New Testament manuscripts. The New Testament is not complete however, as everything after Hebrews 9:14 is lost.[30]

Apart from these two very important uncials, there are five others that are also quite important textually: A 02, C 04, D^{ea} 05, W 032 and Θ 038.

- *Codex Alexandrinus*, A 02. The codex was presented to King Charles I of England in 1627 by Cyril Lucar, Patriarch of Alexandria. The king, in turn, presented the codex to English scholars. The codex is now housed together with the Sinaiticus in the British museum. The codex contains all of the New Testament but with some rather large portions missing; all of Matthew up to Matthew 25:6 is lost together with pages containing portions of John (6:50-8:52) and II Corinthians (4:13-12:6). Handwriting experts showed that the *Codex Alexandrinus* was written in the style employed in Alexandria around the 5th century CE.[31]
- *Codex Ephraemi*, C 04. This 15th century manuscript is actually a *palimpsest*. It's original text, much of the New Testament, but with considerable gaps (and completely missing II Thessalonians and II John), was erased during the 12th century and then used for writing the text of the sermons of St. Ephraemi. The original text was uncovered, through the use

---

28   *Codex* is simply a technical term for loose sheets bound together. All modern books can be called codices.

29   Bentley, *Secrets of Mount Sinai*: p96-99
Davidson & Leaney, *Biblical Criticism*: p225
Metzger, *The Text of the New Testament*: p42-46
Parmalee, *Guidebook to the Bible*: p161-162

30   Metzger, *The Text of the New Testament*: p 47-48
Parmalee, *Guidebook to the Bible*: p160-161

31   Metzger, *The Text of the New Testament*: p 46-47
Parmalee, *Guidebook to the Bible*: p160

of chemical reagents, in 1840-1841 by Tischendorf (the discoverer of the Codex Sinaiticus).[32]

- *Codex Bezae*, D^{ea} 05. This is a 5th century manuscript with Greek and Latin texts facing each other on opposite pages. The codex was presented by French scholar Theodore Beza (1519-1605) to Cambridge University in 1581. It contains most of the four gospels and Acts with some portions of III John. The four gospels are arranged in the so-called "Western" order (Matthew, John, Luke and Mark).[33]
- *Washington Codex*, W 032. This is a 5th century manuscript consisting of the four gospels arranged in the same manner as the Codex Bezae. The manuscript was bought by Charles Freer and is now housed in the Freer Museum in Washington, D.C.[34]
- *Codex Koridethi*, Θ 038. This is a 9th century codex, written by a scribe widely believed to be unfamiliar with Greek. It contains the four gospels with some gaps. Its name was derived from its place of discovery: a church in the town of Koridethi in the mountainous region of Caucasus. The text is now housed in Tiflis, Georgia.[35]

Miniscule manuscripts are the most numerous: numbering more than 2,800. Of these, about 80% attest to the late full-blown *Byzantine* text type (see below) and are of little value in textual research. However, about 10%, according to Kurt and Barbara Aland, offer evidence of earlier text. Some of these more important ones include:[36]

- *Family 1*. This consists of the following minuscule manuscripts: 1, 118, 131, 209 and 1582. All these date from the 12th of the 14th century.
- *Family 13*. This consists of manuscripts 13, 124, 174, 230, 346, 543, 788, 826, 828, 983, 1689 and 1709. Dated from the 11th to the 15th century.
- *Manuscript 33*. A 9th century manuscript, known as "Queen of the minuscules", for its perceived textual value. Housed at *Bibliothèque Nationale* in Paris, it contains all of the New Testament except the book of Revelation.

---

[32]   Aland, K. & Aland B., *The Text of the New Testament*: p109
       Metzger, *The Text of the New Testament*: p48-49
[33]   Metzger, *The Text of the New Testament*: p49
[34]   Aland, K. & Aland B., *The Text of the New Testament*: p113
       Metzger, *The Text of the New Testament*: p56-57
[35]   Aland, K. & Aland B., *The Text of the New Testament*: p118
       Metzger, *The Text of the New Testament*: p58
[36]   Aland, K. & Aland B., *The Text of the New Testament*: p128-129
       Metzger, *The Text of the New Testament*: p61-62

EARLY VERSIONS OF THE NEW TESTAMENT

Versions are translations of the Bible into other languages. Translations of the New Testament appear as early as circa 180 CE. Three early versions are of some importance to understanding the textual history of the New Testament: the Old Latin, Old Syriac and Coptic Versions.[37]

Old Latin (OL) versions, called as such to differentiate it from Jerome's Vulgate, first appeared probably around the end of the second century CE. Extant OL manuscripts date from the 4th to the 13th century. There are, extant, about 50 manuscript fragments of OL, none of which contains the complete New Testament.[38]

The famous *Vulgate* is a Latin translation of the Old and New Testament from the original languages by Jerome (c342-420). The Vulgate, undoubtedly an achievement of a high order, was *the* Bible for Western Europe for a thousand years. Perhaps due to its popularity, many attempts were made to "correct" or "purify" Jerome's text. Today the more than 8,000 extant manuscripts of the Vulgate show numerous cross contamination of all textual types. Thus the Vulgate is not considered of much help in discovering the original text of the New Testament.[39]

The Old Syriac is the term given to the two earliest manuscripts of Syriac translation. These are dated to 4th and 5th centuries. These two manuscripts are the Syr[c], called the Curetonianus after its discoverer William Cureton and the Syr[s], named the Sinaiticus after its place of discovery.[40]

The standard Bible of the Syrian Church is the *Peshitta*. The Peshitta, of which there are 350 extant manuscripts, contains 22 books of the New Testament but lacks II & III John, II Peter, Jude and Revelation - which the Syrian Church does not accept as canonical. Like the Vulgate, the Peshitta betrays the work of many hands (attempted corrections and revisions) and is of limited significance textually. Other Syriac versions include the Harklensis/Philoxeniana (Syr[h]), which may have some textual significance, and the Palestinian Syriac.[41]

Coptic is an ancient Egyptian language written with Greek alphabets (with additional letters). There are seven known Coptic dialects: Sahidic, Bohairic, Fayyumic, Akhmimic, Subakhmimic, Middle Egyptian and Protobohairic. Versions in the first two dialects are normally considered the most important. The oldest Coptic manuscripts found are fragments that date from the 4th century consisting of texts from the gospels.[42]

---

[37] Epp & Fee, *Studies in... NT Textual Criticism*: p5
[38] Metzger, *The Text of the New Testament*: p72
[39] Epp & Fee, *Studies in... NT Textual Criticism*: p6
Metzger, *The Bible in Translation*: p35
Metzger, *The Text of the New Testament*: p76
[40] Aland, K. & Aland B., *The Text of the New Testament*: p193-194
Metzger, *The Text of the New Testament*: p69
[41] Aland, K. & Aland B., *The Text of the New Testament*: p194-200
Epp & Fee, *Studies in... NT Textual Criticism*: p6
Metzger, *The Bible in Translation*: p28
Metzger, *The Text of the New Testament*: p79-82
[42] Aland, K. & Aland B., *The Text of the New Testament*: p200-201

Two other versions deserve mention; the Armenian and Georgian versions. Both these are translations, not from the original Greek, but from other versions. The early Armenian versions (no earlier than the fifth century) were probably based on the old Syriac versions. Later, around the eighth to the twelfth centuries, the Armenian version was revised based on a Greek text. With the exception of the Latin Vulgate, there are more manuscripts of the Armenian version (around 1,500 manuscripts) extant than any other versions.

The old Georgian version was a translation of the old Armenian version. Thus it was a translation of a translation of a translation of the original (Georgian-Armenian-Syriac-Greek). Among the oldest known Georgian manuscripts are the Adysh manuscript (897 CE) designated as Geo[1], the Oppiza manuscript (913 CE) and the Tbet' manuscript (995 CE). The last two are collectively designated as Geo[2].[43]

NEW TESTAMENT TEXT TYPES

While the extant manuscripts are similar to each other in a large part, they are not completely identical. The reason is that these manuscripts were *handwritten* copies made by Christian scribes from older copies. And in manual copying, as we all know, mistakes are often made. In fact, the scribes make all types of errors imaginable, some unintentional and some intentional. Some of the errors and differences between the various manuscripts can be quite major, theologically speaking.[44] The vast majority of these errors occur during the first four centuries CE. Thus the extant manuscripts today are a vast sea of confusion that needs to be sorted out for any sense to be made of them.

Although scribes do make, accidental or deliberate, mistakes, in general most copyists are conservative. After all, they are copying what is to them sacred scriptures. There is a tendency to faithfully copy what they see in front of them. So errors made by an earlier scribe were generally preserved by later scribes who used his manuscript as their "master copy" – or exemplar. Such shared errors, or characteristic readings, enable scholars to group various manuscripts together.

Johann A. Bengel (1687-1752) was the first textual critic to suggest that the ancient manuscripts could be group into text types; groupings of manuscripts with similar characteristic readings. Johann S. Semler (1725-1791) suggested that these manuscripts be divided into three major groups, which he termed the *Alexandrian* (derived from the citations of Origen (c185-254), and preserved in the Syriac and Bohairic versions), the *Eastern* (from the churches in Antioch and Constantinople) and the *Western* (based on the Old Latin versions and citations from the western church fathers).

Metzger, *The Bible in Translation*: p35-37
Metzger, *The Text of the New Testament*: p69-71
[43] Aland, K. & Aland B., *The Text of the New Testament*: p204-205
Metzger, *The Text of the New Testament*: p82-83
[44] We will look at two examples of these later in this chapter under the section "The Case of Unauthentic Texts." For examples of how proto-orthodox Christians deliberately changed the text of the manuscripts of the New Testament to support their theologies against the "heretics" refer to Bart Ehrman's books *The Orthodox Corruption of Scripture* (Oxford UP, 1993) and *Misquoting Jesus* (Harper, 2005).

Next came Johann J. Griesbach (1745-1812) who refined earlier ideas and suggested three textual families. The Alexandrian (represented by the uncials C, L and K), the Western (represented by the uncial D) and the later Byzantine text (represented by the uncial A and a great mass of the minuscules).[45]

In 1881, B.F. Wescott (1825-1901) and F.J.A. Hort (1828-1892), published their groundbreaking work, *The New Testament in the Original Greek*. They divided the manuscripts into four basic groups: the Syrian, the Western, the Alexandrian and the Neutral. The Syrian is essentially what is today known as the Byzantine text. They considered the Syrian text, represented mainly by Codex Alexandrinus (A 02) in the gospels and the bulk of the later minuscules, to be a conflation of earlier textual families and are useful mainly for "recitation" and not for "diligent study"; in other words, of very little textual value. The Western Text, represented by Codex Bazae in the gospels and Acts (D[ea]) and the Old Latin versions, is of early origins, perhaps as early as just before mid second century CE. The Alexandrian Text, represented by codex Ephremi (C 04), minuscule 33 and the Coptic versions, is characterized by a greater degree of polish in its style. This, according to W&H, is due mainly to the influence of its affinity to the great centers of Greek learning. Finally, the Neutral Text, represented by the Codex Sinaiticus ℵ 01, and Codex Vaticanus (B 03), is, as the name implies, the textual group most likely to be the original readings from the autographs. To W&H, readings from the Neutral Text family are accepted as the original text and are only to be rejected when strong evidence exists to the contrary.[46]

The main development since the time of Wescott and Hort is the discovery of the numerous papyri manuscripts from Egypt. These discoveries have tended to confirm their basic position on the textual families (with some minor changes) and on the lateness (and low textual value) of the Byzantine text.[47]

The generally accepted position on the textual families and their major manuscript witnesses are given in figure 6.1 and table 6.1 respectively on the next page. The manuscripts of a certain text type are not completely identical but they are similar enough to each other that grouping the manuscripts into three (or four) types can be done quite easily.

Figure 6.1:
Relationship of the
Text Types

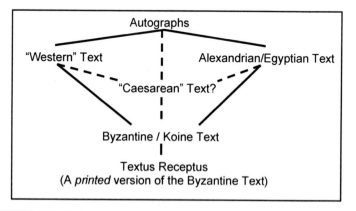

---

[45] Metzger, *The Text of the New Testament*: p112-119
[46] Metzger, *The Text of the New Testament*: p130-134
[47] Epp & Fee, *Studies in... NT Textual Criticism*: p12
       Metzger, *The Text of the New Testament*: p137

Text Types Witness	Alexandrian / Egyptian	"Western"	Caesarean	Byzantine / Koine
Early Papyrus	P[75], P[66], P[46], P[72]	P[48], P[39], P[69]	P[45]	No early papyrus manuscripts
Uncials	ℵ 01, B 03, C 04 and W 032 [in Luke 1:1-8:12 & John]	D 05, W 032 [in Mark 1:1-5:30][48]	Θ 038 W 032 [in Mark 5:31- 16:20]	A 02 [gospels only], Full text of NT only found in 8th century MSS E 06 and Ω 045
Patristic Citations[49]	Origen (c185- 254), Didymus (c313- 398), Athanasius (296- 373), Cyril of Alexandria (d.444)	Irenaeus (c130- 200), Clement (c96), Tertulian (c160- 225), Cyprian (d.258)	Origen [in Mark], Eusebius (260- 340), Cyril of Jerusalem (c315-386)	Chrysostom (c347-407), Theodoret (c393-466)
Early Versions	Coptic (Sahidic & Bohairic)	Old Latin, Syr[s], Syr[c], Syr[h]	Old Armenian, Old Georgian	-
Minuscules	MSS 33	MSS 383, 614	Family 1, Family 2, 565 and 700	The majority of minuscules

Table 6.1: Major Witnesses of the Various Text Types[50]

The Alexandrian / Egyptian text type is the new name for the Neutral text of Wescott and Hort. Gordon Fee explains the characteristics of this text type:

> [C]ontains readings that are terse, somewhat rough, less harmonized and generally "more difficult" [i.e. from a doctrinal viewpoint-PT] than those of other text types, though on closer study they regularly commend themselves as original. Furthermore, it is consistently so across all the NT books, with a minimal tendency to harmonize an author's idiosyncrasies with the more common Greek patterns. All these facts preserve the impression that this text type is the product of a carefully preserved transmission.[51]

---

[48] That some manuscripts should consist of more than one text type is not really surprising. It is always possible that the exemplars used for making the manuscripts could have originated from different places and may not be a single manuscript. For instance, because many of the early New Testament books circulated separately, it is possible that the scribe copied one book (say the gospels) from one text type and another book (say the Pauline epistles) from another exemplar that comes from a different text type.

[49] These are citations of the New Testament passages from the writings of the early church fathers.

[50] Epp & Fee, *Studies in... NT Textual Criticism*: p7-8
Metzger, *The Text of the New Testament*: p213-216

[51] Epp & Fee, *Studies in... NT Textual Criticism*: p7

The name "Western" text is now almost invariably given with the inverted commas. This is due to the fact that its geographical range is wider than the original term suggests, for manuscripts and citations of church fathers from the East (e.g. Clement) are known. The "Western" text type:

> [I]s particularly marked by some long paraphrases and long additions, as well as harmonistic tendencies and substitutions and synonyms. In fact, the Western text of Acts is about ten percent longer than other texts and almost certainly reflects an early revision...There are several instances, especially in some striking "omissions" but in other places as well, where scholars have cogently argued that the Western text preserves the original NT text.[52]

The existence of a third early text type, the Caesarean, is disputed by some scholars. The reason for the dispute is simple, what is distinctive about the text type is that it contains a mix of "Western" and Alexandrian readings.[53]

The Byzantine text type, as can be seen from the table above, appears late in the history of NT manuscripts. Codex Alexandrinus, (c475), is the earliest manuscript witness of this text type, and even here, it is only a witness for the gospels. The earliest full witnesses are from two 8th and 9th century uncial manuscripts. The Byzantine text type has very low value as a textual witness to the original autographs. Bruce Metzger summarized this thus:

> [R]eadings which are supported by only Koine or Byzantine witness...may be set aside as almost certainly secondary. The reason that justifies one in discarding the Koine type of text is that it is based on the recension prepared near the close of the third century by Lucian of Antioch, or some of his close associates, who deliberately combined elements from earlier types of text. Despite the fact that it appears in a large majority of Greek manuscripts (for it was adopted as received text of the Greek Orthodox Church), the abundance of witnesses numerically count for nothing in view of the secondary origin of the text type as a whole.[54]

The characteristics of Byzantine readings tend to confirm this secondary origin:

> Most readings peculiar to this text are generally recognized to be of secondary nature. A great number of them smooth out grammar; remove ambiguity in word order; add nouns, pronouns, and prepositional phrases; and harmonize one passage with another. It's many conflate readings (e.g. Mark 9:49), where the Byzantine text-type combine the alternative variants of the Egyptian and Western texts, also reflect this secondary process.[55]

This whole exercise is done to help scholars arrive as close as possible to the original writings, or *autographs*, of the biblical authors. This grouping of manuscripts allows

---

[52]   Epp & Fee, *Studies in... NT Textual Criticism*: p7

[53]   Epp & Fee, *Studies in... NT Textual Criticism*: p7-8
       Metzger, *The Text of the New Testament*: p214-215

[54]   Metzger, *The Text of the New Testament*: p212

[55]   Epp & Fee, *Studies in... NT Textual Criticism*: p8

one to consider the genealogy of the textual witnesses.[56] The value of this classification into text types is that it allows the textual critic to *weigh* the manuscripts rather than to merely *count* them. For example, if ten manuscripts agree against one, but the former group is known to be derived from a common original, the numerical preponderance counts for nothing. The grouping of manuscripts into text types also allows for their general characteristics to be used for evaluating various readings when the internal evidence of the texts is ambiguous.[57]

THE *TEXTUS RECEPTUS*

The term *Textus Receptus* refers to *printed* editions of Greek New Testaments that are traced ultimately to the editions published in the 16th century. The beginnings can be traced to the Dutch Humanist Desiderius Erasmus (1469-1536).

Erasmus published five editions from 1516 to 1535. The Greek text was based on only about half a dozen minuscule manuscripts of the Byzantine text. Even worse, he relied mainly on *two* of these - both dating from the 12th century. The oldest (and best) of the texts available to him, a 10th century manuscript, he rarely used because he was afraid of what seems to him like an erratic text!

Erasmus only had *one* manuscript for the book of Revelation. This manuscript was missing the last page and thus he had no access to the last six verses of the book. Erasmus then used the Latin Vulgate, *translated these verses into Greek* and included it in his Greek New Testament! Needless to say, the Greek readings of Erasmus on these six verses have no parallel anywhere among the Greek manuscripts. However, these last six verses are still present in current editions of the Textus Receptus.

Erasmus used the Latin Vulgate as a corrective text for his Greek edition. For instance, the question of Paul in Acts 9:6 ("And he trembling and astonished said, Lord, what wilt thou have me do?") is not found in *any* Greek manuscript. It is an addition made by Erasmus into his Greek New Testament imported from the Vulgate.

---

[56]   It needs to be mentioned that not all scholars accept the grouping of the manuscripts into these regional text types. One notable example among textual critics was Kurt Aland. His argument seems to be that as early papyri manuscripts of the various text types (e.g. P45, P46, P66, P75) are found in the same location (Egypt) at the same time (second to third centuries), this invalidates the idea of the regional text types or at least the idea that the text types existed in the second and third centuries. However, it has been pointed out that the papyri manuscripts actually provide hard evidence for some of Wescott & Hort's conjectures on the ancestors of the text types. For instance, some of the manuscripts could actually be "fossilized" evolution of the text types; e.g. P75, or something like it, could be an early ancestor of the Alexandrian text type with P66 representing an early revised form of it. Some could be the early ancestor the "Western" type (e.g. P45). That they are all found in the same place should not constitute a problem since we know that informal mail services during Greco Roman times could transport documents throughout the eastern Mediterranean region within a few short weeks.

    (see Epp & Fee, *Studies in... NT Textual Criticism*: p92 & Epp, E.J., "The Papyrus Manuscripts of the New Testament", Chap 1 in Ehrman & Holmes, *The Text of the New Testament in Contemporary Research*: p8-9)

[57]   Metzger, *The Text of the New Testament*: p130-131

Incidentally, this passage became a part of the Textus Receptus and was used in the translation of the King James Version.

The infamous *Johanine Comma* (see next section) was included by Erasmus in the third edition of his Greek New Testament based purely on *one* Greek manuscript he found. It appears now that the manuscript was written in 1520 by a Franciscan monk who took the disputed words from the Latin Vulgate.

Although Erasmus' text was undoubtedly faulty, subsequent editors essentially kept to the same text.

Robert Stephanus (1503-1559) printed four editions from 1546 to 1551. Stephanus' third edition followed the text of Erasmus very closely. The fourth edition (1551) - is noteworthy for its division of the biblical books into chapters and verses, a system still in use today.

Theodore Beza (1519-1605) published nine editions from 1565-1604. The "importance" of Beza's work lies mainly in the fact that his editions differed very little from Erasmus' text. This is a bit surprising, considering the fact that Beza had in his possession the Codex Bezae, a 5th century manuscript! As a result, the text of Erasmus became even more entrenched.

The term *Textus Receptus* came from the second edition (in 1633) of a Greek New Testament published by brothers Bonaventure and Abraham Elzevir. In the preface to this edition, the editors wrote, *Textum ergo habes, nunc ab omnibus receptum: in quo nihil immutatum aut corruptum damus* [What you have here, is the text which is now received by all, in which we give nothing changed or corrupted.].

The Textus Receptus also strengthened its reputation from the fact that it was used by major translations into the vernacular. The second edition of Erasmus' Greek NT became the basis for Martin Luther's German translation. The third edition of Stephanus (1550), which was based on Erasmus' third edition, became the basis for the translation of the King James Version.[58]

Partly because of the advertising boast by the Elzevir brothers, its use for translations into major European languages, and its blessing by the Pope, the *Textus Receptus* became for Protestants everywhere the inspired word of God. The Textus Receptus was used by Luther in his 1520 German translation of the Bible, and by English scholars to produce the "Authorized Version" or "King James Version" of 1611. Erasmus text was also blessed by Pope Leo X (1475-1521). Soon the text itself became so entrenched that scholars and laymen were not allowed to question its accuracy. When the Swiss clergyman, Johann Jakob Wettstein (1693-1754) published a new edition of the Greek New Testament which deviated from Textus Receptus, he was duly deprived of his holy orders. The Textus Receptus remained the main Greek New Testament text used by scholars and translators until the end of the 19th century. It was only towards the end of the 19th century that the evidence accumulated became so overwhelming that Christian scholars had to reluctantly admit that the Textus was inaccurate and was based on manuscripts written far later than the period of the

---

[58] Aland, K. & Aland B., *The Text of the New Testament*: p3-9
Epp & Fee, *Studies in... NT Textual Criticism*: p10
Metzger, *The Text of the New Testament*: p98-106

original texts. So for a period spanning four centuries the Textus Receptus, faults and all, reigned supreme. [59]

Yet, we have seen that the *Textus Receptus* is a text based on a small sample of the late and unreliable Byzantine text. Today most critical Bible versions (such as the RSV and the NRSV) no longer use it as the basis of their translations.

THE CASE OF UNAUTHENTIC TEXTS

Although no longer used by critical editions, the issue of the inaccuracy of the Textus Receptus is still with us. There is a group of fundamentalist Christians who call themselves "King James Only" advocates, who continue to see the KJV not just as a translation but *the* inspired word of God. Here we will look in detail at some of the flaws in the Textus Receptus and the peculiar problem it raises for Christian apologists.

Edward Gibbon (1737-1794) in his most famous work *The Decline and Fall of the Roman Empire* (1788), pointed out that the church fathers defeated heretics by forged testimonies. These fathers went so far as to alter the text of the Holy Scripture itself. He pointed out one passage in particular:

I John 5:7-8 (KJV)
For there are three that bear record *in heaven, the Father, the Word and the Holy Ghost, and these three are one. And there are three that witness on earth,* the Spirit, the Water and the Blood and these three agree in one.

This passage, known as the *Johanine Comma*, had long been used by Christians to prove the truth of the doctrine of the Trinity. Gibbon pointed out that this text (the italicized portion above) was never quoted by the earliest church fathers, nor does it appear in any Greek manuscript earlier than the 15th century. In fact the earliest appearance was in Latin manuscripts around 400 CE and its earliest quotation was from the western theologian Priscillian (late 4th century CE). In short it was a later insertion into the Bible.

Why then did Christian scholars continue to accept it although it was obviously false? Gibbon claimed that Erasmus knew the passage was false but kept it out of prudence and that both the Catholic and Protestant Churches stuck to the spurious text out of "honest bigotry". In other words, the churches were trying to defend the doctrine of the Trinity by fraudulent means!

Since the end of the 19th century, the Johanine Comma is no longer included in modern translations of the Bible. However, there are still passages in the Bible that continued to be included in these modern translations although all evidence point towards them not being in the ancient manuscripts.

The first passage is the story of the woman taken in adultery which was included in the Textus Receptus in John 8:1-11. This passage, known as the *Pericopae Adulterae,* is absent from the earliest manuscripts. Nowhere does it appear in the

---

[59]   Bentley, *Secrets of Mount Sinai*: p33-34, 170
        Bruce, *The Books and the Parchments*: p186-187
        Martin, *New Testament Foundations I*: p166-168

Codex Vaticanus and the Codex Sinaiticus and most of the later Greek manuscripts also omit it. In some manuscripts, it appears not in the Gospel of John but in Luke (after Luke 21:38)! The passage is absent from all the earliest translations of the Bible - the Syriac, the Coptic and the Armenian. The passage was unknown to Christian writers before Ambrose (340-397) and Augustine (354-430). These considerations show conclusively that we have here another late and fraudulent insertion into the Bible. That it is still not taken out from the Bible today is a modern example of what Gibbon called "honest bigotry".[60]

Another passage that is known to be a late insertion is Mark 16:9-20. This passage is found neither in the Vaticanus nor the Sinaiticus. It is also noticeably absent from the Syriac and Armenian manuscripts. One can perhaps understand why fundamentalist Christians are hesitant to throw this passage out, despite the compelling proofs of its lateness and unauthenticity.[61] *The fraudulent passage in Mark is the very portion that describes the resurrection of Jesus.*

OVERWHELMING MANUSCRIPT EVIDENCE?

One of the most often heard assertions of fundamentalists is that the sheer number of New Testament manuscripts somehow shows that it is "special", is historically accurate and, as such, is the word of God.

Two books cited most commonly in support of this claim are Lee Strobel's *The Case for Christ* (1998) and Josh McDowell's *Evidence that Demands a Verdict* (1979).[62] McDowell's chapter on this is based on citations from various works, primarily from Bruce Metzger, a much-respected scholar in the field of textual criticism, but interspersed with quotations from more conservative scholars such as F.F. Bruce, Norman Geisler and William Nix. Strobel's chapter is presented as an interview with Bruce Metzger, again interspersed with quotes from more conservative scholars. Let us look at what these fundamentalists have to say.

We are told, first and foremost, of the *sheer number* of New Testament manuscripts available in the original language, Greek: now numbering at 5,664.[63] We are then told that, in comparison, the other major work of antiquity, Homer's *Iliad*, has only 643 surviving manuscripts. Then we are told that the earliest extant copy of the *Iliad* is datable to 400 BCE, which is approximately five centuries later than the date of the original autograph (circa 900 BCE).[64] By comparison, we are shown that

---

60   Bentley, *Secrets of Mount Sinai*: p29-31, 130
    Howell-Smith, *In Search of the Real Bible*: p13, 60
    Livingstone, *Dictionary of the Christian Church*: p274

61   See chapter 15 for more detail on the textual evidence against the authenticity of Mark 16:9-20.

62   McDowell, *Evidence that Demands a Verdict*: p39-53
    Strobel, *The Case for Christ*: p70-94

63   Strobel, *The Case for Christ*: p81

64   Actually this dating for Homer's work, 900 BCE, given in McDowell's book (p43) is nowadays recognized to be too early. It is now generally accepted that the date in which the *Iliad*, in its present form, was put in writing was around 700 BCE.(see Roberts, *Pelican History of the World*: p181)

the earliest extant manuscript evidence of the New Testament, has been dated to 125 CE which is only 25 years away from the time of writing.[65]

Finally, in both books, we are treated to quotations from fundamentalist and conservative scholars, waxing lyrical about the resulting significance of these statistics. Let us look at some of these:

- We are told that the sheer number confirms the textual integrity of the New Testament:[66]

  > The number of manuscripts of the New Testament, the early translations from it, and of quotations from it in the older writers of the Church, is so large that it is practically certain that the true reading of every doubtful passage is preserved in some one of other of these ancient authorities. *This can be said of no other ancient book in the world.*

- We are told that this guarantees the *purity* of the New Testament text:[67]

  > The New Testament, then, has not only survived in more manuscripts than any other book from antiquity, but it has survived in a purer form than any other great book-*a form that is 99.5 percent pure.*

- We are assured that none of these remaining variants affect basic Christian doctrine in any substantial way:[68]

  > [The great majority of New Testament] has been transmitted to us with no, or next to no variation; and even in the most corrupt form in which it has ever appeared, to use the oft-quoted remarks of Richard Bentley, "the real text of the sacred writers is competently exact;...nor is one article of faith or moral percept either perverted or lost..."

- Finally, we are told that all these unparalleled features of the manuscripts collection hint at *divine* guidance:[69]

  > If we compare the present state of the New Testament text with that of any other ancient writing, we must...declare it to be marvelously correct. Such has been the care with which the New Testament has been copied-a care which has doubtless grown out of true reverence for the holy words-*such has been the providence of God in preserving for His Church in each and every age a competently exact text of the scriptures*, that not only is the New Testament unrivalled among ancient writings in the purity of its text as actually transmitted and kept in use, but also in the abundance of testimony which has come down to us for castigating its comparatively infrequent blemishes. [Emphasis mine-PT]

---

[65] McDowell, *Evidence that Demands a Verdict*: p39, 43

[66] Sir Frederick Kenyon, *Our Bible and the Ancient Manuscripts* (1941) quoted in McDowell, *Evidence that Demands a Verdict*: p45

[67] Norman Geisler and William Nix, *A General Introduction to the Bible* (1968) quoted in Strobel, *The Case for Christ*: p85

[68] Benjamin Warfield, *Introduction to the Textual Criticism of the New Testament* (1907) quoted in McDowell, *Evidence that Demands a Verdict*: p44

[69] Warfield (op.cit.) quoted in McDowell, *Evidence that Demands a Verdict*: p45-46

On Textual Purity and Historical Veracity

Before we start looking at each of these claims, we need to make an obvious point that is often missed out by fundamentalists. An often-made assertion by *lay* fundamentalists (note none of the authors quoted above explicitly made this claim) is that the large number of surviving manuscripts and their relative lack of deviations *prove* that the New Testament is "true". This is patently false. *At best* all these claims about the sheer number of manuscripts and their faithful reproduction can do is to show that the New Testament as we have it today is what the original authors wrote. *It does not follow from this that what they had written is true.*

Since this rather obvious point does not seem to have permeated fundamentalist circles yet, let us illustrate this with an example.

Suppose we find a couple of old manuscripts of a document of an ancient, now-defunct, religion. The two manuscripts are more or less identical except for a few verses. Let us say that there is one verse where there is a discrepancy which cannot be resolved easily. This verse [when translated into English] is given in the two manuscripts as:

> Manuscript "A"   : THE MOON IS MADE OF *SWEET* CHEESE.
> Manuscript "B"   : THE MOON IS MADE OF *SWISS* CHEESE.

Suppose that at a later date more manuscripts of this document dating to times earlier than these two manuscripts were found. Upon studying these new finds, it is found that they all support the reading given in Manuscript "B". This means that textual scholars can now be certain that the verse, in its original form, reads "The moon is made of *Swiss* cheese." We have now reached a state of *textual purity* as far as this verse is concerned. It is uncontaminated by later additions, deletions or emendations and we *know* that this was what the original author of the manuscript wrote down.

Note however, that textual purity does not equate to factual veracity or to epistemological truth. The statement that "The moon is made of *Swiss* cheese" is *still false.*

This point is so often missed by fundamentalists and evangelicals that even the renowned textual scholar, Bart Ehrman, had to assert this in his textbook *The New Testament: An Historical Introduction to the Early Christian Writings* (2000):

> At one time or another, you may have heard someone claim that the New Testament can be trusted because it is the best attested book from the ancient world, that because there are more manuscripts of the New Testament than of any other book, we should have no doubt concerning the truth of its message. Given what we have seen in this chapter, it should be clear why this line of reasoning is faulty. It is true, of course, that the New Testament is abundantly attested in the manuscripts produced through the ages, but most of these manuscripts are many centuries removed from the originals, and none of them perfectly accurate. They all contain mistakes-altogether many thousands of mistakes. It is not an easy task to reconstruct the original words of the New Testament.
>
> Moreover, even if scholars have by and large succeeded in reconstructing the New Testament, this, in itself, has no bearing on the truthfulness of the message. It

simply means that we can be reasonably certain of what the New Testament authors actually said, just as we can be reasonably certain what Plato and Euripides and Josephus and Suetonius all said. Whether or not any of these ancient authors said anything that was *true* is another question, one we cannot answer simply by appealing to the number of surviving manuscripts that preserve their writings.[70]

With this little point made and out of the way, we will now examine the other claims based on the sheer number of manuscripts.

Analysis of the Statistics

As is usual with fundamentalist claims, once one looks beneath the surface, cracks appear. There are a few rather inconvenient (for the fundamentalist) facts that are normally omitted from these claims.

Firstly, many of the early manuscripts are extant only in *fragments*. Sometimes "one manuscript" can consist of no more than a single scrap of paper! Renowned textual scholar, Bruce M. Metzger, added the following *caveat* when presenting this data in his book *The Text of the New Testament: Its Transmission Corruption and Restoration* (1992):

> Lest, however, the wrong impression be conveyed from the statistics given above regarding the total number of Greek manuscripts of the New Testament, it should be pointed out that most of the papyri are relatively fragmentary and that only about fifty manuscripts (of which the Codex Sinaiticus is the only Uncial manuscript) contain the entire New Testament.[71]

Let us elaborate what is being said here.

- Up to the 9th century there is only *one* complete manuscript of the New Testament, the Codex Sinaiticus (4th century CE). Only two other uncial manuscripts come close to having the complete New Testament, the Codex Alexandrinus (5th century CE), [in which the first 25 chapters of the Gospel of Matthew is missing, a couple of chapters of the Gospel of John and eight chapters of II Corinthians] and the Codex Ephremi (5th century)[missing completely II Thessalonians and II John.].[72]

- There are *less than sixty* complete (or almost complete) manuscripts of the New Testament extant; 59 to be exact. We have seen the three uncials above. The 56 remaining complete manuscripts of the New Testament are minuscules manuscripts. All these are late and date from the 9th century CE and later.

---

[70]   Ehrman, *Introduction to the New Testament*: p449
[71]   Metzger, *The Text of the New Testament*: p34 n3
[72]   Aland, K. & Aland B., *The Text of the New Testament*: p107-109
       Metzger, *The Text of the New Testament*: p48

- Most of the extant manuscripts are fragmentary. Let us give some example of the papyri manuscripts. P[1], a third century manuscript, consists of only 17 verses from the Gospel of Matthew (1:1-9, 12, 14-20). P[2], a 6th century manuscript, consists of three verses from John (12:12-15) and six verses from Luke (7:22-26, 50). Even the famous P[52], from the John Rylands library, the earliest fragment of the New Testament, consists only of five verses from the Gospel of John (18:31-33, 37-38). Out of the 96 catalogued papyri manuscripts, 68 contain 20 verses or less. Only thirteen of the papyri manuscripts contain more than 40 verses. The situation with the uncial manuscripts is not much different. Of the 299 extant uncial manuscripts, 195 have only two folios or less. (A *folio*, by the way, is a parchment folded in the middle to make four pages)[73]

Secondly, calling the New Testament *a book* and then comparing with Homer's *Iliad* which, in every sense of the word, *is a single* book by a *single* author[74] is, to say the least, disingenuous. For, as we have seen in chapter one, the New Testament is a *compilation* of many books by various authors. We also know that many of the books were initially circulated independently or in collections smaller than the New Testament. The manuscript collection attests to this fact. As the Alands noted in their book, *The Text of the New Testament*,[75] many of the manuscripts in codex form come in various configurations that do not include the complete New Testament:

- Full New Testament (3 uncials, 56 minuscules - as we have seen above)
- All of the New Testament except Revelation (2 uncials, 147 minuscules)
- All of the New Testament *minus* the gospels (1 uncial, 75 minuscules)
- Gospels with Revelation (11 minuscules)
- Gospels, Acts & Catholic Epistles (2 papyri, 1 uncial, 8 minuscules)
- Gospels, Acts, Catholic Epistles & Revelation (2 minuscules)
- Pauline Epistles & Revelation (6 minuscules)
- Acts, Catholic Epistles, Revelation (3 minuscules)
- Gospels & Pauline Epistles (5 minuscules)
- Acts, Catholic Epistles (18 papyri, 29 uncials, 40 minuscules)
- Acts, Catholic & Pauline Epistles (8 uncials, 265 minuscules)
- Pauline Epistles (26 papyri, 58 uncials, 138 minuscules)
- Revelation (5 papyri, 7 uncial, 118 minuscules)
- Gospels (43 papyri, 184 uncials, 1896 minuscules)

To simply add up these and then claim that "the" New Testament has more than 5,000 manuscripts is, as Austin Powers would say, "just not cricket".

What do we get when we compare *individual books* within the New Testament with the *Iliad*? Let us take the Book of Revelation as an example. There are only 287

---

[73] Aland, K. & Aland B., *The Text of the New Testament*: p77, 98, 99, 103

[74] Although there is some controversy whether the *Iliad* is the work of a single person or of many different redactors, the poem is without doubt a single work, which talks about a single event, The Trojan War.

[75] Aland, K. & Aland B., *The Text of the New Testament*: p78-81

extant, complete and incomplete, manuscripts of this book, far below Homer's *Iliad* of around 650. The Book of Acts is found in 573 manuscripts; still less than the *Iliad*. When *Acts* is combined with the catholic epistles as a single work, this number is increased to 662 - more or less the same as the *Iliad*. If we take the entire Pauline corpus as a book, this comes up to 792 manuscripts, not very far above the *Iliad*. Only when we look at the gospels, do the numbers get significantly higher (2361 extant manuscripts).[76] Broken down in this way, as it should be, the numbers no longer look that impressive.[77]

Thirdly, the comparison is a fabricated one in that it is made with books from Greek and Roman cultures only. The Quran can boast of even more manuscripts than the New Testament. The library of Astan-i Quds-i Razavi in Mashhad, Iran alone houses 11,000 manuscripts of the Quran in Arabic. This is already double the extant New Testament manuscripts. Some of these manuscripts date from the 9th century CE, or only three centuries after the death of Muhammad (570-632 CE). Thus if sheer number of manuscripts mean that there is something "special" about the document, then the Quran must be "more special" than the New Testament![78]

While we are comparing the New Testament with the Quran, let us look at the time between the earliest manuscripts and the time of the composition of the autographs. We have seen above that the oldest complete New Testament, the Codex Sinaiticus, dates from the 4th century CE, or about two and a half to three centuries after the original autographs. The oldest securely dated complete manuscript of the Quran is dated to the 9th century CE. It is, also, around two and a half centuries removed from Muhammad's time, comparable to the Sinaiticus. Furthermore, fragments of the Quran[79] have been dated back to as early as the early 8th or even 7th

---

[76] The reader may notice that the numbers don't add up to 5,000+ and is considerably less than this. There are two reasons for this. Firstly, there is some overlap between the manuscripts, i.e. that some New Testament manuscripts may contain Pauline epistles with Revelation, some have gospels with Acts etc. The reader may also notice that this reason actually brings *down* the total. Indeed, there are only about 3,200+ New Testament manuscripts. Now comes the second reason. The 5,000+ figure is derived from adding about 2,200+ *lectionaries* to the total. Some 200 of these lectionaries contain only scattered New Testament text and according to Kurt and Barbara Aland "should not have been included in the total". These are, so to speak, "grand fathered" into the total manuscript numbers. The earliest extant lectionary is dated to the 4th century CE. Only 32 of these 2200+ manuscripts can be dated to before the 9th century. (Aland, K. & Aland B., *The Text of the New Testament*: p163-170)

[77] Aland, K. & Aland B., *The Text of the New Testament*: p78-83

[78] Geoffrey Roper (ed), World Survey of Islamic Manuscripts, 1992, Volume I, London 1992: pp481-486 (quoted in the website The Quranic Manuscripts in Museums, Institutes, Libraries & Collections: http://www.quran.org.uk/ieb_quran_manuscripts.htm, accessed on October 12, 2002)

[79] It should be noted that the Quran is not without its textual problems. A couple of good reference works on this issue are: Michael Cook, *The Koran: A very Short Introduction*, Oxford, London 2000 and Ibn Warraq, *The Origins of the Koran*, Prometheus, New York 1998.

century CE, again, comparable to the earliest of the New Testament papyrus fragments.[80]

In short, the statistics with respect to the New Testament manuscripts are not unparalleled historically.

The New Testament is Not Variant Free

Strobel subtitled the section of his book, *The Case for Christ*, dealing with the manuscripts as "A Wealth of Evidence". So has this "wealth of evidence" of textual data confirmed the traditional biblical texts, like the *Textus Receptus* underlying the King James Version (KJV)? Let us first look at this evidence with respect to the variant verses in the New Testament.

Strobel mentioned that he had "seen estimates" of 200,000 variants in the New Testament. But he immediately allayed his readers fear by stating that this is an illusion, for a "single word misspelled in two thousand manuscripts" is "counted as two thousand variants". He then went on, as we have seen above, to quote Geisler and Nix as saying that the text of the New Testament is "99.5% pure".[81]

A better way to approach this is to look at the totality of verses in the New Testament and see how many of these verses have variants. Thus even if there are 100 variant manuscripts on a particular verse, we will simply count this as a single variant verse. Given this definition, how many verses in the New Testament have variants? The Table 6.2 below, adapted[82] from Aland's *The Text of the New Testament*, shows the full story.

---

[80]   Cook, *The Koran*: p122

[81]   Strobel, *The Case for Christ*: p84-85

[82]   Note that the figures given in the table actually *underestimate* the number of variant verses. The variants are computed based on the differences in the *printed editions* of the New Testament, namely the editions of Tischendorf (1872), Wescott-Hort (1881), von Soden (1913), Vogels (1922), Merk (1933), Bover (1943) and Nestle-Aland25. It is certain that even those verses that are the same for all these editions may have textual variants but the scholars are in agreement as to which constitute the actual reading. It should also be noted that Aland presented the table with the intent of showing how much *agreement* there is among the manuscripts than is "generally recognized". Presumably textual scholars have quite a pessimistic view of the New Testament such that even if 1/3 of the verses have variants, it is considered a positive sign.

Group of Writings	Total Number of Verses	No. of Verses with Variants	% of Verses with Variants
The Gospels	3769	1713	45.4%
The Acts	1006	329	32.7%
Pauline Epistles	2032	495	24.4%
The Catholic Epistles	735	220	29.9%
Revelation	405	191	47.1%
Total	**7947**	**2948**	**37.1%**

Table 6.2 Variant Verses in the New Testament[83]

It can be seen above that the most corrupted works (in terms of variant verses) in the New Testament are the Book of Revelation and the Gospels. Virtually *half* of the verses in these works have variants. Even the *least corrupted* corpus, the Pauline epistles, has almost 25% variant verses. In total *more than a third* of the verses in the New Testament have variants. One could justly ask: Could these variants be mainly insignificant ones, consisting of spelling errors, copying errors etc? And could it be that the New Testament can still be considered to have "survived in...a form that is 99.5% pure"?

The science of modern *textual criticism* utilizes the evidence from this manuscript base to try and get as close to the text of the original autographs as possible. The result of all this research into the evidence of the manuscripts are the Nestle-Aland *Novum Testamentum Graece*, 27th edition (normally abbreviated as Nestle-Aland[27]) and the United Bible Societies' *Greek New Testament* fourth edition (GNT[4]). Both these editions have the same underlying Greek text. These are referred to as "critical editions" as the text is based on the critical scientific evaluation of all the extant New Testament manuscripts.

Do these new editions enable one to get closer to the autographs of the New Testament? Yes, they do. Do these editions confirm the traditional text of the King James Version? Definitely NOT!

Let us just consider how today's critical edition differs from the text underlying the King James Version.

For starters, we have seen elsewhere, modern textual criticism has shown that the ending of the Gospel of Mark (16:9-20), the Johanine comma (I John 5:7-8) and the *pericopae adulterae* in John 7:53-8:11, do not form part of the original text of the New Testament.

Kurt and Barbara Aland, the editors of both the Nestle-Aland[27] and the GNT[4], in their book *The Text of the New Testament*, gave a list of New Testament verses that have been *relegated* to the apparatus (i.e. in the footnotes) of the modern *Greek New Testament*. Relegated verses mean that these are no longer considered authentic by textual scholars. These verses are Matthew 5:44, 6:13, 16:2b-3, 17:21, 18:11, 20:16, 20:22, 20:23, 23:14, 25:13, 27:35 ; Mark 7:16, 9:44, 9:46, 11:26, 15:28; Luke 4:4, 9:54-56, 17:36, 23:17, 24:42; John 5:3b-4; Acts 8:37, 15:34, 24:6b-8, 28:16, 28:29; Romans 16:24. As the reader can check for himself, many of these verses have significant content in them.

---

[83]   Aland, K. & Aland B., *The Text of the New Testament*: p29

The Alands provided more verses which are still left in the text but placed in brackets to show their doubtful authenticity. These include Mark 10:7, 10:21, 10:24, 14:68; Luke 8:43, 22:43-44; Romans 16:25-27.[84]

We note also that modern textual studies have resulted in the deletion or changes in many portions of verses that used to be in the KJV. Some of the affected verses are Matthew 1:25, 8:29, 16:20, 17:20, 20:16, 21:12, 25:13, 27:35, Mark 1:2, 6:1, 10:21, Mark 10:24, Luke 2:14, Acts 6:8, Romans 1:16, I Corinthians 10:28, Ephesians 3:9, Colossians 2:2, I Timothy 1:7, James 5:16, I John 4:3, Revelations 1:11. A reader can easily compare these verses by comparing the KJV (based on the *Textus Receptus*) next to the NRSV (based on the latest critical edition of the *Greek New Testament*).[85]

A cursory count of the variants shown above - those that are unauthentic, doubtful, or rendered differently in the new Greek New Testament compared to the traditional KJV - gives the number to be around 100 verses. And this does not exhaust all the significant textual variants in the New Testament.

Thus, when Strobel quotes Geisler and Nix to say that the New Testament *has survived* in a form that is "99.5% pure", the message he conveys is that, at any time in its history, regardless of the underlying Greek text, Christians had had access to essentially the original text of the New Testament. This is also what the quote above by Benjamin Warfield says: namely that God preserved "for His Church in each and every age a competently exact text of the scriptures".

However, as we can see above, this claim is simply not true. (Note that 0.5% errors amount to 40 verses. We have already shown more than twice this amount of differences between the KJV and the GNT[4].)

Some of the Variants Impinge on Christian Doctrine

Further, it is obvious that these deletions, omissions and changes to the traditional text trouble many fundamentalists. Since the 1970s, the proponents of the "Majority Text"[86] and "the King James Only" have mounted a concerted effort to resist the findings of the textual critics. Far from providing comfort to believers, the new "wealth of evidence" has caused a backlash within fundamentalist circles.[87]

That such a backlash occurs calls to question one of the claims above; that there is "no article of faith or moral precept" that is threatened by this textual data. There are actually a few traditional practices and beliefs that have been called into question due to the textual evidence.

One example is from the last 12 verses of Mark.

---

[84] Aland, K. & Aland B., *The Text of the New Testament*: p297-312
[85] Aland, K. & Aland B., *The Text of the New Testament*: p282-297
Metzger, *The Text of the New Testament*: p219-246
White, *The King James Only Controversy*: p156-186
[86] The "Majority Text" is essentially the Byzantine Text described earlier. It is basically the reading shown in the majority of manuscripts regardless of the age of the manuscript. Thus an old second century manuscript reading may carry less weight than 100 medieval minuscule manuscripts. In other words, the manuscripts are simply *counted* and not *weighed*.
[87] Wallace, Daniel, "The Majority Text Theory: History, Methods and Critique", in Ehrman & Holmes, *The Text of the New Testament in Contemporary Research*: p282-296

Mark 16:17-18
 And these signs will accompany those who believe;...*they will pick up snakes with their hands, and if they drink any deadly thing, it will not hurt them*; they will lay their hands on the sick, and they will recover.

Many Pentecostal churches still practice carrying poisonous snakes and drinking poison during worship as a show of their faith. That this practice is dangerous cannot be doubted. *Freethought Today* (Vol 15 1998 No.9) reported that during the last hundred years, there have been around 75 reported deaths in the U.S. among fundamentalists due to snake handling. Yet, as the textual evidence show, the passage promising they will not get hurt is spurious! This is an example of a precept (which is "a rule of action") that has been affected due to the textual evidence.

Let us look at another, weightier, example - the Johanine comma:

I John 5:7-8
For there are three *that bear record in heaven, the Father, the Word and the Holy Ghost, and these three are one. And there are three that witness on earth,* the Spirit, the Water and the Blood and these three agree in one.

Remember that modern textual evidence shows that the italicized words above are not found in the earliest manuscripts. In other words, they do not form part of the original autograph of I John. Yet this statement is the *clearest and most direct support of the doctrine of the Trinity* in the New Testament.

Some fundamentalist, while accepting the lack of authenticity of this passage, normally claim that there are other passages that support the doctrine of the Trinity. They would normally cite passages such as this:[88]

II Corinthians 13:13
The grace of the Lord Jesus Christ, the love of God, and the communion of the Holy Spirit be with all of you.

(Other such similar passages such as Matthew 28:19, I Corinthians 6:11, 12:4-6, II Corinthians 1:21-22.) However, as Gerd Lüdemann points out,[89] these are, strictly speaking, *triadic*, not *trinitarian*, formulas. That the formula was not taken to mean a triune godhead can be seen from the fact that the first official definition of the trinity was not found in Christian theology until 381 CE! While it is certainly *possible* to read backwards through the prism of modern Christian theology to take these passages as trinitarian, in reality the meaning is not explicit in the text. The closest modern meaning for this triadic formula would be the English phrase "fighting for king and country". As we know, the phrase is in no way meant to show the unity of king and country but simply that one stands as a symbol for the other. Thus the triadic formula, in its primitive meaning, simply implies that Jesus, like the king, stands as a symbol for something greater. The Holy Spirit is something that emanates, like breath from a human, from God. As the *Macmillan Compendium: World Religions* explains:

---

[88]   Strobel, *The Case for Christ*: p84-85
[89]   Lüdemann, *Heretics*: p187, p310 n635

[E]xegetes and theologians agree that the New Testament does not contain an explicit doctrine of the Trinity. God the Father is the source of all that is (Pantokrator) and also the father of Jesus Christ. "Father" is not a title for the first person of the Trinity but a synonym for God. Early liturgical and creedal formulas speak of God as "Father of our Lord Jesus Christ"; praise is to be rendered to God through Christ (see opening greetings in Paul and deutero-Paul). There are other binatarian texts (e.g. Rom 4:24, 8:11; 2 Cor. 4:14; Col. 2:12; 1 Tm. 2:5-6, 6:13; 2 Tm. 4:1) and a few triadic texts (the strongest are 2 Cor. 13:13 and Mt. 28:19; others are 1 Cor 6:11, 12:4-6; 2 Cor. 1:21-22; 1 Thes. 5:18-19; Gal. 3:11-14) Christ is sent by God and the spirit is sent by Christ so that all may be returned to God.[90]

Thus, take away the Johanine comma, and you take away the *only* verse in the New Testament which explicitly teaches the triune godhead.

Conclusions on "Overwhelming Manuscript Evidence"

We can make the following conclusions about the claim of the special status of the New Testament based on the "overwhelming" number of manuscripts.

1. While it is true that the more manuscripts, the closer one may get to the original texts, it does not follow that what the original texts say are therefore "proven true".

2. The counting of the manuscripts and its comparison with the works of Greek literature is misleading. Even a single scrap of papyrus with one or two verses is counted as "one manuscript". Furthermore, the New Testament is not a book, but a compilation of various books and epistles that once circulated independently.

3. Far from showing the New Testament is variant-free, the manuscripts show that almost 40% of the verses in the New Testament contain variants.

4. Some of the variants do affect Christian doctrine.

THE NEW TESTAMENT CANON

The time has now come for us to ask the same question as we did on the Old Testament: how did the books in the New Testament came to be regarded as canonical? What about books that were excluded? What were their reasons for exclusion?

The first generations of the church fathers such as Ignatius (d. c110), Papias (60-130) and Justin (c100-c165) were more concerned with the canon of the Old Testament than that of the New. One reason is, of course, that they could appeal to the living oral tradition that surrounded them.[91] Another reason is that some of the New Testament books were not yet written during their lifetimes!

---

90   *Macmillan Compendium: World Religions*: p1122
91   Davidson & Leaney, *Biblical Criticism*: p230

In fact the impetus towards providing a definitive list of canonical books for the New Testament came from a heretic[92] named Marcion (d.160). He was a native of Sinope in Asia Minor who made his way to Rome in 140 and began preaching what he believed to be the original good news. He taught that many of the early Christian literature were corrupted by Jewish ideas. He rejected the entire Old Testament. Marcion accepted only the ten epistles of Paul (Galatians, I & II Corinthians, Romans I & II Thessalonians, Laodiceans [?], Colossians, Philemon and Philippians) and a "purified" version of Luke's gospel. Marcion's teaching was immensely popular and he became an immediate concern for his rivals.[93]

Irenaeus (c130-c200), Bishop of Hippo, argued against Marcion's inclusion of only one gospel with a curious piece of logic – *since there are four winds, there should be four gospels*! This is what he actually wrote:

> Against Heresies 3:11:8
> It is not possible that the Gospels can be either more or fewer in number than they are. For, since there are four zones of the world in which we live, and four principal winds, while the Church is scattered throughout all the world, and the "pillar and ground" of the Church is the Gospel and the spirit of life; it is fitting that she should have four pillars

Irenaeus then drew up a list of writings he considered canonical. His list consisted of 22 books of which 21 are present in today's New Testament. But noteworthy are the books he left out: Philemon, II Peter, II & III John, Hebrews and Jude. Interestingly, his list included a book no longer present in the New Testament: *The Shepherd of Hermas*[94] - a book he clearly designate as "scripture." Thus the first formal list of canonical books drawn up in the second half of the second century (around 180) does not completely tally with the modern canon.[95]

The next list came from the so-called Muratorian Fragment, discovered in Milan by L.A. Muratori who published it in 1740. The fragment is dated to around 200 CE. The fragment presents a list of what its author considered to be inspired or canonical

---

[92] Terms such as heretic and orthodox are retroactive. In the lifetimes of these figures involved, every party calls itself the orthodox and labels every other as heretics. We will come through this term *heretic* many times in this book applied to Christian scholars who lost the theological battle for survival. Hence, to the uninitiated, reading the history of Christian theology, it would seem as if the orthodox party always triumphed against the heretic. Whereas, in reality, heretics simply means losers in the theological battle.

[93] Bentley, *Secrets of Mount Sinai*: p170
Bruce, *The Books and the Parchments*: p108
Davidson & Leaney, *Biblical Criticism*: p230
Metzger, *The Canon of the New Testament*: p90-99
McDonald, *The Formation of the Christian Biblical Canon*: p154-161

[94] The book is the treatise of Hermas to whom an angel appeared in the form of a shepherd and communicated with him in various visions. The work inculcates the need for penance and the possibility of forgiveness for post baptismal sin.

[95] Bentley, *Secrets of Mount Sinai*: p170
Bruce, *The Books and the Parchments*: p109
Davidson & Leaney, *Biblical Criticism*: p230
Metzger, *The Canon of the New Testament*: p153-156

books. The list rejects The Shepherd of Hermas, saying that it was a recent book. One of the books it did add to the canonical list does not inspire confidence in the believer. It is a book very few Christians know of today and is called *The Apocalypse of Peter*.[96] Again, we find some books in today's canon missing from the Muratorian Fragment: I & II Peter, Hebrews, James and III John. The exclusion of the epistles of Peter is remarkable for a Roman document (if Peter did die in Rome and wrote the epistle attributed to him). The exclusion of the epistles of Hebrew and James, both of which are known in Rome at least a century before the list is curious.[97]

The next canonical list came from Origen (c.185-254) who in 230 CE defined what he believed to be the canon of scripture for the New Testament. He included the four gospels, Acts, Paul's thirteen epistles, I Peter, I John and Revelation. He also mentioned that the following books were under dispute: Hebrews, II Peter, II & III John, James, Jude, the *Epistle of Barnabas*[98], *The Shepherd of Hermas*, *The Didache*[99] and the *Gospel According to the Hebrews*.[100] The last four books are no longer in the canon today.[101]

We have now reached the period of the uncial script. In the extant manuscripts that we have, the disagreements as to which books should be included in the New Testament and which should be excluded are evident here as well. We find in Codex Sinaiticus the inclusion of *Shepherd of Hermas* and *the Epistle of Barnabas*. Both works were placed in the codex that in no way showed that the compiler wanted them to be separated from the rest. The Codex Alexandrinus contains the two *Epistles of Clement*,[102] supposedly written by Clement, Bishop of Rome, to the Corinthian Church around 95 CE.[103]

We can conclude then, that by the beginning of the 4th century, some books that are now included in the New Testament canon had their canonicity doubted. Some other disputed books somehow never made it into the canon. These disputed books were: Hebrews, Revelation, the Epistles of James, II Peter, II & III John, The

---

[96] *The Apocalypse of Peter* describes how Peter was granted a vision of heaven and hell.

[97] Bruce, *The Books and the Parchments*: p109-110
      Davidson & Leaney, *Biblical Criticism*: p230-231

[98] *The Epistle of Barnabas* was a theological tract that strongly attacked Judaism and claims to find in the Old Testament testimonies for Christianity.

[99] *The Didache* is a short Christian manual on morals and church practice.

[100] *The Gospel according to the Hebrews* was the gospel used originally by the Nazarene sect. It was composed in Aramaic and contains certain sayings of Jesus not recorded in the canonical gospels. The consensus among scholars today is that some passages in this gospel, although based on different traditions from the canonical gospels, are of historical value.

[101] Bruce, *The Books and the Parchments*: p113
      Metzger, *The Canon of the New Testament*: p135-141

[102] The First Epistle of Clement dealt with the problem of the hierarchical structure of the early church. Its immediate concern was the deposing of some presbyters in the Corinthian Church. The second epistle is a homily on Christian life and the duty of repentance.

[103] Bentley, *Secrets of Mount Sinai*: p176
      Bruce, *The Books and the Parchments*: p111
      Metzger, *The Canon of the New Testament*: p65, 187

Shepherd of Hermas, The Didache, The Epistle of Barnabas and The Epistles of Clement.

Then a process that can be called religious forgery began to take place. Books which somehow managed to attach themselves to the names of apostles (the tradition of apostolic authorship rears its ugly head again!) were eventually thought to be inspired based on that "fact": Hebrew was attributed to Paul; Revelation and the II & III John to John the apostle, the epistles of James and Jude to the brothers of Jesus; and the epistles of Peter to Simon Peter himself.[104] As we have seen in the previous chapter, these attributions are false. Most of the books that were left out never had the luck to strongly attach themselves to the names of apostles and never made the cut. So the inclusion of some of the books in the New Testament was based on the mistaken belief in apostolic authorships. In should be mentioned here that in no way were the books that finally became canonical invariably written earlier than the non-canonical ones. Thus the non-canonical *Didache, 1 Clement* and the *Epistle of Barnabas* all date to the second half of the first century, while the canonical II Peter and Jude date to the middle of the second century.

The first list of all the 27 books of the New Testament to the exclusion of all others appeared in the Festal Letter written by Athanasius (c296-373), Bishop of Alexandria to the Egyptian Churches in the year 367. In the letter Athanasius told his bishops that these 27 books are to be regarded as canonical. Athanasius' list was confirmed by a council under Pope Damasus in 382 CE. However, many churches in the east continue to disagree with the Athanasian canon. The Book of Revelation, for instance, was not considered divinely inspired until well into the 8th century. We find in Codex Claromontanus, a 6th century manuscript, that the Hebrews was omitted from it while the epistle of Barnabas was included and placed between the epistle of Jude and the book of Revelation.[105]

Even today we find some Christian churches, *with very old roots*, have different books in the New Testament. The Ethiopian Church has an expanded canon of 38 books in their New Testament. Included in their list of canonical books are *the Shepherd of Hermas, 1 & II Clement and the Apostolic Constitutions.*[106] The East-Syrian Nestorian Church, on the other hand, has a canon of only 22 books. The canon excludes II Peter, II & III John, Jude and Revelation from their New Testament. [107]

It is clear from our short survey above that the New Testament canon as we know it was by no means universally accepted by all Christians since the beginning. Books that were accepted by some churches as canonical were rejected by others as uninspired. Doubtless the false tradition of apostolic authorship helped many of the books that eventually became included in the canon. We are certain too that ludicrous arguments, *a la* Ireneaus and his "four winds therefore four gospels" logic, must have played a role in the acceptance and rejection of the various books. Thus the

---

[104] Parmalee, *Guidebook to the Bible*: p134
[105] Bentley, *Secrets of Mount Sinai*: p170-171
Bruce, *The Books and the Parchments*: p112
Livingstone, *Dictionary of the Christian Church*: p88
[106] The *Apostolic Constitutions* is a collection of religious law that most scholars believe is of Syrian origin.
[107] Metzger, *The Oxford Companion to the Bible*: p104

development of the canon of the New Testament was in no way miraculous or inspired.

* * * * *

We have looked at the formation of the Old and New Testament canon. The selection process included the utilization of faulty logic, the fraudulent attribution of apostolic authorship and even political considerations. It was a process which does not inspire confidence in the list of canonical books. We have also looked at the much-touted claim of fundamentalists that the preponderance of New Testament manuscripts "proves" that the Bible is something special and have found such assertions to fly in the face of available evidence.

Excursus A
LIBERALS AND THE BIBLE

Most mainline Protestant Churches today subscribe to some form of liberal-modernist theology. Liberal or modernist theologians are those who would accept that the Bible is not inerrant. They would also acknowledge that many, if not most, of the stories related about Jesus in the gospels are not historical. Many of them would probably reject the Trinitarian doctrine of God and some would even dispense with belief in the existence of God altogether. Strange as it may seem to the average person, these theologians still consider themselves Christians.

These theologians would happily admit to most of the findings in this book but would certainly dismiss them as "insignificant" objections to their faith. Our aim in this excursus is to examine how liberals view the Bible and Jesus. But before we begin our investigations, an historical summary of the liberal-modernist movement would be of great benefit in appreciating this phenomenon.

HISTORY OF LIBERAL THEOLOGY

From a theological point of view, the 19th century inherited a great number of problems from the preceding centuries. Thus the skepticism of philosophers such as David Hume (1711-1776) and to a certain extent, Immanuel Kant (1724-1804) presented many difficulties for Christian theologians. In his book, *An Enquiry Concerning Human Understanding* (1748), Hume demonstrated the philosophical implausibility of miracles. And in his posthumously published *Dialogues Concerning Natural Religion* (1779), Hume showed that the traditional arguments for God's existence, especially the argument from design, cannot lead to the conclusions believers want them to. Immanuel Kant, in his monumental masterpiece, *Critique of Pure Reason* (1781), showed that none of the traditional arguments for God's existence have any validity.

Even more troubling to theology than philosophy was *natural* philosophy, or, as it eventually became known, science. Science was making embarrassing encroachments into what had traditionally been regarded as the theologians' turf. The Copernican revolution showed that the sun, not the earth, was the center upon which everything in the then known universe revolves. It took away the earth's, and thus man's, place from the center of the universe. It became harder to believe how man could be the crowning glory of creation when he is placed in an insignificant corner of the universe.[1]

The plight of the theologians continued to pile up in the 19th century. The publishing of Charles Darwin's (1809-1882) treatise on evolution, *The Origin of Species* (1859) meant that science had gone one step further against the theologian. The theory of evolution presented by Darwin showed that man is an evolved animal, no more and no less. If evolution is true, and the evidence marshaled by Darwin in

---

[1]   Hordern, *A Layman's Guide to Protestant Theology*: p31-33

his book was compelling, then Genesis is false; far from being created in God's image, mankind bore all the marks of an animal ancestry.

Within Christendom, the development of biblical criticism, especially in its "higher" form, began to show that the Bible was not a unique document. Using critical historical methods common in the study of other historical documents, the higher critics showed that the first five books of the Bible were not written by the Hebrew prophet, Moses, as was traditionally believed. These books show traces of at least four separate documents. They also showed that some prophetic books such as Daniel were actually written *after* the events it purports to prophesy about. Even the New Testament was not spared. It began to be seen that the gospels were not written close to the events they describe but were written decades and perhaps even up to a century later. The fundamental result of higher criticism was that it revealed that the belief in Bible infallibility was no longer tenable.[2]

Thus by the second half of the 19th century, it was clear to most theologians that it could no longer be "business as usual" for their profession; the monolithic fabric of Christian theology was torn, never again to be mended. Christian theology bifurcated into fundamentalist/conservatism on one side and liberal-modernism on the other.[3] The fundamentalists took the overtly irrational route and rejected all scientific findings that contradicted the literal reading of the Bible. Higher criticism was condemned as a tool of the devil.[4] The liberals on the other hand rationally accepted the findings of science and biblical criticism. They tried many different methods to keep their faith meaningful and alive by employing various interpretative methods on the Bible and the traditional concepts of orthodox theology.

The first steps of liberal[5] theology were made by the German theologian Friedrich Schleiermacher (1768-1834). In trying to win back the educated classes to Christianity, he taught that the debate over proofs of God's existence, biblical inerrancy and miracles are, at best, peripheral issues. The most important issue, according to Schleiermacher, was the feeling present in a believer in experiencing God. Another German theologian, Albrecht Ritschl (1822-1889), preached that faith,

---

[2]   Hordern, *A Layman's Guide to Protestant Theology*: p40-42

[3]   While this section concerns mainly Protestant liberal theology, it should be mentioned that there was a similar movement in the Roman Catholic Church towards the end of the 19th and early 20th century, which was also called "Modernism". Its advocates openly accepted the findings of biblical criticism and generally rejected the traditional Catholic scholastic theology. This group was eventually suppressed by an Encyclical in 1907 by Pope Pius X. [Bullock, *Dictionary of Modern Thought*: p540, Livingstone, *Oxford Dictionary of the Christian Church*: p341] Although Roman Catholic scholarship is nowadays quite "liberal", its scholars tend to treat central Roman Catholic dogma (e.g. Mary's Perpetual Virginity, Jesus Resurrection) with kid gloves and tend not to study these critically.

[4]   In fact, this whole book up to now has been mainly a critique of the fundamentalist position.

[5]   The term "liberal" is used loosely here to refer to theologians of the liberal-modernist tendencies: this would include those the systematic theologians normally group under liberalism, modernism, neo-liberalism, neo-orthodoxy, Christian existentialism, empirical theology, radical theology and crisis theology to name a few. Their similarity lies in their acceptance of biblical criticism and their rejection of fundamentalist doctrines.

not reason, must be the bedrock of true religion. Religion, to him, concerns value judgment whereas reason, which includes science and higher criticism, concerns matters of fact. Thus, even if biblical criticism shows that stories about Jesus' virgin birth, his miracles and his pre-existence are false, it does not change the value of the person Jesus. The important thing about Jesus, according to Ritschl, was that he led mankind to the "God of values"; in other words, Jesus made his followers conscious of the highest values of life. Ritschl's views were popularized by another German theologian Adolf von Harnack (1851-1930). Harnack criticized most of traditional Christian dogmas and blamed the apostle Paul for corrupting the simple teaching of Jesus by changing the religion *of* Jesus to a religion *about* Jesus. Harnack denied the miracles in the gospels and taught that Jesus never claimed to be divine. Harnack taught that Christianity can be reduced to a few simple elements: the belief in God the Father and the gospel of which Jesus was the "personal realization." Towards the end of his life, Harnack even campaigned for the ejection of the Old Testament from the Christian canon.[6]

The conservative-fundamentalists hit back in a way that has become a hallmark of their style: in the US, they resorted to political action to remove liberal preachers from the pulpits of Protestant churches and liberal professors from their academic postings in theological seminaries. They had some initial successes but eventually in the third decade of the 20th century, due primarily to the sheer number of non-fundamentalist theologians, they were forced to retreat into the small denominations and their related seminaries.[7]

Despite this victory against the fundamentalist, it was quite clear, even to theologians steeped in the liberal tradition, that liberalism cannot continue in its course. That would eventually lead to a complete repudiation of the whole Bible and the entirety of the tenets of Christianity: the surefire path to atheism. What was needed was a shift of focus, so to speak; to put the fruits of critical thinking in soft focus and to concentrate on "squishy" issues such as the problems of human existence. This they found in the writings of the 19th century Danish theologian Soren Kierkegaard (1813-1855). His philosophy, which eventually became known as *existentialism*, ostensibly dealt with the problems of human existence. He taught that human existence cannot be rationalized. Therefore God, being inextricably linked with our existence, cannot be rationalized by an objective system of rational truths. Thus being a Christian means embarking on a leap of faith in the dark, to commit one's whole life to Christ.[8]

Thus when the Swiss theologian Karl Barth (1886-1968) reacted to the more "extreme" doctrines preached by the liberals and affirmed much of traditional theology such as the doctrine of the trinity and the belief of Jesus Christ as the incarnate Word of God, he did not repudiate higher criticism. He merely shifted the focus away from this into existentialist issues. In line with many liberal theologians, he did not believe that reason has much use in the field of theological thought.[9]

---

[6]   Cunliffe-Jones, *Christian Theology Since 1600*: p144-145
      Hordern, *A Layman's Guide to Protestant Theology*: p44-49
[7]   Hordern, *A Layman's Guide to Protestant Theology*: p52-54
[8]   Hordern, *A Layman's Guide to Protestant Theology*: p113-118
[9]   Bullock, *Dictionary of Modern Thinkers*: p43-44

Another important theologian in the liberal tradition was the German Rudolf Bultmann (1884-1976). Bultmann was certainly one of the greatest New Testament scholars of the 20th century. He was renowned for introducing two powerful tools into biblical criticism: "Demythologization" and "Form Criticism". According to him, and his followers, the myths in the Bible were an obvious reflection of the worldview of the early Christians. As they stand, the myths in the Bible can no longer be honestly believed by modern man. Thus, these myths: such as the belief that supernatural beings (Satan, angels, demons and God) regularly interfere in the natural working of the world and that Jesus was a pre-existent being sent to a sacrificial death to atone for man's sins are all not objective history. They are myths which reflect the early Christians' understanding of the world. Demythologization was a program of getting to the *kerygma*, or the proclamation, of the early Christians behind the myths. In this sense, he differs from the early 20th century liberals that simply jettisoned the myths form their theology. Form criticism is the method that aids in the demythologization process. Recognizing that the stories in the Bible were originally handed down orally and that oral tradition has certain structural forms, the form critics were able, in many cases to find the historical setting in which the stories were first told. Form criticism showed that much of the stories about Jesus in the gospels, even the non-mythical ones, were not historical and were the results of the early Christian community belief or expectation about him. Yet from this position Bultmann, like Barth, affirmed his belief in Jesus via an existentialist viewpoint. He claimed that all the Christian need to know was that Jesus once existed and that he was crucified. It is irrelevant whether the stories about Jesus in the gospels were true or false. What was important about these stories was that it showed what the *idea* of Jesus meant to the early Christians who first circulated those stories. For Bultmann, the gospels present, not an historical or scientific truth, but an existential one.[10]

Bultmann's contemporary, Paul Tillich (1886-1965), developed his own existentialist brand of theology. The interesting aspect, for our purpose, is Tillich's assertion that God, as he is formulated by traditional Christian theology, does not exist.[11]

The development of liberal thinking eventually led to thinkers such as Dietrich Bonhoeffer (1906-1945). He believed that traditional Christianity has outlived its usefulness and called for a "religionless Christianity." Bonhoeffer, who died in a Nazi concentration camp, seemed to believe that there is no afterlife, no message of personal salvation in the Bible. Bonhoeffer, and his intellectual heirs, repudiated the traditional body of the Church, its liturgy and its metaphysics and called for a complete secularization of Christianity.[12] This "radical theology" as it came to be called, is the modern flag bearer of Christian liberalism.

Cunliffe-Jones, *Christian Theology Since 1600*: p146-147

Hordern, *A Layman's Guide to Protestant Theology*: p130-149

[10]   Bullock, *Dictionary of Modern Thinkers*: p111-112

Cunliffe-Jones, *Christian Theology Since 1600*: p150-151

Hordern, *A Layman's Guide to Protestant Theology*: p130-149

[11]   Hordern, *A Layman's Guide to Protestant Theology*: p170-190

[12]   Hordern, *A Layman's Guide to Protestant Theology*: p210-229

Zaehner, *The Hutchinson Encyclopedia of Living Faiths*: p126-127

With this we end our short excursion into the historical background of modernist-liberal theology. It should be mentioned that the liberals did not reach their position by abstruse theological reasoning: they were *forced* by external circumstances - the findings of science, comparative religions, enlightenment philosophies and historical criticism - to resort to such a method of reasoning for the only other available alternatives are the collapse into complete irrationality of fundamentalism and the theological resignation of atheism. Our main concern here is to examine the validity of the fundamental epistemological assumptions of the liberal theology. We will examine below the liberal views on the Bible and Jesus.

LIBERAL VIEWS ON THE BIBLE

The fundamentalists believe that everything in the Bible, except when the allegorical intent is clear, is literally true. To these biblical literalists, there really was an Adam and an Eve, there really was a worldwide Noachian flood and there really was a resurrection event in the first century CE. While the fundamentalists are ultimately wrong on all these claims, they are right on one important issue: the Bible was written by the authors with an overt intention of conveying historical facts, not myths.

The position of the liberals on the Bible can be divided into two broad, not necessarily mutually exclusive, categories: the first is that the biblical myths convey symbolic truths; the second is that the Bible is a very human and fallible document but *some* portions are inspired by God and these show the way to the truth. We will look at each of these positions in turn.

Bultmann's position is a good representation of the first position. Demythologization admits openly that many of the stories in the Bible are not true literally. Form criticism attempts to find the symbolic truths behind these myths. Just in case the reader thinks that this position is uncommon, I will give below a quote from a report published in 1938 by the Commission on Christian Doctrine - a report sanctioned by the Anglican Church:

> Statements affirming particular facts may be found to have value as pictorial expressions of spiritual truths, even though the supposed facts themselves do not actually happen. In that case such statements must be called symbolically true...It is not therefore of necessity illegitimate to accept and affirm particular clauses in the Creeds while understanding them in this symbolic sense.[13]

The report above, probably on purpose, never made it clear which clauses of the Anglican creeds were to be understood in the symbolic sense.

The second position asserts that the Bible, while being fallible - with many parts untrue and some unacceptable - is, in general, the inspired word of God. In their book, *The Bible Without Illusions* (SCM Press, London, 1989), two English liberal theologians, R.P.C. Hanson and A.T. Hanson adumbrated this idea. Below is a summary of their position as given by Carl Lofmark:

---

[13]   quoted in *Knight, Honest to Man*: p172

They recognized that the Bible contains errors and cannot be divinely inspired, that its world view is "pre-scientific" and its accounts of history mainly myths, legend or fiction, that its miracles never happened and that parts of it is unedifying if not disgusting. They see that it is no good trying to read symbolic truths or higher significance into much of Numbers, Leviticus and Deuteronomy or even into the second epistle of Peter. They agree that the Bible text is unreliable and the original words (including the words of Jesus) have often been altered. Yet they still believe that the Bible's "general drift" or "impression" is a "true witness to the nature of God." The unedifying texts are "balanced" by others, which reveal the truth. Deep significance is not found everywhere in the Bible, but only in its "high spots" (p138). They disapprove when God commands the massacre of the Amelekites (I Samuel 15) or Elijah slaughters the priests of Baal (I Kings 18), but the story of 2 Samuel 12, where Nathan condemns King David for his treatment of Uriah, reveals "an insight into God's nature" (p93). This approach is eclectic: they select from the Bible those passages which they find edifying and construct from those passages their own impression of the Bible's "general drift," while rejecting the bulk of what the Bible contains. Only the better parts are a true witness to the nature and purpose of God.[14]

With regards to the "myths-symbolic truths" position, the first thing that comes to mind is that Christians for two millennia had always believed that the Bible, where there is no hint of allegory, is literally true.[15] Now if the modern liberals assert that the many parts of the Bible cannot be taken literally, they are saying that for close to 2,000 years Christians have failed to understand God's true message. It is up to these brilliant 20th century liberals to discover it. Put in this way, the liberals' position sounds smug and pretentious - even ludicrous.

The second problem is that the question remains as to *which* passages are to be taken literally and which are to be taken symbolically. If the clear intent of the biblical authors is rejected as the method of selection (which leads to the fundamentalist position), then it leaves the door wide open for selecting which passage should be symbolic and which should not. Thirdly, *how* are those passages to be interpreted symbolically? There is no guide or generally accepted method of symbolic interpretation. How does one know which symbolic interpretation is correct? All the prominent theologians, Barth, Bultmann, Tillich and Bonhoeffer, disagree on many broad categories in their interpretation of the biblical message. Fourthly, just because the stories are *defined* as symbolic by the liberals, it does not mean that the issue of the criterion of truth has been successfully avoided. What happens when two liberal theologians come up with two mutually exclusive symbolic truths from the same biblical passage? How is one to chose from the symbolic truths of the Bible and, say, the symbolic truths mentioned in the Hindu scriptures? And

---

14   Lofmark, *What is the Bible?*: p61-62

15   While there were a few early Christian theologians such as Clement of Alexandria (c150-220) and Origen (c185-254) who tried to interpret the Bible figuratively; they methods were that the Bible contains layers of truths with the literal meaning being the surface layer. There was no explicit rejection of the literal messages. At any rate, the allegorical interpretations by these theologians never gained widespread acceptance in the Church. [Chadwick, *The Early Church*: p107-108 Smith, *Atheism, Ayn Rand And Other Heresies*: p93]

finally, many so-called interpretations of the symbolic truths of the bible are actually *devoid of any cognitive meaning*. Take for instance an Ascension Day sermon written for an English newspaper by an Anglican bishop:

> [The ascension of Jesus is] not a primitive essay in astrophysics, but the symbol of creative intuition...into the abiding significance of Jesus and his place in the destiny of man. It might be called a pictorial presentation of the earliest creed, Jesus is Lord...Creed and scripture are saying in their own language that here is something final and decisive, the truth and the meaning of man's life and destiny-truth not in theory but in a person-life in its ultimate quality, that is God's life.[16]

From the above passage, only one thing is clear; the good bishop does not believe that the ascension story as depicted in the first chapter of the Acts of the Apostles is to be taken literally. But apart from this, it is very difficult to fathom what it is he is trying to say and how what he is trying to say is derived from that story told in three verses in Acts. The rest of the passage is, literally, *meaningless*. It should be mentioned here that if one reads the book of Acts it can clearly be seen that in no way was the story meant by the author to be taken in any other except in its literal sense. The author was wrong, of course, for there was no heaven above the clouds for Jesus to ascend to. But while we can forgive the author of Acts for his lack of knowledge of astrophysics, it is hard to know what to do with the bishop.[17]

As for the "take some and leave some" approach to the Bible, the central question remains: if some parts of the Bible are false or unacceptable, what guarantee do we have that the other parts are true or of any special value? And even if these other parts are true, how does this make the Bible any different from the sacred scriptures of other religions? If the scriptures of other religions are to be dismissed as a collection of myths, legend, some history and some moral teachings; shouldn't the same be done for the Bible? Thus the moment one admits that some parts of the Bible are untrue or unacceptable, the position of the Bible as the inspired word of God becomes impossible to defend. For it becomes more probable that where the biblical authors got it right, whether it be an historical fact or a profound moral insight, they got it right because they were bound to hit the jackpot once and a while amidst so many mistakes.[18] In many cases these liberal theologians simply do not think about the passages that trouble them in the Bible. Take for instance this passage from the book *The Christian Agnostic* (Abingdon Press, Nashville, 1965) by the American liberal theologian Leslie Weatherhead :

> ...when Jesus is reported as consigning to everlasting torture those who displease him or do not "believe" what he says, I know in my heart that there is something wrong somewhere. Either he is misrepresented or misunderstood...So I put his alleged saying in my mental drawer awaiting further light. By the judgment of the court within my own breast...I reject such sayings. [19]

---

16   quoted in Knight, *Honest to Man*: p173
17   Knight, *Honest to Man*: p173
18   Lofmark, *What is the Bible?*: p62-63
19   quoted in Smith, *Atheism, The Case Against God*: p79

The question here is simple: if he could use his own judgment to accept and reject biblical passages, why rely on the Bible at all?

LIBERAL VIEWS ON JESUS

This leads us into the liberal theologians' views of Jesus. It is obvious that since the late 19th century these theologians, by whatever fashionable names they call themselves, whether liberal, neo-liberals, neo-orthodox or modernists, have ceased to believe that the main events of the gospels are historical: the virgin birth and the associated nativity stories, the miracles and the resurrection accounts are all accepted as mythological with no grounding in history. Take for instance this comment by the Episcopal Bishop of Newark, John Shelby Spong in his book, *Resurrection: Myth or Reality* (1994):

> As I first studied the birth narratives, it was clear that no major scholar of any persuasion took them literally...how long could the educated folk of the twentieth century continue to be literal about such things as the conception that occurred for a couple when both were well beyond menopause, the visit of the angel Gabriel, a pregnancy without a male agent, an angelic choir that sang in the sky, a star that roamed through the heavens, shepherds that have no trouble finding a baby in a city crowded with people called for a special census, and a king named Herod who would rely on three men he never met before to bring him an intelligence report about a pretender to his throne who was said to have been born just six miles away? If the divinity of Jesus was attached to the literal details of the birth tradition, then it was a doomed concept.[20]

What sort of meaning do theologians find in the nativity story then? Well here is one interpretation of this symbolic truth:

> The virgin birth stories are mythical attempts to express the meaning of Jesus for faith. They say that Christ comes to us from the action of God.[21]

One is tempted to do a double take over here. If the myths are unhistorical, what does it mean then when it is asserted that "Christ comes...from the action of God"? Just what "action of God" is the passage referring to, if not the virgin birth? It is obvious that the above statement on the supposed message of the virgin birth tells us nothing.

But it is mainly on the resurrection that the liberals spun their yarn of meaningless words. It is obvious that *all* the major liberal theologians do not take the resurrection account literally: i.e. they all accept that it is historically false. Karl Barth, for instance, denied that historical verification is of any importance to the "verdict of God" which is the resurrection.[22] Paul Tillich's theory of the resurrection is called the "restitution"; so-called because the resurrection, as Tillich understands it is "the restitution of Jesus to the dignity of the Christ (Jesus is one with God) in the minds of his disciples." This according to Tillich is an "ecstatic" experience of the

---

[20]   Spong, *Resurrection: Myth or Reality*: p14, 18

[21]   Hordern, *A Layman's Guide to Protestant Theology*: p205

[22]   Hordern, *A Layman's Guide to Protestant Theology*: p142-143

disciples.[23] It is obvious that Rudolf Bultmann, although he believed in the actual historicity of the crucifixion, was convinced that the resurrection was not an historical event. One of Bultmann's theological disciples has this to say about the resurrection:

> the resurrection is to be understood neither as outward or as inward, neither mystical nor as a supernatural phenomenon, nor as historical.[24]

Now, one may ask, if the resurrection is not any of the above, then it can only mean that the resurrection cannot be understood in *any* sense.[25] Take another example, this one from Bishop Spong in his book *Resurrection: Myth or Reality*. Claiming that he has found the *Midrash* as a method of understanding the symbolic truths of Jesus' life, he proceeds to explain what the method does:

> It was a way to think mythologically about *dimensions of reality* for which *the language of time and space were simply not appropriate*. It is an attempt to gather rational words and concepts around those moments where *eternity broke into the consciousness of men living in time.*[26] [Italics added]

What is actually meant by "dimensions of reality" that cannot be appropriately described by the language of time and space? Dimension is a term used in science and everyday speech to refer to measurable things: thus time can be measured by a watch and space can be measured by a ruler. Now the "language of time and space" obviously means the realm of measurable things. Therefore, the good bishop is saying that his theology talks about "dimensions of reality" that cannot be measured. Now, *dimension*, by definition, implies the realm of the measurable. A "dimension of reality" that cannot be measured is simply nonsense talk![27]

The last sentence is even more intriguing: what can it possibly mean to say that "eternity broke into the consciousness of men living in time?" The use of words like "eternity", "consciousness" and "time" tends to delude one that something really profound is being uttered. But let us break the passage down into its constituent parts. In everyday speech, "eternity" means, whether literally or figuratively, "time without end". "Broke into the consciousness of" can only mean "forced an understanding of." "Men living in time" simply means "some men;" since all men, by definition, "live in time." Thus the passage simply means "The understanding of time without end was forced onto some men." So while we would not say that this is meaningless; it is, at best, a trivial statement with no profundity. Examples of sentences like these are plentiful in liberal literature.

The liberals trip all over themselves to avoid saying the actual truth: *that if the resurrection is not historical, traditional Christianity, in any form, is no longer valid.* This, naturally, is the skeptic's position. The liberals added that the resurrection is to be understood in a different sense, but just exactly what sense is not clear. Their writings contain so much garbled speech that it is difficult to see even if they agree or

---

23   Hughes (ed), *Creative Minds in Contemporary Theology*: p461-462
24   MacKinnon et.al., *Objections to Christian Beliefs*: p77
25   MacKinnon et.al., *Objections to Christian Beliefs*: p78
26   Spong, *Resurrection: Myth or Reality*: p16
27   Clements, *Science Vs. Religion*: p146

disagree with one another! The central issue is this: if the resurrection is unhistorical, simply *proclaiming* it as true in another sense does not mean that the proclamation has successfully absolved the burden of proof from the liberals. Most of the liberal interpretation involves accepting the resurrection as some kind of internal revelation of the disciples. This experience, they proclaim, is what really matters, not the actual historical fact of resurrection. But why should it, we ask? Why should the hallucinations of a few ill educated first century Galilean peasants be of any significance and be treated any differently from other hallucinations all over the world and throughout history? Because it is about Jesus? Take away the historical claims about his supposed supernatural powers, his miracles and his resurrection, what do we have? A first century xenophobic, fanatical Galilean peasant who thought the world was going to end.[28] If it takes the theologians so many volumes to reinterpret his teaching for the 20th century and still only come up with, at best, a very vague collections of doctrines, why not just dispense with it altogether? The liberal theologians will, no doubt, have an answer or answers ready for these questions; but chances are only *they* will understand it.

* * * * *

In short modernist-liberal theology has no rational basis whatsoever. Their continued attempts to couch their ideas in vague terms reveal what can only be described as an intellectually dishonest streak and an unwillingness to face the common sensical truth - that the natural and historical sciences have shown that Christianity, as it has been understood for 2,000 years, is false.

---

[28]   See chapter 13 for a critical evaluation of the teachings and person of Jesus.

Excursus B
NOT ALL VERSIONS
ARE CREATED EQUAL

From the first complete translation of the English Bible in 1382 (normally attributed to John Wycliffe [c1330-1384]), there are today literally hundreds of English translations of the Bible. These translations, normally called *versions*, are usually directly translated from the original languages of the Bible. Yet not all the translations are equally reliable.

Older versions, for instance, are less reliable because they had access only to less reliable source documents. As we have seen in chapter 6, the *King James Version*, or Authorized Version, or KJV for short, which was first published in 1611, was based on the Greek Text of Erasmus known as *The Textus Receptus*. Most modern versions, however, are based on newly discovered, more ancient, texts as well as scientific textual studies. So in general, modern versions are more reliable than older ones.[1] Some examples of good modern translations include the *New Revised Standard Version* (NRSV), its precursor the *Revised Standard Version* (RSV), the *New English Bible* (NEB) and paraphrased *Good News Bible* (GNB).

Our interest here is in a particular subset of modern versions: those coming from evangelical publishers. Some examples of such translations include *The Book*, *The Living Bible* and *The New International Version (NIV)*. Apart from textual evidence one additional consideration looms large in these versions: their belief in biblical inerrancy. Given below is the quote taken from the Translator's Preface of the NIV:

> In working towards these goals, the translators were united in their commitment to the authority and infallibility of the Bible as God's word in written form.[2]

As the ex-fundamentalist preacher and songwriter, Dan Barker, remarked:

> This is hardly an objective agenda for a team of translators! Imagine if freethinkers publish a new bible translation, prefacing it with a statement that we are "united in our commitment" to bash and disprove "God's word".[3]

The NIV is *the* best selling English Bible today. Since its first introduction in 1973, this evangelical version has sold more than 215 million copies worldwide.[4] Since the average fundamentalist will very likely be using this version, it is important to understand how the translators' belief in biblical inerrancy affects their rendition of the Bible.

---

[1]   Metzger, *Companion to the Bible*: p758-763
[2]   NIV, p: xxxix
[3]   Barker, *Losing Faith in Faith*: p269
[4]   http://en.wikipedia.org/wiki/New_International_Version – accessed on October 1, 2007

REMOVING CONTRADICTIONS BY QUOTING OR USING LESS AUTHORITATIVE TEXTS

Some alterations seem to have been made to remove contradictions from the main text. One example comes from a contradiction long known to exist between the texts of II Kings and II Chronicles:

> II Kings 24:8 NRSV
> Jehoiachin was *eighteen* years old when he became King; he reigned three months in Jerusalem
>
> II Chronicles 36:9 NRSV
> Jehoiachin was *eight* years old when he began to reign; he reigned three months and ten days in Jerusalem.

The NRSV did not even have a footnote at II Chronicles 36:9, implying that the main textual traditions supported this reading, although it is in contradiction to the passage in II Kings. Let us see how the NIV presents these passages:

> II Kings 24:8 NIV
> Jehoiachin was *eighteen* years old when he became King and he reigned in Jerusalem for three months.
>
> II Chronicles 36:9 NIV
> Jehoiachin was *eighteen* years old when he began to reign and he reigned in Jerusalem for three months and ten days.

See how the contradiction has disappeared! Have there been new discoveries in archaeology or textual criticism since the publication of the NRSV (in 1989) that the NIV took advantage of? No. The NIV referred to here is a 1989 edition and is similarly based mainly on the *Biblia Hebraica*, like the NRSV. The truth is found in a very small footnote at the bottom of the page in which this passage appears. This is what the footnote says:

> *One* Hebrew manuscript, some Septuagint manuscripts and Syriac, most Hebrew manuscripts *eight*. [emphases added – PT]

Thus the footnote implicitly admits that the balance of evidence favors *eight* not *eighteen*. So why was the latter chosen to be in the main body of the text? Look at the excerpt from the preface again. Now one can see the relevance of Dan Barker's comments. This tendency to make contradictions in the original texts disappear by translating it away can be found in other passages in the NIV. Another example is from II Kings 8:26 / II Chronicles 2:22. Here II Kings 8:26 gives Ahaziah's age of ascension to the throne as 22 while II Chronicles 2:22 says he was 42 when he became King. All the major modern versions support this. Yet the NIV has simply translated away this contradiction by changing the age given in II Chronicles to 22!

REMOVING DIFFICULTIES BY TRANSLATING IN "SOFT FOCUS"

Sometimes we find that words are paraphrased to remove obvious difficulties that exist in the original Hebrew text. Take one instance of the warning of God to Adam in Genesis 2:17. This is how three different versions of the Bible present the verse:

Genesis 2:17 KJV
But of the tree of the knowledge of good and evil, thou shalt not eat it: for in the day that thou eatest thereof thou shalt surely die.

Genesis 2:17 Good News Bible
[E]xcept the tree that gives knowledge of what is good and what is bad. You must not eat the fruit of that tree; for if you do, you will die the same day.

Genesis 2:17 NRSV
[B]ut of the tree of the knowledge of good and evil you shall not eat, for in that day that you eat of it you shall die.

The various translations above give us an idea of what the original Hebrew is saying: that if Adam were to eat the fruit *he'll die on that very day*. The problem is that Adam *did* partake of the fruit (Genesis 3:6). However, he did *not* die, in fact he lived to a ripe old age of 930 (Genesis 5:5)!

The way NIV skirted this difficulty is interesting, watch:

Genesis 2:17 NIV
[B]ut you must not eat from the tree of knowledge of good and evil, for when you eat of it you will surely die.

Can you see the theological rabbit being pulled out of the hat? Yes, by translating the passage in the "soft focus" mode the *specific* curse to die on the very same day is no longer there. Thus a difficulty is removed!

REMOVING REPREHENSIBLE PASSAGES BY MISTRANSLATION

Some passages in the Bible sound reprehensible. Given below is the passage taken from II Kings where the prophet Elisha used his powers to curse and kill 42 children. Just to give the sense of the Hebrew we will give three different translations:

II Kings 2:23-24 KJV
And he went up from thence unto Bethlehem and he was going up by the way, there came forth little children out of the city, and mocked him, and said unto him, Go up, thou bald head; go up, thou bald head. And he turned back, and looked on them, and cursed them in the name of the Lord. And there came forth two she bears out of the wood, and tare forty and two children of them.

II Kings 2:23-24 GNB
Elisha left Jericho to go to Bethel, and on the way some boys came out of a town and made fun of him. "Get out of here, baldy!" they shouted. Elisha turned round, glared at them, and cursed them in the name of the Lord. Then two she-bears came out of the woods and tore forty-two of the boys to pieces.

II Kings 2:23-24 NRSV
He went up from there to Bethel; and while he was going up on the way, some small boys came out of the city and jeered at him, saying, "Go away, baldhead! Go away, baldhead!" When he turned around and saw them, he cursed them in the name of the Lord. The two she-bears came out of the woods and mauled forty-two of the boys.

The passage doesn't put Elisha (or God) in good light for both seemed to be responsible for the murder of 42 children. That "little boys" or "small children" are meant can be seen from the original Hebrew. According to Strong's Exhaustive Concordance of the Bible the original Hebrew word for "little" used here is *qatan*, which means small in number or young in age, and the word for "children" here is *naar*, which means a boy (or a girl) from infancy to adolescence. In other words, the passage was talking about "little children". We can see that the above three versions have been quite faithful to the original Hebrew despite the theological difficulties.

The NIV however, translated the same passage thus:

II Kings 2:23-24 NIV
From there Elisha went up to Bethel. As he was walking along the road, some *youths* came out of the town and jeered at him. "Go on up, you baldhead" they said. "Go on up, you baldhead!" He turned round, looked at them and called down a curse on them in the name of the Lord. Then two bears came out from the woods and mauled forty-two of the *youths*.

The italics are mine, but it's just to emphasize the major change in meaning that has happened by using "youths" instead of "little children" or "small boys". "Youths" today can mean young men in their early twenties. Suddenly Elisha's act does not look *that* bad. It looks like some gangsters taunted him and he defended himself. Yet as we see above, "youth" was not meant in the original Hebrew; as the other versions attested. Thus by twisting two words completely out of its original meaning the NIV has managed to skip over another theological difficulty.

LEAVING ERRORS IN TRANSLATION UNCHANGED

Sometimes the editors of the NIV keep dubious translations from older versions. Let us look at one famous example. This concerns the messianic prophecy of the virgin birth. *Matthew* proclaimed that Jesus' birth was in fulfillment of an Old Testament prophecy:

Matthew 1:22-23
And this took place to fulfill what the Lord had said through the prophet: "The virgin is with child and will give birth to a son, and they will call him Immanuel-which means 'God is with us.'"

The prophecy referred to by the Matthean passage above is in found Isaiah 7:14. This is how the passage looks in the King James Version:

Isaiah 7:14 KJV
Therefore the Lord himself shall give you a sign; Behold a *virgin* shall conceive, a bear a son, and shall call his name Immanuel.

At first glance, this looks like an amazing fulfillment of prophecy. Unfortunately, the KJV's use of *virgin* here is a *well-known error in translation.*

The Hebrew word in Isaiah 7:14 of the Masoretic Text, wrongly translated as *virgin* above, is *almah*. Now *almah* does not carry any explicit notion of virginity, meaning simply a young woman of marriageable age. Had *Isaiah* actually wanted to convey the prophecy of the virgin birth he would have used the word *bethulah*, which does carry the explicit meaning of virgin.

As we will show in chapter 11, Matthew used the Greek translation of the Old Testament, the Septuagint, which erroneously translated *almah* as *parthenos*. Now *parthenos* does mean "virgin". The correct Greek word that should have been used by the translators of the Septuagint was *neanis*. Thus Matthew's proclamation was based on a *mistranslation* of the Hebrew word *almah*.

In fact in modern, more reliable versions, the correct translation for Isaiah 7:14 is used. Two examples:

Isaiah 7:14 GNB
Well then, the Lord himself shall give you a sign: a *young woman* who is pregnant will have a son and will name him Immanuel.

Isaiah 7:14 NRSV
Therefore the Lord himself shall give you a sign. Look, the *young woman* is with child and shall bear a son, and shall name him Immanuel.

The Good News Bible even provides a footnote explaining this:

YOUNG WOMAN: The Hebrew word here translated "young woman" is not the specific term for "virgin", but refers to any young woman of marriageable age. The use of "virgin" in Mat. 1.23 reflects a Greek translation of the Old Testament, made some 500 years after Isaiah.[5]

The implication of the above translation is enormous. It implied that Matthew *erroneously* attributed a non-existent prophecy to Jesus by utilizing a less than perfect translation of the Hebrew Bible.[6] Let us look at how the NIV presents the same passage:

---

[5]   Good News Bible (ABS 1976): p673 footnote
[6]   See chapter 7 for a more detailed analysis of this virgin birth prophecy.

Isaiah 7:14 NIV
Therefore the Lord himself will give you a sign: The *virgin* will be with child and
will give birth to a son, and will call him Immanuel.

Amazingly, there *isn't even a footnote* explaining why *virgin* was used! Again, the
implication is obvious. The adherence of the editors/translators of the NIV to biblical
inerrancy made them perpetuate an obvious translation error in Septuagint in order to
"keep" the prophecy!

ALTERING THE TRANSLATION
UNTIL IT COMES OUT RIGHT

Sometimes the errors in the extant Hebrew text are so obvious that one cannot get it
right with simply changing a word here and there: a major overhaul is required. One
such example is this passage in II Chronicles:

I Chronicles 3:22-24 (NRSV/RSV/KJV)
22 ...And the sons of Shemaiah: Hattush, Igal, Bariah, Neariah, and Shaphat, *six*.
23 The sons of Neariah: Elioenai, Hizkiah, and Azrikam, three.
24 The sons of Elioenai: Hodaviah, Eliashib, Pelaiah, Akkub, Johanan, Delaiah,
     and Anani, seven.

The relevant line is verse 22. It gives five names for the sons of Shemiah but gives the
total as six! This type of mistake is one which an inerrant Bible is supposed to be free
of.

This is how the NIV translated the verses above:

I Chronicles 3:22-24 (NIV)
22 ...Shemaiah *and his sons*: Huttush, Igal, Bariah, Neriah, and Shaphat - six in all.
23 The sons of Neriah: Elioenai, Hizkiah and Azrikam – three in all.
24 The sons of Elioenai: Hodaviah, Eliashib, Pelaiah, Akkub, Johanan, Delaiah, and
     Anani – seven in all.

With this translation, the error noted in verse 22 above magically disappears! However, to
accomplish this sleight of hand, the original verse has been completely mutilated. In the
original Hebrew text, the format of verse 22 is exactly the same as verses 23 and 24; they
all start with "And the sons of..." – as the NRSV, RSV and KJV correctly translate. It is
obvious that, in all three verses, the Chronicler *is counting only the sons* without including
the fathers. However, by twisting the words around in verse 22, from "And the sons of
Shemaiah" to "Shemiah and his sons," it looks as though the Chronicler's count of six
now includes the father! Yet this translation is illegitimate and is made purely to rid the
Bible of the "difficulties" fundamentalists fear so much.

ADDING WORDS INTO THE BIBLE TEXT

On the last page of the Christian Bible we find this warning:

> Revelation 22:18
> I testify to everyone who hears the words of the prophecy of this book, if anyone adds to them, may God add to him the plagues which are written in this book.

Yet this admonition does not to carry any weight with the editors of NIV; words not found in the biblical manuscripts are quite freely added when biblical inerrancy seems to be threatened. In his recent book *The Bible in Translation* (2001), the respected textual scholar of Princeton Theological Seminary and chairman of the NRSV translation committee, Bruce M. Metzger, had this to say about this aspect of the NIV:

> It is surprising that translators [of the NIV] who profess to have a "high view of scripture" should take liberties with the text in omitting words, or, more often, by adding words that are not in the manuscripts...in Jeremiah 7:22 the translators have inserted the word "just" for which there is no Hebrew authority. In the New Testament at Matthew 13:32 concerning the mustard seed, they inserted the word "your" ("the smallest of all your seeds") and the word "now" in I Peter 4:6 ("the gospel was preached even to those who are now dead.") - neither of which is in the Greek text. In I Corinthians 4:9, we find in the NIV a quite considerable elaboration of what Paul actually wrote: "God put us apostles on display *at the end of the procession*, like men condemned to die *in the arena* (the two additions have been italicized here).[7]

Professor Metzger did not elaborate on *why* these textually indefensible additions were made. However, the theological implications are clear. Let us look at a couple of the passages Metzger cited:

First, let us look at Jeremiah 7:22, in which the "Lord Almighty" speaks:

> Jeremiah 7:22 NRSV
> For in the day that I brought your ancestors out to the land of Egypt, I did not speak to them concerning burnt offerings and sacrifices.

> Jeremiah 7:22 NIV
> For when I brought your forefathers out of Egypt and spoke to them, I did not *just* give them commands about burnt offerings and sacrifices.

Remember that Metzger mentioned that there is *no* Hebrew manuscript that supports this reading in NIV (i.e. the addition of "just"). Note that this addition changes *the whole meaning of the passage*, from negative to positive. The reason the NIV translators did so, is easy to see. For God *did* command the Israelites during the exodus from Egypt about burnt sacrifices. One example:

Exodus 20:22-24 NRSV

---

[7]   Metzger, *The Bible in Translation*: p140-141

> The Lord said to Moses: Thus you shall say to the Israelites:"...You need make for me only an altar of earth and *sacrifice* on it your *burnt offerings*..."

It is obvious then, that in the original Hebrew manuscripts, a blatant contradiction exists. Here was a passage (Jeremiah 7:22) that *explicitly* mentioned that God did not give any command on burnt offerings during the exodus that clearly contradicts Exodus 20:22-24 which *equally explicitly* provides a commandment from God about burnt offerings and sacrifices. Thus to save their doctrine of biblical inerrancy, the translators added the word "just" to avoid this very contradiction!

The change made to the passage from Matthew 13:32 is even more blatant. Let us compare the NRSV and the NIV again here:

> Matthew 13:31-32 NRSV
> He [Jesus] put before them another parable: "The kingdom of heaven is like a mustard seed that someone took and sowed in the field; it is *the smallest of all seeds...*

> Matthew 13:31-32 NIV
> He told them another parable: "The kingdom of heaven is like a mustard seed which a man took and planted in his field. Though it is the smallest of all *your* seeds...[italics added-PT]

The extant Greek manuscripts have Jesus here saying that the mustard is the smallest of *all* seeds, as the NRSV faithfully translates. However, this statement, that the mustard seed is the smallest of all seeds, is a *gross botanical error.* For while it is true that mustard seeds are small, they are not the smallest. The orchid seed, for instance, is even smaller.[8] The fundamentalist translators of NIV cannot have the divine Jesus being shown to make such a mistake, so they add the word "your" to "seeds," implying that Jesus was merely talking about the seeds available to this audience! Again, it is important to note that the translators had added a word *not found* in the extant Greek manuscripts.

* * * * *

These examples should be enough to caution anyone about thinking that all Bible versions are the same. Some have theological preconceptions *built-into* the translation. [9]

---

[8] According to the *Guinness Book of World Records,* the smallest seeds are those of the epiphytic orchids. Each seed weighs in at approximately 0.0000008 grams!

[9] Other fundamentalist versions such as *The Book* (and the *Living Bible,* on which *The Book* is based) have similar methods of skirting through theological difficulties. Those who are interested to explore this further can consult the book *Fundamentalism: Hazards and Heartbreaks* by Rod Evans and Irwin Berent published by Open Court publishing.

Part Two
JESUS

I believe that Christ was a man like ourselves; to look upon him as God would seem to me the greatest of sacrileges.

Leo Tolstoy (1828-1910)

If I had the power that the New Testament narrative say that Jesus had, I would not cure one person of blindness, I would make blindness impossible; I would not cure one person of leprosy, I would abolish leprosy.

Joseph Lewis (1889-1968)

Chapter Seven
METHODOLOGIES, ASSUMPTIONS &
HISTORICAL BACKGROUND

PRELIMINARIES

To study the life of Jesus one needs to be familiar with the primary sources relating to him and the general historical environment of the period which he lived. The major sources on the life of Jesus are the canonical gospels, the Acts of the Apostles and the authentic Pauline epistles. There are also extra-biblical sources that make references to Jesus and to the general environment of first century Palestine.

However, we cannot simply read from these sources, paraphrase the stories found therein and assume that what we have then come up with is "history." We need to be able to *critically* evaluate these sources in order to be able to determine what is historical and what is not. In order to ensure the validity of our findings we first need to be clear about our methodologies and assumptions in evaluating these sources.

In this chapter, we will concern ourselves with these preliminary issues relating to the historical method, its methodologies and assumptions and how it will relate to the study of Jesus. We will also be familiarizing ourselves with the general history of first century Palestine. Finally, we will look at contemporaneous extra-biblical sources that made references to Jesus.

ON THE HISTORICAL METHOD

How does one evaluate the general trustworthiness of an historical document? Fundamentalists sometimes claim that the only fair treatment of their sacred writings is to accept its witness at face value until they are proven false. This view is commonsensical; after all, we trust the stories told to us by friends and do not generally second-guess them. They also claim that a critical evaluation of their scriptures is unfair as historians are generally less critical of their (secular) sources than modern scholars are of the New Testament. While such a claim may be true in the past, it is manifestly untrue today; a critical evaluation of sources is the basis of all modern scientific historical analysis. This is how the famed historian and philosopher of history, R.G. Collingwood, framed the issue:

> I will begin by stating what may be called the common sense theory of it [i.e. history]...According to this theory, the essential things in history are memory and authority...History is...believing someone else when he says that he remembers something. The believer is the historian; the person believed is called his authority.

> This doctrine implies that historical truth, so far as it is at all accessible to the historian, is accessible to him only because it exists ready-made in the ready-made statements of his authorities. These statements are to him a sacred text...He must therefore on no account tamper with them. He must no mutilate them; he must not add to them; and above all he must not contradict them...The authority may be garrulous, discursive, a gossip and a scandal monger; he may have overlooked or forgotten or omitted facts; he may have ignorantly or wilfully mis-stated them; but

against this defects the historian has no remedy. For him, on the [common sense] theory, what his authorities tell him is the truth, the whole accessible truth, and nothing but the truth.[1]

As Collingwood added, such as "common-sense" theory needs "only to be stated to be repudiated". Accepting sources as completely sacrosanct means that no history is possible – for we are asked to swallow wholesale what is told to us, regardless of the authors' agenda or their own accessibility to the events they are reporting. All we would have are conflicting sources telling conflicting stories – much as it is when fundamentalist religions clash.

What is required, according to Collingwood, is *historical criticism.*

> As natural science finds its proper method when the scientist, in Bacon's metaphor, puts Nature to the question, tortures her by experiment in order to wring from her answers to his own questions, so history finds its proper method when the historian puts his authorities in the witness box, and by cross-questioning extorts from them information which in their original statements they have withheld, either because they do not wish to give it or because they do not possess it...

> [The historian] has it in his power to reject something explicitly told to him by his authorities and to substitute something else...[T]he criterion of historical truth cannot be the fact that a statement is made by an authority. It is the truthfulness and the information of the so-called authority that are in question...

> We know that the truth is to be had, not by swallowing what authorities tell us, but by criticizing it; and thus the supposedly fixed points between which the historical imagination spins its web are not given to us ready made, they must be achieved by critical thinking.[2]

In their book *From Reliable Sources: An Introduction to Historical Methods* (2001), historians Martha Howell and Walter Prevenier spelt out some of the critical evaluation required in the study of historical manuscripts:

> Sources must be carefully located in time and place: when was it composed, where and in what country, in what social setting and by which individual? Are these apparent "facts" of composition correct?...[T]he source must be checked for authenticity...[3]

Then there are the internal criteria or *source criticism*, with the appropriate caveats, with which such sources must be evaluated:

> These include questions about the intended meaning of a source – was the author of the text in the position to know what he reported? Did he intend an accurate report? Are his interpretations "reliable"? These are questions which nineteenth century historians concentrated, and these scholars developed very sophisticated tools for addressing them...If used carefully, with full knowledge of their limitations, the

---

[1]   Collingwood, *The Idea of History*: p234-235

[2]   Collingwood, *The Idea of History*: p237-238, 243

[3]   Howell & Prevenier, *From Reliable Sources*: p43

tools can help us make good use of sources, make them produce meaning in responsible ways.[4]

The tools which Howell and Prevernier spoke of in the passage above can be summarized into seven points:[5]

1. **Genealogy** - Are copies of extant documents accurate representations of the original autograph if this no longer exists?[6]

2. **Genesis** – Who wrote it, when and where was it written? The *significance* of such information may also be important.

3. **Originality** - What possible earlier sources were used by the author and what if any were the redactional changes made to it?

4. **Interpretation** – What is the meaning and intent of the document? An ostensibly straightforward report about some supposed historical incident may be written with the intention of providing a certain faction's viewpoint.

5. **Authorial Authority** – Was the author an eyewitness to the events he or she reports, or was he or she retelling a second, third or fourth hand account? "The greater number of intermediaries between the original telling of an event and the version that our source contains, the more chance there is of distortion."

6. **Competence** – What was the psychological state of the author? How selective was the reporting? What prejudices may be inherent in the report? What were the outside influences that may have affected the reporting? What was the mindset of the author? Was he gullible? Skeptical?

7. **Trustworthiness** – Does the personality of the author – as far as we can tell – provide us with confidence in the accounts being reported? "People – and thus sources – lie…sometimes consciously but sometimes unconsciously. Here historians are interested not so much in the lie, as in the more subtle form of falsehood, the suppression or shading of knowledge…"

Thus modern historical methods mean that sources cannot be accepted blindly and must be critically evaluated.[7] This will have to be done with the sources relating to the life of Jesus.

---

[4] Howell & Prevenier, *From Reliable Sources*: p60

[5] Howell & Prevenier, *From Reliable Sources*: p61-68

[6] This is the province of textual criticism, something which was looked at in chapter 6.

[7] One of the major flaws of Richard Bauckham's recent book *Jesus and The Eyewitnesses* is the eschewing of such principles of historical criticism. In page 486 of that book, Bauckham noted that *"Testimony should be treated as reliable until proved otherwise."* Even if documents can be shown to be that of an eyewitness, the need to evaluate his competence and trustworthiness is not discarded. Bauckham seems to want history to

CRITERIA OF AUTHENTICITY

In addition to the above, critical historians have additional criteria to evaluate the details of Jesus' life given in the primary sources. These criteria are sometimes given in slightly different forms by various historians but in general they can be summarized into these few points:[8]

1. **Multiple Attestation** – Events or sayings attested in more than one *independent* source are more likely to be historically accurate. That Jesus normally taught in parables is independently attested in the Gospel of Mark, Q, M and L[9] and the Gospel of Thomas.[10] That these sources are independent of each other and they all say the same things give critical historians confidence in asserting that the historical Jesus did teach in parabolic forms. Independence is a very important criterion here. If multiple sources say the same thing but that can all be shown to be derived from only one source, then the criterion of multiple attestations does not apply.

2. **Dissimilarity / Offensiveness** – When something mentioned of Jesus is at odds with the general cultural environment, or what the early Christians believed about him, or is something that may sound offensive to them, we have again something which is very probably historically authentic. It is extremely unlikely that the early Christian tradition would construct a story about Jesus that would be difficult to explain within the context of their beliefs. For instance, as we will see in chapter 12, Jesus' baptism by John the Baptist (Mark 1:9-11) was something that caused difficulties and embarrassment for the early Christians. Since by the time the gospels were written, the early Christians already believed Jesus to be more than a mere man. His submitting to baptism by John would mean that he required cleansing for his sins – something that they would not have accepted. Thus most historians are convinced that Jesus' baptism by John is an historical fact. The flip side of this criterion is that if something is reported of Jesus that fits *too well* the situation of the early Christians, then it is highly probable that *that* story may be a fictional concoction of the community.

---

revert to a pre-enlightenment, non-critical, acceptance of authorities. Of course, such a view guarantees that the gospels will be accepted as "the gospel truth"!

[8]   Funk et. al., *The Five Gospels*: p16-34
Lüdemann, *Jesus After 200 Years*: p4-6
Powell, *The Jesus Debate*: p52-56

[9]   Q is the term generally used by scholars to refer to the special sayings source used independently by Matthew and Luke. M is the source specific to Matthew and L is the source specific to Luke. See chapter 9 for more detailed discussions on these sources.

[10] The gospel of Thomas is a sayings gospel generally dated to the first half of the first century, making it a near contemporary to the canonical gospels of Luke and John. Many scholars believe that some of the sayings within this gospel provide an independent source to the authentic Jesus. We will be discussing the gospel of Thomas within the topic of apocalyptic eschatology in chapter 13.

Similarly, we become suspicious of the historicity of a reported saying or act of Jesus that seems to fit too well the redactional agenda of the author.

3. **Verisimilitude** – In a way this is a "check" on the previous criterion. Something attributed to Jesus that is very different from the history, language and culture in which he lived is also very likely unauthentic. Thus the saying in Mark 10:11-12, where Jesus is supposedly prohibiting a woman's right to divorce, is generally accepted as unauthentic as Jewish law does not allow the woman to initiate such a procedure. It is important to add that verisimilitude alone is never adequate to establish a report as authentic. Historical fiction is filled with verisimilitudes but is still fiction nevertheless. Thus this criterion is more often applied negatively – if something is anachronistic it is unhistorical; however, it does not follow that something which is free from anachronisms is therefore proven to be historical.

4. **Oral Form** – The earliest traditions about Jesus were passed on by word of mouth. Studies have shown that oral tradition is most reliably preserved when it takes the form that is short, memorable and provocative. This is exactly the kind of sayings, teaching and stories we generally find in the synoptic gospels (i.e. Matthew, Mark and Luke). This also means that the form and content of Jesus' teaching that we see in the Gospel of John, long, meandering sayings that are extremely hard to memorize, are very likely unhistorical.

5. **Coherence** – This is an expansional criterion, used to include reports regarding Jesus that cannot be deduced with certainty from any, or a combination of, the above criteria. The basic assumption here is that if something which is reported of Jesus is consistent with or fits well with what is reported of him from more assured reports – it *may* be historical.

We will be applying these criteria throughout our study of the accounts of Jesus' life.

EPISTEMOLOGICAL ASSUMPTIONS

It is also important to note the working epistemological assumptions that go with the historical methodologies and criteria outlined above. There are three fundamental epistemological assumptions that will have to be clarified. The first has to do with certainty. The historical sciences cannot achieve the certainty that we can derive from the hard sciences like physics and chemistry. Indeed, even in the hard sciences there is, philosophically speaking, never *complete* certainty. However, the lack of complete certainty does not mean anything goes. Thus it is important to know the difference between the concepts of *possibility* and *probability*. Since there is no absolute certainly, the final decision has to come from an evaluation of the evidence.

This brings us to the second assumption - the criterion we use to evaluate these probabilities. There is a fundamental assumption in all historical judgment that *the present as key to the past.* Since this criterion has been caricatured and criticized by fundamentalists and by conservative scholars, it is important for us to examine its validity.

Finally, when there are competing explanations, all of which seem to explain the phenomenon equally well, we need a rule that will help us decide which among them is most likely to be the correct one. This rule is known as Ockham's Razor.

We will be looking at all these three fundamental assumptions below.

On Possibility and Probability

Many fundamentalists have what is called *certitude*. According to *Webster's New World College Dictionary*, *certitude* is the feeling of "absolute sureness or conviction". Now *certitude* is different from *certainty*. *Webster's* gives *certainty* as the "*state* or *fact*" of being certain". The difference is this: the latter is an *objective* statement of a situation while the former is a *subjective* description of one person's views. Thus *feeling*, "knowing in your heart", that one is right (certitude) is different from being able to *demonstrate it* (certainty).

Where can we find certainty? Strictly speaking, the only certainties we have are in the fields of mathematics and logic. But these are mental constructs and their deductive certainty comes from the fact that we *define* certainty into it. Thus "1+1 = 2" is certainly true because we defined "2" as the next number after "1."[11] Mathematics and logic also allow us to pronounce, with certainty, the *impossibility* of some concepts. These include concepts like a square circle or a four sided triangle. The reader will note that it is simply not possible to *imagine* these! In other words, we can be *certain* that square circles and four sided triangles cannot exist.

When it comes to the empirical world, this kind of certainty disappears. Let us take, as an example, this statement of fact:

The sun will rise from the east tomorrow.

This is, admittedly, a rather quaint geocentric rendering but it would suffice for our current purpose. Our belief that this statement is true comes from the fact that all our experiences in the past and in recorded history have shown that the sun has risen from the east without fail. Furthermore, our collection of the *habits* of nature summarized in physics (conservation of angular momentum and the law of gravitation) supports this fact.

However, as David Hume (1711-1776) showed a long time ago, all these findings, in support of our certainty that the sun will rise from the east tomorrow, are taken from the *past*. There is no *logical* contradiction in thinking that the future may be different. For instance, I can say:

*The sun will rise from the **west** tomorrow*

---

[11] One should note, as Godel's incompleteness theorem shows, that even here the knowledge [within a single deductive system] will always be incomplete. Note also that "1+1 = 1" is also "certainly true" in Boolean algebra!

and can imagine it, in a way that I cannot imagine a four sided triangle! So, strictly speaking, anything that is not logically contradictory is, in principle, *possible*.

That's not where the analysis ends though. For if we believe anything is possible than we have no way of deciding anything. The reason why we take the fact that the sun will rise from the east tomorrow as virtually certain is that our past experiences, coupled with our knowledge of science and history, give us a high confidence level (a very high probability) that the event will happen again tomorrow. Indeed, I would classify anyone denying this as being delusional. Thus we are justified in saying that this is one thing that approaches certainty. Note how *possibility*, apart from setting an initial counter-example, plays no role at all in the decision making process.

Similarly, historical reconstructions are all done on the basis of evaluation of the evidence and the probability of the various scenarios. This is how *reason* works, in science, in history and in life.

Unfortunately, this is not the case with fundamentalist apologetic "reasoning". Almost invariably, fundamentalist apologists "reason" from the basis of *possibility*.

One example of this is from the recent fundamentalist bestseller, Lee Strobel's *The Case for Christ* (Zondervan 1998), in discussing the conflicting genealogies of Jesus in Matthew and Luke (Matt 1:1-16 and Luke 3:23-32).[12] Strobel quoted conservative scholar Craig Blomberg[13] as suggesting "two options" to "resolve" this difficulty: the first option is that Luke's genealogy is of Mary, while Matthew's is of Joseph, the second "option" is the "levirate" explanation, i.e. that while both genealogies traces Joseph's ancestries, one traces the legal ancestry (levirate) while the other traces his biological one. These options, according to Strobel, provide "rational explanations" and give a "reasonable harmonization" of the gospel accounts.

Note the fallacy here. Blomberg was merely providing additional *possibilities* (which are mutually exclusive!) that *may* account for the discrepancy in genealogies. The third possibility, that this actually is a contradiction, has not been proven wrong (i.e. shown to be improbable). Thus most critical scholars would take these possibilities as the starting point for analysis (i.e. to look into the probability of various explanations) not as the ending or the resolution of the problem, as Blomberg and Strobel clearly intended it to be.

The root cause of the fallacy is simple. Embedded within this method of "reasoning" is the belief (certitude) that the Bible is inerrant and the moment there are *possible* explanations for the various "difficulties", the problem is considered solved! This is not how things work in reasoned discourse. Remember that it is "possible" that the sun may rise from the west tomorrow! To show why their explanation is more likely to be true, they have to provide evidence why it is to be preferred over other accounts. Merely *suggesting* a possible explanation does not mean the problem is resolved.

This "defense from possibility" permeates fundamentalist thought on the Bible and the "historical" Jesus. We leave the last word to Dr. Robert Miller, a fellow of the *Jesus Seminar*:[14]

---

12   We will be discussing these conflicting genealogies in detail in chapter 11.
13   Strobel, *Case for Christ*: p60-61
14   The Jesus seminar, founded in 1985 by New Testament scholars Robert Funk (1926-2005) and John Dominic Crossan, is a research group consisting of more than one

[T]he concept of possibility is not very helpful in historical matters. Endless historical scenarios can be concocted, and virtually all of them are possible, even the weirdest and most fantastic. That's why to say that a certain scenario is possible almost always is to say nothing about it at all.

...But it's crucial to make the distinction between possibility and probability because very different criteria apply in each case. To be historically possible, something only needs to be imaginable. However, for something to be historically probable means that there is some evidence for it. Not everyone in the historical Jesus discussion seems aware of this distinction, for we often read statements like "Isn't it possible that Jesus...?" Fill in the blank with any scenario you like, no matter how you like: the answer will always be yes.[15]

The Present as Key to the Past

Fundamentalists and conservative theologians complain of a "naturalistic presupposition" of the historical sciences. By introducing this as an "unconscious bias" of secular historians, they claim that this immediately dismisses all claims of miracles from any historical consideration and, by such prejudice, the central claims of Christianity are simply rejected, *a priori*, without much analysis.

It is true that historians work on the principle that can be construed as "naturalistic", so it is important to see why this is so and whether the fundamentalists' critique is fair.

One of the most important principles of critical historical thinking is this: *the present is the key to the past*. This is simply another way of saying that the past is in many ways analogous to the present. Without such an assumption *historical thinking becomes impossible*. Let me give an example. We have a saying of Jesus, given in Mark within the context of paying taxes to the Roman Empire, that is generally accepted by most scholars to be an authentic saying of Jesus:

Mark 12:17
"Render to Caesar the things that are Caesar's, and to God the things that are God's."

This saying fits many of the criteria we mentioned earlier.

- It is *multiply attested*, since we not only find it in Mark, but also (probably independently) in the Gospel of Thomas (100:1-4)

---

hundred biblical scholars who come together twice a year to study, discuss and decide on issues such as what the historical Jesus actually said and did. The main innovations of the Jesus seminar consist in their use of voting to decide on these issues and the very *public* nature of their seminars. Of course many of their findings do not conform to the traditional Christian beliefs about Jesus and, as expected, they have experienced a strong backlash from more conservative scholars. While I do not agree with everything the seminar concludes [see chapter 12 on the historicity of the "apocalyptic Jesus"], this seminar has advanced the study of Jesus considerably and have done a great service to the public by showing that not all theologians are Bible thumping fundamentalists or evangelicals!

[15] Miller, *The Jesus Seminar and Its Critics*:p39

- It fulfils the criterion of dissimilarity. It does not fit too well with the beliefs of the early Christians. The early Christians, starting with Paul (Romans 13:1-7) came out on the side of paying the civil authorities their due. Although Christians from early on interpreted this saying to mean that paying taxes is okay, the saying – taken by itself - does not seem to say one way or another whether one should pay taxes or not; only that one should be able to know the difference.[16]

However, there is another, more *fundamental,* assumption that enables the criteria of authenticity above to be used. To spell it out may sound silly but it is important to do so. This is the assumption that when Jesus opened his mouth to speak and is heard by those around him, the laws of physics and facts of human biology as we know them continue to apply. In other words, his voice box vibrates, which in turn changes the air pressure in it, which then propagates out from his mouth as sound waves. These sound waves travel through the air and reaches the ears of those who were around him, their ear drums vibrates, sending signals to their brains which are then interpreted as spoken words.

Thus our *fundamental assumptions* are that the laws of physics and our knowledge of the biology of human speech and hearing derived from modern studies holds. Thus at the very fundamental level we *assume* that, like today, when someone opens his mouth to speak, people around him would hear what he is saying. Suppose someone says, "Well we were not there to verify this and for all we know the world 2,000 years ago follows different laws of physics and that human biology functions differently." Note that if we allow such an objection *carte blanche* then we cannot say *anything* about history at all. We have no way of evaluating evidence (all of which assumes things we know to be true today) from the past – since all anyone needs to invoke is the stock objection: *"naturalistic presuppositions!"*. For "naturalistic presupposition" is simply this: what we see happening today, how things are interconnected, are how things are in the past.

Does such an assumption lead to an *a priori* bias against the Christian claims? The answer is no. As we shall see in chapter 12, extraordinary events, *even miracles,* in principle, can be proven true if the evidence is strong enough.

If historians have any bias, it is an *evidential* one. That means no claim can be accepted as true unless the evidence supporting it is strong enough. This sounds reasonable enough but is unacceptable to the fundamentalist. Since by rallying around the banner against "naturalistic presuppositions" they want the *arbitrary* right to assert *when* the laws of nature holds (as in the case when Jesus spoke or did things that are later retold by witnesses - as we have shown in the example above) and when they do not (when miracles are "reported" in the Bible to have happened).

How then do fundamentalists believe their claims to be true without considering the evidence? The answer is in their own presupposition: *biblical inerrancy.* As Robert Price rightly noted,[17] the argument is not between "naturalism" and "supernaturalism", it is between accepting the Bible as true without question versus approaching it rationally as we would any other historical document. The case of

---

[16] Funk, et. al., *The Five Gospels*: p102
[17] Robert Price, "By the Time He Stinketh", Price & Lowder (ed), *The Empty Tomb*: p419

miracles is a good example. Fundamentalists want to accept all claims of the miraculous in the Bible as true.[18] Yet we know that other religions and cultures have their own miraculous claims. Even within Christendom, there are claims of spectacular miracles – such as the sun dancing in Fatima in 1917, a supposed miracle witnessed by a crowd of 70,000 people – that are not accepted as such by all Christians.[19] Yet, most of the time, when asked about miracles not mentioned in the Bible in debates with skeptics, their response has invariably been that – they have not studied them![20] This is perhaps the only response available, since if they ever try to systematically reject these miracles, the very tools they use would be used against their claims of miracles in the Bible.

Yes, there are suppositions in critical historical methodology. The fundamental supposition is *evidential*. We construct historical knowledge based on *evidence*. We do not assert anything we have no evidence for. In the consideration of evidence, we work, rationally, from the known to the unknown. What is known is what we see today; the assumption, that the present is the key to the past, is essential to being able to do history. If this assumption is removed, history, as we know it, becomes impossible.

Ockham's Razor

Closely related to the above issue is the philosophical concept of Ockham's Razor named after the 14th century logician William Ockham (*c.* 1295–1349). The razor,

---

18 See chapter 12, in the section "On Miracles," for a more detailed analysis on the proper methodology when dealing with accounts of miracles.

19 Most fundamentalists believe that the Mariology in the Catholic Church is (or at least is very close to) a form of polytheism. The miracle in Fatima which was tied to visions of the Virgin Mary would not have been considered "kosher" by fundamentalists. For a more detailed analysis of the "miracle of the sun" at Fatima, see chapter 12 in the section "On Miracles."

20 One such example is that of Christian apologist Micheal Horner. Horner is fond of claiming that skeptics and critical historians have an "anti-supernatural bias" against reports about miracles in the Bible. In his debate with skeptic Farrell Till in 1995, the latter presented him with accounts of miracles from non-Christian writers (Josephus, Suetonius), modern day "Elvis-sightings" and Mormon claims about Joseph Smith and the golden plates and asked for his opinion on their historicity. Horner, who obviously does not believe such miracles, replied that he hadn't "checked into" them. A year later, in another debate, this time with atheist Dan Barker, Horner was once again asked by Till in the Q&A session about these non-biblical reports of miracles and whether he had evaluated them historically. Once again Horner replied that he hasn't "yet done that." The full transcripts of both debates as well as Farell Till's comments can be found in the Internet Infidels website [accessed on October 2, 2007]:
The Horner-Till debate:
http://www.infidels.org/library/modern/farrell_till/horner-till/
The Horner-Barker debate:
http://www.infidels.org/library/modern/dan_barker/barker_horner.html
Farrell Till's comments on Horner's position on miracles:
http://www.infidels.org/library/magazines/tsr/1997/2/2claim97.html

also known as the law of parsimony, says that *"entities should not be multiplied beyond necessity."* What this means is that in cases where we have two explanations that equally explain a phenomenon or an historical incident, the explanation that requires the least assumptions is to be preferred.

This "economy of thought" is more than just a philosophical fiat, for there are sound reasons why it is to be preferred from an epistemological standpoint. It comes from the recognitions that all explanatory theories and hypothesis need initial assumptions. All assumptions by their very nature are uncertain and the addition of further assumptions simply increases the uncertainty to the edifice of the explanation. In other words, the more assumptions we make initially, the higher the probability that the theory or hypothesis may turn out to be wrong.[21]

This is an important concept in our evaluation of the stories of the miraculous and in the stories of Jesus' resurrection.

HISTORICAL BACKGROUND

Like all documents, the documents concerning the life of Jesus, namely the gospels of Matthew, Mark, Luke and John, did not appear in an historical vacuum. The biography of any historical person cannot be detached from its historical setting. To attain a rational understanding and appreciation of the gospels it is important therefore to have at least a working knowledge of the historical situations and circumstances surrounding the life of Jesus and the writing of the gospels.

The most convenient point for a background historical summary of these events would be the year 39 BCE. It was in that year that the Idumean, Herod "The Great" (c73-4 BCE) was appointed the "confederate king" of the Jews by the Roman senate. He took control of Jerusalem two years later and started his reign as King of the Jews in 37 BCE.

Herod, however, was not popular with the Jews. He was too Hellenized and too pro-Roman for the average Jew. However, it was Herod who initiated the rebuilding of the temple in Jerusalem in 20 BCE. Herod meant it to be the grandest temple of all, for which he hoped to be remembered by his Jewish subject. He did not live to see its completion for he died in 4 BCE and the temple was not finished until 63 CE.

Historically, Herod is connected to Jesus in many ways. Jesus was very likely born during the last years of Herod's reign. It was this Herod whom the Gospel of Matthew alleged ordered the massacre of all male babies under two years old as an attempt to get rid of Jesus. It was also the temple that Herod built which Jesus referred to as his father's house when he drove out the money changers.[22]

After Herod's death, the Roman Emperor, Augustus (63 BCE–14 CE), divided the province of Palestine into four separate districts or *tetrachies*. (See Figure 7.1 below) Three of these four districts were given to Herod's three sons:[23] Herod Philip (d. 34 CE), Herod Archelaus (d. 18 CE) and Herod Antipas (died circa 40 CE). Philip and Antipas were called "tetrarchs" which means ruler of one fourth of a province.

---

21   Losee, *A Historical Introduction to the Philosophy of Science*: p38-39
22   Martin, *New Testament Foundations I*: p61-62
      Livingstone, *Dictionary of the Christian Church*: p239, 502
23   The fourth tetrarchy, Abilene, was ruled by Lysanias, who had no relation to Herod.

Archelaus was called "ethnarch" or provincial governor. Philip was given the territories of Iturea, Gaulatinus, Trachonitis and Auranitis. Archelaus was given the territories of Idumea, Judea and Samaria. Herod Antipas was given the territories of Galilee and Paraea. It was Archelaus' reign in Judea that, according to Matthew, forced Joseph to bring Mary and Jesus to Galilee after their brief sojourn in Egypt (Matthew 2:22).

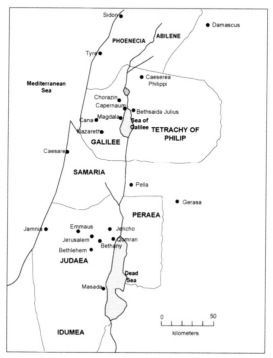

Figure 7.1: Palestine during the time of Jesus

Philip had a quiet reign. When he died in 34 CE, he left no heir and his tetrarchy was passed over to the Roman legate of Syria. Things were less peaceful for the other two Herods. Herod Archelaus' rule coincided with a rise in messianic fervor among the Jews and the Samaritans. This fervor, which boiled over into minor uprisings, was dealt with severely by Archelaus. His oppressive rule made the Romans fear a widespread Jewish revolt. As a result, in 6 CE, Augustus banished him to Vienne. After that his tetrarchy became a province administered directly by a Roman procurator or governor.

Herod Antipas, of the three, was the one most like his father. An event concerning Antipas that was narrated in the gospels involved what was, to the Jews of that time, an illicit affair. It involved Antipas and Herodias, the wife of his brother, Philip. This sister-in-law induced Antipas to leave his wife, which he did. Herod then married Herodias, an incestuous union in Jewish eyes. It was the condemnation of this action by John the Baptist that led to his imprisonment and execution (Mark 6:14-29). It was under Herod Antipas' reign that Jesus grew up in Galilee. It was also to this Herod that Luke says Pilate sent Jesus for interrogation (Luke 23:6) during his trial in Jerusalem. Herod Antipas remained as tetrarch until 39 CE when he was banished to Lyons in Gaul.[24]

After Judea was made a Roman province in 6 CE, the Roman legate in Syria, Publius Sulphicus Quirinius (c51 BCE–21 CE) ordered a census there to determine the taxable properties in Judea. This measure provoked a popular Jewish revolt that was led by one Judas of Galilee.

The armed rebellion failed and around 2,000 of the rebels were crucified.[25] The forces of Judas of Galilee became known as the *Zealots*, which came from the Greek *zelos* (rebellion) or as *Cananaeans*, from the Aramaic *qanan* with the same meaning. Some of Jesus' apostles were Zealots: Simon the Cananaeans and, probably, Judas Iscariot.[26]

The uprising convinced Rome of the need for more direct rule over the unruly province. A Roman procurator, Coponius, was appointed to rule over Judea. The next historical figure of interest is Pontius Pilate, the fifth Roman procurator of Judea. He held this office from 26 to 37 CE. The whole span of Jesus' ministry is within the tenureship of Pilate. According to the gospels it was he who ordered, albeit reluctantly, the execution of Jesus (Mark 15:1-15). Pilate's successor, the sixth procurator, was Marullus, who held the post from 37 to 41 CE.[27]

Marullus' successor however, was not a Roman procurator but another Idumean named Herod. This Herod also appeared in the narrative documents of the New Testament (in the *Acts of the Apostles*). His name was Herod Agrippa I (10 BCE-44 CE). Agrippa was the grandson of Herod the Great through his father Aristobolus, who was Herod's second son. For some services rendered to the Emperor Claudius, Herod Agrippa was made the king of the entire region of Palestine once ruled by his grandfather in 41 CE. His rule was short though, for he died suddenly in 44 CE. It was Herod Agrippa who had James the son of Zebedee, and probably his brother John, executed in 44 CE. It was also this Herod that imprisoned Peter (Acts 12:1-3).[28]

After the death of Herod Agrippa in 44 CE, he was succeeded by the seventh procurator, Fadus. In his eight years as procurator, Fadus kept good control of the Judean political climate. His successors did a poorer job. Fadus successor was Felix became the eighth procurator in 52 CE. It was during Felix's term that Paul the apostle was arrested and detained for trial. Felix's successor, Festus held the office for only two years, from 60-62 CE.[29]

It was during the procuratorship of Festus that Paul was sent to Rome to appeal his case. Paul spent two whole years under house arrest in Rome. According to the

---

[24] Craveri, *The Life of Jesus*: p63-64
      Martin, *New Testament Foundations I*: p65-66
      Livingstone, *Dictionary of the Christian Church*: p239
[25] Crucifixion as a method of death sentence was reserved for crimes of a *political* nature, such as revolution against the Empire.
[26] Craveri, *The Life of Jesus*: p77,154-155
      Martin, *New Testament Foundations I*: p66
[27] Martin, *New Testament Foundations I*: p66
[28] Asimov, *Guide to the Bible*: p1033-1035
      Craveri, *The Life of Jesus*: p152
      Livingstone, *Dictionary of the Christian Church*: p239
[29] Martin, *New Testament Foundations I*: p68

Acts of the Apostles, he "without hindrance...preached the kingdom of God and taught about the Lord Jesus Christ."(Acts 28:31).

Actually, Paul's timing could not have been worse. It was around this time that the Roman Emperor Nero (37-68 CE) started to lose his mental equilibrium and became insane. The first eight years of his reign, from 54-62 CE, saw an enlightened reign, under guidance of the stoic philosopher Seneca (c4 BCE-65 CE). Having gone mad, Nero killed Seneca by ordering him to commit suicide. The emperor then had his wife, Octavia, murdered to please his mistress, Poppaea. This mistress, who was pregnant, was also murdered: kicked to death by the insane emperor.

Then in 64 CE, a great fire, lasting a week, raged over central Rome. Nero then used the burnt-out land to build a new palace, the Domus Aurea. Not surprisingly, the finger of suspicion as to the cause of the fire fell upon Nero. He looked for a scapegoat and found a convenient one in the Christians. He began a systematic persecution of Christians in the city of Rome. The terror that befell the Christians included being used as living torches and being thrown to beasts in the amphitheater. It was in this persecution, circa 64-67 CE, that, according to tradition, both Paul and Peter were martyred.[30]

Meanwhile back in Palestine, after the death of Festus in 62 CE, there was a brief period before his successor took office. The High Priest, Ananus, a Sadducee,[31] took the opportunity to indict James, the brother of Jesus and brought about his death in 62 CE. When Albinus became the tenth procurator later that year, the political situation in Judea was reaching a fever pitch. Jewish revolutionaries, called *sicarii*, men of the dagger, were launching terrorist attacks all throughout the Judean countryside. His attempts at suppressing them met with little success. The next procurator, Florus, took office in 64 CE. He was probably the worst possible person to hold the post; greedy and corrupt with no empathy for the Jews of Palestine. All the sporadic protests of the Jews finally coalesced into a full scale revolt.[32]

In 66 CE a race riot between the Jews and the Gentiles erupted in Ceasarea. The Gentiles slaughtered 20,000 Jews within an hour. This slaughter, together with the arrests of Jews by the order of Florus, effectively emptied Ceasarea of any Jewish resident. Florus handled subsequent events poorly: he desecrated the Jewish temple and attempted to extort the Jews by ordering them to pay him 17 gold talents from the Temple funds for protection. This sequence of humiliating events united the Jews; the Zealots were joined by all the major Jewish sects. In May of that year the Zealots

---

[30]   Armstrong, *The First Christian*: p168
       Cary & Scullard, *A History of Rome*: p359, 634
       Roberts, *History of the World*: p266

[31]   The Jewish religion during the first century CE consisted of four main sects or factions. These sects are the Sadducees, the Pharisees, the Zealots and the Essenes. The Sadducees consisted of the wealthy and land owning, many of whom are priests. Its members are situated mainly in Jerusalem. The Pharisees consisted of lay religious teachers. It was they who kept the faith of Israel alive outside Jerusalem. Modern Judaism is derived from the theology of the Pharisees. The Zealots are Jews committed to open rebellion against Rome. The Essenes was the monastic sect in Judaism. The ruins at Qumran where the Dead Sea Scrolls were discovered are generally believed to be an Essene monastery.

[32]   Martin, *New Testament Foundations I*: p68-69

attacked the Roman garrison stationed outside Jerusalem. The garrison, which was led by Cestius Gallus, the legate of Syria, was routed by the Jewish insurgents. This initial morale boosting victory initiated open rebellion against the Romans all over Palestine.[33]

Nero sent one of his best generals, Vespasian (9-79 CE), to quell the rebellion. The general's first move was to wipe out the Jewish resistance in Galilee, which he did successfully. In one of these battles, he captured a Jewish military commander, Joseph ben Matthias (37-c100 CE). This Jew eventually went over to the Roman side, was awarded Roman citizenship and changed his name to Flavius Josephus. It is to Josephus' voluminous writings after his defection that we owe much of our knowledge of the conditions of first century Palestine and the Jewish Revolt. His *History of the Jewish War* in seven volumes presents an eyewitness account of the Jewish Revolt. His *Antiquities of the Jews*, a 20 volume work, traces the history of the Jews from the moment of creation until the Jewish revolt. Among his other writings include *Autobiography* and *Against Apion*.[34]

Meanwhile, Vespasian continued to mop up the Jewish resistance in Paraea, Samaria and Idumea. He was poised for an attack on Jerusalem when the news of Nero's death reached him. He made his way back to Rome where he became the new emperor. The task of attacking Jerusalem fell on the shoulders of his son, Titus (c40-81 CE). The siege of the holy city of the Jews took place in April 70, at the time of the Jewish Passover festival when Jerusalem was filled with pilgrims. The Jews stubbornly defended the city for several months. Finally famine, fatigue and the vastly superior Roman army took their toll on them. Jerusalem finally fell in September of 70 CE. The Romans entered Jerusalem and killed everyone they found. The loss of life in Jerusalem was horrendous. More than *one million* Jews died during the siege. The whole city was leveled, including its walls. The Temple, the symbol of Judaism, was destroyed.[35]

With the fall of Jerusalem the main force of the Jewish revolt was no more. The rest of the operation consisted of mopping up the remaining insurgents. The last Jewish stronghold was in fortress of Masada, west of the Dead Sea. Masada was stubbornly defended by the Jews but it too, fell in 74 CE. The Jews in Masada, upon realizing that Roman victory was imminent, committed mass suicide. When the Romans finally made their way into the fort, to their surprise they found only one woman alive. With the fall of Masada, the Jewish revolt ended.[36]

The Jewish revolutionary war marked a turning point for Christianity (and Judaism). Doubtless, many of the Jewish Christians, who were called Nazarenes, died during the war. Some of them, acting on an oracle, managed to flee Jerusalem and escaped to Pella in Transjordan.

---

[33] Cary & Scullard, *A History of Rome*: p367
      Schonfield, *The Passover Plot*: p186
[34] Martin, *New Testament Foundations I*: p69, 75-76
      Livingstone, *Dictionary of the Christian Church*: p280
[35] Craveri, *The Life of Jesus*: p333
      Martin, *New Testament Foundations I*: p70
      Schonfield, *The Passover Plot*: p185
[36] Martin, *New Testament Foundations I*: p70

The Nazarenes, the followers of Peter and James, were, by logical extension, the true followers of Jesus. Before the revolt, they were caught in the middle between the Gentile Christians and the Jews. They could not fully accept the Gentiles because they still believed that Jesus never abrogated the law. To them, a follower of Jesus must first be a Jew. The Jews in turn could not accept the Nazarenes because of their beliefs in Jesus. The Roman destruction of Jerusalem made the Jews even more eager to foster unity among themselves to the exclusion of others. The Nazarenes, with their association of Gentiles, began to be shunned by the orthodox Jews. Tension between the Nazarenes and Jews led in many cases to the former being expelled from synagogues.[37] By the time of the second Jewish revolt in 132-135 CE the break between the Nazarenes and Judaism was completely severed.[38]

The destruction of Jerusalem was viewed by the Gentile Christians from a different angle. To them it was proof of God's punishment to the Jews for rejecting the savior. As the number of Gentile Christians grew, Jewish Christianity, with its insistence on adherence to the law, was pushed into the background. The die was cast. The Nazarenes, now known mainly to proto-orthodox Christians by the name *Ebionites*, the poor ones, were branded as a heresy.[39] The Nazarenes/Ebionites were active mainly to the east of the Roman Empire and survived in remnants there until the advent of Islam.[40]

With the exclusion of the Nazarenes from the Jewish synagogue worship and the labeling of the same as "heretics" by the Gentile followers of Jesus, the way was cleared for the complete separation of Christianity from Judaism.

With this we end our brief excursion into the historical background of the New Testament times.

---

[37] Until recently, it was believed that this was done through a liturgical "test clause" known as the *birkat ha-minim*, that was introduced by the rabbis around 90 CE. The *birkat ha-minim* is a congregational prayer that curses the "heretics and Nazarenes." Anyone keeping silent during this part of the worship would automatically reveal that he is a Nazarene. Recent scholarship, however, has questioned the historicity of this reconstruction. [see Boyarin: *Border Lines*: p67-73] However, it remains the case that Jewish Christians were expelled from synagogues on many occasions around the end of the first century and the first half of the second. (see John 9:22, 12:42; 16:2 & Justin's *Dialogue with Trypho* 16:4, 47:4, 47:4 & 96:2).

[38] Martin, *New Testament Foundations I*: p70

[39] Although many scholars, based on an uncritical reading of the patristic evidence, still believe that the Nazarenes and Ebionites were two separate sects, with the former being accepted by Gentile proto-orthodox Christians as a "legitimate" (i.e. non-heretical) form of Jewish Christianity [see Ray Pritz, *Nazarene Jewish Christianity* (Magnes Press 1988)], a careful consideration of the evidence shows that both are simply different names for one Jewish Christian group. [see Petri Luomanen, "Ebionites and Nazarenes", *Jewish Christianity Reconsidered* (Fortress, 2007)]

[40] John Gager, "Did Jewish Christians See the Rise of Islam?" Becker & Reed, *The Ways That Never Parted*: p361-372

NON-CHRISTIAN SOURCES ON JESUS

We now examine the contemporaneous references to Jesus from sources outside Christianity. If authentic, these sources can be used to corroborate or augment the information found in the New Testament.

ROMAN SOURCES

Our first candidate is the Roman historian, Cornelius Tacitus (c55-c117). In his book *Annals*, which covered the history of Rome from the death of Augustus (14 CE) to the death of Nero (69 CE), he related the story of the Neronian persecution of the Christians. He narrated how Nero tried to blame the burning of Rome in 64 CE on "the common people called Christians." He went on to explain that the Christians "derived their name and origin from Christ, who, in the reign of Tiberias, had suffered death, by the sentence of the procurator Pontius Pilate."

This passage may well be authentic and actually penned by Tacitus himself. However, its authenticity is not, in itself, proof of its reliability. It is important to know the *source* of his information.

A suggestion had been made that there could have existed the report of Jesus' execution, perhaps penned by Pilate himself, filed in the Roman archives; and that this is where Tacitus derived his information. Two considerations make this suggestion dubious. Firstly, we find that Tacitus was using the name "Christ" as though it was the proper name for Jesus. Christ was a title that the early Christians frequently used to refer to Jesus. The Roman archives, if it did contain any references to the execution of Jesus would have used his proper name, *Yeshua* or *Iesus*, but definitely not *Christ*. Secondly, the title the historian gave to Pontius Pilate - procurator - is an anachronism. We know from an inscription discovered in Judea, a dedication of a building by Pilate to Tiberius, that his title was *perfect* not *procurator*. In fact, the title of Roman provincial governors was only changed to procurator from the time of Claudius in 41 CE. Pilate was governor in Judea from 26 to 37 CE; thus at no time during that tenure could he had held the title ascribed to him by Tacitus. At any rate, the archives, as Tacitus tells us, were not available to private individuals, himself included.

The above considerations show that Tacitus was merely echoing popular opinion about Jesus and had no independent source of information. Thus, as a separate historical evidence for Jesus, the passage in the *Annals* has no value.[41]

The evidence of another Roman historian, Suetonius (c70-140), is equally worthless as an independent authentic historical witness to Jesus. In chapter 25 of his book *Life of Claudius*, he wrote: "He drove out of Rome the Jews who were perpetually stirring up trouble at the instigation of *Chrestus*." The event he was describing took place around 50 CE. At that time Jesus was obviously already dead. The Christians referred to Jesus as their (spiritual) leader and Suetonius took it

---

[41] Guignebert, *Jesus*: p13
      Hoffman, *Jesus Outside the Gospels*: p59-60
      Wells, *Did Jesus Exist?*: p14
      Wilson, *Jesus: The Evidence*: p51

literally that their leader was alive and was the chief instigator. His erroneous use of the title *Chrestus* as though it was a proper name again points to the fact that he got his information from popular opinion and not independent historical testimony.[42]

There is thus no certain independent verification of Jesus in the Roman sources available to us.

JEWISH SOURCES

For the Jewish sources the first major candidate would be the writings of Philosopher Philo of Alexandria (c20 BCE – 50 CE). He was a full contemporary of Jesus, who probably lived from c6 BCE to c30 CE. We find in Philo's philosophy, Jewish ideas mixed with Greek thought. It was Philo who introduced the concept of Logos, which he called the Son of God, the Paraclete, the mediator between God and man. Philo was also someone who maintained an active interest in the welfare of Israel. If there was a Jew who thought of himself as the Son of God and the Logos (as the Gospel of John tells us Jesus did) and miraculously rose from the dead, it is highly improbable that Philo would not have heard of him. Yet in more than fifty works of Philo known to us today, there is not a single allusion to Jesus or to his followers.[43]

The second candidate would be Justus of Tiberias, a Jewish historian and contemporary of Josephus, who was himself born in Galilee around the time of Jesus' crucifixion. Justus grew up and lived among men who, we would think, were still freshly imbued with Jesus' and his disciples' preaching. It is therefore extremely surprising that in his two great works, a history of the war of independence and a chronicle of events from Moses to Agrippa II (d. 100 CE), not a single reference was made to Jesus. Photius, the 9th century Byzantine theologian, who knew both books, commented on this fact with astonishment.[44]

THE TESTIMONIUM FLAVIANIUM

The final witness is that of Flavius Josephus (37-c100CE). In his *Antiquities of the Jews*, written around 94 CE, we actually find *two* references to Jesus. We will review this in more detail than the rest as what these passages say or imply is important.

In the 18th volume of the book we find the following remarkable passage:

Antiquities 18:3:3
Now there was about this time Jesus, a wise man, *if it be lawful to call him a man*; for he was a doer of wonderful works, a teacher of such men as receive the truth with pleasure. He drew over to him both many of the Jews and many of the Gentiles. *He was [the] Christ.* And when Pilate, at the suggestion of the principal men amongst us, had condemned him to the cross, those that loved him at the first

---

42   Guignebert, *Jesus*: p13
     Wilson, *Jesus: The Evidence*: p51
     Hoffman, *Jesus Outside the Gospels*: p60-61
43   Graham, *The Jesus Hoax*: p145-146
     Guignebert, *Jesus*: p16
44   Graham, *The Jesus Hoax*: p145-146
     Guignebert, *Jesus*: p16

did not forsake him; *for he appeared to them alive again the third day; as the divine prophets had foretold these and ten thousand other wonderful things concerning him.* And the tribe of Christians, so named from him, are not extinct at this day.

The above passage has been referred to so often in academic circles that it has been given a name: the *Testimonium Flavianum* (Latin for "Witness of Josephus"). The question of its authenticity has been debated in academic circles since the 16th [!] century. Scholarly positions on this issue span from asserting the passage to be completely true to dismissing the whole passage as a Christian interpolation.[45] The current "scholarly consensus,"[46] is that although the passage contains obvious Christian interpolations, some parts of it are nevertheless genuine.

Here Jacob Neusner's dictum "What we cannot *show*, we do not *know*"[47] is apt. Scholarly consensus really means nothing if the evidence for or against a certain position is not strong. Let us consider the evidence for ourselves.

Based on all his extant writings, Josephus was manifestly not a Christian. From his own *Autobiography,* we know that Josephus was trained as a Pharisee. The phrases italicized in the above passage are certainly those that no Jew would have made, except one that is on the verge of conversion to Christianity. No sensible scholar today accepts the authenticity of the passage as it stands. It is claimed however, that by taking away the italicized portions, which they admit must have been added by an overzealous early Christian copyist, we can actually come to the original passage as written by Josephus, which goes something like this:[48]

Antiquities 18:3:3 ("Excised" Version)
Now there was about this time Jesus, a wise man, ...; for he was a doer of wonderful works, a teacher of such men as receive the truth with pleasure. He drew over to him both many of the Jews and many of the Gentiles. ... And when Pilate, at the suggestion of the principal men amongst us, had condemned him to the cross, those that loved him at the first did not forsake him; .... And the tribe of Christians, so named from him, are not extinct at this day.

---

45 Mason, *Josephus and the New Testament*: p172-173
    Setzer, *Jewish Responses to Early Christians*: p106
    Wilson, *Related Strangers*: p184

46 The "consensus" has actually "ding-donged" quite a few times within the last few decades. Samuel Sandmel in *Judaism and Christian Beginnings* (1978 p395) wrote that "Most modern scholars regard the passage as completely a Christian interpolation into Josephus". Mark Allan Powell in his summary of historical Jesus scholarship entitled *The Jesus Debate* (1998 p39) mentioned that "most scholars" accept the passage minus the "editorial additions".

47 Neusner, *Rabbinic Literature and the New Testament*: p10

48 Crossan, Jesus, *A Revolutionary Biography*: p161-162
    Guignebert, *Jesus*: p16
    Wilson, *Jesus: The Evidence*: p52-54

This is the position of many scholars today. To this excised passage, or some variant of it, is normally added the "scholarly" insight as to how *neutral*, and even "surprisingly friendly", the passage is.[49]

That "insight" should have probably given these scholars a clue to the actual situation. For even in its excised form, it simply does not sit well together with the rest of the section in *Antiquities*. Below is a summary of the relevant sections surrounding the *Testimonium*:

18:3:1   Trouble between the Jews and Pontius Pilate over his exhibition of the images of Caesar in Jerusalem that the natives considered sacrilegious. Pilate backed down when he saw that the Jews, who came in "multitudes", would rather be killed than transgressed their laws.

18:3:2   Pilate had apportioned some money from the Temple to pay for the building of an aqueduct. The Jews again protested – this time "many ten thousands" of them. This time, unlike the first incident when Pilate let them off, he had the Jews massacred by placing some of his men in the crowds with hidden clubs. In the commotion that followed many protestors were clubbed to death.

18:3:3   *Testimonium Flavianium.*

18:3:4   Seduction of a married Roman woman, Paulina, by one Mandus who pretended to be a god in the Temple of Isis while performing the deed. The Emperor Tiberius (who was emperor from 14 CE to 37 CE) upon hearing of this, demolished the temple of Isis and executed - by crucifixion - the priests who colluded on this deception.

18:3:5   Four Jews conspired to cheat a Roman woman who was a convert into Judaism. On the pretext of collecting money for the temple in Jerusalem, they took money from her and spent it on themselves. Upon hearing of this, Tiberius had all the 4,000 resident Jews banished from Rome.

18:4:1   Pilate brutally suppressed a rebellion consisting of "a great multitude" of Samaritans at Mount Gerizim.

As Steve Mason points out, all the incidents above, except the *Testimonium Flavianium*, deals with "outrages", "uprisings" and "tumults."[50] Yet the 18:3:3 is merely about someone who was executed and who had some followers "to this day." Furthermore, immediately after this third paragraph (i.e. in 18:3:4), the fourth paragraph starts with: "About the same time also *another sad calamity* put the Jews into disorder..." An obvious question arises: what does Josephus mean by *another* sad calamity? The fourth paragraph follows the paragraph about Jesus. Was Jesus

[49]   Brown, *Introduction to the New Testament*: p834-835
Crossan, *Jesus: A Revolutionary Biography*: p161-162
Ehrman, *The New Testament*: p198
Powell, *The Jesus Debate*: p38-39
Wilson, *Related Strangers*: p184-185
Wilson, *Jesus the Evidence*: p52-54
Setzer, *Jewish Responses to Early Christians*: p106-107
Vermes, *The Changing Faces of Jesus*: p258-259
[50]   Mason, *Josephus and the New Testament*: p164

the sad calamity? Or was it his being risen from the dead? Or was the continued existence of Christians at the date of writing the "sad calamity"? In short, the initial sentence in the fourth paragraph does not make sense given the current forms of the *Testimonium* (either in the form we find it in our available manuscripts of *Antiquities* or in the scholars' excised version).[51]

What does the textual evidence tell us? Like most ancient documents, we do not have the original manuscript of *Antiquities*. The earliest extant manuscripts date to the 9th and 10th centuries CE. The manuscripts with this particular portion of the *Testimonium* date even later – from the 11th century. The evidence from the citations of the church fathers seems to indicate a rather late origin of the passage as we now know it. We find no reference to the above passage until the time of Eusebius (c260-c340). Eusebius who wrote *The History of the Church* in the early 4th century, quoted Josephus in that work (*History of the Church* 1:11:7) in exactly the way we read it in the extant manuscripts today. Yet it is amazing, had this passage been anything like we have seen, that no Christian writer earlier than Eusebius quoted it. We do not see this, for instance, in Justin Martyr's (c100-c165) work *Dialogue With Trypho.* In chapter 7 of the *Dialogue,* written around 135, we read that the Jew Trypho accused Christians of "having accepted a groundless report, invent a Christ for yourselves". Had Josephus' passage been known to Justin, he would surely have triumphantly referred to this work; a writing by another Jew (albeit a traitor of sorts!) about the historicity of Jesus. We even find the church father Origen (c185-253) telling us, in his *Commentary on Matthew* (10:17) and *Against Celsus* (1:47), that Josephus did not believe that Jesus was the messiah. An unlikely statement, had the passage above existed during Origen's time.[52]

This does not mean that Josephus wrote nothing about Jesus, it only showed that whatever Josephus had written about Jesus, it was not in a form that the early church fathers, prior to Eusebius, would have liked. It is very likely that Josephus *did* write something about the Jesus. This evidence comes from another passage in *Antiquities* (20:9:1). It relates the death of James, the brother of Jesus:

> Antiquities 20:9:1
> Festus was now dead, and Albinus was but upon the road; so he [Ananus] assembled the Sanhedrim of judges, and brought before them *the brother of Jesus, who was called Christ, whose name was James,* and some others, [or, some of his companions] and when he had formed an accusation against them as breakers of the law, he delivered them to be stoned.

Some Jesus mythists[53], realizing the weakness of the evidence for the *Testimonium*, tried to argue that Josephus wrote nothing about Jesus and that the italicized portion represents a Christian interpolation. But the above passage is not that easy to explain away. G.A. Wells, suggested that the phrase "the brother of Jesus who was called

---

51 Mason, *Josephus and the New Testament*: p165
    Wells, *The Jesus Myth*: p202-204
52 Mason, *Josephus and the New Testament*: p167-168
    Wells, *The Jesus Myth*: p202-204
    Wells, *The Jesus Legend*: p49
53 "Jesus mythists" are those who assert that the historical Jesus never existed.

Christ" was originally a marginal note by a Christian scribe that was later innocently included into the main text by a later copyist.[54] But this is dubious. For one thing, the marginal note explanation would mean that this "James" (Hebrew "Jacob"), which was a very common name at that time, would be left unidentified in the main text, something unlikely. Having identified this James as the brother of Jesus, *this* Jesus, in turn, needs to be identified, for Josephus' writings consist of more than twenty different individuals with that name. Calling this person by his "nickname", in other words, the "so-called Christ" clarifies the identity of James completely.[55]

We noted above that Origen made no direct reference to the *Testimonium*, yet he did mention that Josephus wrote about James in the same passage:

> Against Celsus 1:47
> For in the 18th book of his *Antiquities of the Jews*, Josephus bears witness to John as having been a Baptist, and as promising purification to those who underwent the rite. Now this writer, *although not believing in Jesus as the Christ*, in seeking after the cause of the fall of Jerusalem and the destruction of the temple, whereas he ought to have said that the conspiracy against Jesus was the cause of these calamities befalling the people, since they put to death Christ, who was a prophet, says nevertheless-being, although against his will, not far from the truth - that these disasters happened to the Jews as a punishment for the death of *James the Just, who was a brother of Jesus (called Christ)* - the Jews having put him to death, although he was a man most distinguished for his justice.

This passage is strong confirmation that the wording as found in Antiquities 20:9:1 is original to the text. Furthermore, the fact that Jesus is just mentioned almost in passing as "the one called Christ", means that this character has been introduced earlier, for the term "Christ" would not have been something immediately familiar to his readers.[56]

If Josephus wrote something earlier than the reference to James, does it not follow then that the *Testimonium* (or at least in its excised form, shorn of all obvious Christian interpolations) must have been what Josephus actually wrote? However, as we have noted above, the passage is *too friendly* for it *not* to be used by Christians earlier than Eusebius. Furthermore, as we have seen above, Origen wrote in Against Celsus 1:47 that Josephus did not believe that Jesus was the messiah. As SGF Brandon pointed out, the word Origen used *apiston*[57] (which was translated as "not believing") actually implies an *active rejection* of Jesus as the messiah. This excludes the possibility that Josephus simply did not make any remarks of Jesus' messiahship, but that Josephus wrote actively *against* it. Thus a "surprisingly friendly" *Testimonium* simply does not accord with the evidence of the church fathers.[58]

---

[54]   Wells, *Did Jesus Exist?*: p11
[55]   Mason, *Josephus and the New Testament*: p166
       Painter, *Just James*: p134-135
[56]   Mason, *Josephus and the New Testament*: p166, 172
[57]   The word stems from *apistos* which means "unbelieving" or "without confidence in" something.
[58]   Brandon, *The Fall of Jerusalem and the Christian Church*: p111
       Mason, *Josephus and the New Testament*: p167-168

What we can conclude is this: Antiquities 20:9:1, the reference to "Jesus, the one called Christ", as the brother of James is authentic. It also tells us that Josephus must have written more about this Jesus. However, what he had written could not have been too friendly or even neutral to Christians (i.e. not in the form of the *Testimonium* known to us, nor the standard scholarly construction) since no church father referred to it until the 4th century (Eusebius) and Origen, a century earlier, actually mentioned that Josephus *rejected* Jesus' messiahship. It is tempting to speculate[59] what the original form of the *Testimonium* might have been, but for our purposes it is enough to say that the most we can get from Josephus is that it gives strong evidence for the existence[60] of Jesus, that he had a brother named James and that he was called the Christ (or messiah). We cannot know if any of the details in the *Testimonium* is not an interpolation – what he actually wrote is lost to us.[61]

* * * * *

In this chapter we have seen that one cannot escape a critical evaluation of the gospels. The methods and assumptions used are the same as that used in other historical studies.

External attestations to Jesus are found only in the writings of Josephus.

---

59   It *is* tempting to speculate, so we will succumb to it here. If you look at Antiquities 18:3:4, immediately after describing Jesus, Josephus interrupted the whole sequence (which had been about the problems under Pilate) to discuss the story of a Roman matron who was a follower of Isis. This interlude makes no sense in the present context. Yet if you recall the story: it was about *a woman tricked into having sex with someone she thought was a god.* This brings to mind the story about the virgin birth and Mary! Furthermore, the *crucifixion* of the temple priests for religious charlatanism seems to echo what we would expect of a nonbelieving Jew's view of the crucifixion of Jesus. Thus 18:3:4 could be anecdotes Josephus had used to illustrate what he actually wrote in 18:3:3 – i.e. that there were elements of fraud and charlatanism in the story relating to Jesus! Such a *Testimonium* would square away the Origen's statement that Josephus *rejected* the messiahship of Jesus. (see Brandon, *Jesus and the Zealots*: p362-363, Eisenman, *James the Brother of Jesus*: p65-66 and Robertson, *The Bible and Its Background Volume II*: p30-31)

60   I do not subscribe to the position of the Jesus mythists: that Jesus is a myth and that he never existed historically. Paul mentioned that Jesus had brothers: Galatians 1:18-19; I Corinthians 9:5-6. The contexts of these passages show that he meant *brothers* in the normal sense of the word and not in any metaphorical sense. Furthermore, I Corinthians 9:5-6 also implies that his brothers were out preaching about the same time as Paul. This means that Jesus was a near contemporary of Paul. Attempts by Jesus mythists to discredit these passages mainly fall into two categories: either the term "brothers" is some kind of honorific title unknown to us or that they are late interpolations into the text. Both are unsatisfactory. For one thing, saving a postulate (Jesus did not exist) by making up still another postulate (that "brothers" means something else) that has no evidential support sounds more like fundamentalism than rationalism. Secondly, the earliest manuscripts available to us (dating to around 200 CE) contain these passages and no external evidence suggests that they are late additions.

61   Mason, *Josephus and the New Testament*: p174

Chapter Eight
AUTHORSHIP OF THE GOSPELS
-EXTERNAL EVIDENCE

AUTHORSHIP OF THE GOSPELS

We have seen in the previous chapter that extra-biblical sources on Jesus do not tell us much beyond the fact of his existence and that he had a sibling named James. We now turn to the New Testament. Although some allusions exist in the epistles of Paul, the main bulk of information concerning the historical Jesus comes from the four gospels: Matthew, Mark, Luke and John. The traditional attributions of authorship of these four gospels were made based on the belief that the men who wrote them knew either Jesus directly or one of his close associates: Matthew and John were apostles of Jesus, Mark was Peter's interpreter and Luke was Paul's traveling companion. If these traditional attributions of authorship are true, especially for Matthew, Mark and John, they would certainly add weight to the argument for the general trustworthiness of these works. In this and the next chapter we will analyze both the external attestations by the church fathers and the internal evidence of the gospels to determine whether these gospels actually were written by whom Christian tradition believed them to be.

THE ANONYMOUS NATURE OF THE GOSPELS

The first thing that strikes us about the gospels is that there is nothing in any of them that explicitly names their authors. Although some fundamentalists still claim, without evidence, that the names of the gospels were attached to the gospels from the beginning,[1] the evidence is quite compelling that these gospels *initially circulated anonymously* and the names that are now attached to them were only given in the second century CE.

Anonymous Quotes

The first strand of evidence is from quotations of the gospels by the early church fathers. Prior to the year 150[2], quotations from, or allusions to, the gospels were always made anonymously.[3]

---

[1]   For an example of the fundamentalist flight of imagination on this, see Carsten Thiede's *Jesus: Life or Legend?* (1990, p57-62)
[2]   Starting with our discussion of the church fathers, I will largely dispense with the use of the designations "CE / BCE" (Common Era / before Common Era) – since it is obvious that we are discussing a time after the beginning of the Gregorian calendar. We will only use CE sparingly and mainly for the years in the first century of the modern era.
[3]   Sanders & Davies, *Studying the Synoptic Gospels*: p9-10

- Clement (c. 96) in his epistle to the Corinthians (I Clement 13) referred to the sayings of Jesus that can be found (in slightly different forms) in various places in the Gospel of Matthew (5:7, 6:14, 7:12, 7:1-2).

- Ignatius (d. c110) in his epistle to the Smyrneans made a reference to the baptism of Jesus with the words "in order that all righteousness might be fulfilled", an exact quotation from Matthew 3:15.

- In the Epistle of Barnabas 4:14 (c130-135), the author noted that "it is written, many are called, but few are chosen", an exact quotation from Matthew 22:14.

In all the above examples, the source of the quote is not mentioned. In the case of Clement, it may be possible that he was referring to a living oral tradition about the sayings of Jesus. In the cases of Ignatius and Barnabas, it is quite certain that they were quoting from the gospel we now know as Matthew. Yet at no time did they refer to their source(s) by that name.

It was with Justin Martyr (c100-c165), together with his near contemporary, Papias (c60-c130)[4], that changes from anonymity started to take place.[5] From Justin's works we find references to "Memoirs of the Apostles" as *written* documents recounting the acts and sayings of Jesus. Justin was also one of the first (after Marcion[6] c.140) to use the term "gospel" to refer to these documents. Prior to these two, the term was used to mean only the "good news" that was preached by the Christians. Here are two quotes from Justin's works:[7]

First Apology 66:3 (c155)
For the apostles, in the memoirs composed by them, which are called Gospels, have thus delivered unto us what was enjoined upon them; that Jesus took bread, and when He had given thanks, said, "This do ye in remembrance of Me, this is My body;" and that, after the same manner, having taken the cup and given thanks, He said, "This is My blood;" and gave it to them alone. [a quote from Luke 22:19]

---

[4] The year of Papias' death is normally given as 130-140, however, this is far from certain and it could have been as late as 150.

[5] Papias, around the middle of the second century, mentioned gospels of Matthew and Mark but did not quote any passages from them. We will be discussing Papias' statements in the next section.

[6] The first person to actually use the term "gospel" (Greek = *euangelion*) in referring to a *written* document, instead of its original meaning which was "good news" or "glad tidings" (*eu* [= good/happy] + *angelia* [= message]), was Marcion (d. c.160) who used it to refer to his version of Luke. See Koester's *Ancient Christian Gospels*: p35-36 for a more detail discussion on Marcion's use of the term "gospel". Incidentally, the word "gospel" is derived from the Anglo-Saxon word *God-Spell*. *God-spell* originally meant, literally, a story from God, but has always been understood in a popular sense as "glad tidings" or "good news." (Craveri, *The Life of Jesus*: p94).

[7] Koester, *Ancient Christian Gospels*: p37-43

Dialogue with Trypho 100:1 (c160)
[I]n the Gospel it is written that He said: 'All things are delivered unto me by My Father;' and, 'No man knoweth the Father but the Son; nor the Son but the Father, and they to whom the Son will reveal Him.' [Matthew 11:27]

Thus Justin was the first church father to cite quotations from the gospels and referring them as *originating from the apostles*. Justin did not explicitly name the author of any gospel but there is one instance where he may have come close:

Dialogue with Trypho 106:3 (c160)
And when it is said that he changed the name of one of the apostles to Peter; and when it is written in the *memoirs of him* that this so happened, as well as that he changed the names of other two brothers, the sons of Zebedee, to Boanerges, which means sons of thunder.

This is a citation of a passage from Mark:

Mark 3:16-17
Simon whom he surnamed Peter; James the son of Zebedee and John the brother of James, whom he surnamed Boanerges, that is, sons of thunder.

This passage shows that Justin knows of the Gospel of Mark (or some harmony in which this passage is contained). The whole question lies around whether the "him" in the *memoirs of him* refers to Peter or to Jesus. If "him" refers to Peter, it would mean that the tradition of Mark's gospel being closely related to Peter is known to Justin. If "him" refers to Jesus, as I think more likely, it simply means that Justin had access to the gospel either in the form of a harmony of the gospels or an anonymous narrative. Whatever the case may be, Justin still did not explicitly mention the names of any other gospel (if he indeed had more than one).

Justin's writings can be considered the historical dividing line between the complete anonymity of the gospels of his predecessors and the complete certainty of their authorship of his successors.

The first *explicit* references to the supposed authors of all the four gospels were made only towards the end of the second century; by Irenaeus (c130-c200). Thus we see him making references to the gospels according to Mark, Matthew, Luke and John in *Against Heresies* (c180):

Against Heresies 3:10:5
Wherefore also Mark, the interpreter and follower of Peter, does thus commence his Gospel narrative: "The beginning of the Gospel of Jesus Christ, the Son of God..." [Mark 1:1]

Against Heresies 3:16:2
And Matthew, too, recognizing one and the same Jesus Christ, exhibiting his generation as a man from the Virgin, even as God did promise David that He would raise up from the fruit of his body an eternal King, having made the same promise to Abraham a long time previously, says: "The book of the generation of Jesus Christ, the son of David, the son of Abraham." [Matthew 1:1]

Against Heresies 3:10:1
Luke also, the follower and disciple of the apostles, referring to Zacharias and Elisabeth, from whom, according to promise, John was born, says: "And they were both righteous before God, walking in all the commandments and ordinances of the Lord blameless." [Luke 1:5-6]

Against Heresies 3:11:1
John, the disciple of the Lord...thus commenced His teaching in the Gospel: "In the beginning was the Word, and the Word was with God, and the Word was God." [John 1:1]

After Irenaeus explicit quotations to named gospels became common. In Clement of Alexandria's (c150-c215) *Stromata 1:21* [or Miscellanies], he quoted from Matthew 1:17 and explicitly noted it as from "The Gospel According to Matthew". And it was also after this time that we find full-scale treatises on specific gospels. Hippolytus (c170 – c236) wrote a work defending the apostolic authorship of John, and Origen (c185-254) published commentaries on Matthew and John.[8]

We can summarize the evidence of gospel quotations of the early Christians as follows. From the end of the first century (c96) until the middle of the second century (c155), the gospels were *always* quoted anonymously.[9] Around that time we find (in the works of Justin) references being made to the written sources being "Memoirs of the Apostles" or simply "Gospel" - but still with no specific apostolic names attached to any of these. There *may be* a specific citation of the Gospel of Mark in Justin's *Dialogue* (106:3) - if this is the case, the explicit citation of the Gospel of Mark as a gospel related to Peter was made around 160. It was only around the year 180, in Irenaeus' *Against Heresies*, do we find explicit references to the names of each gospels with passages quoted from them. After this explicit references became common in the writings of the church fathers.

Ancient Book Titles

The second strand of evidence that the gospel initially circulated anonymously is in the title of the works themselves. If you look at a Greek New Testament today you will find these headings on top of each gospel: *Kata Matthaion, Kata Markon, Kata Loukan* and *Kata Ioannen*; which mean simply "According to Matthew", "According to Mark", "According to Luke" and "According to John".

The alert reader will immediately notice something amiss about this. The four gospels were all written with differing styles and theological perspectives. It is unlikely in the extreme that all four authors would "hit" upon the same form of title, i.e. the "According to..." The titles look like they were placed later on already existing works by people who were treating these writings *as a group*. This consideration is

---

8   Metzger, *The Canon of the New Testament*: p135-137, 150

9   It is not the case that these authors quoted *everything* anonymously. Both Clement (I Clement 47) and Ignatius (Ephesian 12) attributed epistles to Paul. Barnabas referred to the book of Daniel by name (Barnabas 4) and attributed the Psalms to David (Barnabas 10). So the way they all anonymously quoted the gospel is something which requires explanation.

enough to lead one to doubt that the titles as we have them today originally accompanied these writings when they circulated as independent works.

There is a further clue in the quotations from Irenaeus given above. Note that in his quotes of the gospels he referred to the *first verse* of all of them when introducing the works. (For Luke it was the fifth verse because the first four verses were merely the preface to Theophilus) In effect he was saying, "Mark's gospel is the one that begins with 'The beginning of the Gospel of Jesus Christ, the Son of God'; Matthew's gospel is the one that begins with 'The book of the generation of Jesus Christ, the son of David'" and so on. Why this identification with the first verse? The most obvious answer is this - during his time, the practice of putting the suprascript titles *Kata Markon* or *Kata Matthaion* had either yet to be started or to gain widespread use.

Evidence from ancient works confirms this. The titles of ancient books were normally taken from the first line of their text, normally referred to as the *incipit*. Thus in anonymous works, like some of the books of the Hebrew Bible, the titles were taken from words in the first line of the text. For examples, *Genesis* is known in Hebrew as *Beresit* which is the first word of the first book of the Tanakh "*Beresit bara elohim...*" (In the beginning God created...[Genesis 1:1]), *Shemoth*, the Hebrew name for the book of Exodus, is the second word of the first line (the first word is simple "and these" - thus would not be an appropriate title) and *Wayiqra* ("And he called...") is the first word of Leviticus and so on.

The anonymous style of the gospels of Mark, Matthew and John was obviously based on the example set by the Jewish Bible. Even Luke, although he started his work with a preface typical of Hellenistic histories, reverted back to the anonymous writing style typical of the rest. Charles Hedrick, Professor of Religious Studies at Southwest Missouri State University, has suggested that the earliest titles of the gospels were probably taken from the first line of their text. Thus the gospel we now know as Mark was called simply "The Beginning of the Gospel of Jesus Christ" (from Mark 1:1), the gospel according to Matthew was "The Book of Generation of Jesus Christ" (Matthew 1:1), Luke was known as "In the Days of Herod" (Luke 1:5 - ignoring the prologue) and John was referred to as "The Testimony of John" (John 1:19 - again ignoring the prologue). Note, by the way, "John" here refers to John *The Baptist*). For the fourth gospel, the title could equally have been "In the Beginning Was the Word".[10]

Furthermore, we have direct evidence that the early Christians did use the *incipit* as the title. In his complaint against the Valentinians, Irenaeus wrote that "[T]hey have arrived at such a pitch of audacity, as to *entitle* their comparatively recent writing 'The Gospel of Truth'" (Against Heresies 3:11:9). This is very likely to be one of the Gnostic gospels discovered at Nag Hammadi, which showed the same

---

[10]   Some conservative scholars argue that the gospels *must* have the names of the authors attached to them from early on else it would lead to confusion when a particular church started to have more than one gospel. However, it can be seen that with the *incipit* as titles, the gospels would be fully differentiated from each other without necessary knowing the names of the authors.

Valentinian theology. This gospel starts thus: *"The Gospel of Truth* is a joy for those who have received from the Father of truth the gift of knowing him..."[11]

Indeed, we can see from these considerations that Irenaeus - in the four quotations of the gospels given above - was simply giving his readers the *titles* of the canonical gospels as he knew them.

Conclusion to Anonymity of the Gospels

Let's recap. From the end of the first until the mid second century, the gospels were *never* referred to by the names we now know them. Around 155, Justin Martyr began to refer to "Memoirs of the Apostles" and to written "gospels" and *perhaps* to the Gospel of Mark as the "Memoirs of Peter". The year 180 marks the *first time* all four gospels were first explicitly named and quoted (by Irenaeus). Following that the practice took hold and later references begin to cite the gospels from which the passages are taken. The suprascript titles found in today's gospels ("According to Mark" etc) were not part of the original manuscripts. Ancient scrolls were more popularly identified by the *incipit*: the first line of the work.

EVALUATION OF THE PATRISTIC EVIDENCE

The traditional attribution of authors to the gospels came from the writings of the church fathers. It is now time to critically evaluate these citations.

Mark

The earliest attempt to give the names of the authors of some of the gospels came just before the middle of the second century. This is the witness of an early Christian named Papias (c60 – c130), bishop of Heirapolis. He wrote a now lost work entitled *Interpretations of the Oracles of the Lord*. The full text of this work is now lost and only some portions of it are available in fragments quoted by later Christians. The actual time of his writing is unknown with most scholars placing it around 130, but it could well be as late as 150. This is what Papias wrote - as quoted in Eusebius's (c275-339) *History of the Church*:[12]

> Quoted in *History of the Church* 3:39:15
> And the presbyter said this: Mark the interpreter of Peter, wrote down exactly, but not in order, what he remembered of the acts and sayings of the Lord, for he neither heard the Lord himself nor accompanied him, but, as I said, Peter later on. Peter adapted his teachings to the needs [of his hearers], but made no attempt to provide a connected narrative of things related to our Lord. So Mark made no mistake in setting down some things as he remembered them, for he took care not to omit

---

11   Hedrick, *When History and Faith Collide*: p25
       Robinson, *The Nag Hammadi Library*: p37
12   Helms, *Who Wrote the Gospels?*: p1-3
       Koester, *Ancient Christian Gospels.*: p32-34
       Sanders & Davies, *Studying the Synoptic Gospels*: p8-9

anything he heard nor to include anything false. As for Matthew, he made a collection in Hebrew of the sayings and each translated them as best they could.

Papias' source for this information was one *Presbyter John*. Who was this mysterious person? We do not know. We *do know* that he was not one of the apostles, as earlier in the same work Papias wrote this:

> Quoted in *History of the Church* 3:39:3-4
> And whenever anyone came who had been a follower of the presbyters, I inquired into the words of the presbyters, what Andrew or Peter had said, or Philip or Thomas or James or **John** or Matthew, or any other disciple of the Lord, and what Aristion and the **presbyter John**, disciples of the Lord, were still saying.

Note that the presbyter John is *not* included in the list of the apostles and is not to be confused with the apostle John who was mentioned earlier in the sentence and in the past tense.

Whatever the case may be as to the reliability of this tradition (which we will consider below), Papias' testimony tells us that the name Mark was attached to the gospel around 130-150.

Were there later Patristic attestations to the Gospel of Mark? There certainly were. However, in considering these there is a very important fact to keep in mind: *the church fathers copied from their earlier predecessors*. This only made sense, for it was unlikely that an older work would have survived if later "orthodox" fathers did not consider them worth preserving. Carried further, this means that if an earlier church father was held in high regard, his successors would accept the authority of what he wrote. However, they were not faithful copyists. They also normally felt free to expand, comment or extrapolate from their sources.[13] As the renowned New Testament scholar B.H. Streeter noted:

> Irenaeus (c130-200) derived materials from Papias (c60-130), Hegesippus (c110-180) and Justin Martyr (c100-c165); Clement of Alexandria (c150-215), Tertullian (c160-c225) and Hippolytus (c170-c236) used Irenaeus; Origen (c185-254) read most of his predecessors; and Eusebius (c260-c340), the real "father of Church history", used all these earlier writers. Jerome (c342-420)...copied and improved upon Eusebius. But even Eusebius rarely, if ever, perceived that a later writer was merely repeating, with his own comments or conjectural amplification, the statement of an earlier writer; and he thus sets their evidence side by side, as if they were independent witnesses who corroborated one another's testimony.[14]

What Streeter is saying here is important to keep in mind. If we have more than one Patristic citation of a particular "fact", it does not necessarily mean that we therefore have *independent attestations* of that fact. This is especially so when we know that they had access to earlier materials and that they tend to add to or revise the sources with their own comments or conjectures. To see if this is the case with later witnesses to the authorship of Mark, let us look at these citations in detail:

---

13   Streeter, *The Primitive Church*: p16
14   Streeter, *The Primitive Church*: p17

- **Irenaeus** (c130-200) (Against Heresies 3:1:1) added that Mark wrote his gospel "after the departure" (i.e. death) of Peter.

- **Clement of Alexandria** (c150-215) (quoted in History of the Church 6:14:6-7) contradicted Irenaeus and added his own statement that Mark wrote his gospel while Peter was alive and when he (Peter) heard of the gospel "he neither directly forbade nor encouraged it."

- **Origen** (c185-254) (quoted in History of the Church 6:25:8-9) said that Mark "composed it according to the instructions of Peter."

- **Eusebius** (c260-c340) who faithfully recorded the witnesses above, followed Clement's account but then added that when Peter heard about the gospel he "was pleased with the zeal of the men, and that the work obtained the sanction of his authority for the purpose of being used in the churches. " (History of the Church 2:15:2-6)

- **Jerome** (c342-420) in his letter to Hedibia (Letter 120) mentioned that Peter narrated while Mark noted down what he said.

Let us analyze each of these attestations to see if any of them form an *independent* testimony to Papias.

Origen's testimony is simple. Saying that Mark wrote his gospel according to "Peter's instructions" amounts to no more that paraphrasing what Papias had wrote - which was that he noted down "Peter's teachings". Therefore, we have no independent testimony from Origen.

Irenaeus' added the point that Mark wrote after Peter's death. This again is inferable from Papias' statement - since Mark, we are told there, wrote down what he "remembered" of Peter's teachings. The implication being that Peter was no longer around the gospel was composed.

With Clement, Eusebius and Jerome we begin to see a tendency to make the gospel ever more reliable. Clement, contradicting Irenaeus and Papias wrote that Mark wrote the gospel while Peter was still alive and that Peter "heard" the gospel. Eusebius added to this that Peter was "pleased" with what he heard and actually gave "sanction" to it. This directly contradicts what Clement had wrote, which was that Peter "neither directly forbade nor encourage" the spread or reading of the gospel.

Jerome's statement is interesting, for he has taken the exaggeration of the reliability of the gospel accounts to still greater heights. Note that it is no longer the case that Peter approved of the writing which Mark wrote from memory but that the apostle is now being described as *dictating* his memoirs to Mark. Did Jerome have access to information hitherto unavailable to the other church fathers? Unlikely. Look at what he wrote in *On Illustrious Men* (c392):

On Illustrious Men 8
Mark the disciple and interpreter of Peter wrote a short gospel at the request of the brethren at Rome embodying what *he had heard Peter tell*. When *Peter had heard this*, he approved it and published it to the churches to be read by his authority as Clemens in the sixth book of his Hypotyposes and Papias, bishop of Hierapolis, record.

Note how this detail completely contradicts his Letter to Hedibia. Here he wrote that Mark wrote what he *had heard* Peter tell - it was not dictated to him and that Peter heard of the gospel only later and approved it.

There is another disturbing fact about his statement here. He cited his sources as Clement and Papias. Yet the point about Peter approving and publishing the work directly contradicts what Clement himself had written - which was that Peter was "neutral" to the gospel ("neither forbade nor approve"). His source for that was Eusebius. He had simply added Eusebius' account to Clement's and removed the latter's contradictory remarks.

Jerome's handling of the traditions available to him tells us that we should be cautious of later patristic citations that seem to add more information than that found in earlier writings. He has no more sources than what we have available - he referred to Papias and Clement and doubtless also used Eusebius. Most importantly what comes out of this is his *tendency to exaggerate*. Note that from his various sources he selected the information that increased and heightened the reliability of the gospels, not worrying about the contradictions. Thus, as Streeter remarked, we catch Jerome in an act of "conscious exaggeration" in his letter to Hedibia.[15]

We can summarize the status of the Patristic attribution for the authorship of the Gospel of Mark. For Mark, the only evidence comes from around 130-150CE, through Papias; *all later Patristic attributions were directly dependent in him and did not have any additional information to offer*. This means that there is only a single strand of evidence for the attribution of the second gospel to Mark.

It is now time for us to evaluate the evidence of Papias. Can we trust his testimony?

This is what Eusebius wrote about Papias:

> History of the Church 3:39:11-13
> The same writer gives also other accounts which he says came to him through unwritten tradition, *certain strange parables and teachings of the Saviour*, and *some other more mythical things*. To these belong his statement that there will be a period of some thousand years after the resurrection of the dead, and that the kingdom of Christ will be set up in material form on this very earth. I suppose he got these ideas through *a misunderstanding of the apostolic accounts*, not perceiving that the things said by them were spoken mystically in figures. *For he appears to have been of very limited understanding, as one can see from his discourses.*

Eusebius evidently did not think very high of Papias, calling him "stupid" (i.e. someone "of very limited understanding"). Some scholars have asserted that Eusebius' assessment was merely directed at Papias' eschatology – his belief in the millennium, and not on his whole work. Yet the last line of the excerpt above - "as one can see from his discourses" - clearly shows that the assessment was meant of Papias as a whole.

From the extant fragments of Papias' writings we can conclude that Eusebius' assessment of the second century church father is largely correct. In the fragment preserved by Apollinarius of Laodicea, a 4th century Christian bishop, Papias wrote

---

15   Streeter, *The Primitive Church*: p17-18

about Judas' suffering after his betrayal of Jesus. Conflating the accounts of Matthew (27:3-5) and Acts (1:18-19), it tells of how Judas, who survived the hanging and having his insides falling out, walked around with a massively swollen head, sunken eyes and bloated genitalia. His body was flowing with pus, emanating of worms while exuding a terrible stench. When he died, his stench polluted the place such that it became uninhabitable. [16] This is the stuff of legend, the type of *folkloric expansion* one sees in ancient writers whenever they describe the suffering of the wicked.[17] It is not history.

In another fragment, this one preserved by Philip of Side (c380 - c439), we hear of the daughters of Philip who drank snake venom with no ill effects, of a woman resurrected and of those who were raised by Jesus surviving until the early second century![18] Another excerpt, this time found in Irenaeus' *Against Heresies* (5:33:3-4), has Papias quoting as a saying of Jesus about the millennium what was actually an excerpt from the Jewish pseudepigrapha (2 Baruch 29:3-6)!

In other words, Papias was a teller of tall tales, a man unable to evaluate the difference between fact and fiction, between history and myth.

Most critical scholars are of the opinion that the testimony of Papias regarding the authorship of this gospel is not reliable.[19] This is what E.P. Sanders, Professor of Religion at Duke University and Margaret Davies, Lecturer in New Testament at University of Bristol (UK) wrote in their textbook *Studying the Synoptic Gospels*:

> The connection of the name Mark with the Second Gospel, then, depends on Papias and on the view that when he referred to a gospel written by Mark he meant Mark as we have it. If, as seems probable, this is the case, it may still be questioned whether Papias' information or guess was correct. This cannot be decisively proved one way or another. The key fact to recall is that the tradition about Mark does not surface until approximately 140, *which on balance must make us doubt that Papias had an old and reliable tradition.*[20]
> [Emphasis added-PT]

---

[16] Fragment 3, from *The Apostolic Fathers* Translated By J. B. Lightfoot & J. R. Harmer (source: http://www.textexcavation.com/papias.html#apollinarius)

[17] Josephus in Antiquities 17:6:5 described Herod the Great's suffering before his death to include putrefied genitals, emanation of pus and worms and bad stench. Acts 12:23 describes the death of Herod's grandson, Herod Agrippa I by stating that he was struck by an angel and was "eaten by worms." [see Maccoby, *Judas Iscariot and the Myth of Jewish Evil*: p82-84]

[18] Fragment 5, from *The Apostolic Fathers* Translated By J. B. Lightfoot & J. R. Harmer (source: http://www.textexcavation.com/papias.html#philipside)

[19] Richard Bauckham in his book, *Jesus and The Eyewitnesses* (Eerdmans 2006 p13), simply asserted that Papias was a reliable witness who works according to the proper historiographic conventions of his day while calling those who reject the church father's witness as "prejudiced." The evidence provided above was not considered at all in his book! Considering how pivotal Papias' witness was to his claim that the gospels contain eyewitness accounts, this is quite surprising.

[20] Sanders & Davies, *Studying the Synoptic Gospels*: p12

Matthew

Papias also wrote about Matthew and this has been a source of contention ever since. Let us look at what he wrote again:

> Quoted in *History of the Church* 3:39:15
> As for Matthew, he made a collection in Hebrew of the *sayings* and each translated them as best they could.

Note that Papias said Matthew made a collection in *Hebrew* of the *sayings* (Greek: *ta logia*) of Jesus. Many scholars are not convinced that this is a reference to the canonical Gospel of Matthew. There are four main reasons for this skepticism.[21]

- The gospel as we have it today was unmistakably first written in Greek and not Hebrew.[22] Both the Greek literary style and the gospel's use of earlier Greek sources (Mark and Q)[23] definitely exclude the possibility that it was written originally in Hebrew.

- If according to Papias "each translated them as best they could", we would expect to see many differing translations of Matthew in the extant manuscript tradition. No different translation of any work would hit upon exactly the same construction of sentences and the same choice of words each time. Yet the extant manuscripts all show that they are copied from (ultimately) the same *Greek* source.

- Papias wrote that Matthew only recorded "the sayings" of Jesus. The canonical Gospel of Matthew is a narrative consisting of both sayings and acts of Jesus. To say that Papias may have meant "sayings" to mean "narrative" is unlikely. For in the case of Mark, Papias wrote that the second evangelist wrote down "what he remembered of *the acts and sayings* of the Lord". Had he meant the same for Matthew one would have expected him to describe it in the same manner.

- Finally, note that in the case of Mark, Papias had commented that his narrative was not in order. Now the canonical Matthew shares the same narrative framework as Mark; had Papias meant his *logia* of Matthew to be the same as our first gospel, his lack of comment on the order of this gospel is hard to explain away.

These four arguments provide compelling argument against the document referred to by Papias being identical with the canonical Matthew. As Werner Kümmel, in his standard textbook of the New Testament admitted:

---

[21] Koester, *Ancient Christian Gospels.*: p316-318
Sanders & Davies, *Studying the Synoptic Gospels*: p10

[22] By "Hebrew", Papias probably meant Aramaic - the language spoken by the Jews in Palestine at that time. However, we will continue to use "Hebrew" for our discussion.

[23] See the next chapter for the evidence that the Gospel of Mark and Q were sources used in the composition of the Gospel of Matthew.

We must concede that the report that Mt was written by Matthew "in the Hebrew language" is utterly false, however it may have arisen. All that remains of the tradition passed on Papias is the name, Matthew.[24]

The most likely explanation for this is that the "sayings" Papias was referring to is *not* the canonical Matthew but a collection of sayings with little or no accompanying narrative, much like Q or the Gospel of Thomas - a different *genre* altogether.

Let us now look at later Patristic attribution of the authorship of the Gospel of Matthew:

- **Irenaeus** (c130-200) (Against Heresies 3:1:1) wrote that "Matthew published his gospel among the Hebrews in their own tongue" when Peter and Paul were still preaching in Rome, thus indicating that the gospel is earlier than Mark - which he mentioned as being written only after "Peter's departure." Irenaeus, writing around the end of the second century, was the first to mention that Matthew's was the first gospel to be written.

- **Clement of Alexandria** (c150-215) (quoted in History of the Church 6:14:6) did not specifically mention Matthew but only notes that "the gospels containing genealogies" were written first. The only gospels containing genealogies are Matthew and Luke. Thus by the time of Clement, around the early third century, the belief that Matthew is the earliest gospels may already be entrenched in the tradition.

- **Origen** (c185-254) (quoted in History of the Church 6:25:4) wrote that he "learned by tradition that the first [gospel] was written by Matthew" and that it was "published in the Hebrew language."

- **Eusebius** (c260-c340) (History of the Church 3:24:6) had this to add "For Matthew, who had at first preached to the Hebrews, when he was about to go to other peoples, committed his Gospel to writing in his native tongue."

- **Jerome** (c342-420) (Lives of Illustrious Men 3) noted that "Matthew...composed a gospel of Christ at first published in Judea in Hebrew" and that it was "afterwards translated into Greek" though he did not know by whom. What is interesting is that Jerome claimed to seen the Aramaic or Hebrew Matthew and that he was *permitted to copy it.* He further added that a copy can still be found during his time in the library at Caesarea. He even claims in his *Commentary on Matthew* that he had actually translated it!

We can see that the main information about the *Logia* of Matthew - that it was written in Hebrew - was taken from Papias. That this is identical to the canonical Matthew and that it was the earliest gospel was the information added by Irenaeus, about fifty years after Papias. Later patristic citations, such as Clement of Alexandria, Origen and Eusebius merely repeated these two with some paraphrasing and extrapolation.

---

[24] Kümmel, *Introduction to the New Testament*: p120-121

Jerome is another matter. He claimed *to have seen, copied and actually translated an original Hebrew Gospel of Matthew*! How are we to evaluate this? We start by noting that Jerome had a habit of exaggerating: both in his presentation of evidence (as in the case of Mark above - where he had Peter *dictate* the gospel to Mark) and in his portrayal of his own achievements.[25] Thus we cannot simply take his claim at face value. Indeed, a series of considerations lead us to conclude that this is just another empty boast by Jerome:[26]

- Eusebius had full access to the library of Caesarea and it is unlikely in the extreme that he would have kept silent about the existence of a Gospel of Matthew in Hebrew there. Yet we hear nothing about such a work from Eusebius.

- The quotations of Jerome's supposed translation of the Hebrew "Matthew" is identical to that of Origen's translation of a *Gospel According to the Hebrews*. It is unlikely that Jerome would have hit upon the exact phrases in his translation.

- The extant fragments, of the *Gospel According to the Hebrews* translated by Origen, showed considerable deviations from the canonical Matthew and cannot be the same work. That Jerome seemed unaware of this most likely means that he never had direct access to a Hebrew gospel.

We can conclude that Jerome never translated any Hebrew gospel and that his citations were merely passages plagiarized from Origen's work. Furthermore, had Jerome actually had access to the gospel he would have noted the considerable deviation from the canonical Matthew - something he never even mentioned. In other words, the most likely possibility in this case is that Jerome never had anything close to full access to any Hebrew gospel (perhaps he had just glanced at it or heard it described to him). His attestation here is of no value.

To summarize, the earliest *unambiguous* attribution of the first gospel in the canon to Matthew is by Irenaeus around 180 CE, almost a century after the work was written. Its attribution seems to be partly based - erroneously - on Papias' remark about *a different* document - a collection of sayings by Jesus. Furthermore, although we have evidence that passages from the first gospel were cited (as we have seen

---

[25] Jerome is known to be particularly boastful and normally claimed to have accomplished more than what he had actually achieved. A couple of examples should suffice. In his book *On Illustrious Men* (392) Jerome claimed that he had finished translating the Old Testament from the Hebrew when in actuality he did not accomplish this task until another fifteen years later (c406). He made similar claims about translating the whole Septuagint (the Greek OT) into Latin. There are only a few books in the Septuagint which we have extant of Jerome's translations. And these were the few books he generally referred to when asked about the translation. Indeed when Augustine asked him for a copy of his translation of the Septuagint, he simply used the excuse every schoolboy uses: he lost it!

[26] Kelly, *Jerome*: p158, 159, 302,334
Philipp Vielhauer & Georg Strecker, "Jewish Christian Gospels", *New Testament Apochrypha I*, Schneemelcher (ed): p142-4

above), there is no sign of any tradition *assigning* the first gospel to Matthew in the intervening half a century period between Papias and Irenaeus.

Furthermore, whatever information Irenaeus had with him did not help him to note that the information given by Papias could not have referred to the canonical Matthew. This all leads us to conclude that Irenaeus did not have any additional information than that available to Papias and that it was he who took the latter's statement about Matthew's *logia* to mean the canonical gospel. He was probably also the source about Matthew being the earliest gospel published.[27]

The explanation that best fit all the facts is that the traditional attribution of the second gospel to the apostle Matthew rested on Irenaeus' misreading of Papias.

Luke

As far as we can tell from the available fragments of the writings of Papias, he did not mention anything about the Gospel According to Luke. While it was widely attested later that Marcion used an abbreviated Luke around 140, and some passages from Luke may have been quoted by Justin (either directly or as part of a harmony of gospels), it was not until Irenaeus around 180 that we see the gospel being directly referred to by name:

> Against Heresies 3:1:1
> Luke also, the companion of Paul, recorded in a book the Gospel preached by him

There is no explicit attestation to the third gospel earlier than this. The *earliest report* that Marcion (c 140) used a "mutilated Luke" also came from Irenaeus (Against Heresies: 1:25:1). Marcion was an extreme Pauline and certainly equated the gospel he used with the gospel preached by Paul - but there is no evidence that Marcion identified the work as Luke's. Indeed, Tertullian (c160 - c225), in his work *Against Marcion* (4:2), criticized the heretic for *not* naming the author of his gospel. [28]

Later attestations did not add any new or more reliable information:[29]

- **Muratorian Canon** (c200) noted that "Luke the physician, after the ascension of Christ, after Paul had taken him as a learned person, wrote in his own name according to his [Paul's] perspective."

- **Clement of Alexandria** (c150-215) (quoted in History of the Church 6:14:6) did not specifically mention Luke but only notes that "the gospels containing genealogies" were written first: meaning Matthew and Luke.

- **Tertullian** (c160 - c225) in Against Marcion 4 reported that Marcion abbreviated and modified the Gospel of Luke to come up with his gospel. Tertullian also added that Luke's gospel "was subsequent to the others" (Against Marcion 4:2) - meaning that it was the latest of all the gospels.

---

27   Sanders & Davies, *Studying the Synoptic Gospels*: p10-11
28   Koester, *Ancient Christian Gospels*: p334-335
      Metzger, *The Canon of the New Testament*: p92
29   Schneele, *The History and Theology of the New Testament Writings*: p240

- **Origen** (c185-254) (quoted in History of the Church 6:25:3-6) - according to Eusebius - noted in his *Commentary on Matthew* that he "knows only four gospels" [the four in the canon] and that Luke wrote the third gospel, the one "commended by Paul", mainly for Gentile converts.

- **Eusebius** (c260-c340) (History of the Church 3:4:7) wrote "Luke, who was of Antiochian parentage and a physician by profession, and who was especially intimate with Paul and well acquainted with the rest of the apostles, has left us, in two inspired books, proofs of that spiritual healing art which he learned from them. One of these books is the Gospel, which he testifies that he wrote as those who were from the beginning eye witnesses and ministers of the word delivered unto him, all of whom, as he says, he followed accurately from the first. The other book is the Acts of the Apostles which he composed not from the accounts of others, but from what he had seen himself."

As is the case with the attestation of the other two gospels, later "witnesses" were fully dependant on earlier ones. We get contradictory information whenever the later witnesses tried to add to their attestation. Thus Tertullian said Luke was written "subsequent to all the others" (that it was the last to be written) while Clement (as quoted by Eusebius) said that it, together with Matthew, were the earliest gospels! The information given by Eusebius cannot be considered to constitute him having any additional sources as it could be derived from someone reading Luke and The Acts of the Apostles - since it is generally accepted that the same author wrote both books - and the epistles of Paul.

The information that Marcion used Luke (or a mutilated form of it) cannot be used to attest for the *name* being used to identify the third gospel. As we have noted above, Tertullian (Against Marcion 4:2) specifically condemned Marcion for *not* mentioning Luke's name as the author of the gospel he used.[30]

We can summarize the case for the third gospel in the canon thus: up to 180, there was no linkage of the name "Luke" to it. Thus Irenaeus - around 180 - formed the datum for identifying the author of the third gospel with Luke, companion of Paul.

John

As in the case of Luke, the name John was not mentioned by Papias in connection to any narrative or logia of Jesus. Again, as in the case of Luke, the first attribution of authorship of the fourth gospel to the apostle John came from Irenaeus in the year 180:

---

[30]   Metzger, *The Canon of the New Testament*: p92

Against Heresies 3:1:1
[also quoted by Eusebius in his *History of the Church* 5:8:4]
Afterwards, John, the disciple of the Lord, who also had leaned upon His breast, did himself publish a Gospel during his residence at Ephesus in Asia.

Since the "afterwards" came after the description of the other three gospels, Irenaeus was obviously stating that John's was the last gospel to be written.

By around 200, Irenaeus' assertion had gained general acceptance.[31] Subsequent testimonies of the church fathers were all dependent on his account and did not add anything new to the tradition - nor were they likely to have had access to any independent tradition.

- **Clement of Alexandria** (c150-215) (quoted in History of the Church 6:14:7) wrote that John was the last of the gospels to be published and "perceiving that the external facts had been made plain in the Gospel, being urged by his friends, and inspired by the Spirit, composed a spiritual Gospel".

- **Theophilus of Antioch** (fl. c190) in his work *To Autolycus* 2:22 wrote this "And hence the holy writings teach us, and all the spirit-bearing [inspired] men, one of whom, John, says, "In the beginning was the Word, and the Word was with God." [It is unclear if it is the *apostle* John that was meant.][32]

- **Origen** (c185-254) (quoted in History of the Church 6:25:8) - according to Eusebius - wrote that John "who reclined upon the bosom of Jesus", "left us one gospel". He too, like earlier writers, mentioned that John was the last gospel written.

- **Eusebius** (c260-c340) (History of the Church 3:24:5) noted that John wrote "after Mark and Luke had already published their gospels". Since he also noted that Matthew wrote first, this meant that John was the last gospel to be written.

It is clear that all these later testimonies were dependent on Irenaeus. How reliable then, is his testimony? We should note that the tradition that John lived to a great age and that he published his gospel during the time of Trajan (98-117) also came from Irenaeus.[33]

Against Heresies 2:22:5 [also 3:3:4]
[T]hose who were conversant in Asia with John, the disciple of the Lord, [affirming] that John conveyed to them that information. And he remained among them up to the times of Trajan.

---

[31] Schneele, *The History and Theology of the New Testament Writings*: p471
[32] Some scholars, e.g. R. Alan Culpepper in *John* (p122-123) claimed that Theophilus formed the earliest witness to a "John" being the author of the fourth gospel. Most other scholars, e.g. Bruce Metzger, Lee M. McDonald, dated him later than Irenaeus, to around 188 or 190. The opinion of the majority of scholars, as far as I can tell, is that Irenaeus provided the earliest attestation to the apostolic authorship of John.
[33] Culpepper, *John*: p123

Against Heresies 3:3:4
Then, again, the Church in Ephesus, founded by Paul, and having John remaining among them permanently until the times of Trajan, is a true witness of the tradition of the apostles.

Thus the idea of gospel authorship and John's residence in Ephesus during his old age are tied together. All the witnesses copied this connection that John's gospel was the last to be written.

The major pillar of this is the claim by Irenaeus that he was in the direct chain of transmission of apostolic tradition. In his *Letter to Florinus* (quoted in History of the Church 5:20:5-6), he wrote that he was a student of Polycarp (69-155 CE) as a "boy" and that his teacher was a disciple of the apostle John. He was to make the same assertion in his major polemic, *Against Heresies* (3:3:4): namely that Polycarp was appointed bishop by the apostle John.[34]

Yet both aspects of Irenaeus' claims, that Polycarp knew the apostle John and that the latter appointed Polycarp bishop of Smyrna rest on extremely shaky grounds. First there is the complete silence about the presence of John in Asia in the writings of the earlier apostolic fathers such as Ignatius (d. c110) and Polycarp (c 69 - c 155).

Ignatius was fond of connecting the various cities he was addressing to the apostles of Jesus. For instance when he wrote to the Romans, he mentioned both Peter and Paul in connection to that city (Romans 4). In his epistle to the Ephesians he mentioned that Paul remembered them in his epistles. (Ephesians 12). It is in this epistle to the Ephesian that we would expect Ignatius to mention John. The letter was written from *Smyrna*, the residence of Polycarp, the bishop supposedly appointed by John, to the city of *Ephesus*, where John was supposedly still living, or, at worst, had just passed away. That he mentioned only Paul in connection with Ephesus is strong evidence that Ignatius knew of no such tradition linking John with either Ephesus or Smyrna.

Similarly, in Polycarp's epistle to the Philippians the only apostle he mentioned was Paul:

Polycarp's Epistle to the Philippians 3, 11
For neither I, nor any other such one, can come up to the wisdom of the blessed and glorified Paul. He, when among you, accurately and steadfastly taught the word of truth in the presence of those who were then alive. And when absent from you, he wrote you a letter

...

"Do we not know that the saints shall judge the world?" as Paul teaches. But I have neither seen nor heard of any such thing among you, in the midst of whom the blessed Paul labored, and who are commended in the beginning of his Epistle.

Polycarp's mention of Paul was in connection with the latter "accurately and steadfastly" teaching the correct doctrine. This occasion would have been the perfect time to introduce *his* credentials for teaching the correct doctrine if indeed he was a

---

[34]   Actually Irenaeus wrote in Against Heresies 3:3:4 that Polycarp was appointed bishop by "the apostles in Asia." Although he used the plural form here, the only apostle he mentioned by name in connection with Polycarp was John.

disciple of John, an apostle of Jesus. If Polycarp actually was a disciple of John, and was appointed Bishop of Smyrna by the apostle,[35] this silence cannot be easily explained away.

Second, Papias' own writing completely contradicts what Irenaeus claimed. According to Irenaeus, Papias, like Polycarp, was also a disciple of the apostle John. As we have seen in the excerpt preserved in Eusebius' *History of the Church* (3:39:3-4),[36] by the time of Papias' writing John the apostle was already dead. The only John he mentioned having met was one *presbyter* John, who - as indicated in Papias' own writing - was clearly a separate person from the *apostle* John. There is no indication that Papias ever met the apostle John.[37]

Thus Irenaeus' claim of apostolic authorship hinges upon the connection of John's residency at an old age in Asia Minor. Yet we are virtually certain from the evidence given above that this tradition is *false* and is based on a case of mistaken identity between John the *presbyter* and John the *apostle*.

---

[35] It should also be mentioned here that there is an alternate tradition of Polycarp's succession to the bishopric of Smyrna that does not involve his appointment by John. This tradition is preserved in two 4th century documents *The Apostolic Constitutions* (c370) and the *Life of Polycarp* (c400). Both documents, which are independent of one another, agree on the fact that Polycarp was not the first bishop of Smyrna and that there were at least two or three bishops before him. For more detailed exploration of this issue refer to B.H. Streeter's *The Primitive Church*: p89-97.

[36] See note 34 above.

[37] It should also be mentioned that there is an *alternate* tradition in the early Church that John the son of Zebedee died early, together with his brother James. The church historian Philip of Side (c. 380 - c. 439), in his 36 volume *Christian History* quoted from the second volume of Papias' now lost *Interpretation of the Oracles of the Lord* which goes like this:

> Papias said in his second book *that John the Evangelist and his brother James were slain by the Jews.*

We are told in Acts 12:1-3 that James the son of Zebedee was put to death by Herod Agrippa around 44 CE with no mention being made of John. Interestingly, Acts stopped making any mention of John after Acts 8:25 which narrated his return, together with Peter, from a missionary trip to Samaria.

We find evidence to corroborate John's death, together with his brother James, in Mark's Gospel in the pericope which had the brothers Zebedee asking Jesus for exalted positions in the coming kingdom for themselves in Mark 10:35-40. Jesus' reply that "*You shall indeed drink the cup that I drink*" (Mark 10:39) is obviously a prophecy of their deaths as martyrs. Now we know that Mark generally put prophecies in the mouth of Jesus *after* they had come true - a couple examples of such a technique include Jesus' prophecies about Peter's denial (Mark 14:54, 66-72) and about the fall of Jerusalem (Mark 13:1-2). This strongly suggests that by the time Mark was written, around 70 CE, the tradition available to the evangelist indicated that John was already dead.

[Culpepper, *John*: p170-174

Ranke-Heinemann, *Putting Away Childish Things*: p220-221]

We mentioned above that after Irenaeus, the proto-orthodox tradition quickly settled on the apostle John as the author of the fourth gospel. Yet Irenaeus' predecessors and contemporaries do not share the same opinion.

Perhaps the most poignant case is that of Justin Martyr (c100-c165). Justin claimed that the book of Revelation was written by the apostle John. As we have noted above, Justin had already started calling some gospels (either Matthew, Luke and Mark), or a harmony of these, *Memoirs of the Apostles*. In other words, there is already a felt need to attribute apostolic origins to extant writings that support their proto-orthodox theology. We know that Justin had been to Ephesus, yet he made no mention of the apostle John having lived there or that he wrote a gospel. Justin, as we recall, wrote 30 years prior to Irenaeus and would surely had had access to people who *knew* the apostle John when he visited Ephesus - had it actually been the case that John was a resident there.[38]

A proto-orthodox contemporary of Irenaeus, the Roman presbyter Gauis (fl c 200) in his treatise *Dialogue with Proclus* rejected the apostolic origin of the fourth gospel on literary-historical grounds and attributed the authorship to the Gnostic Cerinthus. That Gauis' objection to Johanine scholarship was not an isolated opinion can be seen from the fact that another Roman presbyter, Hippolytus (c170-c236) had to defend the Johanine authorship.[39] The important point here is that even as late as 200 CE, the apostolic authorship of the fourth gospel was still being disputed.[40]

Conclusion on the Traditional Attribution of Apostolic Authorship

Two important facts arise from our analysis of the traditional attribution of apostolic authorship to the gospels:

- The whole tradition of apostolic authorship of the gospels rested on the testimonies of *only two persons*: Papias and Irenaeus. All later attributions were dependent on these two and do not offer independent support for the tradition.

- The attributions were late, being first made between *60 to 100 years* after the gospels were first written.

In the case of Mark, everything hinges upon Papias' testimony, around 130-150 CE (or 60 to 80 years after Mark was written). Papias based his testimony on one Presbyter John. We do not know the value of the Presbyter's testimony and Papias was probably not the type of person who would have the intelligence to verify the information independently. The length of time elapsed from the time the gospel was written to this first attestation leads us to treat the tradition with extreme skepticism.

In the case of Matthew, we *do not* have a testimony from Papias, since he was definitely referring to another document and not the canonical Gospel of Matthew. Thus for Matthew, Luke and John - all we have is the testimony of Irenaeus around 180 CE. It is important to let the implication of this fact sink in. Despite the relatively

---

[38]   Culpepper, *John*: p112-114
[39]   Davidson & Leaney, *Biblical Criticism.*: p268
[40]   Culpepper, *John*: p121

voluminous surviving Christian literature from the end of the first century onwards, *the first attribution of apostolic authorship to the gospels of Matthew, Luke and John were made almost a century after these gospels were written.* Furthermore, we can tell from the writing of Justin Martyr around 155 CE that appeal to apostolic writings were already beginning to take on an importance not felt prior to that point. Had the tradition been floating around at that time, it would surely have made it into at least *some* surviving manuscripts. That it did not point us to the conclusion that the tradition of apostolic authorship was relatively new during the time of Irenaeus.

We are pretty certain that Irenaeus *misinterpreted* the sources for attributing the authorship of the gospels of John and Matthew. Irenaeus' mistake in confusing the two *Johns* in Papias' led to him attributing the fourth gospel to the apostle John. He mistook Papias' description regarding a *logia* written by Matthew to mean a narrative gospel. His attribution of the authorship of the third gospel was, as we shall see below, based on pure guesswork.

THE TRADITIONAL ATTRIBUTION OF AUTHORSHIP: SECOND CENTURY GUESSES

As have seen in the previous section, the gospels initially circulated anonymously and were not pinned to any particular author until well into the second century. Two questions come to mind. First, why did the names of the evangelists started surfacing only around the middle of the second century and not earlier? Second, how did Papias and Irenaeus get the specific names of the authors for each individual gospel?

The mid-second century stands out for few good reasons. One of the main reason lies with Marcion (d. c160). A native of Asia Minor, he traveled to Rome in 139 and, as a result of his large donation to the church there, gained considerable influence. Marcion taught that the Jewish scriptures could not be the work of the God of Jesus. He came up with an alternate scripture which consisted of ten epistles of Paul and one gospel (a form of Luke). Five years after arriving in Rome, he called for a meeting with leaders of the Roman Church and presented his ideas. However, the elders did not take his theology well and branded Marcion, a "heretic." Traveling back to Asia Minor, Marcion was wildly successful in spreading his beliefs there. His collection is widely believed to be the first attempt at forming a Christian "canon" of scripture.[41]

Around that time, other groups of Christians - Gnostics, Montanists, and Ebionites - were also making contesting claims about apostolic succession in their preaching and in their writings.

Thus there was a very strong felt need on the *proto-orthodox*[42] side to confer apostolic origins to the writings in their possession. Given this background, the timing of the assertions of Papias and Justin about apostolic writings makes sense.[43]

The second question was: why the names *Matthew, Mark, Luke and John*? As we will see in the next chapter, internal evidence of the gospels shows that these

---

[41] Ehrman, *Lost Christianities*: p104-109
[42] Bart Ehrman's term for the side that ultimately won the theological battle of control over how Christianity would develop
[43] Ehrman, *Lost Christianities*: p234-235

attributions are spurious. So how did they settle for these four names? The answer is simple: they *guessed.*

Note that we do not need to *speculate* that they guessed, we *know* - in the case of the Gospel of Luke - exactly how one of them did it!

In *Against Heresies* 3:14:1. Irenaeus explained how he got the name "Luke" as the author of the third gospel. By referring to the "we-passages" in Acts (16:10-17; 20:5-15; 21:1-18; 27:1-28:16), he noted that the writer was a companion of Paul. Then noting from II Timothy 4:10-11 - which is "set" during Paul's imprisonment in Rome (see II Timothy 1:16-17) - in which "Paul" wrote "Only Luke is with me", and tying that to Acts 28:16 which states that "we came into Rome", he came up with author to Acts and hence also the third gospel (since they are obviously written by the same person) - namely "Luke the Physician" (Colossians 4:14). Since he never referred to any tradition as the basis for his identification - we can conclude that this was actually how he got the name for the author of the third gospel.[44]

The example of Luke provides an important clue to how the traditional names were derived. Due to Papias, the name *Matthew* floated in the proto-orthodox mindscape as having written something. A later Christian, perhaps Irenaeus himself, connected the dots between the first gospel and the tax collector Matthew. The dots were simple and similar to the way it was done with Luke. The gospels of Mark (Mark 3:14-19) and Luke (Luke 6:13-16) listed "Matthew" as one of Jesus twelve apostles. Yet in the episode on the calling of the tax collector, both Mark 2:14-15 and Luke 5:27-29, named him Levi son of Alphaeus. Only the first gospel called him Matthew (Matthew 9:9-10). Who better to know the "real" name of this man than if the author is that very person?[45]

When it comes to the gospel John, an unnamed "beloved disciple" figures prominently (John 13:23-25; 20:2-8, 21:21-23). There is also a claim made in the epilogue of the gospel that this disciple was the one who wrote the gospel (John 21:24). Furthermore, the beloved disciple seems to be a companion of Peter. Adducing from verses in Acts (Acts 1:13; 3:1-4; 3:11; 4:13; 4:19; 8:14) which shows that John the son of Zebedee was a companion of Peter and added that to the fact that John was never explicitly named in the fourth gospel, led the second century Christian detective(s) to conclude that he must have been the author of this work. Again, it may have been Irenaeus that did this guesswork, or he may have been the one to connect this with the fact that he remembered being told of a "John" - whom he mistook for the apostle - who lived in Ephesus in the early second century.[46]

For the case of Mark, we recall that Papias got his information from John the Presbyter. Note that it is not impossible for someone named *Mark* to have written the gospel, after all *someone* actually did write it! And *Mark* [Latin = *Marcus*] was an exceedingly common name during that time.[47] Many early Christians around that time

---

[44] Sanders & Davies, *Studying the Synoptic Gospels.*: p.14
      Schnelle: *The New Testament Writings*: p240
[45] Sanders & Davies, *Studying the Synoptic Gospels.*: p14-15
[46] Sanders, *The Historical Figure of Jesus*: p65
[47] Just think of famous contemporaries with that name. We have the Roman Emperor *Marcus* Aurelius (121-180 CE), the Roman general *Marcus* Antonius (83 - 30 BCE) and

would have had that name.[48] Thus, it is possible that the Presbyter - around 130 - heard that the author of the second gospel was of that name. However, "Mark" was not the name of an apostle. So either the Presbyter or Papias, did the best he could to bring the otherwise anonymous author into as close an association to an apostle as possible. He put together the tradition [reflected in the accounts from Acts 12:12 and I Peter 5:13] that seems to suggest that Peter had a junior companion named John Mark and connected it with the gospel written by an otherwise unknown Mark.[49]

* * * * *

We can conclude from all this that the traditional identification of the evangelists: Matthew the apostle, John Mark the interpreter of Peter, Luke the travel companion of Paul, and John the son of Zebedee, were nothing more than *second century guesses* of the church fathers. These guesses were brought on by polemical needs in their battle against heretical sects. Unfortunately, as we shall see in the next chapter *they guessed wrong*.

---

one of the conspirators in the assassination of Julius Caesar, *Marcus* Junius Brutus (85 - 42 BCE).

48   Martin, *New Testament Foundations I*: p213
49   Sanders & Davies, *Studying the Synoptic Gospels.*: p13

Chapter Nine
AUTHORSHIP OF THE GOSPELS
- INTERNAL EVIDENCE

INTERNAL EVIDENCE

In the previous chapter we have seen that the traditional names of the authors of the gospels were reliant on the testimonies of Papias (c60-130) and Irenaeus (c130-c200). The gospels initially circulated anonymously. They were probably known, or differentiated, based on the *incipit*, or the first line of the gospel. Their names were guesses first made probably by these two church fathers.

Whether their guesses are correct or not will depend on the evidence we can find within the gospels themselves. This is the task we have in front of us.

THE SYNOPTIC GOSPELS

Anyone who has read the gospels will notice that Matthew, Mark and Luke report many common incidents and sayings of Jesus and that they all share a common narrative framework. It was the German New Testament scholar, Johann Griesbach (1745-1812) who introduced the term "synoptics," from the Greek word for "seen together," for these three gospels. John's gospel, on the other hand, has a different framework and describes different events. It also devotes much space to long speeches of Jesus which are very unlike those reported in the synoptics. No attempt at harmonization has ever worked.[1] The Gospel of John will be treated separately later in this chapter.

Irenaeus (Against Heresies 3:1:1) was also the first to give a chronological sequence of the writing of the four gospels: Matthew wrote first, followed by Mark, Luke and, finally, John. This tradition of Matthew's primacy was repeated throughout Christian history. The church father, Clement of Alexandria (c150-c215), said that the earliest gospels were those with Jesus' family tree. We find Jesus' genealogies in Matthew and Luke but not in Mark. Another church father, Origen (c185-254), said that the first gospel was written in Hebrew by Matthew. Augustine (354-430), one of the most important theologians of early Christianity, stated that Mark copied and abbreviated Matthew. It is because of this tremendous *weight* of tradition that it became established as a "fact" that Matthew was the earliest gospel and that its author was one of the twelve apostles. However, as we have noted in the previous chapter, B.H. Streeter (1874-1937) pointed out that the church fathers read one another's work, with the later ones merely copying and expanding the works of their predecessors with no new information. This weight of tradition is really nothing more than the church fathers uncritical acceptance of the assertions of their ecclesiastical forerunners.[2]

---

[1]   Wilson, *Jesus: The Evidence*: p31
[2]   Bentley, *Secrets of Mount Sinai*: p140-142
     Streeter, *The Primitive Church*: p16-18

Indeed, this "weight of tradition" really does not mean anything, for the claim of Matthean priority is *demonstrably untrue*. The next section examines the compelling case for *Markan* priority.

THE PROOF OF MARKAN PRIORITY

The traditional belief that Matthew was the earliest gospel written was finally shown to be false in 1835 by the German philologist and textual critic, Karl Lachman (1793-1851). He amassed evidence showing that the Gospel of Mark was the earliest of the synoptics and that the authors of Matthew and Luke copied extensively from it. Since then it has been further refined by other scholars such as H.J. Holtzman (1832-1910) and B.H. Streeter (1874-1937). This explanation of the similarities and differences found in the synoptics (known as "the synoptic problem") is now called "The Two Source Hypothesis"[3] (TSH) and now accepted by most scholars to be the solution to the synoptic problem. The main alternative to this is the Griesbach Hypothesis (GH), named after Johann Griesbach who postulated that Matthew was the common source of Mark and Luke.[4] In presenting the evidence for the two-source hypothesis we will be looking at how it could be explained by the alternate hypothesis proposed by Griesbach. There are three main groups of evidence: the pattern of the internal contents, the order of the gospels and the redactional changes.

Pattern of Internal Contents

The Gospel of Mark consists of 661 verses. Both Matthew (1,068 verses) and Luke (1,149 verses) are comparatively larger works. Of the 661 verses found in Mark, Matthew repeats about 600 verses, while Luke uses about 350, some of which differ from the verses used by Matthew. From Mark's 661 verses only 31 verses did not appear in some form or another in Matthew and Luke. In terms of vocabulary, of Mark's 11,205 words only 132 have no parallel in Matthew (which has 18,293 words) and/or Luke (19,376 words). 97.2% (10,721 words) of the words in Mark have a parallel in Matthew, while 88.4% (9,743) of Mark have a parallel in Luke. Looked at another way, 59% of Matthew's and 51% of Luke's language repeat Mark's words. When Luke is quoting the sayings of Jesus from Mark, the similarity in words rises to 69%.

Mark's gospel can also be divided in another, more natural way, into separate episodes or pericopae. With this method we can divide Mark's gospels in 88 separate episodes. Of these 88 only three - Mark 4:26-29 [the seed growing of itself], 7:31-37 [healing of the deaf mute], 8:22-26 [healing of the blind man]- are not found in the other two gospels.[5]

---

[3]   The hypothesis is that both Matthew and Luke used *two* main sources for their respective gospels: Mark and a now lost sayings collection called "Q" [from the German word *Quelle* for "source"]. See the later section in this chapter on "Q."

[4]   Brown, *An Introduction to the New Testament*: p114-115
     Stein, *Studying the Synoptic Gospels*: p50

[5]   Bentley, *Secrets of Mount Sinai*: p141
     Brown, *An Introduction to the New Testament*: p111

These statistics make the use of Matthew (or Luke) by Mark extremely unlikely. Why would Mark, if he was copying one of the other ignore about 41% of Matthew and almost half of Luke? Why ignore the stories of the virgin birth, the birth of John the Baptist and the Sermon on the Mount? The latter is especially hard to explain if Mark has Matthew in front of him. Mark[6] placed a heavy emphasizes on Jesus' teachings in his gospel – the noun or verb for "teach" can be found throughout (e.g. Mark 1:21-22, 2:13, 4:1-2, 6:2, 8:31, 12:35) – for him to ignore a whole chunk of Jesus teaching (Matthew 5:1-7:29) is inexplicable.[7]

The counter argument that Mark was meant as an abridgement of Matthew (or Luke) - originally suggested by Augustine (354-430) - does not work. While it is true that Mark is shorter overall, this pattern is not seen in individual episodes. In comparing 51 stories in common between these gospels, Robert H. Stein has shown that Mark has the longest account in 21 of these, with Matthew having the longest in 11 and Luke in 10. In the other nine, where the longest and second longest differ by only three words or less, Mark is always one of the two longest account. This pattern is difficult to explain within the context of the GH – why would Mark abridge the length by reducing the number of episodes but expand the individual episodes he retained? Within the context of the TSH the explanation comes naturally. Both Luke and Matthew had additional stories that they included in their gospel. They generally abbreviated Mark's episodes so that while the stories in Mark are included in their gospels, it allows space for the others.[8]

The Order of the Gospels

The *order* of Mark's narrative is supported most of the time by the gospels of Matthew and Luke. In those cases where either Matthew or Luke diverged from Mark's order, the other is usually found supporting it. There is *no* case where Matthew and Luke agreed with each other in their order against Mark. Whenever both Matthew and Luke diverged from Mark they also diverged from one another. Where Matthew's order agrees with Luke, it begins and ends with the pattern of events in Mark. Mark's order is basic to the other two gospels.

Many of Mark's verses are found in both Matthew and Luke: these are referred to as the "Triple Tradition". While there are about 200+ verses that Matthew and Luke have in common which are not found in Mark. This is known as the "Double Tradition".[9] In those stories that Matthew and Luke share with Mark (whether it is

---

Kummel, *Introduction to the New Testament*: p56-57

Martin, *New Testament Foundations I*: p140

Stein, *Studying the Synoptic Gospels*: p50-52

[6] I am using "Mark" here to mean simply "the [unnamed] author of the second gospel". It does not mean that I am in agreement with the traditional attribution of this gospel to John Mark, interpreter of Peter. The same holds for my use of "Matthew", "Luke" and "John" throughout this book.

[7] Stein, *Studying the Synoptic Gospels*: p55

[8] Bentley, *Secrets of Mount Sinai*: p142

Stein, *Studying the Synoptic Gospels*: p52-55

[9] For an explanation of this "Double Tradition" see the section on "Q" below.

just one of them with Mark or as part of the triple tradition) we find that they always have the same sequence as Mark. Yet when it comes to the "Double Tradition", their order diverged from each other completely. This is hard to explain if Luke knew Mark *and* Matthew. Why would he only keep the sequence of Markan material, but juxtapose the Matthean material anyway that suits him? The same argument holds also if we assume Matthew knew Luke and Mark. The order of the synoptics tell us not only that Mark's order is fundamental to the synoptics but that Luke and Matthew are works that are independent of one another.[10]

Table 9.1 on the next page provides us with such an example.[11] Note that all three gospels follow the same order initially. However, at Mark 2:23-28 Matthew diverges in his order. The asterisk in Table 9.1 shows where the divergence began.

Episode	Matthew	Mark	Luke
Healing of the Paralytic	9:1-8	2:1-12	5:17-26
Calling of Matthew	9:9-13	2:13-17	5:27-32
About Fasting	9:14-17*	2:18-22	5:33-39
The Lord of the Sabbath	12:1-8#	2:23-28	6:1-5
The Withered Hand	12:9-21	3:1-6	6:6-11
Crowds Follow Jesus		3:7-11	6:17-19*
The Twelve Apostles	10:1-4	3:13-19	6:12-16
Beelzebub	12:22-32	3:23-30	11:14-20
Jesus Renounces Family	12:46-50	3:20-21; 3:31-35	8:19-21
The Sower	13:1-9	4:1-8	8:4-8#
Kingdom not for Everyone	13:10-13	4:9-12	8:9-10
The Sower Parable Explained	13:18-23	4-13-20	8:11-15

Table 9:1 The Markan Order

Table 9.2 below gives this Matthean divergence. From 9:35 to 11:30 Matthew went his own way. Luke shared many of the same episodes as Matthew here but they are not at all in the same order. The Matthean story returned to the Markan sequence at Matthew 12:1: indicated by the "#" sign in Table 9.1. Note that all this time while Matthew was merrily going his own way Luke was following the Markan order.

10   Ehrman, *The New Testament*: p78
11   Kümmel, *Introduction to the New Testament*: p57-58

Episode	Matthew	Mark	Luke
The Harvest is Great	9:35-38	6:6b ; 6:34	8:1, 10:2
Commissioning the Twelve	10:1-16	6:7; 3:13-19; 6:8-11	9:1, 6:12-16, 9:2-5, 10:3
Fate of the Disciples	10:17-25	13:9-13	12:11-12, 6:40, 21:12-19
Nothing is Concealed	10:26-33		12:2-9
Divisions within Households	10:34-36		12:51-53
Conditions of Discipleship	10:37-42		14:25-27, 17:33
John the Baptist	11:2-19		7:18-35
Woes	11:20-24		10:12-15
Thanksgiving	11:25-30		10:21-22

Table 9.2 Matthean Divergence

Similarly Luke diverged from the Markan order after 6:19 and do not join back the main Markan sequence until 8:4. [See Table 9.3 below for the Lukan divergence] There are parallel episodes with Matthew but they do not share the same order. Note again that while Luke left the order, Matthew can be found to be supporting the Markan order.

Episode	Matthew	Mark	Luke
Sermon on the Plain			6:20-49
The Centurion	8:5-12		7:1-10
The Widow's Son			7:11-17
John the Baptist	11:2-19		7:18-35
Woman with Ointment	26:6-13	14:3-9	7:36-50
The Ministering Woman			8:1-3

Table 9.3 Lukan Divergence

The German New Testament scholar, Werner Kümmel called the evidence from order "decisive" for establishing Markan priority. In other words, it showed clearly Matthew's and Luke's dependence on Mark.

Redactional Changes

Sometimes we find that Mark contains theologically "difficult" passages which were smoothed over by Matthew and/or Luke. Take for instance the excerpt below from chapter 10 of Mark:

Mark 10:17-18 (RSV)
And as he was setting out on his journey, a man ran up and knelt before him, and asked him, "Good Teacher, what must I do to inherit eternal life?" And Jesus said to him, "Why do you call me good? No one is good but God alone."

Here we see Jesus is depicted as expressly denying any claim to divinity, a factor which, by the time Matthew came to be written, was already starting to gain ground in Christianity. We see how Matthew altered Mark's account:

Matthew 19:16-17 (RSV)
And behold, one came up to him, saying, "Teacher, what good deed must I do, to have eternal life?" And he said to him, "Why do you ask me about what is good? One there is who is good. If you would enter life, keep the commandments."

Note that Matthew has changed the question and taken out the "good" before "teacher". He has also altered Jesus reply such that it no longer reads like a straightforward denial of his divinity. It is easily conceivable how Matthew could have altered Mark for theologically motivated reasons. It is inconceivable how Mark could have altered the Matthean version to reach his. Again, the evidence point towards Matthew copying from Mark and not vice versa.[12]

In many passages in his gospel, Mark portrayed Jesus with human emotions and gestures; Jesus is sometimes amazed or sorrowful, angered or grieved. By the time Matthew and Luke came to be written it had become difficult for the author to view Jesus Christ as a man with human emotions. They thus altered any passage they find in Mark that has Jesus displaying them. Take for instance the episode below:

Mark 10:13-16
They were bringing to him little children, that he should touch them, but the disciples rebuked those who were bringing them. But when Jesus saw it, *he was moved with indignation*, and said to them, "Allow the little children to come to me! Don't forbid them, for the Kingdom of God belongs to such as these. Most certainly I tell you, whoever will not receive the Kingdom of God like a little child, he will in no way enter into it." *He took them in his arms*, and blessed them, laying his hands on them.

Now let us look at how Luke and Matthew altered this episode to fit with their own preconceived theology.

Matthew 19:13-15
Then little children were brought to him, that he should lay his hands on them and pray; and the disciples rebuked them. But Jesus said, "Allow the little children, and don't forbid them to come to me; for the Kingdom of Heaven belongs to ones like these." He laid his hands on them, and departed from there.

Luke 18:15-17
They were also bringing their babies to him, that he might touch them. But when the disciples saw it, they rebuked them. Jesus summoned them, saying, "Allow the little children to come to me, and don't hinder them, for the Kingdom of God belongs to such as these. Most certainly, I tell you, whoever doesn't receive the Kingdom of God like a little child, he will in no way enter into it."

---

[12] Bentley, *Secrets of Mount Sinai*: p143-145
Schenelle, *The New Testament Writings*: p169

Notice how both Luke and Matthew omitted Mark's phrase, "he was moved with indignation," a very human emotion. The two evangelists also omitted the human gesture of Jesus taking the children in his arms. Matthew gives only the laying of hands, an impersonal religious gesture. Again, we can explain why Luke and Matthew would have changed the account in Mark, given the development of Christology in primitive Christianity. It would be harder to explain why Mark would have made those changes given this evolution of the image of Jesus.[13]

Mistakes in copying the Markan account by the other two evangelists also betray the second gospel as the source for them. The episode on Herod Antipas and John the Baptist which can be found in Mark 6:14-29 and Matthew 14:1-13 provide us with a couple of examples of these.

In an attempt to create a more elegant version of Mark, Matthew tripped all over himself and produced a flawed version. Mark's account above tells of King Herod having John imprisoned because of his wife's demand (Mark 6:17). But he also *respected* John and *liked* listening to him (Mark 6:20). When Herodias' daughter demanded John's head, Herod's reaction of being "greatly distressed" makes sense (Mark 6:26), as he did not want to kill John, but in view of the situation had no choice.

When we look at Matthew, we see that he had twisted the story such that it is now slightly different from Mark's. Unlike in Mark, where Herod was said to like and respect John, Matthew said that Herod *wanted* to kill the Baptist from the beginning but "feared the people". (Matthew 14:5) Matthew then reverted to Mark's account and said that Herod was "greatly distressed" when he heard the girl's request (Matthew 14:9). But describing Herod as being "greatly distressed" does not make sense in Matthew's account for we are told that Herod *wanted* to kill John from the beginning. In Matthew's story, the request of the daughter of Herodias' would have made an excellent excuse to have John killed. In short, Matthew by setting out to create an improved version of Mark, ended with a blunder of inconsistency.[14]

Another minor mistake is in the title used by Herod Antipas. His official title was *Tetrarch*, as Matthew 14:1 rightly denotes. Mark consistently used the more popular, but incorrect, title; king. (e.g. Mark 6:14) but later on in the passage Matthew forgot this and simply put "king" instead of "tetrarch" (Matthew 14:9, Mark 6:26), betraying Mark as his source.

A comparison of the grammar of the three gospels leads us to the same conclusion. We find in Mark a roughness in style and grammar not seen in Matthew and Luke. The preservation of Aramaic words in Mark (e.g. 3:17 *boanerges*, 5:41 *talitha cumi*, 7:11 *corban*, 7:34 *ephphatha*. 14:36 *abba*) is also generally considered to be further proof of the primitiveness of Mark. [15]

All these considerations, taken together, provide a compelling case for Markan priority. They show us that Mark wrote first and the other two evangelists, independently, somehow got a hold of a copy of his gospel and incorporated it into their gospels. We have already remarked earlier on the "Double Tradition" −

---

[13] Parmalee, *Guidebook to the Bible*: p111
[14] Bentley, *Secrets of Mount Sinai*: p142-143
[15] Stein, *Studying the Synoptic Gospels*: p56-66

passages which Luke and Matthew share in common that are not found in Mark. What can we say about this?

THE SECOND SOURCE OF MATTHEW AND LUKE

When we have eliminated all Markan material from Matthew and Luke we still find another 220 or so verses that both these gospels have in common. We see that in more than a few cases these common passages have almost exact verbal correspondence. One example:

Matthew 3:7-10	Luke 3:7-9
But when he saw many of the Pharisees and Sadducees coming for his baptism, he said to them, "You offspring of vipers, who warned you to flee from the wrath to come? Therefore bring forth fruit worthy of repentance! Don't think to yourselves, 'We have Abraham for our father,' for I tell you that God is able to raise up children to Abraham from these stones. "Even now the axe lies at the root of the trees. Therefore, every tree that doesn't bring forth good fruit is cut down, and cast into the fire."	He said therefore to the multitudes who went out to be baptized by him, "You offspring of vipers, who warned you to flee from the wrath to come? Bring forth therefore fruits worthy of repentance, and don't begin to say among yourselves, 'We have Abraham for our father;' for I tell you that God is able to raise up children to Abraham from these stones! Even now the axe also lies at the root of the trees. Every tree therefore that doesn't bring forth good fruit is cut down, and thrown into the fire."

Although the evangelists had placed the episode of John the Baptist sermon in different contexts (in Matthew it was a warning to the Pharisees and Sadducees while in Luke it was a general warning to all the Jews) the word for word correspondence of the preaching rules out independent oral sources. The common source must be a written one. And since both Matthew and Luke were written in Greek (thus the word for word correspondence is in Greek) the original source must be in Greek as well. For it is most improbable that both Luke and Matthew would have hit upon so exact a translation from an original source document in Hebrew or Aramaic.[16]

This common source for Luke and Matthew is normally referred to as "Q". The normal explanation for this is that it comes from the German word *Quelle* which means "source" or "spring". Table 9.4 on the next page lists the common verses from Matthew and Luke generally agreed by scholars to have come from Q. These verses contain mainly of Jesus' sayings with almost no narrative at all.[17]

The original Q is now lost but there is very little doubt that it once existed. Some scholars have raised the question as to why such an important document was allowed to disappear. The discovery at Nag Hammadi in Egypt in 1945 of Gnostic gospels previously unknown to modern scholars such as *The Gospel to the Egyptians*

---

16   Guignebert, *Jesus*: p13
      Martin, *New Testament Foundations I*: p143
17   Guignebert, *Jesus*: p35
      Parmalee, *Guidebook to the Bible*: p111

and *The Gospel of Truth* show how completely a gospel could be suppressed when it becomes associated with a heretical sect.[18] The recent discovery of the *Gospel of Judas* is another example. A possible, but by no means the only possibility, answer to this is that Q could have eventually become associated with a heretical sect (the Nazarenes?) and was eventually suppressed and suffered the same fate as the above Gnostic writings.

To forgo the Q hypothesis, it must be postulated that either Luke copied Matthew or Matthew copied Luke. This is extremely unlikely. A comparison of Tables 9.1 and 9.4 show that there is little correspondence between Luke and Matthew in their order of presentation of the Q material. If both Matthew and Luke followed the order of Gospel of Mark so closely, why would they ignore the other's arrangement of the Q material so completely? This lack of correspondence suggests that the two evangelists did not have access to the other's gospel. Both independently used Mark and Q as their source material. This also strengthens the case for Q being almost completely a collection of sayings with no narrative – as there is no chronological order in a collection of isolated sayings.[19]

Sayings/Episodes	Luke	Matthew
I: The Preparation		
A. John's Preaching of Repentance	3:7-9	3:7-10
B. The Temptation of Jesus	4:1-13	4:1-11
II: The Sayings		
A. Beatitudes	6:20-23	5:3,4,6,11,12
B. Love to One's Enemies	6:27-36	5:39-42,44-48,7:12
C. Judging	6:37-42	7:1-5;10:24;15:14
D. Hearer and Doers of the Word	6:47-49	7:24-27
III. Narratives		
A. The Centurion's Servant	7:1-10	7:28;8:5-10,13
B. The Baptist's Questions	7:18-20	11:2-3
C. Christ's Answer	7:22-35	11:4-19
IV. Discipleship		
A. On the Cost of Discipleship	9:57-60	8:19-22
B. The Mission Charge	10:2-16	9:37-38;10:9-15;11:21-23
C. Christ's Thanksgiving to the Father	10:21-24	11:25-27;13:16-17
V. Various Sayings		
A. The Pattern Prayer	11:2-4	6:9-13
B. An Answer to Prayer	11:9-13	7:7-11
C. The Beelzebub Discussion and Its Sequel	11:14-23	12:22-30
D. Sign of the Prophet Jonah	11:29-32	12:38-42
E. About Light	11:33-36	5:15;6:22-23

---

18 Pagels, *The Gnostic Gospels*: p15

19 The case for Q, unlike Markan priority, is not exactly settled yet. There are some prominent scholars, although in the minority, who do not accept the existence of Q as proven. These include William Farmer (see his book *The Synoptic Problem: A Critical Analysis*, Western North Carolina Press 1976), E.P. Sanders (*Studying the Synoptic Gospels*, SCM Press 1992), Michael Goulder (*Luke: A New Paradigm*, Sheffield Academic Press, 1994) and Mark Goodacre (*The Case Against Q*, Trinity Press International, 2002).

VI. Discourse Against the Pharisees		
A. Against the Pharisees	11:37-12:1	Chapter 23
VII. Sayings		
A. About Fearless Confession	12:2-12	10:19,26-33;12:32
B. On Cares About Earthly Things	12:22-34	6:19-21,25-33
C. On Faithfulness	12:39-46	24:43-51
D. On Signs for This Age	12:51-56	10:34-36;16:2-3
E. On Agreeing with One's Adversaries	12:57-59	5:25-26
VIII. Parables		
A. On the Mustard Seed and Leaven	13:18-21	13:31-33
IX. Other Sayings		
A. Condemnation of Israel	13:23-30	7:13,14,22,23;8:11-12
B. Lament Over Jerusalem	13:34-35	23:37-39
C. The Wedding Feast	14:15-24	22:2-14
D. Cost of Discipleship	14:26-35	10:37-39;5:13
E. On Serving Two Masters	6:13	6:24
F. On Law and Divorce	16:16-18	11:12-13;15:18,32
G. On Offence, Forgiveness and Faith	17:1-6	18:6,7,15,20-22
H. The Day of the Son of Man	17:23-27,33-37	24:17-18,26-28,37-41

Table 9.4: The probable contents of Q[20]

OTHER SOURCES OF MATTHEW AND LUKE

The Gospel of Matthew consists of slightly more than 1,000 verses, we have accounted for the source of about 800 of these (600 from Mark and 200+ from Q), the remaining 200+ verses are materials peculiar to Matthew. These include some sayings of Jesus (in chapters 5-7 [not found in Luke] and the final parable in chapter 25) and some narratives (the events surrounding the birth and resurrection of Jesus in Matthew chapters 1 to 3 and 28). It is here we see Matthew's literary style taking free rein. This strongly suggests that either Matthew used oral sources for these or composed it himself. Scholars use the letter "M" to refer to this special source of Matthew.[21]

The Gospel of Luke has about 1100 verses of which more than 500 verses, or about half the gospel, cannot be traced to either Mark or Q. As in Matthew, it is in these extra verses that we find Luke's unencumbered style. The distinctive Lukan words and phrases occur more frequently in these 500+ verses than anywhere else in his gospel. This again strongly suggests Luke's sources to be either from the oral community tradition or his own creative mind. The letter "L" is normally used to designate this Lukan special source.[22]

That some of Luke's sources are from oral tradition we can have some certainty. Luke shares many episodes and details with John which are not paralleled in the other two gospels. These similarities (see Table 9.5 below) do not have the close verbal correspondence that we see in the synoptics but share analogous outlines. Analogous

[20]   Martin, *New Testament Foundations I*: p150
[21]   Guignebert, *Jesus*: p14
       Martin, *New Testament Foundations I*: p152
       Wilson, *Jesus: The Evidence*: p38
[22]   Caird, *Saint Luke*: p19
       Wilson, *Jesus: The Evidence*: p38

events are placed in different contexts. For instance, the miraculous catch of fish was placed by Luke in Galilee early in the ministry of Jesus (Luke 5:1-11). John, however, placed this miracle after the resurrection (John 21:1-4). Another example is the story of the anointing of Jesus by a woman (Luke 7:36-38; John 12:1-8). The words used are very similar but Luke said that the anointing was done by a prostitute in the house of a Pharisee while John said it was done by Mary, a close friend of Jesus, in her own house. The stories must have reached the evangelists either detached from their original setting or distorted by oral transmission. All these point to allied sources of oral transmission for Luke and John.[23]

EPISODES	LUKE	JOHN
1. There was a second Judas among the twelve.	6:16	14:22
2. The betrayal was Satan's entry into Judas Iscariot.	22:3	13:27
3. The slave lost his *right* ear in Gethsemane.	22:50	18:10
4. Pilate three times declared Jesus' innocence.	23:4,16,23	18:38;19:4,6
5. The tomb that Jesus was laid in had never been used.	23:53	19:41
6. *Two* angels appeared on the morning of the resurrection.	24:4	20:12
7. Jesus first resurrection appearance was in *Jerusalem*.	23:33-49	20:19-23
8. The miraculous catch of fish.	5:1-11	21:1-4
9. Jesus anointed by a woman.	7:36-38	12:1-8
10. Jesus' friendship with Mary and Martha.	10:38-42	11:1-44
11. The story of Lazarus.	16:19-31	11:44-47
12. Other disciples apart from the women who saw the tomb.	24:24	20:3-10

Table 9.5: Similarities between John and Luke[24]

THE AUTHOR OF MARK

We have seen above that Matthew and Luke were heavily dependent on the Gospel of Mark. Who was the author of the second gospel in the New Testament then? As we have seen in the previous chapter, Papias (c60 - c130), on the authority of one John the Presbyter, claimed that the author of this gospel was Mark, Peter's interpreter. Tradition has further tied this Mark to the John Mark mentioned in the Acts of the Apostles (Acts:12:12;13:5,13;15:37,39), the epistles of Paul (Colossians 4:10;II Timothy 4:11; Philemon 24:1) and the first epistle of Peter (I Peter 5:13). We note in Acts that it was to Mark's house in Jerusalem that Peter came after his escape from prison (Acts 12:12). Mark also joined Paul and Barnabas on their mission to Cyprus (Acts 12:25;13:15). Mark was also the center of disagreement between Paul and Barnabas; Paul not liking the fact that Mark deserted them in their mission in Cyprus earlier. Paul and Barnabas parted company with Mark going to Barnabas on another mission to Cyprus (Acts 15:37-39). We have seen from chapter 5 that I Peter was a late document and was not written by the apostle of that name. Yet by the time of its writing the tradition of the connection between Peter and John Mark was already so strong that Peter is made to call Mark his "son" (I Peter 5:13).[25]

---

23   Caird, *Saint Luke*: p20
24   Caird, *Saint Luke*: p20
25   Martin, *New Testament Foundations I*: p212

A closer examination of the gospel, however, shows that the traditional attribution of authorship to John Mark is *false*. The gospel contains numerous mistakes about Palestinian geography and customs which a native such as John Mark would not have made.

As our first example, consider this passage:

Mark 7:31 (RSV)[26]
Then he [Jesus] returned from the region of Tyre, and went *through* Sidon to the Sea of Galilee, through the region of the Decapolis.

There is no hint of any prolonged tour in the narrative. The verse above suggests that Sidon is between the road from Tyre to the Sea of Galilee. However, look at the map of Palestine in Figure 9.1 on the next page. The Sea of Galilee is to the *southeast* of Tyre while Sidon is to the *north* of the city. It is simply not possible to go *through* Sidon from Tyre to reach the Sea of Galilee. As David Barr, Professor of Religion at Wright State University remarked: "the itinerary sketched in 7:31 would be a little like going from New York to Washington, D.C. by way of Boston"! What is worse, it is a known historical fact that there was no direct road from Sidon to the Sea of Galilee during the first century CE. There was, however, one from Tyre to the Sea of Galilee.

There are thus two geographical errors in the above passage. Firstly, the author obviously does not know the relative positions of Sidon, Tyre and the Sea of Galilee. Secondly, he does not know that there was no direct road between Sidon and the Sea of Galilee during the time of Jesus. Such a widely traveled native of Palestine such as John Mark (as our New Testament sources assure us that he is) could not have made such a blatant mistake[27] about Palestinian geography.[28]

---

[26]   Modern translations such as the New Revised Standard Version (NRSV), the Revised Standard Version (RSV) the Good News Bible and even the fundamentalist New International Version (NIV) accurately translates the Greek as meaning Jesus went *through* Sidon. However, older versions of the Bible such as the King James Version (KJV) and the New King James Version (NKJV) have the passage translated thus:

> Mark 7:31 (KJV, ASV, WEB)
> And again, departing from the coasts of Tyre *and* Sidon, he came unto the Sea of Galilee...

With this reading the geographical error is eliminated. Unfortunately this reading is not supported by textual evidence. We have seen earlier that the Greek text on which the King James Version was based, the *Textus Receptus* [or the *Majority Text* in the case of the NKJV], was inaccurate in many places and is no longer used today as the underlying Greek text for modern translations.

[27]   Attempts by fundamentalists to explain this difficulty amount to no more than 'arguing from authority'. One example is Lee Strobel's fundamentalist bestseller *The Case for Christ*. In recounting his interview with John McRay (introduced with a "PhD" next to his name!), when the issue of Mark 7:31 was raised, all Strobel could muster to defend Biblical inerrancy here was simply to note that McRay "pulled a Greek version of Mark off his shelf" and opened "large maps of ancient Palestine" and then:

> Reading the text in the original language, taking into accounts the mountainous terrain and probable roads in the region...McRay traced a

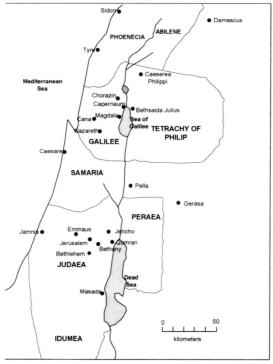

Figure 9.1: Palestine during the time of Jesus

Another mistake occurred in the episode on the healing of the demoniac. This incident occurred in the region of the Gerasenes, or Gerasa. Mark 5:1 makes Jesus cross the Sea of Galilee to reach Gerasa, implying that Gerasa was a city close to the lake:

Mark 5:1
They came to the other side of the sea, to the country of the Gerasenes.

Similarly in Mark 5:13 Jesus allowed the demons to leave the man and enter the herd of pigs nearby which then rushed headlong through a precipice into the lake:

---

logical route on the map corresponding precisely with Mark's description. "When everything is put into the appropriate context," he concluded, "there's no problem with Mark's account." [Strobel, *The Case for Christ*: p134]
And that's it! Without explaining how the route was "logical" and exactly what "Greek text" McRay read, this is supposed to convince readers that the problem is resolved! Needless to say this "argument" fails to convince skeptics.

28 Nineham, *Saint Mark*: p203
Wilson, *Jesus: The Evidence*: p34
Barr, *New Testament Story*: p240

Mark 5:13

At once Jesus gave them permission. The unclean spirits came out and entered into the pigs. The herd of about two thousand rushed down the steep bank into the sea, and they were drowned in the sea.

From these verses it is obvious that Mark meant Gerasa to be a town situated near the Sea of Galilee. However, look at the map in Figure 9.1 again. Gerasa is more than *thirty miles* to the southeast of the Sea of Galilee!! There is not even a hint of any lake nearby.[29] As the scholars of the Jesus Seminar so deliciously remarked:

> Gerasa is located approximately thirty miles to the southeast of the Sea of Galilee, not exactly a convenient location for the drowning of the pigs. Matthew relocates the demoniac to Gadara, which is only six miles from the lakeshore. Later scribes tried other remedies to accommodate the pigs.[30]

Again, such a basic mistake in Palestinian geography could not have been committed by a well-traveled native such as John Mark.[31]

Enough geography![32] Let us look at the mistakes in the second gospel about Jewish customs. Given below is an excerpt from Mark where Jesus is quoted as making some pronouncements on divorce:

---

[29] Again, fundamentalists have tried to rescue this. They point to an archaeological find. The ruins of a small town called Khersa (or Kursa or Kersa) , on the east coast of the Sea of Galilee, which according to Craig Blomberg (quoted in Strobel's *Case for Christ:* p60) could be the origin of the use of the name *Gerasa*. This explanation has two problems. Firstly, there are *no cliffs overhanging the lake* in this small town! This would be required for the pigs to jump down from. Secondly, as there *was* a town called Gerasa during the time of Jesus, Mark's use of this term, even if he had meant Khursa, would still imply that he was ignorant of Palestinian geography. [Nineham, *Saint Mark:* p153]

[30] Funk, et.al. *The Acts of Jesus:* p79

[31] Nineham, *Saint Mark:* p266
Wilson, *Jesus: The Evidence:* p34

[32] For those of you that need more of this, there are a few further examples of geographical errors in Mark:

- **Mark 8:22-26**: The pericopae of the healing of the blind man was mentioned by Mark to have occurred at Bethsaida, which he referred to as a "village". But it is well known that Bethsaida during the time of Jesus was a large and prosperous town. [Nineham, *Saint Mark:* p219]

- **Mark 10:1**: Jesus is supposed to have gone from Capernaum to the territory of Judea and "across the Jordan" river. As the reader can see by looking at the map in figure 6.1, the statement by Mark is geographically problematic. Firstly, none of Judea is to the east of Jordan (which would be what "across the Jordan" from Capernaum would mean). Secondly, to get from Capernaum to Judea, Jesus would have had to cross the Jordan twice (avoiding the traditionally antagonistic Samaritans) or not at all (directly southwards through Samaria). The passage implies a single crossing, leading him nowhere. [Funk, et.al. *The Acts of Jesus:* p111; Nineham, *Saint Mark:* p63]

Mark 10:11-12
He [Jesus] said to them, "Whoever divorces his wife, and marries another, commits adultery against her. If a woman herself divorces her husband, and marries another, she commits adultery."

Jesus last sentence implies that women had the right to divorce her husband. But according to Jewish law, a woman had no right of divorce whatsoever.[33] In Roman law a woman had that right. The author of Mark had simply and mistakenly assumed that this is so for Jewish law as well. Again, the author of Mark shows an ignorance of the conditions of Palestine which is really impossible for a native of the country to make.[34]

Another example of Mark's ignorance is from the explanation he included for his readers regarding ritual cleansing:

Mark 7:3-4
For the Pharisees, and all the Jews, don't eat unless they wash their hands and forearms, holding to the tradition of the elders. They don't eat when they come from the marketplace, unless they bathe themselves, and there are many other things, which they have received to hold to: washings of cups, pitchers, bronze vessels, and couches.

This passage by Mark has been the subject of considerable debate among Jewish and Christian scholars. Jewish scholars have pointed out, based on the evidence of the *Talmuds*, that the washing of hands before meals was obligatory only on priests and not on lay people like the Pharisees and scribes. While it may be possible that some, or even many, Pharisees submitted to this ritual voluntarily, it is certainly cannot be said that *all the Jews* were following this. Thus Mark had made a mistake in generalizing a custom that was simply not practiced by all during the time of Jesus.[35]

The above errors in Palestinian geography and Jewish customs should rule out John Mark as the author of Mark. The evidence also rules out Papias' story of the author's close relation with Peter and that he wrote down what Peter said. Peter could hardly have made the mistakes we have seen above. In short, like so many books in the Bible, we do not know the identity of the author of Mark. As early as Papias' time (early second century) the real author was no longer known. Of course, as we mentioned in the previous chapter, the author *could* have been named Mark, as it was an exceedingly common name in those days. But we know nothing of him.[36]

- **Mark 11:1**: The passage has Jesus traveling from Jericho (Mark 10:46) *via* Bethpage and Bethany when it should have been in reverse order. We treat this particular error in more detail in chapter 14.

[33] It is pointless to say that Jesus was instituting divorce for women, as his whole pronouncement is one that is geared against divorce in general.

[34] Nineham, *Saint Mark*: p266
Wilson, *Jesus: The Evidence*: p34

[35] Nineham, *Saint Mark*: p193

[36] Kummel, *Introduction to the New Testament*: p97
Martin, *New Testament Foundations I*: p213

If the author of Mark was neither an eyewitness nor a follower of an eyewitness, how did he get his material? The structure of the gospel reveals to us how he got this. With a few exceptions, the episodes in Mark seem to be completely *independent* units. In Mark the different episodes are attached together by link passages that are normally one or two sentences long. As an example of this, let us look at chapter three of this gospel which contains five separate episodes.

Link Passages	Episodes
Mark 3:1	Mark 3:2-6
He entered again into the synagogue…	[Healing of the shriveled hand]
Mark 3:7	Mark 3:8-12
Jesus withdrew to the sea …	[Healing of the multitudes]
Mark 3:13	Mark 3:14-19a
He went up into the mountain…	[Appointment of the 12 apostles]
Mark 3:19b	Mark 3:20-30
He came into a house…	[Answering the scribes]
Mark 3:31	Mark 3:31-35
His mother and his brothers came…	[Renunciation of his family]

Table 9:6 Isolated Episodes in Mark 3

The one noticeable thing from a reading of Mark 3 is how isolated from each other the episodes were. The link passages "He entered…the synagogue", "he withdrew to the lake," "he went up the mountain" etc., mean that there is no organic connection between one episode and another. Jesus could, after all, "withdrew to the lake" and *then* "entered the synagogue" later. The order of the episodes could easily be interchanged without doing any damage to the narrative as a whole. There is no organic connection between the separate incidents. They are almost like snapshots placed side by side in a photo album.

This very strongly suggests that the stories relating to Jesus came to Mark in isolated anecdotes from separate sources. Where could these stories come from? It is very probable that most of these stories were circulated orally among the followers of Jesus. Some of the episodes were probably even used in the worship of the early Christians and were written down earlier. The Gospel of Mark therefore is, more likely than not, the compilation of the early Christian community tradition about Jesus.[37]

We have demonstrated that both Matthew and Luke copied extensively from Mark. We have also shown that the author of Mark displayed ignorance of Palestinian geography and culture that rule out the author being a native of that country. We have also shown that the mistakes committed in Mark were very unlikely to have come from Peter, as it would have been if the tradition that Peter was the direct source behind this gospel was correct. We can conclude that the author is neither an eyewitness, nor a native of Palestine nor even a close acquaintance of an apostle. He was at least three times removed from the original eyewitnesses (i.e. eyewitnesses - oral tradition - written sources – Gospel of Mark).

---

[37]   Nineham, *Saint Mark*: p27-28

THE AUTHOR OF MATTHEW

Our finding that the author of the second gospel was not Mark, the interpreter for Peter, has immediate implications for the authorship of Matthew.

We have already shown earlier that the Gospel of Matthew is an anonymous work. Nowhere in the gospel does the author identify himself. As we have seen from the previous chapter, Papias' witness cannot be used to claim that the name Matthew was already attached to the first gospel by 130 and that the first unambiguous attribution of its authorship to the apostle Matthew cannot be traced earlier than Irenaeus in 180.

Today it is considered a settled issue among critical historical scholars that author of the first gospel, whoever he was, was *definitely not* the apostle Matthew.[38] (For ease of reference we will continue to refer to this "anonymous author of the third gospel" as "Matthew.") Let us review the reasons for this.

Matthew's Use of Mark

The most important issue is in Matthew's use of Mark. We have demonstrated above that Matthew copied extensively from the second gospel in the canon. We have also shown that the author of the Gospel of Mark was neither an eyewitness, nor a native of Palestine nor even a close acquaintance of an apostle. Thus the reliance of a supposed eyewitness (the apostle Matthew) on the accounts of a non-eyewitness (the anonymous author of Mark) at least three times removed from the original eyewitnesses is, in the words of Raymond E. Brown, a conservative Catholic theologian, simply "implausible."[39]

The changes in details that Matthew made of Mark are not those that an eyewitness would make. The changes betray an author with a theological agenda. As J.C. Fenton noted in his commentary on Matthew:

> [A] study of Matthew's use of his sources does not show us a man correcting one
> source from first hand knowledge of events. In the author of this Gospel, we have

---

[38]   Barr, *New Testament Story*: p277
Bentley, *Secrets of Mount Sinai*: p142
Brown, *An Introduction to the New Testament*: p210-211
Ehrmann, *The New Testament*: p84
Kümmel, *Introduction to the New Testament*: p120-121
Mack, *Who Wrote the New Testament?*: p162
Martin, *New Testament Foundations* I: p238-240
Parmalee, *Guidebook to the Bible*: p103
Schenelle, *The New Testament Writings*: p219-220
Wilson, *Jesus: The Evidence*: p34

[39]   Brown, *An Introduction to the New Testament*: p210-211
Ehrmann, *The New Testament*: p84
Kümmel, *Introduction to the New Testament*: p120-121
Schenelle, *The New Testament Writings*: p219-220

an editor, an arranger of material, rather than someone who is revising in the light of accurate historical information.[40]

Let us take a few examples here. The most obvious is in the call to discipleship of Matthew.

> Mark 2:14-15 (Luke 5:27-29)
> As he passed by, he saw Levi, the son of Alphaeus, sitting at the tax office, and he said to him, "Follow me." And he arose and followed him. It happened, that he was reclining at the table in his house, and many tax collectors and sinners sat down with Jesus and his disciples, for there were many, and they followed him.

> Matthew 9:9-10
> As Jesus passed by from there, he saw a man called Matthew sitting at the tax collection office. He said to him, "Follow me." He got up and followed him. It happened as he sat in the house, behold, many tax collectors and sinners came and sat down with Jesus and his disciples.

Note that the *only change* is the name of the person from Levi to Matthew. If the Gospel of Matthew really was written by the apostle of that name, one would expect a vivid eyewitness account of his own personal call to discipleship. Yet, all we have is a slavish and wooden word-for-word copying of Mark. This is, according to Bart Ehrman, "difficult to believe" if the author was actually Matthew.[41]

Furthermore, many of the actual changes the author of Matthew made to the accounts in Mark is done not for providing a more vivid eyewitness account but done in order to show that the events in the life of Jesus fulfill prophecy. Let us look at a couple of examples. In the episode on the triumphal entry, Mark (11:1-11) [also Luke 19:29-35 and John 12:12-16] had Jesus entering Jerusalem riding on a young donkey. Matthew (21:1-7) had Jesus perform the impossible task of sitting on *two* donkeys! This could not have been an eyewitness account. The change was made because the author of this gospel misunderstood Zechariah 9:9 to mean that Jesus *had* to ride in on two donkeys.[42] Similarly in the crucifixion scene, his changing Mark's (15:23) *myrrh* to *gall* (Matthew 27:34) was clearly done to "fulfill" an Old Testament prophecy (Psalm 69:21).[43]

Another important piece of evidence is the case of the story of John the Baptist's martyrdom. The story is told in Mark 6:17-30 but retroactively. This can be seen from Mark 6:14-16 where Herod feared that Jesus was John the Baptist raised from the dead. The story that followed this retroactive tale was the feeding of the 5,000 (Mark 6:31-44) which chronologically follows Herod's hearing about Jesus (Mark 6:14). Matthew's fondness for adding connective links between the individual episodes provided in Mark led him to make a mistake here. Although he copied Mark's remark about Herod having already killed John (Matthew 14:2), he did not notice that in Mark the feeding of the 5,000 did not take place immediately after John was buried,

---

40   Fenton, *Saint Matthew*: p14
41   Ehrmann, *The New Testament*: p84
42   We will discuss this alleged acrobatic feat of Jesus sitting simultaneously on two donkeys in chapter 14.
43   Fenton, *Saint Matthew*: p18

but later than that and therefore erroneously added the connecting link "Now when Jesus heard this [about the burial of John], he withdrew from there in a boat to a lonely place apart." (Matthew 14:13). This was the beginning of the feeding of the 5,000 in Mark. Any eyewitness would never have made such a mistake. But a non-eyewitness hurriedly copying his source certainly could![44]

The Form, Content and Structure

Many other details in the gospels exclude the possibility that its author was the apostle Matthew.

- Both the Greek literary style and the gospel's use of earlier Greek sources (Mark and Q) means that the gospel was originally written in Greek; something unlikely to have come from a Palestinian Jew like Matthew.[45]

- As many scholars have pointed out the structural form of the gospel is systematic and artificial. Matthew had essentially inserted five chunks of sayings materials (Matthew Chapters: 5-7; 9-10; 13; 18; 23-25), mostly from Q, into the Markan narrative. Such a structure is non-biographical and weighs against the gospel being the work of an eyewitness.[46]

- The theology in *Matthew* is such that would be relevant only to Christians living around the turn of the first century. For instance his emphasis on church discipline (Matthew 18:15-20) does not make sense within the context of the times of Jesus. This makes sense only at a time when the church was more fully developed.[47]

Conclusion on the Authorship of Matthew

The first gospel in the canon could not have been written by the apostle Matthew because:

- It relied heavily on the work of a non-eyewitness (Mark).

- The changes it made to the accounts in Mark are not what one would expect from an eyewitness.

- It was written in Greek and relied on Greek sources (Mark and Q)

---

[44] Kümmel, *Introduction to the New Testament*: p107
[45] Koester, *Ancient Christian Gospels*: p316-318
      Kümmel, *Introduction to the New Testament*: p121
      Sanders & Davies, *Studying the Synoptic Gospels*: p10
[46] Ehrmann, *The New Testament*: p253
      Fenton, *Saint Matthew*: p15
      Kümmel, *Introduction to the New Testament*: p106-107, 121
[47] Kümmel, *Introduction to the New Testament*: p121
      Martin, *New Testament Foundations* I: p242

- Its structure is artificial and speaks against it being autobiographical.

- Its theology is more suited to the situation facing the church around 80-100 CE.

THE AUTHOR OF LUKE-ACTS

Since it is generally accepted by most scholars that the Gospel of Luke and the Acts of the Apostles were written by the same person, we will be searching for the identity of the author by looking at the evidence in these two books of the New Testament. We will follow scholarly convention and use the term "Luke-Acts" to refer to these two books together.

We have seen from chapter 8 that the name "Luke" was first attached to the third gospel relatively late; in 180 CE by Irenaeus. It was also Irenaeus who first guessed that Luke was the author based on the "we-passages" found in Acts and linking it with three verses in the Pauline epistles that mentioned a "Luke" who was a physician and Paul's travel companion. The traditional claim of Lukan authorship therefore rests on three assertions:

- That Paul had a constant traveling companion named Luke.

- That Acts shows evidence of being written by a close companion of Paul (whoever he or she is).

- That the "we-passages" *prove* the case that what we have is the eyewitness accounts of a traveling companion.

We will look at these three points in order.

Luke as Paul's Constant Traveling Companion

Luke was referred to in three verses in the Pauline corpus. These are:

Colossians 4:10-14
Aristarchus, my fellow prisoner, greets you, and Mark, the cousin of Barnabas (concerning whom you received commandments, "if he comes to you, receive him"), and Jesus who is called Justus, *who are of the circumcision.* These are my only fellow workers for the Kingdom of God, men who have been a comfort to me. Epaphras, who is one of you, a servant of Christ, salutes you, always striving for you in his prayers, that you may stand perfect and complete in all the will of God. For I testify about him, that he has great zeal for you, and for those in Laodicea, and for those in Hierapolis. *Luke, the beloved physician,* and Demas greet you.

II Timothy 4:10-11
Demas left me, having loved this present world, and went to Thessalonica; Crescens to Galatia, and Titus to Dalmatia. *Only Luke is with me.* Take Mark, and bring him with you, for he is useful to me for service.

Philemon 1:23-24
Epaphras, my fellow prisoner in Christ Jesus, greets you, as do Mark, Aristarchus, Demas, and *Luke,* my fellow workers.

Note that *everything* that is normally mentioned about Luke is given in these three passages. The fact that he was a Gentile is derived from the fact that in Colossians Luke was named after the men "*who are of circumcision*" were introduced: implying that Epaphras, Luke and Demas were Gentiles. We are also told there that he was a physician. In II Timothy, which is set during Paul's imprisonment in Rome (II Timothy 1:16-17), we are told that "only Luke" is with Paul. In other words, we are told that he was with him till (near) the end. In Philemon, we are simply introduced to Luke as a "fellow worker" of Paul.[48]

However, the derivation of information about Luke from these Pauline epistles is of dubious value. II Timothy is almost universally regarded by critical-historical scholars as a "pseudepigrapha" or, to put in bluntly, a *forgery*: a document written by someone else *pretending* to be Paul.[49] Similarly, a substantial majority of scholars also think that Colossians is pseudepigraphical.[50]

Thus the only certain information we have about Luke is that of Philemon 1:23-24. Here all we know is that Paul referred to Luke as a "fellow worker". We do not know if he was a Gentile, or that he was a physician or that he traveled frequently with Paul. All these additional "facts" are derivable only from Colossians and II Timothy, and since these are forgeries, we are in no position to know how reliable they are as far as Paul's companions were concerned.[51]

Thus the name "Luke" is only one of the names of the many people who were, either occasionally or often, with Paul during some of his missionary work. There is no way to single out that name as *the* companion who wrote Luke-Acts.

The Author of Luke-Acts as a Traveling Companion of Paul

Whatever the case may be with regards to the name or identity of the author, can it at least be concluded that the author *must* have been a companion of Paul? No. A number of factual errors in Acts which weigh heavily against the author being a companion of Paul:[52]

- There are a number of serious discrepancies in the portrayal of Paul in Acts and what we can derive from his authentic epistles. Here we will give a summary of some of the major points:

    o **Number of trips Paul made to Jerusalem**

---

[48]   Ehrmann, *The New Testament*: p138
        Kümmel, *Introduction to the New Testament*: p180-184
        Schnelle: *The New Testament Writings*: p240-242
[49]   See chapter 5.
[50]   Brown, *An Introduction to the New Testament*: p610, 675
        Ehrmann, *The New Testament*: p138
        Schnelle, *The New Testament Writings*: p240-242
[51]   Akenson, *Saint Saul*: p135-136
        Ehrmann, *The New Testament*: p138
[52]   Ehrmann, *The New Testament.*: p262-265
        Kummel, *Introduction to the New Testament*: p180-184
        Schnelle, *The New Testament Writings*: p240-242

Acts say five, Paul noted only three (Acts 9, 11, 15, 18:22, 21 versus Galatians 1:18, 2:1 and the (planned) visit to Jerusalem in Romans: 15:25).

○ **Paul's first meeting with the apostles**

Paul mentioned that he only visited the apostles in Jerusalem three years after his conversion (Galatians 1:16-19) but the narrative in Acts showed that he went to Jerusalem a short time after his conversion. (Acts 9:1-26)

○ **Paul in Jerusalem**

According to Acts, Paul took an active part in the execution of Stephen in Jerusalem (Acts 7:58, 8:3) where he would certainly have been seen by at least some Christians there. Yet Paul in Galatians 1:22 mentioned that when he visited Jerusalem for the first time after his conversion he was "still unknown by sight to the Churches of Judea."

○ **Paul as a miracle worker**

Acts portrayed Paul as a miracle-worker (Acts 13:6-12; 14:8-10; 20:7-2). Yet Paul's epistle do not contain much claim of miracle working and in the rare case where it is raised, it seems to be mentioned in a clearly defensive tone (II Corinthians 12:1-12) - implying that the criticism of his opponents was that his miracles were not impressive.

○ **Paul as an outstanding orator**

In Acts Paul is portrayed as an outstanding orator able to command the attention of philosophers, unruly crowds and Roman prosecutors alike. (Acts 17:22-31 21:40-22:21; 24:1-21) Yet Paul admitted that he had been criticized of having "weak bodily presence" whose speech making skills was of "no account" (II Corinthians 10:10).

○ **Paul as an apostle**

Paul presented himself as an apostle (I Corinthians 9:1-3; Galatians 2:8). Acts give the criteria to be an apostle to include being one of the twelve and having eaten and drunk with the risen Jesus (Acts 1:21-25; 10:41) - thus leaving Paul out.

○ **Paul's attitude towards the law**

Acts portrayed Paul as a loyal and practicing Jew. (e.g. Acts 16:1-3; 16:4; 18:18;18:21, 20:16) Yet in his epistles Paul's position on the law is more complicated (I Corinthians 9:21; Galatians 2:1-6, 11-14; 2:21, 5:4 Philippians 3:5-9)

• In Acts 15:2-21 James was portrayed as the mediator between Paul and the Pharisees but in Paul's own account (Galatians 2:9) James was placed squarely on the side which opposes Paul.

• Acts 10:1-11:18 stated that the mission to the Gentiles was started by Peter, yet in Galatians 2:1-10 Paul is called to defend his mission to the Gentiles against the "three pillars" (James, John and *Peter*). Why would he have to defend a mission to the Gentiles when Peter had already started it?

These mistakes *rule out* the possibility that the author personally knew the apostle to the Gentiles.

The "We-Passages" in Acts

Now if the author of Luke-Acts was not a companion of Paul how do we explain the so-called "we-passages" (Acts 16:10-17; 20:5-15, 21:1-8 and 27:1-28:16)? Let us begin by taking a look at one such passage:

> Acts 20:37-21:1
> They all wept a lot, and fell on *Paul's* neck and kissed him, sorrowing most of all because of the word which *he* had spoken, that they should see *his* face no more. And they accompanied *him* to the ship. When it happened that *we* had parted from them and had set sail, *we* came with a straight course to Cos, and the next day to Rhodes, and from there to Patara.

Probably desensitized by biblical narratives, we no longer notice how *odd* the above passage actually is. The third person singular ("Paul", "he") shifts suddenly and without warning into a first person plural ("we"), the moment the sea voyage starts. One would expect, perhaps something more natural like, "Paul came to the ship and I, with the other brothers, were waiting for him and we set sail". Instead the change happens in midstream, as it were. [53]

As Stanley E. Porter, Professor of New Testament at McMaster Divinity College, admits:

> An admitted difficulty for any analysis of the book of Acts, it must be conceded, is that *there is apparently no significant parallel yet found* in any major Greek historian, including earlier classical authors and the later Oxyrhynchus historian, that evidences a similar use of anonymous first person plural embedded within a third person narrative. [54] [Emphasis added]

This means that far from *proving* that the author of Luke-Acts was a companion of Paul, the way in which the "we-passages" are embedded within Acts is actually quite *puzzling*. There is something artificial about the whole construct.

Note that the "we-passages" in Acts are limited only to stories which involve *travel by sea*. It would indeed be strange if the author was only present during sea voyages and nowhere else in Paul's ministry.

In an important paper, Vernon Robbins[55] showed that there was *a literary convention* at the time Acts was written. Although, in general, historiographical writing was done in an informal third person (i.e. "he," they," "Paul" etc), this changed when scenes relating to sea voyages were involved. With examples from Mediterranean literature (Roman and Greek) around the time of the writing of *Luke-*

---

[53]   Ehrmann, *The New Testament*: p138-139
[54]   Porter, *Paul in Acts*: p23-24
[55]   Vernon Robbins, "By Land and By Sea: The We-Passages and Ancient Sea Voyages", *Perspective in Luke-Acts*, Charles Talbert (ed) 1978

Acts, Robbins showed that the "we-passages" is a stylistic device designed to add vividness and excitement to the account of sea voyages.

One of the examples Robbins amassed is the tale of *The Voyage of Hanno the Carthaginian* (c third or second cent BCE). Note how the narration starts in the third person and then shifts abruptly to the first person plural when the sea voyage starts:

> The Carthaginians decided that *Hanno* should go past the Pillars and found Carthaginian cities. *He* set sail with sixty pentekontas (fifty-oared ships) carrying thirty thousand men and women with provisions and other necessities. After passing the Pillars of Hercules and sailing for two days beyond them *we* founded the first city, which was named Thymiaterion.[56]

Thus the use of the first person plural *may* mean the author of the narrative was present during the events described but *it could also equally mean that he was not*.[57] For our purposes here, we can say that the "we" in the "we-passages" can no longer be straightforwardly used as evidence that the author was a travel companion of Paul.[58]

It remains to be explained why not *all* the accounts of sea voyages in Luke-Acts are in the first person plural (e.g. Acts 13:13). Marrianne Bonz, managing editor of *Harvard Theological Review*, has argued in her book *The Past as Legacy: Luke-Acts and the Ancient Epic* that the "we-passages" serves an important rhetorical function. They begin only *after* the Jerusalem council (15:22-29) where, significantly, full equality was given to Gentiles. The whole of Acts now move away from a focus on Jerusalem and the Jewish Christian church towards the Gentile mission. As Bonz continues:

> Once introduced the "we" group serves as a peripheral or vicarious participant in all of the elements of Paul's active ministry: proclamation [e.g. Acts 16:13], the breaking of bread [Acts 20:7] and its salvific results - even acceptance by James and the body of Jerusalem elders [Acts 21:17-18]. Most importantly the group accompanies Paul to Rome [Acts 28:16], the dramatic climax of the narrative journey and the geographical and theological symbol of the fulfillment of the missionary prophecy.

---

[56] Text from Wilfred Schoff's *The Periplus of Hanno* 1912
(www.barca.fsnet.co.uk/**hanno**-voyage.htm accessed on May 5, 2003)

[57] Predictably, Vernon Robbin's paper has been criticized quite extensively by conservative theologians. Their criticisms have normally centered on the claim that the parallels presented by Robbins are "somewhat inexact" (Joseph Fitzmeyer) or "not similar enough" (Stanley E. Porter). Yet as we see in Porter's admission above, there exist *no parallel at all* with any historiographical work of an anonymous eyewitness who shifts from third person to first person singular without explanation. It is important to note that Fitzmeyer, despite his criticism, did not dismiss the existence of such a literary convention altogether. [Ref: Porter, *Paul in Acts*: p23-24, Powell, *What are they saying about Acts?*: p34]

[58] Barr, *New Testament Story*: p324
Mack, *Who Wrote the New Testament*: p230-231
Schenelle, *The New Testament Writings*: p267-268
Wells, *The Historical Evidence for Jesus*: p146-149

The "we" passages do not represent historical, eyewitness accounts...the "we" references serve as a rhetorical shorthand for the Pauline Christians - those who are vicariously privy to Paul's example and who, as heirs to his legacy, have been called by him to continue his unfinished mission. They are Luke's intended audience, whose participation of the ongoing drama of God's salvation plan is signaled by the words of the Lukan prologue: "concerning the events that have been fulfilled *among us*." [Luke 1:1][59]
[Verses from Luke and Acts added - PT]

Vernon Robbins reached more or less the same conclusion in his paper. Thus we can discern the reasons why "we" was used in those passages in Acts. Firstly, by using a literary convention it adds "vividness" to the picture and secondly, since the "we" meant, like "us" in Luke 1:1, the Gentile Christians, the "we" function as a metaphor representing Gentile Christians in their spiritual journey. Therefore, the presence of the "we-passages" in Acts cannot be used against the evidence we have seen earlier that the author of Acts could not have been a companion of Paul.

Conclusion on the Authorship of Luke-Acts

The evidence speaks against Luke as the author of Luke-Acts:

- A "Luke" is referenced only once in the genuine Pauline epistles, and all we know of him is that he was a "fellow worker" of Paul. Every other bit of information about him: that he was a Gentile, a physician and a constant companion of Paul came from the two spurious epistles and cannot be confidently counted as historical.

- The mistakes in historical events and discrepancies of the portrayal of Paul (when compared to the Pauline epistles) specifically excludes a companion of Paul (whoever he may be) as the author of Luke-Acts.

- The "we-passages" do not imply the writing of an eyewitness. Its form (switching from third person to first person plural) is puzzling and there is no known historical parallel outside the genre of sea-voyage narratives. The best explanation is that it was used as a rhetorical shorthand for "all Gentile Christians".

THE GOSPEL OF JOHN

The Gospel of John differs from the synoptics in many substantial ways. It recounts stories about Jesus that does not appear in the other three. Its whole framework of Jesus' ministry also differs substantially from the synoptics. In the synoptics, Jesus ministry begins only after John the Baptist was imprisoned (Mark 1:14; Matthew 4:12), John showed the two prophets preaching together (John 3:24). While the synoptics timetable of Jesus' ministry can be fitted into a single year, John makes the ministry last for three years (according to the fourth gospel, Jesus celebrated the Passover with his disciples thrice: John 2:13; 6:4; 11:55). The synoptics identified

---

59   Bonz, *The Past as Legacy:* p173

Galilee as the main location of Jesus' ministry. John placed Jerusalem as the principle location. The synoptics recorded only a single trip to Jerusalem by Jesus while John had him going to the holy city five times (John 2:13; 5:1; 7:10; 10:22; 12:1).[60]

Even the figure of Jesus presented in John is different, and indeed irreconcilable, with that presented in the synoptics. The Jesus of history was a Jew, but the Jesus presented in John does not sound like one. The Jewish scholar, Hyam Maccoby (b.1924) sums this up very nicely:

> In the synoptics' account Jesus is still a recognizably Jewish figure, sparing in words and human and concrete in approach; in John, Jesus has become a Greek: voluble, full of abstractions, mystical.[61]

Not only is Jesus presented in the Gospel of John as a non-Jew, he is even recognizably anti-Jewish. In his debates with "the Jews" he called them the sons of the devil (John 8:43) and speaks of Jewish Law as "your Law" as though it wasn't his. (John 8:17)[62]

His method of preaching is also different. Whereas in the synoptics he preaches in parables and in short compact sayings, in John the method is with long discourses. If one were to read only the Gospel of John one would never guess that the parable was a common method in Jesus' teachings (John 20:2-6 being a rare example).[63]

In the synoptics we find that Jesus kept his messiahship a secret at the beginning only to reveal it after Peter's confession at Ceasarea Phillipi (Mark 8:27-30; Matthew 16: 13-20; Luke 9:18-21) but in John his special status is made known almost from the beginning. In John, Jesus calls himself "The resurrection and the life", "the bread of life" (John 6:35) and "the light of the world" (John 8:12). There is no such utterance attributed to Jesus in the synoptics.[64]

The chronological order in the fourth gospel is irreconcilable with that given in the synoptics. One example is an incident that is given in all four gospels: the Cleansing of the Temple (Mark 11:12-19; Matthew 21:12-13; Luke 19:45-48; John 2:12-22). The story involves Jesus and the merchants and moneychangers outside the temple. The merchants actually serve a useful function for the Jewish temple worship. Jewish Law specified that, in certain cases, a worshipper could bring an offering of doves (Leviticus 12:8; 14:22). The moneychangers provide Jewish pilgrims from foreign lands clean money for payment of the temple tax (Exodus 30:13ff). Jesus was, for some reason, angry at these merchants and called them robbers (Mark 11:17). John describes the subsequent happening:

---

60   Guignebert, *Jesus*: p27
      Martin, *New Testament Foundations I*: p271
61   Maccoby, *Revolution in Judea*: p245-246
62   Wilson, *Jesus: The Evidence*: p42
63   Livingstone, *Dictionary of the Christian Church*: p275
      Mack, *Who Wrote the New Testament*: p177
64   Davidson & Leaney, *Biblical Criticism*: p266
      Martin, *New Testament Foundations I*: p280

John 2: 15-16
He [Jesus] made a whip of cords, and threw all out of the temple, both the sheep and the oxen; and he poured out the changers' money, and overthrew their tables. To those who sold the doves, he said, "Take these things out of here! Don't make my Father's house a marketplace!"

This event must have caused quite a commotion and could not have failed to produce unpleasant consequences for the Galilean prophet. In the synoptics, Jesus was dead within a week of the incident. John incomprehensibly placed this event in the *beginning* of Jesus' ministry; and made him preach for another three years with impunity![65]

That he makes use of traditional material cannot be denied: the parallel episodes found in both John and Luke and the story of the cleansing of the Temple above, among others, should be sufficient to prove this. But John did not faithfully transmit these traditional stories but used them to weave his own theology. Take for instance this saying of Jesus:

John 8:12
Again, therefore, Jesus spoke to them, saying, "I am the light of the world. He who follows me will not walk in the darkness, but will have the light of life."

The reader should try and imagine being present in this scene where the Galilean prophet was uttering this statement about himself. The scene would be unbelievable, and the prophet will look like one on the verge of insanity. The sayings put into the mouth of Jesus by John are too unrealistic for it to have ever been uttered. G.A. Wells showed how these statements could have been invented by John. There is some traditional material about discipleship, typified by Peter's statement that he has left everything to follow Jesus. (Mark 10:28). There is also another passage from the Old Testament:

Isaiah 9:2
The people who walked in darkness have seen a great light. Those who lived in the land of the shadow of death, on them the light has shined.

Thus, John used fragments from tradition and scriptures (i.e. the Old Testament) and weaved them together with his own theological imagination.[66]

In summary, John's material differs substantially from the synoptics and all the evidence points to his changing his sources freely with none of the (relative) restraint we see in the synoptics. As Marcello Craveri aptly puts it:

The fourth gospel is of exceedingly little worth as a historical document and the Christian theologians themselves describe it as "pneumatic"-that is, spiritual-Gospel because it can be accepted only as a philosophical Christological dissertation.[67]

---

[65]   Guignebert, *Jesus*: p418
[66]   Wells, *Historical Evidence for Jesus*: p130
[67]   Craveri, *The Life of Jesus*: p312

We have discussed the Gospel of John at considerable length. It is now time to pause a little and consider the implications of our findings. In the synoptics we note that Mark very probably depended on traditional material. Both Luke and Matthew, while allowing themselves some artistic and theological license, generally tried to preserve the witness of their sources, be it Mark or Q. We do not find this in John. He uses the traditional material rather freely and disagrees on many points with the synoptics. Thus it should be concluded here, as do the majority of critical historical scholars,[68] that John, as an historical source for the life of Jesus, is the least reliable of the four gospels. In the discussions of the historical evidence for Jesus in this book John will be used rather sparingly and when it is quoted, a higher level of skepticism must be applied to it.

THE AUTHOR OF JOHN

Who was the author of *John*? Tradition has it that it was written by the apostle John, the son of Zebedee, who is identified with "the beloved disciple" mentioned on at least four occasions in the gospel (John 13:23-25; 19:26f, 20:2-8 and 21:7f). This would make the gospel an eyewitness account. However, several considerations show that this attribution is extremely improbable.

Firstly, it is important to note that nowhere in the 20 chapters of the gospel is the author identified with anyone named John.

Secondly, the identity of John, son of Zebedee with the person referred to as "the beloved disciple" is based primarily on parallel passages in the synoptics. For instance it is argued that John is depicted as Peter's companion in Acts (Acts 1:13; 3:1-4; 3:11; 4:13; 4:19; 8:14), the beloved disciple also appears with Peter in the fourth gospel (John 13:23-25; 20:2-8, 21:21-23 and, possibly, 18:15f). [69]

Appealing to parallel passages in the synoptics cuts both ways. For there are many parallel scenes in the synoptics in which the beloved disciple is *not* mentioned when we would have expected him to be, given the importance of his role depicted in the fourth gospel. These episodes are the last supper, the crucifixion and the empty tomb.

In the last supper, Peter is made to ask the "beloved disciple" to inquire from Jesus who the traitor was after Jesus revealed that it will be one of the twelve (John 13:18-26). The incident, as described in the other gospels had the disciples inquiring among themselves who the betrayer was (Mark 14:19; Matthew 26:22; Luke 22:23).

In the scene of the crucifixion, Jesus is said to have handed his mother to the care of the "beloved disciple" (John 19:25-27). This episode is nowhere to be found in any of the synoptics' account of the crucifixion. Indeed, we are explicitly told by Mark that "*all* of them (Jesus' disciples) deserted him and fled" (Mark 14:50).

---

68   Lüdemann, *Jesus After 2000 Years*: p416
      Sanders, *The Historical Figure of Jesus*: p57, 72-73
69   John 18:15-16 mentioned an unnamed "the other disciple, who was known to the chief priest" who was with Peter outside the courtyard of the chief priest during the interrogation of Jesus. In the story of race to the empty tomb (John 20:2), "the other disciple" is identified as "the one whom Jesus loved". However, it is by no means clear that "the other disciple" at the empty tomb is to be identified with "the other disciple" at the courtyard of the high priest.

In the episode of the empty tomb, the "beloved disciple" is made to race Peter to the empty tomb and even outran him (John 20:3-5). Again, nowhere in the synoptics do we find the "beloved disciple" or anybody apart from the women (and Peter in Luke 24:12) to have seen the empty tomb. This episode provides a clue as to how the stories concerning the beloved disciple are constructed. In the episode on the resurrection, John's account is very similar to Luke's where Peter, alone, ran to the tomb after hearing the news from Mary Magdalene (Luke 24:12). The expression in John 20:3 was "Peter went forth". The verb here is singular in Greek and seems to show that John's traditional material only has Peter alone running to the tomb. But the evangelist clumsily adds "and the other disciple, and they went toward the tomb." Far from being an eyewitness account, this shows that the character of the "beloved disciple" is merely an impromptu insertion by the author into his traditional source material.[70]

There is a passage in the fourth gospel that would also seem to *exclude* John, the son of Zebedee as the "beloved disciple". Recall that sometimes the "beloved disciple" is also referred to as "the other disciple" and is never named (e.g. 21:21-23 and, possibly, 18:15f). If this indeed is an alternate designation, then the disciples who were present during the resurrection appearance at the Sea of Tiberias were given in John 21:2 as Peter, Nathaniel, *the sons of Zebedee* and two "other disciples". Given the premise of not naming the beloved disciple, it is more probable that he was among the "two other disciples" than one of the sons of Zebedee.

We should also note, for what it is worth, that Acts 4:13 mentioned John (with Peter) to be "uneducated and ordinary" which, according to Bart Ehrman, means that he was *illiterate*.[71] It is unlikely that John the son of Zebedee, an illiterate Galilean fisherman, could have produced such a theological work.

Thirdly, the gospel is anonymous for the first 20 chapters. It also seems probable that this chapter was the end of the original gospel, as the following verse testifies:

John 20:30-31
Therefore Jesus did many other signs in the presence of his disciples, which are not written in this book; but these are written, that you may believe that Jesus is the Christ, the Son of God, and that believing you may have life in his name.

This sounds very much like a concluding paragraph of the gospel. Prior to this point, no claim is made that the beloved disciple himself wrote the gospel. Indeed, one passage seems to explicitly rule him out as the direct author of the gospel:

John 19:35
He who has seen has testified, and his testimony is true. He knows that he tells the truth, that you may believe.

---

[70] Culpepper, *John*: p72-76
Kümmel, *Introduction to the New Testament*: p234-236
Marsh, *Saint John*: p23-24
Wells, *Historical Evidence for Jesus*: p128-129
[71] Ehrman, *The New Testament: A Historical Introduction*: p.161

The "beloved disciple" was described earlier (John 19:26) as being the only disciple present at the crucifixion (besides the women), so it is reasonable to assume that "he" here refers to him. However, the third person construction of the sentence more naturally means that, whoever this disciple is, his *witness* is being claimed for the gospel *not* his authorship.

Chapter 21 restarts rather abruptly with: "Afterwards Jesus appeared again..." It is only here that the author is explicitly identified as the mysterious "beloved disciple":

> John 21:24
> This is the disciple who testifies about these things, and wrote these things. We know that his witness is true.

The first person plural "we" in the above verse, as well as the abrupt beginning mentioned earlier, show that chapter 21 is definitely a later addition to the gospel. And it is also clear that the beloved disciple had died when this chapter was written, as we can surmise from this passage:

> John 21:21-23
> Peter seeing him, said to Jesus, "Lord, what about this man?" Jesus said to him, "If I desire that he stay until I come, what is that to you? You follow me." This saying therefore went out among the brothers that this disciple wouldn't die. Yet Jesus didn't say to him that he wouldn't die, but, "If I desire that he stay until I come, what is that to you?"

The explanation provided in John 21:23 above only makes sense if the beloved disciple had already died when that passage was penned. Thus the claim that the "beloved disciple" wrote the gospel was made in a chapter that was definitely not written by him![72]

Even if we have shown that the author was not John the son of Zebedee, what about the claim that it was written by an, albeit anonymous, eyewitness? This is unlikely in the extreme, as Udo Schnelle, Professor of New Testament at Halle, Germany noted:

> The different way in which the life of Jesus is portrayed, the independent theology, the numerous special traditions and the thought world explicitly oriented to the post-Easter perspective point to the conclusion that the Fourth Gospel was not composed by an eyewitness of the life of Jesus. He was a *theologian of the later period* who, on the basis of comprehensive traditions, rethought the meaning of Jesus' life, and interpreted and presented it in his own way.[73]

We can now summarize the evidence *against* identifying the author of the fourth gospel as John, the son of Zebedee:

---

[72]   Brown, *An Introduction to the New Testament*: p369
Ehrman, *The New Testament*: p161
Kümmel, *Introduction to the New Testament:*: p234-236

[73]   Schnelle, *The History and Theology of the New Testament Writings*: p474

- Nowhere in the gospel is the author's name given as John.

- The identification of the "beloved disciple" with "John, the son of Zebedee" is false. The very method used for this - parallel passages in the synoptics - can be used to *exclude* the identification.

- There is no explicit claim, in the first 20 chapters, of any authorship by the "beloved disciple" whoever he was.

- The claim was made in chapter 21 was that of another hand and was penned after the death of the "beloved disciple".

- The *content* of the fourth gospel explicitly excludes it as an eyewitness account.

The author of John, like that of the three gospels, is therefore anonymous. We can be reasonably certain that it was *not* John the apostle.

* * * * *

We have looked at the internal evidence of gospel authorship. In each and every case we saw that the traditional attribution of these works to Mark, Matthew, Luke and John is spurious. The authors are unknown to us. We do know however, that they were not (otherwise anonymous) eyewitnesses and they recorded accounts that are a few times removed from the actual eyewitnesses.

Chapter Ten
DATING THE GOSPELS

NO DATES OF PUBLICATION

It is a pity that the gospels did not come with the dates of their publication as modern books do. In this chapter we will attempt to find approximate dates of composition for the four gospels based on external and internal clues. The external clues come from the attestations of the early church fathers and the earliest extant manuscript fragments. The original document had to have already been in existence earlier for it to be cited in the writings of a church father or for a copy of the manuscript to be made. Thus the external evidence provides us with the *terminus ad quem*, the latest possible date of composition for the particular piece of writing. The internal evidence comes from the *content* of the gospels themselves. If a gospel describes an event that is datable historically, it will tell us the earliest possible date – the *terminus a quo* - for its composition; since a report, or allusion to an event, could not have happened before the event itself.[1]

While it is possible for us to have some level of certainly that the composition falls between these two dates (the *terminus ad quem* and the *terminus a quo*) getting a more accurate dating – i.e. a single date of publication for each of the gospels – is impossible given the available evidence. In this chapter we will try to provide as narrow a range between these two dates as possible. We will also be looking at attempts, generally by evangelicals, to date the gospels very early.

MARK'S DATE OF COMPOSITION

We know Papias (quoted earlier) spoke about the Gospel of Mark and its origin around 130. This is the earliest direct historical reference to this gospel. Thus the year 130 sets the upper limit for Mark's date of composition. The question now lies on the other end. What is the earliest possible time for the composition of that gospel? As the gospel contains account of the death of Jesus it obviously must be written after that. So our first approximation tells us that Mark was written sometime between the years 30 and 130 CE. But a hundred year span as a possible time of composition is quite unsatisfactory.

Irenaeus, around 180, told us that Mark wrote the gospel in Rome after the "departure" of Peter and Paul. The word "departure" is generally taken to refer to the deaths of the two apostles. Christian tradition held that Peter and Paul were in Rome together and both perished there during the Neronian persecution of Christians around 64 to 67 CE. If the tradition available to Irenaeus is reliable, this would make the earliest date for the composition of Mark around 64 CE. In fact some scholars date the composition of Mark to around 65 CE, assuming that Mark started work on his

---

[1]   There is, of course, the specific problem of *prophecies* attributed to Jesus in the gospels. Since a prophecy is supposed to be a prediction *before* the actual occurrence of an event – this could cause some difficulty with evaluating the *terminus a quo*. We will be looking at this issue later in the chapter.

gospel immediately after Peter's death and that it took him a few months to complete the gospel.[2] The year 65 can be considered the "best case" scenario for Christians who prefer an early a date as possible for the gospel composition.

However, we have seen in the previous two chapters that the tradition of Mark's connection with Peter is false. The evidence from the gospel itself favors a date later than 65 CE. First let us take a look at a passage from Mark.

> Mark 13:1-2
> As he was leaving the Temple, one of his disciples said to him, "Look, Teacher! What massive stones! What magnificent buildings!" "Do you see all these great buildings?" replied Jesus, "Not one stone here will be left on another; every one will be thrown down."

The saying clearly refers to the destruction of the temple in Jerusalem. We know that the Jerusalem Temple and, in fact, the whole city, was destroyed by the Romans in 70 CE. This is *prima facie* evidence that this work is written after the fall of Jerusalem. Some scholars, eager to preserve at least one gospel to be written before the cataclysm of 70 CE, have argued that this could be a prophecy that actually came true. Taken singularly, it is not impossible that Jesus could have made this prediction about Jerusalem's fall,[3] or even that Mark could have faithfully recorded Jesus' prediction before the event.

Other considerations, however, show that, like all "apocalyptic" predictions, this too is made *after* the fact. For the whole outlook of the Markan gospel could not have made sense if the author was not aware of the destruction of the temple. For instance, in this gospel, Jesus is made to say that he will "build a temple without hands" (Mark 14:58). This is precisely what the various strains of Judaism, including the one that eventually became Christianity, tried to do *after* 70 CE! In other words, the fact that Jesus became, so to speak, a replacement for the Temple could not have made sense theologically if the temple was still standing.[4] Furthermore, the whole of chapter 13 of Mark consists of what is known as the "Little Apocalypse". As professor of New Testament, Robert M. Price pointed out, it is a characteristic of such *genre* that they make "predictions" after the fact, in order to allow them to explain why God allowed such catastrophes to take place.[5] Mark's whole theological stance seems to be one that assumes that the temple has already been destroyed.

---

[2]   Cuppitt & Armstrong, *Who Was Jesus?*: p41
Eusebius, *The History of the Church*: 2:25
Nineham, *Saint Mark*: p41

[3]   Predicting Jerusalem's ruin was an extremely popular pastime among the prophets of the OT (see Micah 3:2, Jeremiah 26:18). Josephus mentioned of a "Jesus ben Ananias" who started his prophecy of the fall of Jerusalem four years before the war began - around 62 CE. [Jewish War: 6:5:3]

[4]   Akeson, *Saint Saul*: p76-77
Mack, *Who Wrote the New Testament?*: p152-153
Schnelle, *The New Testament Writings*: p202

[5]   Price, *The Incredible Shrinking Son of Man*: p32

Thus we can say, in agreement with most critical historical scholars, that Mark was written *after* 70 CE but before 130 CE. The upper limit here is actually too high. We will return to this after we look at the other two synoptic gospels.

MATTHEW'S DATE OF COMPOSITION

The earliest historical reference (albeit indirect) to the Gospel of Matthew is contained in the epistles of Ignatius, Bishop of Antioch (d. c110). We do not know much about Ignatius. We know that around 110 he was taken under heavy guard from Syria to Rome where he was fed to wild animals in the Coliseum. We also know that along his way to Rome, he wrote at least seven letters to the churches of Ephesus, Magnesia, Tralles, Rome, Philadelphia, Smyrna and to Polycarp (c69-155), Bishop of Smyrna. In his letters we find references to the Star of Bethlehem and several sayings of Jesus that are to be found only in the Gospel of Matthew (12:33; 15:13; 19:12). This is generally taken to mean that Ignatius had access to the Gospel of Matthew; although there is no excluding the possibility that he had access to a tradition parallel to the one Matthew used. The former assumption, however, is more likely and we can conclude with some certainty that Matthew was written before 110. This date sets the upper limit for Matthew's composition.[6]

We also have in Matthew references to the fall of Jerusalem. One is a direct copy from Mark (Mark 13:1-2 = Matthew 24:1-2) about the destruction of the Temple in Jerusalem.

Another clear-cut reference to the fall of Jerusalem is in the Parable of the Wedding Banquet:

Matthew 22:1-10
Jesus answered and spoke again in parables to them, saying, "The Kingdom of Heaven is like a certain king, who made a marriage feast for his son, and sent out his servants to call those who were invited to the marriage feast, but they would not come. Again he sent out other servants, saying,' Tell those who are invited, "Behold, I have made ready my dinner. My cattle and my fatlings are killed, and all things are ready. Come to the marriage feast!"' But they made light of it, and went their ways, one to his own farm, another to his merchandise, and the rest grabbed his servants, and treated them shamefully, and killed them. *When the king heard that, he was angry, and sent his armies, destroyed those murderers, and burned their city.* Then he said to his servants, 'The wedding is ready, but those who were invited weren't worthy. Go therefore to the intersections of the highways, and as many as you may find, invite to the marriage feast.' Those servants went out into the highways, and gathered together as many as they found, both bad and good. The wedding was filled with guests."

This parable is in the form of an allegory. It makes no sense in itself. Why would the invited guests have to kill the servants who were only asking them to attend a banquet? And why would the king *burn the city* of the invited guests just because they won't attend his wedding banquet. The allegory can only be understood when the reader knows what the figures in it stand for. The king is God who had invited

---

6   Fenton, *Saint Matthew*: p11

some selected guests, the Jews, to a wedding banquet. The rejection of the king's invitation resulted in the destruction of the city of the guests. This is another obvious allusion to the fall of Jerusalem: the Jews rejected Jesus and the destruction of the city was just punishment from God. The opening of the invitation to the other people obviously referred to the Gentiles who accepted Jesus' teaching.[7] Thus these verses show that Matthew too was written after 70 CE. This is consistent with our earlier finding about the primacy of Mark; if Mark was written after 70, then Matthew, who used Mark as one of his sources, must have been written after that as well.

There are further considerations which show that Matthew was composed quite some time after 70 CE. Firstly, we note that although the author of the gospel knew about the fall of Jerusalem, the gospel as a whole was not pre-occupied with the event. In Matthew 24:6 Jesus is made to tell his disciples not to be troubled when they hear of wars because "the end is not yet." This suggests that he was already removed from that event by a reasonable passage of time.

Secondly, we know that the early Jewish Christians, who still considered themselves Jews, were at odds with the emergent Rabbinic Judaism and were competing with them for followers.[8] The "scribes and Pharisees" are particularly singled out as the enemies of the Matthean community. One poignant example is this passage presented as a saying of Jesus:

> Matthew 23: 1-8
> Then Jesus spoke to the multitudes and to his disciples, saying, "The scribes and the Pharisees...don't do their works; for they say, and don't do...They ...love the place of honor at feasts, the best seats in the synagogues, the salutations in the marketplaces, and to be called 'Rabbi, Rabbi' by men. But don't you be called 'Rabbi,'..."

It is obvious that this polemic was against the *leadership* of an opposing group – not against all Jews. Especially significant is the command not to call each other "Rabbi."[9] This flies against what we know from the other gospels, where Jesus is addressed by such this title very frequently:

> Mark 9:5 (see also Mark 10:51, 11:21 & 14:45)
> Peter answered Jesus, "Rabbi, it is good for us to be here..."

> John 1:48-49 (see also John 1:38, 3:2, 4:31, 9:2, 11:8, 20:16)
> Nathanael said to him, "How do you know me?" Jesus answered him, "Before Philip called you, when you were under the fig tree, I saw you." Nathanael answered him, "Rabbi, you are the Son of God! You are King of Israel!"

---

7   Fenton, *Saint Matthew*: p11, 347
8   Two recent works have shown that the Matthean community was *Jewish* Christian: Anthony Saldarini's *Matthew's Christian-Jewish Community*, University of Chicago 1994 and David C. Sim's *The Gospel of Matthew and Christian Judaism*, T&T Clark 1998
9   In Matthew only Judas is made to call Jesus "rabbi" (Matthew 26:25,49)

During the time of Jesus the title "Rabbi" meant no more than a respectful form of address. That the Jesus of Matthew is made to tell his followers not to be called "Rabbi" can only mean that the evangelist was writing at a time when such a title was already being "hijacked" by another group. This happened in the decades following 70 CE with the forerunners of what later became Rabbinic Judaism where the term is used primarily to refer to religious officials.[10]

Another example is where Matthew refers to his opponents' places of worship as "*their* synagogues" (Matthew 4:23; 9:35; 10:17; 12:9; 13:54) as though he wants to distinguish Jewish synagogues from the Christian places of worship. Such development - the appropriation of titles and the separation of places of worship - as David C. Sim commented, "did not take place overnight" and we have to allow at least a decade or two to pass before it would have reached such a state. Based on such considerations most scholars date Matthew, at the earliest, to around 85 CE.[11]

LUKE'S DATE OF COMPOSITION

The earliest historical reference to the third gospel was in 140 CE by the heretic Marcion who championed this work, albeit in an altered form. This sets the *terminus ad quem* of the Luke's composition at 140. There are, of course, references to the destruction of the Jerusalem Temple copied from Mark (Mark 13:1-2 = Luke 21:5-7). More details regarding the fall of Jerusalem were provided in two other passages:

Luke 19:41-44
When he [Jesus] drew near, he saw the city and wept over it, saying, "If you, even you, had known today the things which belong to your peace! But now, they are hidden from your eyes. *For the days will come on you, when your enemies will throw up a barricade against you, surround you, hem you in on every side*, and will dash you and your children within you to the ground. *They will not leave in you one stone on another*, because you didn't know the time of your visitation."

Luke 21:20-24
"But *when you see Jerusalem surrounded by armies*, then know that its desolation is at hand. Then let those who are in Judea flee to the mountains. Let those who are in the midst of her depart. Let those who are in the country not enter therein. For these are days of vengeance, that all things which are written may be fulfilled. Woe to those who are pregnant and to those who nurse infants in those days! For there will be great distress in the land, and wrath to this people. *They will fall by the edge of the sword*, and *will be led captive into all the nations. Jerusalem will be trampled down by the Gentiles*, until the times of the Gentiles are fulfilled.

---

10   Sim, *The Gospel of Matthew and Christian Judaism*: p118-122
11   Brown, *An Introduction to the New Testament*: p217
      Fenton, *Saint Matthew*: p11
      Koester, *Introduction to the New Testament Vol II*: p177
      Martin, *New Testament Foundations I*: p71
      Schnelle, *The New Testament Writings*: p222
      Sim, *The Gospel of Matthew and Christian Judaism*: p40

Note the *details* which correspond exactly with contemporary accounts of the action of Titus on Jerusalem. We have the siege of Jerusalem ("when your enemies will throw up a barricade against you, surround you, hem you in on every side" and "when you see Jerusalem surrounded by armies") the complete destruction of the city by the Romans ("they will not leave in you one stone upon another" and "Jerusalem will be trampled down by the Gentiles"), the slaughter of innumerable Jews ("they will fall by the edge of the sword") and the capture of many Jews ("will be led away captive into all the nations"). As Kümmel pointed out, such detailed correspondences could only have been formulated *after the event* of Jerusalem's destruction. [12]

As we have shown in the previous chapter, Luke is dependent on Mark, which itself a post-70 CE work; the Lukan date of composition must be later than this by quite a few years. Up until recently, most scholars are content to place Luke as more or less contemporaneous with Matthew – around 85-90 CE.[13] Yet of late, more and more scholars are assigning the composition of Luke to dates later than this - to around 100 CE and even as late as 120 CE.[14] The arguments used for suggesting a late first century or early second century composition include: Luke's generally positive attitude towards the Romans implies a time after the persecution of Christians by Domitian (who died in 96 CE) [Patterson]; the genre affinities between Luke-Acts and the various apocryphal Acts and Hellenistic novels prevalent in the second century CE suggest a similar period of composition [Price]; and the prefaces to Luke-Acts show that the author belonged to the third generation of Christians [Koester]. Although these arguments have some force behind them, there is a more certain way to anchor Luke-Acts as a late first century or early second century work. This comes from comparing Luke-Acts with the works of Flavius Josephus (c37 CE - c100 CE).

That there is some sort of a relationship can easily be seen by anyone familiar with the two authors' works. For instance, we find some historical references in Luke that could have been taken from the writings of Flavius Josephus. Luke's references to the census by Quirinius (Luke 2:1-3) and to the massacre of the Jews by Pilate (Luke 13:1) were given in Josephus' *Antiquities of the Jews* (18:1 & 18:3:2).

So the next question is this: how goes this "relationship"? Did Luke rely (either "copied" or "remembered") on Josephus? Or did Josephus copy Luke? Or could the relationship be explained simply by the authors sharing a similar cultural milieu and having access to similar sources? Although many scholars are skeptical of any direct dependence of Luke-Acts on Josephus,[15] Steve Mason, Associate Professor of Humanities at Vanier College, York University, Ontario has recently amassed what I believe to be powerful reasons for believing that Luke was "familiar" with Josephus'

---

[12]   Kümmel, *Introduction to the New Testament*: p150
[13]   Barr, *The New Testament Story*: p329
       Brown, *An Introduction to the New Testament*: p273-274
       Kümmel, *Introduction to the New Testament*: p151
       Schnelle, *The New Testament Writings*: p202
[14]   Koester, *Introduction to the New Testament Vol II*: p314
       Mack, *Who Wrote the New Testament?*: p167
       Patterson, *The God of Jesus*: p22
       Price, *The Incredible Shrinking Son of Man*: p33
       Sanders & Davies, *Studying the Synoptic Gospels*: p5-6
[15]   Sanders & Davies, *Studying the Synoptic Gospels*: p18

works.[16] Mason's work has recently been further extended by Richard Pervo[17] and Joseph Tyson.[18] We will review the evidence below.

Historical Errors in Luke

The strongest line of evidence for Luke's dependence on Josephus is when the former commits historical errors.

The first example is the speech he attributed to the Pharisee Gamaliel:

> Acts 5:36-37
> For before these days Theudas rose up, making himself out to be somebody; to whom a number of men, about four hundred, joined themselves: who was slain; and all, as many as obeyed him, were dispersed, and came to nothing. *After this man,* Judas of Galilee rose up in the days of the *enrolment* [i.e. census], and drew away some people after him. He also perished, and all, as many as obeyed him, were scattered abroad.

By referring to *the* census, Luke was obviously alluding to the events in 6 CE and he had this census *following* the revolt by Theudas. Josephus had described in his book, *Antiquities of the Jews,* the events of Theudas within the procuratorship of Fadus, who was procurator in the years 44-46 CE, i.e. four decades *after* the revolt by Judas the Galilean. Yet Luke had Theudas' revolt happening *before* that of Judas the Galilean.[19]

The explanation that there was another Theudas before Judas the Galilean is weak, for there is no historical attestation to a Theudas that preceded Judas the Galilean. To have two revolutionaries with the same name doing the exact same things would make for an uncanny coincidence. This explanation is even less likely when we consider the fact that the name Theudas is a very uncommon name.[20]

We find in Antiquities 20:5:1-2 the probable source of Luke's mistaken sequence of events. In it, Josephus first described the incident with Theudas under Fadus. Then in describing the exploits of Fadus' successor, Tiberius Alexander, he mentioned that the latter had slain the *sons* of Judas the Galilean. He went on to explain that Judas the Galilean was the one who caused the revolt under Quirinius.

We can easily see how someone who may have read Josephus sometime in the past had confused the sequence of events from memory and had Judas following Theudas; following the sequence of writing but not the chronological one.[21]

Crucially, as Richard Pervo points out, the author of Acts does not just share historical data with Josephus but also the latter's historical *interpretation.* Josephus is the only historian known to us who traced the roots of the first Jewish revolt in 70 CE

---

[16] Mason, *Josephus and the New Testament*: p185-225
[17] Pervo, *Dating Acts*: p149-201
[18] Tyson, *Marcion and Luke-Acts*: p14-15
[19] Note also that Luke placed this speech of Gamaliel before the conversion of Paul which is narrated in chapter 8 of Acts – thus placing this oration sometime between 30-33 CE. However, as we have seen, the revolt by Theudas happened during the reign of Fadus. Thus we have situation where Gamaliel was talking about a revolt that *had yet to occur*!
[20] Pervo, *Dating Acts*: p156
[21] Mason, *Josephus and the New Testament*: p208-211

to the Roman census in 6 CE. Josephus, in his description of the Roman census under Quirinius in 6 CE, tied the revolt following this to a unified group of revolutionaries under Judas the Galilean (Antiquities 18:1:1-6, Jewish War 2:8:1). That he did this is in line with his whole strategy of trying to exonerate *most* Jews from the blame of the revolt of 70 CE. In other words, he wanted to show that the revolts were a result of the agitation of *some groups* within Palestine and not a spontaneous ethnic uprising. As part of this, Josephus presented the census in 6 CE and the revolt following it as a watershed event and in many ways a precursor to the revolt six decades later. Yet modern studies have thrown doubts on this version of events; there were *many* different revolutionary movements in first century CE Palestine, ranging from peasant to (probably) even aristocratic ones. Thus it was Josephus who put emphasis on the census and the revolt following it by Judas the Galilean, another historian with a different axe to grind would not have placed similar emphasis on this census or on one person.

This thesis is peculiar to Josephus. That Luke followed this interpretation and literary arrangements of Josephus, while screwing up the chronological order, point to the dependence of the former on the latter.[22]

The second example involves the account of an Egyptian prophet. This is how the story goes in Acts, where it is weaved into a narrative of Paul's mission. Paul, after being rescued by the Roman garrison from a mob of angry Jews (Acts 21:27-32), spoke to them in Greek, wherein the Roman tribune asked of him:

Acts 21:38
"Do you know Greek? Aren't you then the Egyptian, who before these days stirred up to sedition and led out into the wilderness the four thousand men of the Assassins [Greek = *sicarion*]?"

That Luke had a mistake here is obvious. Josephus was the first person, as far as we now, to use the term *sicarii* [a word borrowed from Latin for short daggers: *sicae*] as a technical term to describe a Jewish revolutionary group. The terms fits aptly the description of them by Josephus (see next paragraph), i.e. as assassins. You would not expect these people to follow a prophet into the wilderness! Luke on the other hand betrays a very confused use of the word and for him to place the *sicarii* in the desert indicates that he knew of their name but not exactly *who* these people were. Thus, it is obvious that Luke had erroneously used the term that he *borrowed* from somewhere.

Now, let us look at Josephus' accounts (in both *Antiquities* and *Jewish War*). In Antiquities 20:8:5, Josephus describes the men of the *sicarii* (whom he named as such in Antiquities 2:8:10) as being men who carry very short, easily concealable, daggers who mingled with the crowds during festivals and stabbed their opponents in broad daylight. Then following this, as a separate account, in Antiquities 20:8:6, Josephus mentioned some "impostors and deceivers" who persuaded the multitude to follow them into the desert. Then he described, *again as a separate account* immediately following this (Antiquities 20:8:6), the unnamed Egyptian who "led the multitude" to the Mount of Olives.

---

[22]   Mason, *Josephus and the New Testament*: p205-206
        Pervo, *Dating Acts*: p159-160

So too in his *Jewish War,* we find the same sequence of events, again describing them as separate incidents with different people. In War 2:13:3-5, the *sicarii,* the mob being led out into the desert and the case of the Egyptian prophet were described in quick succession. Josephus was careful not to conflate these three accounts as one, for he mentioned that the *sicarii* were guerillas, while the Egyptian was a "false prophet".

In Luke's narratives in *Acts,* all these three accounts have been conflated into one. It was the *Egyptian* who led the *Sicarii* out into the *desert!* This can easily be explained by the postulate that Luke had read Josephus sometime in the past and simply confused the three separate accounts as one. It is not easily explainable any other way. For instance, if Luke did not know Josephus, it would require the occurrence of a large number of simultaneous coincidences for this to happen: he would somehow have to link the Egyptian with the *sicarii* and then *connect* the Egyptian with the desert. The idea that Josephus copied Luke would be even more absurd. This would require that Luke first used a term (*sicarii*) he did not fully understand in a context that was completely wrong and then for someone like Josephus who *knew* about *sicarii* to use an obviously erroneous and highly abbreviated passage as his source.[23]

Reference to the Same Names

We find that Luke hit upon the exact same persons that Josephus tied to certain events.

As we have seen above, Josephus considered the census of 6 CE as an important event. We will see in the next chapter that Luke made some historical guffaws in his tying Jesus' nativity to the census in Quirinius. For now we only need to point out that Luke, too, placed much emphasis on the census (Luke 2:1-3), as the watershed event during the birth of Jesus (it was in Luke's gospel, *the reason,* why Joseph and Mary had to go to Bethlehem). Furthermore, in the sequel to the Gospel of Luke, he alluded to the very same name Josephus had used when referring to the revolt after the census: Judas the Galilean (Acts 5:37).

Josephus mentioned that there were *many* "deceivers and imposters" who led the Jewish people into revolt. He gave, as examples, three personalities: Judas the Galilean, who appeared circa 6 CE as we have seen above; Theudas, who led a group of revolutionaries (circa 44-46 CE), tried to miraculously part the Jordan river and was beheaded by the Roman governor Fadus (Antiquities 20:5:1); and an unnamed Egyptian prophet, who wanted to bring down the walls of Jerusalem by a miracle, who had his followers killed by the soldiers of Felix, the Roman procurator from 52-59 CE.

Interestingly, of all the names of the "many deceivers and impostors", these are the very three names Luke used in his narratives in Acts (Acts 5:36-37 and Acts 21:38). This strongly suggests again that Josephus' works were Luke's only sources for that period.[24]

---

23   Mason, *Josephus and the New Testament*: p211-213
24   Mason, *Josephus and the New Testament*: p205-210

Note too that in these cases, it is Josephus that had the fuller accounts. Luke's narratives normally had no more than one or two sentences. As is the normal rule, the copier normally abbreviates his source, not the other way round.

Uncanny Parallels

Many of the details in the Gospel of Luke have parallels in Josephus's works. The story narrated in Luke 2:41-52 tells of how Joseph and Mary took the twelve-year-old Jesus to Jerusalem for the Passover festival and lost him for three days. They finally found him in the temple where he was discussing religious matters with the teachers of the law. They were "amazed at his understanding and his answers." (Luke 2:47). We are told in *The Life of Flavius Josephus* that at fourteen he was "commended by all" for his love of learning and that the "high priests and principal men" came to him to seek his "opinion about the accurate understanding of points of the Law".

In Luke 9:52-53, an incident is told in which the Samaritans stopped Jesus and his Galilean followers from entering the village because Jesus was with an entourage heading for Jerusalem. This incident parallels very closely the incident in *Antiquities* 20:6:1 where Josephus relates how some Galileans on the way to Jerusalem were refused entry into a Samaritan village by its inhabitants.

Another instance is in Luke 7:1-10 which tells of Jesus healing the centurion's servant. Luke also added that the centurion was a friend of the Jews (Luke 7:4). The centurion reminds one of the story in Josephus' *Jewish War* 2:10:4 in which the Roman legate of Syria was a friend of the Jews. When Emperor Gauis wanted to place his statue at the temple, the legate explained his predicament to the Jews, "For I am under authority, as well as you." This quote is very similar to the one Luke put in the mouth of the centurion: "For I myself am a man under authority." (Luke 7:8)

It is easier to explain that Luke utilized these events from the various books of Josephus than to imagine it the other way round, that Josephus utilized one book (Luke's gospel) and "remembered" to put bits and pieces of it into his various writings.[25]

Similarities in Unique Vocabulary

The similarities in usage of certain words in Josephus and Luke could not be attributed to chance.

During Roman times, Judaism was increasingly being seen as a "superstition" or a "religion" by outsiders. The Romans held philosophy to be a higher ideal than superstition or religion. One of the main themes of Josephus' works was a monumental attempt to redefine Judaism in philosophical terms familiar to the Romans. Thus he used the word *schools* (*haireseis*, the singular form is *hairesis*) to describes the various factions within Judaism; presenting them as philosophical schools rather than religious sects. Thus the Pharisees, the Sadducees and the Essenes were presented as various *schools* within Judaism. (Antiquities 18:1:2-5). It is important to note that we do not know of any contemporaneous authors that used this

---

[25]   Schonfield, *The Passover Plot*: p245-246

term for the various Jewish sects. Josephus nomenclature was thus, original and unique.

Yet Luke used the very same term *haireseis* to describe the Pharisees and Sadducees (Acts 5:17, 15:5 and 26:5). In Acts 5:17, Jesus followers were opposed by the "school of the Sadducees". In Acts 15:5 it was some believers who were from the "school of the Pharisees" who insisted that new converts be circumcised. Unlike Josephus, who weaved the term within the context of aim of presenting these sects as respectable philosophical schools, Luke's use of the term is nonchalant as though it was self evidently appropriate.

The point then is this, Luke used the term *heireseis* to describe the various sects within Judaism as though it was already a term already a commonly used one, not as one who invented it. Yet apart from Luke, the terminology was unique to Josephus.

In Acts 26:5, Luke had Paul call the Pharisees, the "most precise school" among the Jews. Yet this word "precision" is also one of Josephus' key terms in describing the Pharisees (Jewish War 1:5:2, 2:8:14, Antiquities 17:2:4, Life of Josephus 38).

Again, outside of Luke-Acts, the description of the Pharisees as the most "precise school" is unique to Josephus. Josephus' use of this is easily understandable in view of his overall aim. Luke's use is, as above, like one who has borrowed the term from elsewhere.

As Steve Mason asks: "If Luke did not know of Josephus' work, how did this language suggest itself to him?"[26]

Conclusions on Luke-Acts reliance on Josephus

All these cannot be explained by Josephus having copied Luke, or that they both shared similar sources as Richard Pervo explains:

> [N]early every item of "modern" history [i.e. post Septuagint - PT] to which Luke refers to can be found in Josephus. This may not be remarkable. Yet, when Luke calls Jewish parties philosophical "sects," when he views the census of 6 CE as a watershed event; when he introduces such characters as Judas, Theudas, "the Egyptian," and sicarii; it is appropriate to introduce the adjective "remarkable."[27]

The conclusion that Luke used the works of Josephus (*Jewish War, Antiquities of the Jews* and the autobiographical *The Life of Flavius Josephus*) means that Luke's literary works (the gospel and the Acts of the Apostles) must be written later than Josephus'. Josephus completed his autobiography (the latest of his three works mentioned here) circa 95 CE. This means that the earliest date possible for the composition of Luke's gospel is 95 CE. Thus Luke's date of composition is between 95 to 140 CE.

---

[26]   Mason, *Josephus and the New Testament*: p214-223
[27]   Pervo, *Dating Acts*: p198

JOHN'S DATE OF COMPOSITION

When was the Gospel of John written? The upper limit is provided by a papyrus manuscript fragment measuring only 6 cm by 9 cm discovered in Egypt. Also known as p^{52}, this fragment is now kept in the John Rylands library. It contains two verses of the gospel on one side (John 18:37-38) and three verses on the other side (John 18:31-33). Based on paleography – comparison with the writing of other known manuscripts - it is usually dated with an ostensible precision to the year 125. Conservative theologians and evangelicals have milked this apparently precise dating to the hilt. Some have even claimed that it could have been produced as early as the end of the first century, thus pushing the composition of John even earlier than anyone had ever suggested. However, paleographical analysis cannot provide such precision and dates provided by recent paleographical analysis range from 110 to 200! Udo Schnelle have suggested that the best compromise date would be the rather conservative (given the range) "mid-point" of 150. Thus we can say that, approximately, the year 150 sets the absolute upper limit for John's composition.[28]

Since John is not clearly dependent on Mark, it is important to note that, like the rest of the gospels, it too is a post 70 CE work. We find clear allusions to the destruction of the temple and the fall of Jerusalem in these two verses:

John 2:19
Jesus answered them, "Destroy this temple, and in three days I will raise it up."

John 11:47-48
The chief priests therefore and the Pharisees gathered a council, and said, "What are we doing? For this man does many signs. If we leave him alone like this, everyone will believe in him, and the Romans will come and take away both our place and our nation."

As we have already seen in our dating of Mark above, the theme of replacing the Temple with Jesus is an idea simply that cannot be made before the Temple was destroyed. Indeed, the historian Donald Akenson had said that "the entire structure of the Gospel of John…is nothing less than a description of a temple religion without the Temple."[29] The idea of the destruction of Jerusalem and the Jewish nation being due to the rejection of Jesus by the Jews is also another common theme in early, post-70 CE, Christianity.[30]

---

[28]   Bentley, *Secrets of Mount Sinai*: p159
Cuppitt & Armstrong, *Who Was Jesus?*: p18-19
Ehrman, B., "The Text as Window: New Testament Manuscripts and the Social History of Early Christianity", Chp 22 in *Ehrman & Holmes, The Text of the New Testament in Contemporary Research*: p371 n4
Schnelle, *The New Testament Writings*: p477 , 477 n119
Wilson, *Jesus, The Evidence*: p28

[29]   Akenson, *Saint Saul*: p75

[30]   Udo Schnelle wrote in *The New Testament Writings*, John 11:48 "presupposed" the destruction of Jerusalem.

However, the Gospel of John was written much later than 70 CE. One clue lies in the passage in John chapter 9, it involves the story of a man born blind who was healed· by Jesus: The Jews were skeptical and inquired about this man from his parents:

> John 9:19-22 (also John 12:42 and 16:2)
> "Is this your son, who you say was born blind? How then does he now see? His parents answered them, "We know that this is our son, and that he was born blind; but how he now sees, we don't know; or who opened his eyes, we don't know. He is of age. Ask him. He will speak for himself." His parents said these things because they feared the Jews; *for the Jews had already agreed that if any man would confess him as Christ, he would be put out of the synagogue.*

I have purposely italicized the last sentence to make it stand out from the rest of the passage: it says that Christians were being systematically excluded from synagogues. This passage could not be referring to the situation during the time of Jesus. While there were undoubtedly some early Christians who were harassed by the Jews before this, by and large the early Christians shared the same worshipping place with the Jews without much trouble. This is attested to by Luke and Acts. After the ascension of Jesus, the apostles were said to worship continually in the Temple (Luke 24:53).

Therefore, such an expulsion could only have happened quite some time after 70 CE when the emergent Rabbinic Judaism was vying with the Jewish-Christians for religious dominance. Many scholars are of the opinion that such evictions could only have happened, at the earliest, around the turn of the first century.[31]

Added to this, external evidence also points to a late date. There is no reference whatsoever among the early church fathers - such as Papias (c60-130), Ignatius (d. c110) and Polycarp (c69-c155) - to the Gospel of John. This, in the opinion of many scholars, points to a date around 100 CE.[32]

Q's DATE OF COMPOSITION

We have seen in the previous chapter that both Matthew and Luke very probably had access to a source document – referred to by scholars as Q. Since this document, if it exists, would obviously predate both gospels.

The dating of the source document Q is uncertain. Scholars used to put 50 CE as the date for the composition of Q.[33] For a few reasons, this is almost certainly a

---

[31] Barr, *New Testament Story*: p371-372
   Ehrman, *The New Testament*: p158
   Vermes, *The Changing Faces of Jesus*: p9
   Wells, *Historical Evidence for Jesus*: p126-127
[32] Brown *An Introduction to the New Testament*: p334
   Cadoux, *The Life of Jesus*: p15
   Martin, *New Testament Foundations I*: p282
   Schnelle, *The New Testament Writings*: p 476-477
   Wells, *Historical Evidence for Jesus*: p127
[33] Cuppitt & Armstrong, *Who Was Jesus?*: p31
   Schonfield, *The Passover Plot*: p228

bit too early. Firstly, we do not find any references to it in the epistles of Paul, which was written between 51 CE and 64 CE. Secondly, there is a section in Q known as Jesus' Lament over Jerusalem that is almost certainly a reference to the fall of Jerusalem in 70 CE.

> Luke 13:34-35 (Matthew 23:37-39)
> "Jerusalem, Jerusalem, that kills the prophets, and stones those who are sent to her! How often I wanted to gather your children together, like a hen gathers her own brood under her wings, and you refused! *Behold, your house is left to you desolate.* I tell you, you will not see me, until you say, 'Blessed is he who comes in the name of the Lord!'"

Thus Q, in the form that it was used by the authors of Matthew and Luke,[34] must be a post-70 CE document.[35]

DATING OF THE GOSPELS – CONCLUSION

Turning back to Mark, its upper limit of 130 CE should now be modified based on what we found the dating of the other gospel to be. If both Luke and Matthew composed their gospels independently, as was probably the case, the fact that they both used Mark must imply that this gospel must have been in circulation for some time. But for how long? We don't know. But let us say that it takes at least five years for the gospel to be circulated before it first comes into the notice of Matthew. Since Matthew was probably written sometime around 85-110 CE, the latest possible date for Mark's composition would be around 105 CE.

The most likely dates for the four gospels as we have them are as follows:

Mark	70-105 CE
Matthew	85-110 CE
Luke	95-140 CE
John	90-150 CE

As we have mentioned at the beginning of the chapter, to settle on accurate single dates of composition is quite impossible but, as a short hand, we can use these dates

---

[34]   In recent years the theological world has seen a resurgence of interest in the study of Q. A popular hypothesis among scholarly circles is that Q went through three different stages of documentation (called Q1, Q2 and Q3) with Q1, a collection of aphorisms by Jesus, being the sayings most likely to be authentic. Q2, which contained the apocalyptic sayings of the coming of the kingdom, is taken as the second strata added by the "Q people" and is considered non authentic. Q3 depicts a few minor additions that were believed by theologians to have been added after the fall of Jerusalem in 70 CE and definitely further away from the historical Jesus. The reader can find a summary of the findings in the book by Button L. Mack *The Lost Gospel: The Book of Q and Christian Origins* (1993). Yet this hypothesis is not accepted by all scholars. [For such views see Raymond Brown *An Introduction to the New Testament*: p120-122]

[35]   Mack, *Who Wrote the New Testament?*: p53

below - which roughly correspond to our analysis above and to the current "scholarly consensus:"[36]

Mark	70 CE
Matthew	90 CE
Luke	95 CE
John	100 CE

ARGUMENTS FOR EARLY DATING OF THE GOSPELS

We have shown that the gospels are all post-70 CE documents. Late dates of gospel composition do not make fundamentalists feel comfortable, since the reliability of the texts then become questionable. Thus, apologists have argued for earlier dates. In the remaining part of this chapter we will be looking at three arguments for early dates of gospel composition.

THE ARGUMENT FROM UNFULFILLED PROPHECIES

John A.T. Robinson (1919-1983), was a New Testament scholar and an Anglican bishop. Robinson was well known for his work on liberal theology, having argued in his book *Honest to God* (1963) that God does not exist "out there" but within the depth of human existence.[37] It therefore came in as a bit of a surprise when his book *Redating the New Testament* (1976) argued for a pre-70 CE dating of the gospels. He argued that *Matthew* could have been written as early as 40 CE with *John* even earlier. Basically there are two main reasons why he argued for a pre-70 CE composition:

- Unfulfilled Prophecies: Robinson claims that there are prophecies supposedly made by Jesus that were unfulfilled. Had the gospels been written after 70 CE the authors would have fudged or changed the prophecies to make those look like they came true or leave out the prophecies altogether.

- Brevity of Prophecies on Destruction of the Temple: Robinson claims that the lack of details in the prophecies of the destruction of the temple argues for it being an actual *prediction* rather than something written after the fact.

One of the examples given by Robinson involves a failed eschatological prophecy made by Jesus:

---

[36] This is based on my own survey of 30 books by New Testament scholars reporting on the consensus. The dates vary a little but the tendency is to leave Mark around 70CE, Matthew around 85-95 CE, Luke to around the same time as Matthew but with a trend towards a later date. John is normally placed the last around 90-110.

[37] Whatever *that* may mean – see Excursus A.

297

Mark 13:24-27 (Matthew 24:29-31; Luke 21:25-28)
But in those days, after that oppression, the sun will be darkened, the moon will not give its light, the stars will be falling from the sky, and the powers that are in the heavens will be shaken. Then they will see the Son of Man coming in clouds with great power and glory. Then he will send out his angels, and will gather together his chosen ones from the four winds, from the ends of the earth to the ends of the sky.

Jesus supposedly ended this discourse with the statement below:

Mark 13:30 (Matthew 24:34-36; Luke 21:32-33)
Most certainly I say to you, this generation will not pass away until all these things happen.

The above, Robinson argues, is a mistaken prophecy. For the world as we know it obviously did not end. Now if Jesus, and his original disciples, had already been dead a long time when the gospels were written, the evangelists would have left this out. Thus he argues for an early date of composition for the gospels, before the Jewish revolt of 66-70 CE.[38]

This argument is flawed. While I do not disagree that the above is an example of a failed prophecy, I do disagree with the use of that passage to date the gospels as pre-70 CE documents. To bring more clarification on the matter, we see that Jesus actually uttered a similar statement in another passage:

Mark 9:1 (Matthew 16:28; Luke 9:27)
Most certainly I tell you, there are *some* standing here who will in no way taste death until they see the Kingdom of God come with power.

Note the statement about *some* of the people being alive when Jesus returns. This is already evidence of fudging; we would expect some of the people in Jesus' generation to be alive after 70 CE and even some (though very few) to be alive around the end of the first century. Thus the argument from unfulfilled prophecies in no way favors a pre-70 CE date of composition for the gospels.[39]

On the lack of details on the prediction of the destruction of the Temple, Robinson pointed to this passage (which we have already seen above):

Matthew 22:1-10
Jesus answered and spoke again in parables to them, saying, "The Kingdom of Heaven is like a certain king, who made a marriage feast for his son, and sent out his servants to call those who were invited to the marriage feast, but they would not come. Again he sent out other servants, saying,' Tell those who are invited, "Behold, I have made ready my dinner. My cattle and my fatlings are killed, and all things are ready. Come to the marriage feast!"' But they made light of it, and went their ways, one to his own farm, another to his merchandise, and the rest grabbed his servants, and treated them shamefully, and killed them. When the king heard that, he was angry, *and sent his armies, destroyed those murderers, and burned*

---

38   Wilson, *Jesus: The Evidence*: p43-44
39   Wells, *Historical Evidence for Jesus*: p113

their city." Then he said to his servants, 'The wedding is ready, but those who were invited weren't worthy. Go therefore to the intersections of the highways, and as many as you may find, invite to the marriage feast.' Those servants went out into the highways, and gathered together as many as they found, both bad and good. The wedding was filled with guests.

Here Robinson argues that the description italicized is very brief and that *Matthew* would certainly have added more details had this been written after 70 CE. However, this argument is flawed. For Matthew did not make up the whole paragraph above from whole cloth. In fact he copied it from *Q*. We know this for a fact because Luke has a similar parable (Luke 14:15-24) that *does not* have the italicized portion above. What does this tells us? It tells us that Matthew inserted one line into an already pre-existing story in *Q*. He was constrained by the pre-existing structure he found there. His addition had the effect of "updating" the parable to include the destruction of Jerusalem and thus fulfils its task.[40]

Thus Robinson's arguments for a pre-70 CE date of compositions for the gospels are far from convincing and we are not surprised that his views are not accepted by any consensus of scholars.[41]

THE ARGUMENT FROM "EARLY" GOSPEL FRAGMENTS

Carsten Thiede (1952-2004) was a professor of comparative literature who got side-tracked half-way through his career into investigating early Christianity. He was a man whose conservative bent often times got in the way of his better judgment. For instance, he claimed in his book *The Quest for the True Cross* (2002) that the *Titulus Crucis* [Latin for "Title of the Cross"], a medieval Roman relic, was actually from the headboard of the cross of Jesus![42] However, in 2002, carbon dating conducted on behalf of the University of Arizona showed that the wood from the *Titulus* can be dated to around 980-1146 – a thousand years too late for it to have been from the cross of Jesus.[43]

In the same spirit, Thiede wrote three books, *Jesus: Life or Legend?* (1990), *The Earliest Gospel Manuscript?* (1992) and *The Jesus Papyrus* (1996), in which he claimed that very early fragments of the gospels Mark and Matthew had been found in Qumran and in a library in Oxford!

The so-called *Qumran Mark* was discovered by a Jesuit papyrologist Jose O'Callaghan in 1972 in the seventh cave at Qumran. It is a very small papyrus fragment, measuring only around 35 cm long by 25 cm wide. O'Callaghan claimed that the fragment was from Mark 6:52-53. Since the cave is known to have been sealed in 68 CE, this shows that Mark must have been written prior to the caves being sealed, perhaps as early as 50 CE. Thiede tried to revive this claim in his books.[44]

---

[40]   Wells, *Historical Evidence for Jesus*: p123
[41]   Wilson, *Jesus: The Evidence*: p44
[42]   John 19:18-22 describes how Pilate had the words "Jesus of Nazareth, the King of the Jews" in Hebrew, Latin and Greek inscribed on the headboard of Jesus' cross.
[43]   Francisco Bella & Carlo Azzi, "14C Dating of the Titulus Crucis," *Radiocarbon*, Vol: 44 #3, 2002, p685-689
[44]   Thiede, *Jesus, Life or Legend*: p90

Let us look at the fragment itself. First we will note that it is *very small*, it consists of five lines with only *one* complete word. What is the word? The most banal of all words, the Greek *kai*, which means "and". Apart from these three alphabets or letters, there are six other well-preserved single letters, two imperfect letters that could be reconstructed with some certainty, six defective letters on which reconstruction is problematic and two unreadable letters. To summarize, only one complete word ("and"), sixteen scattered Greek alphabets about half of which are nearly illegible.

Much of the criticism by scholars on this claim lays precisely in this, the fragment is *so ambiguous* that you could fit anything you want into the clear letters and make up "likely possibilities" for the rest of the illegible ones and the blank portions. In other words, the eyes of faith make them see things that are not there. Let us look at an example:

Mark 6:53 (transliterated from the Greek) goes like this: *kai diaperasantes epi ten gen elthon eis Gennesaret kai prosormisthesan* ("and when they had passed over, they came into the land of Gennesaret, and drew to the shore.")

Now if this fragment is from Mark 6:52-53, after *kai* we would expect the fragment to have a *delta* (Greek: Δ equivalent to the Roman "d"), yet at this point we have one of the well preserved letters and it shows...a *tau* (T)! The next letter, should be an *iota* (I) but here we have an imperfectly preserved letter that extends below the line, (much like a modern "j" or "g" or "p" goes below the line). Now the Greek *iota* is like our modern "i", it *does not* extend below the line. The papyrologist T.C Skeat opines that it is most likely a *rho* (Greek: P = Roman "r") - which does tend to extend below the line. So what you really have is *kai tr...*,[45] to make this into *kai diaperasantes* requires a lot of faith![46]

It is not surprising then when we hear what Burton Mack, John Wesley Professor of New Testament at the School of Theology at Claremont, has to say about this:

> Thiede's Dead Sea Scrolls scenario is preposterous; his theory about the Markan fragment among the Dead Sea Scrolls has been discredited.[47]

The English textual critic J.K. Elliot had called *The Earliest Gospel Manuscript?* by Thiede "a publication cashing in on human gullibility."[48]

The other "proof" of early gospel composition is the three papyrus fragments that had been kept at the Magdalen College Library of Oxford since 1901. These fragments contain partial texts from the 26th chapter of the Gospel of *Matthew*

Thiede, *The Jesus Papyrus*: p87

[45] Reading Thiede's book *Jesus: Life or Legend?*, without knowing the fragmentary nature of the letters, tends to lead one to imply that the word "diaperasantes" is in the fragment with only the "d" being changed to a "t"!

[46] Metzger, *The Text of the New Testament*: p264-265
Wells, *The Jesus Legend*: p153-154
Wells, *The Jesus Myth*: p9-10

[47] Mack, *Who Wrote the New Testament*: p9

[48] quoted in Wells, *The Jesus Legend*: p155

(Matthew 26:7-8, 10, 14-15, 22-23, 31, 32-33). The fragments are well known and scholars have reliably dated these fragments to the *end* of the second century.

Thiede initially made the claim, reported in the London *Times* in 1994, that the fragments are from the mid first century, i.e. circa 50 CE. He then promised to follow up this sensational claim with a more "scholarly" paper. Yet when his paper was published in a German academic journal of papyrology in 1995, he was only able to argue for a *late* first century dating of the fragments.[49] Since we have seen that *Matthew* was written circa 90 CE, dating the fragments to the late first century is not *that* sensational. However, even this claim has been found wanting by experts.[50]

Thiede's main arguments are that:

- The script (handwriting) is similar in style to some Greek texts found in Pompey Herculaneum and in Qumran which are dateable to the first century CE.

- A similar fragment of Christian writing has been found in Qumran, the Qumran Mark dateable to before 68 CE.[51]

We have seen that Thiede's Qumran Mark is a figment of his (and Father O'Callaghan's) imagination. Many scholars expert in handwriting analysis of that era have shown Thiede's claim to be spurious. In the same German magazine, but in a later volume, the German textual critic Klaus Wachtel replied to Thiede's paper and showed that the style of the Magdalen fragments is the type that exists from the end of the second century to the 5th century. As an example of this, Biblical Uncial style (of which the Magdalen fragment is an early example) normally has each letter isolated from one another. Yet the characters in the Qumran text, as even Thiede admits, are "very close to each other, occasionally even connected." This distinction, Wachtel mentioned, is very significant. The style of isolated letters is one of the reasons why scholars can, with certainty, date the Magdalen fragment to the end of the second century.[52]

Let us look at the main reasons why scholars date the Magdalen Fragments to the end of the second century:

- The fragments are of papyrus (basically a kind of paper). Parchments began to be used after circa 200. Therefore, these fragments probably date from before 200.

---

[49] Why this change in claim? Surely if he can get a paper published with his initial claim of mid first century he could change the whole world of biblical studies as we know it. G.A. Wells in his book *The Jesus Myth* says this: "Articles published in academic journals such as the Bonn *Zeitschrift* are carefully refereed, and so authors do not find it easy to use these journals as a forum for extravagant claims". [Ref. Wells, *The Jesus Myth*: p6] In other words, when you have to write for an audience of experts it becomes harder to try and pull wool over their eyes!

[50] Shorto, *Gospel Truth*: p257-258
Wells, *The Jesus Myth*: p5-8

[51] Thiede & D'Ancona, *The Jesus Papyrus*: p132

[52] Wells, *The Jesus Myth*: p6-8

- The fragments are from a codex (i.e. loose papers bound into book form) as opposed to a scroll (which is paper rolled into, well, a scroll). The shift from scrolls to codex took place during the second century. Thus, the fragment must date from *after* the first century.

- The fragments are similar in style to other fragments of New Testament texts from the second and third centuries. The writing style fits the style that began towards the end of the second century.

- A second century dating also fits with what we know of the spread of early Christian writing.[53]

The first three reasons converge towards the end of the second century as the date for the writing of fragments. While the last is an important reminder that there is a mass of other evidence that must be accounted for if Thiede's argument is to have any credence. Let's quote from Burton Mack again:

> From a critical scholar's point of view, Thiede's proposal is an example of just how desperate the Christian imagination can become in the quest to argue for the literal facticity of the Christian gospels.[54]

THE ARGUMENT FROM THE ENDING OF ACTS

Another favorite argument among fundamentalists for early dates of the composition of the gospels is taken from the ending of the Acts of the Apostles. This is how it ends (with Paul in Rome):

> Acts 28:30-31
> Paul stayed two whole years in his own rented house, and received all who were coming to him, preaching the Kingdom of God, and teaching the things concerning the Lord Jesus Christ with all boldness, without hindrance.

The argument is deceptively attractive. The tradition is that Paul died in the persecution of Christians by Nero circa 64 CE. Had the author of Acts known about Paul's death he would certainly have written about it. That he did not, can only mean that he was writing at a time *before it happened*. Paul probably reached Rome around 60 CE. Since Acts mentioned "two whole years" after that, this makes the date of composition of the work to be around 62 CE. It is generally accepted that the author of the Gospel of Luke and Acts are the same person. And in Acts 1:1, the author referred to his "first book about Jesus", thus making the gospel earlier than this. This would make the date of composition of Luke at a slightly earlier date - perhaps around 60 CE. Since it is well known that Luke incorporated large portions of Mark into his gospel, Mark must have been written even earlier, perhaps as early as the late 50s.[55]

---

[53] Mack, *Who Wrote the New Testament*: p9
      Wells, *The Jesus Myth*: p7
[54] Mack, *Who Wrote the New Testament*: p10
[55] Strobel, *The Case for Christ*: p41-42

Like all fundamentalist arguments, this assertion is not a new. Although when one reads books like Lee Strobel's *The Case for Christ* (1998), one is given the impression that these are explosive new lines of evidence that mainstream scholars have not considered. Actually this dating is the *traditional* date given by Christian apologists. For instance, in the first half of the 20th century, *The Papal Biblical Commission* decreed that, due to this passage, the Acts of the Apostles was written by Luke around 62 CE. That pronouncement was binding on Catholic scholars for a few decades. It was also suggested by NT scholar Adolf von Harnack (1851-1930) in his book *The Date of the Acts and of the Synoptic Gospels* (1911).[56]

However, among critical historical scholars, a pre-70 CE composition of *Luke-Acts* is a thoroughly discredited concept. Let us now examine the reasons.

Firstly, the claim that the author of Acts did not know that Paul died in Rome is demonstrably *false*. We are given this information obliquely in the book of Acts. We see in Acts 20:25, Paul is supposed to have told the people of Ephesus that they "will never see my face again". That this was taken to mean that Paul will die soon is made obvious a few verses later:[57]

> Acts 20:29, 36-38
> [Paul speaking] "For I know that after my departure, vicious wolves will enter in among you, not sparing the flock"... When he had spoken these things, he knelt down and prayed with them all. They all wept a lot, and fell on Paul's neck and kissed him, sorrowing most of all because of the word, which he had spoken, *that they should see his face no more.*

That Paul will meet the emperor Nero himself is also alluded to in Acts. This is what Luke had Paul say to his fellow seafarers:

> Acts 27:21-24
> When they had been long without food, Paul stood up in the middle of them, and said, "Sirs, you should have listened to me, and not have set sail from Crete, and have gotten this injury and loss. Now I exhort you to cheer up, for there will be no loss of life among you, but only of the ship. For there stood by me this night an angel, belonging to the God whose I am and whom I serve, saying, 'Don't be afraid, Paul. *You must stand before Caesar.* Behold, God has granted you all those who sail with you.'"

As A.N Wilson pointed out in his book *Paul: The Mind of the Apostle* (1997):

> The interesting thing about this speech, from the narrative point of view, is that, in Luke's terms, it is clearly true, or meant to be taken as true. Angels often appear in Luke's works - to announce the incarnation of Christ to the virgin, to proclaim his birth to the shepherds of Bethlehem, to proclaim his resurrection, to release Peter from prison. They do not lie, for they are messengers of God. So we can assume that the author of Acts believes, and wants us to believe, that Paul is indeed

---

[56]   Guignebert, *Jesus*: p22
        Powell, *What are They Saying About Acts*: p36, 121n61
        Williams, *The Acts of the Apostles*: p13
[57]   Schnelle, *The New Testament Writings*: p243

destined, not merely to reach Rome and to be tried, but that he will come face to face with Nero himself.[58]

Secondly, note that the last verses of Acts actually mentioned that Paul lived freely "for two whole years". There is actually no other way to interpret that (especially in the light of the verses alluding to Paul's death at the hands of Nero above) statement except that after two years a change happened and that this was Paul's condemnation and subsequent execution.[59]

Thirdly, we know that Luke used Mark as one of his sources. And Mark, as we have shown earlier in this chapter, is a post 70 CE document. Since Luke copied Mark, the Gospel of Luke must therefore be later than 70 CE. Furthermore, as we saw earlier, the Gospel of Luke had very detailed allusions to the siege and fall of Jerusalem that the only viable explanation is that it was written after the event. Since Acts was written after Luke, it too must be a post 70 CE document.

Finally, we look at *why* Luke ended Acts the way he did. Actually even a cursory thought should suffice to show that Luke could not have ended Acts with Paul's death. For, unlike Jesus, who was believed to have risen from the dead, Paul did not. Ending it with Paul's death would go against the whole grain of his work, which was primarily a summary of the *triumph* of the faith which spread from Jerusalem to Rome.[60] The fitting end would have been the *parousia* itself. However, since that had yet to happen at the time of writing, Paul's triumphal preaching was a satisfactory intermediate end.[61] As Werner Kummel explained in his classic *Introduction to the New Testament* (1975):

---

[58] Wilson, *Paul*: p246

[59] Wells, *The Jesus Myth*: p31

[60] Many evangelical apologists claim that the ending of Acts if extremely "odd" if it ignores such major events such as Paul's subsequent re-arrest and execution – thus the only *possible* explanation is that it has to be written before the fact. Yet we know that writers of history (or of fictionalized or dramatized history) sometimes do this. The most current example I can think of is the movie "Ali" directed by Michael Mann.   The show chronicles the heavyweight champion's life from around 1964 (his fight with Sonny Liston) up until his 1974 win over George Foreman in Kinshasa, Zaire. Now we know that Ali's life after his 1974 victory was anything but bland and would certainly have made for good drama – for instance he lost the heavyweight title in 1978 and regained it again later that year. Later in his life he was to suffer from Parkinson's disease (diagnosed in 1984). The movie mentioned nothing of these subsequent events. If we use the same logic as the fundamentalist apologists, we would have concluded that the movie must have been shot after the Kinshasa victory (1974) but before he lost the heavyweight crown, in 1978. Yet the movie, starring Will Smith as the incomparable heavyweight, started production in 1999 and was released in 2001! The reason why the movie ended in 1974 was simple, its point was not to chronicle all of Ali's life but to show the part of Ali's life that was intertwined with the radical politics of the 60's and 70's, namely his involvement with the civil rights movement of that time. The 1974 bout enables the movie on a triumphant note. This is exactly what Luke did with Acts. Acts was not meant to be a biography of Paul but an account of how the Christian faith spread from Jerusalem to Rome.

[61] Barr, *New Testament Story*: p 325

[I]n Lk 24:46f already the risen Lord proclaims as the meaning of both writings, not only the suffering and resurrection of Christ, but also the preaching "to all people, beginning from Jerusalem". And the same risen Lord (Acts 1:8) conveys to the disciples more precisely the charge "You will be my witness in Jerusalem and in all of Judea and in Samaria and to the ends of the earth." The theme of 1:8 is carried through in Acts and the declaration in 28:31 that Paul in Rome "preaches the kingdom of God and teaches about the Lord Jesus" to all who come to him...strikes a "triumphal note....," which corresponds precisely to the author's aim in Acts and proves to be the intended end of the book.[62]

Let us recap why the argument from the ending of Acts does not work.

- The basic assertion that the author of Acts did not know about Paul's subsequent fate is wrong. There are allusions to Paul's death and his "meeting" with Nero in Acts.

- The fact that Acts said Paul preached without hindrance for "two whole years" implied that something happened after that. In this case the arrest and trial under Nero.

- We know from an independent line of evidence that Mark is a post 70 CE document. Since Luke copied Mark, it must be a later work than Mark.

- Furthermore, the Gospel of Luke added many details to the basic "prophecy" of Jerusalem's fall in Mark that it is ludicrous to assume that it was written before the event.

- The ending in Acts is actually a very reasonable compromise ending, given that the ultimate end, the *parousia*, was not yet available and ending his work with Paul's death would have been anti-climactic. Thus, even with Luke knowing Paul's subsequent fate, the way Acts ended is understandable.

These then are the reasons why the majority of critical historical scholars do not accept the dating of Acts as 62 CE. That evangelical "scholars" continue to use Acts 28:30-31 as an argument for early dates for the composition of the gospels shows the bankrupt state of their "scholarship."

THE ORAL TRADITION

Now if the traditional date of 30 CE as the death of Jesus is accepted, the dating of the synoptics shows that the earliest gospel, Mark, did not appear until *at least four decades* after that. In the case of Matthew, Luke and John, these were written more than *sixty years* after the events they purport to describe.

How were the stories concerning Jesus passed down through the four to six decades? The answer is obvious, the stories and sayings of Jesus were mainly handed down orally. How reliable is this tradition?

Most fundamentalists, while admitting to the existence of a period of oral transmission, claim that the time elapsed from Jesus' life to the writing of the gospels

---

[62]   Kümmel, *Introduction to the New Testament*: p164

was too short for any false or erroneous material to have been included. Besides, they normally add, people who knew Jesus were around during the time of the gospels' publication.[63] Had it contained false materials, these eyewitnesses would have surely pointed it out. Another implied assumption here is that the eyewitnesses who started the transmission were themselves telling the stories as they actually occurred. Furthermore, they claim, based on the evidence of how the *Mishnah*[64] was memorized by the Jewish rabbis, the followers of Jesus, who were all Jews, must have been very adept at memorizing the words and deeds of Jesus.[65]

The Apostles as Guarantors of the Gospel Tradition

First let us look at the claim that eyewitnesses served as guarantors that the stories circulating about Jesus were authentic. Who among these eyewitnesses were around to check the veracity of the gospels when they were published? Peter, as Christian tradition tells us, died in the Neronian persecution of 64-67 CE. James (and probably John as well)[66] the son of Zebedee was killed in 44 CE by Herod Agrippa (Acts 12:2). These were the three "inner circle" of Jesus' apostles. For the rest, the remainder of their lives rests on conjecture and speculation. Tradition supplied them all with martyrs' deaths but as will be shown in chapter 12 some confusion as to the names of the apostles had already arisen by the time the gospels were put to writing. So little is known about them that we can't even be certain of *their identities*, let alone assume that they were the guarantors of the truth of the gospels. Apart from Peter, James and John, the witnesses of the apostles are dubious.

As for the minor disciples of Jesus (Luke says there were 70 or 72 : Luke 10:1), the uncertainties concerning their existence (70 or 72 is another symbolism in Jewish numerology and it appears only in Luke-Acts) argue against their being used as the assurance of the gospels' veracity.

As for those who heard him preach, they were confined mainly to Galilean peasants and some pilgrims during the Passover in Jerusalem in 30 CE. Many in his audience would not have sufficient knowledge about Jesus' ministry to be in a position to question any tradition about his life. Even for those who do (say some interested Galilean peasants who followed Jesus around the villages and towns of Galilee) how many of them would have been around when the gospels were written? The average life expectancy for a man during the Roman era was only 36 years.[67] Assuming that the worthwhile eyewitnesses were adults during the ministry of Jesus, they would have been around 60 years old by the (earliest possible) time Mark was published around 70 CE. So given the life expectancy of 36, clearly many would

---

63   McDowell, *Evidence that Demands a Verdict*: p62
64   The Mishnah is a collection done around 200 CE by Jewish Rabbis of the hitherto orally transmitted sayings of the Jewish sages from the Tannaitic period (50CE-200 CE).
65   This argument springs from the works of Birger Gerhardsson. He drew a parallel between the transmission of the oral Torah and the oral transmission of traditions and sayings of Jesus. For a critical summary of Gerhardsson's thesis see *The Oral and the Written Gospel* by Werner H. Kelber (Indiana University Press, 1997) p8-14
66   For evidence regarding the early death of the apostle John see note 37 in chapter 8.
67   Kendig & Hutton, *Life Spans*: p8

have been dead by then. To add on to this, the conditions before the publication of the gospels were a tumultuous one for Palestine; the Jewish revolt of 66-74 CE clearly took its toll on the natives of that land. It should be remembered that in Jerusalem alone more than one million Jews perished. Galilee, the home of many of the supposed eyewitnesses, was not spared as Josephus himself tells us:

> Jewish War 3:10:9
> The Romans never ceased, night or day, to devastate the plains and to pillage the property of the country folk, invariably killing all capable of bearing arms and reducing the inefficient to servitude. Galilee from end to end became a scene of fire and blood; from no misery, no calamity was it exempt.

Later in the war, many Galileans were slaughtered along the shore of the Sea of Galilee, Josephus adds:

> Jewish War 3:10:9
> One could see the whole lake red with blood and covered with corpses, for not a man escaped. During the following days the district reeked with a dreadful stench and presented a spectacle equally horrible. The beaches were strewn with wrecks and swollen carcasses.

Many of the eyewitnesses and even followers of Jesus would certainly have perished in this war. As for those who did survive, and doubtless some did, how much reliance can be placed on the testimony of old and broken men? As Hugh Schonfield (1901-1988) wrote:

> There is something further to be said about the survivors of the war. Early rabbinical literature reveals an inevitable consequence of the conflict, and of the troubled period preceding it, which has to be taken into account. Many, especially of the older generation, were gravely impaired in health and memory. People whose testimonies were of importance about past events and practices make contradictory statements, got dates mixed and persons and events confused. It was very natural, but most unfortunate.[68]

If this happened to the Jewish elders, it would undoubtedly had happened to the followers and eyewitnesses of Jesus. Those few who remained alive were probably traumatized by the war, unable to relate accurately the events of Jesus' life.

As Jesus confined his teachings mainly to Galilean backwaters, it is unlikely that many among his followers would have traveled widely. Furthermore, Christian tradition attributes the location of the gospels' composition *outside* Palestinian soil: Mark in Rome, Matthew in Alexandria (or Antioch), Luke in Antioch and John in Ephesus. Of these few remaining broken and confused eyewitnesses, how many would have been around the location of the gospels when they were first composed to vouch for their veracity? How many would travel around the Mediterranean telling *their* version of the story as opposed to the gospels?

---

[68]   Schonfield, *The Passover Plot*: p186-187

Some scholars have argued[69] that the evidence of the later rabbinic practice of *mechanical* memorization of oral tradition implies that the followers of Jesus employed such methods to reliably preserve, almost verbatim, the teachings and acts of Jesus. Such claims are fundamentally flawed. As the Jewish scholar Jacob Neusner has emphasized, we have no evidence that the form of oral transmission indicated in the Mishnah dates much earlier than 200 CE. He also provided evidence that, in many cases, the rabbis *simply made up sayings and stories and attributed them to earlier sages!*[70] The much-touted *verbatim* oral preservation skill of the Rabbis is a mere figment of some modern scholarly imagination.[71]

It gets worse. Unlike the rabbis, the apostles and most of the people who were witnesses to Jesus' sayings were unschooled and illiterate (Acts 4:13). It is highly unlikely that they would have been trained in the rabbinic method of memorization. Studies of oral tradition show that stories told orally normally incorporate mnemonic devices to help the memory as well as the telling of the stories. Such devices, at best, preserve information that was relevant to the *sitz im leben* of the teller of the stories, his audience and the pertinent issues of his community, and never convey the full information available to him. The mechanical memorization techniques employed by the rabbis are not evident in the teachings attributed to Jesus in the gospels.[72]

The guarantee of reliable eyewitnesses so often cited by the fundamentalists disappears before our very eyes.

Time Elapsed Too Short for Mythologization

What about the claim that the time elapsed between the lifetime of Jesus and the publication of the gospels was simply too short for any falsification or mythologization to creep into the oral transmission? This claim is simply wrong. We know of many cases, from studies of oral tradition worldwide, where stories became embellished and mythologized within a short period of time. Let us look at three examples, one of a person reminiscing a past event (i.e. as an eye witness and a participant), another of a person who was still alive when stories about her started circulating and the last about a person who was well loved by those who may not know much about the details of his life.

The first involves the meeting of Gioacchino Antonio Rossini (1792-1868), an Italian composer, with Ludwig van Beethoven (1770-1827). Rossini first told the story of their meeting a few years after the death of the great Austrian composer. He went to Beethoven's house and found difficulty in getting admitted. And when he did get it, did not manage to talk to Beethoven at all as the latter did not have a good command of Italian. However, upon retelling by Rossini, the story became more and more embellished until in its final form, we are told of how the Austrian master

---

69   A major proponent of this view on the high reliability of the gospel tradition is Birger Gerhardsson (see *The Reliability of the Gospel Tradition*, Hendrickson 2001)

70   Neusner, *Rabbinic Literature and the New Testament*: p13, 33, 68-82

71   This is not to say, of course, that everything in the Mishnah and Talmuds are fictional creation of the rabbis. It merely means that one approaches such works with the same skepticism as one would approach the gospels.

72   Kelber, *The Oral and the Written Gospel*: p14-15, 21

received the Italian composer openly and advised him to continue his work and showered praises on his opera *The Barber of Seville*.[73]

The second example involves the legend originating from a small village in Romania, told by Mircea Eliade, in his book *Cosmos and History* (New York 1959). The legend tells the tale of a young suitor who was bewitched by a fairy, who threw him off a cliff a few days before he was to be married. His body was discovered by some shepherds, who took it back to the village. Upon arrival his fiancée spontaneously broke into a beautiful funeral lament.

When a folklorist discovered that the story had only taken place about forty years ago, and that the heroine was still alive, he inquired from her regarding the legend. Her description differs substantially from the popular tale. She described a commonplace tragedy. There was no fairy and no spontaneous funeral lament. Her lover slipped off a cliff but did not die immediately. He was taken back to the village where he soon died. She participated in the funeral rites, which included the customary ritual lamentations.

The collective memory of the village had stripped the story of all historical details and had embellished it with mythical elements. Amazingly, when the folklorist reminded the villagers of the authentic version, they repudiated it and insisted that the old woman's mind and memory were destroyed by her grief. As Eliade wrote: "[I]t was the myth that told the truth; the real story was only a falsification."[74]

The final example is a religious one, taken from Andrew Dickson White's *A History of the Warfare of Science with Christendom* (1876). It involves the famous 16th century missionary, St. Francis Xavier (1506-1552), who spent many years preaching in India, China and Japan.

After the missionary's death, stories of his power to perform miracles began to circulate. He was supposed to be able to cure the sick, raise the dead, turn seawater into fresh and call fire down from heaven. There was even the fantastic story of how after having lost his crucifix at sea, it was miraculously returned to him by a crab.

Perhaps the most remarkable, and certainly the most useful, miracle ascribed to Francis Xavier was the *gift of tongues*. It was claimed that he spoke to various tribes with ease in their own languages. The legend was further developed to the point where it was claimed that when he addressed various native tribes at the same time, each heard the same sermon in their own native language! When this proselytizer was canonized (i.e. made a saint) seventy years after his death, the bull of canonization laid great stress on the new saint's gift of tongues.

The problem with all these stories about Xavier's gift of tongues is that we *know* that they are untrue. Throughout his missionary journeys, he and his fellow missionaries wrote many letters to friends and associates. Many of these are still extant today. In none of his letters do we find any reference to the numerous miracles attributed to him. In fact, throughout his letters he constantly referred to the difficulties he faced in the communication of his faith to the different tribes. He wrote of how he surmounted these difficulties: sometimes by learning just enough of a language to translate the main formulas of the church, by soliciting help from others

---

[73] Vansina, *Oral Tradition as History*: p9-10

[74] Wilken, *The Myth of Christian Beginnings*: p10-11

to patch together some teachings for natives to learn by rote, by a mixture of various dialects, by using sign language, and by using interpreters. Xavier actually related how, on one occasion, his voyage to China was delayed because his interpreter he had hired for the mission had failed to meet him. How much easier his mission would have been had he actually possessed the gift of tongues![75]

It is therefore clear that the miracles attributed to this missionary never happened. References by Francis Xavier in his letters to the actual situation were quickly forgotten and popular memory placed the mythological and legendary elements on center stage. We let Andrew White (1832-1918) sum up this section on mythologization:

> It is hardly necessary to attribute to orators and biographers generally a conscious attempt to deceive. The simple fact is, that as a rule they thought, spoke, and wrote in obedience to the natural laws which govern the luxuriant growth of myth and legend in the warm atmosphere of love and devotion which constantly arises about great religious leaders in times when men have little or no knowledge of natural law, where there is little care for scientific evidence, and when he who believes most is most meritorious.[76]

The passage above could well be applied to the early followers of Jesus. It is thus shown, without a shadow of a doubt, that mythologization *can* occur within a short space of time. It can occur in all situations: where the person telling the story was himself a participant, or where the person the story being told about was still alive (and supposedly able to "refute" false accounts), or where they are told by devotees caught up in the "warm atmosphere of love and devotion" shortly after the death of the person concerned.

* * * * *

The conclusions we can draw from the last three chapters are many. None of the authors of the gospels was an eyewitness to the events in Jesus' life. None of them had any direct access to eyewitnesses. The stories about Jesus came from the community oral tradition and were mainly third or fourth hand accounts. They were put in written form at least four decades after the death of Jesus. There is no assurance that people who knew Jesus were around to correct the falsifications that are present in these writings. And even if some of them were around, the tumultuous events following the Jewish war mean that not much faith can be placed in their testimony. Furthermore, we know from studies of oral tradition that mythologization can set in very quickly in the retelling of stories.

---

[75]   White, *A History of the Warfare of Science with Theology*, Vol II: p5-22
[76]   White, *A History of the Warfare of Science with Theology*, Vol II: p21

Chapter Eleven
THE NATIVITY

THE STORY AS IS

The story of the nativity in the New Testament appears in only two of the four gospels: Matthew and Luke.

The Gospel of Matthew opens with the genealogy of Jesus. It traces his ancestry from his father Joseph through David to Abraham. The main point of the genealogy is to show that Jesus was a descendent of King David.[1] This was supposed to have been a fulfillment of an Old Testament passage which prophesized that the messiah will be descended from that famed Jewish king of antiquity:

> II Samuel 7:12-13
> When your days [i.e. David's] are fulfilled, and you shall sleep with your fathers, I will set up your seed after you, who shall proceed out of your bowels, and I will establish his kingdom. He shall build a house for my name, and I will establish the throne of his kingdom forever.

After the genealogy, the focus is shifted to Mary, a woman pledged to be married to Joseph. Before they had had any sexual relations, Joseph found out Mary was pregnant, or as the gospel puts it "with child through the Holy Spirit" (Matthew 1:19). He wanted to terminate the engagement but had a dream that night which made him change his mind. In that dream, an angel appeared to him, informing him of Mary's miraculous conception. This virginal conception was in fulfillment of another Old Testament prophecy (Isaiah 7:14). Convinced that his dream was a message from God, Joseph married the pregnant girl and when the child was born, named him Jesus. Matthew mentioned that Jesus was born in Bethlehem in Judea. The whole narrative up to now gives no hint that Joseph and Mary were from anywhere else except Bethlehem.

After Jesus was born, "wise men from the east" (Matthew 2:2) came to Jerusalem to look for the newborn king of the Jews. They mentioned that they had seen a star in the east that led them to Judea. Their enquiries reached the ears of King Herod the Great. He was worried about this possible threat to his throne and summoned the chief priests and the teachers of the law to enquire from them where the messiah will be born. They told him Bethlehem was the ordained placed for it was prophesied in the Old Testament (Micah 5:2). Herod then told the wise men to look for the newborn and to inform him of the baby's whereabouts on the pretext that he too would want the worship the new "king of the Jews". So the wise men went to Bethlehem where they found the baby Jesus. Consistent with his story, the wise men found Jesus in Joseph's and Mary's *house* (Matthew 2:11). Upon seeing the baby the wise men gave him gifts of gold, incense and myrrh[2] and worshipped him. They then

---

[1]   Fenton, *Saint Matthew*: p36
[2]   It is probably from these *three* presents that tradition counted *three* wise men.

went back to their own country by another route, having being warned by an angel in a dream not to go back to Herod.

Now an angel appeared to Joseph, again in a dream, telling him to take his family to Egypt, which he did. This was done to save the baby from the murderous schemes of Herod. For Herod, realizing that the wise men had outwitted him, had given orders to slaughter all the baby boys less than two years of age in and around Bethlehem. After Herod died, Joseph took his family from Egypt back to Judea. However, when he heard that Archelaus was reigning in his father's stead, he went to Galilee instead.

Matthew now quoted two passages from the Old Testament to show that, here too, what happened was in fulfillment of the scriptures. He quoted from Hosea 11:1 for the calling of Joseph, Mary and baby Jesus from Egypt and from Jeremiah 31:5 for the prophecy of the slaughter of the babies by Herod. The nativity story in Matthew ends with the author telling us that Joseph and Mary settled down in the town of Nazareth in Galilee.

Luke's story of the nativity narrates two parallel birth stories: one of Jesus and one of John the Baptist. The account kicks off with the annunciation of the birth of John the Baptist to Zechariah, his father-to-be. When Elizabeth, Zechariah's wife, was six months pregnant, the angel Gabriel appeared to a virgin in Nazareth named Mary. The angel announced to her that she was to be the mother of Jesus, "the son of the most high." (Luke 1:32). Mary, seeing that she was a virgin, asked how this was to be. The angel explained that she will be conceived by "the power of the most high." Mary then acquiesced by saying, "I am the servant of the Lord, may it be to me as you have said."

Mary, impregnated by the Holy Spirit, then visited her relative Elizabeth, who was herself pregnant. It was during this visit that she sang her famous hymn, The Magnificat. She stayed at her cousin's place for three months. After Mary left, Elizabeth gave birth to John. Therefore, according to Luke, Jesus was the second cousin of John the Baptist.

Whereas Matthew had Joseph and Mary already living in Bethlehem when she became pregnant, in Luke, both Joseph and Mary were natives of Nazareth. The reason why they had to go to Bethlehem, according to Luke, was due to the Roman census under Quirinius:

> Luke 2:1-2
> Now it happened in those days, that a decree went out from Caesar Augustus that all the world should be enrolled. This was the first enrollment made when Quirinius was governor of Syria...

According to Luke, this census required everyone to register not in their present hometown but in the hometown of their ancestor. And since Joseph, so says Luke, was descended from David, he had to go back to Bethlehem, the town of David, to be registered. And so off he went, taking his heavily pregnant wife with him. When they reached Bethlehem, Mary started having her contractions. Not being able to find any place in the inn, Mary probably gave birth to Jesus in a stable, for the gospel makes reference to Jesus being put in a manger (Luke 2:7), which is a container used for feeding animals.

That night an angel appeared to some shepherds who were keeping watch over their flocks. He announced the news of Jesus' birth to them. On hearing this, they hurried to the place where Jesus was born. After seeing the baby, they went about telling people about their experience.

Luke then described the customary Jewish rituals that Jesus went through: he was circumcised on the 8th day, and presented to the Temple in Jerusalem on the 40th day. After all this, Joseph, Mary and baby Jesus left Judea and went back to Nazareth.

Both the nativity stories of Matthew and Luke share some things in common for sure: the birth in Bethlehem, the virginal conception and birth, the names of Jesus' parents (Mary and Joseph) and the eventual move to the town of Nazareth. However, even in the above cursory presentation of the two nativities, one can sense the differences between them. In Matthew, we are presented with the wise men, the Star of Bethlehem and Herod's slaughter of the innocents. In Luke, we are presented with the census of Quirinius, the birth in the stable, the visitation of the shepherds and the customary Jewish ceremony. The traditional Christian view is that the two evangelists were selectively describing separate events that happened during the nativity. A skeptic may well ask: were they telling different aspects within the same historical event or were they relying on separate, mutually contradictory, traditions on Jesus' birth? And are the individual stories or episodes historical or are they just myths? It is these questions that we concern ourselves with for the rest of this chapter.

THE GENEALOGIES

As was mentioned earlier, Matthew started his gospel by giving the genealogy of Jesus (Matthew 1:1-17) from Jesus to Abraham. Luke also gave a genealogy of Jesus, tracing it all the way to Adam. (Luke 3:23-38). Both these genealogies trace Jesus' ancestry from Joseph's side. By comparing the two genealogies, an obvious difficulty arises: they are not the same! The names given in Luke from Joseph to David do not corroborate with that given in Matthew. In fact, the genealogies disagree even on the name of Joseph's father:

Matthew 1:16
Jacob became the father of Joseph, the husband of Mary, from whom was born Jesus, who is called Christ.

Luke 3:23
Jesus himself, when he began to teach, was about thirty years old, being the son (as was supposed) of Joseph, the son of Heli.

So according to Matthew, Joseph's father was Jacob but according to Luke he was Heli! The discrepancies do not stop here. The messiah is supposed to be a descendant of David. The genealogies are meant to prove this Davidic descent. Yet, we find that the two gospels can't even agree as to which of David's sons Jesus was descended from. Matthew says he is descended through David's son and successor, Solomon. Luke contradicts this by noting that he was descended through another son, Nathan.[3]

Table 11.1 on the next page summarizes in tabular form the generations from Jesus to David as given by both gospels.[4] A quick glance at the table will reveal the glaring inconsistencies in both lists. From Joseph to David, with the exception of Shealtiel and Zerubbabel[5], none of the other names coincide! And worse, Luke has 43 generations from David to Jesus, Matthew lists only 28, giving a discrepancy of 15 generations. Assuming an average of 25 to 30 years per generation, this brings the disparity of about *four centuries* between the genealogies.[6] In short, to put it bluntly, the two genealogies contradict one another at almost every turn.

Matthew 1:1-11	Luke 3:23-31	Matthew 1:1-11 (cont'd)	Luke 3:23-31 (cont'd)
1. *Jesus*	1. *Jesus*	14. Jechoniah	23. Neri
2. *Joseph*	2. *Joseph*	15. Josiah	24. Melchi
3. Jacob	3. Heli	16. Amon	25. Addi
4. Matthan	4. Matthat	17. Manasseh	26. Cosam
5. Eleazar	5. Levi	18. Hezekiah	27. Elmadam
6. Eluid	6. Melchi	19. Ahaz	28. Er
7. Achim	7. Jannai	20. Jotham	29. Joshua
8. Zadok	8. Joseph	21. Uzziah	30. Eliezer
9. Azor	9. Mattathias	22. Joram	31. Jorim
10. Eliakim	10. Amos	23. Jehoshapat	32. Matthat
11. Abiud	11. Nahum	24. Asa	33. Levi
12. *Zerubbabel*	12. Esli	25. Abijah	34. Simeon
13. *Shealtiel*	13. Naggai	26. Rehoboam	35. Judah
	14. Maath	27. Solomon	36. Joseph
	15. Mattathias	28. *David*	37. Joanm
	16. Semein		38. Eliakim
	17. Josech		39. Melea
	18. Joda		40. Menna
	19. Joanan		41. Mattatha
	20. Rhesa		42. Nathan
	21. *Zerubbabel*		43. *David*
	22. *Shealtiel*		

Table 11.1: The genealogies of Jesus in Matthew and Luke

Throughout the centuries, many ingenious attempts has been made by Christians to overcome this obvious contradiction.

---

[3]   Lüdemann, *Virgin Birth?*: p121

[4]   Fenton, *Saint Matthew*: p36

[5]   The names of Shealtiel and Zerubbabel really could not have been omitted by both evangelists given the strong connection of those names with the return from exile (Ezra 5:2)

[6]   Craveri, *The Life of Jesus*: p19
      Guignebert, *Jesus*: p113

APOLOGETIC ATTEMPT #1:
THE LEVIRATE

The first explanation is that the two lists do give the genealogy from Joseph's side but one lists the *legal* heritage while the other gives the *natural or biological* descent. This, they say, is due to the Jewish religious custom of the *levirate* (Deuteronomy 25:5-10). The levirate decrees that if a man died without leaving any offspring, it is the *duty* of the deceased man's brother to impregnate his brother's wife to give the former offspring to perpetuate the family line. In this system, the baby's *biological* father is the living brother but the rights and obligations of the newborn are with respect to the deceased legal parent. Using this law, the ancient apologists claimed that one line of the genealogy gives the actual legal father, the other gives the natural father (from the levirate). The difficulty with this explanation is obvious, we are to suppose that the levirate affected *all* the generations except two (Schealtiel and Zerubbabel) from David to Jesus. As Charles Guignebert (1867-1939), who was Professor of History of Christianity in the Sorbonne, concluded, such an explanation is clearly "absurd."[7]

Another apologetic attempt comes from the third century Christian writer Julius Africanus (c160-c240). According to Africanus, Jacob (Joseph's father as given in Matthew) and Heli (Joseph's father as given in Luke) were brothers. When Heli died childless, Jacob impregnated his sister-in-law, and presto!, both Heli and Jacob are Joseph's fathers; Heli being the legal father while Jacob the biological father via the levirate. The obvious question then is: why do these two brothers have different fathers? Heli's father is Matthat and Jacob's father is Matthan. Africanus' solution here is typical apologetic nonsense: he claimed that Jacob and Heli were *half* brothers![8] They shared the same mother who after the death of her first husband, Matthan, remarried this time to Matthat! The explanation is rather strange and sounds unreal. Did Africanus supply any proof of this? No, but evidence to the early Christians is of no consequence. As Africanus himself wrote:

> This may or may not be the truth of the matter; but in my opinion and that of every fair minded person no one else could give a clearer exposition, and we must content ourselves with it even if it is unconfirmed, as we are not in a position to suggest a better or truer one. *In any case the gospel record is true.*[9]

This was how the inconsistency was reconciled in ancient times; with convoluted explanations based on hypothetical levirate and second marriages. This explanation was eventually abandoned by the Christian apologists.

---

[7]   Guignebert, *Jesus*: p113

[8]   Actually Africanus' claim was that Matthan and *Melchi* were half brothers. His Lukan genealogy probably lacked the names Matthat and Levi. [see Skausaune & Hvalvik, *Jewish Believers in Jesus*: p355-356]

[9]   Eusebius, *History of the Church*: 1:7

APOLOGETIC ATTEMPT #2:
LUKE'S GENEALOGY IS TRACED THROUGH MARY'S ANCESTRY

Around the end of 15th century Annius of Viterbo suggested another alternative explanation to this discrepancy. This "explanation" maintains that the genealogy in Matthew applied to Joseph while the one in Luke applied to Mary! This explanation does not hold water. In the first place, both gospels state explicitly that they are tracing Jesus' ancestors from Joseph's side (Matthew 1:16; Luke 3:23-see above). In fact, Luke - the one the apologists claim traces the ancestry from Mary - *always* refers to *Joseph* whenever he talks about ancestry of David:

> Luke 1:26-27
> Now in the sixth month, the angel Gabriel was sent from God to a city of Galilee, named Nazareth, to a virgin pledged to be married to a man whose name was *Joseph, of the house of David.*

> Luke 2:4
> *Joseph* also went up from Galilee, out of the city of Nazareth, into Judea, to the city of David, which is called Bethlehem, *because he was of the house and family of David*

Furthermore, Luke, by making Mary the relative of Elizabeth (Luke 1:36), whom he gave as a descendent of priestly family of Aaron[10] (Luke 1:5) immediately makes Mary a member of that family.

In the second place, the Jews do not admit to transmission of birthright by the mother, as St. Jerome rightly said, "It is not the custom of the scriptures to count women in their genealogies." A genealogy traced from Mary's side is of no value in determining the descent from David.[11] The fact that this discredited medieval explanation is still the same one used by some believers today only serves to underline the bankrupt state of evangelical Christian theology.

OTHER PROBLEMS WITH THE GENEALOGY

The contradictions remain. Some conservative commentators have tried to explain away this problem by saying that we should still give the genealogies the benefit of the doubt because there are other ancient contemporaneous genealogies that are authentic and that great care was taken to preserve these. However, this defense does not cut it. At best it explains the importance of genealogies in the ancient world and why both Matthew and Luke, independently, felt compelled to present one for Jesus. It does not explain away the discrepancies.[12]

So, at best, only one of these genealogies can be true, at worst, both could be false. Can we find out one way or the other? Yes we can!

---

[10] Aaron, according to tradition, the brother of Moses was the first member of the priestly line, all descendents from Aaron were also appointed priests (Exodus 28)

[11] Guignebert, *Jesus*: p107,114

[12] Lüdemann, *Virgin Birth?*: p122

Let us look at Matthew's genealogy first. For reasons unknown to us today, but probably with some important spiritual significance for the author and his readers, Matthew presents an impressive piece of numerology concerning the ancestors of Jesus:

Matthew 1:17
So all the generations from Abraham to David are fourteen generations; from David to the exile to Babylon fourteen generations; and from the carrying away to Babylon to the Christ, fourteen generations.

From David to the "exile" ends with Jeconiah. The numerical significance perhaps lies in Matthew trying to show that every fourteen generations something spectacular happens: for fourteen generations after Abraham was David and fourteen generations after that was the exile and so fourteen generations after the exile the messiah was born. There is probably something symbolic in the number 14 and it could be that 14 is 7 x 2, and 7 is a number that appears very often in Matthew.[13] All this sounds impressive. To help in our analysis, Table 11:2 below gives the names in Matthew's list in tabular form.

From Abraham to David (Matthew 1:2-6a)	From David to the Exile (Matthew 1:6b-11)	From the Exile to Christ (Matthew 1:12-16)
1. Abraham	**1. David**	**1. Jechoniah**
2. Isaac	2. Solomon	2. Shealtiel
3. Jacob	3. Rehoboam	3. Zerubbabel
4. Judah	4. Abijah	4. Abiud
5. Perez	5. Asa	5. Eliakim
6. Hezron	6. Jehoshapat	6. Azor
7. Ram	*7. Joram*	7. Zadok
8 Amminadab	*8. Uzziah*	8. Achim
9. Nahshon	9. Jotham	9. Eluid
10. Salmon	10. Ahaz	10. Eleazar
11. Boaz	11. Hezekiah	11. Matthan
12. Obed	12. Manasseh	12. Jacob
13. Jesse	13. Amon	13. Joseph
14. David	14. Josiah	**14. Jesus**
	15. Jechoniah	

Table 11.2: "Fourteen" Generations

Whether Matthew meant "generations" in the sense of counting the number of names or whether it is in terms of "begats" (i.e. "A begats B who begats C" has three names but two begats) his scheme doesn't really work. For in terms of names we do have fourteen from Abraham to David and from the exile (Jechoniah) to Jesus but we have *fifteen* names from David to the exile (Jechoniah). It does not help if we take "generations" to mean "begats" – for now we have only *thirteen* generations for Abraham to David and from the exile to Jesus. Note also that this problem is not solved by removing names which are counted twice (David and Jechoniah), for if

---

[13]   7 demons (Matthew 12:45), 7 loaves (Matthew 15:34), 7 baskets (Matthew 15:37), 7x forgiveness (Matthew 18:21), 7 brothers (Matthew 22:25) & 7 woes (Matthew 23)

these are remove David from the second column and Jechoniah from the third column we have 14-14-13. In essence we have 41 names when we need 42. Whichever way we look at it, the scheme is not 14-14-14.[14]

Furthermore, Matthew has been less than honest in making the genealogy fit his numerological scheme. In the second list of fourteen generations (from David to Jeconiah) we have the seemingly innocent verse:

Matthew 1:8
Joram became the father of Uzziah.

These are the seventh and eighth name in the second column of table 11.2 above. Matthew had skipped *three* generations from Joram to Uziah to keep his nicely balanced numerology. For we know from the Old Testament that Joram was actually the great great grandfather of Uzziah:

II Kings 8:24 (II Chronicles 22:1)
Joram slept with his fathers, and was buried with his fathers in the city of David; and *Ahaziah his son reigned in his place.*

II Kings 11:2 (II Chronicles 22:11)
... Joash the son of Ahaziah...

II Kings 14:1 (II Chronicles 25:1)
... Amaziah the son of Joash...

II Chronicles 26:1 (II Kings 15:1)
All the people of Judah took *Uzziah*, who was sixteen years old, *and made him king in the room of his father Amaziah*

So the actual genealogical relationship between Joram and Uzziah is Joram-Ahaizah-Joash-Amaziah-Uzzaih. Matthew has left out three generations (Ahaziah, Joash and Amaziah) to make the genealogy conform to his numerology.

There is another mistake in Matthew's list:

Matthew 1:11
Josiah became the father of Jechoniah and his brothers, at the time of the exile to Babylon.

Jeconiah is just another form of the name Jehoiachin and we know from the Old Testament that Josiah was Jeconiah's *grandfather*:

II Kings 23:34 (II Chronicles 36:4)
Pharaoh Necoh made Eliakim the son of Josiah king in the room of *Josiah* his father, and changed his name to *Jehoiakim*

---

[14] Lüdemann, *Virgin Birth?*: p60, 122
Miller, *Born Divine*: p79

II Kings 24:6 (II Chronicles 36:8)
So *Jehoiakim* slept with his fathers; and *Jehoiachin* [=Jechoniah] his son reigned in his place.

The genealogy is Josiah-Jehoiakim-Jechoniah; Matthew had left out the middle name. Again, this name was probably left out to make the whole list fit his numerological scheme.

Now if we include all the names that Matthew missed out, we get fourteen generations from Abraham to David, and we get eighteen generations from David (but not counting David again) to the exile (to Jechoniah and not counting his name for the next section) and only thirteen generations from the exile to Jesus. Neither a pretty nor satisfying numerological relationship![15]

The conclusion regarding Matthew's handling of the genealogy is most aptly stated by Guignebert:

> It is not a case of accidental forgetfulness or casual inaccuracy; the redactor has simply cut out anything that interfered with the regular pattern of the symbolic structure by which he professed to prove that Jesus had fulfilled the divine promises made to his ancestor Abraham, and had accomplished the sacred destiny of the race of David. The prosaic facts of history mattered little to him.[16]

While the early genealogies had their source in the Old Testament, the generations after the exile from Abiud to Joseph is taken from a source no longer known to us. Bearing in mind the way Matthew used available material it is not impossible that some of these names could well be fictitious.

Let us now have a look at Luke's genealogy. Luke's list is in reverse order compared to Matthew. While Matthew started with Abraham and worked his way down to Jesus, Luke started his Jesus and worked his way up to Adam. In Luke 3:35-36, it is stated that Shelah was the son of Cainan who, in turn, was the son of Arphaxad:

Luke 3:35-36
... the son of *Shelah*, the son of *Cainan*, the son of *Arphaxad*,...

So, according to Luke, Shelah was the *grandson* of Arphaxad. However, the Hebrew Old Testament explicitly stated that Arphaxad was the *father* of Shelah.

Genesis 10:24
Arpachshad became the *father* of *Shelah*....

Only in the Greek Septuagint do we find the name Cainan inserted between Arphaxad and Shelah.

---

[15] Asimov, *Guide to the Bible*: p777-778
Guignebert, *Jesus*: p109-110
Miller, *Born Divine*: p77-81

[16] Guignebert, *Jesus*: p110

There is however, another name that did not appear in any extant text known to us, i.e. neither in the Hebrew Bible nor in the Greek Septuagint. That name appears in Luke 3:27, Rhesa

> Luke 3:27
> the son of *Joanan*, the son of *Rhesa*, the son of *Zerubbabel*

Rhesa, in the above passage is the father of Joanan and the son of Zerubbabel. This makes Joanan the grandson of Zerubbabel. Now Joanan is just another form of the name Hananiah and we know from the Old Testament that he was the *son* of Zerubbabel.

> I Chronicles 3:19
> The sons of *Zerubbabel*: Meshullam, and *Hananiah [=Joanan]*...

There is no such person as Rhesa and Luke had simply inserted another generation to the list.

It remains an open question whether Luke's mistakes in inserting the names of Rhesa and Cainan were accidental or purposeful. It should be noted that the number of generations from God to Jesus in Luke's list is 77 and we know that the messianic number is 7. So perhaps Luke, like Matthew, dabbled in numerology.

Matthew traces Jesus' lineage through the Davidic kings, so we can compare his list with those from the books of Kings. Luke on the other hand has a list, with the exception of Nathan (son of David), Zerubbabel, Shealtiel and Joseph, consisting of totally unknown names. We do not know where Luke got these names from. It should also be mentioned that even with known names we have discrepancies between the two lists. In Matthew the father of Shealtiel was given as Jeconiah [Jehoaichin], in Luke the father is given as Neri.[17]

Let us conclude what we have found out about the genealogies. Some of the names in the genealogies are taken out from the Old Testament. Even from this known source, we find that both Matthew and Luke used the source rather freely to fit it into their theological schemes. Where the source in unknown we find they contradict one another. The conclusion is obvious: both the genealogies are works of fiction.

THE VIRGIN BIRTH

Both Matthew and Luke stated that Jesus' conception was not a commonplace one. In these gospels Mary was a virgin who became pregnant, not through sexual intercourse, but through the "power of the Holy Spirit" (Matthew 1:18; Luke 1:34-

---

[17]   Asimov, *Guide to the Bible*: p938
Caird, *Saint Luke*: p19
Guignebert, *Jesus*: p110
Miller, *Born Divine*: p73-75

35). The Gospel of Matthew explicitly mentioned that this virgin pregnancy[18] took place in fulfillment of the scriptures:

Matthew 1:22-23
Now all this has happened, that it might be fulfilled which was spoken by the Lord through the prophet, saying, "Behold, the virgin shall be with child, and shall bring forth a son. They shall call his name Immanuel;" which is, being interpreted, 'God with us.'"

Matthew is quoting the book of Isaiah (7:14) from the Septuagint. The word for *virgin* is rendered in the Greek Bible as *parthenos*. This word carries the explicit meaning of virgin. However, if we are to look at the Bible in its original Hebrew, from the Masoretic Text, the word used there is *almah*. Now the nearest English translation for *almah* is a *young woman* and does not carry with it any strong connotation of virginity. To show how far *almah* is from the meaning of virginity, I have quoted below some passages from the Old Testament where the word was used:

Genesis 20:17
Abraham prayed to God. God healed Abimelech, and his wife, and his female servants [*almah*], and they bore children. For Yahweh had closed up tight all the wombs of the house of Abimelech, because of Sarah, Abraham's wife.

Genesis 21:12-13
God said to Abraham, "Don't let it be grievous in your sight because of the boy, and because of your handmaid [*almah*]. In all that Sarah says to you, listen to her voice. For from Isaac will your seed be called. I will also make a nation of the son of the handmaid [*almah*], because he is your seed."

The word *almah* was used in the above passages to refer to a female slave. In Genesis 21:12-13, the *almah* referred to was Hagar who had already borne Abraham a son (Genesis 16:15). Let us look at two more passages in which the word almah is used. The word is left untranslated, so the reader will get a direct sense of its meaning by reading the sentence.

Songs of Solomon 6:8
There are sixty queens and eighty concubines, and *almah* without number.

Proverbs 30:18-19
"There are three things which are too amazing for me, four which I don't understand: The way of an eagle in the air; the way of a serpent on a rock; the way of a ship in the midst of the sea; and the way of a man with an *almah*."

In these two passages we have *almah* as an occupant of a harem and as the object of a man's physical sexual attention. Clearly, the passages above could not have been referring to *virgins*. So while the use of the Hebrew word can sometimes mean a

---

[18] Recently Robert Miller, Professor of Religion at Juniata College, has argued in this book *Born Divine: The births of Jesus and other sons of God* (Polebridge 2003) that a careful, unprejudiced, reading of Matthew reveals that the first gospel never suggested a virgin birth! (p195-206).

young girl of marriageable age, as for instance, when it is applied to Rebecca before her marriage to Isaac (Genesis 24:43), it is also used to mean a slave woman and sometimes even for women in a harem.

If the author of Isaiah wanted to make clear the prophecy was meant for a virgin birth, he would not have used the word *almah* for all the ambiguity that it entails. He would have chosen the Hebrew word that does explicitly mean a virgin: *bethulah*. This word would have been the Hebrew equivalent for the Greek *parthenos*. The Greek equivalent for *almah* should actually be *neanis*, which means young woman.

Matthew's assertion of the virgin birth being prophesied in the scripture is therefore based on a *mistranslation* of the Hebrew word for a young woman. The virgin birth is nowhere prophesied in the original Hebrew. [19]

In fact, if we look at the passage in Isaiah within its entire context, it looks even more unlikely to be any sort of a messianic prophecy. It arose in a conversation between the prophet Isaiah and Ahaz, the King of Judah. It was a time of national danger and the king feared a new attack from the alliance of Syria and Israel. The two combined force had just failed to take Jerusalem (Isaiah 7:1). Isaiah wanted to assure Ahaz that God is on Judah's side. From this point on let us follow the biblical narrative:

> Isaiah 7:10-17
> Yahweh spoke again to Ahaz, saying, "Ask a sign of Yahweh your God; ask it either in the depth, or in the height above." But Ahaz said, "I will not ask, neither will I tempt Yahweh." He said, "Listen now, house of David: Is it not enough for you to try the patience of men, that you will try the patience of my God also? Therefore the Lord himself will give you a sign. Behold, the *almah* will conceive, and bear a son, and shall call his name Immanuel. He shall eat butter and honey when he knows to refuse the evil, and choose the good. *For before the child knows to refuse the evil, and choose the good, the land whose two kings you abhor shall be forsaken.* Yahweh will bring on you, on your people, and on your father's house, days that have not come, from the day that Ephraim departed from Judah; even the king of Assyria.

Trying to fit Jesus into the passage above is impossible. What does the prophet mean when he said that the savior will eat butter and honey? Or that there was a time in Jesus' life when he does a not know how to refuse the evil and choose the good? Yet the prophecy above is obviously meant to be taken as a whole.

The whole passage suggests that the prophecy had a more immediate meaning. It is enough to note the section I have italicized above, which connects the child to be born with the immediate events (i.e. the defeat of the two kings). The prophecy was obviously meant by Isaiah to reassure Ahaz that the kings of Syria and Israel will

---

[19]   Brown, *Birth of the Messiah*: p145-148
Cuppitt & Armstrong, Who Was Jesus?: p46
Guignebert, Jesus: p123
Lüdemann, *Virgin Birth?*: p122
Warner, Alone of All Her Sex: p19
Wilson, Jesus: The Evidence: p19, 48

soon be defeated or rendered powerless. In modern terms the prophecy will go something like this:

> If a woman gets married today and conceives a child, from now until his birth [i.e. around nine months] conditions will be so much improved [butter and honey] that he will be able to be given a name that signifies a good omen, *Immanuel* or "God is with us". And by the time the child begins to understand and distinguish between good and bad [around two to three years] the two enemies of King Ahaz will be vanquished by the king of Assyria.

The emphasis of the prophecy of Isaiah was not on the *mode of conception* of the child but on the *speediness* in which king Ahaz's enemies will be defeated. The child was used as a chronological benchmark, so to speak, for the Judean king to confidently estimate the timing of the approaching events.

In fact the child being prophesied was probably[20] the one referred to in the next chapter:

> Isaiah 8:3-4
> And I went to the prophetess, and she conceived and bore a son. Then the Lord said to me, "Call his name Mahershalalhashbaz; for before the child knows how to cry 'My father' or 'My mother', the wealth of Damascus and the spoils of Samaria will be carried away before the king of Assyria.

Immanuel was obviously a symbolic name, after all the Christians were never bothered that Jesus was not called by that name. But the name of the child above Mahershalalhashbaz, is significant here, for it is another symbolic name which means "haste-spoil, speed-booty"; it connotes the calamity which was to befall the kings of Israel and Syria, is the *exact opposite* of Immanuel, which connotes the converse fortune for Judah. And before the child can utter "mama" and "papa", Ahaz's enemies will be defeated: exactly what was predicted in Isaiah 7:10-17.

It is therefore obvious that the passage from Isaiah viewed in its full context has nothing to do with Jesus or any messianic prophecy. Only by taking the passage out of context and by the mistranslation of the Hebrew word *almah* could it be twisted to refer to Jesus. In short, there was no Old Testament prophesy of the virgin birth.[21]

The question arises: did Matthew invent the story of the virgin birth based on the mistranslation of Isaiah or did he or some other early Christian read into Isaiah a tradition that was already circulating among the believers at that time Matthew was

---

[20] Raymond Brown in his book *The Birth of the Messiah* (Doubleday, 1993) disagreed that the prophet's wife is the almah being referred to in Isaiah 7:14. However, the Catholic theologian admitted that the prophecy is essentially one that uses the upcoming birth of a baby as a "chronological benchmark" for the defeat of Ahaz's enemies. (see *The Birth of Messiah*, p147-148)

[21] Asimov, *Guide to the Bible*: p531-533
Brown, *Birth of the Messiah*: p145-148
Craveri, *The Life of Jesus*: p36-37
Cadoux, *The Life of Jesus*: p27-30
Guignebert, *Jesus*: p122
Miller, *Born Divine*: p93-94

written around the end of the first century CE? The former is unlikely as Luke seems to have written about the virgin birth independently of Matthew. Hence it is more likely that Matthew was writing down (and perhaps embellishing it with additional details from his own creative mind) what was community tradition regarding Jesus circulating among the believers at that time.

Parthenogenesis or virgin birth is, among human beings, to say the least, an extremely unlikely occurrence. This is not to reject the idea out of hand but simply to point out that anyone making such a claim is making an extraordinary assertion. The burden of proof lies squarely with the party that asserts that such an event had occurred in history. And *extraordinary claims demand extraordinary proof.* We have seen that the Bible can contain error, inconsistencies and downright falsehoods, it is therefore not enough to assert that just because it is in the Bible it must be true.

Let us now get back to the virgin birth. Now most of the people who knew Jesus during his ministry knew him as an adult, so they are pretty useless as witnesses in this case. From the people who should have known him before his ministry, we get a reaction that positively suggests that the miracle of *parthenogenesis* never happened. For example, as Mark reveals, when Jesus started preaching, his family, including his mother, went to call him back because they thought he was "out of his mind" (Mark 3:21). Now why on earth would Mary, of all people, think her son "out of his mind" when he started preaching when she had been a willing and knowing party to the first miracle in the messiah's life? What about the people whom Jesus grew up with? They were the next best candidates to have knowledge about his special birth. What did they do when he started preaching? According to Mark they rejected his teachings (Mark 6:1-6).

In fact the earliest sources on Jesus are silent on the issue of the virgin birth; we see nothing in Paul's letters (AD51-64) and Mark's gospel (cAD70) about Jesus' miraculous conception. This silence is actually strong testimony against the historicity of the virgin birth. For both Mark and Paul were convinced believers and had it occurred or had they heard about it, they would surely have written something about it. In fact a natural reading (i.e. without any theological preconception) of Paul's letter to the Galatians showed that the "apostle to the gentiles" believed Jesus came into the world like everyone else:

Galatians 4:4
But when the fullness of the time came, God sent out his Son, born to a woman, born under the law.

The message conveyed by Paul here is that Jesus was a normal Jewish child called by God.[22]

Our next early source is from the Jewish Christians, the Nazarenes or Ebionites. The Jewish Christians never accepted the story of the virgin birth. We know this through references of their beliefs by the early church fathers such as Justin Martyr, Jerome, Irenaeus and Origen.[23] Now we know from how myths developed that stories

---

[22] Cadoux, *The Life of Jesus*: p27
    Guignebert, *Jesus*: p119
[23] Maccoby, *Revolution In Judea*: p286

tend to get more fantastic upon retelling not the other way round. That the Jewish Christians' did not believe in the virgin birth is strong evidence that they were adhering to an older, unembellished tradition. Furthermore, we have strong reasons to believe that the Nazarenes or Ebionites were the theological descendents of James, the brother of Jesus. It is this group of Christians, more than any other early Christian sect, that could have claimed to be direct eyewitnesses to the events in Jesus' life.[24]

The virgin birth is myth not history.

THE EVOLUTION OF THE CONCEPT OF VIRGIN BIRTH

It is also important to note that apart from the fact that the virgin birth was not prophesied in the Old Testament, but as an *asexual* form of reproduction, it is also an idea that is foreign Jewish theology. There are six times in the Old Testament where God is described as miraculously helping in the conception of a child but at no time does it mean the absence of sexual intercourse. In Genesis 17:15-21; 21:1-3 God helped the 90 year old Sarah, long past child bearing age, conceive – giving birth to Isaac. But sexual relations between Sarah and Abraham are clearly assumed. In Genesis 29:30-32, Leah was cured of her infertility by God, and again here the implication is that she had sexual relations with her husband Jacob. Similarly Rebecca, Rachel and Hannah became pregnant because God answered their prayers (Genesis 25:21, 30:22, I Samuel 1:10-11, 19-20). In the story of Samson (Judges 13), God's intervention in his birth also assumes normal intercourse between the husband and wife.[25]

However, when we look over at the side of the Gentiles, the world where Christianity was to flourish, we see something completely different. Miraculous virgin birth and divine incarnation are common place ideas. For example in the Greek myth, Perseus was born of the virgin Danae. Danae was conceived by the God Zeus who took the form of a shower of gold.[26]

And in almost all the popular mystery religions[27], the beliefs of the uneducated masses, the divine personalities are born of virgins. For example, Mithra, a derivative of the Persian sun-worship, whose cult rivaled Christianity during the first few centuries of its existence, was conceived when God himself, in the form of light, entered a virgin. Phoenecian mythology had Adonis being born of the virgin Myrrh. Parthenogenesis was also the explanation for the birth of the Phyrgian deity, Attis from his mother Cybele.[28]

The popular culture also ascribed to many famous men miraculous, divine and, sometimes, even virgin birth. The emperor Augustus, the reigning sovereign during the time of Jesus, was reputedly miraculously begotten when a snake descended upon his mother in the temple of Apollo. Romulus, the legendary founder of Rome, was

---

[24] A recent book that treats this subject of the Ebionites as the descendents of the original mother church in Jerusalem is *How Jesus Became Christian* (2008) by Barrie Wilson.

[25] Miller, *Born Divine*: p235-236

[26] Craveri, *The Life of Jesus*: p33-34

[27] The pagan religions were referred to as mystery religions because they took the form of mysteries which were only revealed to the initiated.

[28] Freke & Gandy, *The Jesus Mysteries*: p37

also believed that have been born of a vestal virgin. Alexander the Great was conceived, according to popular tradition, by a bolt of lightning that descended upon his mother.[29]

How was the bridge formed between these two alien cultures with differing views of divine intervention in childbirth? The answer lies in one phrase, common to both cultures, but understood differently: *son of God*.

In the Jewish world the term *son of God* does not carry with it the idea of divine fathering. The term can be found in numerous passages in the Old Testament. In II Samuel 7:14 and Psalm 2:7, David is referred to as God's son. In Isaiah 45:11 and Hosea 11:1, the term is used to describe the Israelites in general. In Jewish apocryphal literature we find that even a righteous person can be called a son of God (Wisdom of Solomon 2:10-20, Sirach 4:10). From there, we can gather that the term can be applied to kings, righteous men and even Israelites in general. The term in Jewish theology is an *honorific* title. We find this influence very clearly in early Jewish Christianity, when Paul repeats what was probably taught to him by James and Peter:

> Romans 1:3-4
> [C]oncerning his Son, who was born of the seed of David according to the flesh, *who was declared to be the Son of God with power*, according to the Spirit of holiness, *by the resurrection from the dead, Jesus Christ our Lord*

Read the passage very carefully. This is one of the earliest extant Christological statements, earlier than those in gospels - which were all written twenty to sixty years after this. Here we are told that Jesus was appointed (i.e. "declared") the son of God *by his resurrection*. He became son of God not at birth but after his resurrection. There is no hint of a divine begetting.[30]

The term *son of God* is also very widely used in the Hellenistic world but with a completely different meaning. For here, as we have seen from the examples above, it really does literally mean *fathered by a god*. Thus we find Alexander, Augustus, Romulus, Hercules, Plato and Pythagoras were all called sons of God because their fathers were believed to be gods![31]

This shared phraseology allowed the "jump" of understanding Jesus' title from the Jewish honorific concept into the pagan concept of actually being fathered by God. With this equation, it is inevitable that in the vulgar Greco-Roman culture - where mystery religions, Greek mythologies and general cultural tendencies tend to assume that a person's greatness is a sign of divine origin - the person of Jesus, a *Jewish* "son of God" was transformed into a *Hellenistic* one.[32]

The conclusion regarding the virgin birth is inescapable: it has no historical foundation and arose as an infusion of pagan mythology into early Christianity

---

[29]   Craveri, *The Life of Jesus*: p33
       Knight, *Honest to Man*: p119
       Knight, *Humanist Anthology*: p29
       Miller, *Born Divine*: p138-144
[30]   Miller, *Born Divine*: p223-228
[31]   Lüdemann, *Virgin Birth?*: p72-73
[32]   Guignebert, *Jesus*: p122

facilitated by a common, but differently understood, phrase, *son of God*, in both cultures.

THE MYTH OF MARY'S PERPETUAL VIRGINITY

Apart from a belief in the virgin birth, two main branches of Christianity, the Roman Catholic and Eastern Orthodox Churches, hold that Mary remained a virgin for life. Note that this belief does not simply say Mary never had sex throughout her whole life. It also maintains that Mary's hymen remained intact even after her birth! This is what the *Catechism of the Catholic Church 499* says about the matter:

> The deepening of the faith in the virginal motherhood led the Church to confess Mary's real and perpetual virginity even in the act of giving birth to the Son of God made man. In fact, Christ's birth "did not diminish his mother's virginal integrity but sanctified it."[33]

Apart from this obvious impossibility, a natural reading of the gospels will show that none of their authors ascribed to Mary a perpetual virginity. Let us look at a couple of passages from Matthew and Luke.

> Matthew 1:24-25
> Joseph arose from his sleep, and did as the angel of the Lord commanded him, and took his wife to himself; and didn't know her sexually *until* she had brought forth her son. He named him Jesus.

> Luke 2:6-7
> It happened, while they [Joseph and Mary] were there, that the day had come that she should give birth. She brought forth her *firstborn son...*

From the above it is implied that Joseph did have sex with Mary after the birth of Jesus and that there were subsequent children born to these two. After all to say that you did not do A *until* B happened would naturally suggest that you did do A afterwards. And to call a child the *first born* from the vantage point of Luke (i.e. who wrote around 60 to 70 years after the death of Jesus) means that Joseph and Mary subsequently had more children. As the New Testament scholar Charles Guignebert asserted: "the term "first born"...immediately suggests the birth of younger children."[34]

This dovetails nicely with the information from the gospels and the epistles of Paul that Jesus had brothers and sisters. The passage below from Mark tells us that Jesus had a large family, at least four brothers and two sisters, when he makes the people of Nazareth ask of Jesus:

---

[33] Quoted in Lüdemann, *Virgin Birth?*: p12
[34] Guignebert, *Jesus*: p130

Mark 6:3 (Matthew 13:55) [also Mark 3:31-32 (Matthew 12:46-50)]
Isn't this the carpenter, the son of Mary, and brother of James, Joses, Judah, and Simon? Aren't his sisters here with us?"

Even John, the most mystical of all the gospels, does not deny the fact that Jesus was not the only child:

John 2:12 [also John 7:3]
After this, he went down to Capernaum, he, and his mother, his brothers, and his disciples; and they stayed there a few days.

Paul's epistles also clearly show Jesus had brothers:

Galatians 1:18-19
Then after three years I went up to Jerusalem to visit Peter, and stayed with him fifteen days. But of the other apostles I saw no one, except James, the Lord's brother.

I Corinthians 9:5
Have we no right to take along a wife who is a believer, even as the rest of the apostles, and the brothers of the Lord, and Cephas?

Roman Catholic theologians have been fighting this obvious and natural interpretation of the gospel passages with tortuous and *ad hoc* explanations that will convince only those who already want to believe. Let us look at some of their apologetic attempts.

In explaining Matthew 1:24-25, the Catholic theologian Raymond E. Brown in his book *The Birth of the Messiah* (Doubleday 1993) stated that the Greek usage of "until" (Greek: *heos hou*) "*often* has no implication at all about what happened after the limit of "until" was reached." and that "The immediate context favors a lack of future implication here, for Matthew is concerned *only* with stressing Mary's virginity before the child's birth…"[35] [italics added].

It is important to note this is merely a "possibility" defense – something we have looked at in chapter 7 of this book. "Often" does not imply "always" or even "more often than not". In other words, what he omits to say is that equally often, *heos hou* does imply a future event. As for the context of Matthew, this is again a theological sleight of hand. If Matthew is concerned *only* in stressing Mary's virginity before the birth of Jesus, this means that Matthew, at best, says *nothing* about Mary's perpetual virginity. Furthermore, since "until" in Greek or English does sometimes imply a future event after that "until", had Matthew believed in the perpetual virginity of Mary, he would certainly have chosen to phrase the passage differently in order to avoid the misinterpretation that Mary ceased being virgin after the birth of Jesus.[36]

His defense of Luke 2:6-7 is equally ad hoc. The problem here is that there is a nice Greek word that Luke could have used if he wanted to show that Jesus was Mary's only child: *monogenes*. That he used instead *prototokos* (first born) requires some apologetic shuffling. Citing a Greek tombstone dating to 5 BCE which states

---

35   Brown, *Birth of the Messiah*: p132
36   Lüdemann, *Virgin Birth?*: p71

that a woman died after giving birth to her "firstborn," he again stress that the term *firstborn* "need not imply the birth of subsequent children." And that the reason why Luke used the term "firstborn" was because he wanted to show that Jesus had the privileges and positions that Hebrew culture gives to the eldest child.

Note again that all the above is another "possibility" defense. Yes, it is *possible* that the term firstborn may not imply subsequent children, but more often than not it *does* imply this very thing! The additional statement that Luke wanted to show Jesus had the rights and privileges of the eldest child does not cut it. For an only child is by definition the eldest and would get the same rights and privileges. Had Luke believed in the perpetual virginity of Mary, he would have phrased that passage differently to avoid a misinterpretation based on a natural reading of that term. That he did not means that the idea of perpetual virginity never occurred to him.

On these defenses we must ask one more question: if the idea of Mary's perpetual virginity is not implied (but according to the Catholic theologians not explicitly repudiated) in Matthew 1:24-25 and Luke 2:6-7 (and nowhere else in the New Testament) then *where* did the idea come from in the first place? As we will see below it evolved much later than the time of the evangelists.

As to the matter of brothers and sisters there were two traditional explanations tried by Orthodox (Eastern) and Catholic (Western) branches of Christianity to reconcile this passages with their own theology. These two explanations are called, respectively, the Epiphanian View and the Hieronymian view.

The Epiphanian View

The Eastern Church came up with the idea that the brothers and sisters mentioned in the gospels were *children of Joseph from a prior marriage*. This explanation became known as the *Epiphanian View*, after the 4th century father, Epiphanius (c315-403), bishop of Salamis.

This view is mainly based on the apocryphal *Protoevangelium of James*. This mid second century work of hagiographic piety testifies to the growing fascination with Mary's virginity in early Christianity.[37] Joseph was portrayed as an old widower with children when the chief priest entrusted the twelve year old Mary to his care. For this is what Joseph said upon being told of this:

> Protoevangelium 8:12-13[38]
> And the high priest said, "Joseph, you are the person chosen to take the virgin of the Lord, to keep for him." But Joseph refused, saying "I am an old man, and have children, but she is young, and I fear lest I should appear ridiculous in Israel."

That Mary was a virgin *post partum*, that is *after* the birth of the baby Jesus, was poignantly shown by the following episode. Salome, who was skeptical of Mary's

---

[37] Ferguson, *Encyclopedia of Early Christianity*: p955
[38] The text of the Protoevangelium and well as the chapter and verses are taken from *The Lost Books of the Bible and the Forgotten Books of Eden*, Meridian Books, New York 1974. (I have slightly updated the archaic English.) Other editions of this may have different chapter and verse references.

continued virginity, was told to "try it herself". She did and found her offending hand withered as a result!

> Protoevangelium 14:15-22
> And the midwife said to her, "Salome, Salome, I will tell you a most surprising thing which I saw. A virgin has given birth, which is a thing contrary to nature." To which Salome replied, "As the Lord my God lives, unless I receive particular proof of this matter, I will not believe that a virgin has given birth." Then Salome went in and the midwife said, "Mary, show yourself, for a great controversy is risen concerning you." And Salome received satisfaction. But her hand was withered and she groaned bitterly.

The *Protoevangelium* also claimed James as its author and established him as the *elder* brother of Jesus. In the appendix to the work we read this:

> Protoevangelium, Appendix
> I, James, wrote this history in Jerusalem; and when the disturbance was I retired into the desert place, until the death of Herod.

Origen (c185-254), whose piety extended to him castrating himself after reflecting on Matthew 19:12, was an early supporter of the Epiphanian view. Citing both the Protoevangelium (which Origen referred to as "The Book of James") and a now lost portion of *The Gospel of Peter*, Origen mentioned this in his *Commentary on Matthew*:

> *On Matthew*: 10:17
> But some say, basing it on a tradition in the Gospel according to Peter, as it is entitled, or The Book of James, that the brethren of Jesus were sons of Joseph by a former wife, whom he married before Mary. Now those who say so wish to preserve the honor of Mary in virginity to the end ... And I think it in harmony with reason that Jesus was the first-fruit among men of the purity which consists in chastity, and Mary among women; for it were not pious to ascribe to any other than to her the first-fruit of virginity.

Another prominent supporter of the Epiphanian view was, naturally, Epiphanius (c315-403) himself. In his *Panarion*, a "medicine chest" for use against heresies, Ephiphanius mentioned that Joseph's first wife died after bearing him six children, with James being the eldest. He also added that Joseph was 80 years old when he was betrothed to Mary; by then, presumably, he was too old to have sex. (Panarion 78:7:1-78:8:2)

It seems hardly necessary to refute such a charming fantasy! However, for completeness' sake we need to look at why almost everyone looks at this view with skepticism.

- The earliest evidence for this came from the mid second century *Protoevangelium*. The Protoevangelium was authored by someone who obviously had no knowledge of Palestinian geography and Jewish customs. Its narratives are a conflation of the canonical works of Matthew and Luke. It bears, according to John Painter, "deep marks of legendary development". The work is a derivative work of piety. Its author was not an eyewitness and did not have any access to reliable historical information.

- As Origen's statement above makes clear, the purpose for accepting this view is purely apologetic in nature. It *harmonizes* with the then prevailing view with respect to chastity. This *ad hoc* nature of the explanation invites extreme skepticism.

- In the Gospel of Luke 2:6-7, the idea of Jesus being Mary's *firstborn* loses much of its force if he was also not Joseph's first-born. For inheriting the kingdom of David must surely go to the eldest *in the family*. If Jesus had elder brothers through Joseph's previous marriage, Luke's phraseology loses much of its force. The fact that Luke phrased it the way he did can only mean that he knew of no such tradition, of Jesus having an older brother, at the time of his writing (c 100 CE).[39]

The Hieronymian View

Not satisfied with just the perpetual virginity of *Mary*, the Western Church went a step further and suggested that *Joseph* was a virgin as well. Therefore, it was no longer permissible for Joseph to have had sexual intercourse with a hypothetical earlier wife! The "brothers and sisters" were claimed to be "cousins" of Jesus. This "cousin hypothesis" was first put forward by Eusebius, Bishop of Caesarea (c260-c340). This suggestion is normally called the *Hieronymian View*, after Jerome (c342-420), whose full name was Eusebius Hieronymous, since it was he who fleshed out this hypothesis.

Jerome did not like the Epiphanian view because it was based, in his opinion, on spurious works such as *The Protoevangelium of James*. He sought to derive the idea of Mary's perpetual virginity from canonical sources alone. Jerome's argument, put forward in his *Against Helvidius*, written in 383, is a four step process.

- First, he cited Paul in Galatians:

  > Galatians 1:18-19
  > Then after three years I went up to Jerusalem to visit Peter, and stayed with him fifteen days. But of the other apostles I saw no one, except James, the Lord's brother.

  Jerome takes the statement above to mean that James was one of the twelve apostles.

- Second, in the list of the twelve apostles given in Mark 3:13-19 (and Matthew 10:1-4), there were two James's, one being the son of Zebedee and the other being the son of Alphaeus. Since we know that John the son of Zebedee could not be James the brother of the Lord, this means that

---

[39]   Bernheim, *James, Brother of Jesus*: p19-20
       Chilton & Neusner, *The Brother of Jesus*: p13-16
       Craveri, *The Life of Jesus*: p66-67
       Guignebert, *Jesus*: p129-130
       Painter, *Just James*: p198-201

James the son of Alphaeus was the one known as James, the brother of the Lord! However, since Alphaeus is not Joseph, this leaves the term "brother" still unexplained, so there are a couple more steps to go.

- Third, in the scene of Jesus' crucifixion both Mark and John gave a list of women who were present there:

  Mark 15:40

  There were also women watching from afar, among whom were both Mary Magdalene, and Mary the mother of James the *less* (Greek=*mikrou*) and of Joses, and Salome

  John 19:25

  But there were standing by the cross of Jesus his mother, and his mother's sister, Mary the wife of Clopas, and Mary Magdalene.

Although modern translations add "the wife" to Clopas, the original Greek is missing that term and the phrase could easily be read, ambiguously, as "Mary of Clopas". Jerome understood John 19:25 to mean that Mary of Clopas was the *sister* of Jesus' mother, also called Mary.

Now Mary of Clopas given in John's gospel is to be identified with Mary, the mother of James the Less and Joses given in Mark's. As for the identity of James the Less, Jerome claimed that it makes no sense to call someone *lesser* unless there is another *greater*. The only other "greater" James was the son of Zebedee. Now, Jerome added, comparisons of "greater" and "lesser" are done between two people only, not three. This James the *Less*, Jerome argued, must be the second James among the apostles. This makes Mary of Clopas the mother of James, brother of the Lord.

- Therefore, the James the Less and Joses of Mark 15:40, are to be identified with the names given in Mark 6:3:

  Mark 6: 3 (also Matthew 13:55-56)

  Isn't this the carpenter, the son of Mary, and brother of James, Joses, Judah, and Simon? Aren't his sisters here with us?" They were offended at him.

Thus, the four names and the two girls were not the children of Jesus' mother, Mary, but of her sister, also called Mary!

- Finally, Jerome explained the use of the term "brother". Citing examples from the Bible, Jerome noted that the term could be taken to mean brother *by nature, by kinship, by race or by love.* As "brother" could mean any of these things, in this particular reconstruction, it obviously means that James and the rest were *cousins* of Jesus, being the children of Mary's sister, Mary. To this is normally added the argument that the Hebrew language lacks specific nouns for kinfolk. The Hebrew word *ah* (Aramaic: *aha*) can mean brother, stepbrother, cousin, nephew; in general it can mean any blood relative.

This, in a nutshell, is the Hieronymian view. The construction is, it must be admitted, intricate and ingenious and it is, in principle, *possible*. But reminding the reader about the difference between possibility and probability as shown in chapter 7, the argument rests on many highly improbable suppositions:

- Equating Paul's use of the term *apostle* to be synonymous with *the twelve* is highly speculative. For Paul's use of the former term seems to cover a wider group of followers. He called himself an apostle (I Corinthians 9:1-3). In I Corinthians 15:5-7 he seems to differentiate between *the twelve* and *all the apostles*. The former having a more restricted use than the latter.

  I Corinthians 15:5-7

  [A]nd that he appeared to Cephas, *then to the twelve*. Then he appeared to over five hundred brothers at once, most of whom remain until now, but some have also fallen asleep. Then he appeared to James, *then to all the apostles*.

- The identity of James the Less with James the son of Alphaeus is a crucial link in Jerome's argument, yet it is based purely on conjecture. It is hard to explain why Mark, who counted James, son of Alphaeus, should fail to make the identification in relating the son of Mary at the crucifixion to the apostle.

- The Greek *tou mikrou* more probably means "the small" rather than "the less". If this indeed is the case, the use of the term in a comparative sense is nonexistent. Furthermore, nowhere in the gospels is James the son of Zebedee referred to as "the greater".

- Another necessary supposition is the identity of "Mary of Clopas" and "Mary the mother of James the Less and Joses". Yet, again, this is pure conjecture. Jerome himself did not argue too strongly for this, being content, he wrote, only to assert that Mary the mother of James and Joses was *not* Mary, the mother of Jesus. However, without that crucial identification, Jerome's whole argument falters! For the identity of Mary of Clopas as the sister of Mary, mother of Jesus, provides the whole foundation of James being the *cousin* of Jesus.

- The vague term "Mary of Clopas" presents another problem, it could mean Mary wife of Clopas or Mary mother of Clopas. (Indeed, as I mentioned above, most modern translations describe Mary as the wife of Clopas.) The former would be a problem for Jerome's linkage. Although later Catholic theologians had tried to argue that even if Mary is the wife of Clopas, the name could be another form of Alphaeus as both could be derived from the Aramaic form *Chalphai*. It is by no means certain that Clopas and Alphaeus come from the same Aramaic name. It is another conjecture made to cover up the earlier one. Note how suppositions are piled upon suppositions!

- The suggestion that Mary, mother of Jesus, had a sister also called Mary is, on the surface absurd. Yet, this is another crucial supposition for Jerome's argument. Some Catholic theologians have tried to argue that Mary, mother of Clopas is actually the sister of Joseph and therefore the sister-in-law of Mary, mother of Jesus. Here again, another supposition is added, that "sister" can mean "sister-in-law".

- While it is highly unlikely that siblings would have identical names ("this is my brother Darrell and my *other* brother Darrell") it is certainly likely that many people during the time of Jesus shared the same names. Relatively few Jewish names were used during that period. The names Jacob (=James), Judah (=Jude), Simeon, Joseph (=Joses?) are names of patriarchs and were very popular during that time. The fact that some unrelated people have similar names does not provide enough reason to base a theory of identity on.

- Furthermore, it is by no means clear that John meant "Mary the mother of Clopas" to be an expansion of "the sister of Jesus' mother". The Greek text could easily be read as referring to two separate persons: one being Mary of Clopas and the other being the (unnamed) sister of Mary, mother of Jesus.

- Finally, we look at the linguistic argument. The "paucity of familial terms" in Hebrew is a red herring, since the New Testament was written in *Greek* not Hebrew. In Greek there are separate nouns for brothers and cousins. The Greek word for brother is *adelphos* (plural = *adelphoi)* and for cousin is *anepsios* (plural = *anepsioi).* All the evangelists used *adelphoi* to describe his brothers. Had they been convinced that James, Joses, Judas and Simon were not Jesus' brothers, they would have used the word *anepsioi* to avoid any confusion. This is especially true for Paul who wrote in Greek for Gentiles. We see that in Paul's letters to the Galatians he too referred to James as Jesus' brother and to the fact that Jesus had more than one brother. (See above quote on Galatians 1:18-19 and I Corinthians 9:4) The Catholic theologian J.P. Meier studied 343 passages in the New Testament in which the word *adelphos* appeared. He concluded that, when it is not used figuratively or metaphorically, it always referred to a biological or legal relationship between full brothers or half brothers: i.e. *not* cousins. The further attempt to claim that in the Septuagint, the word *adelphos* is sometimes used to translate for "cousin" is weak. For the occurrence of such translation is very rare in the Old Testament and the context normally remove any ambiguity in the kinship.

It can be seen that the Hieronymian view relies heavily on a series of improbable conjectures, *all of which must be true* for the hypothesis to work. Take away one link and the whole chain breaks. To get the probability of the view being true, the probability for each difficulty being somehow true is *multiplied* to the next. If we allow each of the seven difficulties above (which in itself does not exhaust all the difficulties with the theory) a 50% chance of being true (a very generous assumption), the chances of the Heironymian view being correct is less than 1% or less than 1 in 100. Now that's a long shot!

In conclusion, there is absolutely nothing to suggest that Mary remained a virgin perpetually.[40]

---

[40]   Bernheim, *James, Brother of Jesus*: p20-29
        Chilton & Neusner, *The Brother of Jesus*: p16-20
        Craveri, *The Life of Jesus*: p66-67
        Guignebert, *Jesus*: p129-130
        Painter, *Just James*: p213-220

The fact that Catholic theologians still insist on this doctrine should convince all that reason has very little to do with theology. Looking at the theological explanations for the genealogies and for the perpetual virginity brings to mind what the American novelist Frank Yerby (1916-1991) wrote: *Theology is a mild form of insanity.*[41]

THE BIRTHPLACE OF JESUS

Both Matthew and Luke stated that Jesus was born in Bethlehem in Judea. However, the different ways in which both gospels connect Jesus' birth to that Judean town arouse suspicion. In Matthew, the impression we get is that both Mary and Joseph were already living in Bethlehem during the time of the annunciation and the conception:

> Matthew 1:24-2:1
> Joseph arose from his sleep, and did as the angel of the Lord commanded him, and took his wife to himself; and didn't know her sexually until she had brought forth her firstborn son. He named him Jesus. *Now when Jesus was born in Bethlehem of Judea ...*

Note that no mention is given of any traveling between Joseph taking Mary home as his wife and the birth of Jesus. In fact anyone reading the nativity story in Matthew alone will conclude that Joseph and Mary were natives of Bethlehem as is confirmed by the passage below (after the flight of Joseph and his family to Egypt):

> Matthew 2:19-23
> But when Herod was dead, behold, an angel of the Lord appeared in a dream to Joseph in Egypt, saying, "Arise and take the young child and his mother, and go into the land of Israel, for those who sought the young child's life are dead." He arose and took the young child and his mother, and came into the land of Israel. *But when he heard that Archelaus was reigning over Judea in the place of his father, Herod, he was afraid to go there. Being warned in a dream, he withdrew into the region of Galilee, and came and lived in a city called Nazareth;* that it might be fulfilled which was spoken through the prophets: "He will be called a Nazarene."

Especially in the view of the earlier passage, the one above gives definite proof that Joseph wanted to return to his home town of Bethlehem but was prevented from doing so by the fact that Archelaus was the new tetrarch. His making Nazareth a home came after this.

In Luke, however, we are told that both Mary and Joseph were living in the Galilean town of Nazareth before the annunciation:

---

[41] Yerby, *Judas, My Brother*: p504

Luke 1:26-27
Now in the sixth month, the angel Gabriel was sent from God to a city of Galilee, named Nazareth, to a virgin pledged to be married to a man whose name was Joseph, of the house of David.

So Luke makes Mary and Joseph natives of Galilee. The event that made them travel to Bethlehem was the Roman census under Quirinius. According to the evangelist, the Roman census required all to register in the town of their ancestors. Since David was from Bethlehem, Joseph had to travel to Judea to register himself.

Luke 2:1-7
Now it happened in those days, that a decree went out from Caesar Augustus that all the world should be enrolled. This was the first enrollment made when Quirinius was governor of Syria. *All went to enroll themselves, everyone to his own city. Joseph also went up from Galilee, out of the city of Nazareth, into Judea, to the city of David, which is called Bethlehem,* because he was of the house and family of David; to enroll himself with Mary, who was pledged to be married to him as wife, being pregnant. It happened, while they were there, that the day had come that she should give birth. She brought forth her firstborn son.

Luke's version is historically suspect for at least three reasons. Firstly, while the Romans do periodically conduct census at different times in various locations, there is simply no evidence that there ever was a simultaneous worldwide census either under Caesar Augustus or anyone else.

Secondly, the *method* of taking the census, by herding everyone to register in the towns of their ancestors, is unheard of in the history of the Roman Empire. The Roman censuses were always taken for economic purposes, to determine the amount of taxable income of the residents of their provinces. These censuses were taken at the place of residence not the ancestral hometown. Furthermore, the census, if conducted in the manner described by Luke, was extremely impracticable: each and every Israelite will have to recall the residence of their ancestors who lived when Joshua partitioned the land of Palestine among the twelve tribes, i.e. an event that occurred more than 1,000 years before the census! And why would Joseph haul Mary along with him to Bethlehem, when she was already in an advanced stage of pregnancy? The distance from Nazareth to Bethlehem is about 100 kilometers and would have taken an exhausting ten days or so on donkey-back. The fact that Mary was not even required for the census further compounds this problem.

Thirdly, while there was one historical census when Quirinius was governor of Syria *it happened ten years after the death of King Herod.* But according to both Matthew and Luke, Jesus was born during the reign of Herod the great (Matthew 2:1, Luke 1:5). And even here Josephus tells us (Antiquities 18:1:1) that the census by Quirinius was for the province of Judea only and was purely for evaluating the possession of the residents there for taxation purposes. As Joseph was a resident of Nazareth in Galilee, there would have been no need for him to be involved in this census under Quirinius. [We will review this third discrepancy in more detail later in this chapter.] [42]

---

[42]   Brown, *The Birth of the Messiah*: p549

In short, Luke's whole scenario is unconvincing and, especially his description of the method of the Roman census, without any historical support.

Assuming that Luke did not have the audacity to invent his whole account of the Nativity, it is probable that both Matthew and Luke received different and, perhaps still amorphous, traditions regarding the birth of Jesus. For instance, it is possible that the tradition stated only that Jesus was born in Bethlehem not how his parents got there. Both Matthew and Luke then simply added details to the story as they see fit. Could this tradition of the birth in Bethlehem be based on historical fact? It is certainly possible but highly unlikely. Had it been historical, one would expect more substantial points of agreement between the stories told by both evangelists. Furthermore, the birth in Bethlehem supposedly fulfilled an Old Testament passage. This is explicitly stated in Matthew:

Matthew 2:4-5
Gathering together all the chief priests and scribes of the people, he [King Herod] asked them where the Christ would be born. They said to him, "In Bethlehem of Judea, for thus it is written through the prophet, 'You Bethlehem, land of Judah… for out of you shall come forth a governor, who shall shepherd my people, Israel.'"

Matthew was quoting from Micah 5:2.

Micah 5:2
But you, Bethlehem Ephrathah…out of you one will come forth to me that is to be ruler in Israel

It was highly probable that the early Christians searched, or rather ransacked, the Old Testament to look for references to Jesus. Then having found the verse in Micah, concluded that Jesus *must* have been born in Bethlehem. Indeed, John 7:41-43 showed that for some believers theological reasoning alone is sufficient to conclude that the messiah *must* be born in Bethlehem:

John 7:41-43
Others said, "This is the Christ." But some said, "What, does the Christ come out of Galilee? Hasn't the Scripture said that the Christ comes of the seed of David, and from Bethlehem, the village where David was?"

The theological reasoning is straightforward: the messiah must be a descendent of David (Isaiah 11:1), and David was from Bethlehem (I Samuel 16:8) and the new King will come from this town (Micah 5:2).

The very fact that the birth in Bethlehem fulfils an Old Testament prophecy makes the whole tradition of doubtful historicity. This *caveat* is an accepted principle of historical criticism, as the theologians Don Cuppitt and Peter Armstrong stated in their book, *Who Was Jesus?*:

Craveri, *The Life of Jesus*: p44
Crossan, *Who is Jesus?*: p23
Freed, *The Stories of Jesus' Birth*: p119
Guignebert, *Jesus*: p30-32
Miller, *Born Divine*: p180-181

So our first principle of historical criticism must be: be wary of any details in the gospels which have close parallels in the Old Testament[43]

Our suspicion as to the basic non-historicity of the account of the birth in Bethlehem is further aroused by the fact that apart from the nativity stories in Matthew and Luke, there is no evidence elsewhere in the New Testament to support the assertion that Jesus was born in Bethlehem. We find in Mark, the oldest of all the gospels, passages that seem to imply the birthplace of Jesus as Nazareth in Galilee:

Mark 6:1
He [Jesus] went out from there. He came into his own country...

The Greek work translated above as "own country" is *patris* which means one's native place or home town, city or country. The whole section covered in the early chapters of Mark show Jesus preaching in the towns and villages of Galilee, so his native place must be a town in Galilee. In the first verse referring to Jesus in Mark, this is how he was introduced:

Mark 1:9
It happened in those days, that Jesus came from Nazareth of Galilee, and was baptized by John in the Jordan.

Anyone reading these passages in Mark, without any references to Matthew or Luke will doubtless conclude that Jesus was born in Nazareth in Galilee. Furthermore, we find that in all the three synoptics, Jesus was henceforth referred to as "the Galilean" or "the Nazarene" with no further reference being made to his birth in Bethlehem.

And in the passage we have just seen above - John 7:41-43 - a scene is narrated where people doubted Jesus' messianic status because they believed that the messiah *had to come* from Bethlehem. Surely John would have shown that the Jews' doubts were based on their own ignorance about Jesus' ancestry and place of birth had he believed that Jesus was of the house of David and born in Bethlehem. The passage strongly suggests that John was relying on a tradition about Jesus that included neither the descent from David nor the birth in Bethlehem. That John believed that Jesus came from Nazareth can be surmised from this passage below:

John 1:45-46
Philip found Nathanael, and said to him, "We have found him, of whom Moses in the law, and the prophets, wrote: Jesus of Nazareth, the son of Joseph." Nathanael said to him, "Can any good thing come out of Nazareth?"

As Robert Miller in his book *Born Divine: The Births of Jesus and Other Sons of God* (2003) pointed out, John is normally of the habit of interjecting his narrative to

---

[43]   Cuppitt & Armstrong, *Who Was Jesus?*: p45

explain things he thought his readers may not understand.[44] This would be a perfect occasion for him to interject and explain that Jesus did not come from Nazareth and that Nathanael's question was moot. That he did not is strong evidence that he believed Jesus was from that Galilean town.

There are thus strong reasons to believe that Jesus was born in Nazareth. Mark and John clearly believed Jesus was from there. Both Matthew and Luke came up with contradictory ways to get Jesus to Nazareth after their respective nativities. Furthermore, the fact that his alleged birth in Bethlehem could be deduced entirely from Old Testament messianic prophecies is strong evidence against the historicity of such a story. In conclusion, the tradition of Jesus' birth in Bethlehem is not historical.[45]

It is also important to note, despite Matthew's determination to show that Jesus' nativity fulfils the scriptures, he is not beyond twisting Old Testament passages when they do not suit his paradigm. Let us look at the passage and its supposed fulfillment again:

> Matthew 2:5-6
> They said to him, "In Bethlehem of Judea, for thus it is written through the prophet, 'You Bethlehem, land of Judah, *are in no way least* among the princes of Judah: for out of you shall come forth a governor, who shall shepherd my people, Israel.'"

Matthew was quoting from Micah. But note that the original passage was *slightly* different:

> Micah 5:2
> But you, Bethlehem Ephrathah, *being small* among the clans of Judah, out of you one will come forth to me that is to be ruler in Israel; whose goings forth are from of old, from everlasting.

Note how the evangelist had tried to elevate the status of Bethlehem by changing Micah's "being small..." to "are in no way least". Matthew has changed the text of the Old Testament to say the *exact opposite* of what it means! This provides an important insight into how the early Christians treated the Old Testament "prophecies". They were willing to "correct" prophetic writings in order to conform to their view of the world. In this case it is obvious that they wanted to increase the prestige of Bethlehem as the birthplace of Jesus.[46]

---

[44]   See for examples John 2:21 when he explains that Jesus was talking about his body and not the temple; John 8:27 when he injected that the Pharisees did not understand that Jesus was speaking about his father in heaven.

[45]   Guignebert, *Jesus*: p90
Miller, *Born Divine:* p181-183

[46]   Allegro, *The Dead Sea Scrolls*: p150-151
Freed, *The Stories of Jesus' Birth*: p76-77
Miller, *Born Divine:* p112-113

THE SLAUGHTER OF THE INNOCENTS

According to Matthew's gospel, once Herod realized that he had been tricked by the wise men, he ordered the slaughter of all male babies less than two years of age living in or around Bethlehem:

> Matthew 2:16-18
> Then Herod, when he saw that he was mocked by the wise men, was exceedingly angry, and sent out, and killed all the male children who were in Bethlehem and in all the surrounding countryside, from two years old and under, according to the exact time which he had learned from the wise men. Then that which was spoken by Jeremiah the prophet was fulfilled, saying, *"A voice was heard in Ramah, lamentation, weeping and great mourning, Rachel weeping for her children; she wouldn't be comforted, because they are no more."*

Historically, Herod, to put it mildly, did not have a peaceful reign. His many sons and wives were involved in bitter rivalry for his throne. Herod was not a man to hold family relations sacred. He had three of his sons executed for conspiracy. He executed his brother-in-law, Joseph. At the urging of Joseph's widow, Salome, he murdered his own wife, Mariamme. If he treated his own family badly, his opponents and enemies were given even more ferocious handling. He murdered the Jewish High Priest, Aristobolus III and 45 members of the Sanhedrin[47] for their support of the Hasmoneans. These are just samplings of Herod's atrocities. There was a well-known Greek pun, attributed to Caesar Augustus, which goes something like "It is better to be Herod's pig [Greek = *hus*] than his son [*huios*]." In order to present himself as a Jew, he kept his meals kosher, i.e. pork-free; he did not slaughter pigs but had three of his own sons killed. He was therefore a kind of man that *could* have committed the crime Matthew attributed to him.

The atrocities listed above are taken from Josephus' *Antiquities of the Jews*. From Josephus' own writings, we can tell that he hated Herod, for he obviously took pleasure in noting down every crime and atrocity that was attributed to the Idumean king. Many of the crimes described by Josephus were far less "wicked" than the slaughter of the innocents described by Matthew. Now Josephus' list was very detailed. Had the slaughter actually occurred it would have been an event well known enough for the Jewish historian to have heard of it. Yet the silence of Josephus and the absence of any reference to it in any contemporary secular writings (Jewish, Greek or Roman) cannot be explained if the event was historical. The conclusion forces itself on us, *it never happened.*

Note also that Matthew 2:16-18 claimed that this fulfilled an Old Testament prophecy of Jeremiah (31:15). We noted earlier how the early Christians used the Hebrew scriptures as a happy hunting ground for allusions to their savior, sometimes, as in the earlier case of Isaiah 7:14, lifting verses out of context in order to do so. This is another example. The passage in the Old Testament is not a prophecy about the future but a story about the Israelites being deported into exile. Ramah was the

---

[47]   The Sanhedrin is the supreme religious council of ancient Israel.

stopover town for the deportees before they are shipped out into exile. Let us look at the passage in full:

> Jeremiah 31:15-17
> Thus says Yahweh: *A voice is heard in Ramah, lamentation, and bitter weeping, Rachel weeping for her children; she refuses to be comforted for her children, because they are no more.* Thus says Yahweh: Refrain your voice from weeping, and your eyes from tears; for your work shall be rewarded, says Yahweh; and they shall come again from the land of the enemy. There is hope for your latter end, says Yahweh; and **your children shall come again to their own border.**

The italicized portion was the one lifted out by Matthew but note the last line in boldface. According to the passage Yahweh promised that her children will return again to their own country! There is no prophecy here, merely the metaphorical weeping of an important figure in Judaism (Rachel was dead long before the exile) for a national calamity. Let us repeat the difference again. Rachel was not weeping about babies but about the Israelites as her (metaphorical) "children" and she was not weeping about their *deaths* but about their *deportation*. It was a story about the exile and has nothing to do with a prophecy of a future massacre of babies.[48]

Furthermore, the story in Matthew is very similar to the Old Testament story of the baby Moses' escape from the pharaoh slaughter of the Israelite children:

> Exodus 1:15-16
> The king of Egypt spoke to the Hebrew midwives, of whom the name of the one was Shiphrah, and the name of the other Puah, and he said, "When you perform the duty of a midwife to the Hebrew women, and see them on the birth stool; if it is a son, then you shall kill him; but if it is a daughter, then she shall live."

Just like the escape of Moses from the clutches of the pharaoh's slaughter, so was Jesus to escape from the grip of Herod's massacre. The parallel in these two stories is strongly suggestive of Matthew's dependence on the Exodus episode for this portion of his nativity.[49]

As an aside, it is interesting to consider this pericopae from the framework of the problem of evil. Note that in this story, God intervened by revealing to the wise men in a dream not to go back to Jerusalem so that Herod would not know where exactly the baby Jesus was. It was because of not knowing this exact location that Herod had all the male babies below two years of age in Bethlehem slaughtered. And also it was revealed to Joseph in a dream to take Mary and Jesus and flee to Egypt to avoid this massacre. As the 19th century critical historical scholar David Strauss (1808-1874) pointed out, God, if he wanted to avoid the massacre of the innocents, could easily have intervened supernaturally at the *beginning* by making the wise men avoid

---

48   Miller, *Born Divine:* p114-115
49   Asimov, Guide to the Bible: p795-796
     Cuppitt & Armstrong, Who Was Jesus?: p46
     Freed, *The Stories of Jesus' Birth*: p102
     Miller, *Born Divine:* p184
     Wilson, Jesus: The Evidence, p48

Jerusalem altogether and head on to Bethlehem directly. That way Herod would never have heard of the birth of the messiah![50]

Let us pause to consider the facts: the massacre of the male babies by Herod as described in Matthew is an event without any historical corroboration; it fulfils an Old Testament prophecy (which in itself makes the whole episode suspect); and it closely parallels the story of Moses' escape from the clutches of the pharaoh. To all these facts there is only one answer: the episode is a work of theological fiction, based on the story of Moses in Exodus, composed either by Matthew himself or the early Christian tradition to fulfill what was thought to be an Old Testament prophecy about the messiah.

THE "RETURN" TO NAZARETH

Another problem conveniently overlooked by believers is the basic incompatibility in the narratives of Matthew and Luke regarding the "return"[51] of Joseph and his family to Nazareth.

According to Matthew, Joseph and Mary went there direct from Egypt, as they dared not return to Judea because of Archelaus.

> Matthew 2:19-23
> But when Herod was dead, behold, an angel of the Lord appeared in a dream to Joseph in Egypt, saying, "Arise and take the young child and his mother, and go into the land of Israel, for those who sought the young child's life are dead." He arose and took the young child and his mother, and came into the land of Israel. *But when he heard that Archelaus was reigning over Judea in the place of his father, Herod, he was afraid to go there. Being warned in a dream, he withdrew into the region of Galilee, and came and lived in a city called Nazareth*; that it might be fulfilled which was spoken through the prophets: "He will be called a Nazarene."

According to Luke, Joseph went to Jerusalem from Bethlehem for Mary's purification ceremony and from there went back to Nazareth:

> Luke 2:22,39
> When the days of their purification according to the law of Moses were fulfilled, they brought him up to Jerusalem, to present him to the Lord... When they had accomplished all things that were according to the law of the Lord, they returned into Galilee, to their own city, Nazareth

Nowhere in earlier passages had Luke even implied that Mary and Joseph went back to Nazareth first after the birth of Jesus. According to Luke, Joseph, Mary and Jesus went to Jerusalem from Bethlehem and then returned to Nazareth from the ancient capital. The itinerary based on Matthew was Bethlehem-Egypt-Nazareth,

---

50   Lüdemann, *The Virgin Birth?*: p81-84

51   I have put the word return in inverted commas because only in Luke was it made explicit that Joseph and Mary were originally from Nazareth. No such allusion is discernable in Matthew (as was discussed earlier).

while that of Luke was Nazareth-Bethlehem-Jerusalem-Nazareth. The two itineraries are therefore incompatible.

Some theologians had, as usual, tried to twist the story in Matthew to such an extent where they claimed that Joseph went to Jerusalem from Egypt and then went on to Nazareth after the Temple offering. So the "unified" itinerary becomes: Nazareth-Bethlehem-Egypt-Jerusalem-Nazareth. Apart from the fact that Matthew had explicitly stated that Joseph did not return to Judea from Egypt (Matthew 2:22) a problem of timing arises.

Luke says that Joseph and his family went back to Nazareth after the purification ceremony. Jewish Law requires that the purification of the mother is to be done forty days after the birth of the baby:

> Leviticus 12:1-6
> Yahweh spoke to Moses, saying, "Speak to the children of Israel, saying, 'If a woman conceives, and bears a male child, then she shall be unclean seven days; as in the days of her monthly period she shall be unclean. In the eighth day the flesh of his foreskin shall be circumcised. She shall continue in the blood of purification thirty-three days. She shall not touch any holy thing, nor come into the sanctuary, until the days of her purifying are completed. But if she bears a female child, then she shall be unclean two weeks, as in her period; and she shall continue in the blood of purification sixty-six days. When the days of her purification are completed, for a son, or for a daughter, she shall bring to the priest at the door of the Tent of Meeting, a year old lamb for a burnt offering, and a young pigeon, or a turtledove, for a sin offering.'"

So to reconcile the two nativities (and ignoring the basic incompatibility we have noted above) every event must be fitted into these forty days. Now Luke says that Jesus was circumcised and given his name on the eighth day (Luke 2:21) and Matthew narrated about the story of the visit of the wise men only *after* Jesus was named. So, in effect the visit of the wise men, the slaughter of the innocents, the flight into and the return from Egypt all took place within a period of only 32 days![52] This is clearly impossible, for the journey to and from Egypt itself would have taken at least that long. Perhaps God had his remote controller on fast forward?

This event of leaving Egypt for Nazareth was, according to Matthew, in fulfillment of two prophecies. One, as we have seen above, was that Jesus was to be called a *Nazarene* (Matthew 2:23), the other was noted a little earlier in the gospel:

> Matthew 2:14-15
> He [Joseph] arose and took the young child and his mother by night, and departed into Egypt, and was there until the death of Herod; that it might be fulfilled which was spoken by the Lord through the prophet, saying, *"Out of Egypt I called my son."* [Hosea 11:1]

Like the earlier prophecy fulfillments referred to by Matthew – these two are problematic. The first prophecy noted by Matthew [in 2:23 - "He shall be called a Nazarene"] cannot be found anywhere the Old Testament![53] There is nothing in any

---

52   Craveri, *The Life of Jesus*: p60
53   Miller, *Born Divine*: p115

of the books of the Old Testament which says that the messiah will be called a Nazarene. The second prophecy is supposedly lifted from Hosea 11:1. But a quick look at the passage will show that it has nothing to do with a future event:

> Hosea 11:1-2
> When *Israel* was a child, I loved him, and *out of Egypt I called my son*. The more I called them, the more they went from me; they kept sacrificing to the Baals and burning incense to idols.

This is certainly straining the idea of prophecy to the extreme. The passage refers to *Israel* as God's son. The whole passage (Hosea 11:1-7) refers to an event in the past, the Exodus from Egypt, and to God's intention to *punish* Israel for their lack of faith! Matthew has lifted his "prophecy" out of context from a passage that has nothing to do with the messiah.[54]

To summarize matters, Matthew's tale about the sojourn in Egypt cannot be historical for three reasons: firstly, it "fulfils" prophecy, secondly, he had an agenda to use Jesus' life to symbolize what happen to Israel in the past[55] and thirdly, this trip is not alluded to anywhere else in the New Testament.[56]

ON HEROD AND QUIRINIUS

It is easy to lend an aura of authenticity to one's story by adding, as a kind of backdrop, historical persons and events. This is what writers of historical fiction do to create verisimilitude. Done properly it adds to our enjoyment and also to our understanding of the actual historical period. However, sometimes we come across bungling writers who get their history and dates mixed up; irritating the informed reader and misleading the uninformed one. Luke most definitely belonged to the class of bungling authors of historical fiction. This is especially clear in his attempts to connect Jesus' birth to worldwide events of that time.

According to Matthew and Luke, Jesus was born during the reign of Herod the Great (Matthew 2:1, Luke 1:5ff).[57] Now we know from secular sources that Herod

---

[54] Bradlaugh, *Humanity's Gain From Unbelief*: p137
      Miller, *Born Divine*: p113-115
[55] The slaughter of the innocent mirrors the nativity story in Moses and the travel in and out of Egypt recalls the Exodus.
[56] Miller, *Born Divine*: p167
[57] Matthew states this unambiguously:

Matthew 2:1
Now when Jesus was born in Bethlehem of Judea in the days of King Herod

Matthew even attributed the trip to Egypt as an escape from Herod's massacre (Matthew 2:13-16). Although we cannot find a singular statement in Luke as we find in Matthew 2:1, his position is also that Jesus was born during the reign of King Herod. We are first told about the announcement of the birth of John the Baptist was made to his father Zecharias during the reign of King Herod the Great (Luke 1:5-25). We are told that when Zecharias' wife, Elizabeth, was six month pregnant, the annunciation to Mary took place (Luke 1:26-38).That Mary was pregnant before John was born can be deducted from Luke 1:42 where Elizabeth is quoted as blessing the fruit of Mary's womb.

was definitely an historical figure. We also know, with some accuracy, the actual date of Herod's death: towards the end of March in the year 4 BCE. This is because Josephus recorded the execution of 42 people who had staged an unsuccessful revolt against the Idumean. There was an eclipse of the moon that occurred during the night of this execution (Antiquities of the Jews 17:6:4). This allows for precise astronomical calculations which set the date of execution as March 13, 4 BCE. Now we are told that Herod died a few days after this execution, which makes his death around the second half of March 4 BCE.[58] Thus, based on the gospel narratives, Jesus must have been born before or around 4 BCE.

However, Luke's excuse for bringing Joseph and Mary to Bethlehem was the Roman census of Quirinius (Luke 2:1). While we have problems with Luke's description of the method of the census (as was discussed earlier), the census itself was undoubtedly an historical event for Josephus described a Jewish revolt that resulted from this census. The date of the census, like the death of Herod, can also be dated with some precision. Josephus clearly states that the census took place 37 years after Caesar defeated Antony at Actium, which was fought on September 2, 31 BCE (another precise dating based on astronomy) based on our present system of reckoning. This means that census under Quirinius took place in the year 6 CE. We also know, from Roman sources, that Quirinius was legate (or governor) of Syria between Volusius Saturninus and Caecilius Creticus Silonus, which makes his tenure last for six years, from 6 CE to 12 CE. These dates are therefore consistent with Josephus' reckoning.[59]

Now Luke said that it was this census that forced the pregnant Mary to leave Nazareth to travel to Bethlehem with Joseph. We have seen earlier that both gospels state that Jesus was born during the reign of Herod the Great (i.e. 4 BCE). However, Herod had been *dead for ten years* when the census took place in 6 CE. This fundamental inconsistency shows that Luke had resorted to *fiction* to tie in the nativity with historical events.

The dates for the death of Herod (4 BCE) and the census under Quirinius (6 CE) are historically unassailable. So how do the fundamentalist apologists try to wriggle their way out of this? The normal "explanation" was that the census referred to by Luke was an *earlier* census than the one mentioned by Josephus. And to maintain their beloved dogma of biblical inerrancy, they had also suggested that Quirinius was twice governor of Syria, once in 6 CE to 12 CE and once earlier, during the reign of Herod.[60]

However, this apologetic attempt fails. Let us list out the historical facts against such an explanation.

Firstly, there is no historical documentation of a census under Roman auspices earlier than 6 CE in Judea. As mentioned above, the Roman census is taken primarily for taxation purposes. It only became necessary in Judea in 6 CE after Archelaus was deposed and the province of Judea came under direct Roman rule. Before this Judea was a "client kingdom", i.e. under Roman domination but not under direct Roman rule. No Roman census in a client kingdom had ever been recorded. At any rate

---

[58]   Craveri, *The Life of Jesus*: p61-63

[59]   Guignebert, *Jesus*: p97, 100

[60]   McDowell, *Evidence That Demands a Verdict*: p71

Herod the Great was a very obedient subject of Rome who paid his dues properly. There was no need for Rome to intervene directly with any kind of census in Judea.[61]

An earlier census is also impossible for a few other reasons. As Josephus mentioned, in 6 CE the census provoked a revolt among the Jewish people who had never taken kindly to foreign domination and to censuses. Even when the census was done by King David himself it was not viewed in a favorable light. We have the book of Chronicles attributing David's desire for census to the influence of the devil:

> I Chronicle 21:1
> Satan stood up against Israel, and moved David to number Israel.

A people who had historically been hostile to even their own King taking a census would not submissively allow some foreign power do the same and, according to Josephus, they didn't. If an earlier census had occurred it would have provoked a similar reaction from the Jews that would have been impossible for historians to have missed. Some have suggested that the earlier census was carried out by Herod in accordance with Jewish customs and this would have prevented any riots from the inhabitants of Palestine. This explanation is equally unacceptable. Herod, being an Idumean, was considered by the Jews to be as foreign as the Romans! It simply stretches credulity to assert that there was an earlier census conducted in Judea that went unnoticed by historians.[62]

In desperation, some apologists have pointed to the wording in the Gospel of Luke about the census:

> Luke 2:2
> This was the *first* enrollment [i.e. census] made when Quirinius was governor of Syria.

They argue that the use of the word "first" implies that there was a second census under Quirinius and that this latter census was the one Josephus mentioned in 6 CE. This "first" census mentioned in Luke must have been earlier than the one mentioned by Josephus. In spite of the lack of historical evidence and of the reasons given above, they insist on an earlier census based on this one verse.

Although in general the use of the word "first" does imply "second," in this specific case it does not. There are two reasons why this is so. Firstly, it is quite clear that Luke is aware of only one census as attested by this passage in Acts:

> Acts 5:37 NRSV
> After him, Judas of Galilee rose up at the time of *the* census, and got people to follow him; he also perished, and all who followed him were scattered.

The use of the definite article "the" (Greek = *tes*) for the census clearly shows that Luke knew only one census in Judea. Secondly, the context of this passage clearly

---

[61]   Guignebert, *Jesus*: p100
       Maccoby, *Revolution in Judea*: p50
       Miller, *Born Divine*: p180-181
[62]   Asimov, *Guide to the Bible*: p925-926

does not imply a "second." Its meaning in such contexts is that this is something *unique* that has not been done before. The use of the word "first" (Greek = *protos*) in Luke 2:2 means that it was the *first census conducted by the Romans in Judea*. Its use in this sense does not necessarily imply that there was a second census. We can see such a similar use in Josephus' *Antiquities*.

> Antiquities of the Jews 7:3:2
> It was David, therefore, who *first* cast the Jebusites out of Jerusalem ...
> [or - David was *the first* to drive the Jebusites out of Jerusalem...]

Since the Jebusites were never driven out of Jerusalem a second time, the use of the term "first" means that David's feat was, until that time, unique. It does not imply that the Jebusites were driven out a second time from Jerusalem after David. This is exactly the same way the word is used in Luke 2:2.[63]

The second point of the conservative apologists is that Quirinius was governor of Syria twice, once in 6 CE and once earlier, during the reign of Herod the Great. This suggestion (apart from the obvious need to save the faith of the apologists) was based on a fragmentary inscription found in Antioch that supposedly referred to Quirinius as the governor of Syria at an earlier date than 6 CE.[64]

However, this explanation is, as usual, flawed.[65] The suggestion that the inscription could be understood to refer to Quirinius a governor was first made by the apologist Sir William Ramsey (1851-1939). The inscription simply mentioned that Quirinius was honored for his role in achieving a military victory. It was Ramsey who *guessed* that Quirinius' reward for his role was an earlier appointment, prior to 6 CE, as governor of Syria. Nothing in the inscription even suggests this. It is not surprising that most historians are of the opinion that the inscription *does not* provide any evidence to support the assertion that Quirinius was governor of Syria earlier than 6 CE.[66]

Furthermore, from Josephus we know most of the Roman governors of Syria during that time. Table 11.3 below shows the governors of Syria from 23 BCE to 7 CE. Two Roman governors of Syria during the last years of Herod's reign were C. Sentius Saturninus, who held the post from 9 to 6 BCE, and P. Quintilius Varus was his successor from 6 to 4 BCE. And it was Quintillus Varus who, as governor, suppressed the uprising that occurred *after* the death of Herod.

---

[63] Brown, Birth of the Messiah: p668

[64] McDowell, *Evidence That Demands a Verdict*: p71

[65] Note that to prove the narrative in Luke correct the apologists have to show two things to be historically true: first that there was an earlier Roman census in Judea and second that Quirinius was also governor of Syria during that census. We have seen that the idea of an earlier census is totally without historical support and goes against all that we know of the Roman Empire. Thus even if the apologists succeeded in proving that Quirinius was governor of Syria twice, the first problem still remains.

[66] Brown, *The Birth of the Messiah*: p550-551
Cary & Scullard, *A History of Rome*: p630
Price, *The Incredible Shrinking Son of Man*: p61

Years of Governorship	Name of Governor
23-13 BCE	M.Agrippa
13-11 BCE	?
c. 10 BCE	M. Titius
9-6 BCE	C. Sentius Saturninus
6-4 BCE [*after* the death of Herod]	P. Quintilius Varus
c. 3-2 BCE	?
1 BCE to c. 4 CE	Gauis Caesar
4-5 CE	L. Volusius Saturninus
6 CE – after 7 CE	P. Sulpicius Quirinius

Table 11.3 The Governors of Syria Between 23 BCE to 7 CE[67]

There are only two "blanks" in the list of governors between 23 BCE to 7 CE; once between 13-11 BCE and another time between 3-2 BCE. The latter gap is of no consequence since by then Herod was already dead.[68]

Quirinius' career is relatively well documented in our primary sources. Tacitus' *Annals of Imperial Rome* (3:22-23, 3:48), Suetonius' *Tiberius* (49), Strabo *Geography* (12:6:5) and Josephus' *Antiquities of the Jews* (17:13:5, 18:1:1) all mentioned some aspects of his career. From these we know that he was born sometime before 50 BCE and that he died in 22 CE. We know that he was already consul of Rome by 12 BCE. He was in Asia Minor between 12 – 6 BCE where he fought the war against the Homonadenses. He was the governor of Pamphylia-Galatia between 6 to 1 BCE. He was serving as the adviser for Gauis Caesar for several years before 4 CE. Josephus mentioned Quirinius several times when he became governor of Syria in 6 CE (Antiquities 17:13:5, 18:1:1). So we read of Quirinius career spanning 20 years from 12 BCE to 6 CE, yet not once was he mentioned as taking over the governorship of Syria at an earlier date.[69]

These details tell us that Quirinius could not have been governor during the years we have "gaps" in the list of the Roman governors of Syria; in 13-11 BCE he was consul of Rome, while the years 3-2 BCE were spent as governor of Pamphylia-Galatia.

To summarize, no historical record supports a Roman census in Judea earlier than 6 CE. And there is absolutely no possibility of Quirinius being the governor of Syria during the reign of Herod the Great. Luke has presented two events (Herod and the census) as though they were historically simultaneous when they were not. Luke's attempt at creating verisimilitude for his fictional account fails.

---

[67] Adapted from Brown, *The Birth of the Messiah*: p550

[68] Brown, *The Birth of the Messiah*: p550
Caird, *Saint Luke*: p28
Guignebert, *Jesus*: p100-101

[69] Brown, *The Birth of the Messiah*: p550
White, *From Jesus to Christianity*: p33-34

THE DATE OF JESUS BIRTH

The discussions above should show why the date of Jesus' birth cannot be establish with any certainty. If Jesus was born during the reign of Herod the Great then it must have been before or around 4 BCE. If he was born during the Roman census then it must have been in 6 CE. These two dates are not the only discrepancies in determining the birth date of Jesus. Luke states that Jesus was about 30 years old when he began to preach (Luke 3:23) and that was during the "fifteenth year of the reign of Tiberias Caesar" (Luke 3:1). Now we know that Augustus Caesar died in 14 CE and that Tiberias was his successor. The 15th year of his reign would be around 29 or 30 CE. This sets his birth date around 1 BCE or 1 CE. In John we have a passage that implies that Jesus was close to 50 years old during the time of his ministry:

> John 8:57
> The Jews therefore said to him, "You are not yet fifty years old, and have you seen Abraham?"

Since there is nothing symbolic about the number (or age) 50, it is likely that John meant the passage to show that Jesus was in his (probably late) forties. This will bring the birth date of Jesus to slightly after 20 BCE. In the references above we have five different birth dates of Jesus: c20 BCE (John), c4 BCE (Matthew and Luke), c 1 BCE or c1 CE (Luke), 6 CE (Luke). This date gives a discrepancy of more than a quarter of a century! So much for biblical inerrancy.

Our present system of counting years BC (or BCE) and AD (or CE) was first established by a Scythian monk named Dionysius Exiguus who lived in Rome during the 6th century CE. The Romans had counted the years from the foundation of the city Rome [a.u.c. = *ab urbe condita*]. Around the year 534 CE, Dionysius, aptly titled "The Less", based his calculations entirely on Luke 3:1 and Luke 3:23. He allowed for one year to pass between the commencements of John the Baptist's and Jesus' respective ministries. This makes Jesus' preaching start around the 16th year of Tiberius Caesar's reign, which he set at 30 CE with Jesus being 30 years old (Dionysius ignored Luke's *about*) then. This was the year 754 a.u.c. which he equated with 1 AD (*anno domini* – the year of our lord) or 1 CE. So 1 CE became the year of Jesus' birth. The monk did not have any external means of fixing the date of Herod's death (which was four years earlier – at 750 a.u.c) and the Judean census. Of course, he wouldn't have thought he needed to, as the gospels cannot, in his belief, contain any error. So thanks to a bungling Christian monk, we now figure our dates by BCE and CE with the year 1 CE actually based on an event of uncertain date![70]

---

[70]   Asimov, Guide to the Bible: p937
Asimov, Book of Facts: p372-373
Brown, *The Birth of the Messiah*: p166-167
Craveri, The Life of Jesus: p44
Freed, *The Stories of Jesus' Birth*: p118
Guignebert, Jesus: p103
Miller, *Born Divine*: p179

The next piece of fact should probably no longer come as a surprise to the reader: Jesus was *not* born on December 25th. Neither Luke nor Matthew gave any indication of Jesus' actual birthday. Like many things Christian, the origin of this date comes from the celebration of the pagan religions that nascent Christianity had to compete against. Here too, we see Christianity assimilating portions of paganisms into its structure.

December 25th was the date of the winter solstice.[71] After this, the winter, having reached its peak, slowly gives way to spring. Traditionally, in Roman times, the winter solstice was a period of unrestrained celebration. The celebration was called the *Dies Natalis Solis Invicti* or "the birthday of the unconquered sun." In the pagan religion of Mithraism, which was a form of sun worship, the winter solstice was naturally an occasion of great celebration. The worship of *Sol Invictus*, the Sun God, became so popular that by 274, the Roman Emperor Aurelian (c212-275) gave official sanction to December 25th as the birthday of that God. Christianity in its battle with the pagan religions for converts slowly assimilated their celebrations and beliefs. Christmas day became one of the assimilated celebrations. By the year 354 we already have documents referring to December 25th as the birthday of Jesus. By 440, Christians were celebrating the winter solstice as the birthday of Jesus. By the 6th century, during the reign of Emperor Justinian (527-565), it had become recognized as an official *Christian* holiday.[72]

Christmas, one of the most important dates in the Christian calendar, like so many portions of the nativity, is an assimilated pagan celebration.

MATTHEW'S PROPHECY FULFILMENT

Anyone who has read Matthew's nativity will note how often he tried to tie the events in Jesus' life to Old Testament's prophesies. As we have seen in various sections in this chapter, Matthew referred to an Old Testament prophecy five times in his nativity of Jesus:

1. The virgin birth: Matthew 1:22-23 / Isaiah 7:14

2. The birthplace of Jesus as Bethlehem: Matthew 2:4-5 / Micah 5:2

3. The slaughter of the innocents: Matthew 2:18 / Jeremiah 31:15

4. The return from Egypt: Matthew 2:14-15 / Hosea 11:1-2

5. Jesus' origin from Nazareth: Matthew 2:23 / ??

Let us first review how Matthew used the Old Testament prophecies. The prophecy of the virgin birth is mistranslation of the Hebrew Bible, the term "virgin" is not found in there but in the Greek Septuagint. He had no qualms about lifting passages

---

[71] By the old Roman calendar, in our new slightly modified calendar, the winter solstice falls on December 21.

[72] Asimov, *Guide to the Bible*: p931-932
Asimov, *Book of Facts*: p370
Craveri, *The Life of Jesus*: p47
Keller, *The Bible As History*: p338

completely out of their contexts and treats them as prophecies. The Isaiah prophecy was meant for Ahaz and had nothing to do with events centuries in the future. The cry of Rachel in Jeremiah was meant for the Israelites going into exile, not for the deaths of babies in Bethlehem. The passage about the calling of God's *son* in Hosea refers to the Israelites returning from Egypt during the Exodus. He changed the wording in Micah 5:2 because he did not feel it gave enough prestige to Bethlehem.

How many of these prophecies came true? We have seen that the virgin birth is unhistorical, that Jesus was more likely born in Nazareth not Bethlehem, the massacre of the babies in Bethlehem did not happen and that the whole trip to Egypt was a fictitious invention of Matthew. The only one that "came true" was the fact that Jesus was called a Nazarene. Unfortunately this is the only one where the Old Testament passage cannot be found; i.e. Matthew had "made up" the one prophecy that "came true"![73]

THE REST OF THE NATIVITY

All our earlier analysis has shown that a major portion of the story of the birth of Jesus is unhistorical. Now we shall look at the status of the rest of the nativity episodes in Matthew and Luke.

Matthew 2:1-12 describes the appearance of the wise men "from the east" who came looking for Jesus because they saw a "star in the east". And when they found him, they offered him presents of "gold, incense and myrrh."[74] The problem is, despite diligent research by scholars nobody really knows the identity and the origins of these wise men.[75] As for the star, many suggestions had been made: a nova, a comet and even a planetary conjunction of Saturn and Jupiter. None of these were successful: there was no nova recorded during the period of Jesus' birth; Halley's comet appeared in 12/11 BCE but that was too far back to satisfy most Christian theologians; and the planetary conjunction of Saturn and Jupiter occurred in 7 BCE but the distance between the planets, as viewed from the earth, was still far enough apart for each of the planets to be discernable as separate objects. It was highly unlikely that they could have been mistaken for a single star.[76]

It should also be remembered that the occurrence of heavenly phenomena is a common theme in Greco-Roman legends. For instance, a comet's appearance in the sky during the death of Julius Caesar (c110-44 BCE) was recorded by Suetinus while the same phenomenon that accompanied the birth of Mithridates (c132-63 BCE), King of Pontus, was recorded by the historian Justin.[77]

---

[73] Miller, *Born Divine*: p164-167

[74] The myths that grew on this gospel story were so luxuriant that popular imagination asserted that there were *three kings* (not an uncertain number of wise men) and their names were Melchior, Gasper and Balthazar. These are of course merely more legendary accretions to an already unhistorical story.

[75] Riedel et.al., *The Book of the Bible*: p466

[76] Asimov, *Guide to the Bible*: p791-792
Craveri, *The Life of Jesus*: p58
Miller, *Born Divine*: p102

[77] Craveri, *The Life of Jesus*: p57-58
Lüdemann, *Virgin Birth?*: p84-85

In view of the lack of historical support for the story of the wise men and the star of Bethlehem it is very likely that the whole story was composed by Matthew from Old Testament passages:[78]

On the "star in the east"
Numbers 24:17
A star will come out of Jacob. A scepter will rise out of Israel

On the wise men
Isaiah 60:3
Nations shall come to your light, and kings to the brightness of your rising.

On their presents
Isaiah 60:6
they shall bring gold and frankincense.

As for the significance of myrrh, a good explanation is given in Marina Warner's *Alone of All Her Sex*:

> The myrrh appeared...in the book of Exodus, when the Jews at Moses order mix a chrism with which they anoint the Ark of the Covenant - an apt symbol that the child accepts the wise men's myrrh is the anointed one who will inaugurate the new covenant.[79]

All the above considerations point to the fact that Matthew concocted the whole episode of the wise men, the star and the gifts out of Old Testament passages.

Luke's other episodes of the nativity also have very little claims to historicity. Like Matthew, these episodes can be traced directly to Old Testament passages.

Take for instance, the annunciation of the birth of Jesus to Mary by the angel Gabriel. The dialogue between the virgin and the angel seems to be taken wholly from the Old Testament. The comparison given below shows this clearly:[80]

- The angel greets Mary the same way he (in Daniel the angel's name was also Gabriel) was said to have greeted Daniel:

  Luke 1:28
  "Rejoice, you highly favored one!"
  Daniel 9:23
  "for you are greatly beloved"

- And Gabriel's reassurance to Mary is similar to that he gave Daniel:

---

[78]   Warner, *Alone of All Her Sex*: p6
[79]   Warner, *Alone of All Her Sex*: p6
[80]   Warner, *Alone of All Her Sex*: p11

> Luke 1:30
> "Don't be afraid, Mary"
> Daniel 10:12
> "Don't be afraid, Daniel"

- In another Old Testament passage, an angel greets Gideon in the same words that Gabriel used with Mary:

> Luke 1:28
> The angel said to her, "...The Lord is with you..."
>
> Judges 6:12
> And the angel of the Lord appeared to him and said to him, "The Lord is with you..."

No critical scholar considers the two canticles in Luke, Mary's, *The Magnificat* (Luke 1:46-55) and Zechariah's *The Benedictus* (Luke 1:67-79) to be actual spontaneous outburst of poetry of ordinary people. These canticles are mainly based, respectively, on the Septuagint versions of the *Song of Hannah* (1 Samuel 2:1-10) and on the *Book of Psalms*.[81]

This dependence on the Old Testament for the episodes in the nativity stories is almost total. In fact, as Don Cuppitt and Peter Armstrong pointed out the main outline of the nativity stories can be derived *purely from Old Testament passages*.[82] Table 11.4 gives the nativity episodes and the Old Testament passages that were used as sources by Luke and Matthew.

It is important to think about the implications of this. We know that the early Christians believed Jesus was the Christ or messiah. That belief came first. Following that they believe that his coming and the details of his life must have been foretold in the Old Testament. In cases where they have little or no direct historical information on his life, it is natural, indeed expected, that they would scour through the Bible to look for references to Jesus' life. If a passage is viewed, however vaguely, as messianic by these Christians then it follows, in their worldview that *it must have happened that way*. That almost every detail of the nativity has parallel in the Old Testament is very strong evidence that the entire story is unhistorical.

---

[81]   Miller, *Born Divine*: p44-53
Freed, *The Stories of Jesus' Birth*: p155-170
Warner, *Alone of All Her Sex*: p12-13
[82]   Cuppitt & Armstrong, *Who Was Jesus*: p45

EPISODES IN THE NATIVITY	GOSPEL VERSES	OLD TESTAMENT PASSAGES
The Annunciation	Luke 1:26-38	Daniel 9:23, 10:12 Judges 6:12, 13:3-4
The Magnificat	Luke 1:46-56	I Samuel 1:11, 2:1, 7-8 II Samuel 22:51 Malachi 3:12 etc.
The Benedictus	Luke 1:67-69	Psalm 41:3, 72:18, 105:8-9,45 106:10, 45, 48, 107:10, 111:4, 132:17,
The Virgin Birth	Luke 1:27 Matthew 1:18	Isaiah 7:14
The Birth in Bethlehem	Luke 2:4-6 Matthew 2:1	Micah 5:2
The Wise Men From the East	Matthew 2:1-12	Isaiah 60:3, Isaiah 60:6 Exodus 30:23, Psalms 72:10
The Star of Bethlehem	Matthew 2:2, 9-10	Numbers 24:17
The Slaughter of the Innocents	Matthew 2:16-17	Exodus 1:15-16 Jeremiah 31:5
The Return from Egypt	Matthew 2:13-15	Hosea 11:1

Table 11.5: The Dependence of the Nativity Stories on the Old Testament.

THE CHILDHOOD OF JESUS

Of all the four gospels only Luke contains an account of Jesus' childhood. It is an isolated incident of Jesus in the Temple of Jerusalem.

Luke 2:41-52
His parents went every year to Jerusalem at the feast of the Passover. When he was twelve years old, they went up to Jerusalem according to the custom of the feast, and when they had fulfilled the days, as they were returning, the boy Jesus stayed behind in Jerusalem. Joseph and his mother didn't know it, but supposing him to be in the company, they went a day's journey, and they looked for him among their relatives and acquaintances. When they didn't find him, they returned to Jerusalem, looking for him. It happened after three days they found him in the temple, sitting in the midst of the teachers, both listening to them, and asking them questions. All who heard him were amazed at his understanding and his answers. When they saw him, they were astonished, and his mother said to him, "Son, why have you treated us this way? Behold, your father and I were anxiously looking for you." He said to them, "Why were you looking for me? Didn't you know that I must be in my Father's house?" They didn't understand the saying which he spoke to them. And he went down with them, and came to Nazareth. He was subject to them, and his mother kept all these sayings in her heart. And Jesus increased in wisdom and stature, and in favor with God and men.

A consideration of the details of this story is sufficient to convince us of the fictitious nature of this story. How could Joseph and Mary, presumably *good* parents, not ask where their son was for a whole day? Who fed and clothed Jesus during those three days? How could his parents have not understood Jesus' reply about being in his

Father's house when they both know of his miraculous origin? As Robert Miller noted, in Luke's writing "neither historical accuracy nor realistic story telling has a high priority."[83]

Furthermore, as Gerd Lüdemann points out, the statement in Luke 2:51, that his mother "kept all these sayings in her heart" clearly reveals the author's attempt to explain why this story appeared so late in the tradition. [One can imagine the question from some more skeptical hearers of this story "How come we have never heard of this before?" being answered with the retort, "Well, Mary didn't tell anyone about this until much later."][84]

The numbers used in the telling of the story, 3 (days lost) and 12 (age of Jesus) reveals the artificial nature of the whole story. Three is the messianic figure and twelve was the age of Solomon when he became King. Daniel too came into prominence at twelve years of age. And according to Jewish legend, Moses separated himself from his family at that age. According to Josephus, Samuel became a prophet at age twelve (Antiquities 5:10:4).[85]

Recall from the previous chapter that Luke copied and used some material from Josephus. Here, again, we find that Luke had probably used the Jewish historian as his source again. In Josephus' autobiography, *The Life of Flavius Josephus* he mentioned that he had a precocious childhood and had a wide learning of Jewish religious matters. This is what Josephus himself said of his childhood:

> Life of Flavius Josephus 2
> Moreover, when I was a child, and about fourteen years of age, I was commended by all for the love I had to learning; on which account the high priests and principal men of the city came then frequently to me together, in order to know my opinion about the accurate understanding of points of the law.

Note the point about the high priests and the principle men of Jerusalem consulting him due to his accurate understanding of the law and the story in Luke about the twelve year old Jesus who amazed the teachers of the law with *his* understanding of the Law. Furthermore, we find that Josephus story about Moses' childhood probably influence Luke as well. In Antiquities 2:9:6, Josephus wrote that Moses' "understanding" [Greek = *synesis*] became superior to his age and not in accordance to his "stature" [Greek = *helikia*]. In Luke 2:47 the teachers of the Law were "amazed at his understanding [*synesis*]" and in Luke 2:52 that Jesus increased in "stature" [*helikia*].

We have seen earlier that Luke used the Song of Hannah (I Samuel 2:1-10) as the basis for Mary's *Magnificat*. Hannah was the mother of the prophet Samuel. Luke used Samuel's childhood as the basis for this childhood incident as well.[86]

---

[83]   Miller, *Born Divine*: p66
[84]   Lüdemann, *Virgin Birth?*: p118-119
[85]   Freed, *The Stories of Jesus' Birth*: p148
      Guignebert, *Jesus*: p143
      Miller, *Born Divine*: p69-70
[86]   Freed, *The Stories of Jesus' Birth*: p148-149
      Graham, *The Jesus Hoax*: p195
      Miller, *Born Divine*: p65-67

Luke 2:40	I Samuel 2:21
The child was growing, and was becoming strong in spirit, being filled with wisdom, and the grace of God was upon him.	The child Samuel grew before Yahweh.
Luke 2:52	I Samuel 2:26
And Jesus increased in wisdom and stature, and in favor with God and men.	The child Samuel grew on, and increased in favor both with Yahweh, and also with men.

Table 11.6: Luke's dependence on Samuel.

We can conclude that this story is fictitious and is something either an invention *in toto* by Luke or adapted by him from an unhistorical, and late, tradition.

* * * * *

A final note to add about the nativity is that the oldest extant Christian documents, the epistles of Paul and the Gospel of Mark say nothing about the events surrounding Jesus' birth.[87] All this, taken together, provides a very strong indictment against the historicity of the events depicted in the nativity.

But the Gospel of Mark has, perhaps unwittingly, left a testament that clinches our case. We find in this gospel such behavior from his own family members that we would not expect had they known about the events of the Nativity and its meaning (as Joseph and, especially Mary should have). There is an episode related by Mark that occurred during the beginning of Jesus' ministry that shows how his family (including his mother!) reacted when they heard he had started preaching:

> Mark 3:21,31-35 (NIV)[88]
> When his family heard about this, they went to take charge of him, for they said, *"He is out of his mind."*... Then Jesus' mother and brothers arrived. Standing outside, they sent someone in to call him. crowd was sitting around him, and they told him, "Your mother and brothers are outside looking for you." "Who are my mother and my brothers?" he asked. Then he looked at those seated in a circle around him and said, "Here are my mother and my brothers! Whoever does God's will is my brother and sister and mother."

The gist of the above incident is clear, his family including Mary upon hearing that Jesus had started preaching *thought he had gone mad* and went *to restrain him*. Jesus, angered or perhaps embarrassed by his family's reaction, publicly denounced them.

This passage is most definitely historical. This passage fulfils the criterion we introduced in chapter 7 known as the criterion of *embarrassment*. We find that both Matthew and Luke, both of whom used Mark extensively, omitted it. A later

---

Schonfield, *The Passover Plot*: p24

[87] Cuppitt & Armstrong, *Who Was Jesus*: p45

[88] Many Bible versions tend to obscure the "harshness" of the original Greek so the fact that Jesus' own family thought he was mad is sometimes obscured by the translation. Surprisingly (especially in view of our analysis in Excursus B) the version that comes closest to the original Greek for this passage is the NIV!

Christian scribe, as evidenced by some extant manuscripts, even tried to alter the passage by changing "When *his family* heard about this" in Mark 3:21 to "When *the scholars and others* heard this".[89]

The question here is obvious: why did Mary try to stop Jesus when he started preaching? Didn't she consent to an angel to be the virgin mother of the "son of the most high"? Wasn't it her who sang the Magnificat and said that "all generations will call me blessed" because she will be the mother of Jesus? Only one answer is possible, the historical Mary, who had at least seven children, knew nothing of the angels, the virgin birth, her *perpetual* virginity, the slaughter of the innocents, the visit of the wise men and the star of Bethlehem because these events never happened!

In short, nothing is known about Jesus before his public ministry at (probably) around thirty years of age. All references to him prior to this are legends without any historical foundation.

---

[89]   Funk et. al., *The Acts of Jesus*: p72-73

Chapter Twelve
THE MINISTRY

GENERAL COMMENTS

From the purely legendary accounts of Jesus' nativity and childhood, we come to the public period of his life. One would probably expect this portion of his life to be based on more reliable accounts than the former as there would naturally be more eyewitnesses, and as his fame spread, many would tend to remember him more.[1] Presumably, once he had gained some kind of a following, his immediate disciples would have certainly taken some pains to put to memory what he had taught. However, it should be remembered that the sayings and deeds attributed to Jesus existed mainly in an oral form for at least four decades after his death before they were put into writing in the now missing Q and the Gospel of Mark. These oral traditions must have passed through many different persons before reaching their final written forms. Furthermore, there was no guarantee whatsoever that the early compilers of Jesus' words and deeds knew how to differentiate the authentic from the fictitious accounts. We have already seen some of these discussed in chapter nine. There we have shown that Mark, the earliest of the four gospels, was definitely composed from traditional (not direct eyewitness) sources which already contained mistakes regarding the culture and geography of Palestine. In short, while we may expect more reliable information regarding Jesus from this period of his ministry, we should still tread very carefully to ensure that we do not accept as historical what is mainly legendary or purely mythical.

In fact, uncertainties abound regarding the events described by the gospels regarding Jesus' period of ministry. An example of this uncertainty is in the actual duration of it. While it is not stated explicitly in any of the four gospels, we can gather allusions to the actual length of time Jesus went about preaching by looking for internal clues within these documents. A reading of the synoptics (due to only one celebration of the Passover alluded to and the fact that at no point in the earlier narratives was it hinted that even a year had gone by) tend to show that Jesus career lasted, at the utmost, a single year. In John's gospel however, we find that three Passover festivals were mentioned to have occurred during the ministry (John 2:13; 6:4; 11:55) which showed that the author thought that Jesus' career spanned three years.[2]

From the material derived from Mark's gospel, it has been calculated that three to four weeks would suffice for everything related in Mark, with the exception of

---

[1] Some skeptics such as G.A. Wells have postulated, in books such as *The Historical Evidence for Jesus*, that the Galilean prophet never actually existed!. Proving that Jesus' never existed is no mean task. Wells comes close but, in my opinion, not quite enough. However, the basic facts presented by him, that very little of the information we know about Jesus from the gospels are historical, remains valid. Our basic assumption throughout this book is that Jesus actually existed historically. But note that this is *very* different from saying that everything reported in the gospels about him is true.

[2] Guignebert, *Jesus*: p205

Mark 1:13 where Jesus was said to be in the wilderness for forty days.[3] The minimum time of Jesus' ministry derivable from Mark is therefore around two months. Other estimates range from a few months[4] to the full three years of the Johanine itinerary. The truth is that even such a basic information as the duration of his ministry is no longer available to us. The contradictory information derived from the gospels only served to underline this paucity of certain knowledge about the ministry of Jesus.

There is also another important consideration about the ministry of Jesus that is not often alluded to by Christians; and that is the essentially *rural* nature of his itinerary.[5] The synoptics show that Jesus confined himself to strictly Jewish rural areas. The only exception there is being in the last week of his life that was spent in Jerusalem.

Jesus' headquarters was Capernaum (Mark 1:21; Matthew 4:13; Luke 4:31; John 2:12), a frontier village and customs post on the northwest shore of the Sea of Galilee.[6] From here, his ministry consists of visiting small towns and villages in Galilee:

Mark 1:38-39
He [Jesus] said to them, "Let's go elsewhere into the next towns [Greek = komopoleis], that I may preach there also, because I came out for this reason." He went into their synagogues throughout all Galilee, preaching and casting out demons.

Mark 6:6b
He went around the villages [Greek = *komas*] teaching.

The Greek words used by Mark, *komas* and *komopoleis*, refer to villages of varying sizes.[7]

The overall picture we have from the gospel then is a Jesus that was strictly a rural and insular Galilean peasant. The theologian Don Cuppitt summarized the main reasons why the Galilean should be viewed as such:

...there is much to suggest that Jesus confined himself to a strictly Jewish world. Important trade routes passed through Galilee, and there were several notable Hellenistic cities. But Jesus is not reported as having any contact with these major towns of Sepphoris, Tiberias and Gabara. He sticks purely to Jewish rural areas. The thirty or so words of his vocabulary preserved in the gospels are the brand of Aramaic spoken in Galilee: there is no evidence, and no likelihood, that he knew

---

[3] Nineham, *Saint Mark*: p35
[4] Guignebert, *Jesus*: p211
[5] It has been suggested by some scholars [see White, *From Jesus to Christianity*: p102] that Jesus may have been exposed to an urban setting by the fact that Sepphoris, a large town, was situated only around 6-7 km (4 miles) from Nazareth and that Jesus occupation as a carpenter would have virtually required him to travel to this place quite frequently. Yet the fact remains that there is no tradition of Jesus' activity in this place, neither in the canonical gospels nor in any other extra biblical sources.
[6] Nineham, *Saint Mark*: p73
[7] Nineham, *Saint Mark*: p85

Greek or cared for Gentile culture. There is even a saying in which he orders his disciples to avoid Gentiles and Samaritans (Matthew 10:5). An orthodox Jew traveling between Galilee and Jerusalem went down the Jordan valley via Jericho to avoid Samaria, and Jesus to seem to have at least usually taken this route, for he is strongly associated with Bethany and Jericho.[8]

This rural-Galilean picture of Jesus, if he ever existed, is almost certainly the most historically likely. The level of education and intellectual sophistication of those who heard his preaching and those who followed him could not have been very high. They were very likely ignorant, uneducated, superstitious and uncritical. The Acts of the Apostles (4:13) called Peter and John, two of his foremost disciples, *unschooled and ordinary men.*

Why is this fact relevant to our investigation? It is relevant for a couple of reasons. It tells us that those who first followed Jesus could not have been impressed with him had he preached a philosophically sophisticated doctrine. Some modern liberal scholars attributed such sophistication to his teachings that one wonders how that would have attracted *any* following among Galilean peasants.[9] This is also relevant with respect to our evaluation of eyewitness testimony regarding the events in the life of Jesus. If the original eyewitnesses were credulous and uncritical – it weighs heavily against a positive evaluation of the historicity of miracles reported to have been performed by Jesus.

THE BAPTISM OF JESUS BY JOHN THE BAPTIST

All the synoptics agree that the event which initiated Jesus' ministry was his baptism in the River Jordan by a man known as John the Baptist. Mark's description about John is given below:

> Mark 1:4-6
> John came baptizing in the wilderness and preaching the baptism of repentance for forgiveness of sins. All the country of Judea and all those of Jerusalem went out to him. They were baptized by him in the Jordan river, confessing their sins. John was clothed with camel's hair and a leather belt around his waist. He ate locusts and wild honey.

Prophets like John were not an uncommon sight in first century Palestine. Josephus (*Autobiography* 2) related how he spent three years with the hermit Bannos. To this hermit, purity means living entirely on plant products. For all his clothing and food came only from trees. These religious fanatics, like Bannos and John, all went out into the wilderness. Even John's mode of dressing is the standard Hebrew prophetic attire. We are told in II Kings that the prophet Elijah wore almost the same attire (II Kings 1:8). As for eating locusts, this was not considered an abomination to the Jews (Leviticus 11:22).

---

8   Cuppitt & Armstrong, *Who Was Jesus?*:p62
9   We evaluate some of the interpretations of modern liberal scholars on the teachings of Jesus in the next chapter.

There is nothing peculiar about the person of John the Baptist. He was clearly a product of the social environment of contemporary Palestine and was by no means the only prophet running around preaching about the need for repentance.[10] Apart from the fifteen references[11] to John the Baptist in the gospels there is also independent corroboration from Josephus' *Antiquities of the Jews* (18:5:2).

Antiquities 18:5:2
John, that was called the Baptist: ... who was a good man, and commanded the Jews to exercise virtue, both as to righteousness towards one another, and piety towards God, and so to come to baptism; for that the washing [with water] would be acceptable to him, if they made use of it, not in order to the putting away [or the remission] of some sins [only], but for the purification of the body; supposing still that the soul was thoroughly purified beforehand by righteousness.

Therefore, the existence of John the Baptist is not an issue. In any case, that is not where our interest lies. Our interest in John the Baptist stems from the connection the gospels made between him and Jesus. According to the gospels John was the forerunner who prepared the way for Jesus. This is how Mark describes The Baptist's message:

Mark 1:7-8
He [John] preached, saying, "After me comes he who is mightier than I, the thong of whose sandals I am not worthy to stoop down and loosen. I baptized you in water, but he will baptize you in the Holy Spirit."

It was during one John's baptismal sessions that Jesus came along and had himself baptized by John.

Mark 1:9-11
It happened in those days, that Jesus came from Nazareth of Galilee, and was baptized by John in the Jordan. Immediately coming up from the water, he saw the heavens parting, and the Spirit descending on him like a dove. A voice came out of the sky, "*You* are my beloved Son, in whom I am well pleased."

A few things are worthy of note here. First there is no indication that John recognized Jesus as the messiah or the "one who is more powerful" than he (Mark 1:7) Further, note that the vision described was clearly a personal experience of Jesus: he was baptized, saw heaven opened and heard the voice of God which was addressed to him ("*You* are my son..."). There is no suggestion whatsoever in the passage that anyone else saw the heavens opening or a descending dove or heard the voice from heaven. Many mystics have experienced similar or even more spectacular visions. The Markan account is simple, straightforward and historically plausible.

But the theological difficulty in the above account was noticed by the other evangelists, who wrote their gospels later. John specifically taught that his baptism

---

10   Guignebert, *Jesus*: p152-153
11   The fifteen references are found in Mark 1:2-11,14; 2:18; 6:14-29; 9:30-33 Matthew 3:7-17;11:2-19 Luke 1; 3:7-17; 7:18-27;7:31-35; 16:16 John 1:19-42; 3:22-36; 4:1-3

was for the cleansing of one's sins (Mark 1:5, Luke 3:3) and if Jesus went through the same baptismal rite it clearly implied that he had sinned. Furthermore, accepting the baptism in the way Mark described it also seemed to reduce the status of Jesus to below that of John. As Christianity evolved, the figure of Jesus began to take on a supra-human status. Since it came to be believed that Jesus was the superior of John, the later evangelists were forced to change the account in Mark.

Let us look at how Matthew accommodated the account of the baptism in Mark to fit in with the evolving doctrine concerning Jesus.

> Matthew 3:13-17
> Then Jesus came from Galilee to the Jordan to John, to be baptized by him. *But John would have hindered him, saying, "I need to be baptized by you, and you come to me?" But Jesus, answering, said to him, "Allow it now, for this is the fitting way for us to fulfill all righteousness."* Then he allowed him. Jesus, when he was baptized, went up directly from the water: and behold, the heavens were opened to him. He saw the Spirit of God descending as a dove, and coming on him. Behold, a voice out of the heavens said, "*This* is my beloved Son, with whom I am well pleased."

The portions Matthew added to the Markan account are italicized above. John is here made to recognize Jesus instantly and tried to deter the latter from being baptized. John's testimony to Jesus clearly showed the inferior status of the former. Jesus' reply made the baptism a purely ceremonial one. In one fell swoop, the two theological problems apparent in the Markan account are eliminated in Matthew's. Note also that the personal vision of Jesus has been changed here to a more public proclamation; the personal "*You* are my son..." of Mark has been changed by Matthew to the public "*This* is my son".

Although Luke (3:21-22) followed Mark's account of the baptism, he also made adjustments to his gospel to ensure that John's inferior status is made explicit. This adjustment was made in the nativity story of Jesus where the baby John, still in his mother's womb, leapt for joy, when Mary, pregnant with Jesus, greeted Elizabeth (Luke 1:41-44).

In the fourth gospel the theological evolution had progressed even further:

> John 1:29-36
> The next day, he saw Jesus coming to him, and said, "Behold, the Lamb of God, who takes away the sin of the world! This is he of whom I said, 'After me comes a man who is preferred before me, for he was before me.' I didn't know him, but for this reason I came baptizing in water: that he would be revealed to Israel." John testified, saying, "I have seen the Spirit descending like a dove out of heaven, and it remained on him. I didn't recognize him, but he who sent me to baptize in water, he said to me, 'On whomever you will see the Spirit descending, and remaining on him, the same is he who baptizes in the Holy Spirit.' I have seen, and have testified that this is the Son of God." Again, the next day, John was standing with two of his disciples, and he looked at Jesus as he walked, and said, "Behold, the Lamb of God!"

Note that in the Gospel of John the story of Jesus' baptism is completely omitted. And John the Baptist is now made to immediately and openly acknowledge the status of Jesus. And the vision of the dove, which in Mark is given as a purely personal experience of Jesus, is in the fourth gospel given as the experience of John the Baptist.[12]

Most scholars believe that the baptism of Jesus by John is historical. The reason is based on the "criterion of embarrassment," which we introduced in chapter 7. There are two reasons why this incident should be embarrassing to the early Christians. That Jesus submitted to the baptism means he became a *disciple* of John. That he undertook the cleansing process means that, like any ordinary human being, he *needed* to be cleansed. Since the early Christians considered Jesus to be superior to John, we would expect them to try and spin the fact of his baptism in ways that would reduce the two factors of embarrassment. As we have seen above, Matthew tried to explain away Jesus' need for baptism while the fourth gospel did away with the baptism completely. As for proving Jesus' superiority to John, Matthew had the Baptist telling Jesus that it was he [John] who needs to be baptized by Jesus. The fourth gospel has John recognizing Jesus immediately upon setting eyes on him.[13] Thus, we can conclude with much certainty that Jesus was indeed baptized by John – with all that implies.

Furthermore, the theological alterations by Matthew, Luke and John cannot be considered to be based on any historical recollection. This can be demonstrated by a passage from Q. This passage is placed after the arrest of John by Herod Antipas. (John was executed by Herod not long after this imprisonment.)

> Matthew 11:2-3 (Luke 7:18-20)
> Now when John heard in the prison the works of Christ, he sent two of his disciples
> and said to him, "Are you he who comes, or should we look for another?"

The passage above shows that John only questioned Jesus' status *after* he was imprisoned. He was not sure who Jesus was and actually sent his disciples to ask Jesus if he was "the one who was to come." The contradiction between this passage and the theological alterations of Matthew, Luke and John is glaringly obvious. Why would the John who tried to stop Jesus from being baptized by him (according to Matthew) or who leapt in his mother's womb upon receiving Mary's greetings (according to Luke) or who publicly proclaimed Jesus "the Lamb of God who takes away the sins of the world" (according to John) now fail to recognize who he was?[14]

---

[12] Cadoux, *The Life of Jesus*: p44-45
 Craveri, *The Life of Jesus*: p131
 Nineham, *Saint Mark*: p61
 Sanders, *The Historical Figure of Jesus*: p94
 Schonfield, *The Passover Plot*: p67-68
[13] Akenson, Saint Saul: p80-81
 Craveri, *The Life of Jesus:* p87
 Crossan, *The Historical Jesus*: p232-234
 Funk et. al., *The Acts of Jesus*:p54
 Guignebert, *Jesus*: p157
 Sanders, *The Historical Figure of Jesus*: p94
[14] Caird, *Saint Luke*: p111
 Fenton, *Saint Matthew*, p175

There is a further problem in the gospels' story about John's role. If he was to be the forerunner of Jesus, someone who prepares the way for the Lord (Mark 1:2); his mission would have been complete the moment Jesus steps into the scene. One would expect John's movement to be obsolete and his followers would disband or follow Jesus. Yet this was obviously not the case. The passage above also showed that John kept his disciples to the end of his life.[15]

Even after the death of John, his disciples continued to be a separate and distinct group from the followers of Jesus. Acts 19:1-7 narrates the story of Paul meeting some followers of John in Ephesus, a quarter of a century *after* the death of John and Jesus. These followers had not even heard of Jesus or the Holy Spirit. The followers of John, which eventually became known as the Mandeans, survived until today with small followings in Iraq and Iran. They were often locked in theological conflict with the early Christians - as the polemics of the early Christians testify.[16]

The balance of evidence, therefore, is in favor of the hypothesis that John never preached about he being a forerunner to Jesus.[17]

The considerations above show conclusively that the accounts of Jesus' meeting with John the Baptist, as presented in Matthew and John, are fictional. Luke's nativity account, too, must be consigned to the category of myths. This leaves us with the basic Markan account. The story of the baptism, as told in Mark, sounds plausible - Jesus could well have been one of the many who were baptized *incognito* by John.

Some scholars have argued that even this basic story by Mark is unhistorical. The main argument is that the Q (Matthew 11:2-3; Luke 7:18-20) passage we saw above seems to imply that John had never heard of Jesus.[18] However, that passage can equally be interpreted to mean that John may have known Jesus but did not consider him to be anything special until he started hearing about Jesus' miraculous exploits. Another attempt to argue against the historicity of the baptism is from the sociology of religion. According to this argument, the easiest way for a new religion (or religious group) to relinquish and supplant the old would be to incorporate elements of the latter into it. This was what happened when the Christians incorporated the pagan celebrations during the winter solstice and transformed it into Christmas. This was also what happened to the Kaaba, an old shrine of Arabian paganism which Muhammad transformed into the holiest site of Islam. The best way for the early Christians to fight the Mandeans was to assert that John's work was simply a

---

[15] Mark 6:29 mentioned that John was buried by his disciples after his execution by Herod Antipas.

[16] Asimov, *Guide to the Bible*: p1071
Caird, *Saint Luke*: p111
Craveri, *The Life of Jesus*: p88
Hoffman, *The Origins of Christianity*: p255-256
Wells, *Did Jesus Exists?*: p152
Wilson, *Jesus: A Life*: p102

[17] That John's message was *apocalyptic* is undeniable. This could be in the form of a Davidic messiah, the "son of man" described in Daniel or just a direct intervention by God. So while it is possible John may have believed that someone will come after him, we know from the considerations in the text that he definitely did not consider Jesus to be that one.

[18] Mack, *The Lost Gospel*: p155

preparation for Jesus.[19] This again falters on the fact that had the initial attempt been to show Jesus' superiority over the Baptist, we would expect the earliest account be similar to the Gospel of John (1:29-36 – see above), where there is no mention of baptism and where the Baptist openly recognized Jesus as "The Lamb of God."

So we can conclude the following:

- The baptism of Jesus by John is historical.

- John did not preach about being a forerunner to anyone and that he certainly did not recognize Jesus as anything special.

- Since Jesus submitted to baptism, *he must have accepted the fact that he needed to be cleansed.* Also by submitting to this baptism, *he became a disciple, however minor, to John the Baptist.* In other words, far from revealing he was a divine son of God, this episode clearly shows a Galilean peasant getting caught up in the religious fervor of the times who clearly believe he himself was a human who needed cleansing via baptism and instructions via being a disciple.

THE TEMPTATION IN THE WILDERNESS

According to the synoptics, immediately after his baptism, Jesus went into the wilderness where he was tempted by Satan. This is how Mark describes it:

> Mark 1:12-13
> Immediately the Spirit drove him out into the wilderness. He was there in the wilderness forty days tempted by Satan. He was with the wild animals; and the angels were serving him.

There are three reasons why this short Markan account cannot be historical. Firstly, 40 is a symbolic number, we find that the great flood lasted forty days (Genesis 7:4), that the Israelites wandered in the wilderness for forty years (Numbers 14:33) and that it took forty days to embalm the body of Jacob (Genesis 50:3). Secondly, the wilderness is, according to Jewish tradition, the abode of evil spirits. It was the contemporaneous Jewish belief that the messiah will appear in the last days of the world to take on Satan and win. And finally, the mention of mythical creatures like Satan and angels would immediately cause most skeptics to denounce this passage as mythical, or at best, allegorical. The passage in Mark could have simply been made up by early Christian tradition since it was *expected* of the messiah to overcome temptation by the evil one.[20]

In Q, we find that more mythical elements have been added to the basic Markan story:

---

[19] Hoffman, *The Origins of Christianity*: p256
[20] Craveri, *The Life of Jesus*: p90
 Guignebert, *Jesus*: p159
 Nineham, *Saint Mark*: p63-64
 Wells, *Did Jesus Exists?*: p104

Matthew 4:1-11 (Luke 4:1-13)

Then Jesus was led up by the Spirit into the wilderness to be tempted by the devil. When he had fasted forty days and forty nights, he was hungry afterward. The tempter came and said to him, "If you are the Son of God, command that these stones become bread." But he answered, "It is written, 'Man shall not live by bread alone, but by every word that proceeds out of the mouth of God'" Then the devil took him into the holy city. He set him on the pinnacle of the temple, and said to him, "If you are the Son of God, throw yourself down, for it is written, 'He will put his angels in charge of you.' and, 'On their hands they will bear you up, so that you don't dash your foot against a stone.'" Jesus said to him, "Again, it is written, 'You shall not test the Lord, your God.' "Again, the devil took him to an exceedingly high mountain, and showed him all the kingdoms of the world, and their glory. He said to him, "I will give you all of these things, if you will fall down and worship me." Then Jesus said to him, " Get behind me, Satan! For it is written,' You shall worship the Lord your God, and you shall serve him only.' "Then the devil left him, and behold, angels came and served him.

We will first note that the passage above contains some factual errors: first, the temple in Jerusalem has no "highest point" or pinnacle and second, there was (and is) no mountain high enough for Jesus to see "all the kingdoms of the world" even if we take "the world" to mean only Palestine or one of its tetrachies![21]

It has also been pointed out by some scholars that the Old Testament quotations[22] mentioned by both Jesus and Satan agree with the Septuagint or Greek version of the Bible.[23] It is highly unlikely that this was the version Jesus, a Galilean Jew with probably no knowledge of Greek, would have quoted from.

Not only is the information about Jesus *fasting* for forty days in Matthew not found in Mark, it actually contradicts the latter's account. The tense of the Greek verb in Mark shows that the ministry of the angels is continuous and must have consisted of the angels supplying him with food as the angels did with Elijah (I Kings 19).[24] The idea that Jesus fasted for forty days probably came from the Old Testament.[25] There we find that Moses fasted for forty days on Mount Sinai:

Deuteronomy 9:9

"When I was gone up onto the mountain to receive the tables of stone, even the tables of the covenant which Yahweh made with you, then I stayed on the mountain forty days and forty nights; I did neither eat bread nor drink water."

---

21 Craveri, *The Life of Jesus*: p91
22 All of Jesus' quotes came from Deuteronomy (8:3; 6:16 and 6:13-14 respectively) while Satan's singular quote was taken from Psalms (91:11-22).
23 Fenton, *Saint Matthew*: p63
24 Nineham, *Saint Mark*: p64
    Wells, *Did Jesus Exists?*: p104
25 Craveri, *The Life of Jesus:* p90

Similarly, we find that Elijah fasted for forty days after being fed by the angels:

> I Kings 19:8
> He arose, and ate and drank, and went in the strength of that food forty days and
> forty nights to Horeb the Mount of God.

Comparative mythology tells us that the idea of the holy man being tempted by the Evil One is a prevalent theme in the near and far east. Buddhist scriptures tells of how the Buddha after meditating for four weeks was confronted by the personification of evil, *Mara* who tried to lure him away from his task of attaining enlightenment. Zoroastrian legend tells of how Zoroaster, who was meditating in a cave, met with *Angra-Mainyu*, the god of evil. *Angra-Mainyu* offered Zoroaster the world if he would renounce the god of good, *Ahura Mazda*.[26] It is not asserted here that the Matthean passage was directly influenced by the above myths (although that is not impossible). The point is that the idea of a holy man being tested by personifications of evil is not a foreign one and was, in fact, rather a common one in the socio-religious environment of the evangelists and could have resulted in such myths gaining currency among the early followers of the religion.

In summary, we find a simple account in Mark, which itself could be derived from contemporaneous Palestinian beliefs, being added to and expanded in the Q passage. We also find that the addition could be derived purely from the socio-religious context of the times; people expect their hero to triumph over temptation! The presence of mythical creatures like Satan and angels simply helps to confirm the case that the story of the temptation in the wilderness is not historical.[27]

THE TWELVE APOSTLES

According to all the four gospels and the Acts of the Apostles, Jesus selected a band of disciples, twelve in number, to help him to preach his message. Each of the synoptics supplied a list of the twelve apostles. The list in Acts, as expected, is identical with Luke's but with one omission - Judas Iscariot, who committed suicide after the death of Jesus (Acts 1:18-20). In the Gospel of John, the names of nine apostles can be found interspersed in the narrative. Table 12.1 gives a summary of the four lists.

A glance at the table will show that the four lists are by no means harmonious. The only two lists that tally each other are those of Mark and Matthew. Luke's list differs from these by including a second Judas, a son of James, among the twelve.

---

26   Craveri, *The Life of Jesus:* p92

27   Modernist theologians, of course, accept such passages as mythical. However, they still insist that such passages can convey "spiritual truths." Yet, as we explained in Excursus A, these liberal theologians can't seem to agree just what that "spiritual truth" is! For instance, G.B. Caird takes the third temptation (in Matthew-the second in Luke's) to mean that Jesus rejected the worldly kingdom as it does not lead to God [Caird, Saint Luke: p80-81]; C.J Cadoux, on the other hand, argues that it was not the worldly kingdom that was rejected by Jesus but Satan's method of attaining it - by waging war! [Cadoux, The Life of Jesus: p51-52]

His list excluded the name Thaddaeus found in Mark and Matthew. John's list agree with Luke in including a second Judas but compounds the problem by including yet another apostle not found in any of the three earlier lists, Nathanael.

Matthew 10:2-4	Mark 3:14-19	Luke 6:13-16/Acts 1:13	John (various)
Simon Peter	Simon Peter	Simon Peter	Simon Peter (1:42)
Andrew	Andrew	Andrew	Andrew (1:40)
James s/o Zebedee	James s/o Zebedee	James s/o Zebedee	The sons of Zebedee
John s/o Zebedee	John s/o Zebedee	John s/o Zebedee	(21:2)
Philip	Philip	Philip	Philip (1:43)
Bartholomew	Bartholomew	Bartholomew	
Thomas	Thomas	Thomas	Thomas (20:24)
Matthew	Matthew	Matthew	
James s/o Alphaeus	James s/o Alphaeus	James s/o Alphaeus	
Thaddaeus	Thaddaeus		
Simon the Cananean	Simon the Cananean	Simon the Cananean	
Judas Iscariot	Judas Iscariot	Judas Iscariot	Judas Iscariot (6:71)
		Judas s/o James	Judas (14:22)
			Nathanael (1:45)

Table 12.1: The Apostles of Jesus

Apologists had tried to reconcile these discrepancies. First they claimed that Bartholomew is actually *bar Talmai* (son of Talmai) and that his name is Nathanael. (It is amazing that this explanation, if true, was first mentioned only in the 9th century CE) And then they claimed that Thaddaeus is the surname of Judas son of James. These reconstructions have no evidential support whatsoever. In other words, we do not know if Bartholomew is *Bar Talmai*, and we definitely do not know that Nathanael was the son of one Talmai. We definitely have no reason whatsoever to even believe that Thaddaeus was the surname of Judas son of James. These reconstructions are proposed solely to reconcile the four lists to one another and to save the precious doctrine of biblical inerrancy.[28]

There are more anomalies in the lists. In ancient manuscripts of Mark and Matthew, the name of the tenth apostle is rendered in two different ways: Lebbaeus and Thaddaeus. These names are not interchangeable and represent two distinct names. The balance of evidence[29] from these manuscripts point to Lebbaeus being the original reading in Matthew and Thaddaeus in Mark.[30]

---

[28] Cadoux, *The Life of Jesus*: p105
Craveri, *The Life of Jesus*: p150-151
Nineham, *Saint Mark*: p117
Riedel et.al., *The Book of the Bible*: p437

[29] The editors of the UBS Greek New Testament decided to leave Thaddaeus as the reading for both Mark 3:18 and Matthew 10:3. However, as one of the editors explained the issue was not that simple. While they rated the Thaddeus reading in Mark as "A", meaning they are certain that this was the original reading here, the issue was "more difficult" with the reading in Matthew. There were four different types of reading here: "Thaddaeus", "Lebbaeus", and "Lebbaeus who was called Thaddaeus" and "Thaddaeus who was called

Another difficulty arises with the apostle Matthew. The gospel named after him gave an account of his calling:

> Matthew 9:9-10
> As Jesus passed by from there, he saw a man called Matthew sitting at the tax collection office. He said to him, "Follow me." He got up and followed him. It happened as he sat in the house, behold, many tax collectors and sinners came and sat down with Jesus and his disciples.

The problem with that account is that Mark (copied by Luke) gave exactly the same story but supplied a different name for the tax collector:

> Mark 2:14-15 (Luke 5:27-29)
> As he passed by, he saw Levi, the son of Alphaeus, sitting at the tax office, and he said to him, "Follow me." And he arose and followed him. It happened, that he was reclining at the table in his house, and many tax collectors and sinners sat down with Jesus and his disciples, for there were many, and they followed him.

Luke's account also gave Levi as the name of the tax collector. In all the synoptic lists however, it was Matthew and not Levi who was placed in them. Fundamentalists simply assumed that Matthew and Levi are simply different names for one and the same person. Some had suggested that Matthew was the Christian name taken on by Levi after he followed Christ. This, however, does not resolve the problem. There is no evidence that Matthew was the Greek name for Levi. Matthew is as authentically a Hebrew name as Levi.[31] Note that Mark, by calling Levi the son of Alphaeus makes him very probably the brother of the apostle James son of Alphaeus. Nowhere in the Gospel of Matthew do we find any hint of a family tie between Matthew and James. Mark in his list of the twelve apostles, gave the name of Matthew and not Levi. He surely would have stated that this Matthew was Levi, whose calling he narrated earlier, had that been the case.[32]

Coupled with this uncertainty as to who exactly constituted the original twelve apostles, we are even more uncertain about what their subsequent histories were. In the New Testament, our knowledge of the apostles is mainly limited to Peter and the sons of Zebedee (John and James). According to the gospels Peter, John and James formed the inner circle of Jesus' disciples. They were the only ones present to witness the raising of Jairus' daughter (Mark 5:37; Luke 8:51), the Transfiguration (Matthew 17:1; Mark 9:2; Luke 9:28) and the prayers in the garden of Gethsemane (Matthew 26:37; Mark 14:33).[33]

Outside the gospel and Acts we have the genuine epistles of Paul attesting to Peter and John as the "Jerusalem Pillars" (Galatians 2:9). We also know from Paul

---

Lebbaeus". Finally the editors opted for "Thaddaeus" but rated the reading a "B". (see Metzger, *A Textual Commentary on the Greek New Testament*: p26, 81)
[30] Fenton, *Saint Matthew*: p152
Nineham, *Saint Mark*: p117
[31] Craveri, *The Life of Jesus*: p153
[32] Nineham, *Saint Mark*: p99
[33] Riedel et.al., *The Book of the Bible*: p428

that Peter was married (I Corinthians 9:5), he was the first to see the risen Jesus (I Corinthians 15:5) and that he traveled outside Jerusalem (Galatians 2:11).

Matthew, surprisingly, is mentioned *only once* outside the list of apostles given above, in the short passage in the Gospel of Matthew 9:9-10 which we have shown above. This passage narrates his calling as an apostle followed by Jesus having dinner at his house.

Two apostolic deaths are narrated in the New Testament. Judas Iscariot was the first apostle to have died (Matthew 27:9; Acts 1:18) by committing suicide after the crucifixion of Jesus around 30 CE. The next disciple to have suffered martyrdom was James son of Zebedee (Acts 12:2); he was beheaded by Herod Agrippa around 44 CE.[34]

The apostles Thaddaeus, Simon the Cananean, James son of Alphaeus[35] and Bartholomew appear *only in the list of apostles* given above. All we know about them are their names. Nothing else is written about them in all of the New Testament![36]

There are two other apostles that appear only as names in the Synoptic gospels and Acts: Thomas and Philip.[37] The case with Thomas is the worst: *it was not even a name*! "Thomas" comes from the Hebrew *T'hom*, which means "twin". The seemingly additional surname in John 11:16 translated in the King James as "Thomas who is called Didymus" adds nothing new, for "didymus" is simply Greek for "the Twin"! Modern translations now give this passage as "Thomas who is called 'the Twin.'" There is no evidence in contemporary literature that either Thomas or Didymus were ever used as names during that period.[38]

Andrew is mentioned, in the synoptics, only a little bit more than the other six we have seen above. We are told of his calling (Mark 1:16; Matthew 4:18) and his questioning Jesus at the Mount of Olives (Mark 13:3).[39]

In the New Testament, therefore, except in the Gospel of John, which we will examine immediately below, apart from their names, we are told nothing about six of the apostles - Thaddaeus, Simon the Cananean, James son of Alphaeus, Bartholomew, Thomas and Philip. Even Matthew and Andrew barely get any mention beyond their names in the list of the twelve apostles. These eight apostles are *shadowy* characters - we know nothing much beyond their names.

---

[34] Livingstone, *Dictionary of the Christian Church*: p267
Riedel et.al., *The Book of the Bible*: p435

[35] The identification of James the son of Alphaeus with James the Less (Mark 15:40) or with James the brother of Jesus (Mark 6:3) is pure conjecture. See the analysis of the Hieronymian view on the brothers of Jesus in chapter 11.

[36] Goodspeed, *The Twelve*: p19, 41-44
Riedel et.al., *The Book of the Bible*: p437-438

[37] Not to be confused with Philip, one of the seven Hellenist deacons in Acts (6:5; 8-4-50; 21:8).

[38] Goodspeed, *The Twelve*: p25, 43

[39] Even this meager information is considered suspect by scholars. The Jesus Seminar called the whole backdrop of the 13th chapter of Mark (at the Temple and then at the Mount of Olives) a "fictive setting" and the verses containing the question of Andrew of Peter (Mark 13:3-4) as a continuation of the fictitious narrative framework. (see Funk, et.al., *The Acts of Jesus*: p133-134)

JOHN'S TREATMENT OF THE "SHADOWY" APOSTLES

Three of the shadowy apostles mentioned in the section above, Thomas, Philip and Andrew, are given more prominent roles in the Gospel of John. The passages concerning these apostles in John are as follows:

- **Thomas**
  - John 11:16 **The Raising Of Lazarus**
    Then Thomas who was called the Twin, said to his fellow disciples, "Let us go, so that we may die with him."
  - John 14:5 **Jesus' Farewell Discourse at the Last Supper**
    Thomas says to him, "Lord, we do not know where we are going; how can we know the way?"
  - John 20:24-29 **Story of Doubting Thomas**
- **Andrew**
  - John 1:35-42 **The Call of Andrew and Peter**
  - John 6:8-9 **The Feeding of the Multitudes**
    One of the disciples, Andrew, Simon Peter's brother, says to him, "There is a lad here who has five barley loaves and two fishes. But what are these among so many?"
  - John 12:21-22 **Greek Believers in Jesus**
    Now among those who went up to worship at the festival were some Greeks. They came to Philip, who was from Bethsaida in Galilee, and said to him, "Sir, we wish to see Jesus." Philip went and told Andrew; then Andrew and Philip went and told Jesus.
- **Philip**
  - John 1:29-51 **The Call of Philip and Nathanael**
  - John 6:5-8 **The Feeding of the Multitudes**
    Jesus said to Philip "Where are we to buy bread for these people to eat?"...Philip answered him, "200 denarii would not be enough bread for each of them to get a little."
  - John 12:21-22 **Greek Believers in Jesus**
  - John 14:8 **Jesus' Farewell Discourse at the Last Supper**
    Philip says to him, "Lord, show us the father, and that suffices us"

Many of these incidents given in the Gospel of John in which the names of these apostles are included are demonstrably unhistorical.

For instance, the presence of Andrew (John 6:8-9) and Philip (John 6:5-8) in the miracle of the feeding of multitudes is merely the addition of names to an incident which never happened.[40] The Jesus Seminar called this event "a narrative ritualization of a common practice" of Jesus sharing a common meal of fish and bread with his friends.[41]

Similarly, the appearance of Thomas in the Raising of Lazarus (John 11:16) is fraught with problems. As we will see later in this chapter, the many of the details of the raising of Lazarus were lifted from the Egyptian "pyramid texts". Thomas' cameo

---

[40]   See our treatment on miracles later in this chapter.
[41]   Funk, et.al., *The Acts of Jesus*: p387

is embedded within this fictitious account – making it a virtual certainty that the episode is unhistorical.

His major role in the Doubting Thomas episode (John 20:24-29) of the resurrection narratives also faces similar problems. As we shall see in chapter 15, the evidence shows that the earliest experiences of the resurrection were intangible, hallucinatory "visions." The resurrection appearances of a physically tangible Jesus narrated in the gospels are fictitious accounts concocted by the early Christian community. The story of Thomas touching Jesus' side and putting his finger in the mark of the nails on Jesus is pure fiction.

To summarize, the cameo appearance of Thomas in the Raising of Lazarus (John 11:16) and his starring role in the Doubting Thomas episode of the resurrection narratives are merely addition of his name to fictitious accounts.[42]

On other occasions, the names of the disciples are merely added with questions for Jesus to break the monotony of his long discourses. This is the judgment of the Jesus Seminar on the questions of Thomas (John 14:5) and Philip (John 14:9) in the farewell discourse of Jesus during the last supper:

> In the "farewell speeches", the fourth evangelist attributes to Jesus, he occasionally inserts dialogue in order to relieve the monotony of long, uninterrupted monologues. In this segment Thomas is the foil for the question about the way to the place Jesus is going in v.5. Philip functions as the dolt in v.8. These questions and Jesus' answers are completely alien to the historical Jesus, the crafter of parables, aphorisms, and witticisms. Both the words and the contrived narrative framework deserve a black rating. [i.e. "largely or wholly unhistorical" according to the rating system of the Jesus Seminar-PT][43]

The appearance of the pair, Andrew and Philip, in the episode of the Greeks who were seeking Jesus (John 12:20-22) meets with the same difficulty. The whole story seems to serve as justification for the existence of Gentiles in the second century church when there was no story of Jesus preaching to them. The obviously unhistorical element of a voice speaking out from the sky (John 12:28-29 - akin to the episode of Jesus' baptism in Mark 1:10-11) simply confirms the whole unhistorical nature of the story. The Jesus Seminar rightly rated this episode as unhistorical.[44]

We are left only with the calling of Andrew/Peter (John 1:35-42) and Philip/Nathanael (John 1:43-51).

Let us look at the call of Andrew and Peter first. We have John the Baptist calling Jesus "the lamb of God" and "son of God" (John 1:29-36). The narrative mentioned that Andrew "heard this" and followed Jesus and later convinced Peter to do the same. Yet this is totally implausible. As we have seen earlier, the passage from Q (Luke 7:18-20/Matthew 11:2-3) showed that prior to his imprisonment, John the Baptist never thought Jesus as anything special. To have him pronounce Jesus as "son

---

[42] Funk, et.al., *The Acts of Jesus*: p409-411, 422
      Lüdemann, *Jesus After 2000 Years*: p510, 582
[43] Funk, et.al., *The Acts of Jesus*: p422
[44] Funk, et.al., *The Acts of Jesus*: p415

of God" and "lamb of God" the moment he laid his eyes on Jesus is, to quote Winston Churchill, being a little "economical with the truth".[45]

For the calling of Philip and Nathanael, there are several difficulties which suggest the story as it stands is unhistorical. Firstly, we note that the pair of call stories (Andrew/Peter and Philip/Nathanael) parallels that found in Mark (1:16-20) where we have the pairs of Peter/Andrew and James/John. These strongly suggest that the early oral tradition felt that two stories of the calling of pairs are sufficient for purposes. The oral tradition went through a natural evolution and diverged into two strands where the names of the second pair become Philip/Nathanael in John and James/John in Mark. Secondly, we note that the name, Nathanael, is in itself suspect. As we have seen above, the name is not found in the list of the twelve apostles in the synoptics. The name Nathanael, which means "God gives", is very rarely found in rabbinic writings. According to John March, these factors strongly suggest that John chose this name "more for theological meaning than historical exactitude". So apart from the *name* Philip, which is confirmed by the other sources, very little in the story as narrated by John can be confidently said to be historical.[46]

We can safely conclude that the Gospel of John *adds no new historically reliable information* to the shadowy apostles of the synoptics.

LATER TRADITION ON THE APOSTLES

Outside the New Testament, there is even less reliable information about the twelve apostles. In the words of the historian of early Christianity, Professor Henry Chadwick, in the immediate aftermath of the death and "resurrection" of Jesus:

> *Most of the twelve disciples disappear from history.* Only Peter, John, and James the Lord's brother are more than names.[47] [Italics added]

Another historian who has also written on early Christianity, Paul Johnson, concurs:

> *Only with Peter can we trace any activity*; with John it is barely possible, though we can assume it since he was martyred. And it is quite impossible with the rest. James, Jesus' brother, is an identifiable personality, indeed an important one. But he is not an "apostle", nor one of the "twelve."[48] [Italics added]

To fill this lacuna of stories regarding the apostles, five apocryphal acts were written during the period spanning roughly 150-250 CE. These were *The Acts of Peter, The Acts of John, The Acts of Andrew, The Acts of Thomas* and *The Acts of Paul*.[49] These

---

45   Funk, et.al., *The Acts of Jesus*: p368-369

46   Funk, et.al., *The Acts of Jesus*: p370-371
      Lüdemann, *Jesus After 2000 Years*: p429-433
      Marsh, *Saint John*: p135-136

47   Chadwick, *The Early Church*: p17

48   Johnson, *History of Christianity*: p33

49   We will not be discussing the *Acts of Paul* here as he was not one of the twelve apostles.

are all works written chiefly to entertain, to instruct and to spread Christian propaganda. Very little in these works can be considered historical.[50]

- *The Acts of Peter* is preserved today only in scattered fragments in various languages. That the work is largely a fictional invention can be seen from its obsession with virginity and morbid hatred of sex - a trend that was developing during the time it was written. However, it does seem to preserve some authentic tradition of Peter's martyrdom in Rome. According to this work, Peter was crucified on an upside down cross during the persecution of Nero.[51]

- *The Acts of John* is of little historical value since it confused John the seer of Revelation with the apostle John.[52] John the son of Zebedee is some sort of an enigma. Tradition from the late second century (Irenaeus [c130-c200] and Clement of Alexandria [c150-c215]) asserted that John died in Ephesus during the reign of Trajan which would put his death around the year 98 to 117.[53] There is an alternate tradition[54] however, that placed his death very early; stating that he was martyred, together with his brother James, in 44 CE.[55]

- *The Acts of Andrew* is another work of Christian fiction. Its story of Andrew's martyrdom in Patras Greece is generally considered unhistorical. The tradition that he was crucified on an X-shaped cross (St. Andrew's Cross) is based on an even later tradition; around the 13th century.[56]

- *The Acts of Thomas* narrates the story of Thomas' mission to India. Some scholars, about a century ago, argued for this historicity of this Acts due to mention of an actual Indian King, Gundaphorus in the work.[57] However, this view is no longer held today. The presence of the reference to actual historical personae is due to the fact that during the time the Acts of Thomas was written, there was a lively commercial and cultural exchange between Edessa, where this Acts was composed, and India. There was ample opportunity for the author to pick up historical details to weave into his narrative.[58] One of the main reasons why the Acts of Thomas is

---

50   Goodspeed, *The Twelve*: p146, 163
       Schneemelcher, *New Testament Apocrypha Vol II*: p78-83
51   Goodspeed, *The Twelve*: p157
       Perkins, *Peter, Apostle for the Whole Church*: p141-144
       Riedel et.al., *The Book of the Bible*: p431
52   Goodspeed, *The Twelve*: p152
53   Eusebius: *History of the Church*: 3:23
54   The tradition is attributed to Papias – see note 37 on page 244.
55   Craveri, *The Life of Jesus*: p152
56   Livingstone, *Dictionary of the Christian Church*: p20
       Riedel et.al., *The Book of the Bible*: p433
57   Streeter, *The Primitive Church*: p29-30
58   Schneemelcher, *New Testament Apocrypha Vol II*: p325

considered unhistorical is due to the presence of late Gnostic, Mandean and Manichean influence in the work.[59]

The fact that there was little information available on the twelve apostles can be seen from the excerpt below from Eusebius' History of the Church:

> History of the Church 3:1:1-2
> Meanwhile the holy apostles and disciples of our Savior were dispersed throughout the world. Parthia, according to tradition, was allotted to *Thomas* as his field of labor, Scythia to *Andrew*, and Asia to *John*, who, after he had lived some time there, died at Ephesus. *Peter* appears to have preached in Pontus, Galatia, Bithynia, Cappadocia, and Asia to the Jews of the dispersion. And at last, having come to Rome, he was crucified head-downwards; for he had requested that he might suffer in this way.

It should be recalled that Eusebius (c260-c340) was *the* ecclesiastical historian of early Christianity. He had access to the vast library of early Christian works at Caesarea which he cited and quoted extensively in this book. Yet when it comes to the subsequent career of the apostles, *all he could muster was the same four names as the apocryphal Acts*: Thomas, Andrew, John and Peter! Furthermore, he gave no indication that his list was incomplete or that it was merely an excerpt.[60]

After the publication of these five apocryphal Acts, the next generations of Christian hagiographers concocted even more grotesque and less believable Acts. There were *The Acts of Philip*, *The Acts of Peter and Andrew*, *The Martyrdom of Matthew*, *The Acts of Andrew and Bartholomew* and so on. Schneelmacher's *New Testament Apocrypha Volume II* listed forty of such works. These works were mainly expansions of the original five apocryphal Acts with no historical value.[61]

Needless to say, the traditions regarding the later ministries of the "shadowy" apostles are late and extremely unreliable. For instance, the apostle Matthew was supposed to have been martyred (according to different traditions) in Ethiopia, Persia and Pontus![62]   Like Matthew, Bartholomew also managed to die multiple deaths of martyrdom. He was supposed to have been martyred in India and in Armenia. Contradictory, late and unreliable traditions exist about all the apostles.[63] History knows nothing about them.

CONCLUSIONS ON THE TWELVE APOSTLES

With the exception of Peter, James and John, we know *nothing* about the subsequent careers of the apostles. Even as early as the end of the first century, when the gospels and Acts were first composed, we have clear evidence that information regarding the

---

[59]   Goodspeed, *The Twelve*: p158

[60]   Schneemelcher, *New Testament Apocrypha Vol II*: p19

[61]   Goodspeed, *The Twelve*: p163-164
       Schneemelcher, *New Testament Apocrypha Vol II*: p 426

[62]   Riedel et.al., *The Book of the Bible*: p437

[63]   Brownrigg, *Who's Who in the Bible: The New Testament*: 42
       Ferguson, *Encyclopedia of Early Christianity*: p168

apostles was already hard to come by. We find *fifteen* names for the list of *twelve* apostles. Even if we confined ourselves to the twelve names given in Mark and Matthew the problem is not resolved. For at least six of these names are *nothing more than names*; we know nothing about Thaddaeus, Simon the Cananean, James son of Alphaeus, Bartholomew, Thomas and Philip. With Matthew and Andrew we know only slightly more: that Matthew was a tax collector when he was called and that Andrew was Peter's brother. With Judas, there are problems with the whole story of his betrayal.[64]

Subsequent traditions have no more to add to these. The early apocryphal acts of Peter, John, Andrew and Thomas, contain very little that is historically reliable. The later ones were even worse and are merely fanciful expansions of these earlier works. Even the ecclesiastical historian Eusebius, could do no more than repeat the four names of the apocryphal acts when recounting what he knows about the subsequent careers of the apostles.

Two possibilities present themselves. The number twelve, as we have noted has rich symbolic value in Judaism being equal to the tribes of Israel. This means that the number twelve could be one that tradition *assumed* the number of disciples to be.[65] The other possibility, more damning, I think, to Christian belief, is that *the mission of the twelve was a failure*. We know today that a large part of Christian theology has its roots in the epistles of Paul who was not one of the original twelve apostles. The original apostles, the ones actually hand-picked by Jesus, *made no impact on Christian history whatsoever.*[66]

ON MIRACLES

For the rest of this chapter we will turn our attention towards the miracles attributed to Jesus. All four gospels narrated numerous miracles supposedly performed by the Galilean. What interests us here is whether these reports are historically *probable*. In other words, can it be shown to a high degree of probability that Jesus actually did perform those acts?

Due to the concerted effort by evangelical apologists, it has become fashionable to *accuse* critical historical scholars of philosophical bias whenever miracles recorded in the gospels and Acts are dismissed as unhistorical. Therefore, it is important that we come to grips with the philosophical issues related to these phenomena before we start analyzing the individual miracles.

The word *miracle* is used above as though it is a clearly understood concept, but is it? For example, if you were to get an unexpected pay rise from your boss, does that constitute a miracle? Most people would say no. But what if you prayed for it

---

[64]   See chapter 14 for an analysis of the betrayal of Judas

[65]   Sources hostile to Christianity preserved *different* numbers of apostles. The second century critic of Christianity, Celsus, mentioned that there were ten (or eleven) apostles. (see Origen *Against Heresies* 2:46 & 1:62) The Babylonian Talmud listed only five apostles: Matthai, Nagai, Nezer, Buni and Thoda (Sanhedrin 43a). (See Schneemelcher, *New Testament Apocrypha Vol II*: p17)

[66]   Guignebert, *Jesus*: p221
       Nineham, *Saint Mark*: p115

the night before? Whether you agree or disagree that the above example represents a miracle, it is obvious that we need to at least come up with an unambiguous working definition in order to minimize any linguistic confusion later on in our analysis.

St. Augustine (354-430) gave the definition of miracle as anything that happens *contra quam est nota natura* (in defiance of natural laws known to us).[67] By that definition a miracle is something that occurs in a way that is contrary to what we would expect based on our own experience and on scientific generalizations.[68] There is nothing wrong, *per se*, with the definition above and as a tentative attempt it is acceptable to both believers and skeptics. We can use this working definition to see whether the example given above - about getting a raise - is a miracle. Getting a raise is a rare occurrence, certainly not as often as most of us would like, but it does not require any breaking of any law of nature; therefore, our working definition has helped us to eliminate that example as an actual miracle.

We shall not adopt the dismissive attitude of most rationalist theologians who went overboard with their skepticism and did away with the need for an analysis of the problems of miracles. One such theologian was David Friedrich Strauss (1808-1874) who wrote in the Introduction to his *Life of Jesus* (Tubingen,1837):

> We may summarily reject all miracles, prophecies, narratives of angels and demons, and the like, as simply impossible and irreconcilable with the known and universal laws which govern the course of events.[69]

Strauss was writing close to a century before the advent of Quantum Mechanics and Relativity. These two discoveries led to an overthrow of the Newtonian paradigm which, in turn, led to a philosophically more mature understanding of science. Our understanding of Newton's laws today is not that it is *wrong* but that it is an *approximation* of nature and has its range of validity. Newtonian mechanics break down at the domain of the very small and the very large. In the domain of the very small, that of electrons and atoms, the theory of Quantum Mechanics takes over. While in the domain of the very large, that of galaxies and the universe, Einstein's General Theory of Relativity reigns supreme. But in our everyday domain - of cars, houses and stones - Newtonian mechanics is still used and with invariable success. Even in calculating the trajectory of rockets and satellites, NASA scientists still use Newton's equations as they are accurate enough for their purposes. The Newtonian equations also have the added advantage of being a lot less complicated mathematically than Einstein's.

The philosophically mature understanding of science is that scientific laws are a collection of human *generalizations* on the behavior of nature. These generalizations are based on a vast amount of collected data and are certainly trustworthy. But they are nowhere near the ultimate truth, whatever that may mean. Seen from this vantage point, Strauss' blanket rejection of the extraordinary reminds one of Rudolf Carnap's

---

[67]   *De Civitate Dei XXI:8* quoted in Craveri, *The Life of Jesus*: p122

[68]   Using the above definition, the unexpected pay rise example given above is not a miracle. The reason is that while it is a most unusual occurrence there is nothing in our everyday experience that says it could not happen.

[69]   Stein, *Encyclopedia of Unbelief*: p454

analogy of the cartographer who pronounced the terrain false because it did not agree with his map![70]

On the other extreme, an unquestioning acceptance of the reality of these miracle accounts, which is typical of the fundamentalist attitude, is even more absurd. The statement below, from a fundamentalist work, is typical of such an attitude:

> ...the gospel miracles cannot be discounted because of the extravagant superstitious claims of pagan miracles. Just because some miracles are counterfeit is no proof that all are fraudulent.[71]

Note how "pagan miracles" are easily dismissed as *superstitious claims* while the demand is that the gospel miracles *must be proven false*. Both the extreme positions are irrational. The arch skeptic rejects such miracles categorically without any examination. Our understanding of the nature of scientific laws today does not justify such as attitude. The ardent believer blindly accepts these same accounts as true until they are absolutely proven false. This same believer will, in his turn, dismiss all other non-Christian miracles as "frauds". In short, the fundamentalist Christian is as quick to dismiss the miraculous claims of others as the arch-skeptic.

So how are we to approach the study of miracles? There are three issues involved: firstly, we must be clear of the nature of the claim being made; secondly, we must decide who shoulders the burden of proof; and thirdly, we need to have a workable methodology that takes the first two issues into consideration.

To begin with we must be clear as to exactly what is being claimed when someone says a miracle has occurred. As we have seen from the Augustinian definition, the claim is not the same as a mundane statement like "I went grocery shopping yesterday." The claimant is telling us that something extraordinary, something beyond our ordinary experience, has happened and he or she wants us to *believe* that it did. But such extraordinary phenomena are, by definition, highly improbable. The evidence provided must be over and beyond what we would demand in the case of an ordinary claim that does not require a readjustment of what we already know. So we must follow this dictum: *extraordinary claims demand extraordinary proof.*

So who shoulders the burden of proof when it comes to miracles? Perhaps an example may serve to illustrate the issue better. Suppose someone claims that three-headed flying snakes live on the planet Jupiter – certainly an extraordinary claim. How are we to treat such a claim? Is it the skeptic who must devise a way to send a probe to Jupiter, drop a planetary probe and search the whole planet for these snakes?[72] The answer in this case is an unequivocal "No". The skeptic can say that based on what we understand of evolution and the biological system of reptiles, any kind of snake life form is impossible on the Jovian planet. The believer can say that since the skeptic has not proven his claim false, he is justified in his belief that there

---

[70]   Stein, *Encyclopedia of Unbelief*: p455
[71]   McDowell, *Evidence that Demands a Verdict*: p125
[72]   The reader can easily imagine an unending scenario. After the Plutonian probe had shown no sign of life form the believer can claim that the flying snakes can also make themselves invisible at will and thus remain undetected!

are three-headed flying snakes there. The reader can easily see for himself the absurdity of the believer's position. Basically anyone can make any kind of preposterous claim. Disproving such claims is neither practicable nor necessary. *The burden of proof must fall squarely on the party that makes the positive claim.* So if anyone wants to start making claims about three headed flying snakes on Jupiter, he or she better have solid proof!

What should a rational methodology in the study of miracles, that takes into account the two points above, consist of? Actually such a methodology is well known (and grossly misunderstood)[73] and was first suggested by the Scottish philosopher David Hume (1711-1776). In section X of his book *An Enquiry Concerning Human Understanding*, Hume explained how reports of miracles are to be examined and evaluated.[74] We will mainly be following Hume's methodology here – suitably adapted to *written* testimonies. It is important for us to outline this argument before we examine the stories of miracles in the gospels.[75]

Hume pointed out that stories of the miraculous are, first and foremost, *testimonies*. Hume's gift is the clarity with which he explained how testimonies are evaluated. This evaluation is made based on two opposite sets of considerations. The first is the familiar test of the reliability of the person or persons making the testimony. Here we consider the following points:

1. **Concurrence of witnesses**: When the various witnesses agree with each other, we are more certain of the testimony than when they disagree or contradict one another.

2. **Number of witnesses**: The more the witnesses (and that they concur) the more reliable the testimony becomes. Conversely, the less the number of witnesses, the less reliable it is.

3. **Character of the witnesses**: An unimpeachable witness increases our trust in its reliability. If the witnesses are of doubtful character or even someone anonymous to us, the reliability of the testimony becomes less certain.

4. **Interest of the witnesses**: If the witnesses are disinterested, we have no reason to believe they would make up the story they are telling us. However, if the witnesses have a *vested interest* in the acceptance of their stories, it immediately adds to our suspicion as to the veracity of what we are being told.

5. **Tone of the witnesses**: If the testimony is given in a calm and measured tone, we are more likely to accept the basic veracity of the story then when it is told either hesitantly or in an emotionally vehement manner.

---

[73] Hume has been whether, purposely or inadvertently continuously, misunderstood for the past four centuries. Those who misread him are almost always those who are religiously bent and who wanted the criteria for miracles to be made easier. We will consider one such misreading later on.

[74] Hume, *An Enquiry Concerning Human Understanding*: p100-119

[75] The arguments to follow are based on Hume's work and its modern exposition and defense by Professor Robert J. Fogelin in his book, *A Defense of Hume on Miracles* (Princeton 2003).

To these criteria by Hume we can add a few more – that the witness had no problem with their senses (i.e. not visually or hearing impaired), that they are sane and that they are telling a *firsthand* account (i.e. what they themselves saw not what others told them). This final point is an important consideration when we consider the witness of the gospels.

The other set of considerations in the evaluation of extraordinary claims comes from examining the account itself. In other words, apart from considering the eyewitness(es), we need to consider *the inherent probability of the story that is being told*. This is an important but often missed point in the evaluation of testimonies. For our *belief* in testimonies is not based on any *a priori* principle but on the fact that we are used to finding corroboration, or conformity, between what we are told and what we ourselves normally experience. Peter tells you he saw Jane at the bus stop yesterday. You saw Jane earlier today at the same place and she confirmed having seen Peter at the same place the day before.

However, what happens when the story being told violates this normal conformity?

Let us take an example adapted from Professor Fogelin in his book *A Defense of Hume on Miracles*. This example considers a series of improbable claims which are not, in the normal sense, "miraculous". Using this as our first example shows that the Humean methodology does not treat miracles as something different in kind from other testimonies of the improbable. In other words, there is no inherent bias against claims of the miraculous within this methodology.

Suppose Richard is a good friend of mine and I found him through many years of friendship to be a reliable witness in the characteristics given above: he is a calm, keen observer of events who always tell the truth. One day he tells me he met Woody Allen in a bookshop while on holiday in New York City. This is a bit improbable but certainly such unusual events happen quite often every day. Note however, that the nature of the story itself makes us pause to take stock of it. In other words, the first set of considerations, the evaluation of the eyewitness, is no longer sufficient to decide upon our acceptance of the story as true if the account itself is highly improbable. However, in this case, we will say that the first set (Richard's general veracity) outweighs the second (the improbability of the encounter). However, what happens if from that time on Richard starts to tell of more such chance encounters: on a business trip to London, he met with Hugh Grant in an elevator, on a swing past Australia he met Russell Crowe, on a plane trip back he sat next to the Dalai Lama and so on. [Perhaps we can add the added consideration that Richard's job as grocery clerk would hardly have allowed him to travel so extensively!] Each story, while improbable in itself, could happen to anyone. However, for one person to meet all these people by accident within a period of a few short weeks is extremely unlikely. Now this second set of considerations – the incredibility or low intrinsic probability of the story itself – is in opposition to the first – our belief in Richard's general veracity. In other words, we no longer treat the latter as *sufficient* in accepting the story as true. When it comes to cases such as these, the best that can be achieved, without any further investigation, is a *draw*: we can no longer accept the stories as true but at the same time we do not yet have sufficient evidence to pronounce it false. We are forced to investigate the issue further (if Richard's personal life is of such interest to us). In other words, his claim is extraordinary and, therefore, we demand extraordinary proof.

How is this to be settled then? We demand *more* evidence of Richard than we would ordinarily require. Such a requirement can certainly be met. For one, it could be that his encounters were witnessed by many people. Perhaps he showed you a local Australian newspaper with a picture of him and Russell standing side by side and an autographed copy of a Dalai Lama's book referring to their nice conversation on the airplane. This shows that an improbable account – or even a series of improbable accounts - can be proven true. On the other hand, let us say that Richard was unable to provide you with any of the additional, or extraordinary, evidence you asked for. Perhaps he was even unable to show you his passport (or whether he even has one!). We can say now that the inherently low probability of his accounts trumps our belief in his general veracity and we are justified in tentatively disbelieving his stories. Furthermore, if your own enquiries show that he was busy working at the local supermarket in Muskogee, Oklahoma in those times he was supposedly overseas you would certainly use this as conclusive evidence that Richard was not telling the truth despite your initial belief in his veracity.[76]

The above example shows that the Humean methodology works for all extraordinary claims. Now let us see how this would work against claims of the miraculous.

When it comes to the evaluation of miracles, our first set of considerations, the evaluation of the witnesses, remains the same. The second vantage point comes from our understanding of nature. Hume never claimed that "laws of nature" discovered by man is inviolable. Indeed, Hume himself argued strongly that what we see as causes and effects are no more than the sum total of our previous experiences with such events. However, the regularity of nature is an empirical judgment based on *overwhelmingly* many different types of experiments and observations and one would be wise to start from a position of skepticism whenever such regularities are claimed to have been broken. For example, if someone were to claim that he saw, say, Barack Obama walking on water, our general and intuitive understanding of the surface tension characteristics of water would immediately raise skeptical alarm bells. In such cases the knowledge that such an event is highly improbable is enough for us to dismiss the story as told. In other words, the second set of considerations generally trumps over the first.

If this is the case, can a miracle, which by its very definition is a highly improbable event that contradicts what we know of the laws of nature, ever be proven to be true? The answer, as Hume himself gave, is *yes*.[77] Hume gave such an, albeit

---

[76] The question as to *why* an otherwise honest witness would tell an untruth is, strictly speaking, peripheral to our consideration here. In our hypothetical example, perhaps Richard was merely playing a game on you – with no malice - seeing how far he could stretch the truth before you would catch on.

[77] It is amazing, given that Hume himself gave an example of how a miracle could be proven true, how less able minds continue to misunderstand Hume and claim that Hume's argument is that miracles are *a priori* impossible. (One example is CS Lewis who erroneously claimed that Hume was "arguing in a circle" – see *On Miracles* (1947) p123)

secular, example in his book. We give an updated version here. Let us say that you wake up one summer morning and, looking up the sky, find that the sun has stopped shining! You check your watch, it shows that it is already midday. You call your friends – who all confirm the same thing. You switch on your TV, all the major networks CNN, Fox News, BBC report this event – you see scientists being interviewed confirming that their measurements show that the sun has stopped shining. Just to make sure it is not an elaborate hoax, you call a friend who lives overseas, who tells you there is chaos in the streets. So here is something which is witnessed by people all over the world, by scientists and is reported in all the major news networks with no one claiming anything contrary to it. It is evident then that this event, although highly improbable, actually happened. In other words, the second set of considerations (the story itself), although highly improbable, is trumped by the fact that the first set (the strength of the eyewitness reports) is simply unimpeachable.

Let us summarize our discussion. When considering reports of miracles we have to look at both *who* is doing the reporting – with all the associated factors (is the person trustworthy? Is there more than one witness? etc.) – and *what* is being reported (is the story such as it is highly improbable?).

Before we go on to investigate the miracles in the gospels, let us take Hume's analytical methodology for a "test run" - by analyzing an actual report of a miracle. Ironically one of the most famous, widely reported miracles involves the sun – just like Hume's original hypothetical example. This is the so-called "miracle of the sun" which supposedly occurred in front of 70,000 witnesses in the Portuguese town of Fatima on October 13th 1917. Let us give the basic facts about the case. Three young shepherd children claimed that they had seen apparitions of the Virgin Mary and that she told them to "expect a miracle" at noon on October 13th 1917. News of their vision spread far and wide such that on that day about 70,000 people (estimates vary between 40,000 to 100,000) turned up at a field near the town awaiting the miracle. The general account is that many who were there saw the Sun dancing in the sky and then falling or pulsating in a zigzag manner towards the crowd. Apart from Pope Pius XII, who claimed he too saw the miracle from the Vatican, nobody else outside Fatima[78] saw or noticed anything unusual with the sun that day.[79]

Let us analyze this from the viewpoint of the reliability of the eyewitnesses – the first set of considerations. Although there were many witnesses (point 2 above), they do not concur with one another (point 1): some claimed to have seen a dancing sun, others said they saw the sun spin like a pinwheel and still others saw the sun falling towards the earth.[80] More than half of those who were present did not report seeing anything unusual.[81]

Furthermore, we find that the 70,000 people who were present there were not disinterested witnesses (point 4). They took the trouble to travel to Fatima on that day because they *expected* something special to happen; the three little shepherd children

---

[78] There were some outside the general location of the field in Fatima who claimed to have seen something unusual. But even here the evidence is confused; some sources say these people were two miles (three kilometers), while others claims they were about 40 miles (64 kilometers) away.

[79] Ward, *A Dictionary of Common Fallacies II*: p93

[80] Nickell, *Looking for a Miracle*: p177

[81] Dash, *Borderlands*: p64

had claimed that the apparition of the Virgin Mary had promised a miracle at midday. Their minds were already primed for something spectacular. The "trigger" happened when Lucia, one of three shepherd children, yelled "Look at the sun!" This caused those present to start looking up at the sun, certainly *anticipating* some miracle. And, naturally, they were very emotionally involved (point 5), something which would adversely affect their objectivity.

Finally, as Joe Nickell pointed out, staring at an intense source of light (like the sun) coupled with involuntary eye movement could cause could cause a temporary retinal distortion leading the viewer to think he is seeing a "dancing" or even "pulsating" sun. This means that the very act of looking at the bright sun could impair the vision of those present.[82]

Our analysis of the reliability of the eyewitnesses shows us that the case for a miracle at Fatima is very weak: the eyewitnesses contradict one another, they were emotionally involved and they were expecting to see a miracle. Conditions were also such that their normal vision may have been impaired.

When we consider the other side, the inherent improbability of the story itself, the case against a miracle is even more compelling. A wobbling sun should have been seen by everyone on the same sunlit hemisphere of the earth at that time. Yet scientists report no unusual solar or astronomic activity on that day. Again, no one outside the general location saw or felt anything unusual. Furthermore, the gravitational effects of such a phenomenon, had it really occurred, would have caused untold damage – perhaps even destroying the solar system as we know it.

Putting both sets of considerations together – the unreliable and conflicting eyewitnesses and the inherent improbability of the event – we can safely conclude that whatever caused half of the 70,000 crowd to believe they saw a solar dance, the sun stood still that day.

REPORTS OF MIRACLES IN THE GOSPELS

Now we have to add factors which take into account the specific characteristics of the gospel reports of miracles. As we have seen in chapters 8 through 10, the gospels were not written by first hand eyewitnesses and consisted mainly of stories told by the early Christian communities. The tradition was allowed to flourish and develop for at least four decades before it was put in writing, ample time, as we have shown, for mythologization. In other words, fantastic stories about the founder's exploits could have been purely *made up*.

Even if some of the events did occur, in one way or another, what was the mindset of the eyewitness who saw and, more importantly, interpreted it? They lived in a culture where accepting the miraculous or God's intervention in the affairs of the world was considered normal. As we have seen in the beginning of this chapter, Jesus' followers consisted mainly of ill-educated Galilean peasants. In the minds of these ancient plebs, even a phenomenon such as the sprouting of seeds in the fields, seemed to be a miracle. As Marcello Craveri observed:

---

[82]   Nickell, *Looking for a Miracle*: p178

> It is just such ignorance and fear of all events outside the normal course of things-even of atmospheric and seismic phenomena, such as lightning, thunder and volcanic eruptions-that gave birth in antiquity to the conviction that they were the results of divine intervention.[83]

We know from our everyday experience that human powers of observation are fallible. This is especially true when it is in a heightened emotional state, which almost always accompanies the eyewitnesses of the alleged miracles.[84]

The lesson to keep in mind from the "miracle of the sun" at Fatima is that the presence of even many eyewitnesses does not in any way guarantee the actual occurrence of the event being reported. This is especially more so when the eyewitnesses are of an easily suggestible sort, as the first century Galilean Jews were.

The Miracles Performed by Jesus

We can broadly classify the miracles attributed to Jesus into three main classes: the epiphanies, the healings and the nature miracles. The epiphanies are miracles which concern the revelation of Jesus as he really was – i.e. an agent from God. These include the virgin birth, the star of Bethlehem, the transfiguration and the resurrection. The healings include curing the sick and the deranged, as well as raising the dead. This type of miracle is numerically the most common in the gospels. The nature miracles are the ones where Jesus showed his power over nature. These include the calming of the tempest, walking on water, turning water into wine, the feeding of the multitudes and the cursing of the fig tree.[85]

The total number of miracles described in any detail by the four gospels amount to about forty.[86] It should be noted that the miracles attributed to Jesus are not unique. Similar types of miracles stories were current around his time. We know this for a fact because a Greek satirist, Lucian of Somasota, who lived around 120 to 200, wrote a book poking fun at contemporary tales of the miraculous. In his book, aptly called *Philopseudes* (Lover of Lies), Lucian tells of the gathering of philosophers in Eucrates' house one day when he was ill. There they exchanged the most amazing miracle stories. We hear about the sick man who carries his bed on his back; of the man who walks on water and revives putrefying corpses; and of the sorcerer who can talk to the evil spirit possessing a man, threaten him and finally cast him out. Anyone who has familiarity with the miracle stories of the gospels will notice the similarities between Lucian's stories and the miracles supposedly performed by Jesus.[87]

How do the gospels stand up given the first set of considerations Hume proposed for evaluating the veracity of testimonies? First and foremost, we have seen that *none* of the gospels were written by eyewitnesses. Nor were they written by friends of the eyewitnesses. Indeed, they were put in writing at least forty years after the events

---

[83]   Craveri, *The Life of Jesus*: p123
[84]   Guignebert, *Jesus*: p192
        Howell-Smith: *In Search of the Real Bible*: p36
        Randall & Buchler, *Philosophy: An Introduction*: p169-170
[85]   Cadoux, *The Life of Jesus*: p97
[86]   Guignebert, *Jesus*: p197
[87]   Guignebert, *Jesus*: p194-195

they depict, based partially on oral tradition. Furthermore, we know that the evangelists were not disinterested reporters, they had a *vested interest in their readers believing the story*. We can say that even from the standpoint of this first set of considerations, the strength of the claim for the historicity of miracle accounts in the gospel is quite weak.

It should be added that miracles, given the second set of considerations, are extremely improbable, if not impossible, events. In our examination of the miracle accounts to follow these two sets of considerations must be kept in mind.

Epiphanies

Epiphany stories are very common among the ancient writings about holy men. These events are normally looked upon as a moment where the ultimate truth about the person is revealed in all its glory. We have looked at the epiphanies of Jesus' birth in chapter 11 (the virgin birth, the star of Bethlehem etc.) and found them all to be just myths. We will be examining the story of Jesus resurrection, another epiphany, in chapter 15. This leaves us with one epiphany story, the transfiguration.

In this episode, Jesus took his three main apostles (Peter, James and John) to a mountain. There he was "transfigured" before them. This account is given in Mark 9:2-8 and Matthew 17:1-8. We give these two accounts below – with the additions by Matthew italicized.

Mark 9:2-8
9:2 After six days Jesus took with him Peter, James, and John, and brought them up onto a high mountain privately by themselves, and he was changed into another form in front of them. 9:3 His clothing became glistening, exceedingly white, like snow, such as no launderer on earth can whiten them. 9:4 Elijah and Moses appeared to them, and they were talking with Jesus. 9:5 Peter answered Jesus, "Rabbi, it is good for us to be here. Let's make three tents: one for you, one for Moses, and one for Elijah." 9:6 For he didn't know what to say, for they were very afraid. 9:7 A cloud came, overshadowing them, and a voice came out of the cloud, "This is my beloved Son. Listen to him." 9:8 Suddenly looking around, they saw no one with them any more, except Jesus only.

Matthew 17:1-8
17:1 After six days, Jesus took with him Peter, James, and John his brother, and brought them up into a high mountain by themselves. 17:2 He was transfigured before them. *His face shone like the sun*, and his garments became as white as the light. 17:3 Behold, Moses and Elijah appeared to them talking with him. 17:4 Peter answered, and said to Jesus, "Lord, it is good for us to be here. If you want, let's make three tents here: one for you, one for Moses, and one for Elijah." 17:5 While he was still speaking, behold, a bright cloud overshadowed them. Behold, a voice came out of the cloud, saying, "This is my beloved Son, in whom I am well pleased. Listen to him." 17:6 *When the disciples heard it, they fell on their faces, and were very afraid.* 17:7 *Jesus came and touched them and said, "Get up, and don't be afraid."* 17:8 Lifting up their eyes, they saw no one, except Jesus alone.

We will first look at the Markan account. The formula of six days, the setting of the event on a mountain and the appearance of clouds are such common Old Testament themes that the whole episode immediately gives rise to skepticism. Both Moses and Elijah are said to have received revelation from God on a mountain:

Exodus 24:15-16
Moses went up on the *mountain*, and the *cloud* covered the mountain. The glory of Yahweh settled on Mount Sinai, and the cloud covered it six days.

I Kings 19:8-9
He arose, and ate and drank, and went in the strength of that food forty days and forty nights to Horeb the *Mount* of God. He came there to a cave, and lodged there; and behold, the word of Yahweh came to him, and he said to him, "What are you doing here, Elijah?"

The presence of Moses and Elijah is also understandable on theological grounds. Elijah was the prophet promised by God to be sent to the end of the world (Malachi 4:5) and we shall see later, Mark obviously believed that the arrival of Jesus signifies the arrival of the last days. Moses, being the bringer of the old law, is another obvious choice to appear before Jesus, the bringer of the new law. The neat way into which every element fit into a theological scheme brings further doubts to the veracity of the whole episode.

In fact, an obvious question arises, how did Peter, James and John know that the two people with Jesus actually were Moses and Elijah? For they obviously have never seen them before and would not have known what they looked like. It is easy, if this is a fictional account, to simply assume that they recognized them. But if the episode has any claim of being factual this difficulty must be satisfactorily explained by believers. It is not enough to say that perhaps Jesus introduced them as such. How do we know, if that was indeed the case, that he was not pulling a fast one on the apostles?[88]

The first part of the utterance of God in this episode (Mark 9:7) is also taken from an Old Testament passage:

Psalms 2:7
I will tell of the decree. Yahweh said to me, "You are my son. Today I have become your father."

This is an adoption formula on which the person becomes declared as the son of God and is usually conferred on a newly crowned king.[89]

Let us consider the story of the miracle as told in Mark. From the first set of consideration, we can say that it does not have a very strong case. Firstly, the gospel is not written by an eyewitness, neither was it written by the friend of an eyewitness. It is told by a person who obviously had a vested interest in us believing the story – since he wanted to spread his "good news." When we look at the whole account from

---

[88] It is not enough to say that Jesus couldn't have told a lie for he was the son of God. For this is what the Christians set out to prove. By assuming that here they are committing the logical fallacy of *petitio principii*. See chapter 13 for a discussion on the personality of Jesus.

[89] Guignebert, *Jesus*: p275-276
Nineham, *Saint Mark*: p233-237

the second set of considerations – i.e. by the inherent probability of the story itself, the case that this could be a factual account collapses completely. First note that every detail in the setting could be concocted completely from Old Testament accounts. We have seen in chapter 11 why such details immediately raise suspicion as to the historicity of the account. The early Christians treated the Old Testament as a proof text which predicts the life of Jesus and were fond of looking for details of Jesus' life in Old Testament passages. Secondly, note that the recognition by the apostles of Moses and Elijah smacks of fiction – for how do *they* know what these two Jewish prophets look like.

These two sets of considerations show conclusively that the account in Mark of the transfiguration is a fictional account with no basis in history. The scholars of the Jesus Seminar are correct in attributing the whole story of the transfiguration as "an invention of Mark".[90]

If we now turn to Matthew's account we become even more convinced of its mythical and legendary nature. Matthew's additions to Mark also come from the Old Testament. In Matthew 17:2 the phrase "and his face shone like the sun" was added to the Markan account. This is obviously derived from a similar account in Exodus:

Exodus 34:29
It happened, when Moses came down from Mount Sinai with the two tablets of the testimony in Moses' hand, when he came down from the mountain, that Moses didn't know that *the skin of his face shone* by reason of his speaking with him.

Matthew's addition from verses 6 to 8 comes from the book of Daniel:

Daniel 10:7-12
I, Daniel, alone saw the vision…then was *I fallen into a deep sleep on my face, with my face toward the ground.* Behold, a hand touched me, which set me on my knees and on the palms of my hands. He said to me, "Daniel … *stand upright… Don't be afraid*, Daniel"

Matthew had obviously *embroidered* Mark, not with historical details, but with more Old Testament passages. Now if such embroidery can happen to a *written* account it is even more likely it would have occurred to the oral tradition before Mark recorded them.[91] Believers will have to come up with very compelling evidence before the transfiguration story, as it stands, can be accepted as historical. Our analysis points to it being a fictional creation derived almost wholly from Old Testament passages.

Healings

The miracles of healing are the most numerous of the three classes of miracles attributed to Jesus. It is also the kind of miracle most commonly claimed by modern day evangelical preachers. This is not accidental. "Miracles" of healing are the

---

[90]   Funk et. al., *The Acts of Jesus*: p106
[91]   Guignebert, *Jesus*: p276-278

easiest to perform and get away with. As long as the audience is receptive and gullible almost anything can be interpreted as a healing.

We should define an actual miracle of healing to have occurred when a person is actually cured, without relapse, of an organic (i.e. not psychological or psychosomatic) disease. This involves knowing that the person was actually sick to begin with and knowing that subsequent to the miracle, the cure was complete.

Today we have TV evangelists, psychic surgeons or what-have-you all claiming to perform miraculous cures. Many such modern cases have been studied in detail by scientific, skeptical researches, and not one single case of a miraculous cure has actually been proven.[92]

There are many, inherently more probable, alternate explanations for miraculous healings that must be eliminated as possibilities before such extraordinary claims can be seriously considered. Some of the diseases could well be psychosomatic, and no one would call curing a disease that was never there to begin with a miracle. Some diseases may be real, but the cure during the "healing" is not. For the person involved may feel so exhilarated that he could have thought that he was healed although in reality he was not. Those who suffer from diseases in which the main external manifestation is pain, such as cancer and arthritis, can easily be led to believe they were healed if during that moment of exhilaration they forgot their pain. The symptoms invariably return after the feeling of exhilaration fades away. Another possibility is with diseases that have periods of temporary remissions. The miracle healing session which just happens to take place before one of these periods will be interpreted by the credulous as proof of miraculous cures. These explanations account, for instance, for all the more spectacular and supposedly scientifically verified miraculous healings in Lourdes, France a place held by most Catholics to have been visited by the Virgin Mary.[93] Another possibility is primitive medicine. A shaman applying herbs or some methods of massage which have medicinal value is obviously not a miracle.

Finally, we note that there are documented cases in medical science where someone is actually spontaneously cured of a disease. These occurrences are rare, occur randomly and do not favor the adherence of any religion.

The above possibilities assume the veracity of both the healer and the healed. It must also be kept in mind that a healer wanting to enhance his own prestige could have resorted to trickery and deception. For instance we find some modern Christian evangelists supposedly curing blindness, making the lame walk and even the lengthening of legs! The skeptical investigator and professional magician, James Randi, found that a blind man who was supposedly cured during a "miracle rally" remained blind after it. The lame being able to walk turned out to be nothing more than people who could walk being brought up on stage in wheelchairs specifically rented for the rally. The lengthening of legs turn out to be no more than a trick played with the person's shoes! [94]

---

[92]   Randi, *The Faith Healers*, Prometheus 1989
       Nickell, *Looking for a Miracle*, Prometheus 1993
[93]   Nickell, *Looking for a Miracle*: 145-153
[94]   Randi, *The Faith Healers* : p104-105, 112-113, 150-151

The possibility must be kept in mind that the account of the miracle itself may not be historical. As we should all know by now, popular imagination is filled with stories of miracles attributed to famous men. The account of Francis Xavier in chapter 10 is a good example of this.

Let us now list down the possibilities that might be interpreted as a miracle healing:

1. Psychosomatic illnesses
2. Psychological exhilaration mistaken for cure
3. Temporary remissions
4. Primitive medicine
5. Actual spontaneous remissions
6. Use of deception and trickery
7. Non-historicity of account
8. An actual miracle of healing

Now it is obvious – given Hume's second set of considerations - that the first seven possibilities are *a priori* more probable than the eighth. (Remember that the burden of proof lies with the party that makes the positive claim.) To present a strong case, the believer must be able to give strong reasons why the oftentimes unreliable testimony of the gospels can be trusted as a factual reporting of these accounts and to give compelling reasons why these more likely possibilities are to be rejected in favor of the eighth. If he fails to do so, the miracles are to be rejected as false.

To be able to analyze the miracle healings attributed to Jesus we must first have sufficient information to begin with. In many healing stories in the gospels the information is so minimal amounting to no more than a single sentence. This is particularly common in Matthew and Mark:

> Mark 1:34
> He healed many who were sick with various diseases, and cast out many demons.

> Matthew 9:35
> Jesus went about all the cities and the villages, teaching in their synagogues, and preaching the Good News of the Kingdom, and healing every disease and every sickness among the people.

With such vague information such as the above, no reasoned choice can be made between the alternatives. They must therefore be rejected as having no use in our inquiry.

It should also be pointed out that all the accounts of exorcism cannot be used to prove Jesus' miraculous powers of healing. This is because demon possession can in no way be differentiated, at least in the gospel accounts, from hysteria or even epilepsy. Just as a commanding personality can calm a hysterical person, it is no miracle for Jesus to be able to do that as well.

The first healing we will look at is that of Peter's mother-in-law.

Mark 1:30-31 (Matthew 8:14-15; Luke 4:38-39)
Now Simon's wife's mother lay sick with a fever, and immediately they told him about her. He came and took her by the hand, and raised her up. The fever left her, and she served them.

Note that the information given here is by no means complete. We are not told how serious or what kind of fever the woman had. Again, it is not impossible for Jesus' presence to have exhilarated her to the point where she forgot her probably slight fever. In fact none of the first seven alternatives are ruled out by this account. It is nowhere near the strong case needed to prove that this was an actual miracle of healing.

The episode above suggests that faith and trust in Jesus' powers seems to be a prerequisite for the healing to take place. Part of this faith comes from perhaps the aura of mystery that he surrounded himself with. We see in Mark how Jesus, on returning to his home town to preach, could not shake the familiarity they had with him. As a result he was unable to initiate the healing process:

Mark 6:1-6
He went out from there. He came into his own country, and his disciples followed him. When the Sabbath had come, he began to teach in the synagogue, and many hearing him were astonished, saying, "Where did this man get these things?" and, "What is the wisdom that is given to this man, that such mighty works come about by his hands? Isn't this the carpenter, the son of Mary, and brother of James, Joses, Judah, and Simon? Aren't his sisters here with us?" They were offended at him. Jesus said to them, "A prophet is not without honor, except in his own country, and among his own relatives, and in his own house." *He could do no mighty work there*, except that he laid his hands on a few sick people, and healed them. *He marveled because of their unbelief.* He went around the villages teaching. [95]

The above account has strong claims for being historical for it fulfils the criterion of embarrassment – there is no reason why the tradition would have made up a story about Jesus being unable to perform miracles! Therefore, this passage strongly supports the first and second possibilities discussed above as the main explanation to the historical "healings" performed by Jesus. [96]

In some cases the miracles described seem to rule out psychosomatic diseases, psychological exhilaration and even temporary remissions. One example of this would be the healing of the leper narrated in synoptics:

---

[95]   It is interesting to note that Matthew, while copying Mark's passage above (Matthew 13:54-58) deliberately changed the last verse from Mark's "He *could not* do any miracles there" (Mark 6:5) to his own "He *did not* do any miracles there *because of their lack of faith.*" (Matthew 13:58). This verse has changed Mark's meaning-which was that Jesus was *unable* to perform any miracles- to that Jesus *refused* to perform any miracles. Again, a reminder - if Matthew could so casually falsify a *written* record, how much faith do we have in his veracity with unwritten oral tradition?

[96]   Cadoux, *The Life of Jesus*: p102-104

Luke 5:12-13 (Mark 1:40-44; Matthew 8:1-3)
It happened, while he was in one of the cities, behold, there was a man full of leprosy. When he saw Jesus, he fell on his face, and begged him, saying, "Lord, if you want to, you can make me clean." He stretched out his hand, and touched him, saying, "I want to. Be made clean." Immediately the leprosy left him.

This account, as described above, cannot be historical. The reason is simple. All the gospels put this event in the location of Galilee, very much a province of the Jews. The Jews during the time of Jesus did not permit a leper to live or even wander around in town. The command in the Old Testament is very explicit:

Leviticus 13:45-46 (Also II Kings 7:3)
"The leper in whom the plague is shall wear torn clothes, and the hair of his head shall hang loose. He shall cover his upper lip, and shall cry, 'Unclean! Unclean!' All the days in which the plague is in him he shall be unclean. He is unclean. He shall dwell alone. Outside of the camp shall be his dwelling.

Lepers therefore lived away from towns and settlements. To say Jesus healed a leper in one of the towns in Galilee is obviously a product of an author who either did not know, or did not appreciate, the restriction on lepers. As author Frank Yerby commented:

...this writer attributes the Gospel accounts of the cure of lepers to their writers' total ignorance of Palestinian and age-old Jewish Law. For if their stories of lepers wandering about all over the landscape without let or hindrance for Yeshua [Jesus] to cure miraculously, are not the products of overheated pious imaginations, they are something worse-plain unmitigated lies. Lepers didn't wander around Palestine...Not ever.[97]

Marcello Craveri suggested what probably occurred if this event did have a nucleus of historical fact. It was the responsibility of the priest in those times to go to the leper colony to certify if any of the lepers had been cured. Chapters 13 and 14 of Leviticus give a detailed account of how this procedure is to be carried out. Once a person is pronounced clean or cured by the priest he is then allowed to return to the town. The final ritual purification is to be performed there. Any "leper" in the town would be one that is already completely healed and in need only of final ritual purification. As Craveri pointed out the verb used in the gospels *kathairein* means to *purify* (translated above as "clean"). If it was an actual cure of leprosy the verb would have been *therapeuein* which does mean *to cure* or *to heal*. The event narrated could have originated in an event of purely ritual significance with no miracle involved.[98]

Whatever the case may be, no miracle can be even shown to have occurred here.

The normal healing accounts of Jesus are therefore open to all sorts of more probable naturalistic explanations that cannot be convincingly discounted. We now turn to accounts of Jesus raising the dead. There are three such accounts in the gospels. Two of these are narrated in only one of the gospels and only one is reported

---

97   Yerby, *Judas, My Brother*: p506-507
98   Craveri, *The Life of Jesus*: p108-109

in more than one gospel. This is the raising of Jairus' daughter. We give all three reports below.

Mark 5:22-24, 35-43
5:22 Behold, one of the rulers of the synagogue, Jairus by name, came; and seeing him, he fell at his feet, 5:23 and begged him much, saying, "My little daughter is *at the point of death*. Please come and lay your hands on her, that she may be made healthy, and live." 5:24 He went with him, and a great multitude followed him, and they pressed upon him on all sides...5:35 While he was still speaking, people came from the synagogue ruler's house saying, "Your daughter is dead. Why bother the Teacher any more?" 5:36 But Jesus, when he heard the message spoken, immediately said to the ruler of the synagogue, "Don't be afraid, only believe." 5:37 He allowed no one to follow him, except Peter, James, and John the brother of James. 5:38 He came to the synagogue ruler's house, and he saw an uproar, weeping, and great wailing. 5:39 When he had entered in, he said to them, "Why do you make an uproar and weep? The child is not dead, but is asleep."5:40 They ridiculed him. But he, having put them all out, took the father of the child, her mother, and those who were with him, and went in where the child was lying. 5:41 Taking the child by the hand, he said to her, "Talitha cumi!" which means, being interpreted, "Girl, I tell you, get up!" 5:42 Immediately the girl rose up and walked, for she was twelve years old. They were amazed with great amazement. 5:43 He strictly ordered them that no one should know this, and commanded that something should be given to her to eat.

Matthew 9:18-19, 23-26
9:18 While he told these things to them, behold, a ruler came and worshiped him, saying, "My daughter *has just died*, but come and lay your hand on her, and she will live." 9:19 Jesus got up and followed him, as did his disciples. ...9:23 When Jesus came into the ruler's house, and saw the flute players, and the crowd in noisy disorder, 9:24 he said to them, "Make room, because the girl isn't dead, but sleeping." They were ridiculing him. 9:25 But when the crowd was put out, he entered in, took her by the hand, and the girl arose. 9:26 The report of this went out into all that land.

Luke 8:41-42, 49-56
8:41 Behold, there came a man named Jairus, and he was a ruler of the synagogue. He fell down at Jesus' feet, and begged him to come into his house, 8:42 for he had an only daughter, about twelve years of age, and *she was dying*. But as he went, the multitudes pressed against him...8 :49 While he still spoke, one from the ruler of the synagogue's house came, saying to him, "Your daughter is dead. Don't trouble the Teacher." 8:50 But Jesus hearing it, answered him, "Don't be afraid. Only believe, and she will be healed." 8:51 When he came to the house, he didn't allow anyone to enter in, except Peter, John, James, the father of the child, and her mother. 8:52 All were weeping and mourning her, but he said, "Don't weep. She isn't dead, but sleeping." 8:53 They were ridiculing him, *knowing that she was dead.* 8:54 But he put them all outside, and taking her by the hand, he called, saying, "Child, arise!" 8:55 Her spirit returned, and she rose up immediately. He commanded that something be given to her to eat. 8:56 Her parents were amazed, but he commanded them to tell no one what had been done.

Again, here we have problems with the accounts. It is noteworthy that both Matthew and Luke did not faithfully transcribe the incident as depicted in Mark, but each change it to make the miracle sound more incredible.

Matthew changed the verse in Mark (5:23, copied by Luke 8:42) which mentioned that Jairus' daughter was *dying*, not dead, to say that the girl *had just died* (Matthew 9:18). That this is a *deliberate* alteration by Matthew is shown by the fact that he left out the portion of Mark's narrative where some people came from Jairus' house to inform him that his daughter had died.

Luke, like Matthew, also resorted to sensationalizing the Markan account. While Matthew had the girl dead from the beginning, Luke made the crowd who was laughing at Jesus *know* she was dead when he reached Jairus' house (Luke 8:53).

It is obvious that both Matthew and Luke had altered the basic Markan account to make the miracle more striking. But the fact that they can so freely alter a *written* account should give us food for thought as to what the evangelists would do to an *oral* one.

This leaves us with the basic story as given by Mark. Note that even if we are to *assume* (something which believers must *prove* before the miracle can even begin to be considered seriously) that the story in Mark has an historical basis (in other words, that it is somehow rooted in eyewitness testimony), the account is by no means convincing. In fact, Jesus' statement - "The child is not dead but asleep" (Mark 5:39) - could be taken to mean that he knew the child was not dead. We know today of cases of a form of hysterical trance known as catalepsy. It is a self-induced trance in which the person remains in a fixed position for a long time. This can sometimes be terminated by a sharp word of command.[99] Even if the storyline is historical, a miracle is still not proven.[100]

The scholars of Jesus Seminar believed that a core oral tradition of a simple healing – not resuscitation – lies behind this story. This tradition consisted of three segments. The first involves the call of the Jewish official to heal his daughter (Mark 5:22-23). The second involves Jesus taking the girl by the hand and telling her to rise. (Mark 5:21) The last segment involves the crowd being amazed at what had happened – thus confirming the miracle. (Mark 5:42)[101]

However, there are actually strong reasons for believing that the story of the raising of Jairus' daughter is *not* historical. The name Jairus itself is suspect - for it means "He will awaken"; a name that simply fits too neatly into the whole scene. Further, the whole story simply parallels too neatly an Old Testament story regarding a similar feat performed by the prophet Elisha given in II Kings 4:20-37. The story involves a mother whose son has just died. She sets out for the prophet begging him to resuscitate her child. He followed her to her house and raised the child from the dead.

---

[99] Note that the point here is not to prove that the young girl actually had catalepsy or anything else. Remember that the onus is on the one that makes the extraordinary claim to supply the extraordinary proof. As long as the possibility exists that the girl was not dead or that the story is unhistorical, the miracle is not even shown to be deserving any further examination.

[100] Cadoux, *The Life of Jesus*: p101-102
Guignebert, *Jesus*: p196

[101] Funk, et, al. *The Acts of Jesus*: p82-83

1.   In both cases the weeping parent falls at the feet of the healer.

II Kings 4:27	Mark 5:22
When she came to the man of God to the hill, *she caught hold of his feet.*	...Jairus ... came; and seeing him, *he fell at his feet,*

2.   Messenger(s) return with the announcement that the child is indeed dead.

II Kings 4:31	Mark 5:35
Gehazi ... returned to meet him,...saying, *"The child has not awakened."*	...people came ... saying, *"Your daughter is dead."*

3.   The prophet put almost everybody out and performed the healing in private.

II Kings 4:32-33	Mark 5:38-39
When Elisha had come into the house...He went in therefore, and *shut the door on them both,* and prayed to Yahweh.	He came to the synagogue ruler's house...But he, *having put them all out,*...and went in where the child was lying.

4.   Part of the healing involved the prophet touching the child.

II Kings 4:34	Mark 5:41
He went up, and lay... his hands on his hands.	Taking the child by the hand...

It also shares obvious similarity with still another similar story, this time of the prophet Elijah in I Kings 17:17-24. These similarities provide two important considerations from a Humean methodological standpoint. Firstly, its similarities with the passages in I & II Kings argue against the story being based on eyewitness accounts. It is unlikely that eyewitness accounts could have describe the events in terms so similar to the story in the books of Kings. Secondly, the inherent improbability of the actual raising of a dead child points to the high probability of Mark (or the originator of the story) concocting the story from Old Testament passages. Both considerations tell us that the story as it stands cannot be historical.[102]

The next case of raising the dead is given in chapter 7 of Luke. It is the story of the son of a widow who had died and was raised by Jesus. We know from our discussion in chapter 9 that Luke and Matthew used two major written sources in common, Mark and Q, in constructing their gospels. As this episode is found neither in Mark nor Matthew, it therefore comes from Luke's own special source which, if actually grounded in the tradition, probably reached Luke in oral form. Let us look at the story in full as narrated by Luke:

Luke 7:11-17
It happened soon afterwards, that he went to a city called Nain. Many of his disciples, along with a great multitude, went with him. Now when he drew near to

---

the gate of the city, behold, one who was dead was carried out, the only son of his mother, and she was a widow. Many people of the city were with her. When the Lord saw her, he had compassion on her, and said to her, "Don't cry." He came near and touched the coffin, and the bearers stood still. He said, "Young man, I tell you, arise!" He who was dead sat up, and began to speak. And he gave him to his mother. Fear took hold of all, and they glorified God, saying, "A great prophet has arisen among us!" and, "God has visited his people!" This report went out concerning him in the whole of Judea, and in all the surrounding region.

This miracle made those around him realize that a great prophet had arisen among them. Now even if this story was historical, catalepsy still cannot be ruled out. Neither can we rule out trickery and collusion, on behalf of Jesus and the widow, after all he took his disciples and a large crowd with him (Luke 7:11) and the event happened entirely in public. But we have good reason to believe that the story is not even historical. We have already noted that the event is recorded neither in Mark nor Q. Most importantly, the story is *very* similar to the raising of another widow's son by the prophet Elijah given in I Kings 17: 7-24 This story parallels Luke's narrative on many points:

1. The way the stories start in Greek (for Luke and the Septuagint version of I Kings) is identical: *kai egeneto* (variously translated as "as it came to pass", "soon afterwards" or even "then") (I Kings 17:7; Luke 7:11).

2. A town gate was mentioned where the prophet met the widow.

I Kings 17:10	Luke 7:12
So he [Elijah] arose and went to Zarephath; and when he came to the *gate of the city*, behold, *a widow* was there gathering sticks...	Now when he [Jesus] drew near to the *gate of the city*, behold, one who was dead was carried out, the only son of his mother, and she was *a widow*...

3. It was the widow's son who died and was raised.

I Kings 17:17, 21-22	Luke 7:12, 14-15a
It happened after these things, that *the son of the woman*, the mistress of the house, fell sick; and his sickness was so sore, that there was no breath left in him...	Now when he drew near to the gate of the city, behold, one who was dead was carried out, the only *son of his mother*, and she was *a widow*...
He stretched himself on the child three times, and cried to Yahweh, and said, "Yahweh my God, please let this child's soul come into him again." Yahweh listened to the voice of Elijah; and the *soul of the child came into him again, and he revived.*	He came near and touched the coffin, and the bearers stood still. He said, "Young man, I tell you, arise!" *He who was dead sat up, and began to speak.*

4. The child after he was revived was delivered or given back to the mother.

I Kings 17:23	Luke 7:15b
Elijah took the child, ..., and *delivered him to his mother*	And he [Jesus] *gave him to his mother.*

5. The action convinced the witnesses that the one who performed the act was a man of God.

I Kings 17:24	Luke 7:16
The woman said to Elijah, "Now I know that you are a man of God, and that the word of Yahweh in your mouth is truth."	Fear took hold of all, and they glorified God, saying, "A great prophet has arisen among us!" and, "God has visited his people!"

The other elements of the narrative seems to be derived from Mark's account of the raising of Jairus' daughter (Mark 5:22-24, 35-43). Both refer to the presence of a large crowd (Luke 7:12, Mark 5:38). In both cases Jesus made a comment about the crying and wailing (Luke 17: 13; Mark 5:39). Jesus telling the young man to arise (Luke 17:14) mirrors his command to the girl to get up (Mark 5:41). The only independent detail in the story is the name of the town itself, Nain. Yet this is where we have the final piece of evidence against the historicity of the whole account. Archaeological digs have shown the town of Nain in Galilee *never had a wall* (and hence had no need of a gate). The story of the raising of the widow's son is therefore not historical.[103]   The scholars of the Jesus Seminar concur, stating that "The narrative is the product of Christological imagination and not the transmission of an historical record."[104]

The last case of raising the dead is narrated in John 11:1-44.

John 11:1, 11, 17, 33-44
Now a certain man was sick, Lazarus from Bethany, of the village of Mary and her sister, Martha... He said these things, and after that, he said to them, "Our friend, Lazarus, has fallen asleep, but I am going so that I may awake him out of sleep."...So when Jesus came, he found that he had been in the tomb four days already. When Jesus therefore saw her weeping, and the Jews weeping who came with her, he groaned in the spirit, and was troubled. and said, "Where have you laid him?" They told him, "Lord, come and see." Jesus wept. The Jews therefore said, "See how much affection he had for him!" Some of them said, "Couldn't this man, who opened the eyes of him who was blind, have also kept this man from dying?" Jesus therefore, again groaning in himself, came to the tomb. Now it was a cave, and a stone lay against it. Jesus said, "Take away the stone." Martha, the sister of him who was dead, said to him, "Lord, by this time there is a stench, for he has been dead four days." Jesus said to her, "Didn't I tell you that if you believed, you would see God's glory?" So they took away the stone from the place where the dead man was lying. Jesus lifted up his eyes, and said, "Father, I thank you that you listened to me. I know that you always listen to me, but because of the multitude

---

[103]   Craveri, *The Life of Jesus*: p114
         Helms, *Gospel Fictions*: p63-64
[104]   Funk, et. al., *The Acts of Jesus*: p289

that stands around I said this, that they may believe that you sent me." When he had said this, he cried with a loud voice, "Lazarus, come out!" He who was dead came out, bound hand and foot with wrappings, and his face was wrapped around with a cloth. Jesus said to them, "Free him, and let him go."

In this episode, Lazarus, the brother of Martha and Mary, had already been dead for four days when Jesus raised him from the dead. The body of Lazarus was already decomposing when Jesus raised him (John 11:39).

We have many reasons to doubt the veracity of the story. The first reason is that it appears nowhere else except in the Gospel of John. The second reason is that Luke, who also mentioned Martha and Mary as good friends of Jesus, never mentioned that they had a brother (Luke 10:38-42). It would be amazing that Luke would omit the narration of this certainly most spectacular miracle of all. (Neither does Luke mention that Mary and Martha lived in Bethany) The third reason is that we have a very good idea where the story of Lazarus' raising from the dead probably originated from.

First, we know from chapter 9 that Luke and John shared allied streams of oral tradition and that they reached both evangelists in slightly altered form. There is a parable in Luke, not duplicated in the other two synoptics, that is very probably the source of John's miracle. This parable given in Luke 16:19-31 tells of a rich man and a beggar named *Lazarus* who both died; the rich man went to hell while Lazarus appeared at "Abraham's side". The rich man pleaded with Abraham to *raise Lazarus from the dead* so that he can warn his living brothers about the existence of hell and to make them change their ways. Abraham refused the request saying something like "even if Lazarus is raised from the dead they will not believe." This, in fact, forms the moral of the story. In John's miracle the moral had become "even after Lazarus was raised from the dead, the Jews did not believe".[105]

Second, as Randel Helms pointed out in his book *Gospel Fictions*, there is an uncanny similarity between the details in the story of the resurrection of Lazarus and that of the Egyptian myth about the death of the god Osiris and his resurrection by Horus. The story is told in the "Pyramid Texts", so called because it refers to the inscriptions found on the walls in the pyramids from the Egyptian kings of the Vth and VIth dynasties (circa 26th to 23rd century BCE) Osiris has two sisters, Isis and Nephthys. (Note: Horus is the son of Isis by *parthenogenesis*-i.e. virgin birth) In the legend Osiris lies dead at Heliopolis. Heliopolis was the Greek name for the Egyptian burial ground. This necropolis is known by various names in Egyptian-one of them is "House of Anu". The Semitic form of this would be "Beth-anu" which sounds very close to Bethany. The name Lazarus itself sounds very close to the Semitic rendition of the Egyptian god: El-Osiris.

An examination of the details of both stories betrays many similarities between the resurrection stories of Lazarus and Osiris:[106]

---

[105]   Caird, *Saint Luke*: p20-21
[106]   Helms, *Gospel Fictions*: p94-100

1.   Osiris has two sisters - so does Lazarus.

John 11:1
Now a man named Lazarus was sick. He was from Bethany, the village of Mary and her sister Martha...

The Pyramid Text Utterance 670[107]
they come to Osiris the King at the sound of the weeping of Isis, at the cry of Nephthys...

2.   References to death as a state of sleep and resurrection as a waking up from that sleep.

John 11:33
He said these things, and after that, he said to them, "Our friend, Lazarus, has fallen asleep, but I am going so that I may awake him out of sleep."

The Pyramid Text Utterance 670
O Osiris the King, you have gone, but you will return; you have slept; you have died but you will live.

3.   Osiris, like Lazarus, was dead for four days.

John 11:17
So when Jesus came, he found that he had been in the tomb four days already.

The Pyramid Text Utterance 670
Osiris speaks to Horus, for he has removed the evil on his fourth day.

4.   References to the wailing sisters.

John 11:33
When Jesus therefore saw her weeping, and the Jews weeping who came with her, he groaned in the spirit, and was troubled

The Pyramid Text Utterance 670
they come to Osiris the King at the sound of the weeping of Isis, at the cry of Nephthys, at the wailing of these two spirits.

5.   References to the stench (or absence of) the corpse.

John 11:39

Jesus said, "Take away the stone." Martha, the sister of him who was dead, said to him, "Lord, by this time there is a stench, for he has been dead four days."

The Pyramid Text Utterance 412

O flesh of the king, do not decay, do not rot, do not smell unpleasant.

6.   The tombs were opened before the resurrection.

John 11:38, 41
Jesus therefore, again groaning in himself, came to the tomb. Now it was a cave, and a stone lay against it...So they took away the stone from the place where the dead man was lying.

The Pyramid Text Utterance 665A
The tomb is opened for you, the doors of the tomb chamber are thrown open for you.

---

[107]   The translation of the Pyramid Texts are taken from *The Ancient Egyptian Pyramid Texts* by Raymond O. Faulkner (Aris & Phillips 1987)

7.   The calling out of the corpse

John 11:43	The Pyramid Text Utterance 620
When he had said this, he cried with a loud voice, "Lazarus, come out!"	I am Horus, O Osiris the King, I will not let you suffer. Go forth, wake up.

8.   References to the freeing of the bondage of the corpse.

John 11:44	The Pyramid Text Utterance 703
He who was dead came out, bound hand and foot with wrappings, and his face was wrapped around with a cloth. Jesus said to them, "Free him, and let him go."	O King, live, for you are not dead. Horus will come to you that he may cut your cords and throw off your bonds; Horus has removed your hindrance.

These similarities are simply to numerous for the two myths to be unrelated to one another. The Egyptian myth precedes John's gospel by about 2500 years. How could a myth that old influenced John's gospel? The answer is simple, the myth may be old but it was still very much alive in the socio-religious environment of first century Egypt. Just as Christian myths, already 2,000 years old, are still alive today in the fundamentalist socio-religious culture; the Egyptian myth of Osiris remain basically unchanged even unto the first century CE. Upon conversion into Christianity, the Egyptians took their mythological beliefs - only slightly altered - along with them. As the famous early 20th century Egyptologist, E.A. Wallis Budge (1857-1934) puts it:

> The chief features of the Egyptian religion remained unchanged....down to the period when the Egyptians embraced Christianity…so firmly had the early beliefs taken possession of the Egyptian mind; and the Christians in Egypt, or Copts as they are commonly called, seem never to have succeeded in divesting themselves of the superstitious and weird mythological conceptions which they inherited.[108]

As we saw in the previous chapter, that was how the myth of Jesus' virgin birth gained currency. And, as we shall see in chapter 15, that was how many elements of the myth of the Jesus' resurrection found their way into the gospels. It is obvious that the story of Lazarus' resurrection is a piece of fiction which came out from an amalgam of an early Christian parable and an old Egyptian myth.

In conclusion, there is no authentic proof in the gospel accounts that an actual miracle of healing or of raising the dead ever happened.

Nature Miracles

The nature miracles are the most extraordinary of all the miracles. While miracles of healing may conceivably have some kind of historical root as discussed above, the same cannot be said for nature miracles. If they happened, then the laws of nature have been violated, contradicting the results of thousands of experiments and millions of everyday observations. In other words, from the Humean standpoint, the

---

[108]   Budge, *The Egyptian Book of The Dead*, Dover 1967 p xlix quoted in Helms, *Gospel Fictions*: p96

inherent improbability of this type of miracle is such that the highest level of skepticism must be applied in the evaluation of these accounts.

There is also some evidence that the accounts of the nature miracles do not belong to the earliest traditions concerning Jesus. The earliest sources, Q and (probably) some of Luke's special material, do not have any accounts of nature miracles. The earliest written source of the nature miracle is the Gospel of Mark, which is a post-70 CE document.

The first nature miracle we will look at is one that is for most Christians more of an embarrassment than anything else. It concerns the cursing of the fig tree by Jesus. Given below is Mark's account of the miracle:

> Mark 11:12-14, 20-21
> The next day, when they had come out from Bethany, he was hungry. Seeing a fig tree afar off having leaves, he came to see if perhaps he might find anything on it. When he came to it, he found nothing but leaves, *for it was not the season for figs.* Jesus told it, "May no one ever eat fruit from you again!" and his disciples heard it... *As they passed by in the morning,* they saw the fig tree withered away from the roots. Peter, remembering, said to him, "Rabbi, look! The fig tree which you cursed has withered away."

Mark's account makes Jesus look deranged. It was clearly stated that it was *not the season for figs*. The story was set just before the Passover, around the end of March or early April, when figs are never ripe during that time in Palestine. Any native of the land would not have expected to find fruit on a fig tree at that time. To curse a fig tree for not bearing fruit out of its season is, to say the least, not an act of a sane person. Either the story, as it appears in Mark is unhistorical or Jesus had become insane just before his crucifixion.

If we know look at the same story told in the Gospel of Matthew we will note that this evangelists had changed some elements of the story to make it both more credible and more incredible at the same time:

> Matthew 21:18-20
> Now in the morning, as he returned to the city, he was hungry. Seeing a fig tree by the road, he came to it, and found nothing on it but leaves. He said to it, "Let there be no fruit from you forever!" *Immediately the fig tree withered away.* When the disciples saw it, they marveled, saying, "How did the fig tree *immediately* wither away?"

Note the changes Matthew made to the Markan account. He omitted the line where Mark noted that it was not the season for figs. This made Jesus' reaction after not finding fruit on the tree more credible. Note also how Matthew had sensationalized the miracle. He made the fig tree wither *immediately* which was instantly noted by the disciples. In Mark's account, the tree was found to be withered by the disciples only *on the next morning*. Again, I will ask the tiresome question: how can we trust the gospel accounts of miracles when we see them enhancing and altering their sources to suit their own theologies and preconceptions?

In any case the cursing of the fig tree as depicted by Mark could not be historical. D.E. Nineham had suggested that the story probably originated from some conspicuous withered tree on the road between Bethany and Jerusalem which gave rise to the legend that Jesus had cured it. A likelier possibility is that this story was originally a *parable* about figs (as we find in Luke 13:6-9) that was distorted by the oral tradition.[109]

> Luke 13:6-9
> He spoke this parable. "A certain man had a fig tree planted in his vineyard, and he came seeking fruit on it, and found none. He said to the vine dresser, 'Behold, these three years I have come looking for fruit on this fig tree, and found none. Cut it down. Why does it waste the soil?' He answered, 'Lord, leave it alone this year also, until I dig around it, and fertilize it. If it bears fruit, fine; but if not, after that, you can cut it down.'"

The next miracle is the one of turning water into wine, narrated only in the Gospel of John:

> John 2:1-11
> The third day, there was a marriage in Cana of Galilee. Jesus' mother was there. Jesus also was invited, with his disciples, to the marriage. When the wine ran out, Jesus' mother said to him, "They have no wine." Jesus said to her, "Woman, what does that have to do with you and me? My hour has not yet come." His mother said to the servants, "Whatever he says to you, do it." Now there were six water pots of stone set there after the Jews' manner of purifying, containing two or three metretes[110] apiece. Jesus said to them, "Fill the water pots with water." They filled them up to the brim. He said to them, "Now draw some out, and take it to the ruler of the feast." So they took it. When the ruler of the feast tasted the water now become wine, and didn't know where it came from (but the servants who had drawn the water knew), the ruler of the feast called the bridegroom, and said to him, "Everyone serves the good wine first, and when the guests have drunk freely, then that which is worse. You have kept the good wine until now!" This beginning of his signs Jesus did in Cana of Galilee, and revealed his glory; and his disciples believed in him.

The fact this miracle appears only in John, the least historical of the four gospels, is enough to make us doubt the historicity of the account. In other words, our first set of consideration tells us that the veracity of the witness(es), given that it comes from gospel known to take liberties with historical facts, is suspect. When we consider the inherent probability of the story, the problem of its historicity is further compounded.

The inclusion of Mary (called here "the mother of Jesus") in this story only adds the problem. Now John clearly states that this was the *first* of Jesus' miracles. Now we know from the second gospel that Jesus had performed quite a few miracles[111]

---

[109]   Fenton, *Saint Matthew*: p335-336
   Funk, et.al., *Acts of Jesus*: p122-123
   Nineham, *Saint Mark*: p298-303

[110]   *Metretes* is a unit of volumetric measurement used by the ancient Greeks. It is equivalent to about 39.4 liters or 10 [US] gallons.

[111]   According to the gospel of Mark some of the miracles Jesus performed before his confrontation with his mother were the driving out of the evil spirit in Capernaum (Mark

already when he confronted by this mother during one of his sermons. Mark noted (Mark 3:21-34) that Mary thought that Jesus had gone mad by preaching to the crowds. This is clearly not compatible with the account of the miracle in John. Mary, by asking Jesus to do something about the fact that they had run out of wine and by telling the servants to listen to him, was obviously *expecting* some kind of miracle. And as she would obviously had witnesses this miracle, how could her actions in Mark 3:21-34 be reconciled with this? The answer is that it could not.

Craveri noted that John could have constructed the whole episode from Old Testament passages which included Moses miraculously supplying drinking water to save the Israelites in the desert (Exodus 17:1-7; Numbers 20:1-11), Elijah making it possible for the widow of Zareptath to draw from a tiny cruse an indefinite amount of oil which lasted many days (I Kings 17:10-16) and that of Elisha helping a widow in debt by pouring from one pot enough oil to fill a number of jars (II Kings 4:1-6).[112] Furthermore, many Old Testament texts mention that the time of salvation will be accompanied by free flowing wine. (Amos 9:13-14, Hosea 2:24, Zechariah 8:12).[113]

The story, as a whole, is patently absurd. As even the theologian Nathaniel Micklem admits:

> The story of the turning of the water into wine reads like the apocryphal legend of Jesus, the wonder worker, caused clay birds to fly...Not only is this such wonder-working wholly "out of character", but we are asked to believe that by an act of supernatural power Jesus produced (at the lowest estimate) some 120 gallons of wine and thus manifested his glory, causing his followers to "believe in him"- to believe in him, presumably, as a thaumaturgist.[114]

Micklem also noted that the Greek word John used for servants in the above passage, *daikonoi* (deacons), could probably point to the eucharistic, or liturgical, character of the whole story.[115] The idea of a miraculous transmutation of water to wine is not original to John's gospel. We find such beliefs already current in one of Christianity's early competitors: that of the cult of Dionysus. As Rudolph Bultmann mentioned in his book *The Gospel of John* (1971)

> On the festival day of Dionysos the temple springs at Andros and Teos were supposed every year to yield wine instead of water. In Elis on the eve of the feast, three empty pitchers were put into the temple and in the morning they were full of wine.[116]

There were thus ample non-historical influences that would have "helped" John or the oral tradition construct the story of the miracle at the wedding in Cana. To summarize, apart from the inherent improbability of water turning to wine, other

---

1:21-28), the healing of Simon Peter's mother and "many" at Peter's house (Mark 1:29-34) and the healing of the paralytic (Mark 2:1-12).

[112] Craveri, *The Life of Jesus*: p120-121
[113] Lüdemann, *Jesus After 2000 Years*: p435
[114] Micklem, *Behold The Man*: p77-78
[115] Micklem, *Behold The Man*: p79
[116] quoted in Helms, *Gospel Fictions*: p86

factors – such as the story of a disbelieving Mary in Mark 3:21-34, the presence of Old Testament and pagan parallels, as well as its probable *liturgical* character – confirm that the story is unhistorical. An overwhelming majority of critical historians view this whole story as a fictional creation of John.[117]

The next two miracles, the feedings of the multitudes will be discussed together, for reasons that will soon become clear. The feeding of the 5,000 is given in all four gospels (Matthew 14:13-21; Mark 6:34-44; Luke 9:10-17; John 6:1-13) while the feeding of the 4,000 is included in the first two gospels (Matthew 16:29-39; Mark 8:1-13). Now Matthew and Luke obviously copied these accounts from Mark and offered no independent testimony to it. John obviously had access to a similar tradition of Mark. We will therefore confine our analysis to the accounts in Mark. We give both stories in full below:

Mark 6:34-44
Jesus came out, saw a great multitude, and he had compassion on them, because they were like sheep without a shepherd, and he began to teach them many things. When it was late in the day, his disciples came to him, and said, "This place is deserted, and it is late in the day. Send them away, that they may go into the surrounding country and villages, and buy themselves bread, for they have nothing to eat." But he answered them, "You give them something to eat." They asked him, "Shall we go and buy two hundred denarii worth of bread, and give them something to eat?" He said to them, "How many loaves do you have? Go see." When they knew, they said, "Five, and two fish." He commanded them that everyone should sit down in groups on the green grass. They sat down in ranks, by hundreds and by fifties. He took the five loaves and the two fish, and looking up to heaven, he blessed and broke the loaves, and he gave to his disciples to set before them, and he divided the two fish among them all. They all ate, and were filled. They took up twelve baskets full of broken pieces and also of the fish. Those who ate the loaves were five thousand men.

Mark 8:1-13
In those days, when there was a very great multitude, and they had nothing to eat, Jesus called his disciples to himself, and said to them, "I have compassion on the multitude, because they have stayed with me now three days, and have nothing to eat. If I send them away fasting to their home, they will faint on the way, for some of them have come a long way." His disciples answered him, "From where could one satisfy these people with bread here in a deserted place?" He asked them, "How many loaves do you have?" They said, "Seven." He commanded the multitude to sit down on the ground, and he took the seven loaves. Having given thanks, he broke them, and gave them to his disciples to serve, and they served the multitude. They had a few small fish. Having blessed them, he said to serve these also. They ate, and were filled. They took up seven baskets of broken pieces that were left over. Those who had eaten were about four thousand. Then he sent them away. Immediately he entered into the boat with his disciples, and came into the region of Dalmanutha. The Pharisees came out and began to question him, seeking from him a sign from heaven, and testing him. He sighed deeply in his spirit, and said, "Why does this generation seek a sign? Most certainly I tell you, no sign will

---

[117] Funk, et. al., *The Acts of Jesus*: p372-373

be given to this generation. "He left them, and again entering into the boat, departed to the other side. They forgot to take bread; and they didn't have more than one loaf in the boat with them

Anyone reading the two episodes, with a critical mind and not with a pious "I'll believe anything the gospels says" attitude, will note that the questioning of the disciples in the second episode (Mark 8:4) simply does not make sense. For haven't they just witnessed, no more than a few weeks ago, the earlier miracle of Jesus feeding 5,000 men (Mark 6:34-44)?

The reader will further notice the constant detailed, and often verbal, correspondence that would be extremely uncanny if these are two unrelated accounts. Both episodes have the following similarities:

1. Jesus had compassion for the crowd

    Mark 6:34a

    Jesus came out, saw a great multitude, and *he had compassion on them*

    Mark 8:1b-2

    Jesus called his disciples to himself, and said to them, "*I have compassion on the multitude...*"

2. The disciples mentioned the remoteness of the place

    Mark 6:35

    When it was late in the day, his disciples came to him, and said, "*This place is deserted*, and it is late in the day....*"

    Mark 8:4

    His disciples answered him, "From where could one satisfy these people with bread here *in a deserted place?*"

3. The mention of difficulty in getting enough food to feed the crowd

    Mark 6:37

    They asked him, "*Shall we go and buy two hundred denarii worth of bread*, and give them something to eat?"

    Mark 8:4

    His disciples answered him, "*From where could one satisfy these people with bread* here in a deserted place?"

4. Jesus asked how many loaves they had and the disciples answering with a quantity obviously too small to feed the crowd

    Mark 6:38

    He said to them, "How many loaves do you have? Go see." When they knew, they said, "Five, and two fish."

    Mark 8:5

    He asked them, "How many loaves do you have?" They said, "Seven."

5. Jesus asked the group to sit down on the ground

    Mark 6:39

    He commanded them that *everyone should sit down in groups on the green grass.*

    Mark 8:6a

    He commanded *the multitude to sit down on the ground...*

6.   Jesus gave thanks and gave the pieces to his disciples to distribute to the crowd

Mark 6:41	Mark 8:6b-7
He took the five loaves and the two fish, and looking up to heaven, he blessed and broke the loaves, and he gave to his disciples to set before them, and he divided the two fish among them all.	and he took the seven loaves. Having given thanks, he broke them, and gave them to his disciples to serve, and they served the multitude. They had a few small fish. Having blessed them, he said to serve these also.

7.   The people were described to have been satisfied by what they ate

Mark 6:42	Mark 8:8a
They all ate, and were filled.	They ate, and were filled.

8.   There was more food leftover than there was to begin with

Mark 6:43	Mark 8:8b
They took up twelve baskets full of broken pieces and also of the fish.	They took up seven baskets of broken pieces that were left over.

The similarities between these two accounts are such that it can no longer be denied by rational scholars that these two episodes are divergent accounts of the same story.

Mark probably came across the same story at different stages of development. Note that the account in Mark chapter six is, on all accounts, more incredible than the one in chapter eight. There were more people to feed (5,000 in Mark 6:44 as opposed to 4,000 in Mark 8:9) with less food to begin with (five loaves and two fish in Mark 6:38 compared with seven loaves and a few fish in Mark 8:5 & 8:7). The tradition was obviously developing in a trajectory which makes the story more and more incredible.

The statement of the apostles in Mark 6:37 that 200 denarii would be needed to feed the crowd points to an even earlier, less spectacular account. During the time of Jesus, 200 denarii could not have fed more than a few hundred men. This tells us that there, very probably, was an earlier stage of this legend where the crowd amounted to no more than a few hundred men. In fact, the author of John noticed this discrepancy and changed the words of the disciples to say that 200 denarii "would not buy enough bread for each one to have a bite." (John 6:7).[118]

Very likely, the original source of this story is not any historical event at all but an Old Testament passage where a similar miracle is credited to the prophet Elisha:

II Kings 4:42-44
A man from Baal Shalishah came, and brought the man of God bread of the first fruits, twenty loaves of barley, and fresh ears of grain in his sack. He said, "Give to the people, that they may eat." His servant said, "What, should I set this before a hundred men?" But he said, "Give the people, that they may eat; for thus says

---

[118]   Cadoux, *The Life of Jesus*: p98
Nineham, *Saint Mark*: p205-206
Wells, *The Historical Evidence for Jesus*: p131-132

Yahweh, 'They will eat, and will have some left over.'" So he set it before them, and they ate, and left some of it, according to the word of Yahweh.

Note the structure here is very similar to Mark's: all accounts specify that the number of people to be fed (100 people in II Kings; 5,000 & 4,000 in Mark); the amount of food available was clearly inadequate to feed those present (twenty loaves in II Kings, four and five loaves in Mark); despite protests from the followers the prophets (Elisha in II Kings and Jesus in Mark) ordered them to go ahead and feed the crowd; and, finally, at the end of the meal there was some food left over. [119]

From the considerations above we can even see the stage the myth progressed through: it started with feeding a hundred men in II Kings, to a few hundred men as hinted by the statement regarding the 200 denarii, to 4,000 men and, finally, to 5,000 men. The last two stages of the oral tradition were the ones available to Mark. Seen in this light, it is quite obvious that the story of the miraculous feedings has no basis in history.

The last set of nature miracles involves Jesus' supposed power over natural forces such as the sea and the wind. The first account is of Jesus' power to calm the tempest:

> Mark 4:35-41 (Matthew 8:23-27; Luke 8:22-25)
> On that day, when evening had come, he said to them, "Let's go over to the other side." Leaving the multitude, they took him with them, even as he was, in the boat. Other small boats were also with him. A big wind storm arose, and the waves beat into the boat, so much that the boat was already filled. He himself was in the stern, asleep on the cushion, and they woke him up, and told him, "Teacher, don't you care that we are dying?" He awoke, and rebuked the wind, and said to the sea, "Peace! Be still!" The wind ceased, and there was a great calm. He said to them, "Why are you so afraid? How is it that you have no faith?" They were greatly afraid, and said to one another, "Who then is this, that even the wind and the sea obey him?"

As usual apart from the miraculous element itself, two additional points in the story above makes us doubt its historicity. The gospels themselves tell us that at least four of Jesus' disciples were fishermen: Peter, Andrew, James and John. It is highly unlikely that such experienced seamen, as they must be, would not take the necessary precautions of good seamanship to keep the boat afloat during the storm. The second point reveals the true nature of the story: Jesus accused his disciples of lacking faith when they were frightened by the storm. That accusation is totally illogical in an historical setting. The accusation only makes sense if the story is placed in a theological context. For instance the ability to control the sea was regarded in the Old Testament as a characteristic of divine power:

---

[119] Funk, et. al., *The Acts of Jesus*: p89
Helms, *Gospel Fictions*: p 75-76
Lüdemann, *Jesus After 2000 Years*: p45
Nineham, *Saint Mark*: p178

Psalms 89:9 (Also Psalms 93:3-4;106:8-9; Isaiah 51:10)
You rule the pride of the sea. When its waves rise up, you calm them.

The image of the storm is normally used as a metaphor for the evil forces of the world as the phrase from Psalms below illustrates:

Psalms 69:14 (Also Psalms 69:1-2; 18:16)
Deliver me out of the mire, and don't let me sink. Let me be delivered from those who hate me, and out of the deep waters.

The ability to sleep peacefully in times of trouble is also a sign of perfect trust in God:

Psalms 4:8 (Also Proverbs 3:24)
In peace I will both lay myself down and sleep, for you, Yahweh alone, make me live in safety.

Set in a theological context the story finally makes sense: it teaches of the necessity of faith in times of troubles.[120]

The whole episode could very easily have been constructed out of the basic passage in Psalms below:

Psalms 107:23-30
Those who go down to the sea in ships, who do business in great waters; These see Yahweh's works, and his wonders in the deep. For he commands, and raises the stormy wind, which lifts up its waves. They mount up to the sky; they go down again to the depths. Their soul melts away because of trouble. They reel back and forth, and stagger like a drunken man, and are at their wits' end. Then they cry to Yahweh in their trouble, and he brings them out of their distress. He makes the storm calm, so that its waves are still. Then they are glad because it is calm, so he brings them to their desired haven.

Our considerations show us that the story is unhistorical: it contradicts what we know of the laws of nature (remember Hume's second sets of considerations!), it makes no sense historically, it makes perfect sense theologically, and there are even Old Testament passages that could easily have formed the original nucleus for the episode.

The last nature miracle we will look at is probably the most spectacular of all: that of Jesus walking on water. The account is given in the gospels of Mark, Matthew and John. Again, we will look only at Mark's account, as it is the earliest of the gospels and ostensibly the most trustworthy:

Mark 6:47-51 (Matthew 14:23-33; John 6:16-22)
When evening had come, the boat was in the midst of the sea, and he was alone on the land. Seeing them distressed in rowing, for the wind was contrary to them, about the fourth watch of the night he came to them, walking on the sea, and he would have passed by them, but they, when they saw him walking on the sea,

---

[120] Craveri, *The Life of Jesus*: p115
Nineham, *Saint Mark*: p146-147

supposed that it was a ghost, and cried out; for they all saw him, and were troubled. But he immediately spoke with them, and said to them, "Cheer up! It is I! Don't be afraid." He got into the boat with them; and the wind ceased, and they were very amazed among themselves, and marveled.

As in the case of the calming of the storm, elements in the stories betray the unhistorical nature of the story. To make the disciples cry out in fear when they saw him walking on water simply does not make sense, in the context of the narratives. For haven't the disciples before this had witnessed Jesus' other miracles? They had seen Jesus turn water into wine, calm the tempest with a single command, raised Jairus' daughter from the dead and had just finished seeing him feeding 5,000 people with only five loaves and two fish. One would *expect* such a person to walk on water![121] The details in Mark make the whole scene sound extremely artificial.

Furthermore, note that the cathetical element of the story is similar to the one where Jesus calmed the storm. There are also Old Testament references to the divine ability to walk through or on waters:

Psalms 77:19 (Also Job 9:8; Isaiah 43:16)
Your way was through the sea; your paths through the great waters. Your footsteps were not known.

To summarize, the artificial nature of the story in Mark argues against the source being eyewitness accounts. When we add the fact that the account contradicts what is known about the physics of surface tension of water, we can safely conclude that the story is unhistorical.

As an aside, we find that Matthew, as is his *modus operandi*, tried to make the miracle all the more sensational. After following Mark 6:45-50 closely, Matthew inserted the episode below:

Matthew 14: 28-32
Peter answered him and said, "Lord, if it is you, command me to come to you on the waters." He said, "Come!" Peter stepped down from the boat, and walked on the waters to come to Jesus. But when he saw that the wind was strong, he was afraid, and beginning to sink, he cried out, saying, "Lord, save me!" Immediately Jesus stretched out his hand, took hold of him, and said to him, "You of little faith, why did you doubt?" When they got up into the boat, the wind ceased.

The above passage is clearly an example of how, wherever possible, the evangelist tried to make the story more incredible; contrary to what some apologists had claimed.[122] This insertion by Matthew came not from history but from a Buddhist legend. This legend was already circulating in Egypt and Syria around the second century BCE and must have influenced either Matthew or his sources. Given below is that legend:

---

[121]   Nineham, *Saint Mark*: p180-181
[122]   Wilson, *Jesus: The Evidence*: p85

[A disciple who wanted] to visit the Buddha one evening...found that the ferry boat was missing from the bank of the river Aciravati. In faithful trust in Buddha he stepped into the water and went as if on dry land to the very middle of the stream. Then he came out of his contented meditation on the Buddha in which he lost himself, and saw the waves and was frightened, and his feet began to sink. But he forced himself to become wrapped in his meditation again and by its power he reached the far bank safely and reached his master.[123]

The legend above also tells us that myths about holy men walking on water are not something unique to the Christian tradition. There is therefore no reason to accept the account of Jesus walking on water as having any historical basis.

In short, there is no compelling case for the actual occurrence of the nature miracles as recorded in the gospels.

FINAL WORDS ON THE MIRACLES OF JESUS

Some apologists such as the Anglican scholar, Anthony Harvey, had tried to claim that the main difference between the gospel narratives and other miracle stories of antiquity was that the evangelists "tell the story straight". We have seen from the above examples that this claim is simply *false*: Matthew for instance made the fig tree wither *at once* and pronounced the daughter of Jairus dead before the other evangelists; Luke made the crowds outside Jairus' house *know* that his daughter was dead; and Mark made the disciples sound like idiots when, after witnessing so many miracles, they were still frightened when they saw Jesus walking on water. Whenever possible the evangelists do their very best to make the miracles sound more incredible and make the reaction of the witnesses one of awe and amazement even when such reactions were clearly ridiculous. That the gospel accounts "tell the story straight" is one of the myths of modern fundamentalist apologetics.

During the time of Jesus and the writing of the gospels the uncritical attitude towards miracles was the norm. Jesus was certainly not the only one in antiquity to have miracles attributed to him. This is attested to even by the gospels for they make Jesus warn his disciples thus:

Mark 13:22 (Matthew 24:24)
For there will arise false christs and false prophets, and will show signs and wonders, that they may lead astray, if possible, even the chosen ones.

His miracles too were in no way unique, as Guignebert concludes:

The miracles which Jesus performed, according to the gospel writers, were in no way original; the healing of the lunatics, the expulsion of the devils, extraordinary cures, wonderful powers over nature, and even the resurrection of the dead, all were part of what the faith, both of Jews and of pagans, expected of a genuine worker of miracles.[124]

---

[123] Rudolf Bultmann, *The Gospel of John*, Westminster, Philadelphia 1971: p240 quoted in Helms, *Gospel Fictions*: p81

[124] Guignebert, *Jesus*: p194

In other words, in the credulous environment which Jesus and the evangelists found themselves in, accounts of miracles are bound to proliferate. Just as we reject the reality of pagan miracles, we reject the reality of the gospel miracles.

Furthermore, it should be noted that Jesus' actual "miracles" could not have been very spectacular (apart from the fact that it was not always successful - Mark 6:5) for didn't the towns of Chorazin, Bethsaida and Capernaum witnessed the lion's share of Jesus' miracles and still did not believe? Jesus' "loving" response to those who refused to believe him or his miracles can be found in this passage from the first gospel:

> Matthew 11:20-24
> Then he began to denounce the cities in which most of his mighty works had been done, because they didn't repent. "Woe to you, Chorazin! Woe to you, Bethsaida! For if the mighty works had been done in Tyre and Sidon which were done in you, they would have repented long ago in sackcloth and ashes. But I tell you, it will be more tolerable for Tyre and Sidon on the day of judgment than for you. You, Capernaum, who are exalted to heaven, you will go down to Hades. For if the mighty works had been done in Sodom which were done in you, it would have remained until this day. But I tell you that it will be more tolerable for the land of Sodom, on the day of judgment, than for you."

* * * * *

Jesus started out his career as a *disciple* of John the Baptist. Despite attempts by the evangelists to cover up this fact, the available evidence points to Jesus' discipleship of John as being a fact. He chose twelve apostles – most of them made little impact on Christian history. Later tradition regarding the apostles is generally worthless historically. The stories of the miracles performed by Jesus in the gospels are not historical. Many can be shown to be fictional concoctions based on Old Testament sources. Others can be explained by quite naturalistic means. There is no evidence that actual miracles – which transcend the laws of nature – were performed by Jesus during his ministry.

Chapter Thirteen
THE TEACHINGS AND PERSON OF JESUS

THE SAYINGS OF JESUS

We do not have a very large collection of the sayings of Jesus in the gospels. It has been computed that no more than seven hours are needed for someone to utter all these sayings.[1] If Jesus did preach for a year (the maximum possible time span derivable from the synoptics), or three years (derived from John), or even a few months, he must have uttered a lot more than what is extant today.

With such a small amount of his original teachings available to us, the obvious question arises: is the information available sufficient for us to comprehend his teachings and understand his personality? There is no objective answer to this question. From the very beginnings of critical historical research of the gospels, scholars have been unable to agree on this. The German theologian Adolf von Harnack (1851-1930) assured us, in his book *The Essence of Christianity* (1907), that the synoptics give us:

> a perfectly clear idea of the preaching of Jesus, as regards both its fundamental principles and its particular applications.[2]

Another scholar, the French church historian Pierre Batifol (1861-1929), gave the diametrically opposite view when he asserted that while the synoptics may have given the essential principles of his preaching, the teachings collected are by no means complete:

> On certain points these principles are no more than suggestions, and regarding the fundamental articles of the Christian faith, even these are lacking.[3]

The only conclusion we can make here is that we do not know if the extant sayings of Jesus in the gospels is a representative sample of what he actually taught.

There is a more fundamental question with regards to these sayings attributed to Jesus: are they authentic? Were the words attributed to Jesus in the gospels actually spoken by the Galilean, preserved in the tradition by his apostles and subsequently by their followers? Or were they put into the mouth of Jesus by the early Christians who no longer had access to the original tradition?[4]

---

[1]   Guignebert, *Jesus*: p233
[2]   quoted in Guignebert, *Jesus*: p232
[3]   quoted in Guignebert, *Jesus*: p233-234
[4]   By "authentic" sayings I mean both *ippisima verba* ("the very words") and *ippisima vox* ("the very voice"). The former phrase refers to the exact words as uttered by Jesus, while the latter refers to the fact that what he said may have been paraphrased by the tradition but that the quote is still true to his thoughts or ideas. When a saying of Jesus is judged to

The answer to this is that we know for certain that *at least some* sayings attributed to Jesus were never - or could never have been - spoken by him.

The first example of this is in the episode given in Mark 10:1-12. Here Jesus is shown as debating with the Pharisees on the issue of divorce. After the debate, Jesus and his disciples went to a house where they asked him for clarification on the issues debated. Jesus' reply was:

> Make 10:11-12
> He said to them, "Whoever divorces his wife, and marries another, commits adultery against her. *If a woman herself divorces her husband, and marries another, she commits adultery.*"

The saying of Jesus above, specifically the sentence italicized, makes no sense in the context of Jewish customs during that time. Palestinian women during the time of Jesus simply could not divorce their husbands. They had no such right.[5] This verse reflects Roman marriage law, which allows either the man or the woman to initiate divorce. In other words, this reflects the situation of the Gentile community in which Mark was writing, not the situation of Jewish Palestine.[6] G.A. Wells is right when he said that the utterance was:

> [C]oncocted in a Christian community remote in time and place from the Palestine of AD 30.[7]

The second example involves another debate with the Pharisees where Jesus was supposed to have uttered the following critique of their behavior:

> Mark 7:6-8
> He answered them, "Well did Isaiah prophesy of you hypocrites, as it is written,
>> 'This people honors me with their lips,
>> but their heart is far from me.
>> But in vain do they worship me,
>> teaching as doctrines the commandments of men.'
> "For you set aside the commandment of God, and hold tightly to the tradition of men—the washing of pitchers and cups, and you do many other such things."

Jesus is made here to quote a passage from Isaiah (29:13). He is made to conclude, with the support of the verse in Isaiah, that the Pharisees follow the tradition at the expense of the written law. However, the verses quoted from Isaiah are found, in the

---

be unauthentic, we are saying that he neither said those very words nor uttered anything with the same idea.

[5] It would be ludicrous to say that Jesus was instituting a new rule where women could divorce their husbands, for the passage was one that speaks against *any* form of divorce. Other similar explanations like Jesus "elevating" the status of women are nonsense. How could Jesus say that women can now divorce their husbands and then *immediately* forbid it?

[6] Funk, et.al., *The Five Gospels*: p88-89
Lüdemann, *Jesus After 2000 Years*: p67
Nineham, *Saint Mark*: p266

[7] Wells, *The Historical Evidence for Jesus*: p13

form that allows Jesus to derive this conclusion, only in the Greek translation of the Bible, the Septuagint. In the Hebrew Bible, Isaiah 29:13 differs considerably from the Greek one. We give the two in English for comparison:

Isaiah 29:13 (Septuagint)	Isaiah 29:13 (Hebrew Bible) - NRSV
And the Lord has said, This people draw nigh to me with their mouth, and they honor me with their lips, but their heart is far from me: *but in vain do they worship me, teaching the commandments and doctrines of men.*	The Lord said, "Because these people draws near with their mouth and honor me with their lips, while their hearts are far from me, and *their worship of me is a human commandment learned by rote.*

As Nineham observed:

> It is just the part where the Greek text differs from the Hebrew that affords the point of the quotation here - the "doctrines they teach are but human precepts"...in its Hebrew form the passage would hardly be relevant here.[8]

Now, it is improbable that a rural Galilean Jew would know the Old Testament in Greek. It is even more ludicrous to think that he would try to win an argument with the *Pharisees* by quoting a Greek mistranslation of Isaiah![9] Therefore, the saying attributed to Jesus in Mark 7:6-8 could not have been spoken by him. It most definitely is an addition by the early Christian tradition.

We have looked at two examples of utterances attributed to Jesus which we are *sure* could not have been spoken by him. We will now consider a few more examples of sayings of which authenticity are *doubtful* because they were not original and could have been easily available to the evangelists or the early Christians from a wide variety of sources.

In the seventh chapter of Matthew, Jesus was supposed to have uttered:

Matthew 7:12
Therefore whatever you desire for men to do to you, you shall also do to them; for this is the law and the prophets.

The wording and the idea is almost exactly what is said by an earlier Jewish teacher, Hillel (b. 75 BCE): [10]

---

[8]   Nineham, *Saint Mark*: p195
[9]   Wells, *The Historical Evidence for Jesus*: p13
[10]   Maccoby, *Revolution in Judea*: p266

Babylonian Talmud Shabbat 31a[11]
What is hateful to you, do not do to your fellow man: this is the whole
law, the rest is commentary.

The striking similarity between the above two passages gives a strong indication that
Matthew or his source copied the passage from Hillel (b. 75 BCE) and attributed it to
Jesus.

Another example of an unoriginal utterance is to be found in chapter seven of
John. Here we find Jesus arguing with the Jews about the Sabbath, where he was
supposed to have uttered the following:

John 7:22-23
"Moses has given you circumcision (not that it is of Moses, but of the fathers), and
on the Sabbath you circumcise a boy. If a boy receives circumcision on the
Sabbath, that the law of Moses may not be broken, are you angry with me, because
I made a man completely healthy on the Sabbath? "

We find exactly the same idea adumbrated in the *Talmud*:

Babylonian Talmud Yoma 85b
If circumcision, which concerns one of the 248 members of the body, overrides the
Sabbath, shall not a man's whole body override the Sabbath?[12]

We have seen above that some sayings of Jesus which are definitely unauthentic and
some which are of doubtful authenticity. The existence of such passages means that
we cannot simply take it for granted that all sayings attributed to him in the gospels
were actually spoken by him.

Recently, from 1985 to 1997, a group of biblical scholars got together in what
became known as *The Jesus Seminar*[13] to try to discover the authentic sayings and

---

[11]   References to the rabbinic Literature can be quite confusing for those who do not have
        some background in it. Here is a quick summary. We are interested primarily in the group
        of writings known collectively as the *Talmuds*. These consist of the Mishnah, the Tosefta,
        The Jerusalem Talmud and the Babylonian Talmud. The Mishnah was compiled and put
        into writing around 200-220 CE and consists of oral traditions handed down by the
        Rabbis. The Tosefta (literally "addition"), is an addition to the Mishnah normally
        believed to have been compiled around 220-230 CE. The Jerusalem Talmud consists of
        the Mishnah and Tosefta with the interpretations (*Gemara*) of the Rabbis. It was
        compiled in Palestine around 400-425 CE. The Babylonian Talmud (or *Bavli*) is also an
        interpretive expansion of the Mishnah and Tosefta. It was completed in 500-550 CE.
        When referring to the Talmud an alphabet is given to indicate the document: "m" for
        Mishnah, "t" for Tosefta, "y" for the Jerusalem Talmud and "b" for the Bavli followed by
        the specific tractate, the page (and or paragraph). In the Bavli and additional letter at the
        end "a" or "b" refers to the front or backside of the folio. Thus the reference above
        "Babylonian Talmud Shabbat 31a" would normally be rendered as *b. Shabb. 31 a*. In this
        book we will give the reference to the Talmuds in full for ease of reference.
[12]   quoted in Maccoby, *Revolution in Judea*: p267
[13]   The Jesus Seminar generated a lot of controversy both in the press and among the lay
        public not so much because of the content of its findings but because they did their

deeds of Jesus. Of all the sayings attributed to Jesus, they could only count 18% as being probably spoken by him. This is 18% of *all* the sayings attributed to Jesus, both from canonical and non-canonical sources in the first three centuries CE. Dr. Robert J. Miller, a fellow of the Jesus Seminar, estimated that about 50% of the sayings from Mark, Luke, Matthew and *Thomas* probably have some claims to be derived from actual utterances of Jesus.[14] It is also interesting that almost *all* the sayings attributed to Jesus in the Gospel of John are considered unauthentic by the fellows of the Seminar.

Apart from individual sayings, the long discourses attributed to Jesus in the form they are presented, especially in the gospels of Matthew and Luke, are artificial.[15] For example the twelfth chapter of Luke consists wholly of a long discourse by Jesus, the form of which is definitely artificial. A quick look at the first twelve verses of that chapter will suffice to prove the point:

Matthew 10:1, 5, 24-34	Luke 12:1-12
1 He called to himself his twelve disciples, and gave them authority over unclean spirits, to cast them out, and to heal every disease and every sickness.... 5 Jesus sent these twelve out, and commanded them, saying, "... 24 "A disciple is not above his teacher, nor a servant above his lord. 25 It is enough for the disciple that he be like his teacher, and the servant like his lord. If they have called the master of the house Beelzebul, how much more those of his household! *26 Therefore don't be afraid of them, for there is nothing covered that will not be revealed; and hidden that will not be known.* *27 What I tell you in the darkness, speak in the light; and what you hear whispered in the ear, proclaim on the housetops.* *28 Don't be afraid of those who kill the body, but are not able to kill the soul. Rather, fear him who is able to destroy both soul and body in Gehenna.* *29 Aren't two sparrows sold for an assarion coin? Not one of them falls on the ground apart from your Father's will,*	1 Meanwhile, when a multitude of many thousands had gathered together, so much so that they trampled on each other, he began to tell his disciples first of all, "Beware of the yeast of the Pharisees, which is hypocrisy. *2 But there is nothing covered up, that will not be revealed, nor hidden, that will not be known.* *3 Therefore whatever you have said in the darkness will be heard in the light. What you have spoken in the ear in the inner rooms will be proclaimed on the housetops.* *4 "I tell you, my friends, don't be afraid of those who kill the body, and after that have no more that they can do.* *5 But I will warn you whom you should fear. Fear him, who after he has killed, has power to cast into Gehenna. Yes, I tell you, fear him.* *6 "Aren't five sparrows sold for two assaria coins? Not one of them is forgotten by God.*

debates and discussions in *public*. Many of the things "discovered" (such as Jesus didn't speak some of the sayings attributed to him) are not new. But critical historical scholars of the Bible had in the past failed to make their findings known to the general public. Although the author disagree with some of the conclusions of the Jesus Seminar, this was a first crucial step in the right direction.

14 Miller, *The Jesus Seminar and Its Critics*: p76
15 Guignebert, *Jesus*: p236

30 but the very hairs of your head are all numbered. 31 Therefore don't be afraid. You are of more value than many sparrows.	7 But the very hairs of your head are all numbered. Therefore don't be afraid. You are of more value than many sparrows.
32 Everyone therefore who confesses me before men, him I will also confess before my Father who is in heaven.	8 "I tell you, everyone who confesses me before men, him will the Son of Man also confess before the angels of God;
33 But whoever denies me before men, him I will also deny before my Father who is in heaven.	9 but he who denies me in the presence of men will be denied in the presence of the angels of God.
34 "Don't think that I came to send peace on the earth. I didn't come to send peace, but a sword.	10 Everyone who speaks a word against the Son of Man will be forgiven, but those who blaspheme against the Holy Spirit will not be forgiven.
	11 When they bring you before the synagogues, the rulers, and the authorities, don't be anxious how or what you will answer, or what you will say;
	12 for the Holy Spirit will teach you in that same hour what you must say."

Table 13.1: The artificial form of the discourse

There are really no connections among the various sayings, the individual blocks can easily be discerned: Luke 12:1, 2-3,4-5,6-7,8-9,10,11-12. These individual blocks are artificially strung together. However, some of the verses (Luke 12:2-9) were not strung together by Luke but probably by the compiler of Q, for Matthew 10:26-33 records the same sayings in the same sequence.

The comparison with the different contexts in which these eight verses occur in the two gospels serve to further reveal the artificiality of the discourses. For both evangelists had these verses inserted between completely different utterances![16] Luke 12:22-34 is a part of the discourse that deals with the freedom from earthly cares. This same portion is used in Matthew but not in the same diatribe but in an earlier one (Matthew 6:25-34) and in a different context.

Table 13.2 shows the last six verses of chapter 12 of Luke. We find the elements in the sermon given in Luke to have been given by Matthew as having been spoken by Jesus on two separate occasions.

---

[16] It is simply not probable to assume that Jesus spoke almost exactly the same verses within different discourses. Unless, like the modern politicians, Jesus was reading from written notes or had a ghostwriter!

Luke 12:54-59; 13:1	Matthew 16:1-4	Matthew 5:23-26
54 He said to the multitudes also, "When you see a cloud rising from the west, immediately you say, 'A shower is coming,' and so it happens. 55 When a south wind blows, you say, 'There will be a scorching heat,' and it happens.	1 The Pharisees and Sadducees came, and testing him, asked him to show them a sign from heaven. 2 But he answered them, "When it is evening, you say, 'It will be fair weather, for the sky is red.' 3 In the morning, 'It will be foul weather today, for the sky is red and threatening.'	23 "If therefore you are offering your gift at the altar, and there remember that your brother has anything against you, 24 leave your gift there before the altar, and go your way. First be reconciled to your brother, and then come and offer your gift.
56 *You hypocrites! You know how to interpret the appearance of the earth and the sky, but how is it that you don't interpret this time?* 57 Why don't you judge for yourselves what is right? 58 *For when you are going with your adversary before the magistrate, try diligently on the way to be released from him, lest perhaps he drag you to the judge, and the judge deliver you to the officer, and the officer throw you into prison.* 59 *I tell you, you will by no means get out of there, until you have paid the very last penny.*"	*Hypocrites! You know how to discern the appearance of the sky, but you can't discern the signs of the times!* 4 An evil and adulterous generation seeks after a sign, and there will be no sign given to it, except the sign of the prophet Jonah."	25 *Agree with your adversary quickly, while you are with him in the way; lest perhaps the prosecutor deliver you to the judge, and the judge deliver you to the officer, and you be cast into prison.* 26 *Most certainly I tell you, you shall by no means get out of there, until you have paid the last penny.*

Table 13.2: More discourses.

This artificial form is also evident in the famous "Sermon on the Mount" (Matthew chapters 5 to 7). We find in this sermon some sayings and group of sayings that are repeated in Luke's "Sermon on the Plain" (Luke 6:17-49). However, they are given here in a different order:

Matthew 5:38-42	=	Luke 6:29-30
Matthew 5:43-48	=	Luke 6:27-28,32-36
Matthew 7:1-5	=	Luke 6:37,38,41,42
Matthew 7:12	=	Luke 6:31

Other portions from Matthew's "Sermon on the Mount" appear elsewhere in Luke under different contexts:

| Matthew 6:9-15 | = | Luke 11:1-4 |
| Matthew 6:19-21 | = | Luke 12:33-34 |

We can therefore conclude that the discourses of Jesus as they are presented in Matthew and Luke are not historical. They are inventions of the evangelists who did so by stringing the *logia* together like beads to make a necklace. The discourses are merely collections of various unrelated sayings attributed to Jesus by tradition.[17] As Guignebert commonsensically pointed out (regarding the "Sermon on the Mount" and the "Sermon on the Plain"):

> It is obvious that nobody took notes and that it would have been impossible to remember from merely hearing them the one hundred and seven verses of the discourse in Matthew, or even the thirty verses of that of Luke.[18]

THE INTELLECT OF JESUS

What we can know of Jesus is derivable only from a small collection of short sayings - which may or may not be authentic. The longer "sermons" are, as we have seen above, fabrications of the evangelists. This paucity of information makes it impossible for us to assess with any certainty the intellect of this man. An irritating feature of conservative Christian literature is the often cocksure conclusion their authors have about Jesus' intellectual capability. Take, for example, the pronouncement of the Christian theologian and historian, Philip Schaff (1819-1893):

> such an intellect - clear as sky, bracing as the mountain air, sharp and penetrating as a sword, thoroughly healthy and vigorous, always ready and always self possessed.[19]

Another theologian, Charles Dodd (1884-1973) has this to say:

> [The] whole body of sayings...betray a mind whose processes were swift and direct, hitting the nail on the head without waste of words.[20]

Their conclusion comes, not from a thorough study and understanding of the material, but from dogmatic preconceptions. These rose-tinted views have been challenged by more critical scholars such as Charles Guignebert (1867-1939) who was Professor of History of Christianity in the Sorbonne. His observations on Jesus' intellect are as follows:

> [W]e find in it no abstractions, no theories concerning man, life, the world of God, in short, not the slightest interest in rational and objective knowledge. He observes the world and quite simply records his impressions in what he says.

---

[17]   Guignebert, *Jesus*: p237
[18]   Guignebert, *Jesus*: p237
[19]   Schaff, Phillip, *The Person of Christ*, New York 1913, quoted in McDowell, *Evidence that Demands a Verdict*: p107
[20]   Dodd, *The Founder of Christianity*: p49

Jesus' intellect, according to Guignebert is not that of a keen and lively type but that of a dogmatist:

> When he feels himself opposed by a doubt, he makes no attempt to refute it, for there is nothing for him to say. He neither argues nor discusses, proves nor confutes; he knows the truth and he utters it, and when he realized that it is not believed he grows angry and depressed.[21]

A good example of what Guignebert is saying can be found in the incident where Jesus was preaching in a synagogue in Capernaum (Mark 3:1-6). The crowd was not responsive to Jesus and this was his reaction:

> Mark 3:5
> When he had looked around at them with anger, being grieved at the hardening of their hearts...

Jesus' intellect, as we would expect, is very much a product of his environment:

> [I]t is important to remember that we are dealing, according to the synoptics, with a man of the people, born and brought up amongst humble folk in a little town in Galilee; that he was surrounded by companions of the same class as himself; that he, as a rule, spoke only to audiences of peasants and common people; and that the extent of his culture was bounded by his religious education...We have to do, then, with an ignorant man, not so much because he did not pursue liberal studies, which, as a matter of fact, would have been of little use to him in his Palestinian country, but because he had only a limited horizon. He does not appear to have known anything outside Judaism, and he was familiar only with the social environment of Galilee.[22]

In short, Jesus' mind was *simple* and *rural*. His knowledge of his contemporary world was dismal, as Ernest Renan (1823-1892), the famous 19th century French historian, pointed out:

> That he had no knowledge of the general state of the world is apparent from each feature of his authentic discourses. *The courts of kings appear to him as places where men wear fine clothes* [Matthew 11:8]. The charming impossibilities with his parables abound, when he brings kings and the mighty ones on the stage, prove that he never conceived of aristocratic society but as a young villager who sees the world though the prism of his simplicity.[23]

That Jesus was incapable of deep and abstract thought can be seen in the episode below:

---

[21]   Guignebert, *Jesus*: p248
[22]   Guignebert, *Jesus*: p178
[23]   Renan, *The Life of Jesus*: p44-45

Mark 2:23-26

It happened that he was going on the Sabbath day through the grain fields, and his disciples began, as they went, to pluck the ears of grain. The Pharisees said to him, "Behold, why do they do that which is not lawful on the Sabbath day?" He said to them, "Did you never read what David did, when he had need, and was hungry-he, and those who were with him? How he entered into the house of God when Abiathar was high priest, and ate the show bread, which is not lawful to eat except for the priests, and gave also to those who were with him?"

The scripture cited by Jesus in defense of his disciples' action has very little to do with the present situation. For David and his band of soldiers were hungry and were invited by the High Priest himself. The disciples, on the other hand, were simply strolling along and frivolously picking ears of corn. The fact that Jesus was satisfied with such a defense reveals a rather simplistic intellect.[24]

The balance of evidence, far from proving the remarkable intellect of the Jesus of the fundamentalists, suggests that Jesus was an unsophisticated and ignorant Galilean peasant.

THE PSYCHOLOGICAL PROFILE OF JESUS

We do not have enough certain information to draw a psychological profile of Jesus. However, it is interesting to note that an uncritical appreciation of the reliability of the gospel accounts can lead to some rather bewildering (to Christians) conclusions about Jesus' inner psychology.

In the early years of the 20th century, some psychologists and psychiatrists such as Dr. Charles Binet-Sangle, Professor of Psychology at the University of Paris, Dr. J. Dagonet, a physician at St. Anne's Hospital in Paris and Dr. B. Ball, Professor of Mental Pathology in the Faculty of Medicine in Paris made various diagnosis about Jesus. Given below is a summary of their findings:[25]

1. Jesus suffered from *theomania* (excessive religious devotion) inherited through his parents' devoutness. Theomaniacs studied at the mental hospital at Charenton believe that they are called by God, and that they cannot be harmed and that they will live forever. Mystic visions are also very common among theomaniacs. Jesus seeing the dove coming down on him during his baptism (Mark 1:10-11) is the classic example of the type of mystic vision experienced by theomaniacs. Dr. Dagonet noted that theomaniacs get very easily irritated and will not permit contradiction of their utterances, as Jesus was in Mark 3:5. They often speak in tones of authority. Dr. Ball pointed out that the great religious innovators of history, such as Martin Luther and Muhammad, have always been psychologically abnormal. Coupled with his theomania is his *megalomania*. After all, it is quite incompatible with a sound mind that Jesus would announce himself the future judge of the universe (John 5:27).

---

[24]   Guignebert, *Jesus*: p179
[25]   Craveri, *The Life of Jesus*: p167-168
        Guignebert, *Jesus*: p170-171

2.   Jesus suffered from the *hallucinatory syndrome*. This is proven by the numerous visions he experienced throughout his ministry: on his baptism where he saw the Holy Spirit and heard the voice of God (Mark 1:10-11); during his fact in the desert where he saw Satan himself (Matthew 4:1-11; Luke 4:1-12); and in Gethsemane where he saw angels (Luke 22:43). Surely if anyone today tells us he has heard the voice of God, spoken to the devil and has seen angels, we would be hard put *not* to pronounce him deranged.

3.   He also suffered from *dromomania* (irrepressible wanderlust). This is evident from his frequent journeying, from Nazareth to the banks of the Jordan, from there to the wilderness, then back to Nazareth, to Cana, to Capernaum, to Phoenicia, to Caesarea, to Samaria, to Judea etc.

4.   A detailed analysis by the psychologists and psychiatrists of the sayings of Jesus showed that he was an *egocentric maniac* devoid of profundity of thought, incoherent and often amoral.

5.   They also noted various physiological symptoms that point to an abnormal condition:
   a)   The sweat of blood at Gethsemane (Luke 22:44) shows a defect in his vaso-motor system and is in reality a facial *hematidrosis*.
   b)   The forty day fast in the desert (Matthew 4:2; Luke 4:2) shows that Jesus had problems with his digestive system. The forty day fast was actually an attack of *sitiophobia*.
   c)   The fact that Jesus was incapable of carrying the cross himself (Mark 15:21; Matthew 27:32; Luke 23:26) and the pleuro-tubercular effusion revealed by the lance-thrust (John 19:34) shows that Jesus had problems with his respiratory organs as well.
   d)   Jesus probably had problems with his genital organs as well. We get psychological hints from Jesus' encouragement of castration (Matthew 19:12) and his glorification of sterility (Luke 23:29).

6.   Jesus also suffered from *Oedipism* or a tendency to engage self-mutilation. This is evidenced from his advice to his followers to pluck their eyes and cut their hands to avoid sinning. (Matthew 5:29-30)

7.   And finally, we have the testimony from his family, his mother and brothers (Mark 3:21) and his enemies (Mark 3:22), who all thought that he was *mad*.

In short, the psychologists and psychiatrists thought Jesus as a typical psychotic, a visionary, a paranoid and a megalomaniac. With diseases of the digestive system, the lungs and the genitals, he wasn't too healthy either!

It would be wrong to criticize the competence of these esteemed thinkers in the field of psychopathology. Their diagnosis of Jesus is invalid for a different reason: their lack of appreciation of *source criticism*. That is to say, they do not understand that many of the actions and sayings attributed to Jesus by the gospels are not historical and were actually supplied by the early Christian tradition.

It should be mentioned that my disagreement with their diagnosis is no consolation to believers, especially those who accept everything spoken in the Bible as literally true; for then the psychopathological diagnosis cannot be so easily dismissed. It goes to show that an uncritical acceptance of the complete veracity of the gospels accounts led men trained in the field of psychopathology to conclude that Jesus was a sick madman!

THE PERSONALITY OF JESUS

The personality of Jesus is another subject Christian apologists normally harp upon. Josh McDowell in his book *Evidence That Demands a Verdict*, a typical fundamentalist apologetic, quotes the 19th century historian Philip Schaff to support his case:

> the moral purity and dignity of Jesus [is] revealed in his every word and work and acknowledged by universal consent...A character so original, so uniformly consistent, so perfect, so human, and yet so high above all human greatness.[26]

McDowell also quotes two positive assessments of Jesus' personality by two skeptics,[27] John Stuart Mill (1806-1873) and William Lecky (1838-1903), in a transparent attempt to convey the notion to his readers that Jesus' personality is acknowledged by all, believers and skeptics alike, to be what Philip Schaff says.

However, this impression is untrue; many skeptics do not hold such an elevated assessment of Jesus' personality. This is what the renowned skeptic and philosopher Bertrand Russell (1872-1970) had to say about this:

> I want to say a few words upon a topic...and that is the question whether Christ was the best and wisest of men. It is generally taken for granted that we shall all agree that this was so. I do not myself...I cannot myself feel that either in the matter of wisdom or in the matter of virtue Christ stands quite as high as some other people known to history. I think I should put Buddha and Socrates above him in these respects.[28]

Bertrand Russell is not the only skeptic with such a view. Some of the most famous skeptics such as Charles Bradlaugh (1833-1891), Joseph McCabe (1867-1955), and Margaret Knight (1903-1983) are all of the same opinion. Given below is what Margaret Knight, herself a psychologist but with a greater understanding of biblical criticism than the group we saw earlier, had to say about the personality of Jesus:

> Jesus, in fact, was typical of a certain kind of fanatical young idealist: at one moment holding forth, with tears in his eyes, about the need for universal love; at the next furiously denouncing the morons, crooks and bigots who do not see eye to

---

26 McDowell, *Evidence that Demands a Verdict*: p105-106
27 McDowell, *Evidence that Demands a Verdict*: p105
28 Rusell, *Why I am not a Christian*: p20-24

eye with him. It is a very natural and human behavior. Many great men of history (for example, Socrates) have met criticism with more dignity and restraint.[29]

Were Russell and Knight simply rattling off their own preconceived opinions about Jesus, just like the fundamentalists? The answer is, no. Their conclusions are actually based on the sayings of Jesus contained in the gospels, considered in their proper context and without any preconceived opinion (such as "Jesus is God") about him. Our point here is not to discuss the issue of whether any particular saying of Jesus was actually spoken by him. We are here merely interested in seeing whether Jesus, *as depicted in the gospels*, suits the hyperbole accorded to him by believers.

Knight called Jesus a fanatic in the quotation above. This description is apt. Jesus, as we know, preached a kind of universal love and even extolled his followers to love their enemies:

Matthew 5:43-44
"You have heard that it was said, 'You shall love your neighbor, and hate your enemy.' But I tell you, love your enemies, bless those who curse you, do good to those who hate you, and pray for those who mistreat you and persecute you"

Matthew 19:19
"You shall love your neighbor as yourself."

Luke 6:27-28
"But I tell you who hear: love your enemies, do good to those who hate you, bless those who curse you, and pray for those who mistreat you."

This is all well and good. Jesus was generally tolerant towards self-confessed sinners who believed in him. We see this in Mark 2:15 where we are told that he had dinner with tax collectors and sinners at Levi's house. But this tolerance and love is not universally bestowed on everyone. Jesus was extremely intolerant of people, however good and well meaning, who did not believe in him. A fanatic is convinced he is right, anybody who does not follow or believe in him is an enemy of God, that is that. Jesus was like that. Take, for instance, this instruction he gave to his disciples on people who do not accept his "good news":

Matthew 10:14-15 (Also Mark 6:11)
"Whoever doesn't receive you, nor hear your words, as you go out of that house or that city, shake off the dust from your feet. Most certainly I tell you, it will be more tolerable for the land of Sodom and Gomorrah in the day of judgment than for that city."

And given below is what Jesus said to the villages in Galilee who were not impressed with his teachings or his miracles:

Matthew 11:20-24
Then he began to denounce the cities in which most of his mighty works had been done, because they didn't repent. "Woe to you, Chorazin! Woe to you, Bethsaida! For if the mighty works had been done in Tyre and Sidon which were done in you,

---

[29]   Knight, *Honest to Man*: p26

they would have repented long ago in sackcloth and ashes. But I tell you, it will be more tolerable for Tyre and Sidon on the day of judgment than for you. You, Capernaum, who are exalted to heaven, you will go down to Hades. For if the mighty works had been done in Sodom which were done in you, it would have remained until this day. But I tell you that it will be more tolerable for the land of Sodom, on the day of judgment, than for you."

And some Pharisees, representing the generally better educated class of the Jewish populace, were naturally skeptical of his teachings. And to this lot this was the message from Jesus:

> Matthew 13:13-34
> Woe to you, scribes and Pharisees, hypocrites! For you devour widows' houses, and as a pretense you make long prayers. Therefore you will receive greater condemnation. ..."Woe to you, you blind guides...You blind fools! ..."Woe to you, scribes and Pharisees, hypocrites! ...You blind guides, who strain out a gnat, and swallow a camel! ..."Woe to you, scribes and Pharisees, hypocrites! For you are like whitened tombs, which outwardly appear beautiful, but inwardly are full of dead men's bones, and of all uncleanness. Even so you also outwardly appear righteous to men, but inwardly you are full of hypocrisy and iniquity...You serpents, you offspring of vipers, how will you escape the judgment of Gehenna?

Where is the "love your enemies" attitude in the above quotes? Surely people who are unimpressed with your teachings are not worse than your enemies. For your enemies, by definition, are people who want to do you harm, or at least, would like to see harm come to you. The people who rejected his apostles' teachings may not be like that at all, and like the residents of Chorazin, Bethsaida and Capernaum, may simply have been unimpressed by his miracles and his teachings.[30]

There is a further contradiction in Jesus' attitude towards his enemies, given below is a parable of Jesus where he clearly mentions what he would do to his enemies and people who do not believe in him:

> Luke 19:26-27
> "For I tell you that to everyone who has, will more be given; but from him who doesn't have, even that which he has will be taken away from him. *But bring those enemies of mine who didn't want me to reign over them here, and kill them before me.*"[31]

---

[30] Knight, *Honest to Man*: p25

[31] It might be objected that this is part of the parable and the one who is actually asking for the enemies to be slain was the nobleman who became king in the parable. But it is clear that the nobleman/king who was hated by the citizens in the story was an allegorical figure for Jesus who was rejected by the Jews. So the saying clearly means that Jesus would want his enemies to be slain. Another objection, this one correct, is that the saying is not authentic to Jesus and was put into his mouth by Luke. I agree that this verse is not authentic (see for instance Funk et.al, *The Five Gospels*: p373-375 and Lüdemann, *Jesus After 2000 Years*: p381-382) – however, my point was that Jesus, *as he is depicted in the gospels*, is not someone "above all human greatness" as some fundamentalists have claimed.

The observations of the other skeptic, Charles Bradlaugh narrows in on the fundamental problem of Jesus' preaching:

> It is a mockery to speak as if love could really result from the dehumanizing and isolating faith required from the disciples of Jesus.[32]

There is another passage which shows that Jesus' message of love and forgiveness was not meant to be preached to everyone:

> Mark 4:10-12
> When he was alone, those who were around him with the twelve asked him about the parables. He said to them, "To you is given the mystery of the Kingdom of God, but to those who are outside, all things are done in parables, that seeing they may see, and not perceive; and hearing they may hear, and not understand; *lest perhaps they should turn again, and their sins should be forgiven them.*"

The above statement, if historically accurate[33], is startling. For Jesus is saying that there are some people whom he does not want to understand his message because he does not wish for them forgiveness! How is this to be reconciled with universal love?

Furthermore, Jesus was not one to practice what he preached. Take for instance this teaching of his:

> Luke 6:29
> "To him who strikes you on the cheek, offer also the other"

How did Jesus himself respond to those who strike him? Take a look at this episode from the 18th chapter of John:

> John 18:22-23
> When he had said this, one of the officers standing by slapped Jesus with his hand, saying, "Do you answer the high priest like that?" Jesus answered him, "If I have spoken evil, testify of the evil; but if well, why do you beat me?"

When he was struck by one official during his interrogation by the high priest, instead of offering the other cheek, he protested the first slap!

The cursing of the fig tree (Mark 11:12-14, 11:20; Matthew 21:18-19) and the drowning of the swine (Mark 5:1-20; Matthew 8:28-32) are obviously unhistorical episodes.[34] But if these are accepted as illustrations of what his personality was capable of, it makes the picture of Jesus even worse. The irony of the fig tree incident (from the standpoint of a believer) is well captured by Bradlaugh:

---

[32]   Bradlaugh, *Humanity's Gain From Unbelief*: p77

[33]   The scholars of the Jesus Seminar do not think this saying is an actual historical utterance of Jesus and it was an invention of the Markan community. (Funk et. al. *The Five Gospels*: p55).

[34]   See chapter 12 for the discussion on the miracle of the fig tree.

> Will you urge the love of Jesus as the redeeming feature of his teaching? Then read the story of the fig tree withered by the hungry Jesus. The fig tree was, if he were the all powerful God, made by him; he limited its growth and regulated its development; he prevented it from bearing figs, expected fruit when he had rendered fruit impossible, and in his "infinite love" was angry that the tree had not upon it, what it could not have.[35]

If you remember, Jesus cursed the fig tree because it had no fruit. But the fig tree could not have been expected to have fruit, for it was stated explicitly that it was not the season for figs (Mark 11:13).

In the drowning of the swine, Jesus was in the process of exorcizing a man possessed by demons. The demons asked Jesus not to cast them out of the area but into some 2,000 pigs that were nearby. Jesus agreed to do so. The moment the evil spirits were cast into the pigs, they rushed headlong from the steep bank onto the lake and were drowned. Bertrand Russell's tongue-in-cheek comment about this presents the problem to Christians:

> There is the instance of the Gadarene swine where it was certainly not very kind to the pigs to put the devils into them and make them rush down the hill to the sea. You must remember that he was omnipotent and he could have made the devils simply go away; but he chooses to send them into the pigs.[36]

We also find evidence of racism in Jesus. One example is the passage below where Jesus equated non-Jews to dogs:

> Mark 7:26-27 (Matthew 15:21-29)
> Now the woman was a Greek, a Syrophoenician by race. She begged him that he would cast the demon out of her daughter. But Jesus said to her, "Let the children be filled first, for it is not appropriate to take the children's bread and throw it to the dogs."

We will be discussing this episode in more detail in the next section. The thing to note here is that we now have reason to believe that Jesus was a racist.

Our, albeit brief, look at some of the sayings of Jesus reveal a very different Jesus from the one taught and presented by Christian tradition. The Jesus we discovered was a dark and disturbing figure. This Jesus was an ignorant, bigoted and fanatical Galilean peasant.

THE UNIVERSALITY OF JESUS

Christians today believe that Jesus meant his preaching for all mankind, Gentiles and Jews alike. This belief however, is not supported by a critical study of the genuine utterances of Jesus in the gospels. The authentic traditional material gives a very clear indication that the earthly Jesus, not the Jesus of Christian theology, meant his

---

[35]   Bradlaugh, *Humanity's Gain From Unbelief*: p82

[36]   Russell, *Why I am Not a Christian*: p23

teachings strictly for the Jews.[37] One of the most clear-cut examples of this is his instructions to his disciples as they go out to preach his message:

Matthew 10:5-6
Jesus sent these twelve out, and commanded them, saying, "Don't go among the Gentiles, and don't enter into any city of the Samaritans. Rather, go to the lost sheep of the house of Israel."

By the time this gospel was written – around the end of the first century CE – Gentiles already formed the bulk of the Christian community. It is therefore unlikely that the passage above, which overtly excludes the Gentiles from Jesus' plan, would have been invented by the tradition or the evangelist (criterion of dissimilarity).[38] Hence it is highly probable that the above quote represents an authentic quotation of the historical Jesus.

And in the case already cited earlier about Jesus and the Greek Phoenician woman who asked him to heal her daughter, Matthew made Jesus tell her in no uncertain terms where his sympathies lie:

Matthew 15:24
But he [Jesus] answered, "I wasn't sent to anyone but the lost sheep of the house of Israel."

For the same reason as the above passage, this quotation is very likely an authentic utterance of the historical Jesus. Let us now have a look at the whole episode as Mark presented it.

Mark 8:24-30
From there he arose, and went away into the borders of Tyre and Sidon. He entered into a house, and didn't want anyone to know it, but he couldn't escape notice. For a woman, whose little daughter had an unclean spirit, having heard of him, came and fell down at his feet. Now the woman was a Greek, a Syrophoenician by race. She begged him that he would cast the demon out of her daughter. But Jesus said to her, "Let the children be filled first, for it is not appropriate to take the children's bread and throw it to the dogs." But she answered him, "Yes, Lord. Yet even the dogs under the table eat the children's crumbs." He said to her, "For this saying, go your way. The demon has gone out of your daughter." She went away to her house, and found the child having been laid on the bed, with the demon gone out..

As Nineham pointed out,[39] Jesus' use of the word *dog*, a supreme insult to this day in the Middle East, leaves no uncertainty as regards the distinction between Jew and

---

[37] Craveri, *The Life of Jesus*: p62
     Guignebert, *Jesus*: p317
[38] The Jesus Seminar, despite making the point the historical evidence (see Galatians 2:7-8) that Peter, Jesus' chief apostle, did not accept Gentiles into the movement, nevertheless believed this passage to be unauthentic because it was "not characteristic of Jesus"! Thus these modern scholars claim to understand Jesus better than his chief apostle who knew his teachings when he was alive!
[39] Nineham, *Saint Mark*: p200

Gentile in the eye of Jesus. It did not change the order of salvation, where Jews came first, as Jesus understood it. Jesus' actions and his words in this particular case show that this extension of his miraculous powers was to be an exception rather than the norm.[40]

Another point worth noting is that *there is no recorded preaching or teaching of Jesus to the Gentiles.* It is most unlikely that the gospels would have missed out on narrating Jesus' preaching to the Gentiles had it actually occurred or had it actually been circulated in the early tradition.[41] As was pointed out in chapter 12, all our sources tell us that Jesus confined his travels to purely Jewish areas. We have no evidence that he knew about nor cared for Gentile culture.[42]

There is, however, a supposed instruction of Jesus to his disciples that seems to have negated all we have just said:

> Matthew 28:18-19
> Jesus came to them and spoke to them, saying, "All authority has been given to me in heaven and on earth. *Therefore go, and make disciples of all nations,* baptizing them in the name of the Father and of the Son and of the Holy Spirit, teaching them to observe all things that I commanded you. Behold, I am with you always, even to the end of the age." Amen.

There are, however, many difficulties involved in accepting the above verse as an authentic saying of Jesus.[43] In the first place, it openly contradicts all the earlier verses we have quoted. In the second place the setting for this instruction was on a mountain in Galilee *after* the resurrection of Jesus. As we will see in chapter 15, the resurrection appearances of Jesus as depicted in the gospels are unhistorical. The scholars of the Jesus Seminar were absolutely correct in their conclusion on this passage:

> The commission in Matthew is expressed in Matthew's language and reflects the evangelist's idea of the world mission of the church. Jesus probably had no idea of launching a world mission and certainly was not an institution builder. The three parts of the commission – make disciples, baptize, and teach - constitute the program adopted by the infant movement, but do not reflect directions from Jesus.[44]

Perhaps the most compelling reason for the rejection of the above passage as historical lies in the attitude of Jesus' disciples after his death (and supposed resurrection appearances). We note that after the death of Jesus the disciples remained profoundly Jewish, for they continued to use the temple as their place of worship:

---

[40] Guignebert, *Jesus*: p317
      Nineham, *Saint Mark*: p200
[41] Nineham, *Saint Mark*: p197
[42] Cuppitt & Armstrong, *Who was Jesus?*: p62
[43] Guignebert, *Jesus*: p317
[44] Funk, et.al., *The Five Gospels*: p270

Acts 2:46-47
Day by day, continuing steadfastly with one accord *in the temple*, and breaking bread at home, they [the disciples] took their food with gladness and singleness of heart, praising God, and having favor with all the people

Acts 3:1
Peter and John were going up *into the temple* at the hour of prayer, the ninth hour.

In chapter 10 of the Acts of the Apostles we are told that Peter, the supposed leader of the disciples, needed a vision (Acts 10:9-23) before he can be convinced that a Gentile is not unclean (Acts 10:28). And amazingly the other disciples, who Matthew 28:18-19 told us were with Jesus on that mountain in Galilee, and heard Jesus' injunction, did not condone Peter's actions:

Acts 11:1-3
Now the apostles and the brothers who were in Judea heard that the Gentiles had also received the word of God. When Peter had come up to Jerusalem, those who were of the circumcision contended with [i.e. *criticized*] him, saying, "You went in to uncircumcised men, and ate with them!"

And in Paul's (authentic) epistle to the Galatians, we are told of an incident concerning Peter that clinches our case on the falsity of the passage in Matthew 28:18-19. It involves Peter not daring to eat with the Gentiles when he was warned by James' followers:

Galatians 2:11-12
But when Peter came to Antioch, I resisted him to his face, because he stood condemned. For before some people came from James, he ate with the Gentiles. But when they came, he drew back and separated himself, fearing those who were of the circumcision.

Had Jesus left any instructions to the disciples about preaching to the Gentiles, Peter would not have been so uncertain in his actions. As we can see from Acts 11:1-2 above, the other disciples of Jesus too disapproved of Peter mixing with the Gentiles. It was the *self-proclaimed* apostle Paul, who had never met the human Jesus, who preached the good news to the Gentiles. As Guignebert reasons:

We must ask ourselves whether the companion of Jesus would have dared to contravene his express command and repudiate his example by maintaining this attitude of inveterate hostility to the non-Judaizing Gentiles. On the other hand, if he had expressed any wish on the subject, surely the liberals would have triumphantly appealed to his example and if it had been in their power would have confounded the recalcitrant by quoting his commands.[45]

In other words, the early debate between Paul and Peter would not have occurred had Jesus given clear cut instructions on proselytizing to the Gentiles. The fact that the debate occurred, and heatedly, showed that Jesus never mentioned the Gentiles in his

---

[45]   Guignebert, *Jesus*: p318

preaching. It never occurred to him he had to, the Gentiles did not figure in his understanding of the plan of redemption. He never meant his preaching to go outside of Jews and Judaism.

Jesus never intended to abrogate the Law of Moses, as Christians doubtless believe he did. This is obvious from the passages below:

> Matthew 5:17-20
> "Don't think that I came to destroy the law or the prophets. I didn't come to destroy, but to fulfill. For most certainly, I tell you, until heaven and earth pass away, not even one smallest letter or one tiny pen stroke shall in any way pass away from the law, until all things are accomplished. Whoever, therefore, shall break one of these least commandments, and teach others to do so, shall be called least in the Kingdom of Heaven; but whoever shall do and teach them shall be called great in the Kingdom of Heaven. For I tell you that unless your righteousness exceeds that of the scribes and Pharisees, there is no way you will enter into the Kingdom of Heaven."

> Luke 16:17
> But it is easier for heaven and earth to pass away, than for one tiny stroke of a pen in the law to fall.

The fact that Jesus' immediate disciples continued to practice Judaism (going to the temple to worship God, refusing to eat Gentile food etc) after Jesus' death (Acts 2:46, 3:1) proves that at the very least the essence of the above passage is authentic. Their strict observance of the Jewish Law showed that Jesus, in his teachings, never meant to abolish it.[46]

The considerations above show that Jesus was not a universalist.

THE DIVINITY AND THE MESSIAHSHIP OF JESUS

Most Christians, with the Jehovah's Witnesses being one of the few notable exceptions, believe that Jesus was and is in some way divine. In other words, Jesus is, in some mysterious way, actually God incarnate. The idea of the Trinity, the three persons in one Godhead, was invented by the Christian tradition to accommodate the divinity of Jesus.[47] In this section our main concern is what Jesus claimed about himself. Did the historical Jesus believe himself to be the messiah? If he did, did he consider being a messiah the equivalent of being divine? Did he ever teach that he was divine?

---

[46]   Guignebert, *Jesus*: p302

[47]   A good recent book on how Jesus came to be defined as God in the 4th century CE is *When Jesus Became God* (1999) by R.E. Rubenstein

JESUS' DENIAL OF DIVINITY

We find that even in the Gospel of John, the one with the most tendency to show Jesus as a superhuman being,[48] no clear-cut statement is put into Jesus' mouth regarding his own divinity. For example when the Jews accused him of making himself equal to God, Jesus' reply showed that he did not consider himself to be so:[49]

> John 5:18-19
> For this cause therefore the Jews sought all the more to kill him, because he not only broke the Sabbath, but also called God his own Father, making himself equal with God. Jesus therefore answered them, "Most certainly, I tell you, the Son can do nothing of himself, but what he sees the Father doing ..."

In another example from John, Jesus' rebuttal to the Jews who claimed that he made himself God showed that he (or at least the author of the gospel) did not consider himself divine:

> John 10:33-36
> The Jews answered him, "We don't stone you for a good work, but for blasphemy: because you, being a man, make yourself God." Jesus answered them, "Isn't it written in your law, 'I said, you are gods?' If he called them gods, to whom the word of God came (and the Scripture can't be broken), do you say of him whom the Father sanctified and sent into the world, 'You blaspheme,' because I said, 'I am the Son of God?'"

In this same gospel too, Jesus is shown to have admitted that he was not equal to God:

> John 14:28, 31
> "You heard how I told you, 'I go away, and I come to you.' If you loved me, you would have rejoiced, because I said 'I am going to my Father;' *for the Father is greater than I....* But that the world may know that I love the Father, and *as the Father commanded me, even so I do.*"

Leaving John aside, in the synoptics and the Acts we find many passages that expressly exclude the idea that Jesus was divine and equal to God. In Peter's sermon after the ascension of Jesus, the miracle of God was said to have been achieved not by the power of Jesus himself but by God working through him:[50]

> Acts 2:22 (RSV)
> "Men of Israel, hear these words: Jesus of Nazareth, a man attested to you by God with mighty works and wonders and signs which *God did through him* in your midst, as you yourselves know."

There is even a passage in Mark where Jesus explicitly took precautions to avoid people calling him an equal to God:

---

[48]   We will consider the "I am" sayings attributed to Jesus by John later in this chapter.
[49]   Renan, *The Life of Jesus*: p132
[50]   Craveri, *The Life of Jesus*: p312

Mark 10:17-18

As he was going out into the way, one ran to him, knelt before him, and asked him, "Good Teacher, what shall I do that I may inherit eternal life?" Jesus said to him, *"Why do you call me good? No one is good except one-God."*

Furthermore, we find that Jesus does not claim God's omnipotence. For example he admitted that he did not know exactly when the kingdom will come:

Mark 13:32

"But of that day or that hour no one knows, not even the angels in heaven, *nor the Son*, but only the Father...."

When we consider the above examples, it is important to keep in mind the criterion of dissimilarity. Christian tradition was evolving towards making Jesus more and more superhuman or divine. That these passages – which bucked this trend - survived to make it into the gospels means that they must have been established very early in the Christian tradition. This consideration provides a compelling case that the historical Jesus never considered himself God, or in any way divine.

Apologists have argued that since Jesus claimed the power to forgive sins - which is something only God can do - he must have considered himself God.[51] The episode most often cited to prove this claim is the one on the healing of the paralytic:

Mark 2:3-7

[P]eople came, carrying a paralytic to him. When they could not come near to him for the crowd, they removed the roof where he was. When they had broken it up, they let down the mat that the paralytic was lying on. Jesus, seeing their faith, said to the paralytic, "Son, your sins are forgiven you." But there were some of the scribes sitting there, and *reasoning in their hearts*, "Why does this man speak blasphemies like that? Who can forgive sins but God alone?"

This power to forgive sins, according to the theologians, amounts to a declaration of his divine nature. Marcello Craveri in his *Life of Jesus* points out why such a conclusion is wrong:

First of all, the statement "your sins are forgiven" is (since a disease was considered a divine punishment that could be cancelled by repentance or prayer) the equivalent of "God has pardoned you." This was the formula ordinarily used by priests in such circumstances, speaking as interpreters of God. Hence, it means, not that Jesus had arrogated supernatural power to himself, but only that he had claimed priestly power. Even in the Old Testament there are instances of priests and prophets who made the same statement. Jesus did not say: "I forgive your sins", but he did say in effect: "Your sins are forgiven (and I will stand as warranty for it)" The outrage of the scribes arose only from this pretension of Jesus to a priestly authority that they refused to recognize in him.[52]

---

51   McDowell, *Evidence That Demands a Verdict*: p98
52   Craveri, *The Life of Jesus*: p110-111

It should also be pointed out that the above passage in Mark, as it stands, cannot be fully authentic as it contains artificial elements. Note that the teachers of the law did not utter their resentment but only thought of it ("and reasoning in their hearts"). Now, how is anyone else to know what was on their minds? How was Mark able to formulate *their* (note the plural) thoughts so precisely? As Nineham pointed out, the above passage is just a representation of early Jewish reactions to the Christians' claim that they could forgive sins in the name of Jesus.[53]

"SON OF GOD"

Another argument often used by Christian apologists to establish the divinity of Jesus is to claim that Jesus sees and refers to himself as the "Son of God."[54] We have taken a look at this briefly in chapter 11, it is now time to analyze it in more detail. The term "Son of God" in the Jewish tradition, that is the culture of Jesus, his followers and his audience, did not mean a divine figure. From the occurrence of the term in the Hebrew Bible, the *Tanakh*, we can gather that it can be applied to kings, angels, righteous men and even Israelites in general (to separate them as a chosen race from the rest of the world). Given below are some of the passages:

Reference to a king
II Samuel 7:14
[God speaking to Nathan about David]
"I will be his father, and he shall be my son. "

Psalms 2:7
I will tell of the decree. Yahweh said to me [i.e. David], "You are my son. Today I have become your father."

References to angels
Genesis 6:2
God's sons saw that men's daughters were beautiful, and they took for themselves wives of all that they chose.

Job 1:6
Now it happened on the day when the God's sons came to present themselves before Yahweh, that Satan also came among them.

References to Israelites
Psalm 82:6-7
I said, "You are gods, all of you are sons of the Most High. Nevertheless you shall die like men, and fall like one of the rulers."

Isaiah 45:11
Thus says Yahweh, the Holy One of Israel, and his Maker: "You ask me about the things that are to come, concerning my sons, and you command me concerning the work of my hands!

---

53 Nineham, *Saint Mark*: p91
54 McDowell, *Evidence That Demands a Verdict*: p100-101

Therefore, the term "Son [or sons] of God" during the time of Jesus meant to the Jews someone who had a closer moral and spiritual connection with God than do ordinary men. It was understood by the contemporaneous Jewish culture to be an honorary title. There was no hint of any connection of that title with the divinity of the holder.[55]

We are further confronted with the fact that throughout the synoptic gospels Jesus was made to refer to himself in that term *only twice*. Given below are the passages:

> Mark 13:32
> "But of that day or that hour no one knows, not even the angels in heaven, nor the Son, but only the Father."

> Matthew 11:27 (Luke 10:22)
> "All things have been delivered to me by my Father. No one knows the Son, except the Father; neither does anyone know the Father, except the Son, and he to whom the Son desires to reveal him."

The very fact that the passages in which Jesus refers to himself as the Son of God appear only twice in the synoptics is enough to make us suspicious of the authenticity of the above passages. Furthermore, the two passages actually contradict one another. The passage in Mark shows Jesus admitting that he did not know everything the Father knows. The one in Matthew seems to imply the very opposite!

Indeed, the passage in Matthew does not sound like the Jesus of the synoptics, but the Jesus of the fourth gospel! The language is typically Johanine, compare with these verses below:

> John 3:35
> "The Father loves the Son, and has given all things into his hand."

> John 7:29
> "I know him, because I am from him, and he sent me."

The whole theme fits that of a post-Easter Jesus – the risen Christ as a conduit of knowledge from God and through him to his disciples. Note that the first part of Matthew 11:27 ("All things have been delivered to me by my Father.") is almost exactly the same form as that spoken by the risen Jesus in Matthew 28:18 ("All authority has been given to me in heaven and on earth.")[56]

As Guignebert pointed out, the passage in Matthew, which forms part of the "Prayer of Thanksgiving" (Matthew 11:25-30) has such a rhythmic form that it very probably was part of an early Christian liturgy which was incorporated by Matthew into his gospel.[57] Furthermore, many of the verses of the prayer seem to be taken

---

[55]   Cuppitt & Armstrong, *Who Was Jesus?*: p60
       Guignebert, *Jesus*: p260-261

[56]   Funk, et. al., *The Five Gospels*: p182
       Lüdemann, *Jesus After 2000 Years*: p174-175, 330-331

[57]   Guignebert, *Jesus*: p264

from the apocryphal book of Sirach.[58]   The whole prayer is very likely an early Christian liturgical composition.

To summarize, the post-Easter theme and the liturgical form of the passage provide conclusive evidence that the passage in Matthew 11:27 is not an authentic utterance of the historical Jesus.

Evangelicals refer to Matthew 11:27 as the "Johanine Thunderbolt." This verse supposedly shows that the high Christology of John, which elevates Jesus to divine or near divine status, can also be found in the synoptics.[59] Yet if we take Matthew 11:27[60] and consider it by itself (apart from the strong evidence for its lack of authenticity), it still would not prove what they want it to. Without a forced reading (i.e. without any theological preconception), the verse does not show Jesus claiming to be God. All it tells us is that Jesus considered himself to have a special relationship with God.[61]

There are two more passages to look at. These passages involve statements made to Jesus that he was the Son of God. In the first passage Jesus was replying to an interrogation by the Sanhedrin:

Mark 14:61
But he stayed quiet, and answered nothing. Again the high priest asked him, "Are you the Christ, the Son of the Blessed?" Jesus said, "I am"

The very setting of the passage, the night time trial of Jesus by the Sanhedrin, is enough to make us doubt the reliability of the passage.[62] Furthermore, the *automatic connection* the high priest was supposed to have made between the messiahship and being *the* Son of God - that the Son of God is equivalent in meaning to the messiah - is something that we have shown above to be mistaken. To the Jews of Jesus' time, the Messiah may be *a* son of God, but a son of God can mean anyone with the special relationship with God. In other words, while "a son of God" can mean the messiah it does not mean so exclusively. The high priest was shown to have used the term as though they are completely interchangeable in meaning; in the way the early Christians used it. This cannot be historical.[63] We can therefore confidently reject the passage in Mark 14:61 as an early Christian invention, not an authentic saying of Jesus.

The second passage is found in Matthew's version of Peter's confession at Caesarea Philippi:

Matthew 16:16
Simon Peter answered, "You are the Christ, the son of the living God"

---

58 Sirach 51:1; 51:23; 24:19; 6:24; 6:28; 6:29
59 Bird & Crossley, *How Did Christianity Begin?*: p30-31
60 Note the Luke 10:22 does not give independent attestation to the saying since both Matthew 11:27 and Luke 10:22 are taken from Q.
61 Bird & Crossley, *How Did Christianity Begin?*: p15, 35-36, 127-128
62 See chapter 14 for a thorough discussion on why there are compelling reasons to reject the historicity of the accounts of the nighttime trial of Jesus by the Sanhedrin.
63 Guignebert, *Jesus*: p262

Now we know from chapter 9 that Matthew had two principle sources, the Gospel of Mark and a collection of Jesus sayings we call Q. Matthew (16:13-20) have followed Mark (8:27-30) pretty closely in this episode. We do not find this reference to Jesus being the Son of God in the similar passage in Mark:

> Mark 8:29
> Peter answered, "You are the Christ."

There was no connection made to his divine sonship. The question naturally arises whether Matthew made use of an external reliable source to fill in the additional words from Peter. The answer is that this is most unlikely. For, as we have mentioned above, Matthew had followed Mark closely in accounting the whole episode. Had Matthew had additional information one would expect the information to come to Matthew in such a way that may help him expand on the whole story. Yet Matthew's addition is only on that reply of Peter's to Jesus' query: "Who do you say I am?" and on Jesus' reply to that. It looks more like a deliberate and unauthentic addition to the Markan passage than a rendition of further historical information. So this second passage, like the first, is unhistorical.[64]

As we have seen in chapter 11, the term "son of God" only had the meaning of being an actual divine person who is fathered by a god in the pagan milieu. Great historical figures such as Alexander, Augustus, Romulus, Hercules, Plato and Pythagoras were believed to have been fathered by gods.[65] It is extremely unlikely that Jesus or any of his original disciples would have understood the phrase in such a term.

It is now time to summarize our findings on the phrase "Son of God" and Jesus' connection with it. We found out that in the Hebrew Bible, in the culture Jesus was living in, that the phrase is an honorary one bestowed on people who were believed to have a special relationship with God. The term in no way confers any divine status on the person. Furthermore, we found out that Jesus never unequivocally described himself with such a term. The two passages where he seemed to have accepted that designation are unhistorical. Only in the pagan environment do we find the meaning that the early (Gentile) Christians attached to the term. In short, the earliest sources do not support the contention that Jesus, or his original disciples, believed that he was a divine being with no earthly biological father.

"SON OF MAN"

Another title of Jesus, and one which he did use frequently when referring to himself, is the mysterious sounding "Son of Man". This expression occurs about eighty times in the gospels. Outside the gospels it occurs only once, in the Acts of the Apostles where Stephen, who was about to be martyred, used that phrase:

---

[64] Guignebert, *Jesus*: p265
[65] Lüdemann, *Virgin Birth?*: p72-73

Acts 7:56
"Behold, I see the heavens opened, and the Son of Man standing at the
right hand of God!"

In the Greek of the gospels, the phrase "son of man" (*ho huios tou anthropou*), sounds
unintelligible and reminds one of the secret codes used by the secret societies or
mystery religions of the Greco-Roman world. Christian theologians had traditionally
believed the phrase to be equivalent to their understanding of the term "Son of God"
and from that to mean the Christ.[66]

Before we figure out how Jesus used the phrase, we should note that there are
quite a few sayings attributed to Jesus where we know for certain that the phrase was
placed on the lips of Jesus by the evangelists. We have some examples where both
Matthew and Luke changed an original "I" in Mark to "son of man". Let us look at
one example in which Matthew did the change:

> Matthew 16:13 (RSV)
> "Who do men say that the *son of man* is?"

> Mark 8:27
> "Who do men say that *I* am?"

> Luke 9:18
> "Who do the multitudes say that *I* am?"

We have shown earlier that Luke and Matthew copied from Mark. Here Luke has
kept the original Markan form while Matthew has changed the "I" to the "son of
man". Another example is Matthew 16:28 where the evangelist again changed the "I"
in Mark 9:1 to "the son of Man". Luke, as in the earlier example, kept the original
Markan wording (Luke 9:27).

The third gospel is also not free from such editorial changes. In some passages
from Q, Luke changed the original "I" (preserved in Matthew) to "son of man":

> Luke 12:8
> "I tell you, everyone who confesses me before men, him will the *Son of
> Man* also confess before the angels of God"

> Matthew 10:32
> Everyone therefore who confesses me before men, him *I* will also
> confess before my Father who is in heaven.

Another example of such an editorial change is Luke 6:22-23 / Matthew 5:11-12.[67]

The above examples show that the evangelists were not averse to inserting the
phrase wherever they saw fit. There are also passages where the phrase appears
within contexts of dubious historicity. For example in the story of the Transfiguration
in Mark and Matthew, Jesus was supposed to have used that phrase:

---

[66]   Craveri, *The Life of Jesus*: p111
[67]   Guignebert, *Jesus*: p274-275

Mark 9:9 (Matthew 17:9)
As they were coming down from the mountain, he commanded them
that they should tell no one what things they had seen, until after the
Son of Man had risen from the dead.

The story of the Transfiguration, as we have seen in chapter 12, is in itself historically
suspect. Our suspicion is further confirmed when we see the above passage within
the context of him predicting his betrayal and death. We see this prediction of his
death and the phrase Son of Man coupled together in several other passages (Mark
14:21 / Matthew 26:24; Mark 14:41 / Matthew 26:45; Mark 9:11-13 / Matthew
17:10-13; Mark 10:45 / Matthew 20:28). We will show later in this chapter that his
death was not a part of the teaching of the historical Jesus; being actually a Pauline
amendment to it.[68] We will also see in the next chapter that the betrayal by Judas is
very likely unhistorical. Utterances that betray a theology foreign to the historical
Jesus and to events that are unhistorical could not have originated from the historical
Jesus.[69]

An examination of the sayings of Jesus that are most probably authentic, shows
that when the phrase was used by him, it often means little more than "I" or "man".
The original phrase in Hebrew (*ben adam* – literally son of Adam) or Aramaic (*bar
nasha*) is a poetic expression that means literally "a man born of another man" or,
simply, "man".[70] The Jewish historian Geza Vermes (b.1924) pointed out that in
contemporaneous vernacular Palestinian Aramaic, the term *bar nasha* means "a man",
"the man" or an indefinite "someone". When used by Jesus, the term "son of man" is
a circumlocution which simply means "I" or "this fellow".[71] This roundabout way of
saying "I" or "man" is paralleled, as an example, in the Irish expression "mother's
son" (e.g. "every mother's son of them").[72] This is also what we see in the editorial
changes by Luke and Matthew above, they used "I" and "son of man"
interchangeably when placing this phrase on the lips of Jesus. This tells us that, at
least in those specific cases, the evangelists seem to share the view that sometimes "I"
is all that the term "son of man" means.

Now let us look at some sayings with this phrase which probably did come from
Jesus:

Matthew 8:20 (Luke 9:58)
Jesus said to him, "The foxes have holes, and the birds of the sky have nests, but
the Son of Man has nowhere to lay his head."

The above passage has no meaning if the "Son of Man" is to mean God or the
messiah. How could Jesus be asserting his divinity or his messiahship but at the same

---

[68] The vicarious death of Jesus played a major role in Paul's theology as we can see from
Galatians 1:4; 2:20; Romans 15:3 and Philippians 2:7-8.

[69] Guignebert, *Jesus*: p276

[70] Craveri, *The Life of Jesus*: p111
Guignebert, *Jesus*: p270

[71] Vermes, *The Changing Face of Jesus*: p39, 176
Vermes, *The Authentic Gospel of Jesus*: p234-235

[72] Nineham, *Saint Mark*: p93

time say he has nowhere to lay his head? Jesus was merely expressing the truism that nature is sometimes kinder to animals than to man. It could also be interpreted to mean that whoever intends to follow Jesus must be prepared for a hard life. In either case, the term means no more than "man" or "I".[73]

Another example shows how Jesus used this term to simply mean "this fellow", to emphasize his humanity.

> Matthew 11:18-19 (Luke 7:33-35)
> "For John came neither eating nor drinking, and they say, 'He has a demon.' The Son of Man came eating and drinking, and they say, 'Behold, a gluttonous man and a drunkard, a friend of tax collectors and sinners!' But wisdom is justified by her children. "

Here the only possible interpretation of the passage is that Jesus was saying that the Baptist lived as an ascetic and people condemned him as being possessed. And now he, as a man who eats and drinks like everybody else is called a glutton and a wine-bibber. In other words, it was an unassuming way of referring to himself.[74]

Indeed, we find that such a meaning is the one most commonly found in the Old Testament. In Ezekiel, for instance, this term was employed 94 times. The term was used there to mean either "man", or in reference to the prophet, *in contrast with God*.[75] In other cases it is used to refer to human beings as an insignificant creation of God:[76]

> Job 25:6
> "How much less man, who is a worm, *the son of man, who is a worm!*"

> Psalm 8:4
> What is man, that you think of him? *What is the son of man, that you care for him?*

We will now look into some cases where the phrase seems, at first glance, to mean more than simply "man" or "this fellow". The first is the episode of the healing of the paralytic, which we had discussed a little earlier. Here Jesus was supposed to have uttered thus:

> Mark 2:10 (Matthew 9:6; Luke 5:24)
> "But that you may know that the Son of Man has authority on earth to forgive sins"

As we have noted above, Jesus in this episode did not say "I forgive you your sins" but "Your sins are forgiven." The difference is vital, for in the actual statement it implies merely that Jesus was giving the paralytic a pledge, like priests do, that God

---

[73]   Guignebert, *Jesus*: p277
       Sanders, *The Historical Figure of Jesus*: p246
       Vermes, *The Authentic Gospel of Jesus*: p242
[74]   Guignebert, *Jesus*: p277
       Vermes, *The Authentic Gospel of Jesus*: p243
[75]   Akenson, *Saint Saul*: p45
       Craveri, *The Life of Jesus*: p111
[76]   Funk et. al., *The Five Gospels*: p76

will forgive his sins. The statement in Mark 2:10 is simply an assertion that a man that is close to God can guarantee forgiveness of sins. In no way is it a proclamation of special status, either messianic or divine.[77]

The second instance is the statement which seems to imply that Jesus has authority over the Sabbath:

> Mark 2:28 (Matthew 12:8; Luke 6:5)
> "Therefore the Son of Man is lord even of the Sabbath."

But this in no way conveys special status for Jesus; this is supported by the statement he made just before the above:

> Mark 2:27
> "The Sabbath was made for man, not man for the Sabbath."

What is meant here is simply that the dominion given by God to humankind over all things extends also to the Sabbath. The natural follow-up for this would be "so man is master also of the Sabbath" which is precisely what Mark 2:28 means. The "Son of Man" here means no more than "man".[78]

The third instance is one which shows that by the time the traditional material reached the evangelists the original meaning of "Son of Man" was no longer clearly understood by them.

> Matthew 12:32 (Luke 12:10)
> "Whoever speaks a word against the Son of Man, it will be forgiven him; but whoever speaks against the Holy Spirit, it will not be forgiven him, neither in this age, nor in that which is to come."

As it stands above, this statement of Jesus sounds slightly absurd. It's like saying, insult the messiah (or God) if you like but insult the Holy Spirit and you're in trouble! The original form of the saying is found in Mark where the actual meaning is clear and unambiguous:[79]

> Mark 3:28 (RSV)
> "Truly, I say to you, all sins will be forgiven the sons of men, and whatever blasphemies they utter; but whoever blasphemes against the Holy Spirit never has forgiveness, but is guilty of an eternal sin"

---

[77]   Guignebert, *Jesus*: p278
       Vermes, *The Authentic Gospel of Jesus*: p237
[78]   Funk et. al., *The Five Gospels*: p 49
       Guignebert, *Jesus*: p278
       Vermes, *The Authentic Gospel of Jesus*: p238
[79]   Guignebert, *Jesus*: p277

The most problematic interpretation of the use of the phrase is in an apocalyptic[80] setting which speaks of the "coming" of one "son of man". There are quite a few such sayings attributed to Jesus. Let us look at one:

> Mark 13:24-27
> "But in those days, after that oppression, the sun will be darkened, the moon will not give its light, the stars will be falling from the sky, and the powers that are in the heavens will be shaken. Then they will see *the Son of Man coming in clouds with great power and glory*. Then he will send out his angels, and will gather together his chosen ones from the four winds, from the ends of the earth to the ends of the sky."

Such sayings can be found in disparate sources. We find it in Q (Luke 17:24-30 / Matthew 24:27, 37-39), in Matthew's special source, normally referred to as "M" (Matthew 13:40-43) and in Luke's special source "L" (Luke 21:34-36).[81] This multiple attestation suggests that such sayings are probably authentic.

Before deciding what such saying means, it is important to point out that its origin is from the book of Daniel. Note the similar images used between Mark 13:24-27 and Daniel 7:13-14:

> Daniel 7:13-14
> I saw in the night visions, and behold, *there came with the clouds of the sky one like a son of man*, and he came even to the ancient of days, and they brought him near before him. There was given him dominion, and glory, and a kingdom, that all the peoples, nations, and languages should serve him: his dominion is an everlasting dominion, which shall not pass away, and his kingdom that which shall not be destroyed.

It is quite obvious that the saying in Mark, whether actually spoken by Jesus or not, was influenced by these verses in Daniel. So it is important for us to study this a little further. The translation above from the World English Bible is quite accurate, for the original Aramaic has no definite article in front of the phrase "son of man". Note also it talks of one *like* a son of man. The Jewish Publication Society's (JPS) version reads "one like a human being". This actually gives the clearest meaning of the verse, for it talks about one who *resembles* a human being not necessarily an actual man.

In chapter 7 of the book of Daniel four animals were used – lion, bear, leopard and a ten horned beast – to represent the empires of Babylon, Media, Persian and Greece. (Daniel 7:1-8) The climax is when God, pictured as "one who was ancient of days" overpowers the fourth beast and takes away the dominion of the other three animals. (Daniel 7:9-12). The verses quoted above follow this. Within this context it is quite obvious that the "one like a son of man" is used in contrast to the four animals. Since the four ferocious animals mean the four gentile empires who wreak havoc on the world, most scholars take this "one like a son of man" to be the

---

[80] I am using the term "apocalyptic" to embrace what scholars normally refer to more exactly as "apocalyptic eschatology" – which is the idea that history as we know it will end with a direct divine intervention in the world.

[81] Ehrman, *Jesus*: p129-130

"humane" alternative and to be symbolic of the Jewish people who will take over dominion of the world from them. [82]

If such is the case, and it is the most probable interpretation of that passage, then the verse in Daniel does *not* allude to a coming messiah who will sit in judgment of the world. However, we do know by the end of the first century CE, the interpretation of this Danielic vision has evolved into one which sees "the one like a son of man" as the messiah. In I Enoch - which reached its final form in the latter half of the first century CE – the son of man is one who will sit on the "throne of glory" to judge the whole world. 4 Ezra (also around end of the first century CE) portrays the son of man as one who "flew with the clouds of heaven" who spews fire from his mouth destroying his enemies. The famous Jewish Rabbi Akiba (d. c 135 CE) also recognized the son of man as the messiah. However, between the time Daniel was written (167 BCE) and the fall of Jerusalem (70 CE) we have no independent attestation of the use of the phrase "son of man" in this manner. [83]

Now Jesus lived right smack dab in the middle of this evolution. Was Jesus one of the first to reinterpret Daniel as one that speaks of a coming messiah who will overturn the current order and judge the world? In other words, did Jesus say those things about the son of man in an apocalyptic context? Some scholars seem to think that he did, [84] many others do not. [85]

Fortunately for our purposes we do not need to discuss this issue here. As scholars such as Bart Ehrman and E.P. Samders have pointed out: in those "son of man" saying which has an apocalyptic bent, *Jesus does not seem to be referring to himself.* If one looks at the passage above (Mark 13:24-27), without any preconception, the son of man is spoken of in the *third person* and *the third person pronoun* is used to describe what he will do (i.e. send out his angels, gather his chosen people etc.). Let us look at another example:

Mark 8:38
For whoever will be ashamed of me and of my words in this adulterous and sinful generation, the Son of Man also will be ashamed of him, when he comes in the glory of his Father with the holy angels."

---

[82]   Akenson, *Saint Saul*: p45-46
       Ehrman, *Jesus*: p146-147
       Sanders, *The Historical Figure of Jesus*: p246
       Vermes, *The Changing Faces of Jesus*: p39
[83]   Ehrman, *Jesus*: p 147
       Vermes, *The Changing Faces of Jesus*: p39-40
[84]   Scholars who think the "son of man" sayings in an apocalyptic setting are authentic utterances of Jesus include Bart Ehrman (see *Jesus*: p146) and E.P. Sanders (see *The Historical Figure of Jesus*: p246-247).
[85]   The 70 plus scholars of the Jesus Seminar do not think the use of the phrase "son of man" in an apocalyptic setting is authentic to Jesus. (see Funk et. al., *The Five Gospels*: p75-82). Other scholars who are not part of this group who also think these sayings unauthentic include Gerd Lüdemann (*Jesus After 2000 Years*: p91, 343-345) and Geza Vermes (*The Authentic Gospel of Jesus*: p251-260)

Again, there is no indication that Jesus was talking about himself as the apocalyptic son of man. He seems to be saying here "if you don't listen to me, oh boy, are you in trouble when the son of man comes!" – much in the same way a mother would warn her kids "you won't listen to me, wait till your father gets home!"[86]

Thus, even if the apocalyptic sayings are authentically Jesus', he never referred to himself as *the* son of man in those sayings. If these apocalyptic sayings are not authentically the words of Jesus then we are left with the passages where his use of the phrase is in line with the normal Aramaic meaning of "man" or "I".

It is therefore clear that no special meaning should be attached to the term "son of man" when it is applied to Jesus. It means, in the way Jesus used it, simply "I" or "man". Perhaps it was also intended by Jesus to be a self-deprecating reference to himself. As Ian Wilson said:

> [T]he capital letters with which it appears in modern Christian works give it precisely the opposite inference to that intended.[87]

Jesus, in other words, may have, meant the phrase to be a sign of his *humility* which the Christians misread as a proclamation of his *divinity*.

"THE CHRIST"

What Jesus actually claimed to be, we simply do not know. The information available to us simply tells us that the later Christian assertion that Jesus taught about his own divinity is not supported by the authentic passages in the gospels. We do not even know if Jesus believed himself to be the (Jewish) messiah. Leaving aside the Gospel of John, which historicity is suspect, the synoptics record only *one* instance where he actually claimed he was the messiah:

> Mark 9:41
> For whoever will give you a cup of water to drink in my name, because you are Christ's, most certainly I tell you, he will in no way lose his reward.

Again, the authenticity of the above passage is doubtful, for two very good reasons. The expression "Christ" without the definite article (i.e. *the* Christ) is not found anywhere in the synoptics or the Acts but is a common Pauline phrase, of which the passage below is a typical example:

> I Corinthians 3:23 (Also I Corinthians 1:12 etc)
> [A]nd you are Christ's, and Christ is God's.

The second reason is that we find a parallel verse in Matthew that does not have the term "Christ":

---

[86] Ehrman, *Jesus*: p135, 146
Sanders, *The Historical Figure of Jesus*: p246-247
[87] Wilson, *Jesus: The Evidence*: p152

Matthew 10:42
Whoever gives one of these little ones just a cup of cold water to drink in the name
of a disciple, most certainly I tell you he will in no way lose his reward."

The passage in Matthew is very probably the saying in its original form, while the
tradition Mark was drawing from for this passage already suffered Pauline
emendation.[88]

We will be discussing the interrogation of Jesus by the Sanhedrin and Pilate,
where questions regarding his messianic status were posed, in chapter 14.

THE "I AM" SAYINGS IN JOHN

We have noted earlier that the Gospel of John, the least historical of all the gospels, is
the one that comes closest to making the claim for Jesus' divinity. The most often
cited passages from John are the so-called "I am" sayings. In this gospel Jesus is
quoted to have used the absolute phrase "I am" (Greek: *ego eimi*) - without a
predicate - four times:[89]

John 8:24
"I said therefore to you that you will die in your sins; for unless you believe that *I
am*, you will die in your sins."

John 8:28
"When you have lifted up the Son of Man, then you will know that *I am*."

John 8:58
"Most certainly, I tell you, before Abraham came into existence, *I am*."

John 13:19
"From now on, I tell you before it happens, that when it happens, you may believe
that *I am*."

Before we consider whether these words were actually spoken by Jesus, we have to
ask ourselves what the statement could have meant to the *audience* of the gospel. In
the Greco-Roman world the phrase was widely used to refer to any one of the
multitude of *divine beings* or gods. Among the Jews such a designation could mean
that the person was making the claim of being Yahweh himself. This is what God
supposedly said to Moses:

Exodus 3:14
God said to Moses, "I am who I am."

---

[88]   Guignebert, *Jesus*: p281

[89]   Most translations provide the passages above with the predicate "he" which is not in the
original Greek. We have thus given the passages above as close to the original Greek as
possible.

444

The intended audience of the gospel could have understood these "I am" sayings as either Jesus was *a* divine being who was sent by God (and which has the divine spark in him) or that Jesus was Yahweh himself.[90] In view of the subordinate passages we saw above (e.g. John 5:18-19, 7:16, 14:28-31) the first possibility seems more likely.

The most obvious question with regards to these sayings is whether Jesus actually uttered them. We have strong reasons to believe that he did not and that the passages are the free composition of John.

We find that the character of Jesus as presented in the fourth gospel differs substantially from that presented in the synoptics. We have already alluded to this in chapter 9. Here we will concentrate on the difference with respect to Jesus' proclamation of his own identity.[91] In proclamations regarding himself, Jesus is presented as behaving in very different ways by the synoptics and by the fourth gospel. In the synoptics, when asked about his own person, he is never depicted as commenting on it directly. Indeed, in cases where he was called the messiah by others, he ordered his disciples not to tell anyone about it:

> Mark 8:27-30
> Jesus went out, with his disciples, into the villages of Caesarea Philippi. On the way he asked his disciples, "Who do men say that I am?" They told him, "John the Baptizer, and others say Elijah, but others: one of the prophets. "He said to them, "But who do you say that I am?" Peter answered, "You are the Christ." He commanded them that they should tell no one about him.

This is in complete contradiction to the "I am" sayings above where he is depicted as openly telling people (including the Pharisees and "the Jews") of his (divine) status.

Similarly when challenged about his authority to teach, the synoptics depict him as refusing to answer where his authority lies:

> Mark 11:27-33
> They came again to Jerusalem, and as he was walking in the temple, the chief priests, and the scribes, and the elders came to him, and they began saying to him, "By what authority do you do these things? Or who gave you this authority to do these things?" Jesus said to them, "I will ask you one question. Answer me, and I will tell you by what authority I do these things. The baptism of John - was it from heaven, or from men? Answer me." They reasoned with themselves, saying, "If we should say, 'From heaven' he will say, 'Why then did you not believe him?' If we should say, 'From men' - they feared the people, for all held John to really be a prophet. They answered Jesus, "We don't know." Jesus said to them, "Neither do I tell you by what authority I do these things."

---

[90]   Funk et.al., *The Five Gospels*: p419
       Lüdemann, *Jesus After 2000 Years*: p486
[91]   Sanders, *The Historical Figure of Jesus*: p70
       Vermes, *The Changing Face of Jesus*: p22-24

Note again here the general *reticence* of Jesus in speaking about himself and his status. In John, in the passage with the "I am" sayings, Jesus is depicted as openly telling the Pharisees his authority comes from the Father:

John 8:13-18
The Pharisees therefore said to him, "You testify about yourself. Your testimony is not valid." Jesus answered them, "Even if I testify about myself, my testimony is true, for I know where I came from, and where I am going; but you don't know where I came from, or where I am going. You judge according to the flesh. I judge no one. Even if I do judge, my judgment is true, for I am not alone, but I am with the Father who sent me. It's also written in your law that the testimony of two people is valid. I am one who testifies about myself, and the Father who sent me testifies about me."

Note that the two ways of talking about himself could not simply have been done by the same person concurrently, save perhaps for one on the verge of insanity! For if you have already openly told people (including your "enemies") about your identity, being reticent about it at another time simply does not make sense anymore. It is simply not historically believable that Jesus could have presented himself in *both* a secretive, reticent way *and* an open, proclamative way. One of these depictions has to be unhistorical.

So which is the unhistorical one? We have already given reasons earlier why John's gospel is probably the least historical of the four.[92] Here we will look at the specific reasons why the sayings given in John (including the "I am" sayings) cannot be considered historical.

The whole issue comes in the *style* of Jesus' teachings, which differs substantially between the synoptics and John. In the synoptics, Jesus is depicted as teaching in short and snappy sayings (e.g. Matthew 10:24 "A disciple is not above the teacher, nor is a slave above the master."; Mark 2:27 "The Sabbath was made for man, and not man for the Sabbath."; Luke 6:44 "Figs are not gathered from thorns, nor are grapes picked from a bramble bush.") and in parables (e.g. Matthew 20:1-15 "The Vineyard Laborers"; Mark 4:30-32 "The Mustard Seed"; Luke 10:30-35 "The Good Samaritan").

In John, these are missing and the main style of Jesus' preaching is that of long, extended, metaphorical discourses.

Studies in the transmission of oral tradition have shown that sayings and anecdotes that are most often remembered and retold are those that are short, provocative and memorable. As we have seen, this is precisely how the sayings of Jesus are preserved in the synoptics, in short pithy sayings and in rather colorful

---

[92]   We have already seen in chapter 9 that John's presentation of Jesus career is unlikely to be historical. One poignant example is the incident called the cleansing of the temple, given in all four gospels (Mark 11:12-19; Matthew 21:12-13; Luke 19:45-48; John 2:12-22). All the synoptics agree in putting this event very close to his arrest and execution. This makes historical sense, for the commotion Jesus' caused would certainly have serious repercussions. Yet John had placed this incident at the *beginning* of his career and had Jesus preaching with impunity for another three years!

parables.[93] People also tend to remember the *gist* of stories but not the detailed wording. For instance, we tell the same jokes with slightly different words each time but as long as we remember the form and the punch line the joke "works" as intended. One recent study shows that most people forget the particular wording of a statement they had heard after an interval of only *sixteen syllables* between them hearing it and getting a request to retell it. In other words, we *know* that people remember sayings and anecdotes (although not always faithfully) we also know that people *cannot* remember long discourses from memory alone.[94]

The "I am" sayings are part of the typical long winded, tedious and repetitive sermons given in John. Their *form* is not something which allows for easy oral transmission. They are not witty nor do they have any easily remembered form or structure. The sayings in John are *ramblings* which are not memorable and not *memorizable*. We can conclude that the "I am" sayings in John are not historical and were put into the mouth of Jesus by the evangelist himself.

The scholarly consensus (always excepting fundamentalist "scholars") about the non-historicity of the bulk of Johannine sayings attributed to Jesus can be seen by anyone who takes the time to review the available literature. Part of this is an almost total rejection of the "I am" sayings as historical. Some of the more recent examples include:

- Robert Funk, Roy Hoover & The Jesus Seminar[95]
  [In discussing the "I am" sayings]
  In virtually every case, the reader is being confronted with the language of the evangelist and not the language of Jesus.

- Gerd Lüdemann[96]
  The "I am" saying...with the universal claim which it expresses is unthinkable in the mouth of the historical Jesus.

- Geza Vermes[97]
  [In his discussion of the Johanine tendency to equate Jesus with God-including the "I am" sayings]
  The whole ideology reflects the dreamlike cogitation of a religious contemplative, possibly Jewish, addressing a Gentile confraternity nurtured on Hellenistic mysticism.

John E.P. Sanders, Professor of Religion at Duke University, succinctly describes the situation, with respect to the differences between John and the synoptics, thus:

It is impossible to think that Jesus spent his ministry teaching in two such completely different ways, conveying such different contents, and that there were

---

93 The long discourses in the synoptics (such as the "Sermon on the Mount" [Matthew 5-7] or "The Sermon on the Plain" [Luke 6:20-49] are artificial creations by the evangelists made by stringing together shorter sayings of Jesus. These are fundamentally different from the long discourses in John which are singular complete "sermons". [Vermes, The Changing Face of Jesus: p23] We provided a more detailed look at this in chapter 9.

94 Funk et.al., *The Five Gospels*: p27-29

95 Funk et.al., *The Five Gospels*: p419

96 Lüdemann, *Jesus After 2000 Years*: p405

97 Vermes, *The Changing Face of Jesus*: p47

simply two traditions, each going back to Jesus, one transmitting 50 per cent of what he said and another one the other 50 per cent, with almost no overlaps. Consequently for the last 150 or so years scholars have had to choose. They have almost unanimously, and I think entirely correctly, concluded that the teaching of the historical Jesus is to be sought in the synoptic gospels and that John represented an advanced theological development, in which the meditations on the person and work of Christ are presented in the first person, as if Jesus said them.[98]

The "I am" sayings attributed to Jesus by John are not historical.

CONCLUSION ON THE DIVINITY AND MESSIAHSHIP OF JESUS

In short, Jesus, as far as we can tell, never considered himself divine. The Christological titles "Son of God" means no more than a holy man of God. While "Son of Man" simply means a "man" or "this fellow". We cannot even be certain if Jesus ever considered himself the messiah in the Jewish sense. Finally, the "I Am" sayings in John are not historical utterances of Jesus.

THE TEACHINGS OF JESUS

For the rest of this chapter, we will be looking at the teachings attributed to Jesus. We will concentrate on three major themes: the atonement – the vicarious sacrifice of Jesus for the sins of man, the ethical teachings and the herald of the coming of the kingdom.

THE ATONEMENT

One of the central doctrines of Christian theology is the atonement. The basic teaching of this doctrine is that the death of Jesus on the cross was a vicarious sacrifice that brought about the reconciliation of God and man; the ties between which has been severed since the sin of Adam and Eve in the Garden of Eden. The main question here is this: did the historical Jesus actually teach such a doctrine?

As we shall see, the weight of early Christian tradition, as represented in the synoptics,[99] does not support the idea that Jesus actually taught this doctrine. By the time the gospels were written, the idea of the atonement was already entrenched, albeit in a nebulous form, in Christian theology.[100] The authors of Mark, Matthew and Luke tried their best to include some material which had Jesus supposedly knowing about his impending death and suffering (and understanding its necessity).

---

[98]   Sanders, *The Historical Figure of Jesus*: p70-71

[99]   For our considerations we will ignore the gospel of John for it is the least historical gospel and contains mainly unauthentic utterances of Jesus. See chapter 9 and the section immediately above for why John is considered the least reliable document of the four gospels.

[100]   The doctrine came from Paul, the apostle to the Gentiles. See I Corinthians 15:3-5, Romans 3:25-25, 5:6-14, 6:1-5.

According to the synoptics, Jesus told his disciples three times that he will suffer and die:

> Mark 8:31-32
> He began to teach them that the Son of Man must suffer many things, and be rejected by the elders, the chief priests, and the scribes, and be killed, and after three days rise again. He spoke to them openly....

> Mark 9:31-32
> For he was teaching his disciples, and said to them, "The Son of Man is being handed over to the hands of men, and they will kill him; and when he is killed, on the third day he will rise again." But they didn't understand the saying, and were afraid to ask him.

> Mark 10:33-34
> "Behold, we are going up to Jerusalem. The Son of Man will be delivered to the chief priests and the scribes. They will condemn him to death, and will deliver him to the Gentiles. They will mock him, spit on him, scourge him, and kill him. On the third day he will rise again."

Both Matthew (16:21; 17:22-23; 20:17-19) and Luke (9:22; 9:44; 18:31-32) simply copied the Mark verses and had nothing new to add to them. This means that Mark is the sole source of Jesus having uttered such teachings about his death. We have many reasons to believe that these passages from Mark are unhistorical.

As Gerd Lüdemann pointed out, the character of the language of the three passages is Markan – in other words, it looks like something Mark wrote in his own words than something he got from tradition[101]. It is hard to reconcile the behavior of Jesus' disciples throughout the passion and after the resurrection if Jesus had openly said what the Markan passages alleged he did.[102] Why did the disciples flee if it was part of Jesus' mission to be arrested (Mark 14:50)? Mark's explanation that they did not understand Jesus (Mark 9:32) is weak, given the clear and unambiguous nature of Jesus' pronouncements. Mark also said that the disciples were "afraid to ask" Jesus for clarification on this teaching: why? It is inexplicable that they, who have followed their teacher throughout Galilee, would be afraid to ask for enlightenment regarding his teachings.

The three-fold repetition is another case against the historicity of the passages above. It is obviously artificial. The evangelists were very fond of making up three-fold repetitions: there were *three* temptations of Jesus in the desert (Matthew 4:1-11), *three* prayers by Jesus at Gethsemane (Mark 14:32-42) and *three* denials of Jesus by Peter (Mark 14:30;14:66-72).[103]

The predictions are just *too* accurate not to be a prophecy written after the event. Some scholars have described them (especially Mark 10:32-34) as "reading like a printed program of a passion play."[104] All the main events in the passion are clearly

---

101   Lüdemann, *Jesus After 2000 Years*: p56
102   Cadoux, *The Life of Jesus*: p147
     Nineham, *Saint Mark*: p229
103   Nineham, *Saint Mark*: p248
104   Nineham, *Saint Mark*: p278

predicted (the betrayal, the condemnation by the Sanhedrin, the handing over to Pilate, the mocking by Pilate's soldiers, the crucifixion and the resurrection). Furthermore, the prediction here is made regarding events (except the crucifixion) which we will show in the next two chapters to be unhistorical. And as the scholars of the Jesus Seminar pointed out, it is a common practice of ancient oral cultures to put their own confession of faith into the mouth of their founder.[105] The balance of evidence shows that these prophecies were invented either by Christian tradition or by Mark himself.

There is another passage in the synoptics that seems to indicate that Jesus did teach his disciples about his impending vicarious death:

> Mark 10:45 (Matthew 20:25)
> "For the Son of Man also came not to be served, but to serve, and *to give his life as a ransom for many.*"

The full context in Mark is given in Table 13.3 on the next page. In this episode, James and John tried to get Jesus to recognize them as his chief disciples. It is given in full in Mark 10:35-45 and slightly altered in Matthew 20:20-28 where it was James' and John's *mother* who tried to persuade Jesus to that effect. This episode is also found in Luke 22:24-27 (see the right hand column of Table 13.3). The story in Luke obviously came from a non-Markan source. But the similarity is such that this passage is recounting the same tale as found in Mark.[106] Based on a comparison between the depiction found in Mark and Luke, the above quoted saying of Jesus in Mark cannot be authentic for a number of reasons.[107]

Luke seems to be following a tradition which differs from Mark and is missing precisely that very passage in which the doctrine of the atonement is taught. The passage in Luke ends thus:

> Luke 22:27
> "But I am in the midst of you as one who serves."

These words are, in fact, more in harmony with the whole episode than Mark's. The Markan saying is out of the context of the whole episode. From Mark 10:42 onwards the theme of the passage was on service. The additional words of giving his life as a ransom is not in line with the theme and is really a change from one class of idea (service) to another (ransom).

Furthermore, this reference to Jesus' death as a redeeming act is found only here and *nowhere else* in Mark. This isolation is, in itself, strong evidence for its lack of authenticity. There is no evidence elsewhere in the gospels that Jesus taught of his life and death in terms of sacrifice and ransom.

---

[105] Funk, et.al. *The Five Gospels*: p94

[106] Matthew simply copied and modified Mark and should not be considered an independent witness here.

[107] Nineham, *Saint Mark*: p280-281

We can safely conclude that, in all probability, Jesus did not know about his impending death on the cross and that he did not believe his death was his main mission on earth.

Mark 10:35-45	Luke 22:24-27
35 James and John, the sons of Zebedee, came near to him, saying, "Teacher, we want you to do for us whatever we will ask." 36 He said to them, "What do you want me to do for you?" 37 They said to him, "Grant to us that we may sit, one at your right hand, and one at your left hand, in your glory." 38 But Jesus said to them, "You don't know what you are asking. Are you able to drink the cup that I drink, and to be baptized with the baptism that I am baptized with?" 39 They said to him, "We are able." Jesus said to them, "You shall indeed drink the cup that I drink, and you shall be baptized with the baptism that I am baptized with; 40 but to sit at my right hand and at my left hand is not mine to give, but for whom it has been prepared."	
41 When the ten heard it, they began to be indignant towards James and John. *42 Jesus summoned them, and said to them, "You know that they who are recognized as rulers over the nations lord it over them, and their great ones exercise authority over them. But it shall not be so among you, but whoever wants to become great among you shall be your servant. Whoever of you wants to become first among you, shall be bondservant of all. For the Son of Man also came not to be served, but to serve, and to give his life as a ransom for many."*	24 There arose also a contention among them, which of them was considered to be greatest. *25 He said to them, "The kings of the nations lord it over them, and those who have authority over them are called 'benefactors.' 26 But not so with you. But one who is the greater among you, let him become as the younger, and one who is governing, as one who serves. 27 For who is greater, one who sits at the table, or one who serves? Isn't it he who sits at the table? But I am in the midst of you as one who serves.*

Table 13.3: The Request of James and John

ETHICAL TEACHINGS

Much has been said by Christians and Christian theologians about the supposed originality and beauty of the ethical teachings of Jesus. The quotation below, by the Christian historian, Philip Schaff (1819-1893), is a typical example:

> It is universally admitted...that Christ taught the purest and sublimest of ethics, one which throws the moral precepts and maxims of the wisest men of antiquity far into the shade.[108]

There is only one problem with the statement above: *it is simply not true!* Where his ethical teachings are attractive, they are not original and where they are original, they are repugnant. Take Jesus' preaching on love and forgiveness:

> Mark 12:31
> "You shall love your neighbor as yourself.'"

> Matthew 6:14
> "For if you forgive men their trespasses, your heavenly Father will also forgive you."

> Matthew 7:12
> "Therefore whatever you desire for men to do to you, you shall also do to them; for this is the law and the prophets."

These teachings, while commendable, are not original. We find similar teachings in the Jewish cultural milieu. Hillel (b. 75 BCE), the famous Jewish preacher had already taught such a doctrine:[109]

> Babylonian Talmud Shabbat 31a
> What is hateful to you, do not do to your fellow-man: this is the whole law, the rest is commentary.

We find the same essence in the Old Testament:

> Leviticus 19:18
> You shall not take vengeance, nor bear any grudge against the children of your people; but you shall love your neighbor as yourself.

In other cultures too, we find sages already explicating similar doctrines long before Jesus. The Chinese philosopher, Confucius (551-478 BCE) has this to say in his *Analects*:

> Analects I:6
> A young man's duty is to behave well to his parents at home and to his elders abroad, to be cautious in giving promise and punctual in keeping them, to have kindly feelings towards everyone, but seek intimacy of the good.[110]

In the teaching about love and forgiveness, Jesus had no claim to originality. His teachings here did not set new ground. Even his famous dictum about loving one's enemies is not original for it has Old Testament precedents:

---

[108]   quoted in McDowell, *Evidence that Demands a Verdict*: p127
[109]   Maccoby, *Revolution of Judea*: p266
[110]   Quoted in Knight, *Humanist Anthology*: p2

Matthew 5:44
"But I tell you, love your enemies, bless those who curse you, do good to those who hate you, and pray for those who mistreat you and persecute you "

Exodus 23:4-5
If you meet your enemy's ox or his donkey going astray, you shall surely bring it back to him again. If you see the donkey of him who hates you fallen down under his burden, don't leave him, you shall surely help him with it.

Similar parallels are found in the prevalent cynic and stoic philosophies of first century CE:[111]

Epictetus (fl. circa end of first century CE)
"A rather nice part of being a cynic comes when you have to be beaten like an ass, and throughout the beating you have to love those who are beating you as though you were father or brother to them"

Diogenes (c412-323 BCE)
How shall I defend myself against an enemy? By being good and kind towards him replied Diogenes.

Seneca (c4 BCE -65 CE)
Someone gets angry with you. Challenge him with kindness in return. Enmity immediately tumbles away when one side lets it fall.

Another episode normally quoted by those who want to present Jesus as a moral innovator is found in John 8:1-11, the so-called *Pericopae Adulterae*.[112] The story in the first eleven verses of John tells of a woman who was caught in the act of committing adultery. The Pharisees reminded Jesus that according to the Law she must be stoned. Jesus' answer was:

John 8:7
"He who is without sin among you, let him throw the first stone at her."

Leaving aside any problems of authenticity,[113] even here, Jesus' teaching was not unique or original. The idea behind this saying is that since all have sinned, it is more prudent to reflect on one's own fault before hurling condemnations at each other. His contemporary, the Roman stoic philosopher Lucius Annaeus Seneca (c4BCE -65 CE), taught the same thing in his essay *On Anger*:

---

[111]   Price, *Deconstructing Jesus*: p151
[112]   Knight, *Honest to Man*: p28
[113]   This passage is absent from the earliest manuscripts. Nowhere does it appear in the Codex Vaticanus and the Codex Sinaiticus and most of the later Greek manuscripts also omit it. In some manuscripts it appears not in the gospel of John but in Luke (after Luke 21:38)! All the earliest translations of the Bible, the Syriac, the Coptic and Armenian versions are all agreed in not including the passage. The passage was unknown to Christian writers before Ambrose (340-397) and Augustine (354-430).

No man of sense will hate erring, otherwise he will hate himself. Let him reflect how many times he offends against morality, how many of his acts stand in need of pardon; then he will be angry with himself also. For no just judge pronounce one sort of judgment in his own case and a different one in the case of others. No one will be found, I say, who is able to acquit himself, and any man who calls himself innocent is thinking more of [the absence of] witnesses than [his own] conscience. How much more human to manifest toward wrong doers a kind and fatherly spirit, not hunting them down, but calling them back![114]

There were many thinkers, before and after Jesus who extolled teachings similar to Jesus'. They include, among others Lao Tzu (6th cent BCE), Mencius (4th cent BCE), Epicurus (342-270 BCE) and Marcus Aurelius (121-180 CE). However, there is actually a difference between the teachings of these humanists and those of Jesus. To them, doing good comes spontaneously to the educated because he understands that man is a social animal. But to Jesus, one must do good because the reward is great:[115]

> Luke 6:35
> "But love your enemies, and do good, and lend, expecting nothing back; and y*our reward will be great*…"

> Matthew 6:3-4
> "But when you do merciful deeds, don't let your left hand know what your right hand does, so that your merciful deeds may be in secret, then *your Father who sees in secret will reward you openly.*"

> Matthew 5:12
> "Rejoice, and be exceedingly glad, for great is your reward in heaven."

Reward and punishment are primitive ethical concepts. Just as we do not think highly of any man who refrains from committing a crime only because he is afraid of getting caught, we cannot think highly of ethical teachings which promises reward ("Mummy will give you a lollipop if you stop pestering your baby sister.") for doing good and punishment ("If you don't stop it, you'll be grounded for a week!") for doing evil. This concept, as the examples above show, is one suited for little children and morally maladjusted adults. For this reason, Jesus' ethical teachings are not as complete as the humanist thinkers.

In those teachings of Jesus that do have some claims to originality, they are not the sort one would expect to be read in church. For instance, Jesus teaches abandonment of the family:

> Mark 10:29-30 (Matthew 19:29) (RSV)
> "Jesus said, "Truly, I say to you, there is no one who has left house or brothers or sisters or mother or father or children or lands, for my sake and for the gospel, who will not receive a hundredfold now in this time, houses and brothers and sisters and mothers and children and lands, with persecutions, and in the age to come eternal life.""

---

114   Knight, *Humanist Anthology*: p12
115   Knight, *Honest to Man*: p27

Luke 14:26 (Matthew 10:37-38)
"If anyone comes to me, and doesn't hate his own father, mother, wife, children, brothers, and sisters, yes, and his own life also, he can't be my disciple."

Some of his original teachings are so downright barbaric that even fundamentalists[116] wouldn't take it literally:

Matthew 18:8-9 (Mark 9:43-47)
"If your hand or your foot causes you to stumble, cut it off, and cast it from you. It is better for you to enter into life maimed or crippled, rather than having two hands or two feet to be cast into the eternal fire. If your eye causes you to stumble, pluck it out, and cast it from you. It is better for you to enter into life with one eye, rather than having two eyes to be cast into the Gehenna of fire."

Furthermore, some of his teachings advertised as good and revolutionary are actually quite harmful. Take the oft-quoted passage below:

Luke 6:29-30
"To him who strikes you on the cheek, offer also the other; and from him who takes away your cloak, don't withhold your coat also. Give to everyone who asks you, and don't ask him who takes away your goods to give them back again."

Much praise has been showered on the above teaching, but there is something fundamentally unsound about it. What Jesus was preaching was *not* passive resistance *a la* Mahatma Gandhi or Martin Luther King. By turning the other cheek to one who had just slapped you or by giving your coat to one who had just stolen your cloak, Jesus is teaching one to *actively encourage oppression on themselves*. Charles Bradlaugh's reasoning is absolutely correct:

Surely it is better to teach: "he who courts oppression shares the crime." There is a wide distinction between passive resistance and courting further injury at the hands of the wrongdoer.[117]

It is clear that when the glasses of faith are taken off, the ethical teachings of Jesus is neither unique nor sublimely beautiful. As a teacher of ethics Jesus, contrary to the claims of overzealous historians and evangelicals, cannot be considered one of the greats. At best, he was an "also-ran".

THE COMING OF THE KINGDOM

A convergence of various strands of evidence and a reasoned analysis of the collected sayings of Jesus in the gospels show that the central theme of the teaching of the

---

[116] Recently (April 7, 2004) a man in Sherman, Texas, actually *did* take this command seriously and plucked his own eyeball out! The 21 year old man was in jail for allegedly murdering his estranged wife, his four year old son and the woman's one year old baby. (http://www.cnn.com/2004/US/Southwest/04/07/plucked.eyeball.ap/index.html, accessed on April 2004)

[117] Bradlaugh, *Humanity's Gain from Unbelief*: p60

historical Jesus was the announcement of the coming of the Kingdom of God.[118] There are two major groups of evidence: the contextual environment and the sayings of Jesus. These two groups of evidence together provide, in my opinion, a compelling case that Jesus taught what can be described as an "apocalyptic eschatology". As Dale Allison explains:

> "apocalyptic eschatology" [is] a cluster of expectations – cosmic catastrophe, resurrection of the dead, universal judgment, heavenly redeemer figures, etc. – that developed, often in association with belief in a near end.[119]

We will present the evidence for this here. Since there is a substantial group of liberal scholars who, in the attempt to metaphorically "resurrect" Jesus – to make him "relevant" to the 21st century – have eschewed this interpretation and have championed a non-apocalyptic Jesus, we will look at their objections to the evidence that we will present as well as how they made their case later on in this section.

Jesus' Apocalyptic Eschatology:
Evidence from the Contextual Environment

There are four lines of evidence here, from the general to the specific.

1. Contemporaneous and near contemporaneous literature were chock full of eschatological allusions.

I Enoch (late first century CE) speaks of the destruction of those who "led the world astray", of the appearance of the "son of man" who will sit on his throne of glory and of the passing of everything evil. 4 Ezra (around 100 CE) speaks of the "son of man" who destroys his enemies by setting them ablaze with his fiery breath. Among the Dead Sea Scrolls, documents dating between 150 BCE to 70 CE we find such works as *The War Scroll*, which speaks of a final battle between the "sons of light" and "sons of darkness", *Rule of the Congregation* which calls itself "the rule for all the congregation of Israel in the Last Days", and the self-explanatory *Messianic Apocalypse*. Other contemporaneous documents with apocalyptic themes include *Testament of Moses*, *2 Baruch* and *Apocalypse of Abraham*. Josephus also tells us that the apocalyptic book *Daniel* was very popular during this time. (Antiquities 10:11:7) [120]

Similarly we find many personalities who found ready following with their apocalyptic teaching around the time of Jesus. Josephus tells of a few such persons. In 6 CE, following the census of Quirinius, Judas the Galilean revolted, seeking – he claimed with God's help - to free the Jewish people from the yoke of Roman

---

118   Cuppitt & Armstrong, *Who was Jesus?*: p58
       Guignebert, *Jesus*: p325
119   Miller (ed), *The Apocalyptic Jesus: A Debate*: p93
120   Ehrman, *Jesus*: p 147
       Miller (ed), *The Apocalyptic Jesus: A Debate*: p22
       Sanders, *The Historical Figure of Jesus*: p184-185
       VanderKam & Flint, *The Meaning of the Dead Sea Scrolls*: p209-238

imperialism. (Antiquities 18:1:1) Around 45 CE, Theudas led a large following to the Jordan River promising to part the river just as Moses parted the Red Sea. Unfortunately, he was beheaded by the Roman governor Fadus before he got the chance to prove his prowess (Antiquities 20:5:1). Later, an unnamed Egyptian managed to convince a large group to follow him to the Mount of Olives where he claimed he would make the walls of Jerusalem fall, just like Joshua did to the walls of Jericho. Anticipating trouble, Felix (the Roman governor from 52-60 CE) ordered his men to crush the movement of the Egyptian. Although the Egyptian managed to escape, 400 of his followers were killed by Felix's soldiers. (Antiquities 20:8:6). The obvious religious overtones – claiming God's assistance (in the case of Judas the Galilean) and analogies to parting of the Red Sea and the fall of the walls of Jericho (in the case of Theudas and the Egyptian) - show that these were apocalyptic personalities. These three are just examples of the general religious expectations of that time.[121]

2.   In the New Testament we are told that Jesus was compared to personalities with an apocalyptic outlook.[122]

In Mark 6:14, King Herod thought Jesus was John the Baptist raised from the dead.

> Mark 6:14
> King Herod heard this, for his [Jesus'] name had become known, and he said, "John the Baptizer has risen from the dead, and therefore these powers are at work in him."

In Acts 5:35-39, Rabbi Gamaliel compared the Jesus movement with those of Judas the Galilean and Theudas.

> Acts 5:35-39
> He [Rabbi Gamaliel] said to them, "You men of Israel, be careful concerning these men [i.e. Peter and the apostles], what you are about to do. For before these days Theudas rose up, making himself out to be somebody; to whom a number of men, about four hundred, joined themselves: who was slain; and all, as many as obeyed him, were dispersed, and came to nothing. After this man, Judas of Galilee rose up in the days of the enrollment, and drew away some people after him. He also perished, and all, as many as obeyed him, were scattered abroad. Now I tell you, withdraw from these men, and leave them alone. For if this counsel or this work is of men, it will be overthrown. But if it is of God, you will not be able to overthrow it, and you would be found even to be fighting against God!"

3.   The idea that the present world order is going to end soon, but unexpectedly, and will be replaced by a new one inaugurated by God [or Jesus] permeates the New Testament:[123]

I Corinthians 7:29-31 (RSV) (also I Thessalonians 4:15-17)

---

[121]   Ehrman, *Jesus*: p 117-118

Miller (ed), *The Apocalyptic Jesus: A Debate*: p23

[122]   Miller (ed), *The Apocalyptic Jesus: A Debate*: p23

[123]   Miller (ed), *The Apocalyptic Jesus: A Debate*: p20-21

I mean, brothers, *the appointed time has grown very short*; from now on, let those who have wives live as though they had none, and those who mourn as though they were not mourning, and those who rejoice as though they were not rejoicing, and those who buy as though they had no goods, and those who deal with the world as though they had no dealings with it. *For the form of this world is passing away.*

Hebrews 1:1-2 (RSV) (also Hebrews 9:26, 10:37)
In many and various ways God spoke of old to our fathers by the prophets; *but in these last days* he has spoken to us by a Son,....

James 5:9
Don't grumble, brothers, against one another, so that you won't be judged. *Behold, the judge stands at the door.*

I Peter 4:7 (Also I Peter 1:20)
But *the end of all things is near.*

II Peter 3:10
But the day of the Lord will come as a thief in the night; in which the heavens will pass away with a great noise, and the elements will be dissolved with fervent heat, and the earth and the works that are in it will be burned up.

Revelation 22:20 (Also Revelation 3:3; 16:5)
He who testifies these things says, "Yes, I come quickly."

4. We have seen from chapter 12 that Jesus was very probably a follower of John the Baptist. We are told by the New Testament that both John and Jesus preached the same apocalyptic message:

Matthew 3:1-2
In those days, John the Baptizer came, preaching in the wilderness of Judea, saying, "Repent, for the Kingdom of Heaven is at hand!"

Mark 1:14-15 (Matthew 4:17)
Now after John was taken into custody, Jesus came into Galilee, preaching the Good News of the Kingdom of God, and saying, "The time is fulfilled, and the Kingdom of God is at hand! Repent, and believe in the Good News."

Although Josephus was not specific about John's teachings, he did mention that Herod "feared the influence of John" and that he might "raise a rebellion". (Antiquities 18:5:2) This is a clear indication that John's preaching was related to the changing of the present order and dovetails nicely into the gospel depiction of John's preaching above.

Paul considered himself a follower of Jesus (e.g. Romans 1:1). In Paul's preaching, we see a clear apocalyptic overtone. He expected the end of the present world order to end soon since he mentioned that some of those who read this epistle will still be alive when this happens:

I Thessalonians 4:15-17
For this we tell you by the word of the Lord, *that we who are alive, who are left to the coming of the Lord*, will in no way precede those who have fallen asleep. For the Lord himself will descend from heaven with a shout, with the voice of the archangel, and with God's trumpet. The dead in Christ will rise first, then we who are alive, who are left, will be caught up together with them in the clouds, to meet the Lord in the air. So we will be with the Lord forever.

This is very similar to the "son of man" saying attributed to Jesus:

Mark 13:24-27, 30
But in those days, after that oppression, the sun will be darkened, the moon will not give its light, the stars will be falling from the sky, and the powers that are in the heavens will be shaken. Then they will see the Son of Man coming in clouds with great power and glory. Then he will send out his angels, and will gather together his chosen ones from the four winds, from the ends of the earth to the ends of the sky... *Most certainly I say to you, this generation will not pass away until all these things happen.*

Thus, at least as far as an apocalyptic outlook is concerned, a straight line which can be drawn connecting John the Baptist, Jesus and Paul. It would be very unlikely that the middle connector (Jesus) turned out to be non-apocalyptic when the beginning (John) and ending (Paul) of the series were.[124]

Jesus' Apocalyptic Eschatology: Evidence from the Sayings of Jesus

We find that in the earliest sources, the sayings attributed to Jesus refer to an imminent, cataclysmic, and sudden, destruction of the present world order and the inauguration of a new one known as "The Kingdom of God."[125]

Mark 9:1 (see also Mark 13:24-30 quoted above)
He said to them, "Most certainly I tell you, there are some standing here who will in no way taste death until they see the Kingdom of God come with power."

Mark 13:28-37 (see also Matthew 24:42-50; Luke 12:35-40; 13:25)
"Now from the fig tree, learn this parable. When the branch has now become tender, and puts forth its leaves, you know that the summer is near; even so you also, when you see these things coming to pass, know that it is near, at the doors. Most certainly I say to you, this generation will not pass away until all these things happen. Heaven and earth will pass away, but my words will not pass away. But of that day or that hour no one knows, not even the angels in heaven, nor the Son, but only the Father. Watch, keep alert, and pray; for you don't know when the time is. "It is like a man, traveling to another country, having left his house, and given

---

124 Ehrman, *Jesus*: p 137-139
Miller (ed), *The Apocalyptic Jesus: A Debate*: p21, 84-85
Sanders, *The Historical Figure of Jesus*: p183
125 Ehrman, *Jesus*: p 129-130

authority to his servants, and to each one his work, and also commanded the doorkeeper to keep watch. Watch therefore, for you don't know when the lord of the house is coming, whether at evening, or at midnight, or when the rooster crows, or in the morning; lest coming suddenly he might find you sleeping. What I tell you, I tell all: Watch."

Q (Luke 17:24, 26-30 / Matthew 24:27, 37-39) (see also Luke 12:39 / Matthew 24:44)

[F]or as the lightning, when it flashes out of the one part under the sky, shines to the other part under the sky; so will the Son of Man be in his day. As it happened in the days of Noah, even so will it be also in the days of the Son of Man. They ate, they drank, they married, they were given in marriage, until the day that Noah entered into the ship, and the flood came, and destroyed them all. Likewise, even as it happened in the days of Lot: they ate, they drank, they bought, they sold, they planted, they built; but in the day that Lot went out from Sodom, it rained fire and sulfur from the sky, and destroyed them all. It will be the same way in the day that the Son of Man is revealed.

M: Matthew's Special Source (Matthew 13:40-43)

As therefore the darnel weeds are gathered up and burned with fire; so will it be at the end of this age. The Son of Man will send out his angels, and they will gather out of his Kingdom all things that cause stumbling, and those who do iniquity, and will cast them into the furnace of fire. There will be weeping and the gnashing of teeth. Then the righteous will shine forth like the sun in the Kingdom of their Father. He who has ears to hear, let him hear.

M (Matthew 10:23)

[F]or most certainly I tell you, you will not have gone through the cities of Israel, until the Son of Man has come.

L: Luke's Special Source (Luke 21:34-36)

"So be careful, or your hearts will be loaded down with carousing, drunkenness, and cares of this life, and that day will come on you suddenly. For it will come like a snare on all those who dwell on the surface of all the earth. Therefore be watchful all the time, praying that you may be counted worthy to escape all these things that will happen, and to stand before the Son of Man."

From the above examples it is obvious that Jesus, like John the Baptist before him and Paul after, taught that the world will come to a cataclysmic end and will be supernaturally renewed into "the kingdom of God". The Jewish contemporaries of Jesus, the people he preached to and the scribes and priests he supposedly debated had an essentially eschatological world-view. That is to say, they believed God created the world with a definite purpose in mind. And that since this creation, man, tempted by the forces of evil, had deviated from this purpose. There will therefore be a definite point in time when God will overthrow the forces of evil and establish on this world his originally intended purpose. For the select few of God, this new world will be a life of unending happiness, which is their reward for holding on to God's words. *The Kingdom of God is this new order.* (Whether this Kingdom will be on earth or in heaven has always been debated.)

Many of the Jews living during the time of Jesus believed that this kingdom will be inaugurated soon. Just exactly *how* it will be inaugurated, no one knows for certain but most believe it will be done through an earthly vassal, the *messiah* (Greek: *Christos*), which means "the anointed one". Whatever the case may be, this kingdom of God will be inaugurated, with or without the messiah, by divine action which will result in actual *physical* changes to this world. In all contemporaneous Jewish teachings this external and material kingdom is what is meant. There was no hint that the kingdom was to be understood in the spiritual, non-material, sense.

It is important to note that the gospels have no record of Jesus ever attempting to *redefine* the meaning of the term Kingdom of God. From this we can conclude that he meant this term to have already been familiar and understood by his audience. In other words, the Kingdom of God preached by Jesus was the one expected by his contemporaries, the great apocalyptic eschatological transformation of the world.[126]

That the verses quoted above (Mark 9:1; Matthew 16:28; Luke 9:27 and Mark 13:24-30; Matthew 24:29-34) showed that Jesus expected the kingdom to be inaugurated within the lifetime of the generation of his disciples,[127] perhaps no more than fifty to sixty years after 30 CE. It is also obvious that the early Christians and the authors of most other early New Testament books shared this same opinion about the imminent coming of the kingdom. In fact, Luke tells us that some of Jesus' followers thought that the Kingdom of God would appear during Jesus' trip to Jerusalem:[128]

Luke 19:11
As they heard these things, he went on and told a parable, because he was near Jerusalem, and they supposed that the Kingdom of God would be revealed immediately.

During the lifetime of Jesus, his teaching was that he would announce the coming of the kingdom and accompany its advent. After the death of Jesus, the expectation of the coming of the kingdom was transposed slightly into the *parousia*, that Jesus himself would *return* to bring about a new world order. As was stated above all the early New Testament documents, those written in the first century CE, contain this expectation of a speedy coming of the kingdom. Paul, the author of the earliest documents in the New Testament, said in no uncertain terms that he expected the *parousia* within the lifetime of his followers:

I Thessalonians 4:15
For this we tell you by the word of the Lord, *that we who are alive, who are left to the coming of the Lord*, will in no way precede those who have fallen asleep.

Paul believed that the time of the *parousia* was so near that he advised his followers to eschew worldly things. In I Corinthians 7:29-31 (quoted above) Paul, anxious to focus attention on this eschatological event, tells those who had wives to live as though they had none, those who were mourning to live as though they were not and,

---

[126]   Nineham, *Saint Mark*: p43-46
        Guignebert, *Jesus*: p329-330
[127]   Guignebert, *Jesus*: p344
[128]   Guignebert, *Jesus*: p332

in general, to eschew all worldly dealings. Obviously such an advice could not be practical if he believed the world as we know it would continue.

The conclusion is inescapable, Jesus taught that the end of the world would come during the lifetime of his followers, and the first century Christians, with some minor modifications, believed that it would be so. But the world *did not* end. Jesus, was a failed prophet, his prophecy did not come true. The next two millennia of Christianity were to be spent trying to explain away this central teaching of its nominal founder.

Christianity had to move on despite this failure of the coming of the kingdom. In the second and subsequent centuries, Christian theologians spent many hours and expended much thought trying to modify or reinterpret the clear-cut references of Jesus to the kingdom and its imminent coming to suit their new theology.

These explanations and rationalizations can be divided into three basic categories. The first is the attempt to reinterpret the sayings of Jesus about the imminent coming of the kingdom as not references to the eschatological event at all but references to other happenings. The second is to reinterpret the literal time limit set by Jesus in allegorical or other imaginative ways. The third rationalization is to deny that the coming of the Kingdom was a physical event and to assert that it was a spiritual one!

It is obvious that Mark 9:1 and 13:30 are consistent with each other. Both verses had Jesus saying that the Kingdom of God would come during the lifetime of his followers. To avoid this obvious and natural interpretation some theologians had tried to assert that the two verses were referring, not to the kingdom of God, but to two entirely different things.

In the 4th century, some Christian theologians hit upon the idea that Mark 9:1 could be interpreted as referring, not to the *parousia*, but to the Transfiguration! We have already discussed the Transfiguration in chapter 12. It is obvious that the explanation is absurd in the extreme and amounts to no more than theological wishful thinking. There are two reasons why this why this explanation is absurd. Firstly, if we look at the Transfiguration account as depicted in any of the gospels, it was an event that could hardly have been interpreted as "the kingdom of God come to power". And secondly, if someone says "*some* of you will still be alive when such-and-such a thing happens" the time lapse he is thinking about would be around a few years or a few decades. According to Mark 9:2, the Transfiguration took place *six days* after Jesus said that some of those listening to him will still be alive during the coming of the kingdom. To ask a rhetorical question: how many of the hearers did Jesus expect to drop dead within that six day span such that only *some* of them would be alive at the time of the Transfiguration? [129] The Transfiguration hypothesis simply does not hold water.

The same can be said for the other explanation for Mark 13:30. Theologians have tried to identify this prophecy (Mark 13:5-30) with the fall of Jerusalem; hence representing a fulfilled prophecy of Jesus. This explanation is scarcely more credible or believable. Just looking at verses 24 to 27, where Jesus prophesied about a sun which fails to shine, about stars falling from the sky and about him coming in clouds

---

[129]   Nineham, *Saint Mark*: p236
     Guignebert, *Jesus*: p344

with great power and glory, should suffice to show that there is no way these events can be tied in to the fall of Jerusalem. [130]

Undaunted by the failure of these attempts at reinterpretation, theologians tried another explanation. This time, instead of focusing on reinterpreting the slaying of Jesus as referring to something other than the coming of the kingdom, which they had to accept, they tried to reinterpret the time limit set by Jesus. The theologians tried to reinterpret "this generation" in Mark 13:30 to mean not Jesus' contemporaries but the "generation of the faithful for all time"![131] St. Jerome (c342-420) even went to the absurd length of interpreting "this generation" to mean the whole of the human race![132] Guignebert's comments sums up this second type of attempt:

> Once the literal sense of the passage is abandoned, any interpretation is possible, but it is only the preconceived ideas of the expositors which obscure the plain meaning of the words. [133]

It is impossible to deny that Jesus was talking about the coming of the kingdom and he was setting a speedy time limit for its occurrence.

An apocalyptic framework also provides a basis for making sense of some of Jesus' more abhorrent sayings we noted earlier. For example, the command to eschew family relation (Luke 14:26) makes sense if the premise is that the world in its present form will end. It is time to focus on the imminent coming of God in power.[134] Similarly, cutting out your eye if it offends you (Matthew 18:8-9) is surely more acceptable than having the whole body being thrown into hell once the kingdom of God is established on earth – which is going to happen very soon. In other words, those who do not heed Jesus' word and his precepts will be destroyed in the coming kingdom.[135] It is the *urgency* of the coming of the cataclysm that makes sense of these statements.

Now it is time to look at the third attempt – the idea that Jesus preached a *spiritual* rather than an apocalyptic Kingdom of God.

A Non-Apocalyptic Jesus?

Over the last two decades there have been quite a few liberal scholars – particularly those of the Jesus Seminar - who have attempted to metaphorically resurrect Jesus, to make him relevant for the modern world. The way they set about doing this was to argue *against* an apocalyptic Jesus and *for* a Jesus that was not an apocalyptic prophet. According to these scholars, Jesus was probably "a peasant Jewish cynic" with an egalitarian message (John Dominic Crossan)[136] or "a sage...with a gift for coining memorable aphorisms and creating illustrative narratives" (Stephen

---

[130] Guignebert, *Jesus*: p344
[131] Craveri, *The Life of Jesus*: p335
[132] Guignebert, *Jesus*: p345
[133] Guignebert, *Jesus*: p345
[134] Ehrman, *Jesus*: p170-171
[135] Ehrman, *Jesus*: p154
[136] Crossan, *The Historical Jesus*: p421-422

Patterson)[137] or a Jewish "mystic-healer-wisdom teacher-social prophet-movement initiator" (Marcus Borg).[138]

What these scholars claim is that as a social reformer, Jesus was not teaching about a pending cataclysmic revolution but about a metaphorical form of "eternal life" that is available here and now for all who believed in his message.[139] The central social-existential message of Jesus can be discovered from sayings such as these:

Luke 17:33 (=Matthew 10:39)
Whoever seeks to save his life loses it, but whoever loses his life preserves it.

Luke 14:11 (=Matthew 23:12)
For everyone who exalts himself will be humbled, and whoever humbles himself will be exalted.

Gospel of Thomas 110
He who has found the world (and) become rich, let him renounce the world.

The fundamental message here is that, as a social prophet, Jesus is forcing his hearers to rethink their social and economic assumptions. The first saying (Luke 17:33) tells us that we should give up social conventions and norms and enter into a new form of life offered by Jesus. The second saying (Luke 14:11) adds the point that this new form of life is one in which social conventions are turned upside down – one with a reversal of common values. The third saying follows (Thomas 110) this by questioning the economics of life. To find true value and meaning in life, one has to renounce material, worldly wealth.[140]

This Jesus never preached an apocalyptic destruction of the present world order. This Jesus is the one who said:

Luke 17:20-21
"The Kingdom of God doesn't come with observation; neither will they say, 'Look, here!' or, 'Look, there!' for behold, the Kingdom of God is within you."

Gospel of Thomas 113
His disciples said to him: On what day will the kingdom come? <Jesus said:> It will not come while people watch for it; they will not say: Look, here it is, or: Look, there it is; but the kingdom of the father is spread out over the earth, and men do not see it.

Rather than a future-oriented kingdom, Jesus was advocating a "Kingdom of God" which is a way of life that can be achieved in the here and now.[141]

There are two fundamental pillars in this reconstruction of Jesus. The first is the claim that what we have listed above as the earliest strata of Jesus' sayings (Mark, Q, L & M) - which are apocalyptic in nature - were not the earliest. These scholars claim that the earliest strata are to be found *embedded* in Q and in another sayings gospel

---

[137] Patterson, *The God of Jesus*: p90
[138] Miller (ed), *The Apocalyptic Jesus: A Debate*: p35
[139] Ehrman, *Jesus*: p131
[140] Patterson, *The God of Jesus*: p95-97, 104-105
[141] Patterson, *The God of Jesus*: p94

known as the Gospel of Thomas. The second is that Luke 17:20-21 represents an authentic early saying of Jesus which somehow became lost in the apocalyptic fervor of early Christianity – i.e. missed by Mark, Q and Matthew - only to be rediscovered by Luke towards the end of the first century. [142]

Let us look at these fundamental assumptions in some detail. While most scholars do not doubt that Q once existed as a written document, the claim of a non-apocalyptic Jesus goes beyond this. Based on the work of John S. Kloppenborg Verbin,[143] it is postulated that the Q that can be discovered from the gospels of Matthew and Luke is only the *final* stage of its composition. This saying source supposedly went though a few redactional stages, the earliest stage being a collection of "wisdom sayings" known as "sapiential Q" or simply Q1. It is these sayings which reveal the teachings of Jesus in its original form – and these teaching do not contain an apocalyptic eschatology but that of a Jewish sage who wants to overturn social and economic conventions.

Yet Kloppenborg's work, brilliant as it is, is far from actually proving the case. Other scholars have come up with rival hypothesis which does not posit a pre-apocalyptic stage in the collected sayings of Jesus.[144] Historians such as Donald Harman Akenson and Philip Jenkins have complained about the methodologies involved in the "discovery" of the multilayered Q. Akenson noted that the current "International Q Project" have abandoned the fundamental assumptions with which the very existence of Q was postulated (i.e. that these are sayings which are found in both Matthew and Luke but not in Mark and not in each gospel alone). Indeed, what is derivable as Q now seems to be what fits the fancy of the researchers: including sayings found only in Luke, or parallels between Luke and the Gospel of Thomas![145] Jenkins remarked that the placement of the wisdom tradition as the earliest layer and that of the prophetic as later "looks more like an *a priori* assumption."[146]

The Gospel of Thomas was discovered in 1945 in Nag Hammadi together with other gnostic texts. These texts, written in Coptic, were dated to the 4th century. Some Greek fragments of the same gospel, paleographically dated to around the year 200, were discovered 45 years earlier. The gospel consists of 114 sayings with no narrative. Many of the sayings have close parallels to the canonical gospels but about a third of the text is clearly infused with gnostic ideas. The issue of whether Thomas is based on an independent tradition of Jesus' sayings or on the canonical gospels is hotly debated among scholars with no clear consensus. Due to its similarities with other gnostic texts, its composition is generally dated to the first half of the second century (c 140 CE).[147]

There is no doubt that Thomas is an important find, and certainly contains more authentic sayings of Jesus than the canonical Gospel of John. Whether these are derived from the synoptics or independently attested is another matter. What is

[142] Miller (ed), *The Apocalyptic Jesus: A Debate*: p72-75
[143] *The Formation of Q*, Fortress Press 1987 and *Excavating Q*, Fortress Press 2000
[144] Dale Allison, *The Jesus Tradition in Q*, Trinity Press International 1997
[145] Akeson, *Saint Saul*: p321-328
[146] Jenkins, *Hidden Gospels*: p68-69
[147] Ehrman, *Jesus*: p 71-78
Jenkins, *Hidden Gospels*: p70-72

important is to note that this sayings gospel is *later* than the other sources: Q, Mark, Matthew and Luke. And as a rule of thumb texts that are closer to the events they describe are generally more accurate than later ones. This means that the evidential weight of Thomas is, in general, less than Q and the synoptics.[148]

However, this is where the scholars who favor a non-eschatological Jesus perform their sleight of hand. It is noted that since the gospel is independent of synoptics, it must be drawn from the same well of oral tradition as the latter gospels. This "same well of oral tradition" means that a date of 70-100 [like that of the canonical gospels] must be given for its composition.[149]

This dating ignores a few rather important facts. Firstly, the similarity of the gospel with other Gnostic writings mentioned points to an early second century date of composition. Secondly, the well of oral tradition did not suddenly dry up in the year 100. The tradition that was around in 70-100 was still there in 100-130.[150] The dating of 70-100 is therefore fallacious. It is even claimed that "an earlier edition may have originated as early as 50-60 CE."[151] Historian Donald Akenson has commented on this "downward-dating-creep":

> Thus we have moved from viewing a complete document of the fourth century, to a set of fragments at the end of the second, to a postulated beginning at the beginning of the second century, to a hypothesized origin between the destruction of the Second Temple and the end of the first century, and, finally to a hypothetical source, *of which there is no known physical evidence*, said to have been produced between the mid-first century and the Temple's destruction...these hypothetical documents automatically obtain a privileged position in the chronology of Christian invention that is equal to that of the earliest actual Christian documents that we possess...Warning light.[152]

Finally, we look at the lynchpin verse for the non-apocalyptic Jesus: Luke 17:20-21. It is important to note that the rejection of all the apocalyptic sayings attributed to Jesus is based primarily on *this one passage* from Luke. Therein lies its weakest point: it is not multiply attested, being found only in Luke. Of the synoptics, Luke is the one gospel that seeks to de-emphasize Jesus' apocalyptic utterances (as we shall see below). Thus, there is a high probability that this passage is an invention of Luke and is not based on any oral tradition of Jesus' sayings.[153]

However, even if we give the passage the benefit of the doubt and assume it is a genuine saying of Jesus, it does not really do what supporters of a non-apocalyptic Jesus want it to do. *One single passage two verses long* cannot be used to cancel out the numerous apocalyptic sayings in the gospels. Furthermore, there are problems

---

148   Ehrman, *Jesus*: p87-88
149   Miller (ed), *The Complete Gospels*: p302-303
150   For instance we know that Papias, who lived around 130 was still enquiring into the teachings of Jesus through the oral tradition around him (History of the Church 3:39:3-4).
151   Funk (et.al), *The Five Gospels*: p474
152   Akenson, *Saint Saul*: p93
153   Ehrman, *Jesus*: p177
       Sanders, *The Historical Figure of Jesus*: p176-177

with how the text is interpreted by this group of scholars. Let us look at the passage within its context in Luke:

Luke 17:20-30

Being asked by the Pharisees when the Kingdom of God would come, he answered them, "The Kingdom of God doesn't come with observation; neither will they say, 'Look, here!' or, 'Look, there!' for behold, the Kingdom of God is within you." He said to the disciples, "The days will come, when you will desire to see one of the days of the Son of Man, and you will not see it. They will tell you, 'Look, here!' or 'Look, there!' Don't go away, nor follow after them, for as the lightning, when it flashes out of the one part under the sky, shines to the other part under the sky; so will the Son of Man be in his day... but in the day that Lot went out from Sodom, it rained fire and sulfur from the sky, and destroyed them all. It will be the same way in the day that the Son of Man is revealed.

What follows 17:21 is apocalyptic: note lightning flashing in the sky and the rain of fire and sulfur similar to the one that befell Sodom. There is another issue with the passage. This relates to the translation of *entos humon* as "within you." For within the context of that passage, it is highly unlikely that Jesus would be telling the *Pharisees*, his theological nemesis, that the kingdom of God is within *them*! It is more appropriately translated as "among you" or "in your midst" either suddenly or in the near future.[154] When translated this way, the whole passage including what follows, makes sense. Jesus is telling the Pharisees that the Kingdom of God is bearing down on them and will be coming suddenly and soon.

There is a further weak point in the argument for a non-apocalyptic Jesus, admitted even by its proponents. This weakness in their postulate is with respect to the strongest evidence for an apocalyptic Jesus; the "straight-line" which can be drawn connecting John the Baptist, Jesus and Paul (and others). This means that they would first have to postulate that Jesus was initially a believer in John the Baptist's apocalyptic message but changed his mind midstream. Then for some unexplained reason the early followers of Jesus reverted back to an apocalyptic message![155]

To summarize, the case for a non-apocalyptic Jesus lies on extremely shaky premises: a hypothetical layer (Q1) of a hypothetical document (Q), a Gnostic gospel dating to the early second century is assumed to be based on an earlier edition for which there is no evidence whatsoever and a single saying in Luke which can be better translated to mean that the Kingdom of God - in its full apocalyptic, eschatological sense - is coming soon.

It remains for us to see the main lines of criticism that these scholars have on an apocalyptic Jesus.

John Dominic Crossan complained that an apocalyptic Jesus cannot explain why there was no major loss of faith among the early Christians when the promised apocalypse did not come, as he aphoristically phrased it: "the longer they were wrong,

---

[154]   Bauer, *A Greek English Lexicon of the New Testament*: p269
        Guignebert, *Jesus*: p339-341
        Miller (ed), *The Apocalyptic Jesus: A Debate*: p111-112
[155]   Miller (ed), *The Apocalyptic Jesus: A Debate*: p85

the longer they got strong."[156] This objection carries very little weight. For one thing we know from watching modern millenarian movements (Jehovah's Witnesses, Seventh Day Adventist etc) that mistaken predictions about the end of the world did not mean that the movements cease to exist. They continued; aided by convoluted explanations about how the original prediction may have been misunderstood or how the end had actually happened but in heaven first and so on.[157]

Furthermore, we actually do find evidence that the early Church tried to fudge this "wrongness". See how Luke, written around 100 CE tried to change Mark's account of the coming of the Kingdom (written 30 years earlier):

Mark 9:1
He said to them, "Most certainly I tell you, there are some standing here who will in no way taste death until they see the Kingdom of God *come with power.*"

Luke 9:27
"But I tell you the truth: There are some of those who stand here, who will in no way taste of death, until they see the Kingdom of God."

Luke had omitted the last three words in Mark but this omission speaks volumes. As Luke was writing at a time when the disciples of Jesus were all long dead, there is the rather embarrassing fact that the kingdom had yet to "come with power." By omitting the last three words, Luke has made the prediction vague. Here Jesus is simply saying that the disciples will somehow see "The Kingdom". This he actually had fulfilled later on (Luke 11:20) where he had Jesus say that "the Kingdom of God has come to you".

Here is another one. This is what Mark said Jesus told the high priest during his trial:

Mark 14:62
"*You will see* the Son of Man sitting at the right hand of Power, and *coming with the clouds of the sky.*"

Since the high priest evidently did not live to see the son of man "coming with the clouds of the sky," Luke fudged this saying by removing any reference to any future apocalyptic return and merely makes Jesus say:

Luke 22:69
"*From now on,* the Son of Man will be seated at the right hand of the power of God."

We see this trend to downplay the eschatology continued in the Gospel of John, which was probably composed slightly later than Luke. Here those who believe already have eternal life and will not "come into judgment". (John 5:24) The Gospel of Thomas is well within this trajectory of "de-apocalytisation". Saying 113 quoted above is within this trend, by stating that the Kingdom of God already "is spread out over the earth" but is not seen by men, the message is that the Kingdom of God is no longer a

---

[156]   Miller (ed), *The Apocalyptic Jesus: A Debate*: p54
[157]   Miller (ed), *The Apocalyptic Jesus: A Debate*: p102

physical phenomenon but an inner spiritual form of salvation.[158] Therefore, we do see attempts by early Christianity to correct a "wrong", the longer they were wrong, the more they tried to correct themselves in order to stay strong!

A second objection, and a revealing one, is that of Marcus Borg. He complained that an apocalyptic interpretation "flattens" the teaching of Jesus, making it "one dimensional" and "almost banal." In an apocalyptic framework, the call to overturn social conventions is no longer seen as any attempt at a social revolution but merely that because the time remaining is now short, these considerations (family, money, etc) are no longer that important. Everything reduces to the "simple minded" call "Repent, for judgment is at hand."[159]

It is almost embarrassing to state this: Borg objects to an apocalyptic Jesus because he does not *like* the Jesus that comes out of it. This Jesus does not "sizzle." But historical research is not about whether one *likes* what is discovered, it is about uncovering what really was the case. Indeed, we would *expect* such a "banal" teaching to come from a first century uneducated Galilean peasant whose primary profession was that of a carpenter.

Anticipating such an objection, Borg added this defensive note:

> Let me add that it is simply not my commitment to Jesus and to Christianity that leads me to reject the notion that Jesus' message and vision was banal. There is much evidence that his message is far from banal, indeed that many people found it provocative, disturbing and subversive.[160]

If by "much evidence" he means those acquired from assuming a layered-Q or an early date for the Gospel of Thomas, then we can easily dismiss this - as we have shown above. Who were these "many people" who found Jesus' message "provocative, disturbing and subversive"? His audiences were mainly Galilean peasants and his disciples were uneducated illiterates (Acts 4:13). We would not put too much emphasis on messages such an audience found "provocative, disturbing and subversive."

Borg's objection is revealing because it shows these theological flights of fancy (albeit of the liberal sort) comes from an inner need - as believing Christians but those who could no longer accept the literal story of the virgin birth, the miracles and the resurrection - to make Jesus relevant to the modern world. But historical truth does not come from inner needs, it comes from a rational analysis of the evidence at hand.

Jesus' Apocalyptic Eschatology – Conclusions

What can we conclude about all this? That Jesus expected the world as he knew it to end either within his own lifetime or those of his disciples. He expected a new kingdom of God to be inaugurated after that where all the ills of the present world would be no more. But as Dale Allison so poignantly puts it:

---

[158]   Ehrman, *Jesus*: p130-131
[159]   Miller (ed), *The Apocalyptic Jesus: A Debate*: p47
[160]   Miller (ed), *The Apocalyptic Jesus: A Debate*: p48

Jesus the millenarian prophet, like all millenarian prophets, was *wrong*: reality has taken no notice of his imagination…[161]

* * * * *

We have found out in this chapter that the Jesus that Christianity preaches is very different from what the historical person probably was. His personality can only ne understood within the context of his historical environment. He was probably a xenophobic Jew, a devout believer who could not accept criticism and who promised hellfire on his enemies. He never thought of himself as divine and probably did not claim he was the messiah. In no authentic passage do we find the historical Jesus actually saying that his death would play a central role in God's plan. He taught repentance and about the imminence of the coming kingdom, not about his sacrificial death. Since the kingdom did not materialize, Jesus was wrong. He was a failed eschatological prophet.

---

[161]　Miller (ed), *The Apocalyptic Jesus: A Debate*: p49

Chapter Fourteen
FROM TRIUMPHAL ENTRY
TO CRUCIFIXION

THE SEQUENCE OF EVENTS

In this and the next chapter we will analyze the events in the last week of Jesus' life as they are depicted in the gospels. In terms of verses, all the evangelists devote about one third of their respective gospel to these events: Mark about 36%, Matthew 39%, Luke 31% and John 38%.

As we shall see later, serious discrepancies exist in the narratives of events in the gospels - both in general outline and in the specific details of the individual episodes. However, for convenience's sake, we will give a summary of the final week of Jesus' life based on the Markan framework.

The final act begins on Sunday (five days before the Jewish celebration of Passover which was to fall on Friday that year) when Jesus, riding on a donkey, "triumphantly" entered Jerusalem to the cheers of many people. He apparently did not get much done that day. Upon entering Jerusalem, he went into the temple, looked around and then went back to the town of Bethany (Mark 11:1-11).

The next day, on his way back to Jerusalem, he cursed a fig tree for not having fruit. Then, arriving at the temple, he angrily drove out the moneychangers for making the place a "den of robbers". At dusk they left Jerusalem again, probably for Bethany (Mark 11:12-19).

On Tuesday morning, again on the way to Jerusalem, the disciples of Jesus noticed that the fig tree Jesus had cursed the night before had withered. At the temple Jesus debated with the chief priests, the teachers of the law and the elders. He also preached to the crowds (Mark 11:20-13:37).

On Wednesday, two days before the Passover, Jesus was anointed by an unnamed woman at Bethany. On that day too, Judas went to the chief priests to betray Jesus (Mark 14:1-11).

On Thursday, Passover eve, Jesus and his disciples prepared for the ceremonial meal. At night, which by Jewish reckoning was already the next day, they sat down for the meal. This is the famed "last supper" in popular Christian imagination. After the meal, Jesus and his disciples went to Gethsemane, where he prayed in anticipation of his death. (See Figure 14.1 for the probable location of Gethsemane) Judas then appeared with an armed party and Jesus was arrested. After his arrest, all his disciples fled. Peter stayed behind and followed Jesus at a distance. He was recognized by the high priest's maid but denied that he was a follower of Jesus. Jesus was tried that very night before the Jewish religious council, the Sanhedrin, and was found guilty of blasphemy (Mark 14:12-65).

The next morning, on Friday, the Sanhedrin reached a decision and handed Jesus over to the Roman governor, Pontius Pilate. Pilate could not find Jesus guilty of any crime and wanted to release him using a custom which allowed one condemned prisoner to be released during the Jewish Passover. The crowd chose a man named

Barabas, who was condemned for his part in a recent uprising, instead of Jesus. Jesus was then handed over to be crucified. (Mark 15:1-15).

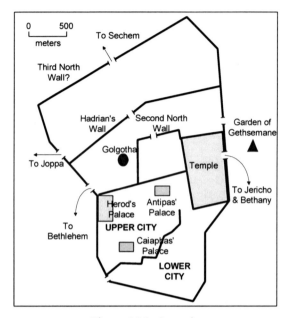

Figure 14.1: Jerusalem

After Pilate handed Jesus over for crucifixion, the Roman soldier forced a man named Simon of Cyrene to help Jesus carry the cross. Jesus was brought to a place called *Golgotha*, which means the Place of the Skull. Before crucifying him, they offered Jesus wine mixed with myrrh which he did not drink. He was nailed to the cross around nine o'clock in the morning. A notice was placed above him on the cross that read: "The King of the Jews." Two robbers were crucified with him who, together with the people gathered there, hurled insults at him. The ubiquitous chief priests and teachers of the law were there too, joining everyone else in mocking the crucified Galilean. At noon, there was darkness until 3 p.m. Then Jesus cried out his last words, "My God, my God, why have you forsaken me?" One man came and offered Jesus a sponge soaked with vinegar for him to drink. Then after uttering a loud cry, Jesus died. At that point, the curtain of the temple was torn in two. The Roman centurion who witnessed the crucifixion declared that Jesus was, indeed, the Son of God. Many of the women followers of Jesus were present at the crucifixion, watching at a distance. Among them were Mary Magdalene, Mary, the mother of James and Joses and Salome. (Mark 15:16-41)

This, in a nutshell, is Mark's version of what happened in the last week of Jesus' life.

Our quest in this chapter is straightforward. We want to find out, as far as possible, whether the events narrated are historical and whether the discrepancies between the various accounts are of any real consequence towards their historicity.

THE TRIUMPHAL ENTRY INTO JERUSALEM

The account of Jesus' entry into Jerusalem as narrated by Mark is fairly straight-forward:

Mark 11:1-11
When they drew near to Jerusalem, to Bethsphage and Bethany, at the Mount of Olives, he sent two of his disciples, and said to them, "Go your way into the village that is opposite you. Immediately as you enter into it, you will find a young donkey tied, on which no one has sat. Untie him, and bring him. If anyone asks you, 'Why are you doing this?' say, 'The Lord needs him;' and immediately he will send him back here." They went away, and found a young donkey tied at the door outside in the open street, and they untied him. Some of those who stood there asked them, "What are you doing, untying the young donkey?" They said to them just as Jesus had said, and they let them go. They brought the young donkey to Jesus, and threw their garments on it, and Jesus sat on it. Many spread their garments on the way, and others were cutting down branches from the trees, and spreading them on the road. Those who went in front, and those who followed, cried out, "Hosanna! Blessed is he who comes in the name of the Lord! Blessed is the kingdom of our father David that is coming in the name of the Lord! Hosanna in the highest!" Jesus entered into the temple in Jerusalem. When he had looked around at everything, it being now evening, he went out to Bethany with the twelve.

Mark 11:1 above says that Jesus "approached Jerusalem and came to Bethphage and Bethany at the Mount of Olives..." His ignorance of Palestinian geography once again shows itself here. Mark's previous passage had Jesus in Jericho (Mark 10:46). The inference is that Jesus was traveling to Jerusalem from Jericho via Bethphage and then Bethany. This, as can be seen from the map given below, is impossible. Bethany is further away from Jerusalem than Bethphage.

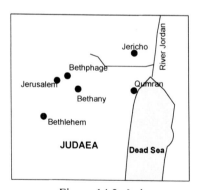

Figure 14.2: Judaea

The correct itinerary should have been Jericho-Bethany-Bethphage.[1] This is the comment from the New Testament scholar D.E. Nineham:

---

[1]   Helms, *Gospel Fictions*: p103

The geographical details make an impression of awkwardness, especially as
Bethphage and Bethany are given in reverse order to that in which travelers from
Jericho would reach them...and we must therefore assume that St Mark did not
know the relative positions of the two villages on the Jericho road...[2]

That this error was noticed early can be seen from the fact that Matthew, who copied
Mark, had changed this passage to remove the error:

Matthew 21:1
When they drew near to Jerusalem, and came to Bethsphage, to the Mount of
Olives, then Jesus sent two disciples.

Note that Matthew had *removed the reference to Bethany completely* from
Mark's account. Again, the most likely explanation is that Matthew noticed Mark's
error and tried to correct it. This oversight, although minor, shows us that Mark's
traditional source for this passage cannot be fully relied on.

In agreement with Mark, both Luke (19:29-35) and John (12:12-16) also
mentioned that in his entry to Jerusalem, Jesus sat on a young donkey. The sitting on
the donkey fulfils an Old Testament prophecy about the manner of how the messiah
will enter the holy city:

Zechariah 9:9
Rejoice greatly, daughter of Zion! Shout, daughter of Jerusalem! Behold, your
King comes to you! He is righteous, and having salvation; lowly, and riding on a
donkey, even on a colt, the foal of a donkey.

An uninitiated person reading the passage of Zechariah above may be slightly
confused by the last two lines; for it seems to imply that the king is riding on *two*
animals: the donkey and its colt. However, this is only an instance of Hebrew
poetical parallelisms, which involve the repetition of the same idea in different words
- mainly for metrical or rhythmical purposes.[3] This basic fact, however, seems to have
escaped the author of Matthew. Given below is Matthew's version of the first part of
the triumphal entry:

Matthew 21:1-7
When they drew near to Jerusalem, and came to Bethsphage, to the Mount of
Olives, then Jesus sent two disciples, saying to them, "Go into the village that is
opposite you, and immediately you will find a donkey tied, and a colt with her.
Untie *them*, and bring *them* to me. If anyone says anything to you, you shall say,
'The Lord needs *them*,' and immediately he will send them. "All this was done,
that it might be fulfilled which was spoken through the prophet, saying, "Tell the
daughter of Zion, behold, your King comes to you, humble, and riding on a
donkey, on a colt, the foal of a donkey. "The disciples went, and did just as Jesus

---

2   Nineham, *Saint Mark*: p294-295
3   Allegro, *The Dead Sea Scrolls*: p151
     Cadoux, *The Life of Jesus*: p180
     Fenton, *Saint Matthew*: p330

commanded them, and brought the donkey and the colt, and laid their clothes on them; and *he sat on them.*

Matthew had obviously read the passage in Zechariah to mean that the messiah will be riding on *two* donkeys. He had actually made Jesus sit on the two animals at the same time! (Try to imagine this!) Note that the last sentence, *he sat on them,* is not just an oversight on Matthew's part, for he had deliberately altered the whole episode to include two animals (the donkey and its colt). To bring this out clearly, the portions where Matthew had changed the singular in Mark to the plural when referring to the animals have been italicized.

Christians of a more conservative persuasion have tried various ways to get out of this obvious difficulty. Some of the earlier attempts involve simply translating away the difficulty. This was the strategy taken by the editors of the King James Version in the 17th century. They translated the Greek *epekathisen epano auton* as "he sat thereon". Most modern Bibles correctly translate the passage as "he sat on them."

In the Catholic *New Jerome Biblical Commentary,* the authors suggested that if their Catholic lay readers find it "difficult" to imagine Jesus sitting on two animals simultaneously they *may* choose to assume that the last "them" in Matthew 21:7 refers to the *garments* (or the cloaks) instead of the donkey and its colt![4] The tentative nature of the suggestion shows that the authors really do not have much to stand on as far as that interpretation goes. However, since this interpretation is also favored by fundamentalists, we have to see why it is wrong.

Firstly, even if we allow, for the sake of argument, that the final "them" refers to the garments, it does not follow that Jesus sat only on one donkey. For just the line before that we are told that the disciples placed the garments *on them* - meaning the two donkeys:

Matthew 21:6-7
The disciples went, and did just as Jesus commanded them, and brought the donkey and the colt, and laid their clothes *on them;* and *he sat on them.*

Even in this case, the cloaks were placed across the two donkeys! However, we do not even need to concede this. There are many reasons why the natural reading that the final "them," refers to the donkey and its colt is the correct one.

1. The prophecy in Zechariah 9:9 tells of the "king" coming riding on the donkey (or donkeys as it may be misinterpreted). Matthew 21.7 was the last line of the description of the process of getting Jesus on the donkey(s). To end the sentence (which was just before the actual entry into Jerusalem) by stating that Jesus "sat on the cloaks" does not make sense and goes against the whole point of the description.

2. The theme of Matthew 21:7 is obviously getting the donkeys ready for Jesus to sit on them, I will give the three lines here again and italicize the main portion referring to the donkeys:

---

4   Brown et.al, *New Jerome Biblical Commentary*: p664

Matthew 21:6-7
The disciples ... brought *the donkey and the colt*,
and laid their clothes *on them*;
and he sat *on them*.

3.   Finally, there is an almost identical construction in Mark, again the only change
      is from the singular to plural for the donkeys. Note that in Mark the *cloaks* are
      still plural while the final line refers to the singular colt:

Matthew 21:6-7	Mark 11:7
The disciples ... brought *the donkey and the colt*,	They brought *the young donkey* to Jesus,
and laid their clothes *on them*;	and threw their garments *on it*,
and he sat *on them*.	and Jesus sat *on it*.

Apart from fundamentalist apologists and conservative Catholic theologians who
concerned about the state of mind of their lay leaders, critical historical scholars are
unanimous in rejecting the interpretation that the final "them" in Matthew 21:7 refer
to the cloaks (or garments).[5]

      That Jesus could negotiate his way by sitting on two animals at the same time is
obviously absurd. Matthew's treatment of the episode gives us an insight into the
mindset of this evangelist. We know from our previous analysis in chapter 9 that
Matthew incorporated a large portion of the Gospel of Mark into his own gospel.
Matthew therefore must have considered Mark to be a reasonably reliable document.
So why would Matthew here alter the Markan account by deliberately replacing a
natural account of the triumphal entry with a more absurd one? The answer to this is
simple. Matthew, like most Christians of his era, believed Jesus to be the Christ or
the messiah. This belief was fundamental to their outlook. Following this they
believed that any Old Testament passages which they interpreted as prophecies of the
coming messiah must therefore have been fulfilled in Jesus' life. The Old Testament
therefore becomes a kind of historical source for events of the life of Jesus. In the
case of the triumphal entry, Matthew understands the passage in Zechariah to mean
that the messiah will be riding on two donkeys. That Mark says otherwise is
inconsequential to him. Mark, at the moment of Matthew's writing, had not yet
achieved canonical status. To Matthew, Mark's narrative, of having Jesus just sitting
on one animal, had to be wrong because the scripture says that there must have been
two!

      This episode will illustrate why a level of skepticism must be applied to any
event narrated in the gospels that deliberately and directly fulfilled an Old Testament

[5]   Allegro, *The Dead Sea Scrolls: A Reappraisal*: p151-152
      Cadoux, The Life of Jesus: p.180
      Cuppitt, *Who was Jesus*: p.44
      Dunn, *Unity and Diversity in the New Testament*: p99
      Fenton, *Saint Matthew*: p.330-331
      Funk et.al. ,*The Acts of Jesus*: p230
      Lüdemann, *Jesus After 2000 Years*: p215
      Ranke-Heinemann, *Putting Away Childish Things*: , p27-28

prophecy. It was very likely in many cases that the evangelist, convinced of his belief that Jesus was the messiah, constructed the episodes based solely on the Old Testament prophecies and not on any historical fact.

Fundamentalists like to point out that the sheer amount of Old Testament passages fulfilled in Jesus' life proves that he was the messiah.[6] What we have seen here shows that the fundamentalists have had their whole understanding turned upside down. The conviction that Jesus was the messiah came first. Then the early Christians began to ransack the Old Testament for passages referring to the messiah to find out more about his life on earth.

If we look back into the passage in Mark, we find that almost every detail of the passage could be traced back to the Old Testament. First, the statement about the Mount of Olives (Mark 11:1). There was widespread Jewish belief current during the first century CE that the Messiah would come to the Mount of Olives. This is based on an interpretation of a passage from Zechariah:

> Zechariah 14:4
> His feet will stand in that day on the Mount of Olives, which is before Jerusalem on the east.

The additional detail about a colt "which no one has ever ridden" (Mark 11:2) is found in the *Septuagint* version of Zechariah 9:9 which adds the description of the colt as *polon neon* (a "new"- i.e. unridden - colt) - the original Hebrew Bible does not add any adjective to the description of the colt. This gives rise to two problems. One, Mark did not take into account the obvious difficulty Jesus would have had sitting on an unbroken and untrained animal.[7] Second, it is highly unlikely, that Jesus would have relied on the *Greek* translation of the Hebrew Bible when figuring out how to fulfill Old Testament prophecies.

The exclamation of the crowd, far from being a natural outburst, is taken from the book of Psalms.[8] Given below are the relevant verses:

Mark	Psalms
11:9	118:25-26
Hosanna!	*Hosanna, O Lord...*
Blessed is he who comes in the name of the Lord!	Blessed be he who enters in the name of the Lord.
11:10	148:1
Hosanna in the highest!	*Praise him* in the highest!

The Hebrew word *Hosanna* in Psalms has been left untranslated above, in order to show the relationship with Mark's passage. The word actually means *save us, we beg you*. It is obvious then that Mark's phrase *Hosanna in the highest!* (Mark 11:10) has

---

[6]   McDowell, *Evidence That Demands a Verdict*: p141-177
[7]   Helms, *Gospel Fictions*: p103
        Wells, *Did Jesus Exist?*: p118
[8]   Helms, *Gospel Fictions*: p104-105

no meaning! Mark had obviously misunderstood the term and thought it meant something like *praise the Lord*. In other words, he misunderstood a cry for help as an expression of joy![7]

The dependence of almost the whole episode of the triumphal entry on the Old Testament, the obvious difficulty that Jesus would have faced riding on an untamed donkey, Mark's mistake about the geography of Jerusalem and his misunderstanding of Hebrew vocabulary all lead us towards one conclusion: the episode is very likely not historical.

THE CURSING OF THE FIG TREE

The miraculous element of the cursing of the fig tree has already been discussed in chapter 12. Here we will only look at the difference in sequences of the event as depicted in the gospels of Mark and Matthew. Both Matthew and Mark say that Jesus cursed the fig tree on the second day of the Passion Week. But whereas Mark said the fig tree was only discovered by the disciples of Jesus to have withered on the next day (Mark 11:20-21), Matthew made the fig tree wither at once and made the disciples notice it immediately. (Matthew 21:18-20) The cavalier manner in which the evangelists change the sequences in their sources does not add to our confidence in their veracity.

THE CLEANSING OF THE TEMPLE

The same discrepancy in sequence exists with the episode of the cleansing of the temple. Let us look at the account as given in Mark:

Mark 11:15-19
They came to Jerusalem, and Jesus entered into the temple, and began to throw out those who sold and those who bought in the temple, and overthrew the tables of the moneychangers, and the seats of those who sold the doves. He would not allow anyone to carry a container through the temple. He taught, saying to them, "Isn't it written, 'My house will be called a house of prayer for all the nations?' But you have made it a den of robbers!" The chief priests and the scribes heard it, and sought how they might destroy him. For they feared him, because all the multitude was astonished at his teaching. When evening came, he went out of the city.

This incident is also narrated in the other three gospels (Matthew 21:12-13; Luke 19:45-47; John 2:13-17). While scholars debate exactly what Jesus did in the temple, it is generally agreed that he caused some kind of commotion while he was there and it was this action that got him arrested and eventually executed.[9]

Yet even here the gospels cannot get their details straight. Mark made the event happen on Monday (Mark 11:12,15) while Matthew and Luke made it happen the day of the triumphal entry itself, i.e. Sunday (Matthew 21:12-17; Luke 19:45-48). The Gospel of John contradicts all these by putting the event at the beginning of Jesus

---

[9]   Funk et.al., *The Acts of Jesus*: p121-122
      Lüdemann, *Jesus After 2000 Years*: p77-78

career, three years *before* the triumphal entry! (John 2:13-35) Again, we have a discrepancy in sequence of events.

THE ANOINTING AT BETHANY

According to Mark, on Wednesday, in the house of one Simon the Leper in Bethany, Jesus was anointed by an unnamed woman (Mark 14:1-9). For once, Matthew followed the sequence of Mark (Matthew 26:6-13). John (12:1-8) too gave an account of the anointing of Jesus that share so many similarities with Mark that it must have originated from a common source and diverge by the distorting process of different oral traditions. There is also a similar account in Luke 7:36-50. We will give the three stories in full first:

Mark 14:1-9
14:1 It was now two days before the feast of the Passover and the unleavened bread, and the chief priests and the scribes sought how they might seize him by deception, and kill him. 14:2 For they said, "Not during the feast, because there might be a riot of the people." 14:3 While he was at Bethany, in the house of Simon the leper, as he sat at the table, a woman came having an alabaster jar of ointment of pure nard-very costly. She broke the jar, and poured it over his head. 14:4 But there were some who were indignant among themselves, saying, "Why has this ointment been wasted? 14:5 For this might have been sold for more than three hundred denarii, and given to the poor." They grumbled against her. 14:6 But Jesus said, "Leave her alone. Why do you trouble her? She has done a good work for me. 14:7 For you always have the poor with you, and whenever you want to, you can do them good; but you will not always have me. 14:8 She has done what she could. She has anointed my body beforehand for the burying. 14:9 Most certainly I tell you, wherever this Good News may be preached throughout the whole world, that which this woman has done will also be spoken of for a memorial of her."

John 12:1-812:1
12:1 Then six days before the Passover, Jesus came to Bethany, where Lazarus was, who had been dead, whom he raised from the dead. 12:2 So they made him a supper there. Martha served, but Lazarus was one of those who sat at the table with him. 12:3 Mary, therefore, took a pound of ointment of pure nard, very precious, and anointed the feet of Jesus, and wiped his feet with her hair. The house was filled with the fragrance of the ointment. 12:4 Then Judas Iscariot, Simon's son, one of his disciples, who would betray him, said, 12:5 "Why wasn't this ointment sold for three hundred denarii, and given to the poor?" 12:6 Now he said this, not because he cared for the poor, but because he was a thief, and having the money box, used to steal what was put into it. 12:7 But Jesus said, "Leave her alone. She has kept this for the day of my burial. 12:8 For you always have the poor with you, but you don't always have me."

Luke 7:36-50

7:36 One of the Pharisees invited him to eat with him. He entered into the Pharisee's house, and sat at the table. 7:37 Behold, a woman in the city who was a sinner, when she knew that he was reclining in the Pharisee's house, she brought an alabaster jar of ointment. 7:38 Standing behind at his feet weeping, she began to wet his feet with her tears, and she wiped them with the hair of her head, kissed his feet, and anointed them with the ointment. 7:39 Now when the Pharisee who had invited him saw it, he said to himself, "This man, if he were a prophet, would have perceived who and what kind of woman this is who touches him, that she is a sinner."7:40 Jesus answered him, "Simon, I have something to tell you." He said, "Teacher, say on."7:41 "A certain lender had two debtors. The one owed five hundred denarii, and the other fifty. 7:42 When they couldn't pay, he forgave them both. Which of them therefore will love him most?" 7:43 Simon answered, "He, I suppose, to whom he forgave the most." He said to him, "You have judged correctly. "Turning to the woman, he said to Simon, "Do you see this woman? I entered into your house, and you gave me no water for my feet, but she has wet my feet with her tears, and wiped them with the hair of her head. 7:45 You gave me no kiss, but she, since the time I came in, has not ceased to kiss my feet. 7:46 You didn't anoint my head with oil, but she has anointed my feet with ointment. 7:47 Therefore I tell you, her sins, which are many, are forgiven, for she loved much. But to whom little is forgiven, the same loves little." 7:48 He said to her, "Your sins are forgiven." 7:49 Those who sat at the table with him began to say to themselves, "Who is this who even forgives sins?" 7:50 He said to the woman, "Your faith has saved you. Go in peace."

Although Mark had the woman anointing Jesus' *head* (Mark 14:3) while John had her anointing his *feet* (John 12:3), the similarities between the two accounts are so numerous that it could not have referred to two separate events. The similarities include:

1. The anointment took place in Bethany (Mark 14:3 / John 12:1)
2. The guests were seated at the table (Mark 14:3 / John 12:2)
3. It was an expensive perfume, made of pure nard (Mark 14:3 / John 12:3)
4. Some people objected to the waste, noted the perfume was worth 300 denarii and that it should have been sold and the money given to the poor (Mark 14:4-5 / John 12:4-6)
5. Jesus defended the woman's action by using the words "leave her alone" (Mark 14:6 / John 12:7)
6. He told the present that the poor will always be with them but that he will not (Mark 14:7 / John 12:8)

These numerous, often verbal, similarities rule out the possibility that Mark and John were describing two different events. Both evangelists could not agree on exactly when it happened. John said it happened six days before the Passover (John 12:1) but Mark said it happened two days before the festival (Mark 14:1).

A look at the passage in Luke will also show that the event has essentially the same source but came to him from yet another strain of the oral tradition. The similarities are between Luke and Mark in some cases and Luke and John in others. They include:

1.   The owner of the house is Simon (Mark 14:3 / Luke 7:40);

2.   The guests were seated at the table (Mark 14:3 / John 12:2 / Luke 7:36),

3.   Jesus was anointed by a woman (Mark 14:3 / John 12:3 / Luke 7:37)

4.   She brought the perfume in an alabaster jar (Mark 14:3 / Luke 7:37);

5.   She anointed his feet and wiped it with her hair (John 12:3 / Luke 7:38)

6.   A mention is made of money although in a form of parable rather than a protest from those present. (Mark 14:5 / John 12:5 / Luke 7:41)

Again, it is obvious that Luke was referring to the same story.[10] Luke however, put this anointing *long before* the triumphal entry, while he was still preaching in Galilee.

The same story is put on three separate locations: John said in was in Lazarus house in Bethany, Mark said it was in Simon the Leper's house in Bethany while Luke said it was in Simon the Pharisee's house in Galilee. The same story is also placed on separate occasions: John said it happened one day before the triumphal entry; Mark said it happened three days after; and Luke said it happened weeks, probably months before that![11]

How dependable are these accounts? All we know is that none of them is completely reliable. Perhaps it happened at another time, another place long forgotten or distorted by tradition. Perhaps it never happened at all.

THE LAST SUPPER

According to the synoptic gospels, the last supper Jesus shared with his disciples was on Passover eve and was a formal Passover meal. The Passover is the most important of the Jewish feasts. It is an eight day festival held from the 14th to the 21st day of the Jewish month of Nisan. The Jewish calendar is a lunar one, which actually allows the Passover to fall anywhere in March or April.[12] The traditional Jewish belief is that this festival is observed to commemorate the Exodus of the Israelites from Egypt under the leadership of Moses.[13]

Many of the Passover observations and indeed the name of the festival itself can be traced to the story in the second book of the Pentateuch. When the pharaoh refused to allow Moses and the Israelites to leave Egypt, ten plagues were sent by God to force the Egyptian monarch to change his mind. The last of these ten plagues was the slaughter of all the first born children of the Egyptians. To ensure that the

---

[10]   This should serve as a good example just how unreliable oral tradition can be. While we can still tell that the stories are the same, many details have been changed and distorted. For Christians to claim that the Bible was inerrant they have to defend that Jesus was anointed three times under very similar circumstances; a clearly absurd proposition.

[11]   Guignebert, *Jesus*: p420

[12]   Summerscale, *The Penguin Encyclopedia:* p449

[13]   It is impossible to know how ancient the celebration of the Passover actually is. II Kings 23:21-23 mentioned that the Passover was not celebrated for hundreds of years "since the days of the judges" until the 18th year of King Josiah (i.e. c622 BCE).

angel of death does not mistake the Israelite households for the Egyptian ones, Moses ordered his people to slaughter a lamb. With the blood of this lamb, they were told to daub their doorposts. Seeing these signs will ensure that the angel of death would *pass over* the household. Later in their hurried escape from Egypt, the Israelites had no time to let their bread rise, so they ate unleavened bread.[14]

On the first evening of the Passover on the 14th of Nisan (technically it is the 15th of Nisan for by Jewish reckoning the new day starts after 6pm) the celebration of the *Seder* takes place. The Seder is a special domestic religious service which includes a ritual meal. This meal contains food which symbolizes the events during the Exodus: the *paschal* lamb which was slain earlier in the evening and the *matzoth* or unleavened bread.[15]

The rules governing the celebration of the Passover are very explicit. They are laid down in the Torah with additional details being codified in the Talmudic tractate *Pesachim*. Given below are some of the rules:

On the length of the festival
Numbers 28:16-17 (Exodus 12:18)
In the first month, on the fourteenth day of the month, is Yahweh's Passover. On the fifteenth day of this month shall be a feast: seven days shall unleavened bread be eaten.

The selection of the paschal lamb
Exodus 12:5-8
Your lamb shall be without blemish, a male a year old. You shall take it from the sheep, or from the goats: and you shall keep it until the fourteenth day of the same month; and the whole assembly of the congregation of Israel shall kill it at evening. They shall take some of the blood, and put it on the two doorposts and on the lintel, on the houses in which they shall eat it. They shall eat the flesh in that night, roasted with fire, and unleavened bread. They shall eat it with bitter herbs.

The prohibition of leaving one's house on Passover night
Exodus 12:22
... and none of you shall go out of the door of his house until the morning...

The prohibition of doing any kind of work on the Passover
Numbers 28:18
In the first day shall be a holy convocation: you shall do no servile work...

Here rabbinical elaboration had extended the prohibition of work to the afternoon of the previous day (Pesachim 4:2).[16] The ritual observations of the Passover, like those for the Sabbath, are very strict and explicit.

All the three synoptic gospels explicitly state that the last meal Jesus had with his disciples was a formal Passover meal:

---

[14]   Riedel et.al., *The Book of the Bible*: p296
        Rosenbaum, *The Desk Concord Encyclopedia*: p934
[15]   Benet, *The Reader's Encyclopedia*: p740
        Rosenbaum, *The Desk Concord Encyclopedia*: p934
[16]   Craveri, *The Life of Jesus*: p361
        Guignebert, *Jesus*: p429-430

Mark 14:12, 16-17 (Matthew 26:17-20; Luke 22:7-14)
On the first day of unleavened bread, when they sacrificed the Passover, his disciples asked him, "Where do you want us to go and prepare that you may eat the Passover?" His disciples went out, and came into the city, and found things as he had said to them, and they prepared the Passover. When it was evening he came with the twelve.

According to the synoptics, Thursday[17] was the 14th of Nisan. However, in the Gospel of John, the last supper was just a normal evening meal on the *13th* of Nisan, *the day before* Passover eve:

John 13:1-2
Now before the feast of the Passover, Jesus, knowing that his time had come that he would depart from this world to the Father, having loved his own who were in the world, he loved them to the end. *During supper*, the devil having already put into the heart of Judas Iscariot, Simon's son, to betray him

According to John, Jesus died while the paschal lamb was being slaughtered (John 19:31). As John agreed that this meal also took place on a Thursday[18], we have a serious discrepancy in our hands. To John, Thursday was the 13th of Nisan while the Synoptics said that it was the 14th. This discrepancy can be seen clearly from Table 14.1.

The inconsistency is also seen in the actual date of Jesus' death. As Jesus was crucified the day after the last supper, this made his death fall on the 15th of Nisan according to the synoptics and the 14th of Nisan according to John.[19]

Date	Synoptics' Chronology	John's Chronology
13 Nisan		Thursday: The Last Supper (normal meal)
14 Nisan	Thursday: The Last Supper (Passover meal)	Friday: Crucifixion
15 Nisan	Friday: Passover & Crucifixion	Saturday: Passover
16 Nisan	Saturday	Sunday: Resurrection
17 Nisan	Sunday: Resurrection	

Table 14.1: Synoptics' & John's chronology[20]

---

[17] The synoptics are all agreed that Jesus died on a Friday (Mark 15:42; Luke 23:54; Matthew 27:62) and that the last supper was held the night before.

[18] For John too said that Jesus died on the day of the preparation for Sabbath (i.e. Friday)-John 19:42.

[19] In the first centuries of Christianity, there was a controversy regarding when to commemorate the actual date of Jesus' crucifixion (and by association his resurrection). The eastern Asiatic churches observed it, according to John's chronology, on the 14th of Nisan. The western churches however, decreed that, based on the Synoptic time table, Jesus was crucified on the 15th of Nisan. The controversy was called the "Quartodeciman" (fourteenth day) controversy. The issue was never fully resolved but in AD325, the Council of Nicaea decreed that Easter would be celebrated on the Sunday immediately following the first full moon that appears after the vernal equinox (March 21st). [Craveri, *The Life of Jesus*: p404, Guignebert, *Jesus*: p426]

If the last supper was an actual historical event why was it that the simple fact whether it occurred on Passover eve or the day before that cannot be agreed upon by the early Christians? Our suspicion as to the historicity of the whole account is further aroused by the fact that both the synoptics and the Gospel of John had theological reasons for their dating of the events.

For John, Jesus was the new *paschal* lamb (*the lamb of God*) and it was fitting that he was sacrificed at the precise moment of the slaughter of the Passover lamb. We will study John's reasons in greater detail in the next chapter. The synoptics' idea was to connect the *Passover meal* to the institution of the Eucharist:[21]

> Mark 14:22-25 (Matthew 26:26-29; Luke 22:17-20)
> As they were eating, Jesus took bread, and when he had blessed, he broke it, and gave to them, and said, "Take, eat. This is my body." He took the cup, and when he had given thanks, he gave to them. They all drank of it. He said to them, "This is my blood of the new covenant, which is poured out for many. Most certainly I tell you, I will no more drink of the fruit of the vine, until that day when I drink it anew in the Kingdom of God."

It is worth noting that the Gospel of John does not contain the above passage. Both accounts of the last supper have different catechistical-liturgical functions: John's with the equating of Jesus with the sacrificial lamb, and Synoptics' with the initiation of the Eucharist.[22]

It should be mentioned that based on Luke 3:1, which states that Jesus started his preaching in the 15th year of the reign of Tiberius Caesar, and the synoptic chronology the most likely year of Jesus' death should be between 29 and 32 CE. However, in none of these years, based on astronomical calculations of the full moon of Nisan, do the 15th of Nisan fall on a Friday (On 29 CE it fell on a Sunday; 30 CE, Saturday; 31 CE Wednesday; and 32 CE Tuesday).[23]

The synoptics add that after the Passover meal Jesus and his disciples left the house and went to the Mount of Olives (Mark 14:26 (Matthew 26:30, Luke 22:39). This is in direct violation of Exodus 12:22 which specifically prohibits leaving the house on a Passover night![24] This makes the whole episode even less believable. For if Jesus and his disciples had wanted to celebrate the Passover, as doubtless the synoptic gospels tell us that they did (Mark 14:12-15; Matthew 26:17-19; Luke 22:7-11), it would have been pointless for them to cavalierly observe some rules and ignore others.

---

20   Craveri, *The Life of Jesus*: p404

21   The *Eucharist* (literally, *Thanksgiving*) was from a very early date a regular and central part of Christian worship. Partaking of the bread and wine, which symbolize the body and blood of the messiah, was called the Eucharistic feast. We know that it is early because it is mentioned in St.Paul's epistle to the Corinthians which predates the gospels by at least two decades (I Corinthians 12:23-25)

22   Craveri, *The Life of Jesus*: p361-405
Guignebert, *Jesus*: p424
Howell-Smith, *In Search of the Real Bible*: p21

23   Craveri, *The Life of Jesus*: p405

24   Craveri, *The Life of Jesus*: p430

In short, the whole relationship of the last supper to the Passover meal, as depicted in the synoptics, is historically suspect.

John's chronology for the last supper is also not without its problems, for he obviously wanted to portray Jesus as the new sacrificial lamb, and by moving the last supper a day back (compared to the synoptics) he could then have Jesus' death coincide exactly with the slaughter of the Passover lamb (see the next chapter). The blatantly theological basis makes its historicity extremely doubtful.

THE AGONY AT GETHSEMANE

After the Passover meal, however inconceivable it was for first century Jews, the synoptic gospels make Jesus and his disciples go to a place call Gethsemane. We will give the account of this incident, as narrated by Mark, in full:

> Mark 14:32-42 (Matthew 26:36-46; Luke 22:39-46)
> They came to a place which was named Gethsemane. He said to his disciples, "Sit here, while I pray." He took with him Peter, James, and John, and began to be greatly troubled and distressed. He said to them, "My soul is exceedingly sorrowful, even to death. Stay here, and watch." He went forward a little, and fell on the ground, and prayed that, if it were possible, the hour might pass away from him. He said, "Abba, Father, all things are possible to you. Please remove this cup from me. However, not what I desire, but what you desire." He came and found them sleeping, and said to Peter, "Simon, are you sleeping? Couldn't you watch one hour? Watch and pray, that you may not enter into temptation. The spirit indeed is willing, but the flesh is weak." Again he went away, and prayed, saying the same words. Again he returned, and found them sleeping, for their eyes were very heavy, and they didn't know what to answer him. He came the third time, and said to them, "Sleep on now, and take your rest. It is enough. The hour has come. Behold, the Son of Man is betrayed into the hands of sinners. Arise, let us be going. Behold, he who betrays me is at hand."

Here is an episode that sounds more like a play or a fictional account than a factual one. For one thing, note that Jesus actually walked some distance away from Peter, James and John before he started praying and that when he came back he found them sleeping! Now, it is only natural to ask; if Jesus was some distance away from his disciples and they were asleep, *who heard Jesus' prayers to his Father*? In other words, where did Mark get his source from? Note also that Jesus was immediately arrested after the episode, so he definitely could not have conveyed it to his disciples. Also the fact that Jesus prayed and went back to his disciple *three* times makes the incident sound very artificial. The answer forces itself on us: the account of the agony of Jesus in Gethsemane is fictional. The whole episode was very probably invented by the pious imagination of the post-apostolic tradition.[25]

There is also an addition to the episode given in Luke that only serves to confirm the conclusion above:

---

[25]   Guignebert, *Jesus*: p411,457
        Nineham, *Saint Mark*: p389

Luke 22:43-44
An angel from heaven appeared to him, strengthening him. Being in agony he prayed more earnestly. His sweat became like great drops of blood falling down on the ground.

Note that no one except Jesus was around to witness this event (remember that Peter, James and John were asleep). Where did Luke obtain the information from? This passage is obviously a fictional addition to an already fictional account.[26]

THE BETRAYAL OF JESUS BY JUDAS

According to all four gospels Jesus was betrayed by Judas Iscariot one of his twelve disciples. The account of the betrayal in Mark is given below:

Mark 14:10-11 (Matthew 26:14-16; Luke 22:1-6)
Judas Iscariot, who was one of the twelve, went away to the chief priests, that he might deliver him to them. They, when they heard it, were glad, and promised to give him money. He sought how he might conveniently deliver him.

Mark 14:43-46 (Matthew 26:47-50; Luke 22:47-48,54)
[After Jesus prayers at Gethsemane] Immediately, while he was still speaking, Judas, one of the twelve, came—and with him a multitude with swords and clubs, from the chief priests, the scribes, and the elders. Now he who betrayed him had given them a sign, saying, "Whoever I will kiss, that is he. Seize him, and lead him away safely." When he had come, immediately he came to him, and said, "Rabbi! Rabbi!" and kissed him. They laid their hands on him, and seized him.

It must be noted at the outset that the whole story of Judas betrayal does not sound natural or believable. For instance, what good does the so-called Judas kiss do? Jesus must have been a very well recognized face in Jerusalem, for he had debated with the chief priests, teachers and the elders just the day before and he had preached in front of large crowds in the Jerusalem Temple courts. So obviously the kiss was not used for the arresting party to recognize Jesus.[27] But then, what other use could the kiss have?

The confusion underlying the betrayal of Judas is further compounded by the fact that we are not told *why* he wanted to betray his master. Some apologists had made the obvious suggestion that it was greed. But this is most unlikely for it would have been more profitable for Judas to actually abscond the common fund (remember that Judas was the treasurer of the group) than to sell his master for the little amount the gospels made it out to be. Other suggestions include that ambition and jealousy. But nothing in the gospels tells us what his ambitions were or who he was jealous of.[28] Some apologists have even suggested that Judas fearing the imminent arrest of Jesus, due to his quarrels with the chief priests and teachers of the law, actually

---

26   Guignebert, *Jesus*: p458
27   Guignebert, *Jesus*: p454
28   Guignebert, *Jesus*: p455

betrayed his master to rid himself of this very fear![29] All these suggestions remain unconvincing. As Guignebert commented:

> We are confronted by nothing but...arbitrary suppositions unsupported by any trustworthy passage. The very number of them [i.e. the explanations of the apologists-PT] is sufficient to discredit them, and they merely vie with another in flights of imagination. Even if we combine all motives, ambition, jealousy, fear and failing confidence, and dress them out in high-sounding epithets, we cannot deduce from them any well-founded and therefore acceptable conclusions. The interminable discussions which we have touched on appear lamentable futile. *The betrayal remains purposeless, useless and unintelligible...*[30]

This is the first problem with the story of Judas' betrayal: it does not seem to have been required (since Jesus was easily recognized) and it does not have a credible motive.

It seems that the story of Judas betrayal was not universal in the early tradition. Paul wrote in his first epistle to the Corinthians that Jesus was betrayed on the night of the last supper but did not mention who the betrayer was:

> I Corinthians 11:23
> For I received from the Lord that which also I delivered to you, that the Lord Jesus *on the night in which he was betrayed* took bread.

In fact it is very likely that Paul's sources told him that the traitor was *not* one of the twelve. For he stated explicitly that Jesus appeared to the twelve after his resurrection:

> I Corinthians 15:5
> ... and that he appeared to Cephas, then to the *twelve*....

Now if Paul knew about Judas' betrayal he would certainly have said Jesus appeared to the *eleven*. The fact that the disciples elected another to replace Judas (Acts 1:26) is of no account here for the election was conducted after Jesus was lifted into heaven (Acts 1:9-11), i.e. after his resurrection appearances. The account of the election in Acts is from the same tradition of the Lukan story of Judas' betrayal, hence its historicity cannot be determined.[31]

There is a further problem with the story of the betrayal in the gospels. The evangelists tried to show us that Jesus knew beforehand who his betrayer was. Matthew, for instance, showed Jesus confidently telling Judas that he is the traitor:

---

[29] Craveri, *Life of Jesus*: p359
[30] Guignebert, *Jesus*: p455
[31] Guignebert, *Jesus*: p457

Matthew 26:21,25
As they were eating, he said, "Most certainly I tell you that one of you will betray me."... Judas, who betrayed him, answered, "It isn't me, is it, Rabbi?" He said to him, "You said it."

For all the foresight the evangelist attributed to Jesus, they seemed to have forgotten a passage from Q that implies that all his twelve disciples will be rewarded. The passage in Matthew probably gives the original rendering in Q, for he makes Jesus tell his disciples:

Matthew 19:28
Jesus said to them, "Most certainly I tell you that you who have followed me, in the regeneration when the Son of Man will sit on the throne of his glory, you also will sit on *twelve thrones*, judging the twelve tribes of Israel.

Unless we have here another case of Matthew making one of the disciples sit on two thrones, like he makes Jesus do with two donkeys, we have here an obvious reference to the idea that Jesus promised each and every one of his twelve disciples a throne in the coming Kingdom of God. It is worth noting that Luke probably realized the basic incompatibility of the above passage from Q with the Judas betrayal. For he altered the saying ever so slightly to avoid the pitfall Matthew fell into:

Luke 22:29-30
I confer on you a kingdom, even as my Father conferred on me, that you may eat and drink at my table in my Kingdom. You will sit on *thrones,* judging the twelve tribes of Israel.

The passage in Luke, by omitting the numbering of the thrones, sounds less natural than the one in Matthew. This serves to confirm our idea that Matthew's passage, at least as far as the last line was concerned, is the original reading in Q.

The Gospel of Peter, fragments of which were discovered in 1884, is a second century work believed by some scholars to contain tradition independent of the canonical gospels.[32] This is how the extant manuscript ends (after the crucifixion of Jesus):

Gospel of Peter 14:58-60
Now it was the last day of the unleavened bread and many went away and repaired to their homes, since the feast was at an end. *But we the twelve disciples of the Lord,* wept and mourned, and each one, very grieved for what has come to pass went to his own home. But, I, Simon Peter, and my brother Andrew took our nets and went to the sea. And there was with us Levi, the son of Alphaeus, whom the Lord... [This is where the extant manuscript ends]

Note that after the crucifixion, the *twelve* disciples of the Lord all went back to Galilee! The passages in Matthew and the Gospel of Peter corroborate the suggestion

---

[32]   One scholar, John Dominic Crossan, even argued that the Gospel of Peter actually *predates* the canonical gospels. See his book *Who Killed Jesus?*, Harper Collins 1995

above that there was an alternative early tradition that did not include the traitor among the original twelve disciples.[33]

As we will see later on in this chapter, there is a marked tendency in the gospels and in early Christian tradition to shift the responsibility for Jesus death from the Romans (crucifixion, after all, was a *Roman* form of execution) to the Jews. The very name of the betrayer, *Judas*, is so close to *Judean* or *Jew* that, given our analysis above, adds to our suspicion as to the historicity of the whole episode.

We can conclude that the core story that Jesus was betrayed by one of the twelve as given in Mark 14, whose name was Judas, is historically suspect.

Mark's story of Judas betrayal, as we see in the passages at the beginning of this section, is quite bare; but both Matthew and Luke added details to the account. While Mark 11:10-11 mentioned that the chief priests promised Judas money, Matthew was more explicit about the actual amount:

Matthew 26:14-16
Then one of the twelve, who was called Judas Iscariot, went to the chief priests, and said, "What are you willing to give me, that I should deliver him to you?" They weighed out for him thirty pieces of silver. From that time he sought opportunity to betray him.

We know that this detail cannot be historical. As Uta Ranke-Heinemann pointed out in her book *Putting Away Childish Things*, the literal translation of Matthew 26:15 would have the high priests "weighing out" (*esperan*) thirty "pieces of silver" (*arguria*). However, this is a major anachronism, for the practice of weighing out pieces of silver and the use of silver pieces as money was no longer current during the time of Jesus.

In Jesus' day there were gold and silver denarii....-but no coin or currency known as "pieces of silver." These had gone out of circulation around 300 years before. Equally anachronistic is the "weighed out." This was customary in Zechariah's time, but by Jesus' day had long been replaced by minted silver coins. (Pinchas Lapide, *Wer war schuld an Jesu Tod?* [1987] pp23-24)[34]

So where does Matthew get this detail from. Remember Matthew and his two asses earlier? This additional detail of thirty pieces of silver comes straight out of the Old Testament; it is a direct quotation from Zechariah:[35]

Zechariah 11:12
So they weighed for my wages thirty pieces of silver.

---

[33]   Craveri, *Life of Jesus*: p274-275
      Maccoby, *Revolution in Judea*: p198
[34]   quoted in Heinemann, *Putting Away Childish Things*: p126
[35]   Craveri, *Life of Jesus*: p358
      Fenton, *Saint Matthew*: p413
      Guignebert, *Jesus*: p455

There is also a mistake in Old Testament reference in Matthew which inadvertently reveals to us the sources he used and how he weaved these together to make up the details in his narrative. Let us look at the story of Judas' death as given in Matthew:

Matthew 27:3-10
Then Judas, who betrayed him, when he saw that Jesus was condemned, felt remorse, and brought back the thirty pieces of silver to the chief priests and elders, saying, "I have sinned in that I betrayed innocent blood." But they said, "What is that to us? You see to it." He threw down the pieces of silver in the sanctuary, and departed. He went away and hanged himself. The chief priests took the pieces of silver, and said, "It's not lawful to put them into the treasury, since it is the price of blood." They took counsel, and bought the potter's field with them, to bury strangers in. Therefore that field was called "The Field of Blood" to this day. Then that which was spoken through *Jeremiah* the prophet was fulfilled, saying,
    "They took the thirty pieces of silver,
    the price of him upon whom a price had been set,
    whom some of the children of Israel priced,
    and they gave them for the potter's field,
    as the Lord commanded me."

The quotation above, which Matthew claimed was found in the Book of *Jeremiah* is actually from *Zechariah*:[36]

Zechariah 11:12-13 (RSV)
Then I said to them, "If it seems right to you, give me my wages; but if not, keep them." And they weighed out as my wages thirty shekels [i.e. pieces] of silver. Then the Lord said to me, "Cast it into the *treasury*" - the lordly price at which I was paid off by them. So I took the thirty shekels of silver and cast them into the treasury in the house of the Lord.

---

[36] This obvious mistake in reference gave a lot of problems to the apologists for an inerrant Bible. It is amusing to look at the convoluted attempts Christians throughout history had tried to reconcile this mistake. St. Augustine in his work *De Consensu Evang* (III 7) said that Matthew knew very well that the sentence came from Zechariah, but he also knew that he was writing at the dictation of the Holy Spirit, and he dared not take the liberty of correcting it. And why did the Holy Spirit dictate an inaccuracy? To show that all the prophets were equally inspired and that it did not matter whether what was said by one was ascribed to another! [Craveri, *Life of Jesus*: p358-359] Attempts by modern apologists are no better. Witness this one by fundamentalist R.A. Torrey:

> There is no record in the book of Jeremiah, of his having uttered this prophecy, but there is no reason whatever to think that we have in Jeremiah all the prophecies he ever uttered, and Zechariah may easily have access to prophecies of Jeremiah *not recorded* in the book of Jeremiah. [Torrey, Difficulties in the Bible: p115]

With such special pleading, even Hitler's *Mein Kempf* can be explained away as an inerrant word of God!

However, the reference to Jeremiah shows the other Old Testament source for Matthew's story:

> Jeremiah 32:9-11, 14
> I bought the field ... and weighed him the money, even seventeen shekels of silver. I subscribed the deed, and sealed it, and called witnesses, and weighed him the money in the balances. So I took the deed of the purchase, both that which was sealed, containing the terms and conditions, and that which was open, ... Thus says Yahweh of Armies, the God of Israel: Take these deeds, this deed of the purchase which is sealed, and this deed which is open, and put them in an earthen vessel (i.e. *pot*)...

From Zechariah, Matthew got the idea of throwing the money into the Temple ("cast it into the treasury"), while from Jeremiah, Matthew got the idea of the purchase of a field with the money. The name "potter's field" was also suggested by Jeremiah, since he had the deed of the purchase of a field being placed into a pot. He weaved them together to make up his narrative, Judas *threw* the *thirty silver pieces* into the Temple and the chief priests used it to *buy a field* called *Potter's field*.[37]

The above mistake by Matthew is actually quite revealing. For it shows us as clear as the case with the two donkeys during the triumphal entry his *modus operandi*. He had conflated two separate Old Testament passages and used these two to construct the story about Judas' actions subsequent to his betrayal.

There are also serious discrepancies in the details given in Matthew and Luke regarding how Judas met with his death and what was done with the money. Let us look at the account in Acts:

> Acts 1:18-20
> *Now* this man obtained a field with the reward for his wickedness, and falling headlong, his body burst open, and all his intestines gushed out. It became known to everyone who lived in Jerusalem that in their language that field was called 'Akeldama,' that is, 'The field of blood.' For it is written in the book of Psalms,
> > 'Let his habitation be made desolate. Let no one dwell therein;'
> > [Psalm 69:25]
> > and,
> > 'Let another take his office.' [Psalm 109:8]

In Matthew 27:3-10 Judas committed suicide by hanging himself – in Acts 1:18-20, Judas fell of a precipice which disemboweled him. Also in Matthew's account, the field was bought by the chief priests, while Acts had Judas himself purchase the field. This disagreement in details has nothing to do with either evangelists having more accurate historical sources but is governed by the fact that they both referred to different Old Testament passages to construct their story.

---

[37]   Craveri, *Life of Jesus*: p358-360
      Crossan, *Who Killed Jesus?*: p73
      Fenton, *Saint Matthew*: p432
      Guignebert, *Jesus*: p456
      Helms, *Gospel Fictions*: p115-116

Acts have to make Judas buy the field himself in order to fulfill Psalm 69:25, which states that *his* habitation or homestead becomes desolate – i.e. it is something *owned* by him. Matthew, in following Zechariah 11:12-13 already had Judas throw the money away, so it was not possible to have him buy the field.[38]

The above tells us that Matthew and Luke got their story on Judas' death not from any historical sources but from oracular readings of Old Testament passages. Recall our earlier statement that the early Christians looked upon the whole of the Old Testament as a source for the events in Jesus' biography. Passages about events which were not even connected directly with any expectation of the messiah are interpreted by them to refer to events in Jesus' life.[39]

The Matthean story of Judas hanging himself has a close parallel in the Old Testament (II Samuel) about another betrayal, in this case one that didn't succeed. It concerned Ahitophel, a renowned sage who betrayed David by going over to Absalom, who had rebelled against the Jewish king. However, his counsel was not accepted by Absalom. As a result, Ahitophel went home and hanged himself. (II Samuel 17:23) The Greek word used by Matthew here (Matthew 27:5), *apegxato* (he hanged himself), is exactly the same as that in the Septuagint for II Samuel 17:23. We find that a passage from Psalms (attributed to David) about this episode had also been used as an archetype in the story of Judas' betrayal.[40]

Psalm 41:9
Yes, my own familiar friend, in whom I trusted, (a reference to Ahitophel) who ate bread with me, has lifted up his heel against me.

This is where the story of Judas' betrayal and his sharing of the last supper with Jesus came from. The Gospel of John in fact had Jesus referring to the above passage in Psalm explicitly:

John 13:18,21
I don't speak concerning all of you. I know whom I have chosen. But that the Scripture may be fulfilled, 'He who eats bread with me has lifted up his heel against me.'... "Most certainly I tell you that one of you will betray me."

Luke's story about Judas' death is taken from the story of the treachery of Joab also in II Samuel:

---

[38] Crossan, *Who Killed Jesus?*: p74
      Howell-Smith, *In Search of the Real Bible*: p21
      Riedel et.al., *The Book of the Bible*: p529

[39] Biblical scholar, Randall Helms calls this method of constructing details of Jesus' life with unrelated stories from the Hebrew Bible "typological fiction." *Typological* because these Old Testament figures are treated as "a 'type' or foreshadowing [*typos*]" of the messiah to come. *Fiction* because these stories were concocted out of whole cloth and have not grounding in history. [Helms, *The Bible Against Itself*: p82-83]

[40] Crossan, *Who Killed Jesus?*: p73, 76-78
      Helms, *Gospel Fictions*: p106, 116

II Samuel 20: 9-10
Joab said to Amasa, "Is it well with you, my brother?" Joab took Amasa by the beard with his right hand to kiss him. But Amasa took no heed to the sword that was in Joab's hand. So he struck him with it in the body, and *shed out his bowels to the ground*, and didn't strike him again; and he died.

The word used in Luke for Judas' death, *exechuthe* "his intestines gushed out" (Acts 1:18), is exactly the one used in the Septuagint for the passage above. Note that the act of Joab coming close to kiss Amasa is an early archetype of the Judas kiss.[41]

Let us now review what we have discovered about the story of Judas' betrayal of Jesus as described in the gospels. We find that there was no strong reason given in the gospel for Judas to betray Jesus. There is evidence in the early Christian writings of an alternate tradition of the betrayal of Jesus which does not include one of his twelve disciples as the traitor. There are also divergent accounts of Judas' death and how the Field of Blood was purchased and got its name. We also discovered all the additional information about Judas from Matthew and Luke could have been derived wholly from Old Testament passages. This is confirmed by Matthew's error in attributing the Old Testament passage to Jeremiah instead of Zechariah. All in all, the betrayal of Jesus by Judas has no strong claim of historicity.

PETER'S DENIAL

After the arrest of Jesus, we are told of his disciples that "They all left him, and fled." (Mark 14:50). Interspersed between the trials of Jesus before the Sanhedrin and Pilate Mark narrates the story of Peter's denial. We give the passages in full here:

Mark 14:54, 66-72
Peter had followed him from a distance, until he came into the court of the high priest. He was sitting with the officers, and warming himself in the light of the fire.... As Peter was in the courtyard below, one of the maids of the high priest came, and seeing Peter warming himself, she looked at him, and said, "You were also with the Nazarene, Jesus!" But he denied it, saying, "I neither know, nor understand what you are saying." He went out on the porch, and the rooster crowed. The maid saw him, and began again to tell those who stood by, "This is one of them." But he again denied it. After a little while again those who stood by said to Peter, "You truly are one of them, for you are a Galilean, and your speech shows it." But he began to curse, and to swear, "I don't know this man of whom you speak!" The rooster crowed the second time. Peter remembered the word, how that Jesus said to him, "Before the rooster crows twice, you will deny me three times." When he thought about that, he wept.

Critical scholars cannot agree whether the story of Peter's denial is historical. Some think it is an historical fact[42] while others think it is a pure Markan invention.[43] Those

---

41   Helms, *Gospel Fictions*: p117
42   Ehrman, *Jesus*: p219
      Nineham, *Saint Mark*: p399
      Lüdemann, *The Resurrection of Jesus*: p95

who argued that the account is historical based their argument on two criteria for authenticity. It is argued that the Christian tradition would not have put one of its early leaders, Peter, in such a bad light if it was not historical (criterion of dissimilarity). The story of the denial is also found to be independently attested in the Gospel of John (18:15-18, 25-27) (criterion of multiple attestation).[44]

Scholars who argued for the passage being unhistorical present the following evidence. The story stands in tension with Mark 14:50 which states that *all* of Jesus disciples, without noting any exception, fled when Jesus was arrested. [45] The whole narrative betrays the literary fingerprints of Mark. It contains a *threefold* denial, something Mark is very fond of. In the Markan narrative we find Jesus' prediction of his suffering (Mark 8:31, 9:31, 10:33), the disciples nodding off of at the Garden of Gethsemane (Mark 14:32-42) and the mocking of Jesus (Mark 14:65, 15:16-20, 15:29-32) all happening in threes.[46] Finally, the verse about the cock crowing is probably unhistorical, as Marcello Craveri noted:

> [I]t would have been impossible to hear a rooster in Jerusalem: there was a specific prohibition in populated areas against keeping such fowls, which were considered unclean, lest they contaminate holy objects.[47]

However, the evidence suggested for rejecting the historicity of the account succeeds only in rejecting the story as it is told in Mark, namely the threefold rejection, the tying up of the incident chronologically following Jesus' arrest and Jesus' trial (where *all* the disciples – surely including Peter - fled) and the cock crowing which deals with a prophecy by Jesus of Peter's denial. The basic core, that Peter once denied Jesus, remained intact. Martin Dibelius had suggested that Peter's story may have originally been told in connection with the resurrection rather than the passion. Just like Paul alluded to a tradition about his past in his epistle to the Galatians:[48]

> Galatians 1:22-23
> I was still unknown by face to the assemblies of Judea which were in Christ, but they only heard: "He who once persecuted us now preaches the faith that he once tried to destroy."

The tradition about Peter's denial could have taken the same form, the original tradition could have gone something like "He who once denied Jesus now proclaims him risen." Everything else is a Markan redaction.

---

43   Craveri, *Life of Jesus*: p384
      Funk et.al, *The Acts of Jesus*: p149
      Price, *The Incredible Shrinking Son of Man*: p195-196
44   Ehrman, *Jesus*: p219
45   Price, *The Incredible Shrinking Son of Man*: p195
46   Funk et.al, *The Acts of Jesus*: p149
47   Craveri, *Life of Jesus*: p384
48   Lüdemann, *The Resurrection of Jesus*: p95

THE TRIAL OF JESUS

All the four gospels seem to agree that Jesus was first tried by Jewish authorities and then by a Roman court before being sentenced to death by crucifixion. On closer examination, these agreements can be seen to be very superficial. We have, in effect, three different sequences of events.

The first sequence is given in the gospels of Mark and Matthew. According to this sequence, Jesus was taken to the high priest's house immediately after his arrest. There, in the middle of the night, the whole Sanhedrin was already assembled waiting to try him (Mark 14:53-54; Matthew 26:57). He was questioned by the high priest, confronted with supposed witnesses and finally condemned to death for blasphemy (Mark 14:55-65; Matthew 26:59-68). The next morning, a Friday and the 15th of Nisan, the Sanhedrin had another meeting where they decided to hand Jesus over to Pontius Pilate the procurator (or governor) of Judea (Mark 15:1; Matthew 27:1-2). He was tried before the procurator who, at the instigation of the crowd, reluctantly handed Jesus the sentence of death by crucifixion (Mark 15:2-15; Matthew 27:11-16).

The second sequence is given by Luke. Luke agreed with Mark and Matthew by stating that Jesus was taken to the high priest's house after he was arrested (Luke 22:54). However, there is no mention in this Gospel of the night time trial of the Sanhedrin. According to Luke, the Sanhedrin only met at day break on Friday. Furthermore, no witness was mentioned as being called. According to the council, Jesus had confessed his blasphemy (Luke 22:66-71). They then handed him over to Pilate (Luke 23:1-2). After a short interrogation, Pilate told the representatives of the Sanhedrin that he could find no basis for their charge (Luke 23:3-5). After finding out that he was a Galilean, Pilate handed Jesus over to Herod Antipas, Tetrarch of Galilee who was in Jerusalem, presumably for the Passover festival (Luke 23:6-7). Herod ridiculed and mocked Jesus but he too found nothing in Jesus' actions that deserved the death penalty (Luke 23:8-15).

The third sequence is given in the Gospel of John. In this version, Jesus was taken after his arrest to the house of the Annas, *father-in-law* of the high priest, Caiaphas (John 18:12-14). No mention is made of the presence of the Sanhedrin in this house or any night time trial. Annas then sent Jesus over to Caiaphas (John 18:19-24). From here, Jesus was taken to the residence of Pilate (John 18:28). Pilate, as in the other versions, could not find Jesus guilty but gave in at the insistence of the crowd and sent Jesus to be crucified. (John 18:28-19:16).

All three versions are incompatible with one another. No mention is made in John of any trial or interrogation by the Sanhedrin. The whole "trial" in John was really just an informal interrogation by Annas alone. Trying to reconcile Mark's (and Matthew's) and Luke's versions is also impossible. In the first place Luke makes the Sanhedrin interrogate Jesus on Friday morning in exactly the same way the gospels of Mark and Matthew made the council do the night before. Given below are the two interrogations:

Mark 14:61-64
[On Thursday night]
Again the high priest asked him, "Are you the Christ, the Son of the Blessed?"
Jesus said, "I am. ... The high priest tore his clothes, and said, "What further need

have we of witnesses? You have heard the blasphemy! What do you think?" They all condemned him to be worthy of death.

Luke 22:66-71
[On Friday morning]
As soon as it was day, the assembly of the elders of the people was gathered together, both chief priests and scribes, and they led him away into their council...They all said, "Are you then the Son of God?" He said to them, "You say it, because I am." They said, "Why do we need any more witness? For we ourselves have heard from his own mouth!"

In the second place, Luke did not give any hint that there was a meeting the night before. In conclusion we have three separate and mutually incompatible accounts of the trial of Jesus.[49]

THE TRIAL BEFORE THE SANHEDRIN

To study the accounts of the trial of Jesus before the Sanhedrin requires us to have a deeper understanding of the working of that Jewish council. Our knowledge of the Sanhedrin comes from the writings of Josephus and Jewish rabbinical literature. The Sanhedrin, as we mentioned, was the supreme court of the Jewish nation. It is composed of 71 members drawn mainly from priestly families and lay families known for their wealth and racial purity. The high priest under the title of Nasi (prince) presided over the assembly.[50] Two major religious parties were influential in the Sanhedrin during the time of Jesus: the *Sadducees* and the *Pharisees*.

The Sadducee constituted the majority party in the Sanhedrin. The high priest himself is a Sadducee. As a religious party, the Sadducees existed between 150 BCE and 70 CE. They do not believe in angels, demons or bodily resurrection. The members are mainly wealthy land owners and people from priestly families. The Sadducees then were people who had a comfortable and good life under the Romans and are the group with most to lose from any disturbance in the equilibrium. They were therefore collaborators with the Romans and supporters of the status quo. History tells us that their fears of disequilibrium were well justified; for after the Jewish revolt of 66 CE to 74 CE, any Jewish privileges granted by the Romans were lost. The Sadducees, as a religious party disappeared after the Jewish War, a direct casualty of that revolt.[51]

The Pharisees formed an influential minority in the Sanhedrin. As a group they appeared in Jewish history about the same time as the Sadducees. These two groups, however, have unbridgeable theological differences. The Pharisees, like the Christians that were to appear on the scene later, believed in angels, demons and the

---

[49]   Guignebert, *Jesus*: p461-463
[50]   Craveri, *Life of Jesus*: p380
        Hinnels, *Dictionary of Religions*: p285
        Nineham, *Saint Mark*: p400
[51]   Hinnels, *Dictionary of Religions*: p279
        Maccoby, *Revolution in Judea*: p71-72
        Martin, *New Testament Foundations I*: p86-87

bodily resurrection. The Pharisees and the Sadducees also differed in their attitude toward the oral law. The Pharisees believed that the Torah is to be supplemented by oral tradition that sought to interpret and develop it. The Sadducees, on the other hand, believed that the written law is a closed and final revelation that requires no further interpretation and elaboration.

Unlike the Sadducees, the Pharisees were a dispossessed party seeking neither political power nor material wealth. As such, they were very popular with the lay people of Palestine. It was through the efforts of the Pharisees that the Jewish faith was kept alive in the towns and villages throughout the land. Judaism, as we know it today, is a direct spiritual descendant of the theology of the Pharisees.[52]

Very strict rules guide the procedures of the Sanhedrin. Just as in modern courts of law, the council has a special meeting place called the *Gazith* (Chamber of Hewn Stone), which is part of the Temple. They do not meet anywhere else. Its sessions start at 9am in the morning and close at 4pm in the evening. An interval of 24 hours must elapse before the conclusion of the testimony and the rendering of a verdict. The Sanhedrin is never convened on Sabbaths, religious holidays and especially the Passover which was the most important feast in the Jewish calendar. This is clearly stated by the Mishnah (Sanhedrin IV:1) and Maimonides (Hilkot Sanhedrin XI:2): "Trails involving capital punishment may not be held on the eve of the Sabbath or a festival." The Sanhedrin also does not hold any meeting at night.[53]

Having equipped ourselves with a basic, albeit brief, understanding of the Sanhedrin, we will now proceed to study the trial of Jesus before the Sanhedrin as accounted in the gospels.

Let us first present the Markan account:

Mark 14:53-65 (Matthew 26:57-67)
[Immediately after Jesus was arrested at Gethsemane][54]
[53]They led Jesus away to the high priest. *All the chief priests, the elders, and the scribes came together with him.* [54] Peter had followed him from a distance, until he came into the court of the high priest. He was sitting with the officers, and warming himself in the light of the fire. [55]Now the chief priests and *the whole council* sought witnesses against Jesus to put him to death, and found none. [56]For many gave false testimony against him, and their testimony didn't agree with each other. [57]Some stood up, and gave false testimony against him, saying, [58]"We heard him say, 'I will destroy this temple that is made with hands, and in three days I will build another made without hands.'" [59]Even so, their testimony did not agree. [60]The high priest stood up in the midst, and asked Jesus, "Have you no answer? What is it which these testify against you?" [61]But he stayed quiet, and answered nothing. Again the high priest asked him, "Are you the Christ, the Son of the Blessed?" [62]Jesus said, "I am. You will see the Son of Man sitting at the right hand of Power,

---

[52] Hinnels, *Dictionary of Religions*: p251
      Maccoby, *Revolution in Judea*: p72-74
      Martin, *New Testament Foundations I*: p86
[53] Craveri, *Life of Jesus*: p380
      Maccoby, *Revolution in Judea*: p202
[54] The verse numbers of the passage are added in here for easy reference in the subsequent discussion.

and coming with the clouds of the sky." [63]The high priest tore his clothes, and said, "What further need have we of witnesses? [64]You have heard the blasphemy! What do you think?" They all condemned him to be worthy of death. [65]Some began to spit on him, and to cover his face, and to beat him with fists, and to tell him, "Prophesy!" The officers struck him with the palms of their hands.

That Mark intended the trial to mean a formal trial before the Sanhedrin cannot be doubted. For this is obviously what he meant when he mentioned that *all* the chief priests elders and scribes came together with the high priest (Mark 14:53) and that the *whole council* sought to find Jesus guilty. (Mark 14:55) This account however, contains difficulties. For one, Mark mentioned that the Sanhedrin met in the house of the high priest while all our other sources on the Sanhedrin tells us that the council does not convene anywhere else except in the Chamber of the Hewn Stone in the Temple.[55] Furthermore, the Sanhedrin was said to have convened immediately after Jesus was arrested and taken to the high priest's house. This was after the Passover supper and the prayer at Gethsemane which makes the council meet around 9 to 10 pm at night. This is again incompatible with what we know of the procedures of the Sanhedrin which disallows nocturnal meetings.[56] To add to the absurdity, this night, if we are to believe the synoptic chronology, was Passover eve and by Jewish reckoning already the 15th of Nisan - Passover itself. As many eminent Jewish scholars have pointed out, this is simply inconceivable, given the strict ruling of no council meetings on the Sabbath, and on religious feast days, such as the Passover.[57] We quote the Jewish scholar, Joseph Klausner from his book *Jesus of Nazareth* (New York 1925):

> [T]he Sadducees themselves would not have conducted even a simple judicial enquiry either on the night of the Passover or the first day of the Passover...the mishnah lays it down that capital cases may not be judged on the eve of a Sabbath or on the eve of a festival to avoid delay should the case not be finished that day, since all trials were forbidden on a Sabbath or a festival.[58]

Another procedural impossibility is given in Mark 14:64 which includes the sentence: *they all condemned him as worthy of death.* This means that the sentence was passed on the same day instead of the prescribed interval of 24 hours.[59] These procedural flaws in the Markan account weighs heavily against any claims of historicity for the episode described there.

---

[55]   Maccoby, *Revolution in Judea*: p202
[56]   Craveri, *Life of Jesus*: p381
        Guignebert, *Jesus*: p463
        Maccoby, *Revolution in Judea*: p202
[57]   Guignebert, *Jesus*: p463
        Maccoby, *Revolution in Judea*: p202
        Nineham, *Saint Mark*: p400-401
        Ranke-Heinemann, *Putting Away Childish Things*: p108
[58]   quoted in Yerby, *Judas, My Brother*: p515
[59]   Craveri, *Life of Jesus*: p381
        Guignebert, *Jesus*: p463

However, procedural flaws are not the only problem with the Markan account of the trial of Jesus. In Mark 14:57-58 we are told that some people came forward with *false* testimony. Yet what they falsely claimed Jesus said, according to Mark, was precisely what the Gospel of John claimed that Jesus did say:[60]

Mark 14:57-58
Some stood up, and gave false testimony against him, saying, "We heard him say, 'I will destroy this temple that is made with hands, and in three days I will build another made without hands.'"

John 2:18-19
The Jews therefore answered him, "What sign do you show us, seeing that you do these things?" Jesus answered them, "Destroy this temple, and in three days I will raise it up."

We also have a passage in Acts (6:14) which seems to imply that the above statement was actually uttered by Jesus.

Another problem with the Markan account is associated with the question asked by the high priest in Mark 14:61. Remember that *Christ* is simply the Greek word for *messiah*. Mark had the high priest made the association of being a messiah with being *the* Son of God. No Jewish priest, let alone the high priest, would have made that connection in the divine sense in the gospels. The Jews simply did not consider the messiahship to have a divine status.[61] Furthermore, the high priest's assertion (Mark 14:64) that Jesus committed blasphemy in his reply (Mark 14:62-63) makes no sense. It was not an offence for a Jew to claim to be the messiah because eventually, according to their belief, someone has got to be him. It is no blasphemy, though of course it could be a mistake, in claiming the title of messiah for oneself.[62] The claim Jesus made, of being seated at the right hand of God, does not necessarily have any divine connotation for himself, as the Jewish scholar Rabbi Morris Goldstein stated:

Use of the phrase "Son of the Blessed" or "Son of God" was no capital crime. The reference to sitting at the right hand of power (Mark 14:62) is not greatly different from King David's allusion to himself sitting at the right hand of God (Psalms 110:1), at all events, it is nowhere indicated as blasphemy.[63]

And finally, Mark 14:65 had members of the Sanhedrin spitting and striking Jesus. This is another patently absurd claim as another Jewish scholar, Hyam Maccoby noted:

---

[60] Nineham, *Saint Mark*: p406
[61] Nineham, *Saint Mark*: p406
       Wilson, *Jesus: The Evidence*: p407
[62] Maccoby, *Revolution in Judea*: p203
       Wilson, *Jesus: The Evidence*: p103
[63] Morris Goldstein, *Jesus in the Jewish Tradition*, Macmillan, New York 1953 quoted in
       Wilson, *Jesus: The Evidence*: p103

As to the reports that members of the Sanhedrin spat on Jesus and stuck him, this is just as incredible in the proceedings of that highly dignified body as if it were reported of the high court of England or the supreme court of the United States.[64]

Almost every point in the Markan account of the nocturnal trial of Jesus is incompatible with what we know of the Jewish council. In short, Mark's account is fiction; and poor fiction at that!

In the morning, according to Mark, the Sanhedrin met again:

Mark 15:1
Immediately in the morning the chief priests, with the elders and scribes, and the whole council, held a consultation, and bound Jesus, and carried him away, and delivered him up to Pilate.

This account is subject to some of the procedural difficulties we have already noted for the night time trial. Namely that it was held on the Passover and that a decision was reached less than 24 hours after the conclusion of the testimony. Another difficulty, a question asked repeatedly by skeptical scholars, is this: if Jesus was condemned for blasphemy (i.e. a crime in Judaism) why was Jesus not sentenced to death by stoning or strangulation in accordance to the Jewish Law?[65] The Torah is unambiguous about this:

Leviticus 24:11-16,23
The son of the Israelite woman blasphemed the Name, and cursed; and they brought him to Moses... Yahweh spoke to Moses, saying, "Bring out of the camp him who cursed; and let all who heard him lay their hands on his head, and let all the congregation stone him. You shall speak to the children of Israel, saying, 'Whoever curses his God shall bear his sin. He who blasphemes the name of Yahweh, he shall surely be put to death; all the congregation shall certainly stone him: the foreigner as well as the native-born, when he blasphemes the Name, shall be put to death... Moses spoke to the children of Israel; and they brought forth him who had cursed out of the camp, and stoned him with stones. The children of Israel did as Yahweh commanded Moses.

Neither Mark nor Matthew attempted to explain why Jesus was handed over to Pilate and sentence to die by crucifixion. For crucifixion was essentially a *Roman* penalty.[66]

In Luke's account, the nocturnal trial in Mark was omitted. However, Luke's story of the trial in the morning is still subject to the same objection as against

---

[64] Maccoby, *Revolution in Judea*: p202
[65] Craveri, *Life of Jesus*: p384
      Guignebert, *Jesus*: p463
      Nineham, *Saint Mark*: p403
      Schonfield, *The Passover Plot*: p141
[66] Guignebert, *Jesus*: p463
      Nineham, *Saint Mark*: p403

Mark's, for the trial was conducted on Passover day itself, something we have seen as impossible. Luke's story of the trial before the Sanhedrin is as unhistorical as Mark's.

John's version is radically different from the synoptics' accounts. First let us look at his passage in full:

> John 18:12-31
> So the detachment, the commanding officer, and the officers of the Jews, seized Jesus and bound him, and led him to Annas first, for he was father-in-law to Caiaphas, who was high priest that year. Now it was Caiaphas who advised the Jews that it was expedient that one man should perish for the people. Simon Peter followed Jesus, as did another disciple. Now that disciple was known to the high priest, and entered in with Jesus into the court of the high priest; but Peter was standing at the door outside. So the other disciple, who was known to the high priest, went out and spoke to her who kept the door, and brought in Peter. Then the maid who kept the door said to Peter, "Are you also one of this man's disciples?" He said, "I am not." Now the servants and the officers were standing there, having made a fire of coals, for it was cold. They were warming themselves. Peter was with them, standing and warming himself. The high priest therefore asked Jesus about his disciples, and about his teaching. Jesus answered him, "I spoke openly to the world. I always taught in synagogues, and in the temple, where the Jews always meet. I said nothing in secret. Why do you ask me? Ask those who have heard me what I said to them. Behold, these know the things which I said." When he had said this, one of the officers standing by slapped Jesus with his hand, saying, "Do you answer the high priest like that?" Jesus answered him, "If I have spoken evil, testify of the evil; but if well, why do you beat me?" Annas sent him bound to Caiaphas, the high priest. Now Simon Peter was standing and warming himself. They said therefore to him, "You aren't also one of his disciples, are you?" He denied it, and said, "I am not." One of the servants of the high priest, being a relative of him whose ear Peter had cut off, said, "Didn't I see you in the garden with him?" Peter therefore denied it again, and immediately the rooster crowed. They led Jesus therefore from Caiaphas into the Praetorium. It was early, and they themselves didn't enter into the Praetorium, that they might not be defiled, but might eat the Passover. Pilate therefore went out to them, and said, "What accusation do you bring against this man?" They answered him, "If this man weren't an evildoer, we wouldn't have delivered him up to you." Pilate therefore said to them, "Take him yourselves, and judge him according to your law." Therefore the Jews said to him, "It is not lawful for us to put anyone to death,"

Note that there is *no* account of any trail before the Sanhedrin in John's account. What transpired was just some hasty overnight interrogation by Annas and Caiaphas. And as John's chronology makes the Passover fall on a Sabbath, the interrogation on Thursday night is not subject to the same objections as the accounts in Mark, Matthew and Luke. The Johanine account is more plausible then that of the synoptics. However, the story in its entirety is still open to a serious objection which casts doubts on its historicity. Note that when the Jews handed Jesus over to the governor, they were told by Pilate to try the Galilean prophet themselves. The Jews objected to this by saying that they had no right to execute anyone. This completely contradicts what we know from other historical sources. It is a historical fact that the Jews did have a right to pass a sentence of death for a religious crime and to execute that sentence but subject to the approval of the Romans. One example is the death of James, the brother of Jesus, related in Josephus' *Antiquities of the Jews* 20:9:1. In the interregnum between the two Roman procurators (Festus had just died and Albinus was on his way to take up his post) the high priest Ananus hastily convened the Sanhedrin and had James and a few others condemned to death. James was then executed by stoning, the standard procedure for blasphemy. Josephus noted that some Jews who were "equitable citizens" went up and protested to Albinus. Their protest was not centered on the execution itself but on the fact that Ananus did it without the *consent* of Albinus.[67] There is even archaeological evidence to support this. Archaeologists discovered incised stone notices of the Jerusalem Temple that warns of the death penalty for any Gentile who trespass the temple's exclusively Jewish areas. These stone notices can be found in the Archaeological Museum at Istanbul and in the Rockefeller Museum at Jerusalem.[68]

In fact, the account of the stoning of Stephen[69] in the book of Acts contradicts the statement in John that the Jews have no right to carry out capital punishment:

Acts 6:12,7:58
They stirred up the people, the elders, and the scribes, and came against him [Stephen] and seized him, and brought him in to the council [i.e. the Sanhedrin] ...
They threw him out of the city, and stoned him.

The fact of the matter is this: had the Sanhedrin actually found Jesus guilty of blasphemy, they could have executed Jesus by stoning.

We have no reason to accept the story of the trial before the Sanhedrin as historical. We have many reasons to reject it as being so: the accounts in the gospels contradict one another, they contradict the tradition regarding the procedures of the Sanhedrin preserved in the Mishnah and the fact that Jesus was not executed by stoning but by the Roman (political) penalty of crucifixion.

Perhaps the most we can conclude is that because Jesus' "cleansing the Temple" caused some commotion there, some members of the Sanhedrin had Jesus arrested and, after a brief interrogation, handed Jesus over to the Romans.

---

[67]   Brandon, *The Trial of Jesus of Nazareth*: p91
         Guignebert, *Jesus*: p463
         Maccoby, *Revolution in Judea*: p204
         Wilson, *Jesus: The Evidence*: p103-104
[68]   Wilson, *Jesus: The Evidence*: p104
[69]   Some historians (see for instance Robin Lane Fox's *The Unauthorised Version* Penguin 1992: page 293) have claimed that this inscription and the example of the stoning of Stephen merely refer to the right of the temple authorities to *lynch* someone to death. It is ludicrous that this could actually be suggested, that *putting someone to death without a formal trial* is permissible to the Roman authorities but giving them a fair hearing was not.

THE TRIAL BEFORE PONTIUS PILATE

According to all four gospels, Jesus was handed over to Pontius Pilate after his Jewish trial. We will look first at Mark's account of the trial by Pontius Pilate:

Mark 15:1-15
Immediately in the morning the chief priests, with the elders and scribes, and the whole council, held a consultation, and bound Jesus, and carried him away, and delivered him up to Pilate. Pilate asked him, "Are you the King of the Jews?" He answered, "So you say." The chief priests accused him of many things. Pilate again asked him, "Have you no answer? See how many things they testify against you!" But Jesus made no further answer, so that Pilate marveled.
Now at the feast he used to release to them one prisoner, whom they asked of him. There was one called Barabbas, bound with those who had made insurrection, men who in the insurrection had committed murder. The multitude, crying aloud, began to ask him to do as he always did for them. Pilate answered them, saying, "Do you want me to release to you the King of the Jews?" For he perceived that for envy the chief priests had delivered him up. But the chief priests stirred up the multitude, that he should release Barabbas to them instead. Pilate again asked them, "What then should I do to him whom you call the King of the Jews?" They cried out again, "Crucify him!" Pilate said to them, "Why, what evil has he done?" But they cried out exceedingly, "Crucify him!" Pilate, wishing to please the multitude, released Barabbas to them, and handed over Jesus, when he had flogged him, to be crucified.

The first thing the reader will note is that Pilate in the passage above seems like a man forced against his will to execute Jesus. He appears to be a nice, albeit weak-willed, man, who tried his best to convince the crowd to allow him to release Jesus. Pilate truly looks like the good guy in Mark. In fact, if we look into the other gospels in the order that they were written (i.e. Mark, Matthew, Luke & John), Pilate became more and more like an innocent man who was forced by the Jews to convict Jesus.[70] Matthew for instance, apart from repeating all of Mark's account, made Pilate wash his hands in a symbolic gesture to assert his innocence:

Matthew 27:24-25
So when Pilate saw that nothing was being gained, but rather that a disturbance was starting, he took water, and washed his hands before the multitude, saying, "I am innocent of the blood of this righteous person. You see to it." All the people answered, "May his blood be on us, and on our children!"

In the Gospel of Luke this process of exonerating Pilate (and indirectly the Romans) of the crime of executing Jesus was carried another step further. In Mark and Matthew, Pilate was made to ask the Jews what crime Jesus had committed which deserved crucifixion (Mark 15:14; Matthew 27:23). This was a rather weak and indirect allusion to Pilate's belief in Jesus' innocence. Luke had Pilate make a *positive* assertion to the Galilean's innocence:

---

[70] Guignebert, *Jesus*: p465

Luke 23:13-16
Pilate called together the chief priests and the rulers and the people, and said to them, "You brought this man to me as one that perverts the people, and see, I have examined him before you, and found no basis for a charge against this man concerning those things of which you accuse him. Neither has Herod, for I sent you to him, and see, nothing worthy of death has been done by him. I will therefore chastise him and release him."

In the same gospel, Pilate is also made to argue more for Jesus and, in fact, does not formally condemn him but abandons him to the Jews:

Luke 23:20-25
Then Pilate spoke to them again, wanting to release Jesus, but they shouted, saying, "Crucify! Crucify him!" He said to them the third time, "Why? What evil has this man done? I have found no capital crime in him. I will therefore chastise him and release him." But they were urgent with loud voices, asking that he might be crucified. Their voices and the voices of the chief priests prevailed. Pilate decreed that what they asked for should be done. He released him who had been thrown into prison for insurrection and murder, for whom they asked, but he delivered Jesus up to their will.

There is another episode, found only in Luke that seems to further absolve Pilate in his role in the crucifixion. While in the gospels of Mark (15:16-20) and Matthew (27:27-31) it was Pilate's soldiers who mocked Jesus, Luke's gospel absolves the Romans even of this affront to Jesus. For in this gospel, instead of the Roman soldiers mocking Jesus it was the Jewish troops who did the deed:

Luke 23:7-11
When he found out that he was in Herod's jurisdiction, he sent him to Herod, who was also in Jerusalem during those days. Now when Herod saw Jesus, he was exceedingly glad, for he had wanted to see him for a long time, because he had heard many things about him. He hoped to see some miracle done by him. He questioned him with many words, but he gave no answers. The chief priests and the scribes stood, vehemently accusing him. *Herod with his soldiers humiliated him and mocked him.* Dressing him in luxurious clothing, they sent him back to Pilate.

As a step in the exoneration of Pilate and the Romans, this passage fulfils its aims amiably but it cannot be historical. For the whole idea that Pilate could have handed Jesus over to Herod Antipas is simply unbelievable. Roman law requires that the case can only be tried by an official in whose jurisdiction the crime was committed. As Craveri concludes:

The statement [that Pilate handed Jesus over to Herod when he found out that Jesus was a Galilean-PT] is not only debatable but undoubtedly false. Juridically, there was no need to extradite the accused from the *forum delicti commissi* to the *forum originis*, because the sole competent judge was the Roman procurator; nor was it in

Pilate's character, if for no other reason than the dignity of his office, to show such deference to the petty Jewish tetrarch.[71]

It is no wonder that Guignebert called the passage in Luke *absurd*.[72]

In the Gospel of John, Pilate is made to repeat, on three separate occasions, the sentence: "I find no basis for a charge against him." (John 18:38;19:4,6) Pilate is made to hand Jesus over for crucifixion only after the Jews threaten Pilate with a denunciation by the emperor:

> John 19:12-16
> At this, Pilate was seeking to release him, but the Jews cried out, saying, "If you release this man, you aren't Caesar's friend! Everyone who makes himself a king speaks against Caesar!" When Pilate therefore heard these words, he brought Jesus out, and sat down on the judgment seat at a place called "The Pavement," but in Hebrew, "Gabbatha." Now it was the Preparation Day of the Passover, at about the sixth hour. He said to the Jews, "Behold, your King!" They cried out, "Away with him! Away with him! Crucify him!" Pilate said to them, "Shall I crucify your King?" The chief priests answered, "We have no king but Caesar!" So then he delivered him to them to be crucified. So they took Jesus and led him away.

This process of exonerating Pilate and the Romans for Jesus crucifixion went beyond the canonical gospels into the apocryphal ones. In the Gospel of Peter, even the actual crucifixion was performed by the Jews. In the Ethiopian Gospel of Gamaliel, the story of Pilate is carried further. In it Pilate regretted having been manipulated by the Jews and actually became a convert to Christianity! In fact the Coptic Church includes Pontius Pilate in its calendar of Christian saints![73]

The Pontius Pilate of the Christian gospels and tradition is therefore a just, kind, albeit somewhat weak man who caved in to the Jewish demands. What do we know about this man from other, secular, sources? That he existed, we have no doubt. There were numerous contemporary references to him, including in the works of Jewish writers such as Philo and Josephus. And in 1961, an inscription bearing Pilate's name as the prefect of Judea was found in Caesarea.[74] Pilate, as we know, was the fifth prefect (i.e. governor) of Judea; holding the post from 26 to 37 CE.

A summary of Pilate's character can be found in the letter of King Agrippa I to Carigula, which was quoted by Philo in *De Legatione ad Caium*

> He [Pilate] feared lest they might in reality go on an embassy to the emperor, and might impeach him with respect to the other particulars of his government, in respect to the his *corruption*, his acts of *insolence*, and his *rapine* and his *habit of insulting people*, and his *continual murder of persons untried and uncondemned*, and his never ending, and gratuitous and *most grievous inhumanity*.[75] [emphasis added]

---

71   Craveri, *Life of Jesus*: p386
72   Guignebert, *Jesus*: p467
73   Craveri, *Life of Jesus*: p392-393
74   Wilson, *Jesus: The Evidence*: p104
75   Maccoby, *Revolution in Judea*: p57-58

In Josephus' writings too, we find further confirmation of Agrippa I's assessment of Pilate. Unlike his predecessors, Coponius (governor 6-9 CE), Ambibulos (9-12 CE), Annius Rufus (12-15 CE) and Valerius Gratus (15-26 CE), Pilate had nothing but contempt for Jewish culture, religion and people. Josephus' *Antiquities* (18:3:1-2) gave a summary of Pilate's experience with the Jews. In two separate incidents, Pilate showed himself to be a man with little respect for the Jews and their religion.

The first incident relates to the image of the emperor on the banners of the Roman soldiers. As the Jews in Jerusalem do not tolerate any graven image in the city, out of abhorrence for idolatry, the previous governors had the soldiers remove this image from their banners before entering the city. Pilate, showing little of respect for the sensitivities of the Jews, ordered his soldiers to enter the city at night and to not remove the image of the emperor. He thought that the Jews would not dare protest once they saw that the image was already there. But the Jews did protest, by sending a massive deputation from Jerusalem to Caesarea, the home of the governor. He initially ignored them and even threatened them with instant deaths by having his soldiers surround the protesting group. However, upon seeing that many of the Jews were willing to die for this, he relented and had the image removed.

The second incident however, did not end without bloodshed. Pilate used the money from the temple tax to build an aqueduct. This was for the public good of Jerusalem, for it would have meant an increase in water supply to the city. The Jews again protested, as it was sacrilegious for the sacred money of the temple to be used for secular purposes. This time Pilate stood his ground. And when the Jews staged a demonstration, he had his soldiers mix with the mob, wearing civilian clothing with clubs hidden underneath. The clubs were then used on the noisy ones first. The resulting confusion caused many deaths; some from the clubbing and some from being trampled by the panicking crowd as they fled from the scene.

Pilate's tenure as governor ended the same way it started, with an act that marked his total lack of compassion for the inhabitants of Palestine. The event that led to his downfall was the appearance of a Samaritan prophet. The prophet gained a large following. Pilate's method of dispelling the crowd around the prophet was typical of his character: he slaughtered them on their holy mountain. About 4,000 Samaritans died in that massacre. When this brutal act was reported to the emperor, Pilate was recalled to Rome in 37 CE. (Antiquities 18:4:1-2).[76]

The character of Pilate as given to us by secular historical sources is completely at variance with that given by the gospels. The Pilate in the gospel was amiable, politically naive and easily intimidated by the Jewish crowd. The historical Pilate, as we have seen, was cruel, headstrong and self-seeking. That this Pilate would have allowed a Jewish mob to have driven his actions is unthinkable. It is obvious that the actual role, if any, Pilate played in the condemnation of Jesus was extensively rewritten to exonerate him and to pin the blame on the Jews. We will discuss, later in this chapter, why this became necessary for the early Christians.

The narrative in the synoptics (Mark 15:6; Matthew 27:15; Luke 23:17) also tells of how Pilate anxious to have Jesus freed, tried to make use of a custom in which

---

[76]   Craveri, *Life of Jesus*: p82
         Maccoby, *Revolution in Judea*: p58
         Martin, *New Testament Foundations I*: p66-67

one prisoner, of the crowd's choice, is released during the Passover. As many scholars have shown, Roman and Jewish sources say nothing about such a custom ever having existed among the Romans either in Palestine or anywhere else.[77] Furthermore, it is unlikely that the Jews, of all people, would have been granted that unique privilege of freeing a prisoner accused of sedition as Palestine was one of the most unruly of the Roman provinces. The revolt against the census in 6 CE would easily have convinced the Romans of that! The quote below by B.H. Branscomd summarizes scholarly opinion about the existence of this custom:

> nothing is known of any such custom as is here described that at the feast of the Passover the Roman procurators regularly released one prisoner, and that the crowd named the individual no matter what his offence had been, is not only without any attestation, but also contrary to what we know of the spirit and manner of Roman rule over Palestine.[78]

In short, the "Passover privilege," as described in the synoptics, is undoubtedly fictional.

Another problem with the account of the trial before Pilate is this: even after the crowd had chosen Barabbas as the prisoner to be released, there was nothing to prevent Pilate from releasing Jesus, if the Roman governor was convinced of his innocence. Remember that in the Markan account (Mark 15:1-15) Jesus was not condemned until after Barabbas was released. There is nothing to prevent Pilate from releasing Jesus anytime before that, for he would not be releasing a condemned prisoner.[79]

Furthermore, the hostile attitude of the crowd is, to say the least, puzzling. According to all four gospels only five days before the trial, during Jesus' entry into Jerusalem, large crowds welcomed him (Mark 11:8; Matthew 21:8; Luke 19:37; John 12:12). And later we are told that the chief priests wanted to arrest Jesus but were afraid of the people:

Mark 11:18
The chief priests and the scribes heard it, and sought how they might destroy him. For they feared him, because all the multitude was astonished at his teaching.

Matthew 26:3-4
Then the chief priests, the scribes, and the elders of the people were gathered together in the court of the high priest, who was called Caiaphas. They took counsel together that they might take Jesus by deceit, and kill him. "

---

[77]   Craveri, *Life of Jesus*: p389
        Guignebert, *Jesus*: p469
        Maccoby, *Revolution in Judea*: p212
[78]   Nineham, *Saint Mark*: p413
[79]   Guignebert, *Jesus*: p469
        Maccoby, *Revolution in Judea*: p213
        Nineham, *Saint Mark*: p416

Luke 22:2

The chief priests and the scribes sought how they might put him to death, for they feared the people.

How this crowd, which had remained favorable to Jesus up to the time of the trial, could have suddenly taken a diametrically opposite position and asked for Jesus' execution is not explained in any of the gospels, and, indeed, is inexplicable.[80]

As in the episode of Jesus' trial before the Jews, we find difficulties and inconsistencies in almost every detail of the account of the trial before Pilate. We find that Pilate's character was different from what history tells us; that the Passover privilege was undoubtedly fictional; that Pilate could have released Jesus had he really wanted to; and in the inexplicable shift in the attitude of the crowd towards Jesus. All these considerations point us to the conclusion that the trial before Pilate, as depicted in the gospels, is unhistorical. Given Pilate's track record, he probably took little interest in the trial and had Jesus summarily executed.

HOW THE STORY OF JESUS' TRIAL COULD HAVE EVOLVED

The accounts of trials of Jesus before the Jewish and Roman authorities seem to have developed in two different directions. The trial before the Sanhedrin developed in a direction that tends to pin the blame of Jesus death more and more on the Jews. The trial before Pilate developed in the opposite way, with less and less blame being put on Pilate and the Romans. Why should this be so? Let us indulge in a bit of informed speculation about how this evolution took place.

The first clue comes from the environment of the early Christians. Certainly most Jews would not have accepted a crucified person as a messiah, for that would invoke the curse of Deuteronomy 21:23 (*for he who is hanged is accursed of God*).

Here, the method of Jesus' death, by crucifixion, made it blasphemous, as far as the Jews were concerned, for the early Christians to claim him as their messiah. The idea probably arose in some of the early Gentile converts that if it was blasphemous for *them* to claim that Jesus was the messiah, it must have been blasphemous for Jesus to do so about himself when he was alive. This could account for the glaring error in the synoptics, which made the Sanhedrin condemn Jesus for blasphemy for claiming to be the messiah. The rejection of many Jews to the message of Christianity would undoubtedly have caused stress in the relationship between the Gentile Christian and the unconverted Jew who does not believe that Jesus was the messiah. The Jewish revolt and the subsequent destruction of Jerusalem in 70 CE must have been interpreted differently by the Christians and the Jews. The Jews probably saw the destruction as God's punishment for straying from his teachings. We can see that they became more and more exclusive in their worship and the available evidence tells us that many Christians were ejected from synagogues in various places around the turn of the first century CE. The Christians, in particular the Gentile Christians, was probably frustrated with the Jews for rejecting Jesus and viewed the destruction of Jerusalem as God's punishment to the Jews for rejecting His Son. At the same time the Romans were friendly or at least tolerant towards the nascent religion. It was

---

[80] Maccoby, *Revolution in Judea*: p213

the Gentiles, which doubtless included many Roman citizens who were more inclined to accept Christianity. There developed a progressive tendency to transfer all the guilt of Jesus' death onto Jewish shoulders. This process was already well on its way when Mark was written and was carried further by the three later gospels. The exoneration continued into the later apocryphal gospels. Partly to exonerate Pilate and partly to satisfy the growing hostility of the Christians towards the Jews, a Jewish trial at least as formal and as decisive as Pilate's was invented.[81]

SIMON OF CYRENE

According to Mark, a man named Simon from Cyrene was forced by the Romans to help Jesus carry the cross to Golgotha:

> Mark 15:21
> They compelled one passing by, coming from the country, Simon of Cyrene, the father of Alexander and Rufus, to go with them, that he might bear his cross

Christian tradition and some modern scholars have asserted that the addition of details such as the names of Simon's sons seems to authenticate the story of the Cyrenian carrying the cross. The tradition had stated that these men, Alexander and Rufus, were men that were known to Mark's audience and as such were a guarantee of the crucifixion accounts. It has further equated them with two persons of the same name mentioned in Paul's epistles - Romans 16:3 mentions Rufus, while I Timothy 1:20 mentions Alexander.[82]

So according to the Markan tradition, it is a vouchsafed historical fact that Simon of Cyrene, the father of Alexander and Rufus, actually helped Jesus carry the cross to the place of crucifixion.

We have, in the Gospel of John, another explicit claim to being an eyewitness account to the crucifixion.

> John 19:35
> He who has seen has testified, and his testimony is true. He knows that he tells the truth, that you may believe.

Now, what did John say about this event? Let us read for ourselves:

> John 19:16-17 (RSV)
> Then he handed him over to them to be crucified. So they took Jesus, and he went out, *bearing his own cross*, to the place called the place of a skull, which is called in Hebrew Golgotha.

Here we have it, a blatant contradiction with the episode in Mark. According to John nobody helped Jesus to carry the cross - he carried it himself. Since both passages

---

81   Nineham, *Saint Mark*: p367-368, 404
82   Craveri, *The Life of Jesus*: p395
      Nineham, *Saint Mark*: p422

contradict one another, at least one of these must be wrong. Could one of these be right?

Let us first look a little closer at the Markan account. That Mark meant Simon to be a Jew we can be sure. Simon (*Shimeon*) is a Hebrew name. Cyrene, a town on the North African coast about 700 kilometers west of Alexandria, was also known to have a large Jewish population.[83]

The passage however, raises many questions that throw grave doubts on its authenticity. As was mentioned in the previous chapter, the synoptic tradition had Jesus crucified on the first day of Passover, a high holy day. No Jew would do any work that day. Yet here, we have Mark telling us that Simon was coming "in from the country", i.e. at work in the fields. This is impossible, given the strict ruling of no work on the Passover.[84]

The attempt to connect the names of the sons with that given in the Pauline epistles is extremely precarious for the names Alexander and Rufus were extremely common during that time.[85] The problem is not resolved when we look at Matthew's and Luke's accounts; both do not have the names of Simon's sons:

Matthew 27:32
As they came out, they found a man of Cyrene, Simon by name, and they compelled him to go with them, that he might carry his cross.

Luke 23:26
When they led him away, they grabbed one Simon of Cyrene, coming from the country, and laid on him the cross, to carry it after Jesus.

As both evangelists above copied Mark, their omission of the "authenticating" detail of Simon's sons is surprising. The possibility cannot be ruled out that the names Alexander and Rufus were later interpolations or insertions into Mark; and the copies of Mark that Matthew and Luke copied from did not have these names.[86] The scholars of the Jesus Seminar, noting that names, places and dates are sometimes added by writers of fiction to achieve verisimilitude, rightly concluded that the whole episode regarding Simon of Cyrene has "no historical value" and is a "piece of Markan fiction."[87]

Let us now turn our attention to John's account. We have shown in chapter 9 that, despite the claim of its author, the gospel is *not* an eyewitness account. John's gospel was written with a very pronounced theological slant. And here too we find the reason why Jesus was made to carry his own cross. During the time of the gospel's composition, the heretical Christian sect of docetic Gnostics was claiming that it was Simon who, transferred to Jesus' likeness, was nailed to the cross. Jesus, who assumed the appearance of Simon, stood near the cross and mocked his

---

[83]   Asimov, *Guide to the Bible*: p892
       Craveri, *The Life of Jesus*: p395
       Nineham, *Saint Mark*: p422
[84]   Craveri, *The Life of Jesus*: p395
[85]   Nineham, *Saint Mark*: p422
[86]   Guignebert, *Jesus*: p481
[87]   Funk, et.al.: *The Acts of Jesus*: p154-155

executioners.[88] John's gospel, which was clearly hostile to the docetics,[89] dealt with this docetist teaching by simply eliminating Simon of Cyrene from the narrative altogether.[90]

Despite claims of historical authentification from both the Markan and Johanine traditions – each contradicting the other - we do not know if Jesus carried his own cross or whether someone else, like Simon of Cyrene, helped him with it.

THE CRUCIFIXION

According to all four gospels, Jesus was crucified in a place called Golgotha or Place of the Skull (Mark 15:2; Matthew 27:33; Luke 23:33; John 19:17). Tradition has it that this location is at the present site of the Church of the Holy Sepulcher, which is a little north of the palace of Herod.[91]

Of the fact that Jesus was crucified we can be reasonably certain. First we know that crucifixion was a well known form of capital punishment used by the Romans on slaves, pirates, political agitators and non-citizens.[92] We also find the tradition of Jesus being crucified in the very earliest Christian documents, the epistles of Paul:

I Corinthians 1:23 (Also 2:2; 2:8)
[B]ut we preach Christ crucified; a stumbling block to Jews, and foolishness to Greeks

Galatians 2:20 (Also 5:24; 6:12,14)
[H]ave been crucified with Christ...

All the gospels mentioned Jesus' crucifixion:

Mark 15:24 (Also Matthew 27:35, Luke 23:33, John 19:18)
Crucifying him...

The crucifixion is thus multiply attested by all the earliest sources. Furthermore, we can apply the criterion of embarrassment to this. The earliest followers of Jesus were Jews, if the story was invented, it was unlikely that they would have chosen a crucified messiah, for the Torah has it that a hanged man is accursed of God:[93]

Deuteronomy 21:23
If a man have committed a sin worthy of death, and he be put to death, and you *hang him on a tree*; his body shall not remain all night on the tree, but you shall surely bury him the same day; for *he who is hanged is accursed of God.*

---

88   Nineham, *Saint Mark*: p422

89   The Docetists believed that Jesus Christ was not truly human and hence did not really suffer on the cross. John's account of the resurrection appearances, which include Jesus showing his wounds to Thomas (John 21:24-31) and Jesus eating fish (John 21:15).

90   Helms, *Gospel Fictions*: 122

91   See the map of Jerusalem in the beginning of this chapter.

92   Hengel, *Crucifixion*: p39-63

93   Guignebert, *Jesus*: p478-479

That this statement - about being "hung from a tree"- also applies to crucifixion can be derived from the fact that the Hebrew word *ets* translated as "tree" here can also be taken to mean "plank." The later Talmuds also accepted the idea that the term can mean a plank or a tree.[94] It is also unlikely that the Gentile converts to early Christianity could have invented this for crucifixion in the Greco-Roman world was considered so offensive as to be "obscene."[95] Paul's statement in I Corinthians 1:23 quoted above, summarizes the *embarrassment* their "theology of the cross" would have caused the early Christians.

These considerations show that the crucifixion itself is an historical fact.[96]

DETAILS OF THE CRUCIFIXION

Saying that Jesus' crucifixion is an historical fact is not the same as saying that the *details* of the crucifixion accounts in the gospels are historical. We have seen in chapter 11 that many of the major episodes of the nativity found in both Matthew and Luke were constructed from Old Testament passages. We have also seen earlier in this chapter, how Matthew changed the account of Jesus' entry into Jerusalem by making him sit on *two* donkeys (Matthew 21:1-7) in order to make Jesus' action fulfill the supposed prophecy in Zechariah 9:9 more exactly. It is the same with the details of the crucifixion scene. Most critical scholars are of the opinion that many of the details of the crucifixion found in the gospels were not the result of eyewitness accounts but were concocted from prophetic passages in the Old Testament.[97]

The Final Drink

According to Mark and Matthew, Jesus was offered something to drink before he was crucified:

Mark 15:23
They offered him wine mixed with *myrrh* to drink, but he didn't take it.

Matthew 27:34
They gave him sour wine to drink mixed with *gall*. When he had tasted it, he would not drink.

The mixture given in Mark, wine with myrrh, could be meant as an attempt to alleviate the pain Jesus was about to endure. The cocktail could have had a sedative effect and lessen his sense of pain. In Matthew however, the mixture had changed to wine with gall. Gall has an extremely bitter taste, so in Matthew the intention seems to be the opposite that of Mark, that it was meant to *add* to the torture of Jesus.

---

[94] Richard C. Carrier, "Burial of Jesus in the Light of Jewish Law", Robert M. Price & Jeffrey Jay Lowder (eds), *The Empty Tomb*: p375

[95] Hengel, *Crucifixion*: p22

[96] For those who think that this is one case where the life of Jesus is prophesied in the Old Testament (i.e. Psalm 22:16) – please refer to Excursus C, section III.

[97] Funk, et. al., *The Acts of Jesus*: p155-158

Since the alcoholic concoctions described by Matthew and Mark are different from each other, both these accounts cannot be true at the same time. We have good reasons to reject both as historical, for there are Old Testament passages which both Mark and Matthew could easily have used as their source:[98]

> Proverbs 31:6
> Give strong drink to him who is ready to perish; and wine to the bitter in soul.

> Psalms 69:21
> They also gave me gall for my food. In my thirst, they gave me vinegar to drink.

Both Luke and John have no reference to this offer of a drink to Jesus before his crucifixion. All four gospels are in agreement that the soldiers offered him wine vinegar to drink just before his death:

> Mark 15: 36 (Matthew 27:48; Luke 23:36)
> One ran, and filling a sponge full of vinegar, put it on a reed, and gave it to him to drink

That this is written merely in fulfillment of Psalm 69:21 (see above) is made clearer in John.

> John 19:28-29
> After this, Jesus, seeing that all things were now finished, that the Scripture might be fulfilled, said, "I am thirsty." Now a vessel full of vinegar was set there; so they put a sponge full of the vinegar on hyssop, and held it at his mouth.

The additional detail by John, that the stick was a stalk of a hyssop plant, shows the Old Testament origins of the passage. The use as a hyssop stalk as a means of conveying the sponge to Jesus' mouth is an almost impossible task - for the plant produces only very slender and fragile stems.[99] John is actually trying to fit in another Old Testament "prophecy":

> Psalm 51:7
> Purify me with hyssop, and I will be clean. Wash me, and I will be whiter than snow.

John's identification of Jesus with the Paschal lamb is also at play here, for hyssop is used for sprinkling the blood of the Paschal lamb on the Hebrew doorposts during the first Passover (Exodus 12:21-22). All the details about giving the drink to Jesus are filled with contradictions and errors. They are derived purely from Old Testament passages, not from eyewitness accounts.

---

[98] Craveri, *The Life of Jesus*: p398
      Guignebert, *Jesus*: p481-482
[99] Craveri, *The Life of Jesus*: p400

The Dividing of the Garments

According to all four gospels, the soldier divided the garments of Jesus among them by casting lots:

> Mark 15:24 (Matthew 27:35; Luke 23:34' John 19:23-24)
> Crucifying him, they parted his garments among them, casting lots on them, what each should take.

That the soldiers could have done this is not impossible. In fact by the reign of Hadrian (117-138) the custom was already established that the ownership of the clothing of the victims of crucifixion was one of the perks of being an executioner! However, the additional detail of the soldiers casting lots to decide who gets which piece of Jesus' garments reveals to us that the actual source of this episode is not history but the Old Testament:[100]

> Psalms 22:18
> They divide my garments among them. They cast lots for my clothing.

The Two Thieves

All four gospels agree that Jesus was not crucified alone (Mark 15:27; Matthew 27:38; Luke 23:32; John 19:18). John said nothing more than that Jesus was crucified between the other two. The synoptic gospels add more details than this. Both Mark and Matthew say that these two convicted criminals joined the crowds in hurling insults at Jesus:

> Mark 15:27,32
> With him they crucified two robbers; one on his right hand, and one on his left...
> *Those who were crucified with him insulted him.*

> Matthew 27:38,44
> Then there were two robbers crucified with him, one on his right hand and one on the left. Those who passed by blasphemed him...*The robbers also who were crucified with him cast on him the same reproach.*

Luke, however, contradicts this account by inserting an edifying tale about one of the robbers who was received by the crucified Jesus into heaven:

> Luke 23:32-33, 39-43
> There were also others, two criminals, led with him to be put to death. When they came to the place that is called The Skull, they crucified him there with the criminals, one on the right and the other on the left....One of the criminals who was hanged insulted him, saying, "If you are the Christ, save yourself and us!" But the other answered, and rebuking him said, "Don't you even fear God, seeing you are under the same condemnation? And we indeed justly, for we receive the due

---

[100]   Craveri, *The Life of Jesus*: p398
Guignebert, *Jesus*: p482

reward for our deeds, but this man has done nothing wrong." He said to Jesus, "Lord, remember me when you come into your Kingdom." Jesus said to him, "Assuredly I tell you, today you will be with me in Paradise."

It is glaringly obvious that Luke's tale cannot be reconciled with the accounts in Mark and Matthew which had *both* the robbers hurling insults at him. Fundamentalists have tried to explain away this contradiction by suggesting that both criminals began by mocking Jesus (as in Mark and Matthew) but one later thought the better of it and rebuked the other criminal for doing so! But as Robert M. Price noted, such an explanation is "just one more lame harmonization." Note that neither Mark nor Luke mentions anything about one of the criminals changing his mind, while Luke was careful not to mention that both started off by criticizing Jesus.[101]

Does the Lukan episode have any claims to historicity? No. It sounds more like a parable than an historical episode. The story also fits nicely into the Lukan agenda of trying to make Christianity acceptable to the Romans. The old saying goes, "it takes one to know one"; by having a criminal recognize that Jesus was not one of them, it allows Luke's Roman audience to see that Jesus' execution, though obscene and horrible, was not deserved.[102]

In fact we have good reason to think that the origin of the tradition that Jesus was crucified between two thieves was not an historical event, but again, an Old Testament passage:[103]

Isaiah 53:12
...*he* poured out his soul to death, and *was numbered with the transgressors*...

Another episode in the crucifixion account shows itself to be of dubious historicity.

The Mocking Crowd

The synoptics' description of the crowd present at Jesus' execution was one that was hostile to the Galilean. Given below is Mark's account of what happened:

Mark 15:29-32
Those who passed by blasphemed him, wagging their heads, and saying, "Ha! You who destroy the temple, and build it in three days, save yourself, and come down from the cross!" Likewise, also the chief priests mocking among themselves with the scribes said, "He saved others. He can't save himself. Let the Christ, the King of Israel, now come down from the cross, that we may see and believe him." Those who were crucified with him insulted him..

---

[101]   Price, *The Incredible Shrinking Son of Man*: p323-324
[102]   Craveri, *The Life of Jesus*: p398-399
        Funk, et. al., *The Acts of Jesus*: p361-362
        Guignebert, *Jesus*: p484-485
        Price, *The Incredible Shrinking Son of Man*: p323
[103]   Craveri, *The Life of Jesus*: p398

D.E. Nineham demonstrated convincingly that, the contents of the passage above show that the evangelist had no historical sources for this.[104]   Firstly, the insults hurled by the passers by amount to no more than a repetition of the charges brought against him by the Sanhedrin (his threat to destroy the temple and his claim of messianic status).   Secondly, the presence of the chief priests and scribes at the scene of the crucifixion *on the first day of Passover* strains our credulity.   Thirdly, many of the details reflect Old Testament passages so closely that it is improbable that these accounts did not stem ultimately from them.   Some of the passages are given below:

> Lamentations 2:15
> All that pass by clap their hands at you. They hiss and wag their head...

> Psalms 22:7
> All those who see me mock me. They insult me with their lips. They shake their heads, saying, "He trusts in Yahweh; let him deliver him. Let him rescue him, since he delights in him."

> Psalms 69:9
> For the zeal of your house consumes me. The reproaches of those who reproach you have fallen on me.

> Wisdom of Solomon 2:17-20 (RSV-Catholic edition)
> Let us see if his words are true and let us test what will happen at the end of his life, for if the righteous man is God's son, he will help him and will deliver him from the hand of his adversaries.   Let us test him with insults and torture, that we may find out how gentle he is, and make trial of his forbearance.   Let us condemn him to a shameful death, for according to what he says, he will be protected.

In fact, the Greek word for *insult* (*oneidizo*) in the Septuagint version of Psalms 69:9 is exactly the same used in Mark 15:32. The exact correspondence between these Old Testament passage and Mark's account points to the fact that Mark's source was not working from the traditional eyewitness material but from a belief that the Old Testament contains predictions about Jesus' life.

Darkness Over the Land

According to the synoptics (but not John), there was an astronomical phenomenon coinciding with Jesus' crucifixion just before his death. Mark said that there was darkness from noon until 3 p.m.:

> Mark 15:33 (Matthew 27:45)
> When the sixth hour had come, there was darkness over the whole land until the ninth hour.

Luke tried to clarify the source of this darkness by saying that it was an eclipse of the sun:

---

[104]   Nineham, *Saint Mark*: p425

Luke 23:44-45
It was now about the sixth hour, and darkness came over the whole land until the ninth hour. The sun was darkened, and the veil of the temple was torn in two.

Luke's account, which clearly described a solar eclipse, is an obvious impossibility. For according to the synoptic gospels, Jesus was crucified on the first day of Passover, the 15th of Nisan. The 15th of Nisan is a full moon night, that is, the moon is on the other side of the earth at the time Luke said a solar eclipse was occurring. For a solar eclipse to happen, the moon must be between the earth and the sun. Luke is here describing an astronomical impossibility - in both senses of the word! Even assuming that the chronology of the gospels was wrong, i.e. that Jesus did not die during the Passover, there is still no report of a solar eclipse in Jerusalem around the few years that Jesus could have died in.[105]

It is obvious therefore that the account of the darkening of the earth, especially the verse in Luke which directly ties it to a solar eclipse, cannot be historical. And, as usual, there were ample passages in the Old Testament that could have been the source of this account (e.g. Exodus 10:22) but perhaps the most apt is found in the book of Amos:

Amos 8:9
"It will happen in that day," says the Lord Yahweh, "that I will cause the sun to go down at noon, and I will darken the earth in the clear day."

The synoptics, if you remember, made the darkness start at the sixth hour (i.e. noon), just as the passage in Amos. In short, all historical and scientific considerations show this episode to be unhistorical. Everything points to its origin in Old Testament passages, not in history.

Jesus' Last Words

All four gospels claimed to have recorded down the last words Jesus uttered before he passed away. We would expect, if their veracity is to be trusted that they all reported Jesus to say the same words. However, this is not the case. The evangelists simply cannot agree on what exactly Jesus said just before he died. We give below each gospel and their report of Jesus' last utterance:

Mark 15:34,37 (Matthew 27:46,50)
At the ninth hour Jesus cried with a loud voice, saying, "Eloi, Eloi, lama sabachthani?" which is, being interpreted, "My God, my God, why have you forsaken me?"... Jesus cried out with a loud voice, and gave up the spirit.

Luke 23:46
Jesus, crying with a loud voice, said, "Father, into your hands I commit my spirit!" Having said this, he breathed his last.

---

[105]   Caird, *Saint Luke*: p253
Craveri, *The Life of Jesus*: p399
Price, *The Incredible Shrinking Son of Man*: p324

John 19:30
When Jesus therefore had received the vinegar, he said, "It is finished." He bowed his head, and gave up his spirit.

Since all the above passages contradict one another, not all of them can be true. And, as usual, each evangelist has theological reasons for putting his own version of Jesus' last words. Mark's source was the book of Psalms:

Psalms 22:1
My God, my God, why have you forsaken me?

Luke's source was another verse from the same book:

Psalms 31:5
Into your hand I commend my spirit.

John's version is in keeping with his portrayal of Jesus throughout the passion - his savior was triumphant. Just as he triumphantly carried the cross himself, he now exclaims the final accomplishment of his mission. As usual none of these accounts have any valid claim to historicity.[106]

The Time of Crucifixion

There are serious discrepancies between the chronologies of the synoptics and John as to the exact time Jesus was crucified. The first we have already pointed out in the previous chapter: to the synoptics Jesus was crucified on Passover itself while to John Jesus was crucified on Passover eve (John 19:14). The second discrepancy involves the timing of events on the day of crucifixion itself. The synoptics had Jesus crucified on the third hour (i.e. 9 a.m.: Mark 15:25):

Mark 15:25
It was the *third hour*, and they crucified him.

There was a darkening of the land from the sixth to the ninth hour. At about 3pm Jesus uttered his last words and died:

Mark 15:33-37 (Matthew 27:45-50; Luke 23:44-46).
When the *sixth hour* had come, there was darkness over the whole land until the ninth hour. At the *ninth hour* Jesus cried with a loud voice...Jesus cried out with a loud voice, and gave up the spirit.

John, however, had Jesus sentenced by Pilate at the sixth hour, i.e. noon, by the time which, according to the synoptics, Jesus had already been hanging on the cross for three hours![107]

---

[106] Guignebert, *Jesus*: p485-486
Helms, *Gospel Fictions*: 123
[107] Cadoux, *The Life of Jesus*: p202

John 19:13-18

When Pilate therefore heard these words, he brought Jesus out, and sat down on the judgment seat at a place called "The Pavement," but in Hebrew, "Gabbatha." Now it was the Preparation Day of the Passover, at about the *sixth hour*. ...So then he delivered him to them to be crucified. So they took Jesus and led him away....to the place called "The Place of a Skull," which is called in Hebrew, "Golgotha," where they crucified him...

This clear cut contradiction cannot be reconciled and further enforce our findings that the details in the account of Jesus' crucifixion have no historical basis.

We reject the Synoptic time table because it is simply too mechanical: Jesus was nailed to the cross on the third hour, on the sixth hour "darkness came over the whole land" and in the ninth hour Jesus died.[108]

We reject John's account because his reason for putting Jesus crucifixion time later was purely theological. He wanted to make the time of Jesus' death coincide with the slaughter of the Passover lamb.[109] As Guignebert noted:

He has placed the death of Jesus at the hour fixed by Jewish custom for the sacrifice of the paschal lamb, *between the two evenings* (Exodus 12:6), that is to say between sunset and twilight, or between the declining (three o'clock) and setting of the sun's orb.[110]

The Events at the Moment of Jesus' Death

According to the synoptics, Jesus' death did go unnoticed by nature. According to Mark, the curtain of the temple was torn in two the moment Jesus died. Luke had the curtain torn just *before* Jesus' died.

Mark 15:37-38

Jesus cried out with a loud voice, and gave up the spirit. The veil of the temple was torn in two from the top to the bottom.

Luke 23:45-46

The sun was darkened, and the veil of the temple was torn in two. Jesus, crying with a loud voice, said, "Father, into your hands I commit my spirit!" Having said this, he breathed his last.

That the curtain was torn into two was an historical fact but not during the death of Jesus. It was most probably torn in two when Titus sacked Jerusalem in 70 CE and had the curtain brought down. This torn curtain was among the spoils of the Temple paraded in Rome to commemorate the victory. It is highly probable that the author of Mark, who was based in Rome, saw this and turned it into an etiological legend.[111]

---

108 Craveri, *The Life of Jesus*: p399
109 Ranke-Heinemann, *Putting Away Childish Things*: p116
110 Guignebert, *Jesus*: p487
111 Price, *The Incredible Shrinking Son of Man*: p324

Matthew reported even more fantastic occurrences – there was an earthquake and many who were already dead came back to life. A kind of first century "Night of the Living Dead":

Matthew 27:51-53
Jesus cried again with a loud voice, and yielded up his spirit. Behold, the veil of the temple was torn in two from the top to the bottom. The earth quaked and the rocks were split. The tombs were opened, and many bodies of the saints who had fallen asleep were raised; and coming out of the tombs after his resurrection, they entered into the holy city and appeared to many.

Surely we are not asked to simply accept Matthew's word for this occurrence of this zombie-fest? We have already seen him to be unreliable in many instances. The account as it is does not tell us who were the "holy men" who raised from the dead, nor who they were that saw them. It should also be noted that this event is not recorded by any contemporaneous historian[112] or even by later evangelists such as John and Luke. I will leave the critique of this ludicrous and unsupported report of Matthew to the American patriot Thomas Paine (1737-1809):

The book ascribed to Matthew says that there was darkness all over the land from the sixth hour to the ninth hour - that the veil of the temple was rent in twain from top to bottom - that there was an earthquake - that the rocks rent - that the graves opened, that the bodies of many saints that slept arose and came out of their graves after the resurrection, and went into the holy city and appeared to many. Such is the account which this dashing writer of the book of Matthew gives, but in which he is not supported by the writers of the other books.

The writer of the book ascribed to Mark, in detailing the circumstances of the crucifixion, makes no mention of any earthquake, nor of the rocks rending, nor of the graves opening, nor of the dead man walking out. The writer of the book of Luke is silent also on the same points. And as to the writer of the book of John, though he details the circumstances of the crucifixion down to the burial of Christ, he says nothing about either the darkness, the veil of the temple, the earthquake, the rocks, the graves, nor the dead men...

It is an easy thing to tell a lie, but it is difficult to support the lie after it is told. The writer of the book of Matthew should have told us who the saints were that came to life again and went into the city, and what became of them afterwards, and who it was that saw them - for he is not hardy enough to say that he saw them himself - whether they came fully dressed and where they got their dresses; whether they went to their former habitation and reclaimed their wives, their husband and their property, and how they were received, whether they entered ejectments for the recovery of their possessions or whether they died again, or went back to their graves alive and buried themselves.

---

[112] As James Crossley noted in his book debate with Micheal Bird, such an event would surely have been recorded by historians such as Josephus had it actually occurred. That all our historical sources are silent on such an incredible event shows beyond a doubt that this story is an invention of Matthew. (Bird & Crossley, *How Did Christianity Begin?*: p57)

> Strange indeed that an army of saints should return to life and nobody knew who they were, or who it was that saw them, and that not a word more should be said upon the subject, nor these saints have anything to tell us![113]

The objections of Thomas Paine are succinct and, I believe, unanswerable. The passage of Matthew, as it stands, cannot be believed. Probably the main reason for concocting this story is the belief in early Christianity that Jesus' resurrection was the precursor – or "first fruits" as Paul put it (I Corinthians 15:23) to the eschatological general resurrection of the dead.[114]

We should note here how the evangelical mind is simply unable to accept the fact that their beloved Scriptures can contain fiction. The evangelical scholar N.T. Wright, in his massive tome (in weight: 3 lbs!)[115] *The Resurrection of the Son of God* (2003), actually tried to argue for the historicity of Matthew 27:51-53:

> Some stories are so odd that they may just have happened. This may be one of them...[116]

Such a "criterion" for historicity is unprecedented in historical research. Wright is saying that if someone can make up a story *just odd enough* – it could be accepted as historical! To this, James Crossley, lecturer in New Testament at the University of Sheffield, asked sarcastically:

> [D]oes this [criterion] apply to sightings of Elvis, stories of fairies or tales of vampires?[117]

Another incident that happened at the point of Jesus' death was the statement by a Roman centurion:

> Mark 15:39 (Matthew 27:54)
> When the centurion, who stood by opposite him, saw that he cried out like this and breathed his last, he said, "Truly this man was the Son of God!"

This statement is most definitely unhistorical. For the concept of the Son of God could not have been intelligible to a Roman soldier.[118] Luke, probably realizing the flaw in Mark, changed the statement of the Roman centurion:

> Luke 23:47
> When the centurion saw what was done, he glorified God, saying, "Certainly this was a righteous man."

---

[113] Paine, *The Age of Reason*: p202-205
[114] Price, *The Incredible Shrinking Son of Man*: p324
[115] Robert M. Price in his review of Wright's book in the *Journal of Higher Criticism* deliciously commented on the unnecessarily long book as "designed to bludgeon us into belief"!
[116] Wright, *The Resurrection of the Son of God*: p636
[117] Bird & Crossley, *How Did Christianity Begin?*: p56
[118] Guignebert, *Jesus*: p488

Luke's change is not based on a more reliable eyewitness account but is consistent with one of his principle goals in writing his gospel. As we have seen in the case of the two thieves, he wanted to make his Roman audience see that Jesus was wrongly condemned and did not deserve the penalty of crucifixion. Having a Roman centurion make the exclamation that Jesus was innocent nicely fits his literary agenda.[119]

John's Special Account of the Crucifixion

Some Christians assert that John, although on the whole unhistorical, may contain eyewitness reports to the death of Jesus.[120] They normally based their claims to two events reported in John and nowhere else. The first involves Jesus handing over the custody of his mother to one of his disciples. The second is the act of the Roman soldiers breaking the legs of the two robbers crucified with Jesus and piercing Jesus' side.

The first event is narrated by John thus:

John 19:25-27
But there were standing by the cross of Jesus his mother, and his mother's sister, Mary the wife of Clopas, and Mary Magdalene. Therefore when Jesus saw his mother, and the disciple whom he loved standing there, he said to his mother, "Woman, behold your son!" Then he said to the disciple, "Behold, your mother!" From that hour, the disciple took her to his own home.

As Craveri pointed out[121] this account cannot be historical because we know from other sources that places of crucifixion were closely guarded and it was not allowed for anyone to go close to them. Hence this conversation, which must require Mary and the beloved disciple to be no more than three meters or so away, could not have occurred.

The second event seems to be a vivid eyewitness account and indeed, the author asserts as much:

John 19:31-35
Therefore the Jews, because it was the Preparation Day, so that the bodies wouldn't remain on the cross on the Sabbath (for that Sabbath was a special one), asked of Pilate that their legs might be broken, and that they might be taken away. Therefore the soldiers came, and broke the legs of the first, and of the other who was crucified with him; but when they came to Jesus, and saw that he was already dead, they didn't break his legs. However one of the soldiers pierced his side with a spear, and immediately blood and water came out. He who has seen has testified, and his testimony is true. He knows that he tells the truth, that you may believe...

The author's claim notwithstanding, the whole episode looks very much like a hastily done insertion. We see that the Jews asked for the legs to be broken and the bodies to

---

[119] Price, *The Incredible Shrinking Son of Man*: p324-325
[120] Wilson, *Jesus: The Evidence*: p110
[121] Craveri, *The Life of Jesus*: p400

be taken down. Pilate, according to John, acquiesced to that. Yet just a few verses later (John 19:38) Joseph of Arimathea was reported to have come later and did the same thing (i.e. asked for permission to remove Jesus from the cross).[122]

The breaking of the legs and the piercing of Jesus' side with the lance clearly fulfills Old Testament prophesies, as John himself admits:

John 19:36-37
For these things happened, that the Scripture might be fulfilled, "A bone of him will not be broken." [Exodus 12:46] [123] Again another Scripture says, "They will look on him whom they pierced." [Zechariah 12:10]

The piercing of Jesus' side and the gushing out of water and blood had been claimed by believers to be an acute observation of a physiological fact.[124] It has been suggested, among others, that the water was actually the pericardial fluid, or that Jesus was suffering from pleural effusion. Unfortunately for the believers, both these suggestions are flawed. Pericardial fluid, could not be found in the quantity described by John, who had the water *flowing* (not trickling) out with the blood. The amount is very small and there is no way it could have been observed to *flow* out from the body.[125] The pleural effusion hypothesis meets the same end. Pleural effusion is the condition in which fluid builds up around the lungs. The common causes are tuberculosis, pneumonia, cancer of the lung, congestive-heart failure or Nephrotic syndrome (a kind of kidney disease).[126] There is no evidence that Jesus was sick during the time of his crucifixion. Furthermore, the human lungs are at sub-atmospheric pressure, so if a man's side is pierced when there is fluid in the pleural cavity, *air will rush in, not* fluid flow out. In fact, in modern medicine, the fluid has to be sucked out under pressure.[127] The source for the fluid flow is not to be found in physiology but in theology: the water represents baptism and the blood represents the Eucharist.[128] The "historical witness" of John vanishes into thin air!

CONCLUSION ON THE GOSPEL CRUCIFIXION ACCOUNTS

As we have seen, the obviously unhistorical nature of the events described and the heavy reliance on Old Testament passages show that *no eyewitness accounts made it into the tradition utilized by the evangelists.* This is probably due to the fact that all his disciples deserted him after his arrest. And perhaps the only reliable line in the

---

[122]   Wells, *The Historical Evidence for Jesus*: p189
[123]   It is important to note that Exodus 12:46 is not a messianic prophecy at all. In fact, the passage doesn't even refer to a human being but to the Passover lamb! That John meant Jesus to be the new paschal lamb cannot be doubted for, as we have seen, unlike the synoptics, he made the time of Jesus' death coincide with the slaughter of the Passover lamb. With such a heavily theological stench it is hard to credit John's passage with any veracity.
[124]   Wilson, *Jesus: The Evidence*: p110
[125]   Wells, *The Historical Evidence for Jesus*: p190
[126]   Personal e-mail exchange with Dr. Ronald Ng, June 26, 2006
[127]   Wells, *The Jesus Legend*: p85
[128]   Guignebert, *Jesus*: p487

last week of Jesus' life is this line from Mark, about what happened after Jesus was arrested:

> Mark 14:50
> They [Jesus' disciples] all left him, and fled.

The tradition that the women followers of Jesus were present during the crucifixion was probably inserted to give a guarantee to the authenticity of the events described. But the artificial nature of this insertion can be seen from the fact that all four gospels simply couldn't agree as to just exactly *who* was present during the crucifixion. Given below is who each evangelist says was there:

> Mark 15:40-41
> There were also women watching from afar, among whom were both Mary Magdalene, and Mary the mother of James the less and of Joses, and Salome; who, when he was in Galilee, followed him, and served him; and many other women who came up with him to Jerusalem.

> Matthew 27:55-56
> Many women were there watching from afar, who had followed Jesus from Galilee, serving him. Among them were Mary Magdalene, Mary the mother of James and Joses, and the mother of the sons of Zebedee.

> Luke 23:49
> All his acquaintances, and the women who followed with him from Galilee, stood at a distance, watching these things.

> John 19:25
> But there were standing by the cross of Jesus his mother, and his mother's sister, Mary the wife of Clopas, and Mary Magdalene.

The proliferation of Marys as witnesses to the crucifixion is a source of confusion. John had three Marys present at the crucifixion, including Jesus' mother. Mark and Matthew did not mention Jesus' mother but another Mary, the mother of James and Joses. This is rather strange as Jesus was mentioned earlier as having brothers named James and Joses (Mark 6:3; Matthew 13:55). Luke was probably aware of these difficulties and avoided it by simply calling those present "the women."

As an interesting note, the only person all three gospels (Mark, Matthew and John) agreed was there was Mary Magdalene. We know of this Mary from Luke:

> Luke 8:1-2
> It happened soon afterwards, that he went about through cities and villages, preaching and bringing the good news of the Kingdom of God. With him were the twelve, and certain women who had been healed of evil spirits and infirmities: Mary who was called Magdalene, from whom seven demons had gone out...

Today we would call a person who was "possessed by demons" as someone who is either insane or psychologically unsound. If the above passage in Luke is historical, it means that the only person the gospels of Mark, Matthew and John agree was present at the crucifixion was someone who we have every reason to believe is mentally unsound! Mary Magdalene is the only person whom all four gospels agree to have been the witness to the resurrection (or at least the empty tomb: Mark 16:1-8) as well! But more of that later.

The lack of agreement as to who the women were makes any appeal to the presence of the women at the crucifixion as the authenticating factor dubious. To conclude what we know of the crucifixion, I quote Guignebert again:

> As a matter of fact, early tradition, with or without the guarantee of the women, was not in a position to do more than assert the essential facts: Jesus was arrested, tried, condemned and executed. Of that alone we are certain.[30]

* * * * *

This chapter has shown that *all* the major events in the few days before Jesus' death: the Passover meal, the betrayal by Judas, the prayer at Gethsemane, and the trials before the Sanhedrin and Pilate, are unhistorical. Even in such simple events such as Jesus' triumphal entry riding on a donkey, there is no agreement as to the *number* of donkeys Jesus was sitting on. As for the cleansing of the temple, although probably an historical event, all four gospels disagree as to *when* it happened: Mark put it on Monday while Matthew and Luke placed the event on Sunday, and John inexplicably put the very same event three years before he died. The story of Jesus' anointing by a woman is given in three different locations and in three different settings; the original form of the story is already lost to us. As for the crucifixion, we can only be confident of the barest detail, namely that Jesus was actually crucified. All the other details are inventions of either the tradition or the evangelists.

In conclusion, most of the details of what happened during the Passion Week are manifestly unhistorical, the rest are historically suspect, at best. As such, we cannot even construct a general outline of what actually happened then. The events that occurred during the last few days of Jesus' life on earth are no longer known to us and, in fact, the details were already forgotten by the time the gospels were written.

Chapter Fifteen
BURIAL
AND RESURRECTION

THE SEQUENCE OF EVENTS

We now turn to the central event of Christianity: the resurrection of Jesus. As the traditional account of the resurrection is very closely tied to the burial account we will analyze these together in this chapter. Before we start with a detailed analysis of the events, we will first give a summary of the episode as depicted in Mark.

It was the day before the Sabbath, Joseph of Arimathea a member of the council (the Sanhedrin), asked Pilate for Jesus' body for burial. The Roman governor, after verifying that Jesus indeed was already dead, granted him the request. Joseph wrapped Jesus' body in linen and then placed him in a tomb cut out of rock. Then he rolled a stone over the entrance of the tomb. The two Marys saw where Jesus was laid. (Mark 15:42-47)

Very early on Sunday morning, the two Marys and Salome went to Jesus' tomb to anoint his body with spices. When they arrived at the tomb they noticed that the stone had been rolled away. They saw a young man dressed in white in the tomb. He told them Jesus had risen and asked the women to tell Jesus' disciples that he will meet them in Galilee. The women ran away from the tomb, frightened and did not tell anyone what had happened. (Mark 16:1-8)

This, in a nutshell, is Mark's version of Jesus' burial and resurrection.

THE BURIAL

The account of Jesus' burial is given in all four gospels. As usual we will give Mark's version in full and use that as the starting point of our analysis.

> Mark 15:42-47
> When evening had now come, because it was the Preparation Day, that is, the day before the Sabbath, Joseph of Arimathea, a prominent council member who also himself was looking for the Kingdom of God, came. He boldly went in to Pilate, and asked for Jesus' body. Pilate marveled if he were already dead; and summoning the centurion, he asked him whether he had been dead long. When he found out from the centurion, he granted the body to Joseph. He bought a linen cloth, and taking him down, wound him in the linen cloth, and laid him in a tomb which had been cut out of a rock. He rolled a stone against the door of the tomb. Mary Magdalene and Mary, the mother of Joses, saw where he was laid.

The fundamentalist apologist, William Lane Craig, argues that there are three reasons why the account of the burial in Mark is historical: first, it is "based on an old source"; second, the accounts of Matthew and John provide "independent attestation" of its historicity; and third, there is no conflicting tradition to this account.[1]

---

[1]   Copan & Tacelli, *Jesus' Resurrection*: p32

Before answering his claims we need to look at the account in greater detail. Many problems and inconsistencies are present in the Markan passage above and in its relation to the same episode in the other three gospels.

The first problem starts with the very first verse of the above passage. "When evening had come" means that it was already sundown (i.e. 6pm) and the new day, which was the Sabbath, had already started. Even if evening can be taken the mean an earlier time [say about 4pm] the problem remains because according to the synoptics that day, Friday, was the first day of Passover. Neither on a Sabbath nor a Passover is any business transaction allowed. Yet we are told that Joseph *purchased a linen shroud on that day*. The wording and arrangement of the passage does not permit the interpretation that Joseph bought the shroud earlier. And the works of laying Jesus in a tomb and rolling a stone to close it are all the kind of labor Jews avoid on the Sabbath and on the Passover.[2] These difficulties led D.E. Nineham to conclude:

> Perhaps the simplest explanation is that the story originates from a cycle of tradition which knew of no chronological tie-up between the crucifixion and the Passover.[3]

What this means, when translated to lay terms is this: the story of Jesus' last few days being closely tied to the Jewish feast of Passover and the story of the burial of Jesus as told in Mark are mutually exclusive; they cannot both be true at the same time. At least one of these must be fictitious and the possibility that both of these being unhistorical is not excluded on logical grounds.

The second problem involves the person of Joseph of Arimathea. According to Mark he was the member of the council, i.e. the Sanhedrin, who was also looking for the kingdom of God. The Gospel of John even made him a *secret disciple* of Jesus (John 19:38). But this is obviously incompatible with what Mark had described earlier:[4]

> Mark 14:55
> Now the chief priests and the *whole council* sought witnesses against Jesus to put him to death, and found none.

If Joseph of Arimathea was in the Sanhedrin, which according to Mark, *unanimously* condemned Jesus, it is unlikely that he would be described as one who was "looking for the kingdom of God." It is even more unlikely that he would be a disciple of Jesus, as John would have us believe.[5] The two evangelists who used Mark as their

William Lane Craig, "John Dominic Crossan and the Resurrection", in Davis, Kendall & Collins, *The Resurrection*: p256-257
[2] Nineham, *Saint Mark*: p433
Guignebert, *Jesus*: p491
[3] Nineham, *Saint Mark*: p434
[4] Guignebert, *Jesus*: p491
[5] As James F. McGrath, Professor of Religion at Butler University in Indianapolis, pointed out in his book, *The Burial of Jesus: History and Faith* (2008), it is historically improbable that Joseph was a secret disciple of Jesus. If he indeed was a "secret" disciple,

source, Matthew and Luke, each tried to modify the story to make it more convincing. Luke added the statement that Joseph had not agreed with the action of the Sanhedrin:

> Luke 23:50-51
> Behold, a man named Joseph, who was a member of the council, a good and righteous man (*he had not consented to their counsel and deed*), from Arimathaea, a city of the Jews, who was also waiting for the Kingdom of God.

This statement in Luke is possible because he had deliberately *avoided* saying earlier that the whole council was present during the trial of Jesus:

> Luke 22:66
> As soon as it was day, the assembly of the elders of the people was gathered together, both chief priests and scribes, and they led him away...

Matthew, to avoid Mark's pitfall, made a more drastic alteration to the identity of Joseph:

> Matthew 27:57
> When evening had come, *a rich man from Arimathaea*, named Joseph, who himself was also Jesus' disciple came.

Anyone reading Matthew's gospel alone (as doubtless its author never originally intended the gospel to be compared to other gospels) will not know that Joseph was a member of the Sanhedrin and the problem in Mark is evaded. The source for Matthew's alteration is, again, not from history but from the Old Testament:

> Isaiah 53:9
> They made his grave with the wicked, and with a rich man in his death.

The problems about the burial accounts do not end here. John, calling Joseph a secret disciple of Jesus, gave him a collaborator, Nicodemus:

> John 19:38-42
> After these things, Joseph of Arimathaea, being a disciple of Jesus, but secretly for fear of the Jews, asked of Pilate that he might take away Jesus' body. Pilate gave him permission. He came therefore and took away his body. Nicodemus, who at first came to Jesus by night, also came bringing a mixture of myrrh and aloes, about a hundred Roman pounds. So they took Jesus' body, and bound it in linen cloths with the spices, as the custom of the Jews is to bury. Now in the place where he was crucified there was a garden. In the garden was a new tomb in which no man had ever yet been laid. Then because of the Jews' Preparation Day (for the tomb was near at hand) they laid Jesus there.

---

why did he not include Jesus' mother Mary and the other women in the burial process? While it is true that the male disciples would have been in danger if they participated in the burial, surely it would have been alright for his mother and his female relatives to take part in it. [McGrath, *The Burial of Jesus*: p78]

John's account contradicts that of the synoptics in a number of important details. In the first place, no mention is made in the other gospels of Joseph having an assistant. In the second place, John had Joseph and Nicodemus *anoint* the body of Jesus, something which is expressly excluded by the Markan narrative. For Mark had the women witness Joseph laying Jesus in the tomb, and then came on Sunday with the specific purpose of anointing Jesus' body:

> Mark 15:46-16:1 (Luke 23:56-24:1)
> He [Joseph] rolled a stone against the door of the tomb. Mary Magdalene and Mary, the mother of Joses, *saw where he was laid.* When the Sabbath was past, Mary Magdalene, and Mary the mother of James, and Salome, bought spices, *that they might come and anoint him.*

It is impossible to try to reconcile John's account with Mark's. For the women would obviously have known that Jesus body was already anointed by Joseph and would not have bought spices to do the same on Sunday.[6]

In addition, it has been pointed out that having 100 pounds of myrrh and aloes would take up a lot of space in the tomb and would have smothered the corpse under a big heap of spice![7]

In fact the whole account of the burial by Joseph of Arimathea has a fatal logical flaw. This was aptly stated by Craveri:

> They [the evangelists] take no account of their own invention. At the very time when the most fanatical followers of Jesus are in flight lest they be accused of complicity, this eleventh hour convert dares to risk expulsion from the Sanhedrin and from his own social circle in order to perform an act of mercy towards the cadaver of a rebel whom everyone had deserted.[8]

We can conclude a few things based on our study above. It is apparent that neither Luke nor Matthew had access to any new source apart from the Markan account. The changes they made were *necessary* from their point of view to correct the inconsistency in their common source – namely describing the whole Sanhedrin as condemning Jesus and then having Joseph as a member of that council. John's account expressly contradicts the account in Mark by having Joseph *anoint* Jesus' corpse.

These considerations show that Craig's second claim, that Matthew's and John's accounts "independently confirm" the Markan account, is simply wrong. Matthew and John had no new sources which corroborate the Markan account. Matthew's account was written expressly to correct what he saw as inconsistencies in the Markan account. John's account flatly contradicts Mark's. As for his first claim, that the Markan account is based on an old source, there is one major flaw: there is simply no evidence of any such source! Michael Goulder, former professor of Biblical Studies at the University of Birmingham, has this to say about Craig's "old source":

---

6   Guignebert, *Jesus*: p492
7   McCane, *Roll Back the Stone*: p99
8   Craveri, *The Life of Jesus*: p403

> Bill [i.e. William Craig] goes on, "The burial is part of very old source material used by Mark." How does he know this? He has no evidence at all for saying the source material was very old: the only evidence before Mark is Paul, and Paul does not mention any detail of the event. The very old source material is just guesswork.[9]

So we can summarize a few things from our analysis above. Mark's is the earliest account of the burial of Jesus in a tomb. The story as it stands in Mark contains some inconsistencies which make its historicity doubtful. The other evangelists show no evidence of having any independent source available to them as the changes made to Mark's account were done for redactional reasons. If the details of story as it stands in Mark is likely to be unhistorical, is there anything we can discover as to what actually happened? There are two major strands of evidence that provides what, in my opinion, is historically the most *probable* account of what happened to Jesus' body.

FIRST CENTURY BURIAL PRACTICE IN PALESTINE

The first major strand of evidence is from what we know happened to bodies of those crucified by Romans. We know from ancient sources that crucifixion is the common form of punishment for criminals and rebels. They tend to leave crucifixion victims on their crosses to serve as a visual deterrence against would be criminals and political agitators. As Martin Hengel noted in his book on crucifixion in the ancient Mediterranean:

> Crucifixion was aggravated further by the fact that quite often its victims were never buried. It was a stereotyped picture that the crucified victim served as food for wild beasts and birds of prey. In this way his humiliation was complete.[10]

This is certainly the case with many victims of crucifixion in Palestine. Josephus recounts three incidents where Jewish rebels were crucified: the Roman governor of Syria, Varus, crucified 2000 Jews who revolted after the death of Herod in 4 BCE (Antiquities of the Jews 17:10:10), in 66 CE at the breakout of the Jewish revolt, the Roman procurator Florus crucified many Jews in a general slaughter which killed 3,600 including women and children (Jewish War 2:14:9) and in 70 CE during the siege of Jerusalem, Titus allowed his troops to crucify in front of the city walls hundreds of Jews who tried to escape (Jewish War 5:11:1). Josephus did not mention whether the bodies were eventually allowed burial, but the implication is that they were not since they were left there to coerce submission of those who were still alive.[11]

---

[9] Michael Goulder, "The Explanatory Power of Conversion Visions" in Copan & Tacelli, *Jesus' Resurrection*: p99

[10] Hengel, *Crucifixion*: p87

[11] McCane, *Roll Back the Stone*: p91

John Dominic Crossan has theorized that this is what exactly happened to Jesus' body. That the corpse was most probably left on the cross and was ultimately devoured by crows and dogs.[12]

However, such a conclusion may be a bit too hasty. The examples from Josephus were all from times of acute political crises and open rebellions.[13] Other evidence shows that when situations were closer to normalcy Jews were in many cases allowed to bury the crucified. Philo mentioned such exceptions:[14]

> Flaccus 83
> I have known instances before now of men who had been crucified when this festival and holiday was at hand, being taken down and given up to their relations, in order to receive the honors of sepulture, and to enjoy such observances as are due to the dead; for it used to be considered, that even the dead ought to derive some enjoyment from the natal festival of a good emperor, and also that the sacred character of the festival ought to be regarded.

Another example is the discovery in 1968 of a crucified skeleton Gi'va ha-Mivtar near Jerusalem. The skeleton was found in a tomb consisting of 35 individuals. That he was found in the tomb is evidence that he was allowed burial.[15] Josephus himself mentioned that Jews in Jerusalem normally bury victims of crucifixion before sunset:

> Jewish War 4:5:2
> [T]he Jews used to take so much care of the burial of men, that they took down those that were condemned and crucified, and buried them before the going down of the sun.

This is mainly on account of the fact that Jewish law requires these bodies of the crucified to be taken down by sunset:

> Deuteronomy 21:22-23
> If a man have committed a sin worthy of death, and he be put to death, and you hang him on a tree; *his body shall not remain all night on the tree, but you shall surely bury him the same day*; for he who is hanged is accursed of God; that you don't defile your land which Yahweh your God gives you for an inheritance.

Such a requirement is also attested in the Mishnah. The Mishnah Sanhedrin 6:4 quoted the above passage from Deuteronomy, adding that Jews do not leave the bodies of executed criminals unburied before sunset.[16] We can conclude therefore that in cases where there is no over-riding need to provide visual deterrence, it is historically probable that bodies of the crucified were allowed *some* kind of burial.

---

[12] Crossan, *Who Killed Jesus*: p187
[13] McCane, *Roll Back the Stone*: p91-92
[14] Lüdemann, *What Really Happened to Jesus*: p23 & 139n20
[15] Crossan, *Who Killed Jesus?*: p167-168
[16] McCane, *Roll Back the Stone*: p64-65

How were such criminals buried? We know from historical sources that such persons were never given honorable burials. In the Old Testament people who disobeyed God's commandments were not allowed such burial:

> I Kings 13:21-22
> Thus says Yahweh, "Because you have been disobedient to the mouth of Yahweh, and have not kept the commandment which Yahweh your God commanded you... your body shall not come to the tomb of your fathers."

We find a similar reference to dishonorable burials for criminals in Josephus' retelling of the biblical story of Achan (Joshua 7):

> Antiquities of the Jews 5:1:14
> This Joshua told the people; and calling for Eleazar the high priest, and the men in authority, he cast lots, tribe by tribe; and when the lot showed that this wicked action was done by one of the tribe of Judah, he then again proposed the lot to the several families thereto belonging; so the truth of this wicked action was found to belong to the family of Zachar; and when the inquiry was made man by man, they took Achar, who, upon God's reducing him to a terrible extremity, could not deny the fact: so he confessed the theft, and produced what he had taken in the midst of them, whereupon *he was immediately put to death; and attained no more than to be buried in the night in a disgraceful manner, and such as was suitable to a condemned malefactor.*

Note the statement that to be buried in a "disgraceful manner" is "suitable" for a condemned person. Such burials for condemned persons are also confirmed in the Mishnah. The Mishnah Sanhedrin 6:5-6 prohibits such persons to be buried "in the burial place of their fathers" but in graveyards for condemned persons. Furthermore, it says that the family members of the dead are "used to not make open lamentations", in other words, these persons are not to be mourned for openly. A dishonorable burial thus consists of two things: a burial away from the family tomb and one in which no open mourning is allowed.[17]

From evidence above we would expect that in cases where Jews were crucified in relatively "normal" or "peaceful" times, the Jewish authorities would have approached the Romans for the bodies of the criminals to be buried. As McCane noted:

> The Jewish leaders were devoutly religious. To imagine that they would discard these traditions, out of indifference or inconvenience, is to misunderstand burial customs in a fundamental way...Thus it is to be expected that someone from the council approached Pilate about the body of Jesus. It is not necessary to...suppose that any of the council members had any secret allegiance to Jesus. It is only necessary to recognize that at least a few of them were involved in the proceedings against Jesus, and that they were devout Jews.[18]

---

[17]   Richard Carrier, "The Burial of Jesus in the Light to Jewish Law" in Price & Lowder, *The Empty Tomb*: p380
McCane, *Roll Back the Stone*: p95-96

[18]   McCane, *Roll Back the Stone*: p96, 98-99

However, such burial would be a *dishonorable* one.

ALTERNATE BURIAL TRADITION IN THE NEW TESTAMENT AND OTHER EARLY CHRISTIAN WRITINGS

Despite Craig's (third) claim that no conflicting tradition exists for Jesus' burial, there *is* such an alternate tradition and, what is more, we find them *multiply attested*. Let us look at a couple of passages in the New Testament:

> John 19:31
> Therefore the Jews, because it was the Preparation Day, so that the bodies wouldn't remain on the cross on the Sabbath (for that Sabbath was a special one), asked of Pilate that their legs might be broken, and that they might be taken away.

> Acts 13:28-29
> "Though they could charge him with nothing deserving death, yet they asked Pilate to have him killed. And when they had fulfilled all that was written of him, they took him down from the tree and laid him in a tomb."

John 19:31 has the people who handed Jesus over to Pilate asking for Jesus' body. The verse in John stands in tension with what was narrated later with Joseph of Arimathea asking Pilate for the body, as Lüdemann noted, John 19:38 "began all over again with Joseph's request."[19] In both the above passages we find exactly what we would expect from our analysis of first century practice among the Jews in Palestine. The Jews who had a hand in Jesus' condemnation were the ones who asked for Jesus' body. Note in Acts 13:28-29 "they" who had him killed were also "they" who took him down from the cross and laid him in a tomb.[20] This tradition fits what we know from the external sources quoted above; that devout Jews would consider it their duty to bury criminals before sunset. This also means that Jesus was very probably dishonorably buried.

The earliest statement about Jesus burial that we have is from Paul's first epistle to the Corinthians (around 53-55 CE):

> I Corinthians 15:3-4
> For I delivered to you first of all that which I also received:
> that Christ died for our sins according to the Scriptures, that he was buried,
> that he was raised on the third day according to the Scriptures,

Paul mentioned only that Jesus was buried with no elaboration as to the manner of his burial. As Gerd Lüdemann pointed out in his debate on the resurrection with William Craig, the statement about his burial belongs in the same section as the statement about his death. His burial reinforces the account that he died and is separate from the statement about his resurrection.[21] This grouping of the verses above is logical and consistent.

---

[19] Lüdemann, *The Resurrection of Jesus*: p43
[20] Lüdemann, *What Really Happened to Jesus:* p22
[21] Copan & Tacelli, *Jesus' Resurrection*: p44

Paul formed a very clear-cut dichotomy in his theology between Jesus' death and resurrection:

> Philippians 2:8-9
> And being found in human form, he humbled himself, becoming obedient to death, yes, the death of the cross. Therefore God also highly exalted him, and gave to him the name which is above every name;

> I Corinthians 1:23
> [W]e preach Christ crucified; a stumbling block to Jews, and foolishness to Greeks

The death of Jesus was a "stumbling block", a form of "foolishness" or *madness*.[22] Jesus' exaltation as we have seen in I Corinthians 15:3-4 *began* with his resurrection, prior to this we have his death as a "stumbling block" and "foolishness." The structure of the passage *excludes* the possibility that Jesus had an honorable burial – for that would imply that his exaltation had already begun. If the burial is part of Jesus' death, it was therefore part of the "folly" or "madness." This is consistent with a dishonorable burial.

Evidence from Christian writings outside the New Testament attests to the presence of this alternate tradition: that the Jews who had Jesus killed were those who took him down and buried him and that his burial was a dishonorable one. We find such references in two early second century texts, the Apocryphon of James and the Gospel of Peter:[23]

> Apocryphon of James 5
> [Jesus speaking] Or do you not know that you have not yet been mistreated and have not yet been accused unjustly, nor have you yet been shut up in prison, nor have you yet been condemned lawlessly, nor have you yet been crucified without reason, nor have you yet been *buried shamefully, as was I myself,* by the evil one?

> Gospel of Peter 6:21
> And then the Jews drew the nails from the hands of the Lord and laid him on the earth.

The Gospel of Peter also added that women were not allowed to mourn for Jesus by the Jewish authorities[24] and planned to do so only in secret on the third day:

> Gospel of Peter 12:52
> [On Sunday morning] And they [Mary Magdalene and her women friends] feared lest the Jews should see them, and said, "Although we could not weep and lament on that day when he was crucified, yet let us now do so at his sepulchre."

---

[22] According to Martin Hengel, the word used by Paul, *moria* (translated as "foolishness") does not denote lack of wisdom or intelligence but is more akin to *mania* ("madness") [Hengel, *Resurrection*: p1]

[23] Peter Kirby, "The Case Against the Empty Tomb", in Price & Lowder, *The Empty Tomb*: p246-248

[24] McGrath, *The Burial of Jesus*: p75

We can conclude that there is a strong alternate tradition of Jesus being buried by the Jews who were not "friendly" to him and that he was buried dishonorably by the very same people who had a hand in his arrest and ultimate crucifixion.

TRAJECTORY OF THE BURIAL ACCOUNT

We find in the gospel accounts a tendency to make the burial less and less dishonorable. Table 15.1 on the next page shows this evolution. The story of the burial of Jesus can be seen above to have evolved towards making his burial more and more honorable. A simple rock tomb has become a *new* tomb in Matthew, an *unused* tomb in Luke and a *new and unused* tomb located in a garden in John. Jesus was simply "wrapped in linen" in Mark. In Matthew it is added that this linen is "clean". While in John we are told Jesus' body was embalmed with 100 pounds of myrrh and aloes! Joseph of Arimathea, who was described in Mark as a member of the Sanhedrin who was also "looking for the kingdom of God," becomes a rich man who was a disciple of Jesus in Matthew and a council member who was "a good and righteous man" in Luke. John added the point that Joseph was a *secret* disciple.[25]

	Burial Account: Jesus' body	Joseph of Arimathea
Mark 15:42-47 (c. 70 CE)	- wrapped in linen shroud and - placed in a rock tomb	- A respectable member of the council (i.e. Sanhedrin) - Looking for the Kingdom of God
Matthew 27:57-61 (c. 90 CE)	- wrapped in *clean* linen shroud and - placed in a *new* rock tomb	- A rich man (No mention made of him being in the Sanhedrin) - A disciple of Jesus
Luke 23:50-56 (c. 95 CE)	- wrapped in linen shroud and - placed in a rock tomb where *no one had yet been laid*	- A member of the council - A good and righteous man - *Who had not consented to the deed of the Sanhedrin*[26]
John 19:38-42 (c. 100 CE)	- wrapped in linen shroud and - anointed with vast quantities of perfume - placed in a *new rock tomb where no one had ever been laid located in a garden*	- A secret disciple of Jesus

Table 15:1 Evolution of the Burial Account

This trajectory continues in the Gospel of Peter.

---

[25] McCane, *Roll Back the Stone*: p101, 105
[26] This statement is possible because Luke avoided saying earlier that the *whole* Sanhedrin condemned Jesus

Gospel of Peter 6:23-24
And the Jews rejoiced, and gave his body to Joseph that he might bury it, since he had seen all the good things that he had done. And he took the Lord, *washed* him, wrapped him in linen and brought him unto *his own sepulchre*, called "Joseph's Garden."

Here we are told that Joseph *washed* Jesus' body and he was placed in the tomb of Joseph's family. Then we are told that the women came to the tomb with the intention of *mourning* for Jesus:

Gospel of Peter 12:50-51
Early in the morning of the Lord's day, Mary Magdalene, a woman disciple of the Lord – for fear of the Jews, since they were inflamed with wrath, she had not *done at the sepulchre of the Lord what women are wont to do for their beloved of them who die* - took with her her women friends and came to the sepulchre where he was laid.

If we recall earlier, a dishonorable burial consists of not being buried in the family tomb and not being mourned. With the Gospel of Peter the trajectory is complete - Jesus is now placed in a family tomb[27] (albeit Joseph's family) and he was to be mourned by the women – his burial is no longer dishonorable.[28]

We have seen how later gospels tried their best to reduce the dishonorable elements in Jesus' burial found in the Markan account. Our question now is this: is the Markan account already on this trajectory or was it the starting point, the historical datum? Note that the Markan burial account did not say that the tomb was new or that it was unused. Jesus' body was probably not the only one in the tomb. If one removes the remark about Joseph of Arimathea as one "looking for the kingdom of God",

---

[27]   In 2007, Discovery Channel aired the documentary "The Lost Tomb of Jesus" in which it was claimed that the family tomb of Jesus has been discovered at Talpiot, a location close to the old city of Jerusalem. A companion book, entitled *The Jesus Family Tomb* co-written by the documentary director, Simcha Jacobovici and space scientist Charles Pellegrino was published around the same time. The documentary and the book claimed that the tomb contained the bones of Jesus, Mary and Mary Magdalene and other relatives of Jesus. One of the consultants to the documentary, James Tabor, is a legitimate biblical scholar. His blog on the Talpiot tomb can be accessed via this URL: http://jesusdynasty.com/blog/category/talpiot-jesus-family-tomb/ [accessed on February 13, 2008]. However, it is unlikely that the claim is correct. At a conference in Jerusalem in January 2008 on Jewish burial practices during the Second Temple period, seventeen prominent biblical scholars and archaeologists issued a joint statement in order to "make it clear that the majority of scholars in attendance – including all of the archaeologists and epigraphers who presented papers relating to the tomb - either reject the identification of the Talpiot tomb as belonging to Jesus' family or find this claim highly speculative."
[The full text of their statement is available at
 http://dukereligion.blogspot.com/2008/01/talpiot-tomb-controversy-revisited.html - accessed on February 13, 2008]

[28]   McCane, *Roll Back the Stone*: p102-103

Mark's description is that of Jesus' dishonorable burial in a common underground tomb reserved for criminals performed by a Torah-observant council member.[29] [30]

This leads us naturally to the next question: was Joseph of Arimathea an historical person? We can immediately see the difficulty involved here, when we note that even the town of Arimathea is probably a fictitious town! As the scholar E. Goldin Hyman pointed out, there is no record in the Old Testament, Torah, Talmud or anywhere else except in the gospels of a place called Arimathea.[31] Attempts to identify the place with Ramathaim (I Maccabees 11:34) and Ramathaim-Zophim (I Samuel 1:1) are based on pure conjecture.[32] How certain can we be of the existence of a person who came from a non-existent town? Some theologians have nevertheless employed some rather convoluted reasoning to enforce the opposite view:

> [Joseph of Arimathea] Apart from this incident, an entirely unknown figure; if he subsequently became a Christian, he does not appear to be a particularly well-known one, *so there would be no obvious reason* for attributing the burial of Jesus to him unless he had in fact been responsible for it.[33] [emphasis added]

The passage above shows how even critical historians, as Nineham doubtless was, could lose their objectivity when dealing with fundamental issues crucial to their faith. There *is* an obvious reason. Our analysis above on Jewish practice and on the alternate tradition of Jesus' burial showed that Jesus very probably was buried by the very people who had a hand in having him executed. This was probably the tradition that Mark had. He was in a dilemma. How to present Jesus' burial in as positive a light as possible given the fact that the tradition known to him, and probably to some in the potential audience of his book, is that Jesus was buried by his enemies? The solution, as John Dominic Crossan suggested, is the invention of an "in-between" character, a member of the council who was *nearly* a disciple of Jesus (i.e. one "also looking for the kingdom of God.").[34]

This also answers Craig's rather naïve rhetorical question about the burial by Joseph in his summary of the debate with Lüdemann:

> So why no burial account of burial by some faithful disciple of Jesus or by his family or by Romans as the direction of a sympathetic Pilate?[35]

The answer is simple: Mark was *constrained* by the tradition available to him. And that tradition stated that Jesus was buried by the same people who had a hand in his

---

29   McCane, *Roll Back the Stone*: p102

30   Of course, to say that Jesus was "buried" by a Torah-observant council member does not mean that the latter actually did the burial himself. He probably arranged for others to do it. Thus to say that Joseph "buried" Jesus would be akin to saying Solomon "built" the Temple. [McGrath, *The Burial of Jesus*: p72]

31   E. Goldin Hyman, "The Case of the Nazarene Reopened", New York 1948 quoted in Yerby, *Judas, My Brother*: p508

32   Nineham, *Saint Mark*: p434

33   Nineham, *Saint Mark*: p434

34   Crossan, *Who Killed Jesus?*: p172-173

35   Copan & Tacelli, *Jesus' Resurrection*: p182

condemnation. The best he could do, like what Matthew, Luke and John did with *his* account, was to nudge and change the tradition in such a way that his redactional purpose is served.

For our purposes it is not important whether the *name* of the Jewish council member who buried Jesus was actually *Joseph*. What is important is that Mark's description of him - as a respected council member who had not consented to their actions and as one "looking for the kingdom of God." - is the evangelist's fictional addition.

CONCLUSION ON THE BURIAL OF JESUS

All the evidence points to the fact that Jesus was dishonorably buried in a tomb reserved for common criminals by Jews who were probably involved in his execution. As is the case with such tombs, Jesus' body would not be the only one interred there.

MATTHEW'S INTERLUDE

Matthew added a further episode between the burial of Jesus and the discovery of the empty tomb. In Matthew 27:62-66 he tells us that the chief priests and the Pharisees asked Pilate to place a guard on the tomb so that the disciples cannot steal Jesus' body and claimed that he was resurrected. To further ensure against the expected theft, they sealed the tomb. This episode is not found in any of the other gospels. Let us first look at the passage in full:

> Matthew 27:62-66
> Now on the next day, which was the day after the Preparation Day, the chief priests and the Pharisees were gathered together to Pilate, saying, "Sir, we remember what that deceiver said while he was still alive: 'After three days I will rise again.' Command therefore that the tomb be made secure until the third day, lest perhaps his disciples come at night and steal him away, and tell the people, 'He is risen from the dead;' and the last deception will be worse than the first." Pilate said to them, "You have a guard. Go, make it as secure as you can." So they went with the guard and made the tomb secure, sealing the stone.

Remember that Jesus died on a Friday, so the "next day" is Saturday – the Jewish Sabbath. We are asked to believe that devout Jews would be holding their meeting with Pilate on a Sabbath day – an improbable proposition. This fact alone proves that the story is fiction.[36]

In the synoptic gospels, Jesus' own disciples were portrayed as not comprehending his words predicting his resurrection on the third day.[37] Yet in this passage we are asked to believe that the chief priests and the Pharisees were not just aware of these sayings of Jesus but completely understood what he meant![38]

---

[36] Lüdemann, *The Resurrection of Christ*: p91
[37] See Mark 8:30-32 (Matthew 16:21-23), Mark 9:9-10 & 9:30-32 (Matthew 17:22-23; Luke 9:43-45)
[38] McGrath, *The Burial of Jesus*: p84-85

There are further problems with the story. For in inserting this episode Matthew had had to alter the straightforward account of Mark, which was supported by Luke. In Mark (and Luke) the women went to the tomb on Sunday morning *to anoint the body of Jesus* (Mark 16:1; Luke 24:1). Matthew had changed this to say that the women simply went *to look at the tomb* (Matthew 28:1). This change was not accidental. The writer of Matthew was probably aware of the inconsistency in his story had he left it the way it was recorded in Mark; for it was most unlikely that the women would have been unaware of the fact that a guard had been put on the tomb.

In fact it can be seen that Matthew's insertion serves a purely apologetic purpose. For after relating the account of Jesus' appearance to the women, he adds another little episode:

> Matthew 28:11-15
> Now while they were going, behold, some of the guards came into the city, and told the chief priests all the things that had happened. When they were assembled with the elders, and had taken counsel, they gave a large amount of silver to the soldiers, saying, "Say that his disciples came by night, and stole him away while we slept. If this comes to the governor's ears, we will persuade him and make you free of worry." So they took the money and did as they were told. This saying was spread abroad among the Jews, and continues until this day.

Now the purpose of Matthew's earlier insertion becomes clear. It was meant as a defense against stories that were circulating among the Jews around the last decade of the first century; i.e. that the disciples stole the body of Jesus.

Not only is the account of the guard at the tomb incompatible with that of the other gospels, the story itself is ludicrous. How is it that Pilate, himself no friend of the Jews, could so readily agree with posting a guard at the tomb? How could the chief priests convince the *Roman* guards of their ability to get them off the hook with the *Roman* governor?

Matthew's story is fundamentally incompatible with the other gospels and is written for a very clear apologetic purpose. Furthermore, the internal logic of the story does not sound plausible. In short, this Mathean interlude is pure fiction.[39]

THE EMPTY TOMB

The "fact" that the tomb Jesus was laid in was empty on that Sunday morning is one of the most often touted "proof" of the fundamentalists for Jesus' actual resurrection. To quote a typical remark by apologist Josh McDowell:

> How can we explain the empty tomb? ...on overwhelming historical evidence Christians believe that Jesus was bodily resurrected...[40]

---

[39] Cadoux, *The Life of Jesus*: p206
      Craveri, *The Life of Jesus*: p403
      Guignebert, *Jesus*: p493
      Lüdemann, *The Resurrection of Christ*: p96-97
[40] McDowell, *More Than a Carpenter*: p92

So what is this "overwhelming historical evidence" the fundamentalists speak of? One would think, based on such overconfident assertions, that the accounts in the gospels support each other to such an extent that it would be impossible to deny the actual historical occurrence of the empty tomb.

According to the harmonized version, "the women" discovered the empty tomb. The obvious question would be: *which women?* Let the gospels speak for themselves:

Mark 16:1
When the Sabbath was past, *Mary Magdalene, and Mary the mother of James, and Salome,* bought spices, that they might come and anoint him.

Matthew 28:1
Now after the Sabbath, as it began to dawn on the first day of the week, *Mary Magdalene and the other Mary* came to see the tomb.

Luke 24:1, 9-10
But on the first day of the week, at early dawn, they [i.e. the women] and some others came to the tomb, bringing the spices which they had prepared...Now they were *Mary Magdalene, Joanna, and Mary the mother of James.* The other women with them told these things to the apostles.

John 20:1
Now on the first day of the week, *Mary Magdalene* went early, while it was still dark, to the tomb, and saw the stone taken away from the tomb.

Mark said that there were three women, namely Mary Magdalene, Mary the mother of James and Salome who saw the tomb empty. Matthew however, said that only the two Marys were there. Luke simply said "the women" he later identified their number as more than three, but the only three names he gave do not coincide with Mark's. According to Luke they were the two Marys and Joanna. John contradicts all these when he mentioned that only one woman witnessed the empty tomb, Mary Magdalene. We have different names and no agreement as to the *number* of women who witnessed the empty tomb.

The "overwhelming historical evidence" begins to crumble: the gospels could not even agree on the fundamental issue as to whom (and how many) the witnesses to the empty tomb were! This is not the only difficulty regarding the accounts of the empty tomb.

In what condition was the tomb actually discovered? Mark says that the stone at the tomb was already rolled away when the women arrived (Mark 16:4). Luke is in agreement with Mark (Luke 24:2). John, too, said that the stone was already removed when Mary of Magdala arrived (John 20:1). Matthew who, if you remember, had the tomb guarded by sentries narrated the accounts in such a way that would lead an impartial reader to conclude that the women witnessed the stoned being rolled away by an earthquake and an angel from heaven (Matthew 28:1-5). This account (of the earthquake and the angel) comes from the same author who mentioned dead people coming to life when Jesus died, an event uncorroborated by the other gospels. The presence of angels, in itself, makes the historicity of the story extremely doubtful.

The evangelists can't even agree on the exact setting in which the news of Jesus' rising was conveyed to the women. Mark said it was a person dressed in white *in the tomb* who told them this:

Mark 16:5-6
Entering into the tomb, they saw a young man sitting on the right side, dressed in a white robe, and they were amazed. He said to them, "Don't be amazed. You seek Jesus, the Nazarene, who has been crucified. He has risen. He is not here. Behold, the place where they laid him!

Matthew said it was an angel who sat on the stone – hence *outside* the tomb - he had just rolled away from Jesus' tomb.

Matthew 28: 2-6
Behold, there was a great earthquake, for an angel of the Lord descended from the sky, and came and rolled away the stone from the door, and sat on it. The angel answered the women, "Don't be afraid, for I know that you seek Jesus, who has been crucified. He is not here, for he has risen, just like he said. Come, see the place where the Lord was lying."

Luke had *two* men in "dazzling clothing" tell the women Jesus had risen.

Luke 24:2-6
They found the stone rolled away from the tomb. They entered in, and didn't find the Lord Jesus' body. It happened, while they were greatly perplexed about this, behold, two men stood by them in dazzling clothing. Becoming terrified, they bowed their faces down to the earth. They said to them, "Why do you seek the living among the dead? He isn't here, but is risen."

John, although in agreement with Luke about the number of angels present, tells a completely different story. Here the two beings did not more than ask Mary why she is crying. The actual announcement of the resurrection was made by Jesus himself.

John 20:11-17
But Mary was standing outside at the tomb weeping. So, as she wept, she stooped and looked into the tomb, and she saw two angels in white sitting, one at the head, and one at the feet, where the body of Jesus had lain. They told her, "Woman, why are you weeping?" She said to them, "Because they have taken away my Lord, and I don't know where they have laid him." When she had said this, she turned around and saw Jesus standing, and didn't know that it was Jesus. Jesus said to her, "Woman, why are you weeping? Who are you looking for?" She, supposing him to be the gardener, said to him, "Sir, if you have carried him away, tell me where you have laid him, and I will take him away." Jesus said to her, "Mary." She turned and said to him, "Rabboni!" which is to say, "Teacher" Jesus said to her, "Don't hold me, for I haven't yet ascended to my Father; but go to my brothers, and tell them, 'I am ascending to my Father and your Father, to my God and your God.'

There is an episode in Luke about Peter running to the tomb when he heard the news from the women (Luke 24:12) that is not found in the other synoptics. To a certain extent Luke's story is corroborated by John. But this evangelist had Peter *race* to the tomb with the beloved disciple (John 20:3-9), whereas in Luke, Peter went to the tomb alone.

Many more loose ends remain. The gospels cannot agree as to what command was given to the women. Mark and Matthew made the angel tell the women to inform Jesus' disciples to meet him in Galilee (Mark 16:7; Matthew 28:10). Luke did not concur with them on this but retained the word Galilee in a different context (Luke 24:6). In John, the command to Mary of Magdala was something entirely different (John 20:17). The message of the angel was not forwarded, according to Mark, for the women did not tell anyone of their experience (Mark 16:8). In Matthew the opposite is the case, for the women were reported to have told the disciples who duly went to Galilee to meet their risen Lord (Matthew 28:8,16).

Hence contradictions exist *in almost every detail* between the four gospels' accounts of the events surrounding the discovery of the empty tomb: they could not agree on who actually witnessed the empty tomb, nor how many witnesses there were; they could not agree if the tomb was guarded or not; they could not agree how many angels (or were they merely men?) the women saw; they could not agree whether it was the angels or Jesus himself who announced his resurrection; they could not agree on the *content* of the message of the angels to the women or whether the message was carried out; and they could not agree whether Peter was a witness to the empty tomb. In fact, the only statement the gospels have in common is this: *the tomb in which Jesus was laid on the night of his death was found empty on Sunday morning.*[41] All the other details contradict each other so blatantly that we have no reason whatsoever to believe any of them to be historically true. Guignebert's observations form an apt summary of the situation:

> In fact everything leads us to believe that the first evangelist [Mark] who related the discovery of the empty tomb said all he knew or thought he knew, and that the others took their point of departure from his account with no new sources at their disposal. They followed him, not faithfully, nor with the idea of elucidating his account by a commentary which respected its integrity, but with that of arranging - or disarranging - it in order to render it more convincing, of embellishing it or merely of altering it, in order to produce an appearance of independent information, for after all none of the discrepancies have any apparent meaning.[42]

Now if the events surrounding the discovery of the empty tomb are historically suspect, how confident are we of this central "fact" of the fundamentalists: that there was actually an empty tomb? It should be remembered that all four gospels were written after the destruction of Jerusalem. Mark, the earliest gospel, was written around 70 CE or forty years after the death of Jesus. In the cases of Matthew, Luke and John, they were written at least twenty years after this, or sixty years after the events they purport to describe. The earliest written sources we have are the epistles of Paul, which were all written in the sixth and early seventh decades of the first

---

[41]   Guignebert, *Jesus*: p496
[42]   Guignebert, *Jesus*: p497

century. We find Paul's account of Jesus' resurrection in his first epistle to the Corinthians:

> I Corinthians 15:3-8
> For I delivered to you first of all that which I also received: that Christ died for our sins according to the Scriptures, that he was buried, that he was raised on the third day according to the Scriptures, and that he appeared to Cephas, then to the twelve. Then he appeared to over five hundred brothers at once, most of whom remain until now, but some have also fallen asleep. Then he appeared to James, then to all the apostles, and last of all, as to the child born at the wrong time, he appeared to me also.

Note in the above passage that there is neither any mention of an empty tomb nor of its discovery by the women. If the discovery of the empty tomb was the essential proof of Jesus' resurrection, Paul's silence in I Corinthians is inexplicable. As the whole of the 15th chapter of this epistle to the Corinthians was a vigorous attempt by Paul to prove to some doubting Thomases there of the reality of the resurrection. For Paul himself had said in the same letter:

> I Corinthians 15:14
> If Christ has not been raised, then our preaching is in vain, and your faith also is in vain.

The appearance of angels to the women announcing the risen Christ would have been especially convincing. Then why didn't Paul say anything about the empty tomb?[43] We have seen earlier in the analysis of the burial account that Acts 13:28-31 preserved an earlier tradition of Jesus' dishonorable burial; this is the passage, redacted as a sermon of Paul:

> Acts 13:28-31
> Though they found no cause for death, they still asked Pilate to have him killed. When they had fulfilled all things that were written about him, they took him down from the tree, and laid him in a tomb. But God raised him from the dead, and he was seen for many days by those who came up with him from Galilee to Jerusalem, who are his witnesses to the people.

Note that there are mentions of appearances but not of an empty tomb and the discovery by the women. One would expect the sermons such as the above to include a sentence regarding this. Yet, like the passage from Paul's epistle, this sermon is silent regarding the empty tomb. In these early testimonies we find no mention of the empty tomb. The balance of evidence strongly suggests that the earliest testimonies of Jesus' resurrection were based on the *appearances* of the risen prophet *not* on the empty tomb.[44]

---

[43]   Guignebert, *Jesus*: p500
       Helms, *Gospel Fictions*: p130
[44]   Cadoux, *The Life of Jesus*: p166
       Guignebert, *Jesus*: p499-500

N.T. Wright tried to argue that, despite what we have seen above, the empty tomb account *is presupposed* in I Corinthians.15:3-4. His argument is based on the premise that Paul's statement that Jesus was "buried and then raised" presupposes the story of the discovery of the empty tomb in the same way that "I walked down the street" presupposes "on my feet". According to Wright, the empty tomb was what alerted the followers that something extraordinary has happened.[45]

Unfortunately this is just another case of a conservative theologian reading into the text what is not there. As Gerd Lüdemann has pointed out the statement about Jesus being buried is tied to Jesus' death, as a way of saying he was really dead and not someone who merely *looked* like he was dead. [46] The passage in I Corinthians 15:3-4 can be naturally divided this way:

Line 1: that Christ died for our sins according to the Scriptures, that he was buried
Line 2: that he was raised on the third day according to the Scriptures

That burial is an indication that the person is really dead can be found from the Talmudic tractate, *Semahot* 1:4-5 which states that preparations for burial can only begin once one is *certain* that death has occurred.[47] The very fact that Jesus was buried confirms to the hearers that he was actually dead and that his resurrection was not a mere resuscitation of someone who had fainted or had feigned death. This fits the whole context better that Wright's hypothesis that the whole tradition of the discovery of the empty tomb is somehow compressed in that one passage "that he was buried."

The gospel accounts were all written after the destruction of Jerusalem when it was no longer possible to ascertain whether there was such an empty tomb or not. The actual location of the tomb, if it ever existed, is no longer known. At present there are *two* locations in Jerusalem that are being claimed by believers to be the actual burial site of Jesus.

Protestant pilgrims favor the tomb discovered at the "Gordon Calvary"- named after the 19th century British general, Charles Gordon, who discovered the site. On the site, situated north of the 16th century Turkish built wall of the city, sits a small hill. The hill has two caves, which viewed from a distance, looked like a skull. However, there is not a shred of evidence in favor of this site as the actual burial site of Jesus. In fact, the tomb claimed to be the actual tomb in which Jesus was laid, has been shown conclusively by experts to be of a later origin.[48]

The other location, at the Church of the Holy Sepulcher was "discovered" by Bishop Marcarius of Jerusalem during the time of Constantine in 326 as a result of "divine revelation." With such an inspiration there was no reason for the discoverer to justify the choice of location![49] In short, no weight can be given to this site

---

45   Wright, *The Resurrection of the Son of God*: p321

46   Lüdemann, *The Resurrection of Christ*: p42, 139n5

47   McCane, *Roll Back the Stone*: p31

48   Millard, *Discoveries From the Time of Jesus*: p126-127

49   The Empress Helena, upon being informed of the discovery, duly found at the site a chip from the original cross, the crown of thorns and the lance which pierced Jesus' side!

allocated by tradition. It certainly was not known before the 4th century.[50] All these considerations had forced theologians, such as C.J. Cadoux, to conclude:

[I]t is impossible to be sure who, if anyone, actually saw an empty tomb.[51]

It should also be kept in mind that Palestinian Jews, as Jesus' original followers were, had no conception of the continuance of the life of the soul without the revival of the body, which was a Greek concept. The disciples of Jesus would have regarded the appearances of Jesus as *proof* that the tomb was empty[52] – or at least empty of Jesus' body [the idea that the tomb was *new and unused* is a later development of the legend as we have seen].

The considerations above show that the story of the empty tomb was a secondary development in the early Christian apologetics for the resurrection of Jesus. It was closely connected to the story of the burial of Jesus, which historicity is also doubtful. We will now look at fundamentalist attempts to "save" the empty tomb.

Fundamentalist apologists tend to mention two factors which they said guarantee the historicity of the empty tomb story. Firstly, it is claimed that women's low social status in Palestinian society means that they "lack qualification to serve as legal witnesses" and any invention of the empty tomb story would not have used them as principle eye-witnesses. [53] Secondly, it is claimed that the fact that the tomb was not venerated means that it was empty. One apologist wrote:

(The early Christians) did not venerate it precisely because it *was* empty. Tombs as such were not venerated. It was the tombs containing remains of the deceased that was venerated.[54]

On the women, remember that the Gospel of Mark mentioned that the women *did not tell anyone else* what they saw:

Mark 16:8
They went out, and fled from the tomb, for trembling and astonishment had come on them. *They said nothing to anyone; for they were afraid.*

This is the ending of the original Mark, as we will see later, the account of the appearances of Jesus in the last twelve verses of Mark is not found in the earliest manuscripts and is a later addition to the gospel. Matthew and Luke both tried to

---

[50]   Craveri, *The Life of Jesus*: p394
        Guignebert, *Jesus*: p493
        Nineham, *Saint Mark*: p422
        Wilson, *Jesus: A Life*: p221
[51]   Cadoux, *The Life of Jesus*: p166
[52]   Cadoux, *The Life of Jesus*: p166
[53]   William Lane Craig, "John Dominic Crossan and the Resurrection", in Davis, Kendall & Collins, *The Resurrection*: p259
[54]   Robert Gundry, "Taming the Debate" in Copan and Tacelli, *Jesus' Resurrection*: p114 n10

correct this "oversight" of Mark and had the women tell the disciples anyway. Their additions are clearly redactional and add nothing of historical value.

The account in Mark does not allow for this. Since the women did not tell anyone, Mark's purpose could not have been to claim them as *reliable* eye-witnesses. This points us to the clue as to why Mark narrated the story this way. Since Mark, written circa 70 CE, is the earliest written source for the empty tomb story, it is likely that he anticipated being confronted by some of his audience with protestations like "Hey, I have been a Christian a long time and have heard lots of stories about Jesus, how come I have never heard of this one about the empty tomb?" So Mark's ending is his way of anticipating this, as if replying "Oh, you know what women are like, brother, they panicked and didn't tell anyone for a long time. That is why nobody has heard of this before."[55] As Gerd Lüdemann noted:

> By intimating that the women fail to relay the message of the resurrection, Mark implicitly identifies himself as the first to proclaim the story of the empty tomb.[56]

As for the argument that the tomb not being venerated means that it was empty, John Barclay, Lecturer of Biblical Studies at the University of Glasgow, noted that this:

> completely backfires: the tomb would not have to contain Jesus' body for it to be venerated (cf. The Holy Sepulchre) and, indeed, the lack of veneration might support the case that the whereabouts of Jesus burial was simply unknown.[57]

Barclay's assertion is to the point. The best evidence that empty tombs *were* venerated is that of the Holy Sepulchre itself. When Jesus' tomb was "rediscovered" in 326 a shrine was immediately put around it and pilgrims have venerated the place since this time.[58] As Joachim Jeremais noted:

> The world of sacred tombs was a real element of the environment in which the earliest communities lived. It is inconceivable that, living in this world, it could have allowed the tomb of Jesus to be forgotten. That is all the more the case since for it the one who had lain in the tomb was more than one of those just men, martyrs and prophet.[59]

The two major arguments for the historicity of the empty tomb dissolve into thin air.

Another recent attempt to argue for this historicity of the empty tomb has been forwarded by N.T. Wright. He claimed that the empty tomb was a *necessary* condition to make the resurrection appearances believable. Without the empty tomb,

---

55   Michael Goulder, "The Baseless Fabric of A Vision", in D'Costa, *Resurrection Reconsidered*: p57-58

56   Lüdemann, *The Resurrection of the Christ*: p87

57   John Barclay, "The Resurrection in Contemporary New Testament Scholarship" in D'Costa, *Resurrection Reconsidered*: p23

58   Millard, *Discoveries from the Time of Jesus*: p128-129

59   quoted in Lüdemann, *What Really Happened to Jesus*: p139

sightings of the risen Jesus "would have been classified as visions of hallucinations, which were well enough known in the ancient world."[60]

Yet, this ignores the fact that in many instances of reported sightings, these visual experiences themselves are accepted as evidence of the reality of the occurrence without any accompanying physical or tangible evidence. We have even in modern times reports of sightings such as that of the Virgin Mary, UFOs, Bigfoot, and Nessie all of which are generally accepted by believers to be evidence for their respective beliefs even without the availability of any other physical evidence. Wright is claiming a level of scientific skepticism on behalf of the "ancients" that is unusual even today. Furthermore, as Gerd Lüdemann pointed out, in the majority of cases the *report* that Jesus was seen alive was sufficient for the would-be believer in those times.[61] That indeed this is the case can be surmised from John 20:29 in the story of doubting Thomas where "those who have not seen and yet believed" are praised for their faith.

We can conclude that the story of the empty tomb is, in all probability, an invention of Mark. How did Mark get the idea of the women at the tomb? As we have seen in chapter 9, Mark was written by and for Gentiles. The invention of the story happened in a culture of worship of pagan gods and of adherence to mystery religions mixed with religions such as Judaism. As Robert Price pointed out, the story developed from the amalgamation of a female mourning cult such as those who worship the slain gods and the ancient *apotheosis* narrative where the hero turns up missing and cannot be found by his companions. The mourning of slain gods can be found in the Old Testament (e.g. Tammuz [Ezekiel 8:14] & Baal Haddad [Zechariah 12:11]) and in the legends of Osiris. The pagan culture was filled with myths of "searching goddesses" such as Cybele, Ishtar, Isis, Aphrodite and Anat. Stories of a missing hero can be found in the legends of Hercules, Aristeaus, Aeneas and Romulus.[62]

It seems very likely that none of Jesus' disciples were witnesses to the events following his arrest.[63] This is firmly supported by the fact that it is in these episodes that the evangelists had to rely on Old Testament passages to reconstruct the events as they thought it might have happened. The stories of Jesus' burial by Joseph of Arimathea and the discovery of an empty tomb by the women are products of the Christian imagination. A fictional expansion of their *hope* historicized. This conclusion has been, albeit reluctantly, accepted by non-fundamentalist theologians. Bishop John Shelby Spong in his book *Resurrection: Myth or Reality?* (1994) had this to say about the empty tombs and the events surrounding it:

> There is a strong probability that the story of Joseph of Arimathea was developed
> to cover the apostles' pain at the memory of Jesus' having no one to claim his body
> and of his death as a common criminal. His body was probably dumped
> unceremoniously into a common grave, the location of which has never been

---

[60] Wright, *The Resurrection of the Son of God*: p686
[61] Lüdemann, *The Resurrection of Christ*: p200
[62] Price, *The Incredible Shrinking Son of Man*: p333-335
[63] Again, Mark 14:50 (They all left him, and fled.) comes to mind. There were no eyewitnesses because all his followers ran away after he was arrested.

known - then or now. This fragment in Paul's sermon in Acts thus rings with startling accuracy...the empty tomb tradition does not appear to be part of the primitive kerygma.[64]

THE RESURRECTION

The first account of Jesus appearance we will look at is the story in the last twelve verses of Mark:

Mark 16:9-20
Now when he had risen early on the first day of the week, he appeared first to Mary Magdalene, from whom he had cast out seven demons. She went and told those who had been with him, as they mourned and wept. When they heard that he was alive, and had been seen by her, they disbelieved. After these things he was revealed in another form to two of them, as they walked, on their way into the country. They went away and told it to the rest. They didn't believe them, either. Afterward he was revealed to the eleven themselves as they sat at the table, and he rebuked them for their unbelief and hardness of heart, because they didn't believe those who had seen him after he had risen. He said to them, "Go into all the world, and preach the Good News to the whole creation. He who believes and is baptized will be saved; but he who disbelieves will be condemned. These signs will accompany those who believe: in my name they will cast out demons; they will speak with new languages; they will take up serpents; and if they drink any deadly thing, it will in no way hurt them; they will lay hands on the sick, and they will recover." So then the Lord Jesus, after he had spoken to them, was received up into heaven, and sat down at the right hand of God. They went out, and preached everywhere, the Lord working with them, and confirming the word by the signs that followed. Amen.

The diligent reader will note that these twelve verses sound very much like a summary of all of Jesus resurrection appearances given in the gospels of Matthew, Luke, John and the book of Acts. This may seem surprising as we have shown in chapter 9 that Mark was written earlier than all of these. But there is really no perplexity here, *for it is in fact proven that these last twelve verses were never part of the original Gospel of Mark and were added in much later.* The proofs are as follows:

I   The style, content and whole character of the last twelve verses are clearly non-Markan. In fact the style, vocabulary and verses are completely different from the rest of Mark.[65] As Nineham pointed out:

> Even a cursory reading will make clear that the passage is not composed of traditional pericopaes such as we have encountered in the gospel proper but of brief resumes of stories and sayings already

---

64   Spong, *Resurrection: Myth or Reality*: p225
65   Nineham, *Saint Mark*: p439,449

reported more fully in other written gospels particularly Luke and Acts.[66]

2   The early church fathers such as Clement of Alexandria (c150-c215), Origen (c185-254) and Tertullian (c160-c225) never quoted any verses from Mark after the eighth verse of chapter 16. In fact down to the year 325 the passage from Mark 6:9-20 was quoted only once, by Ireneaus in 180 CE, in the whole of Christian literature.[67]

3   In the 4th century the Christian historian, Eusebius (c264-340), in his work *Ad Marinum 1* stated that "in the accurate manuscripts Mark ended with the words 'for they were afraid' [Mark 16:8]." This opinion is also shared by the famous fourth century theologian St. Jerome (c340-420).[68]

4   In all the important and earliest extant manuscripts of the Bible - the *Codex Vaticanus*, the *Codex Sinaiticus* and the *Codex Syriacus* - the last twelve verses of Mark are conspicuously missing. All these manuscripts end at Mark 16:8.[69]

5   Some later manuscripts to do have this ending add asterisks to these last twelve verses, probably to show they need deleting. Some even have notes stating that these verses do not appear in older copies.[70]

6   Both Matthew and Luke used the Markan gospel extensively (see chapter 6 for proof of this), both sticking to the basic narrative in that gospel. Yet both Matthew and Luke have completely different accounts of the appearances of Jesus. This also strongly suggests that the copies of Mark used by these evangelists ended at verse eight of chapter sixteen.[71]

All the above considerations present a compelling case for the spuriousness of Mark 16:9-20. There is no longer any respectable scholar that holds the opinion that these verses may be part of the original Mark. The quotation by Ireneaus in 180 CE mentioned above and the fact that it presupposes knowledge of the other gospels suggests a second century origin for these verses.[72]

In fact, from the 4th century onwards there appeared *another* spurious ending to Mark which takes the place of Mark 16:9-20. This ending can be found in some late manuscripts (after the 4th century CE). Given below is that variant ending (placed immediately after Mark 16:8 "for they were afraid"):

---

[66]   Nineham, *Saint Mark*: p450
[67]   Bentley, *Secrets of Mount Sinai*: p178
        Nineham, *Saint Mark*: p449-450
        Guignebert, *Jesus*: p509-510
[68]   Nineham, *Saint Mark*: p449-450
        Guignebert, *Jesus*: p509-510
[69]   Bentley, *Secrets of Mount Sinai*: p178
[70]   Bentley, *Secrets of Mount Sinai*: p179
        Martin, *New Testament Foundations I*: p219
[71]   Nineham, *Saint Mark*: p439
[72]   Nineham, *Saint Mark*: p450

> But they [the three women] briefly reported to those in the company of Peter all they had been told. And after this Jesus himself appeared to them, and sent out by means of them, from the east to the west, the holy and imperishable message of eternal salvation.[73]

Needless to say, Markan authorship is also completely ruled out here as well, both on the lateness of its appearance (after the 4th century) and on linguistic grounds.[74]

These texts (Mark 16:9-20 and the other ending) are as spurious as the Johanine Comma discussed in chapter 6. But because of its early appearance and its acceptance into the Christian canon, which as we saw was not finalized until much later, these verses has been, rather paradoxically, described by the Catholic theologian M.J. Lagrange as "canonically authentic" though not literally authentic (i.e. it was not written by Mark).[75] In other words, the earlier the fraud, the more likely it was divinely inspired!

The fact that most lay Christians are unaware of the fact that the last twelve verses of Mark are bogus bids poorly for the moral integrity of the church leaders who are aware of this fact. Perhaps, like Lagrange, these modern day elders of the churches believe that since the passage is "canonically authentic" there is no reason to destroy the faith of their flock by pointing out that, in very literal sense, this passage is a fraudulent fabrication of early Christian piety!

The importance of this cannot be overstated: *the earliest gospel, Mark, has no account of the resurrection appearance of Jesus.*

THE APPEARANCES OF JESUS AS DEPICTED IN THE GOSPELS

The remaining three gospels all give different and often contradictory accounts of the resurrection appearances of Jesus.

Take the simple question: *who was the first person to see the risen Jesus?* According to Matthew, Jesus first appeared to the two Marys while they were running away from the tomb:

Matthew 28:8-10
They departed quickly from the tomb with fear and great joy, and ran to bring his disciples word. As they went to tell his disciples, behold, Jesus met them, saying, "Rejoice!" They came and took hold of his feet, and worshiped him. Then Jesus said to them, "Don't be afraid. Go tell my brothers that they should go into Galilee, and there they will see me."

According to Luke, the women only saw the angels but did not see Jesus. The first persons to see Jesus were two of his followers (not of the eleven). The story (Luke 24:13-33) recounts how later that Sunday two of Jesus' followers met with a stranger on their way from Jerusalem to Emmaus. They told the stranger about the sad events of the past few days. When they reached Emmaus, they had supper together. During

---

[73]   Bentley, *Secrets of Mount Sinai*: p145
[74]   Nineham, *Saint Mark*: p453
[75]   Nineham, *Saint Mark*: p449

that supper the two finally realized that the stranger was Jesus. Upon this realization Jesus immediately disappeared from their sight. This is the account in full:

Luke 24:13-33
Behold, two of them were going that very day to a village named Emmaus, which was sixty stadia from Jerusalem. They talked with each other about all of these things which had happened. It happened, while they talked and questioned together, that Jesus himself came near, and went with them. But their eyes were kept from recognizing him. He said to them, "What are you talking about as you walk, and are sad?" One of them, named Cleopas, answered him, "Are you the only stranger in Jerusalem who doesn't know the things which have happened there in these days?" He said to them, "What things?" They said to him, "The things concerning Jesus, the Nazarene, who was a prophet mighty in deed and word before God and all the people; and how the chief priests and our rulers delivered him up to be condemned to death, and crucified him. But we were hoping that it was he who would redeem Israel. Yes, and besides all this, it is now the third day since these things happened. Also, certain women of our company amazed us, having arrived early at the tomb; and when they didn't find his body, they came saying that they had also seen a vision of angels, who said that he was alive. Some of us went to the tomb, and found it just like the women had said, but they didn't see him." He said to them, "Foolish men, and slow of heart to believe in all that the prophets have spoken! Didn't the Christ have to suffer these things and to enter into his glory?" Beginning from Moses and from all the prophets, he explained to them in all the Scriptures the things concerning himself. They drew near to the village, where they were going, and he acted like he would go further. They urged him, saying, "Stay with us, for it is almost evening, and the day is almost over." He went in to stay with them. It happened, that when he had sat down at the table with them, he took the bread and gave thanks. Breaking it, he gave to them. Their eyes were opened, and they recognized him, and he vanished out of their sight. They said one to another, "Weren't our hearts burning within us, while he spoke to us along the way, and while he opened the Scriptures to us?" They rose up that very hour, returned to Jerusalem, and found the eleven gathered together, and those who were with them

According to John, Jesus first appeared to Mary Magdalene alone:

John 20:11-18
But Mary was standing outside at the tomb weeping. So, as she wept, she stooped and looked into the tomb, and she saw two angels in white sitting, one at the head, and one at the feet, where the body of Jesus had lain. They told her, "Woman, why are you weeping?" She said to them, "Because they have taken away my Lord, and I don't know where they have laid him." When she had said this, she turned around and saw Jesus standing, and didn't know that it was Jesus. Jesus said to her, "Woman, why are you weeping? Who are you looking for?" She, supposing him to be the gardener, said to him, "Sir, if you have carried him away, tell me where you have laid him, and I will take him away." Jesus said to her, "Mary." She turned and said to him, " Rabboni!" which is to say, " Teacher" Jesus said to her, "Don't hold me, for I haven't yet ascended to my Father; but go to my brothers, and tell them, 'I am ascending to my Father and your Father, to my God and your God.'" Mary Magdalene came and told the disciples that she had seen the Lord, and that he had said these things to her.

And Paul in I Corinthians 15:5 mentioned no appearances to the women but instead said that Jesus appeared first to Peter. This again contradicts all the other three accounts in the gospels of Matthew, Luke and John.[76] There is thus no clear cut answer from the gospels [and Paul's epistles] as to who was actually the first to see the risen Jesus.

Another contradiction arises in *where* exactly did the risen Jesus first meet his eleven apostles. Mark, while not containing any actual account of Jesus appearances, made the angel tell the women that Jesus will meet his apostles in Galilee:

Mark 16:7
"But go, tell his disciples and Peter, 'He goes before you into Galilee. There you will see him, as he said to you.'"

Matthew makes Jesus himself convey that same message to the women (Matthew 28:10-see above). And further adds an episode of the disciples' actual meeting with him on a mountain in Galilee:

Matthew 28:16-20
But the eleven disciples went into Galilee, to the mountain where Jesus had sent them. When they saw him, they bowed down to him, but some doubted. Jesus came to them and spoke to them, saying, "All authority has been given to me in heaven and on earth. Therefore go, and make disciples of all nations, baptizing them in the name of the Father and of the Son and of the Holy Spirit, teaching them to observe all things that I commanded you. Behold, I am with you always, even to the end of the age." Amen.

Matthew made no mention of any meeting of the disciples with the risen Jesus in Jerusalem. The flow of his last chapter implicitly excludes that possibility, for he made Jesus command the women to tell the disciple to go ahead and meet him in Galilee.

Luke, on the other hand, made the first appearance of Jesus to his disciples happen in Jerusalem:

Luke 24:33-36
They rose up that very hour, returned to *Jerusalem*, and found the eleven gathered together, and those who were with them, saying, "The Lord is risen indeed, and has appeared to Simon!" They related the things that happened along the way, and how he was recognized by them in the breaking of the bread. As they said these things, Jesus himself stood among them, and said to them, "Peace be to you."

John did not explicitly mention where the meeting took place, but it is quite obvious that Jerusalem was implied as the appearance took place on that very Sunday evening.

---

[76] Luke 24:34 [the response of the disciples to the story by Cleopas and his companion that "The Lord is risen indeed, and has appeared to Simon!"] might be taken to support the passage in I Corinthians. This in no way solves the problems for the contradiction of whether it was the women, Mary Magdalene alone or Peter who first saw the risen Jesus remains.

John 20:19
When therefore it was evening, on that day, the first day of the week, and when the doors were locked where the disciples were assembled, for fear of the Jews, Jesus came and stood in the midst, and said to them, "Peace be to you."

The New Testament sources can't even agree on the *number and sequence* of the appearances. Given below is a list of the number and sequence of the appearances. It can be seen that there is no agreement whatsoever in the numbers and sequence of appearances:

Matthew

1) 28:9-10	To the two Marys
2) 28:16-17	To the eleven apostles in Galilee

Luke

1) 24:13-32	To the two travelers to Emmaus
2) 24:34	(Statement) To Peter
3) 24:33-39	To the eleven apostles in Jerusalem

John

1) 20:14-18	To Mary Magdalene
2) 20:19-23	To the apostles in a house
3) 20:24-30	To the disciples and Thomas
4) 21:1-23	To the disciples at the Sea of Tiberias

I Corinthians

1) 15:5	To Peter
2) 15:5	To the twelve
3) 15:6	To 500 followers
4) 15:7	To James
5) 15:7	To "all the apostles"
6) 15:7	To Paul

The *duration* of the resurrected Jesus' stay on earth is also something which the gospels cannot agree on. In Matthew, the duration is only a few days needed for the disciples to travel from Jerusalem to Galilee. Luke had the whole resurrection and ascension occur over that one Sunday.[77] Acts contradicts this by asserting that the duration was 40 days (Acts 1:3). John did not explicitly state the duration but made it more than one week (John 21:26).

To summarize, there is no agreement among the New Testament sources as to:[78]

---

[77] Jesus appeared to the two on the way to Emmaus on Sunday evening (Luke 24:13-12). The two traveled immediately to Jerusalem (Luke 24:33). When they found the eleven it was probably late that Sunday night. There Jesus appeared to them (Luke 24:36). After this Jesus led them to Bethany where he was taken up to heaven (Luke 24:50-53).

[78] Guignebert, *Jesus*: p511

1. **The place of Jesus' appearance**. Mark implicitly, and Matthew, explicitly state that Galilee was the exclusive location of the resurrection appearances. Luke and John both assert Jerusalem as the place where the resurrected Jesus was first seen.

2. **The number of appearances.** Matthew mentioned two, Luke implied three, John said four and Paul counted six.

3. **The person who first saw the risen Jesus**. According to Matthew it was the two Marys, according to Luke it was either Peter or the two travelers to Emmaus, John said it was to Mary Magdalene alone and Paul said Peter had that honor.

4. **The duration of the risen Jesus' stay on earth**. Luke said it was one day, Acts put it as forty. John and Matthew had it somewhere in between.

These discrepancies have serious repercussions. We note that there is *some* unanimity in how the gospels tell the story of Jesus' passion yet when it comes to the accounts of the empty tomb and resurrection appearances the evangelists "go off in all different directions." As Roy Hoover, Professor of Biblical Literature at Whitman College pointed out:

> Looked at from the perspective of what we know about how the gospel's authors went about their task of composing their narratives, the variant character of their Easter narratives, especially in contrast to the similarity of their passion narratives, strongly suggests that there is no common tradition behind them. That undoubtedly indicates that their empty-tomb and appearance stories are later in origin than are the testimonies to the appearances of the risen Jesus noted by Paul and that they are intended to make the claim that Jesus had indeed risen believable to popular religious imagination.[79]

The very variant nature of the reports of Jesus' appearances in the gospels speaks against their historicity. It cannot be too heavily stressed that the resurrection appearances are the fundamental sheet anchor of the Christian faith. Without the reality of this, the whole edifice of Christianity (liberal theologians not withstanding) collapses. But here, in a kind of supernatural situation where the burden of proof would be extraordinarily heavy, the gospels and other New Testament sources can't even present us with a harmonious witness to the events surrounding the appearances of the risen Jesus. It goes without saying that no weight can be given to accounts which contradict each other in every major detail.

---

[79] Roy Hoover, "A Contest Between Orthodoxy and Veracity" in Copan and Tacelli, *Jesus' Resurrection*: p135-136

THE NATURE OF THE APPEARANCES

When evangelical Christians talk about the resurrected Jesus, they mean that he was physically raised from the dead. This resurrected Jesus can be touched and can consume food. In other words, his was a tangible presence and not some ghost or spirit (or worse, figments of the disciples' imagination!). These fundamentalist Christians normally refer to the accounts found in Luke and John as evidence of the physical nature of the resurrected Jesus. In Luke, Jesus was made to tell his disciples to touch him to make certain he is real. He was also able to eat:

> Luke 24:36-42
> As they said these things, Jesus himself stood among them, and said to them, "Peace be to you." But they were terrified and filled with fear, and supposed that they had seen a spirit. He said to them, "Why are you troubled? Why do doubts arise in your hearts? See my hands and my feet, that it is truly me. Touch me and see, for a spirit doesn't have flesh and bones, as you see that I have." When he had said this, he showed them his hands and his feet. While they still didn't believe for joy, and wondered, he said to them, "Do you have anything here to eat?" They gave him a piece of a broiled fish and some honeycomb. He took them, and ate in front of them. He said to them, "This is what I told you, while I was still with you, that all things which are written in the law of Moses, the prophets, and the psalms, concerning me must be fulfilled."

In John's account, the resurrected Jesus was also a tangible being who allowed doubting Thomas to touch his hands and his side:

> John 20:24-29
> But Thomas, one of the twelve, called Didymus, wasn't with them when Jesus came. The other disciples therefore said to him, "We have seen the Lord!" But he said to them, "Unless I see in his hands the print of the nails, and put my hand into his side, I will not believe." After eight days again his disciples were inside, and Thomas was with them. Jesus came, the doors being locked, and stood in the midst, and said, "Peace be to you." Then he said to Thomas, "Reach here your finger, and see my hands. Reach here your hand, and put it into my side. Don't be unbelieving, but believing." Thomas answered him, "My Lord and my God!" Jesus said to him, "Because you have seen me, you have believed. Blessed are those who have not seen, and have believed."

In another resurrection account in the same gospel, set by the sea of Galilee, Jesus is described as eating breakfast with Peter and six other disciples (John 21:12-15).

However, we do not find such strong statements of the resurrected Jesus' physical nature in the other two gospels. The Gospel of Matthew contains only two very brief accounts of encounters with the risen Jesus. Let us look at these two in turn. The first encounter with the risen Jesus happened to the two Marys who were running away from the empty tomb:

> Matthew 28:8-10
> They departed quickly from the tomb with fear and great joy, and ran to bring his disciples word. As they went to tell his disciples, behold, Jesus met them, saying,

"Rejoice!" They came and took hold of his feet, and worshiped him. Then Jesus said to them, "Don't be afraid. Go tell my <u>brothers</u> that they should go into Galilee, and there they will see me."

The second passage tells of the disciples meeting Jesus on a mountain in Galilee.

Matthew 28:16-20
But the eleven disciples went into Galilee, to the mountain where Jesus had sent them. When they saw him, they bowed down to him, *but some doubted.* Jesus came to them and spoke to them, saying, "All authority has been given to me in heaven and on earth. Therefore go, and make disciples of all nations, baptizing them in the name of the Father and of the Son and of the Holy Spirit, teaching them to observe all things that I commanded you. Behold, I am with you always, even to the end of the age." Amen.

Note how brief these two accounts in Matthew are compared to the elaborate accounts in Luke and John. In the first passage, the only physical manifestation was that the women were able to clasp Jesus' feet. The second passage has no explicit indication of physicality. Jesus was said to "come to them and spoke to them" briefly. Furthermore, the point made in Matthew 28:17 ("but some doubted") about the presence of doubt among some of his disciples seems to point to a lack of corporeality in the appearance of the risen Jesus.

Finally, the oldest gospel, Mark, does not have any account of the resurrection appearance of Jesus.

This leaves us with one last source on Jesus' resurrection. Unlike the gospels, we do have, in the authentic epistles of Paul, an eyewitness report from someone who actually "saw" the resurrected Jesus. The most important passage from the Pauline epistles on the resurrection is found in I Corinthians 15. Although we have already quoted this passage above, it is of primary importance in our current considerations, so here it is again:

I Corinthians 15:3-8
For I delivered to you first of all that which I also received: that Christ died for our sins according to the Scriptures, that he was buried, that he was raised on the third day according to the Scriptures, and that he appeared to Cephas, then to the twelve. Then he appeared to over five hundred brothers at once, most of whom remain until now, but some have also fallen asleep. Then he appeared to James, then to all the apostles, and last of all, as to the child born at the wrong time, he appeared to me also.

The Greek word translated above as "he appeared to" is *ophthe*. Paul's choice of the word *ophthe* (*he was seen, he was observed*) is significant. We quote Guignebert:

This word does not necessarily imply the actual appearance of a person, but may only indicate an unusual phenomenon...the use of the word *ophthe* in enumerating other visions in the Pauline lists...excludes such details as prolonged conversations, meals and resumption of ordinary life, on which the gospels dwell.[80]

---

[80]   Guignebert, *Jesus*: p523

An example of Paul's experience of the risen Jesus can be seen in this, probably autobiographical, passage:

II Corinthians 12:1-4
It is doubtless not profitable for me to boast. For I will come to visions and revelations of the Lord. I know a man in Christ, fourteen years ago (whether in the body, I don't know, or whether out of the body, I don't know; God knows), such a one caught up into the third heaven. I know such a man (whether in the body, or outside of the body, I don't know; God knows), how he was caught up into Paradise, and heard unspeakable words, which it is not lawful for a man to utter.

Paul's description above shows that his "visions of the Lord" was not something which could be described easily. His euphoric phrases about being "out of body", being "caught up into Paradise" and of having "heard unspeakable words" shows that it was not a simple physical meeting he was talking about.[81]

The Acts of the Apostles provides further indication of such an intangible nature of Jesus' appearance to Paul. Here the account of Paul's vision of the risen Jesus is given in the form of a speech by the apostle:

Acts 22:6-11 (Also Acts 9:3ff; 26:12)
"It happened that, as I made my journey, and came close to Damascus, about noon, suddenly there shone from the sky a great light around me. I fell to the ground, and heard a voice saying to me, 'Saul, Saul, why are you persecuting me?' I answered, 'Who are you, Lord?' He said to me, 'I am Jesus of Nazareth, whom you persecute.' "Those who were with me indeed saw the light and were afraid, but they didn't understand the voice of him who spoke to me. I said, 'What shall I do, Lord?' The Lord said to me, 'Arise, and go into Damascus. There you will be told about all things which are appointed for you to do.' When I couldn't see for the glory of that light, being led by the hand of those who were with me, I came into Damascus."

Nowhere in the accounts given in Acts are we actually told that Paul *saw* the risen Jesus. All he saw was a blinding light and a voice which his companions either did not hear or understand. The experience of Paul, which can be best explained as some kind of *ecstatic vision*, was nowhere near the tangible person of the resurrected Jesus described in the gospels of Luke and John.

If we provide a timeline on the resurrection accounts in the New Testament, we will notice a distinctive evolution in how the resurrection of Jesus was portrayed. The earliest account, the epistles of Paul, written in the 50s, described an intangible resurrected Jesus. The earliest gospel, Mark, written two decades after the epistles of Paul, does not have any narration of the resurrected Jesus. Then circa 90 CE, in the Gospel of Matthew, we find two very brief accounts, only one of which (Matthew 28:8-10) can be unambiguously interpreted as a physical manifestation of Jesus. It

---

81   There is nothing unique about this type of experience. Muhammad, the founder of Islam, was said to have experienced a similar kind of heavenly rapture where he was transported miraculously to the site of the Jerusalem Temple and lifted up into heaven where he spoke to both Moses and Jesus. [Armstrong, *Holy War*: p39]

was only around 100 CE, *or 70 years after the death of Jesus*, that we do find written reports of a tangible resurrected Jesus - in the gospels of Luke and John.

The believer may claim that such stories circulated orally before Luke and John put them in writing. However, is it believable that no one before that - not Paul, not Mark and not, to a certain extent, Matthew, - thought it worthwhile to recount in writing such remarkable stories? This stretches credulity to the breaking point.

At around the same time when Luke and John were written we find the church father, Ignatius (d. c110) retelling such stories in his epistle to the Smyrnaeans:

> Epistle to the Smyrnaean 3-4
> For I know that after His resurrection also He was still possessed of flesh, and I believe that He is so now. When, for instance, He came to those who were with Peter, He said to them, "Lay hold, handle Me, and see that I am not an incorporeal spirit." And immediately they touched Him, and believed, being convinced both by His flesh and spirit. For this cause also they despised death, and were found its conquerors. And after his resurrection He did eat and drink with them, as being possessed of flesh, although spiritually He was united to the Father. I give you these instructions, beloved, assured that ye also hold the same opinions [as I do]. But I guard you beforehand from those beasts in the shape of men, whom you must not only not receive, but, if it be possible, not even meet with; only you must pray to God for them, if by any means they may be brought to repentance, which, however, will be very difficult.

This passage gives us an important clue. It is obvious from the Smyrnaean epistle that Ignatius wasn't just recounting the resurrection appearance of Jesus in a boring sermon-like fashion. He was asserting the *physical* nature of the resurrection *against opponents* ("those beasts in the shape of men") *who believed otherwise*. We know that there was a group of Christians, the Docetists, who first appeared around the end of the first century who taught that Jesus was never truly human and therefore could not have been resurrected in a corporeal form.

It would certainly have been a major coincidence that Ignatius (and Luke and John) had such stories readily available from the oral tradition as a defense against such opponents. A more likely explanation is that these stories were *made up*[82] in the heated battle against other Christians who believed in an intangible resurrected Jesus.[83]

Here we once again bring in the witness of Paul. He in no way considered his vision to be any different from, or inferior to, those experienced by Peter and the other apostles. As he asserted:

> I Corinthians 9:1
> Am I not free? Am I not an apostle? Haven't I seen Jesus Christ, our Lord?

---

[82] This means that the stories could either have been concocted from whole cloth or "padding" added to original stories of visions – as is the case, I believe of the appearance of Jesus to Peter in Galilee – to make the Jesus more tangible.

[83] Michael Goulder, "The Baseless Fabric of a Vision", in D'Costa, *Resurrection Reconsidered*: p56-57

II Corinthians 11:5
For I reckon that I am not at all behind [or *inferior to*] the very best apostles.

For Paul, the seal of apostleship comes from having seen the risen Jesus. In this respect, as is evident in these two passages, he did not consider himself the least bit inferior to the apostles. Such confidence on Paul's part would be very hard to explain if the apostles actually *ate with and touched the resurrected Jesus* while he only had *visions* which he could not properly describe in words. Surely he would not have placed his experience on par with theirs!

The precedent of the Pauline epistle strongly suggests that the appearances witnessed by the original followers of Jesus amount to nothing more than the type described by Paul. We have absolutely no reason to believe that Paul understood Jesus' appearances to the apostles as anything different from his own experience.[84] As Karen Armstrong noted:

> It is interesting to note that Paul makes no distinction between his own vision of Jesus and those apparitions to Peter and the others. Where the gospels show Jesus as physically and inconvertibly present to the apostles, able to eat drink and be touched, Paul, who was writing much earlier, shows the events as entirely similar to his own violent vision, which he compares to an abnormal childbirth. The apparitions to Peter and James and the rest were probably visions like Paul's on the road to Damascus, rather than physical manifestations of the risen Lord. Paul does not suggest that they were any different.[85]

If, as we have seen is very likely, the actual resurrection appearances of Jesus were nothing more than hallucinatory visions, it becomes clear why there were skeptics among the original followers of Jesus as to stories and claims of seeing the risen Christ. We have noted this skepticism in Matthew 28:17. We see this doubt expressed even in the passages from Luke and John given above. Had the appearance of Jesus been in a tangible form it is highly unlikely that such doubts would have arisen.

We can now summarize our findings. Initially, the stories that were in circulation about Jesus' resurrection were like those of Paul's – they never mentioned a Jesus who could be touched and who shared meals with the disciples. Due to the advent of Christian "heretical" groups – such as the Docetists – who denied a physical Jesus, stories about the tangibility of a resurrected Jesus started to appear in the writings of the groups who were opposed to them. We have no reason to believe that the tradition of a corporeal physical resurrected Jesus was part of the earliest Christian tradition. The resurrection appearances of Jesus, as described in the gospels, are not historical.

---

84 Guignebert, *Jesus*: p524
85 Armstrong, *The First Christian*: p55

THE PSYCHOLOGICAL ORIGINS OF
THE RESURRECTION APPEARANCES

We have seen that in I Corinthians 15:5-7, Paul recounted the resurrection appearance of Jesus. According to this Jesus appeared first to Peter and then to the "twelve", then to the "five hundred", to James, to "all the apostles" and finally, to Paul himself. We have seen above that Paul made no distinction between what he experienced and what the rest saw. We can safely call all these *visions* of the resurrected Jesus. In other words, these are *internal experiences* not external supernatural manifestations.

It would be more satisfying if we can also explain the psychological origins of these visions. In other words, what triggered the whole series of "Jesus sightings"? Since Peter, the twelve, James, the "five hundred" and "all the apostles" were all followers of Jesus, we can say that Peter's vision was the "trigger" for the rest of this. Being able to explain why Peter had the vision is the starting point to explain the vision of the rest of Jesus' disciples. Paul's vision had to have a different origin, for he was not a follower and could not have felt what Peter and the rest felt. We have to explain the psychological origins of the appearances to Peter and to Paul; two visions that did not have any external catalyst.

Recently some critical historical scholars such as John Hick[86], Michael Goulder[87] and Gerd Lüdemann[88] have used the findings of modern psychology to analyze and explain the resurrection appearances of Jesus. Hick compares the experiences of the first disciples, in particular Paul's as described in Acts (9:3-8, 22:6-11 & 26:12-18) to modern studies of near death experiences where reports of seeing a bright light or a brightly shining figure seems to be common.[89] Michael Goulder compares these with modern studies of mass hysteria and collective delusions. But by far the most comprehensive attempt to get to the psychological origins of the visions of the apostles has been that of Lüdemann.[90] Our presentation below on the psychological origins of Peter's and Paul's visions is based on Professor Lüdemann's

---

[86] John Hick, *The Metaphor of God Incarnate: Christianity in a Pluralistic Age*, John Knox 1993

[87] Michael Goulder, "The Baseless Fabric of a Vision", in D'Costa, *Resurrection Reconsidered*: p48-61
      Michael Goulder, "The Explanatory Power of Conversion Visions" in Copan & Tacelli, *Jesus' Resurrection*: p86-103

[88] Gerd Lüdemann, *The Resurrection of Jesus: History, Experience, Theology*, Fortress 1994
      Gerd Lüdemann, *What Really Happened to Jesus*, Westminster John Knox 1995
      Gerd Lüdemann, *The Resurrection of the Christ: A Historical Inquiry*, Prometheus 2004

[89] Hick, *The Metaphor of God Incarnate*: p24

[90] As a result of his intensive study into the birth, resurrection of Jesus and the heresies of early Christianity, Lüdemann made a public statement renouncing his Christian faith in 1998, as he could no longer believe what his research has shown to be untrue. As a result Professor Lüdemann was subtly removed from his chair (New Testament) by a renaming of his chair to that of "History and Literature of Early Christianity". The new position would not be one that would attract research funds. In effect this change in name has the effect of stifling his research.

work, while the analysis on the visions of the early community following Peter's vision is based on Professor Goulder's analysis.

The Origin of Peter's Vision

Most scholars agree that Peter must have been one of the first to have seen the risen Jesus. It would otherwise be difficult to understand his primacy among the apostles. This is consistent with the earliest recorded list of the resurrection appearances in I Corinthians 15:5.

Given below is Lüdemann's construction of a psycho-causation profile of the resurrection vision (hallucination) by Peter:[91]

- We are sure that Peter must have mourned Jesus' death.

- We also know, from studies by psychologist of the process of mourning, that mourners, due to their love for the lost one, tend to feel in their minds the presence of the loved one. A successful mourning is when the mourner slowly parts, psychologically, from feeling the presence of the lost one. In other words, their lives slowly return to normal as thoughts about the recently deceased slowly recede into the background.

- However, there are cases where successful mourning is hindered and the feeling of the presence of the loved ones becomes more intense and being unable to bear the pain, the mourner actually "see" the dead person as somehow being alive again. Research at Harvard University on cases like these show unsuccessful mourning is more likely if the following conditions are present:

  o The death is sudden
  o An ambivalent attitude towards the dead person associated with feeling of guilt
  o A dependent relationship between the mourner and the dead.

- We notice that these three factors are all present in Peter's case.

  o Jesus death was sudden.
  o Peter *denied* Jesus just before the latter was executed. This must have caused tremendous guilt in the Galilean fisherman.
  o Peter was a follower of Jesus. He left his work and home to follow him. It was a deeply dependent relationship.

To quote Lüdemann directly:

> The mourning hindered by the three factors mentioned was enormously helped in the case of Peter by a "seeing." The mourning first led to a real, deeper understanding of Jesus, and this in turn helped toward a new understanding of the

---

[91]   Lüdemann, *What Really Happened to Jesus:* p83-94
         Lüdemann, *The Resurrection of the Christ*: p163-166

situation of mourning. Recollections of who Jesus had been led to the recognition of who Jesus *is*. Seeing Jesus thus already included a whole chain of theological conclusions.[92]

We can conclude that Peter's vision of the risen Jesus is very likely the result of an unsuccessful mourning.

The Origin of Paul's Vision

The psychological origins of Paul's own hallucinations (his visions of the resurrected Jesus) are different from Peter's. Remember that we have Paul's own words in his genuine epistles. We are thus able to derive a lot about the inner workings of his mind through his writings.

First let us note that Paul had some kind of illness. He said as much in his epistle to the Galatians:

> Galatians 4:12-14 (RSV)
> Brethren, I beseech you, become as I am, for I also have become as you are. You did me no wrong; *you know it was because of a bodily ailment that I preached the gospel to you at first; and though my condition was a trial to you, you did not scorn or despise me*, but received me as an angel of God, as Christ Jesus.

Paul must have also been frail looking, for this is what he quoted his opponents describing him:

> II Corinthians 10:10
> For, "His letters," they say, "are weighty and strong, but his bodily presence is weak, and his speech is despised."

Now let us look into a very revealing passage from II Corinthians (portions of which we have seen earlier):

> II Corinthians 12:1-10
> It is doubtless not profitable for me to boast. For I will come to visions and revelations of the Lord. I know a man in Christ, fourteen years ago (whether in the body, I don't know, or whether out of the body, I don't know; God knows), such a one caught up into the third heaven. I know such a man (whether in the body, or outside of the body, I don't know; God knows), how he was caught up into Paradise, and heard unspeakable words, which it is not lawful for a man to utter. On behalf of such a one I will boast, but on my own behalf I will not boast, except in my weaknesses. For if I would desire to boast, I will not be foolish; for I will speak the truth. But I refrain, so that no man may think more of me than that which he sees in me, or hears from me. By reason of the exceeding greatness of the revelations, that I should not be exalted excessively, there was given to me *a thorn in the flesh*, a messenger of Satan to torment me, that I should not be exalted excessively. Concerning this thing, I begged the Lord three times that it might depart from me. He has said to me, "My grace is sufficient for you, for my power is

---

92   Lüdemann, *What Really Happened to Jesus:* p94

made perfect in weakness." *Most gladly therefore I will rather glory in my weaknesses, that the power of Christ may rest on me.* Therefore I take pleasure in weaknesses, in injuries, in necessities, in persecutions, in distresses, for Christ's sake. For when I am weak, then am I strong.

Our thinking here will take a few steps to work through:[93]

- Paul is obviously describing one of his visions in this passage.

- Note that he did not attempt to differentiate between his visions and his revelations.

- "A thorn in the flesh", a disease, was given to him to keep him from being too elated by the revelations (or visions).

- This disease, his weakness, was what gave him his visions. For "Christ's power is made perfect in weakness."

- Thus, for Paul, his illness (or the manifestations of its symptoms) and his visions, are inseparably bound together. In other words, he only sees Jesus when he is ill!

Paul's Damascus vision, his first vision of Jesus Christ, must be of a similar nature. What triggered it? Wasn't Paul on the opposite end of the spectrum from Peter and his views completely opposite? For the vision to be coming in from the depth of Paul's psyche we need to show that Paul already had the seeds of belief in him.

Here Lüdemann takes us through the steps, using a psychodynamic approach, in seeing how this is so:[94]

- Many fanatics suffer from inner turmoil. Their basic instincts long to do things their beliefs tell them they cannot.

- This forces them to suppress their instincts.

- This leads to a hatred of their situation.

- This turns into hatred for those who *could* do what they themselves cannot do. For example, the "disgust" most religious fanatics feel towards sex of any kind is but one manifestation of this.

- For some fanatics, a crucial turning point occurs which releases them from previous inhibitions and they become free of their previous shackles.

- In other words, within the inner turmoil, the "emotional dialectic", already lies the new "synthesis" or world view.

Paul's situation parallels these steps very closely:

---

[93] Lüdemann, *What Really Happened to Jesus:* p117-125
[94] Lüdemann, *What Really Happened to Jesus:* p126-129
Lüdemann, *The Resurrection of Christ:* p166-172

- Paul (or Saul) was a fanatic. He was, in his own words full of zeal and faultless in keeping to legalistic requirements to Jewish law (Philippians 3:6).

- Although he claimed to be faultless in following the law, he suffered from inner turmoil and fought to suppress his instincts. The passage below clearly shows this:

  > Romans 7:7-11
  > What shall we say then? Is the law sin? May it never be! However, I wouldn't have known sin, except through the law. For I wouldn't have known coveting, unless the law had said, "You shall not covet." But sin, finding occasion through the commandment, produced in me all kinds of coveting. For apart from the law, sin is dead. I was alive apart from the law once, but when the commandment came, sin revived, and I died. The commandment, which was for life, this I found to be for death; for sin, finding occasion through the commandment, deceived me, and through it killed me.

- His obvious hatred of his own situation is turned outwards towards the Christians. Paul probably saw within the Christian movement the very antithesis of his position towards the law. This is more so in its preaching of a *crucified messiah* in express contradiction to the law (Deuteronomy 21:23 "anyone hung under a tree is under God's curse"). In zeal he persecuted the Christians. (Galatians 1:23)

- This inner turmoil came to a climax on his trip to Damascus where, probably suffering from sunstroke or an epileptic seizure, Paul had his vision which "released" him from his inner turmoil and converted him.

To again quote Lüdemann:

> Paul's appearance did not depend on Peter's vision, since here it was not a follower but an "enemy" of Jesus or his supporters who was affected. Here Paul's biography gives strong indications that his vision of Christ is to be explained psychologically as an overcoming of a smoldering "Christ complex" which led to severe inner (unconscious) conflicts in him and finally released itself in this vision.[95]

Paul's vision arose from an entirely different set of circumstances from Peter's. Paul's vision was a "release" from an inner dialectic tension in his subconscious theological paradigm.

The Sustenance of Subsequent Visions

Our next task would be to explain the subsequent visions described in I Corinthians 15:3-8. These visions are not primary in the sense that people who experienced these visions have already heard of others (such as Peter and Paul) having similar experiences. Michael Goulder labeled the visions of the early disciples, including the

---

[95]   Lüdemann, *What Really Happened to Jesus:* p130

alleged appearance to the 500, as *collective delusions*. Such phenomena have been well studied by modern social psychology and its basic characteristics are known. These characteristics can be found in various UFO sightings, visions of the Virgin in Catholic Mariology and in sightings of creatures such as the Loch Ness Monster and Sasquatch (or Bigfoot).

Basing his study on the *value-added theory* of N.J. Smelser, Goulder compared the characteristics of the resurrection experiences of the early Christians to that of a small community in South Dakota where sightings of Sasquatch suddenly took hold of the community in 1977. There were six factors that brought on and sustained the collective delusions:[96]

1 A close knit community
This allows for rumors to spread easily. The isolation from the outside world means also that excessive skepticism can be kept in check. This was the case with the community in South Dakota and was also the case with the early followers of Jesus.

2 Structural Strain
The society or community must be under some kind of stress. This can be exacerbated by the presence of the lowly educated and people who may be prone to hallucinations. Again, this fits the description of the South Dakota settlements as well as the early church. Remember that the disciples were all running away from the Jewish authorities when Jesus was arrested. They must have been in hiding. They were all poorly educated. (Acts 4:13) The presence of some members – such as Mary Magdalene, who was probably prone to hallucinations (Luke 8:2, Mark 16:9) - is another notable characteristic of the early Christian community.

3 Presence of Generalized Beliefs
Such experiences do not arise out of thin air. Some kind of general belief must already be present. In the case of the South Dakota settlements, the legend of Bigfoot was already part of the local indigenous culture. Among the early Christians there is the apocalyptic expectation that at the end of time, God will raise all from the dead. Jesus is the first sign of this general resurrection. (I Corinthians 15:23)

4 Trigger
There had to be an initial "trigger" that set off the whole series of visions. In the case of the Sasquatch sightings it was the showing of a "B" movie in the summer of 1977 there. In the case of the early Christians, the trigger was the vision of Peter.

5 Sustaining Factors
The series of visions had to be sustained by mobilizing factors. In South Dakota there were the media coverage, the various community actions, the police hunts and the constant meetings over the issue which fed hundreds of sightings of the

---

[96] Michael Goulder, "The Baseless Fabric of a Vision", in D'Costa, *Resurrection Reconsidered*: p53-54

mythical creature. For the early Christians their constant meeting together for prayers (Acts 1:14, Luke 24:52) and then exchanging stories about their resurrection experiences (Luke 24:33-34) could be the sustaining factors.

6 Pay-Off

This is an important consideration. Stories can spread because there was some kind of "pay-off" for those who reported it as happening to them. In the case of the Bigfoot sightings, it is obvious that reporting that you have seen the creature means that you immediately become the center of media attention. In the case of the early church, "seeing the Lord," was an obvious stamp of discipleship (I Corinthians 9:1).

When shown in such a comparative way, we can see that once the initial trigger was done by Peter, we would *expect* the reports of sightings of Jesus would spread like wildfire throughout the early community.

Conclusions on the Psychological Origins of the Resurrection Appearances

We can conclude this section by stating very plainly that there is nothing supernatural about the resurrection appearances of Jesus to his disciples. Once triggered by Peter, the rest of the visions followed well understood principles that govern mass delusions. The appearance to Peter was caused by a failed mourning, while that of Paul was caused by a "Christ complex." No other explanation fits the historical data better and none other require fewer assumptions. There is no need to assume an event unheard of in medical science - the resuscitation of a corpse three days after death. Any explanation which assumes this violates Ockham's razor. As Lüdemann concluded:

> God must no longer be assumed to be the author of these visions, as is still argued frequently, but inconsistently, even by advocates of the vision hypothesis. Rather these are psychological processes which ran their course with a degree of regularity - completely without divine intervention. At the same time this means that the assumption of the resurrection of Jesus is completely unnecessary as a presupposition to explain these phenomena. *A consistent modern view must say farewell to the resurrection of Jesus as an historical event...* We can no longer take the statements about the resurrection of Jesus literally...So let us say this quite specifically: *the tomb of Jesus was not empty, but full, and his body did not disappear, but rotted away.* [97]

"THAT HE APPEARED TO CEPHAS" : A RECONSTRUCTION

We have established that the resurrection appearances of Jesus were purely psychological manifestations – there was no physically resurrected Jesus. However, our natural curiosity demands that we at least try to flesh out (pun intended) this finding and see if we can at least make an educated guess about what actually

---

[97]   Lüdemann, *What Really Happened to Jesus:* p130, 134-135

happened. In this section, we will attempt an, albeit speculative, reconstruction of the probable sequence of events that led to the first resurrection appearance based on the information available to us.

Our first question is: *where* did it happen? We have established that sightings of Jesus around the empty tomb are unhistorical. As we have seen earlier, the gospels disagree on whether it first took place in Galilee (Mark 16:7 and Matthew 28:16-20) or Jerusalem (Luke 24:33-36 and John 20). The tradition of the first sighting taking place in Galilee is more likely to be historical for a few reasons. Firstly, it comes from the earliest source (Mark). Secondly, the Galilean appearance is complete in itself and more consistent with the awkward fact following Jesus' arrest - namely, that his disciples all deserted him after he was apprehended. (Mark 14:50, Matthew 26:56) Finally, the stories of the Jerusalem appearances have clear apologetic motif – to place the appearances of Jesus nearer and closer to the time and place of his death.[98]

Our second question is: *when* did it happen? The formula in Paul's epistle that Jesus was "raised on the third day according to the Scriptures" (I Corinthians 15:4) does not imply that Jesus was actually seen on the third day following his death. The qualifier, "according to the scriptures," shows that there this timing was not based on actual eyewitness accounts but the result of later theological reflection.[99] So we do not know when the first sighting of the resurrected Jesus happened – it could have been a few days or a few weeks after the crucifixion.[100]

We have seen above that it was Peter who had the first vision of the resurrected Jesus. In the gospels there *is* a story of a resurrection appearance to Peter, in the 21st chapter of John. Let us look at the passage in full below:

John 21:1-14
21:1 After these things, Jesus revealed himself again to the disciples at the sea of Tiberias. He revealed himself this way. 21:2 Simon Peter, Thomas called Didymus, Nathanael of Cana in Galilee, and the sons of Zebedee, and two others of his disciples were together. 21:3 Simon Peter said to them, "I'm going fishing." They told him, "We are also coming with you." They immediately went out, and entered into the boat. That night, they caught nothing. 21:4 But when day had already come, Jesus stood on the beach, yet the disciples didn't know that it was Jesus. 21:5 Jesus therefore said to them, "Children, have you anything to eat?" They answered him, "No." 21:6 He said to them, "Cast the net on the right side of the boat, and you will find some." They cast it therefore, and now they weren't able to draw it in for the multitude of fish. 21:7 That disciple therefore whom Jesus loved said to Peter, "It's the Lord!" So when Simon Peter heard that it was the Lord, he wrapped his coat around him (for he was naked), and threw himself into the sea. 21:8 But the other disciples came in the little boat (for they were not far from the land, but about <u>two hundred cubits</u> away), dragging the net full of fish. 21:9 So when they got out on the land, they saw a fire of coals there, and fish laid on it, and

---

[98]   Guignebert, *Jesus*: p501-502

[99]   The passages in the Bible Paul meant were probably:

       Jonah 1:17
       Jonah was in the belly of the fish three days and three nights

       Hosea 6:2
       After two days he will revive us. On the third day he will raise us up

[100]   Guignebert, *Jesus*: p530

bread. 21:10 Jesus said to them, "Bring some of the fish which you have just caught." 21:11 Simon Peter went up, and drew the net to land, full of great fish, one hundred fifty-three; and even though there were so many, the net wasn't torn. 21:12 Jesus said to them, "Come and eat breakfast." None of the disciples dared inquire of him, "Who are you?" knowing that it was the Lord. 21:13 Then Jesus came and took the bread, gave it to them, and the fish likewise. 21:14 This is now the third time that Jesus was revealed to his disciples, after he had risen from the dead. 21:15 So when they had eaten their breakfast, Jesus said to Simon Peter, "Simon, son of Jonah, do you love me more than these?"

There are a few things we should note about this story. In the sequence of resurrection appearances in that gospel, this is the third appearance by Jesus. The story shows that Peter and some of the other disciples had already returned to their previous lives as fishermen.[101] Yet according to the fourth gospel, this is already the third time that Jesus had appeared to them and in the appearance narrated earlier, Jesus had already commissioned them to be apostles of his message (John 20:21-23). It is indeed strange that Peter and the rest would settle back to their earlier life when they had already seen the risen Jesus and had been told to proclaim his message to the world.[102] Even Thomas, who already exclaimed "My Lord and My God" after having touched the wounds of Jesus (John 20:28) seemed inexplicably subdued in this episode. Furthermore, as we have seen in chapter 9, John 20:30-31 seems to be the conclusion of the original form of the gospel with chapter 21 added as an appendix at some later date by (probably) another hand. It is more likely that the story was floating as a separate tradition that was picked up by the author of the 21st chapter of John.

We find further evidence that this was a separate tradition from the fact that almost exactly the same story appears in Luke; not as a resurrection account but rather as a story of the calling of the disciples into Jesus' ministry:

Luke 5:1-11
5:1 Now it happened, while the multitude pressed on him and heard the word of God, that he was standing by the lake of Gennesaret. 5:2 He saw two boats standing by the lake, but the fishermen had gone out of them, and were washing their nets. 5:3 He entered into one of the boats, which was Simon's, and asked him to put out a little from the land. He sat down and taught the multitudes from the boat. 5:4 When he had finished speaking, he said to Simon, "Put out into the deep, and let down your nets for a catch." 5:5 Simon answered him, "Master, we worked all night, and took nothing; but at your word I will let down the net." 5:6 When they had done this, they caught a great multitude of fish, and their net was breaking. 5:7 They beckoned to their partners in the other boat, that they should come and help them. They came, and filled both boats, so that they began to sink. 5:8 But Simon Peter, when he saw it, fell down at Jesus' knees, saying, "Depart from me, for I am a sinful man, Lord." 5:9 For he was amazed, and all who were

---

[101] The statement "I am going fishing" by Peter is not that of a hobbyist who is bored with nothing to do - note that he and some of the other disciples stayed out the whole night trying to catch fish. Remember that Peter was a commercial fisherman. He was essentially saying that he was ready to pick up the pieces of his life again. [Spong, *Resurrection: Myth or Reality?*: p192]

[102] Lüdemann, *The Resurrection of Christ*: p 123
McGrath, *The Burial of Jesus*: p112

with him, at the catch of fish which they had caught; 5:10 and so also were James and John, sons of Zebedee, who were partners with Simon. Jesus said to Simon, "Don't be afraid. From now on you will be catching people alive." 5:11 When they had brought their boats to land, they left everything, and followed him.

Note the similarities between the two accounts:[103]

- The location is the same. Both the Sea of Tiberias and Lake Gennesaret are merely different names for the Sea of Galilee. (John 21:1, Luke 5:1)
- Peter is the main protagonist in both stories.
- In both cases we have an unsuccessful fishing expedition with Peter having caught nothing after being out all night. (John 21:4, Luke 5:5)
- Both accounts tell of Jesus appearing on the scene and then urging them to try again. (John 21:6a, Luke 5:6a)
- After acting upon Jesus' suggestion, they caught a great "multitude of fish". (John 21:6b, Luke 5:6b)

Having established that these two stories have the same origin, the next question is which type of story was it originally? Was it a story of Peter's calling into Jesus' discipleship that morphed into a resurrection account or was it the other way round? Some scholars think that it was originally a resurrection account[104] while some think both are conflations of two initially separate stories: one is about a miraculous catch of fish and the other an "Easter recognition legend."[105] Luke's account is mainly the former, but Peter's cry of guilt (Luke 5:8) seems rather strange for someone who had just met Jesus. It fits the scenario of a resurrection appearance better with Peter's remorse about fleeing after Jesus was arrested in Jerusalem.[106]

That Luke did not use this as a resurrection appearance is also understandable for theological reasons. Luke's presentation of the early church requires that the resurrection appearances all be in Jerusalem. For Luke, this story, set in Galilee, could not be told as it stands in the tradition. He modified it into a story of the calling to discipleship of Peter.[107]

For our purposes, we only need to recognize that there is an old tradition which connects Peter, the Sea of Galilee and his resurrection sighting (i.e. "Easter Recognition of Jesus") which predates Luke and John.[108] The idea that he had gone back to his old life of being a fisherman is supported by the Gospel of Peter which ends thus:

---

[103]   Lüdemann, *The Resurrection of Jesus*: p86-87
[104]   Funk et. al., *The Acts of Jesus*: p489-490
      Guignebert, *Jesus*: p505
      Spong, *Resurrection: Myth or Reality?*: p192
[105]   Lüdemann, *The Resurrection of Christ*: p157
[106]   Lüdemann, *The Resurrection of Jesus*: p86-87
[107]   Guignebert, *Jesus*: p505
[108]   Guignebert, *Jesus*: p506

Gospel of Peter 14:58-60

Now it was the last day of the unleavened bread and many went away and repaired to their homes, since the feast was at an end. But we the twelve disciples of the Lord, wept and mourned, and each one, very grieved for what has come to pass went to his own home. But, I, Simon Peter, and my brother Andrew took our nets and went to the sea. And there was with us Levi, the son of Alphaeus, whom the Lord... .

We do not know if the Gospel of Peter contained any stories about Jesus' resurrection appearances since the available manuscript fragment ends at this point. However, it dovetails with the tradition in John 21 (and Luke 5) that Peter returned to Galilee and resumed his former profession.

We can now make a hypothetical reconstruction of the events that led to the first vision of the resurrected Jesus.[109] We noted in the previous chapter that the stories relating the events subsequent to Jesus' arrest diverge among the gospels. This points to a lack of eyewitnesses and probably means that the disciples fled Jerusalem after his arrest and were not around to find out what exactly happened. This is supported by Mark 14:50 which states that upon the capture of Jesus, the disciples fled. On their way back to Galilee, they may have heard from other Galilean travellers that Jesus had died on the cross and that the Sanhedrin had arranged for his dishonourable burial as a convicted criminal. With their hopes shattered, Peter, and some of the other disciples, went back to their way of life before they had met Jesus - to commercial fishing. It may have been in one of those early misty mornings, when Peter was out fishing, that the combination of his intense love for Jesus, the shattered hopes caused by his master's execution and feelings of guilt for having betrayed him, all came to a head and found release in the form of a vision. We do not know what this vision entailed. It could be that Peter saw an apparition walking by the edge of the sea which he thought was Jesus.[110] Perhaps a stranger came that morning and had bread and fish with him. After the stranger had left, Peter had an epiphany by "recognizing" the person as Jesus.[111] These visions could have been supplemented by dreams where Jesus spoke to him. Peter would have told the rest of the disciples about his experience and, as we have shown above, this triggered a whole series of "Jesus sightings" by the others. He reconstituted the twelve and together with James, the brother of Jesus, would have made their way to Jerusalem to proclaim the "good news." The rest, as they say, is history.   .

---

[109]   My reconstruction is based on the works of these various scholars:
        Guignebert, *Jesus*: p522
        Lüdemann, *The Resurrection of Christ*: p172-173
        McGrath, *The Burial of Jesus*: p105-116
        Spong, *Resurrection: Myth or Reality?*: p242-257
[110]   Spong, *Resurrection: Myth or Reality?*: p249
[111]   McGrath, *The Burial of Jesus*: p114

APOLOGETIC ATTEMPTS

This is a "mopping up" section, dedicated to answering some of the attempts by modern apologists for the resurrection who continue to insist on its historicity.

1. *If Jesus had not been raised, his detractors could simply have pointed to his body in the tomb.*

   According to Acts 2, the disciples started publicly preaching Jesus' resurrection at the Pentecost – or 50 days after Jesus resurrection. Studies on the decay process of corpses have shown that putrefaction starts as early as 2-3 days after death. After 25 days mainly bones and hair remain.[112] Even allowing for variations in decay rate due to temperature differences, it is obvious that by day 50, the body of Jesus, without access to modern forensic tools, would be unrecognizable.[113] The common grave for robbers that Jesus was buried in would have contained the decayed remains of many bodies, it would have been impossible for *anyone* to make any verification.

2. *The resurrection accounts in the gospels showed that Jesus was tangible, ate fish, had his hands touched and was with the disciples for many days. No visions or hallucinations could do this.*

   This simply assumes that the resurrection stories told in Matthew, Luke and John are historical. They are not. The accounts of a tangible Jesus, as narrated in these gospels, first appeared in the last decade of the first century - around 60 years after the death of Jesus. As we have shown above that the earliest accounts of the resurrection, found in the epistles of Paul written 40 years earlier than these gospels, expressly exclude such stories.

3. *Jesus appeared to 500 people at once, this could not be explained as hallucination.*

   I Corinthians 15:6 simply noted that Jesus "appeared to (Greek: *ophthe*) over five hundred brothers at once." Without any further details it is impossible to evaluate this account in depth. Paul's use of the same word *ophthe* means that he did not differentiate these visions from his own. All we need to say is that there are certainly modern parallels to this. The Bigfoot sighting mentioned above is one. The miracle of the "dancing sun" - witnessed by more than 50,000 in Fatima, Portugal in 1917 - is another example.[114] All these can be explained by mass delusion or mass hysteria.

---

[112] Dr. Richard W. Merritt, *Forensic Entomology*
(http://www.cj.msu.edu/~people/forent.html accessed on July 4, 2006)

[113] Jeffery Jay Lowder, "Historical Evidence and the Empty Tomb", in Price & Lowder, *The Empty Tomb*: p289
Lüdemann, *The Resurrection of Christ*: p181

[114] Nickell, *Looking for a Miracle*: p176-181

4.   *The disciples fled in despair when Jesus was arrested (Mark 14:50). The crucifixion of Jesus would have led to the collapse of the early Jesus movement. Only a physical, tangible, resurrected Jesus could have convinced the disciples to continue their mission.*

This reasoning is fallacious. The death of a founder, no matter how tragic, does not necessarily lead to the collapse of the movement. As the Catholic theologian Edward Schillebeeckx pointed out, the movement of John the Baptist continued on among the Jews even after the beheading of the founder – "as if that death entailed no break at all."[115] And as John Hick added:

> [I]n Jewish thinking the death of martyrs were not taken as discrediting them but on the contrary as giving them an even more exalted place in popular esteem and in the divine plan.[116]

THE ASCENSION

The story of Jesus' ascension is told by Luke twice, once in his gospel and then again in the Acts of the Apostle. We give both versions here:

Luke 24:50-53
He led them out as far as Bethany, and he lifted up his hands, and blessed them. It happened, while he blessed them, that he withdrew from them, and was carried up into heaven [Greek = *ouranon*]. *They worshiped him, and returned to Jerusalem with great joy, and were continually in the temple, praising and blessing God. Amen.*

Acts 1:3-11
To these he also showed himself alive after he suffered, by many proofs, *appearing to them over a period of forty days,* and speaking about God's Kingdom. Being assembled together with them, he commanded them, "Don't depart from Jerusalem, but wait for the promise of the Father, which you heard from me. For John indeed baptized in water, but you will be baptized in the Holy Spirit not many days from now." ...*When he had said these things, as they were looking, he was taken up, and a cloud received him out of their sight.* While they were looking steadfastly into *the sky* [Greek = *ouranon*, literally "heaven"] as he went, behold, two men stood by them in white clothing, who also said, "You men of Galilee, why do you stand looking into *the sky* [*ouranon*]? This Jesus, who was received up from you into *the sky* [*ouranon*] will come back in the same way as you saw him going into *the sky* [*ouranon*]." *Then they returned to Jerusalem from the mountain called Olivet,* which is near Jerusalem...

Before delving into the details we will notice that the two accounts contradict each other on a number of points.[117]

---

[115]   Quoted in Hick, *The Metaphor of God Incarnate*: p26
[116]   Ibid: p26
[117]   Copan & Tacelli, *Jesus' Resurrection*: p155

- **Timing of the Ascension**: Luke 24 is a continuous narrative of the events on Easter Sunday. There is no hint that the day is over all the way to the end of the chapter where the ascension takes place. This means that Luke has Jesus ascend into heaven on the *first day* of his resurrection. The account in Acts says that the ascension happens *40 days* after he has been raised.

- **Location of the Ascension**: According to the gospel, the ascent happened at Bethany, while Acts has it happening at the Mount of Olives. Bethany is a small town about three kilometers to the southeast of Jerusalem. The Mount of Olives is a mountain range just outside the city to the east. The two accounts have Jesus ascending into heaven from two separate places.

These contradictions alone tell us that we cannot accept either of the stories at face value. There are further problems with the ascension. Both accounts say Jesus was lifted *up* into heaven. This conforms to ancient understanding of the cosmos that heaven is physically "up there." We find many parallel stories from ancient Mediterranean literature. Cicero's (106 – 46 BCE) *The Republic* narrates a dream of Scipio where he is taken up to the heavens through its various spheres.[118] The historian Livy (59 BCE – 17 CE) tells of how Romulus, the legendary co-founder of Rome was taken up into heaven by a thick cloud.[119] Similar stories of physical ascent into heaven, often times accompanied or carried by clouds, are told of mythical, legendary and historical figures such as Hercules, Empedocles, Alexander the Great and Appolonius of Tyana.[120] Stories of such heavenly ascents are commonplace during the time of Jesus.

It would be wrong to claim that Luke meant the ascension to be taken in a metaphorical sense. As Matthew Baldwin showed, both the vocabulary and narrative elements point to the fact that the evangelist meant a *physical* ascent of Jesus into heaven "up there":

> The vocabulary is drawn from the entire context of Acts 1:1-14. In 1:2 we find ἀνελήμφθη [*anelemphthe*], passive aorist of ἀναλαμβάνω [*analambano*], "he was taken up." In 1:9, we learn that *while they were watching* Jesus, ἐπήρθη [*eperthe*], aorist passive of ἐπαίρω [*epairo*] meaning, "he was lifted up" or "he was raised up" and "a cloud took him before their eyes." The primary meaning of ὑπολαμβάνω [*hupolambano*] stretching back to its use by Herodotus [see Liddell, Scott, Jones Greek Lexicon (Oxford University Press: New York 1992) pg 844] is "to take up by getting under", and here there is more to the suggestion of the idea that the cloud doesn't merely conceal him from their sight, but takes him further our from their sight; they would not be able to see him, standing on the cloud, but the verb implies exactly this, with additional connotations of providing a receptive and protective function. Then in 1:10, we read that "while they were gazing fixedly at his traveling into the sky" ....the two men appear to them. This language is graphic and locative, having the narrative function of describing an ascent of realistic terms.[121]

---

[118]   Cartlidge & Dungan (ed), *Documents for the Study of the Gospels*: p188-194

[119]   Cartlidge & Dungan (ed), *Documents for the Study of the Gospels*: p187

[120]   Ranke-Heinemann, *Putting Away Childish Things*: p144

[121]   Baldwin, *Christ in Orbit*: p20 n31

So clearly Luke meant Jesus' *physical* ascent into heaven. But modern cosmology tells us that there is no heaven "up there," just mainly empty space interspersed with planets, dust, moons, asteroids, stars and galaxies. The story as it is told in Luke is a *myth* and cannot be historical. Yet this presents difficulty for the defenders of the resurrection, for the ascension is very clearly tied to the resurrection in early Christian theology:

> John 3:13
> No one has ascended into heaven, but he who descended out of heaven, the Son of Man, who is in heaven.

> Romans 8:34
> It is Christ who died, yes rather, who was raised from the dead, who is at the right hand of God, who also makes intercession for us.

> Ephesians 1:20
> which he worked in Christ, when he raised him from the dead, and made him to sit at his right hand in the heavenly places

> I Peter 3:21-22
> This is a symbol of baptism, which now saves you - not the putting away of the filth of the flesh, but the answer of a good conscience toward God, through the resurrection of Jesus Christ, who is at the right hand of God, having gone into heaven, angels and authorities and powers being made subject to him.

As Lüdemann pointed out, the sequence – resurrection, ascension and return - are all closely linked. Take out one of these elements and the whole theology collapses.[122] Since it is obvious that Luke's story of the ascension cannot be taken literally given our current state of knowledge, the obvious conclusion is that the whole edifice of the resurrection belief has been completely destroyed. During his debate with William Craig, Professor Lüdemann had to ask the fundamentalist apologist, *twice*,[123] what he thought of the ascension before the former replied. Craig's reply, when it finally came, was a typical fundamentalist *midrashic*[124] attempt to solve an unsolvable problem:

> I believe that Jesus, yes, left this four-dimensional space-time universe...Jesus' body ceased to exist in this four-dimensional space-time manifold that is described

---

122 Copan and Tacelli, *Jesus' Resurrection*: p40
123 Copan and Tacelli, *Jesus' Resurrection*: p40, 52
124 *Midrash* refers to the exegetical method of Rabbinic Judaism. It is a method of expanding their reading of the sacred scripture which may include recasting old stories as new ones or reading "deeper" meanings into existing texts. The former can be seen even in the Old Testament where Moses' parting of the Red Sea (Exodus 14:2-31) is re-casted as the story of Joshua parting the River Jordan (Joshua 3:14-17). The latter method is sometimes used when faced with passages that were clearly at odds with the current state of knowledge or worldview. The Rabbis would then explain and comment on it with various extraneous information which may include legends, sayings, parables and stories of the sages. *Thus it is a method of reading into the text what is not there.*

by the equations of general relativity and special relativity and all the rest. Jesus exited this four-dimensional space-time.[125]

Craig's response showed that he understood the passage literally. However, he had had to add in the idea that the accounts in Luke and Acts only tell the story halfway, and he had to add in the part about leaving our "four-dimensional space-time manifold." In other words, Craig is adding to the narrative what is not in the text and is nowhere even suggested or hinted. This speculative addition is necessary if he is to keep to biblical inerrancy.

Even if we are to accept, for the sake of argument, that Luke left out the juicy bits about Jesus' ascension, it still presents a serious problem for the believer. Craig's midrashic addition to the text means that Jesus actually was taken up physically some distance above the ground, out of sight of the apostles, before he was teleported, *Star-Trek-like*, into another dimension. But Jesus could have been made to "exit this four-dimensional space-time manifold" right there on the Mount of Olives or in Bethany – the *lift-off* was unnecessary. Why then did God choose to *put up a show* by taking Jesus some distance off the ground as though he is going "up to heaven", *in conformance to the prevailing erroneous cosmologies of the day*, when he could have teleported Jesus directly in front of the apostles? In his defense of Craig's response in the book of the debate, Stephen Davis actually suggested that the whole thing was primarily "a symbolic act *performed* [by God] for the sake of the disciples".[126] [emphasis added]

Such an explanation opens up a Pandora's box for fundamentalists. For we are told that in some cases, God could do things to appear in a way that is understandable to the people of a particular period that may not actually be the way things are. So if the ascension is "performance", then what are we to say of the return of the son of man in the clouds? Is that meant to be a performance as well? What about the much anticipated (by fundamentalists) rapture (I Thessalonians 4:16-17)? Would that too be merely a performance?[127] What about the central event, the resurrection itself? Could the whole story of Jesus' resurrection be a performance in which God sent someone else in the place of the dead Jesus to make his symbolic proclamation? What about the virgin birth? To say that an act is performed to suit the viewers' erroneous worldview is to say that the audience is being *deceived*. The absurdity of such an interpretation was already noted almost two centuries ago by David Friedrich Strauß (1808-1874) in his book *Das Leben Yesu* [The Life of Jesus] (1837):

> In order to convince the disciples of Jesus' return to the higher world, even though in fact this world was by no means to be sought in the upper atmosphere, God nevertheless staged the spectacle of this sort of elevation. But this would be turning God into a sleight-of-hand artist.[128]

---

[125]   Copan and Tacelli, *Jesus' Resurrection*: p58

[126]   Stephen Davis, "The Question of Miracles, Ascension and Anti-Semitism", in Copan and Tacelli, *Jesus' Resurrection*: p79

[127]   Baldwin, *Christ in Orbit*: p12-13

[128]   quoted in Ranke-Heinemann, *Putting Away Childish Things*: p143

Like the resurrection, the ascension is an ancient myth told by a people whose understanding of cosmology has been shown to be false.

THE EVOLUTION OF THE MYTH

The new cult of the dead and risen messiah originally had a purely Jewish following. It was when the apostle Paul (not one of the original disciples of Jesus) started preaching around 40 CE that the number of Gentile converts started to swell. We have seen that in the letters of Paul the belief about Jesus' death and resurrection was very basic and undeveloped. In his first epistle to the Corinthians (15:3-8), all he said was that Jesus died, was buried and rose again on the third day *in accordance with the scriptures.* Paul further added that Jesus was seen by Peter, the apostles, James and finally, by himself. Nothing was mentioned as to whether he was actually *seen* on the third day. Nothing was mentioned of the discovery of an empty tomb by the women. Nothing about an ascension into heaven. Where did all these details come from if they are not historical?

As with the case of the nativity, these ideas came from pagan beliefs that were permeating the world of the early Gentile Christians. The new religion preached by Paul had to compete with the class of mystery religions that were popular among the Gentiles during that period. Greek and Roman myths were also part of this cultural milieu.

Christianity's biggest rival during the first few centuries of its existence was Mithraism. Mithraism, the most popular of the mystery religions, had Persian roots and involves the worship of the Sun God, Mithra. During this time, Mithraism was virtually the official religion of the Roman Empire, being very popular especially with the military.[129]

Many rituals and beliefs of Mithraism seemed so closely related to the Christian one that it becomes impossible to deny its influence on nascent Christianity. The Mithraists had a special day dedicated to their god. It was the first day of the week, which they appropriately called Sun-day, the *"day of our Lord"*. Mithra was the God of the upper and nether world and it is he who will judge men's deeds. The Jewish thinker, Philo had already identified the *Logos* with the Sun, it was therefore natural and inevitable that the early Christians should identify Jesus with such a symbol. Sunday became established as the Lord's Day for the Christians as well. From this observance of Sunday, the myth eventually evolved to connect the rising of Jesus with that day. It is worth noting that the Mithraist ritual involve the liturgical representation of *the death, burial (also in a rock tomb!) and resurrection of the god Mithra.*[130]

Other contemporary mystery religions no doubt contributed to the evolution of Christian mythology. The Syrian cult of Adonis also had a large following during the

---

129   Robertson, *A Short History of Christianity*: p37, 41
     Craveri, *The Life of Jesus*: p411
     Hinnels, *Dictionary of Religion*: p216
130   Craveri, *The Life of Jesus*: p411
     Guignebert, *Jesus*: p532
     Robertson, *A Short History of Christianity*: p42

time of early Christianity. Adonis, which means *The Lord* (Hebrew: *Adonai*), was represented in the liturgy *as dying and then rising again on the third day*. And in this liturgy it was *the women who mourned his death and who found him risen on the third day*. The Egyptian cult of Osiris had a similar belief; for it was Osiris who was dead and rose again on the third day.[131]

In the Phrygian myth of Attis, we have his story re-enacted each spring in the form of a *passion play* where an effigy of the deity was *hung on a tree* and then *buried in a tomb. On the third day, while it was still dark*, the tomb is opened and the resurrection of Attis is celebrated with much merriment.[132]

The Markan story of an empty tomb without any resurrection appearances is a well known form of ancient literature called *apotheosis* narratives. In such narratives the hero turns up missing and searches by his companions come up empty handed. It was only from a voice from heaven or through a prophecy recalled that they finally realized he had been taken up to heaven. The story of Apollonius of Tyana is one such example. Apollonius went into a temple and simply disappeared. In another version, a heavenly choir announced his ascension into heaven.[133]

Early Christian liturgy was also clearly absorbed and imported from the mystery religions. The Greco-Roman cult of Dionysius had their God, *born of the virgin*, Semele,[134] being torn to pieces by the Titans. He was then resurrected by his mother. In commemorating his sacrificial death, the devotees *ate bread and wine to represent his body and blood*. The Mithraist too had a Eucharistic celebration very similar to the Christian one. And it was also Mithraism who first came up with the sign of the cross, made on the forehead. It was the supreme symbol of their belief. The worship of Osiris too involves veneration of the Osirian cross, the emblem of their god.[135]

Fundamentalists have tried to explain this away by claiming that it was the pagan mysteries who copied the Christian story. In *The Case for Christ*, Lee Strobel quoted a fundamentalist apologist stating that "given the timing involved" it should be the pagans who plagiarized Christianity.[136] Yet this claim is demonstrably false - for a couple of reasons:

- It is well known that these mystery religion *preceded* Christianity by at least a few centuries. The myth of Adonis was known to the Greeks as early as the 5th century BCE. Attis was introduced to Rome, together with the "Great Mother" Cybele, in 205 BCE.[137] The Egyptian myth of Osiris

---

[131] Guignebert, *Jesus*: p531
   Robertson, *A Short History of Christianity*: p39
[132] Angus, *The Mystery Religions*: p60
   Frazer, *The Golden Bough*: p347-352
[133] Price, *Deconstructing Jesus*: p40-41
[134] Some versions had Dionysius being born of the virgin goddess, Persephone.
[135] Robertson, *A Short History of Christianity*: p42
[136] Strobel, *The Case for Christ*: p161
[137] In a recent debate with Tim Callahan, shown on the evangelical TV show "Faith under Fire," the evangelical apologist Gary Habermas made the claim that the resurrection accounts of Adonis and Attis all date to the second century CE and later. Habermas asserted that these myths could not therefore have influenced the Christian resurrection story. Such a statement flies in the face of the available evidence. As Robert M. Price

dates back to at least 4,000 BCE and was recorded in detail by the Greek biographer Plutarch (c46-120 CE).[138] The Persian Sun-God Mithras was mentioned in the writings of the Greek historian Herodotus (c480-c245 BCE). The cult of Mithraism reached Rome in the first century *BCE*. [139]

- The way the early church fathers defended against the mystery religions showed that they knew these pagan myths antedated the Christian ones. Justin Martyr (c100-c165) claimed that the devil *plagiarized Christianity by anticipation* with the pagan religions in order to lead people from the true faith. He claimed the myth of the virgin birth of Perseus, an ancient Greek legend that preceded Christianity, was pre-copied by the "deceiving serpent" (Dialogue with Trypho: 70). Similarly he asserted that the cultic rites of Mithraism had a diabolical origin (Apology 1:66). Tertulian (c160-

---

pointed out, nowhere are the stories mentioned as *innovations* in these accounts. Although Lucian of Samosata (c125 – 180 CE) was the earliest document we have that explicitly mentioned a *resurrected* Adonis, he was not presenting it as a *new* story. In his *De Dea Syria* (*Concerning The Syrian Goddess*) Lucian was describing the ceremonies he saw in the Temple of Aphrodite in Byblos – in other words, he was describing what was already an entrenched tradition. Similarly, although the extant explicit descriptions of Attis' resurrection date to the common era, we have evidence from pottery dating to pre-Christian times which depicts Attis dancing – the traditional posture of his resurrection. [see Price, *Deconstructing Jesus*: p91]

[138] In the same debate mentioned in note 137 above, Gary Habermas - while admitting that the Egyptian religion of Isis and Osiris is pre-Christian - claimed that there is "no resurrection in ...Osiris... Osiris in particular was not raised." This is another claim which collapses in the face of the evidence. In the pyramid text, a text dating to the third millennium BCE (see chapter 12 for more information on this text) we have this prayer - which clearly points towards the belief in the resurrection of Osiris:

> As truly as Osiris lives, so truly shall his follower live; as truly as Osiris is not dead he shall die no more; as truly as Osiris is not annihilated he shall not be annihilated.

[cf: Freke & Gandy, *The Jesus Mysteries*: p68-69]

As the Egyptologist, E.A. Wallis Budge (1857-1934) wrote in his book *The Papyrus Of Ani*:

> In every funeral inscription known to us, from the Pyramid Texts down to the roughly written prayers upon coffins of the Roman period, what is done for Osiris, is also done for the deceased, the state and condition of Osiris are the state and condition of the deceased; in a word the deceased is identified with Osiris. If Osiris liveth forever, the deceased will liveth forever; if Osiris dieth than will the deceased perish. [Budge, *The Papyrus of Ani*: p56]

The idea that the followers of Osiris will experience the same fate as him is similar to that expounded by Paul about Jesus' resurrection:

> I Corinthians 15:13-22
> But if there is no resurrection of the dead, neither has Christ been raised... But now Christ has been raised from the dead. He became the first fruits of those who are asleep. For since death came by man, the resurrection of the dead also came by man. For as in Adam all die, so also in Christ all will be made alive.

[139] Guirand, *The Larrouse Encyclopedia of Mythology*: p9, 81-82, 220, 314
Benet, *The Reader's Encyclopedia*: p655-656

c225) made the same claim: that it was the devil that provided this "pre-mimicry". That the church fathers would resort to the absurd theory of pre-mimicry (i.e. the copy coming *before* the original) means that they *could not* make the claim that the pagan mystery religions copied from Christianity! Why couldn't they? Because it must have been well known to them and to their audience which came first![140]

The historical origin of the central events of Christianity did not begin with the actual resurrection of a Galilean Jew. It began when Jewish apocalyptic was grafted onto Greco-Roman paganism.

* * * * *

We have analyzed in depth the stories of Jesus' burial and resurrection. The account of the discovery of the empty tomb was a late development and was very probably invented by the author of the second gospel himself. The contradictory accounts of Jesus' resurrection in the gospels and Acts betrays their late, and hence unhistorical, origin in the tradition. Jesus' tangible and physical resurrection appearances were also late developments in the mythologization of the biography of Jesus. The "appearances" of the resurrection Jesus can be best explained as the result of psychological and social-psychological processes in the minds of the early believers. The story of the ascension, closely tied to the resurrection of Jesus and obviously meant to be taken literally, is based on an erroneous ancient cosmology. As there is no heaven "up there", it simply provides another nail in the coffin of the whole resurrection story. Furthermore, we find that the elaboration of details of the resurrection appearances found in the gospels was heavily influenced by stories told in the pagan culture within which the early Gentile Christians lived. In short, the central event of Christianity has no historical foundation.

---

[140]   Freke & Gandy, *The Jesus Mysteries*: p34
Price, *Deconstructing Jesus*: p91-93
Wells, *The Jesus Myth*: p100

Excursus C
WAS THE COMING OF JESUS
FORETOLD IN THE OLD TESTAMENT?

One of the most often stated "proof" offered by fundamentalists of Jesus' status as the messiah or Christ is the claim that details of the Galilean's life were clearly foretold in the Old Testament. This excursus is divided into three major sections. The first section looks at the so-called "messianic prophecies" – passages in the OT which points to specific events or details about Jesus' life. In the second section we look at the passages in Isaiah known as the "Suffering Servant Songs". Finally, we analyze the textual history of Psalm 22:16 to see whether it actually is a specific prediction about the manner of Jesus' death by crucifixion.

I: MESSIANIC PROPHECIES

The fundamentalist apologist Josh McDowell, in chapter 9 of his book *Evidence that Demands a Verdict*, cited 61 passages which he claimed as prophecies in the Old Testament that were supposedly fulfilled in Jesus.[1]

Modern critical historical scholars no longer accept this method of interpreting almost any passage in the Old Testament as foretelling the coming of Jesus. In fact today *very few* passages are interpreted as proper messianic prophecies; these are Isaiah 8:23-9:6; 11:1-9, Zechariah 9:9, Micah 5:1-4 and Isaiah 7:10-17. Even in this short list, the last two are accepted only with major reservations, as the passages refer to people and events in the prophet's own time and the messianic allusions are based on later interpretations.[2]

It should also be mentioned that even this short list of more or less authentic messianic prophecies talked about the coming of the messiah in the Jewish tradition, one who is mainly a *political* leader. *Messiah* is a Hebrew word which means "anointed" and refers to the investiture of the king by anointing with oil.[3]

We will now proceed to look at the prophecies presented by McDowell.

NON-SENSICAL PROPHECIES

Many of the "prophecies" presented by McDowell in his *Evidence* are nonsensical ones. These are passages which, even upon a very cursory inspection, are clearly not prophecies at all. One suspects that these were placed there to simply add "padding" to the number of Old Testament prophecies that were supposedly fulfilled in Jesus. We give below some examples of such "prophecies":

---

[1] McDowell, *Evidence that Demands a Verdict*: p141-166
[2] Soggin, *Introduction to the Old Testament*: p257
[3] Metzger, Coogan, *Oxford Companion to the Bible*:p513-514

Jesus' Pre-Existence (Prophecy No.13)[4]

The prophecy given here is from Micah 5:2. It supposedly predicts Jesus' pre-existence. This is the verse as given in *Evidence*:[5]

> Micah 5:2b
> [O]ut of you one will come forth to me that is to be ruler in Israel; whose goings forth are from of old, from everlasting.

The "fulfillment" of this prophecy is supposedly the passage below:

> Colossians 1:17
> He is before all things, and in him all things are held together.

Note that the author of Colossians (probably not Paul – see chapter 5) is merely *claiming* that Jesus is "before all things". However, merely claiming something and actually showing something to be true are two entirely different things. Only someone who is blinded in the belief of biblical inerrancy can even begin to consider this to be a case of prophecy fulfillment.

That is not the only problem with the passage. Modern translations such as the *New Revised Standard Version* (NRSV) showed no such allusion of the messiah's pre-existence in Micah:[6]

> Micah 5:2b (NRSV)
> from you shall come forth for me, one who is to rule in Israel, whose origin is from of old, from ancient days.

The passage, as read in the NRSV, simply shows that the messiah's *ancestors* are ancient. The *Good News Bible* (GNB) translates this even more clearly:

> Micah 5:2b (GNB)
> but out of one of you I will bring a ruler for Israel, whose family line goes back to ancient times...

Jesus Called Immanuel (Prophecy No.15)

Next McDowell sites the following passage from Isaiah:

> Isaiah 7:14
> "Therefore the Lord Himself shall give you a sign: Behold, a virgin is with child and bear a son, and she will call His name Immanuel".

---

4   The prophecies given are number as they are in McDowell's *Evidence that Demands a Verdict*.
5   McDowell, *Evidence that Demands a Verdict*: p151
6   Callahan, *Bible Prophecy*: p120-121

(We will ignore for the moment some problems with the translation of the passage and with McDowell's rather liberal use of capital letters.) According to McDowell, the above prophecy, that Jesus will be called Immanuel, is *fulfilled* by the following passage:

> Matthew 1:22-23
> Now all this has happened, that it might be fulfilled which was spoken by the Lord through the prophet, saying, "Behold, the virgin shall be with child, and shall bring forth a son. They shall call his name Immanuel;" which is, being interpreted, "God with us."

This is another puzzling assertion. Matthew was merely *repeating* the passage in Isaiah 7:14. Nowhere else in the gospels was Jesus ever referred to by the name Immanuel. Clearly the claim is meaningless and nonsensical.

Jesus as Priest (Prophecy No.17)

The Old Testament passage is this:

> Psalm 110:4
> Yahweh has sworn, and will not change his mind: "You are a priest forever in the order of Melchizedek."

The supposed fulfillment, get this(!), is:

> Hebrews 5:5-6
> So also Christ didn't glorify himself to be made a high priest, but it was he who said to him,…As he says also in another place, "You are a priest forever, after the order of Melchizedek."

Surely the mere quoting of a passage is not the same as its fulfillment!

Seated at the Right Hand of God (Prophecy No.32)

Here the "prophecy" is also in Psalms:

> Psalm 110:1
> Yahweh says to my Lord, "Sit at my right hand, until I make your enemies your footstool for your feet."

The supposed fulfillment:

> Hebrews 1:3
> [W]hen he had by himself made purification for our sins, sat down on the right hand of the Majesty on high

An obvious question is this: how did the author of Hebrews know that Jesus is seated at the right hand of God? He does not. It is merely an unfounded assertion based on his faith in the resurrection. To take this as a fulfillment of a prophecy is surely stretching the idea of prophecy beyond recognition.

These examples can be repeated *ad nauseum*, but I believe the four examples above should suffice.

"MANUFACTURED" PROPHECIES

Certainly, many of the non-prophecies did not originate from McDowell but from the evangelists themselves. The author of the first gospel, for instance, was very fond of *tweaking* the Old Testament verses ever so slightly to make them work as prophecies concerning Jesus. We give two examples of this below.

The Return of Joseph and Mary from Egypt

Surprisingly, this example is *not* in McDowell's list of fulfilled prophecies on Jesus, although *Matthew* explicitly noted that it was in fulfillment of an Old Testament prophecy. McDowell did however, indirectly cite this passage from Hosea when he listed **332** distinct Old Testament passages supposedly fulfilled in Jesus' (from another fundamentalist apologetic) work in the same chapter.

> Matthew 2:14-15
> He arose and took the young child and his mother by night, and departed into Egypt, and was there until the death of Herod; that it might be fulfilled which was spoken by the Lord through the prophet, saying, "Out of Egypt I called my son."

The Old Testament passage Matthew was quoting came from the book of Hosea. Let us look at that passage in its context:

> Hosea 11:1-2
> "When Israel was a child, then I loved him,
> and called my son out of Egypt.
> They called to them, so they went from them.
> They sacrificed to the Baals,
> and burned incense to engraved images.

It takes either a very gullible person, or someone who is bent on believing no matter what, to actually believe that the passage in Hosea above relates to Jesus. For the passage is not even a prophecy at all! The whole passage talks about the calling out of the Israelites from Egypt as narrated in the Pentateuch. *My son* in this passage meant the *whole Israelite nation*. The portions italicized clearly could not be applied to Jesus (*who was sacrificing to Baal and burning incense to idols on the way back from Egypt? Joseph? Mary? Jesus?*), yet the passage is obviously an organic whole.[7] The passage is clearly not a prophecy at all. Matthew had, by selective quotation of the passage, *manufactured* a prophecy.

---

[7]   Bradlaugh, *Humanity's Gain From Unbelief*: p137

Herod's Slaughter of the Children (Prophecy No.12)

We have seen elsewhere[8] that the tale of the slaughter of the innocents is not historical. This fact is enough for us to discard the prophecy below. But there is another reason we are looking at this. The prophecy for this "event" is given in Matthew:

> Matthew 2:16-18
> Then Herod, when he saw that he was mocked by the wise men, was exceedingly angry, and sent out, and killed all the male children who were in Bethlehem and in all the surrounding countryside, from two years old and under, according to the exact time which he had learned from the wise men. Then that which was spoken by Jeremiah the prophet was fulfilled, saying, "A voice was heard in Ramah, lamentation, weeping and great mourning, Rachel weeping for her children; she wouldn't be comforted, because they are no more."

Let us look at the relevant passage in Jeremiah:

> Jeremiah 31:5-7
> Thus says Yahweh: *A voice is heard in Ramah, lamentation, and bitter weeping, Rachel weeping for her children; she refuses to be comforted for her children, because they are no more.* Thus says Yahweh: Refrain your voice from weeping, and your eyes from tears; for your work shall be rewarded, says Yahweh; and they shall come again from the land of the enemy. There is hope for your latter end, says Yahweh; and *your children shall come again to their own border.*

As we have noted in chapter 11, this passage refers to the deportation of the Israelites in exile in Babylon; Ramah being a stopover location for the deportees before continuing their journey. Since Rachel was dead long before the exile, the description of her "weeping" is metaphorical. But the important thing about the whole passage is this: it is not a prophecy about a future massacre but *a message of hope* for the deportees to Babylon, since Rachel's "children" – the Israelites – *will return home.* (see Jeremiah 31:7 above). The passage has nothing to do with babies being slaughtered. It is another example of Matthew taking an Old Testament passage out of context and "manufacturing" a prophecy out of it.[9]

---

[8] See chapter 11.

[9] That these two prophecies are clearly taken out of context is not easily denied. The best Lee Strobel could do in his widely cited (by fundamentalists) book *The Case for Christ* (Zondervan 1998) is quoting a Jewish convert to Christianity, Louis Lapides, as saying "You know I go through the books that people write to try and tear down what we believe. That's not fun to do, but I spend the time to look at each objection individually and then try to research the context and the wording in the original language. And every single time, the prophecies have stood up and shown themselves to be true." (p250) And that's it! No supporting arguments, nothing, were given after that. We are supposed to take the word of one fundamentalist with a master's degree in divinity from an evangelical seminary that it is "all okay!"

"CORE" PROPHECIES?

McDowell also presented eight sets of "core" prophecies which he claimed are "totally beyond human control", i.e., could not have been *deliberately fulfilled*.[10] These eight prophecies relate to:

- Jesus' place of birth.
- The timing of Jesus' birth.
- The virgin birth.
- The betrayal by Judas.
- Death by crucifixion.
- The crowd's reaction at the crucifixion, i.e. mocking, spitting, staring.
- The piercing of the side.
- Burial in a rich man's tomb.

Let us analyze these prophecies in detail.

Jesus' Place of Birth (Prophecy No.10)

The passage supposedly prophesying Jesus' birth is found in the book of Micah:

> Micah 5:2
> But you, Bethlehem Ephrathah,
> being small among the clans of Judah,
> out of you one will come forth to me that is to be ruler in Israel;
> whose goings forth are from of old, from everlasting.

Both *Matthew* (2:1) and *Luke* (2:4-7) mentioned that Jesus was born in Bethlehem. How certain are we that this claim is actually historical? (Remember that we have already shown that the Bible is not inerrant.[11] Just because it was mentioned in these two gospels does not mean it is necessarily true.)

As we have seen in chapter 11 of this book:

- The accounts of how Bethlehem became the birthplace of Jesus in *Luke* and *Matthew* contradict one another. This is a crucial first step; for if the two stories contradict one another, then *at least* one of these must be false.
- There are strong reasons to believe that Jesus was actually born in Nazareth as other passages imply Nazareth as the birthplace of Jesus (see Mark 1:9, 6:1, John 1:45-46, 7:41-43).
- The tradition of Jesus' birth in Bethlehem surfaced late (close to 100 CE; i.e. in Matthew c. 90 and Luke c. 95) and is not found in the earliest gospel

---

[10] McDowell, *Evidence that Demands a Verdict*: p 166
[11] See chapters 2 through 4

Mark (circa 70 CE) nor in the epistles of Paul (circa 50 CE). It is important to appreciate this time frame. It is as though a story about something that happened *before the first world war* (i.e. before 1914), which had not been heard of before, only surfaced today.

Next we note that there is every possibility that the story of Jesus' birth in Bethlehem could have been concocted by the early Christian tradition, not from historical evidence, but from the very Old Testament prophecy which calls for this! Our argument for this goes:

- There was an established tradition in Jewish culture called the *midrash*. It is a method used by the ancient Jewish theologians to interpret and expand the sacred scripture. It is the belief that current events are somehow tied to past sacred events in a very systematic way. That it is present in the Old Testament has been long known to theologians.[12] One example of this should suffice: Moses parted the Red Sea (Exodus 14:22-31) which showed he was God's prophet. To ensure continuation of this prophetic line, the authors of the Old Testament repeated the same archetypal events in Joshua's miraculous parting and crossing over the River Jordan (Joshua 3:14-17), Elijah did the same thing (II Kings 2:7-8) and when Elisha took over the waters parted again (II Kings 2:14). Now we know these events were mythical, the fact that they are repeated in the same form shows the midrash in action. *Mining the Old Testament for allusions to newer sacred stories was not something new.*

- The early Christians, too, treated the Old Testament as "proof text" on Jesus' life. If there was something they wanted to find out about Jesus, searching for it in the Old Testament was the most natural thing to do. For the belief that Jesus was the messiah came first, *then* the belief that Jesus and the major events in his life *must* have been alluded to in the Old Testament. We see this in the passage below in *John* which puts the following words into the mouth of Jesus:[13]

---

[12] Spong, *Resurrection: Myth or Reality*: chapter 1

[13] It is a general consensus among critical historical scholars that Jesus *did not* utter these words. *The Five Gospels* (p416-417) gives the reasons thus:
This lecture on authority [John 5:30-47] is case in the first person, which is uncharacteristic of Jesus' mode of speech...This kind of boasting contravenes the image projected by Jesus who warns his disciples that those who seek to be first will be last (Matt 20:6) and those who promoted themselves will be demoted (Luke 18:14b; compare the parable of the Pharisee and toll collector, Luke 18:10-14a). Rather than authentic words of Jesus, the author of the fourth gospel is presenting his own meditations on the theological significance of Jesus...Jesus is made to claim that the sacred scriptures give evidence on his behalf...it was early Christian practice to search the scriptures for evidence that Jesus' appearance as the Anointed had been anticipated by Moses and the prophets. The Fellows of the Jesus Seminar doubt that Jesus himself indulged in such speculation.

John 5:39
"You search the Scriptures...and these are they which testify about me."

- All the other evangelists shared the same paradigm: that major events in Jesus' life were in fulfillment of Old Testament Prophecies (e.g. Matthew 21:7 [Zechariah 11:12-13]; Mark 14:27 [Zechariah 13:7]; Luke 3:4-6 [Isaiah 40:3-5]).

- The attitude then was that the Old Testament was a *reliable source* for events in the life of Jesus. Proof of this attitude can easily be found. We have seen from the episode of Jesus' triumphal entry into Jerusalem. *Mark, Luke and John* (Mark 11:1-11, Luke 19:29-35 and John 12:12-26) gave a reasonably believable scenario of Jesus making arrangements and then riding into Jerusalem on a donkey. Now *Matthew*, however, had Jesus sitting on *two* donkeys simultaneously (Matthew 21:1-7) instead of one!

We know from our previous analysis[14] that Matthew incorporated a large portion of the Gospel of *Mark* into his own gospel. We must conclude therefore that Matthew considered *Mark* to be a reasonably reliable document. Matthew obviously had Mark's description of the triumphal entry in front of him when he wrote the account. That being the case, why would Matthew here consciously alter the Markan account by deliberately replacing a natural account of the triumphal entry for a more absurd one?

This is because he thought that the passage in Zechariah 9:9 *called for* two donkeys instead of one. Although he was heavily dependent on the Gospel of Mark, he overwrote the obviously more commonsensical story in Mark because *the Old Testament compelled him to do so*! This is a very important point: that to the author of *Matthew*, and the other evangelists also as we shall see below, exact fulfillment of Old Testament prophecies over-rode other considerations[15] even if these were factual and commonsensical descriptions from more contemporaneous source documents (such as *Mark* obviously was to *Matthew*).

---

[14] See chapter 9.

[15] Note that this assertion does not contradict what we had discovered earlier: that the evangelists (including Matthew) were fond of lifting Old Testament stories out of context to construct details in the life of Jesus. For they read the Old Testament in a way, although nonsensical to us today, which allowed them to look at a passage in total exclusion to its surrounding story. In other words, these allusions were *embedded* (much as some fundamentalists believe that some "bible codes" or prophecies were embedded in the Old Testament - e.g. Drosnin's *The Bible Code*) in the Old Testament. We see this in the examples above where Matthew simply lifted out *one line* from Hosea 11:1 ignoring the following line which actually contradicts the way he was planning to use it in this gospel and to construct the story of the return from Egypt and his use of just one paragraph from Jeremiah 31:15 in Herod's slaughter of the innocents ignoring the follow up passage. Thus the belief was that the *relevant passage* must be a prophecy, not the whole document or even the story where that passage was taken from. Let us call this basic relevant passage an "oracular unit". Thus in the case of the two donkeys, Matthew obviously felt that the passage in Zechariah 9:9 was one "oracular unit".

- We have also seen elsewhere that the evangelists sometimes make use of Old Testament passages to *construct* stories about Jesus. Many details of the nativity (which no one claims were messianic) such as Mary's song of praise and the annunciation can be shown to be constructed from Old Testament passages.

- Therefore, the very fact that an Old Testament passage *calls for* the messiah to be born in Bethlehem would have led the early Christians to conclude that Jesus *must* have been born in Bethlehem! We have seen this argument out in the mouth of skeptics in John 7:41-43 who doubted that Jesus is the Christ as they believed he was not from Bethlehem but from Nazareth:

  > John 7:41-43
  > Others said, "This is the Christ." But some said, "What, does the Christ come out of Galilee? Hasn't the Scripture said that the Christ comes of the seed of David, and from Bethlehem, the village where David was?"

- Because the tradition of the birth in Bethlehem surfaced relatively late, it was certainly enough time for oral tradition to develop this myth. We have seen that the old argument that there would have been eyewitnesses to point out this myth if it was untrue is untenable.[16] For there would not have been many eyewitnesses around when (and where) Matthew and Luke were written.

To summarize, the passage in Micah cannot be said to be a fulfilled prophecy because:

- Jesus was probably *not* born in Bethlehem. The accounts of how he was born there given in Luke and Matthew are contradictory.
- It is more likely that he was born in Nazareth.
- The tradition of the birth in Bethlehem surfaced late, almost a *century* after the event was supposed to have happened.
- We also know that the evangelists were not beyond twisting (as was the case with the two donkeys) or even inventing stories (as was the case with the annunciation in Luke) about Jesus from Old Testament passages.
- The very fact that the birth of the future messiah in Bethlehem was *prophesied* in the Old Testament would have led the early Christians to conclude that Jesus *must have been born there.*

---

[16]   See chapter 10 in the section on Oral Tradition.

The Timing of Jesus' Birth

Surprisingly this was not placed by McDowell within the 61 prophecies "fulfilled" in Jesus but placed almost as an afterthought in his "answers to objections" section in chapter 9 of *Evidence*. This is the main passage which supposedly predicted the timing of Jesus' coming:

> Genesis 49:10
> The scepter will not depart from Judah,
> nor the ruler's staff from between his feet,
> until Shiloh comes,
> To him will the obedience of the peoples be.

His argument is quite convoluted. Firstly, for "scepter" read "tribal staff" and for "tribal staff" apply the meaning "national identity". And for "departure of the scepter" read the "removal of the identity of Judah" and the "suppression of judicial power". These are then related to the advent of the Idumean King Herod and to the Sanhedrin's loss of the right to capital punishment under Herod's successor Archelaus in 11 CE. Then *Shiloh* is asserted to mean the *messiah*.[17]

The one thing the reader will note is how extremely subjective the whole line of reasoning is. In other words, the prophecy only begins to work if you read into it hard enough. Let us note where the subjectivities lie:

- His description of the advent of Herod the Great as the first loss of "national identity" is extremely tenuous. He mentioned that Herod took over from the Maccabees who were "Jewish", thus prior to Herod there was still the "national identity". But the passage was clearly describing the *tribe of Judah*. The Maccabees, however, were from the *tribe of Levi*.

- Why should "suppression of judicial power" be taken to mean "departure of the scepter"? And more specifically, why should "suppression of judicial power" be viewed merely as the loss of the right of capital punishment? For the Sanhedrin even then retained substantial judicial powers (as McDowell himself cited) such as excommunication, imprisonment and corporal punishment.

- In fact it is not even historically certain that the Sanhedrin had lost that right to capital punishment. Other evidence points towards the Sanhedrin still *retaining the right*. For example, Acts 7:58 described the stoning to death of Stephen by the Sanhedrin. There is even archaeological evidence to support this. Archaeologists discovered incised stone notices of the Jerusalem Temple which warns of the death penalty for any Gentile who trespassed the temple's exclusively Jewish areas. These stone notices can be found in the Archaeological Museum at Istanbul and in the Rockefeller Museum at Jerusalem.[18]

---

[17] McDowell, *Evidence*: p168-169
[18] Guignebert, *Jesus*: p463

- Next we have the assertion that *Shiloh* is a "code name" for the messiah. The name Shiloh appeared 37 times in the Old Testament. In 36 passages it refers to *a city in Ephraim*. Yet in this one single verse, we are told to accept that Shiloh unambiguously refers to the messiah because "for centuries Jewish and Christian commentators alike have taken the word "Shiloh" to mean a name for the Messiah".

  This ambiguous and tenuous logic is not the only problem here. The Hebrew here in the Masoretic Text is unclear. The phrase "until Shiloh comes" is not the only reading there but could be read as "until he comes to Shiloh" or even "until tribute comes to him". The *Syriac* manuscripts read "until he comes to whom it belongs".[19] In fact the association of one of the readings with the *city* of Shiloh makes for a much simpler explanation for the passage. The prophet Samuel was brought to Shiloh as an infant to be raised by the priests there. (I Samuel 1:21-28) And it was Samuel who *anointed* David as King (or *messiah*) in Bethlehem (I Samuel 16:13).

Most modern critical historical scholars interpret the passage in Genesis 49:9-10 as referring to the dominance of Judah under *David*. Even here it is not considered prophetic but merely provides a clue to the *period in which that portion of Genesis* (normally thought to be part of the "J" Document) was composed.[20]

To summarize:

- The passage in Genesis 49:10's connection with Jesus is non-existent.

- The passage in Hebrew is unclear and could be rendered in several ways.

- The most likely explanation for the text is an allusion to the hegemony of Judah under King David.

The Virgin Birth (Prophecy No.3)

Perhaps the most well known messianic prophecy is this:

Matthew 1:22-23
Now all this has happened, that it might be fulfilled which was spoken by the Lord through the prophet, saying, "Behold, the *virgin* shall be with child, and shall bring forth a son. They shall call his name Immanuel;" which is, being interpreted, "God with us."

Matthew was quoting from Isaiah 7:14. Yet as we have shown in chapter 11:

Maccoby, *Revolution in Judea*: p204
Wilson, *Jesus: The Evidence*: p103-104
[19] See footnote to the text Genesis 49:10 in NRSV
[20] Anderson, *A Critical Introduction to the Old Testament*: p34
Asimov: *Guide to the Bible*: p117
Soggins, *Introduction to the Old Testament*: p75

- The word *virgin* (Greek = *parthenos*) used by Matthew was a mistranslation of the original Hebrew word *almah* which simply means a young woman of marriageable age.

- The passage in Isaiah 7:14 did *not* refer to any future messiah and was merely a prophecy by Isaiah about the impending defeat of Ahaz's enemies. The baby was used merely as a chronological benchmark to measure the fulfillment of this local prophecy.

- Furthermore, the virgin birth, like the tradition of his birth in Bethlehem, was a late development, coming into the scene only towards the end of the first century. There were no allusions to it in earlier documents such as *Mark* and the Pauline epistles.

- We have also shown that elements in the story of the virgin birth were simply imported from the pagan religious milieu of the environment of that time.

Isaiah 7:14 is not a messianic prophecy at all but simply a mistranslated passage taken out of context by the early Christians. Furthermore, the virgin birth is *unhistorical* and was a pagan concept imported into nascent Christianity.

The Betrayal by Judas (Prophecies No. 33 through 36)

These prophecies are presented in *Evidence* thus:

No.33 Betrayal by a Friend

Prophecy	"Fulfillment"
Psalm 41:9	Matthew 10:4
Yes, my own familiar friend, in whom I trusted, who ate bread with me, has lifted up his heel against me.	and Judas Iscariot, who also betrayed him.

No.34 Sold for 30 Pieces of Silver

Prophecy	"Fulfillment"
Zechariah 11:12	Matthew 26:15
I said to them, "If you think it best, give me my wages; and if not, keep them." So they weighed for my wages thirty pieces of silver.	and said, "What are you willing to give me, that I should deliver him to you?" They weighed out for him thirty pieces of silver.

No.35 Money to be Thrown in God's House

Prophecy	"Fulfillment"
Zechariah 11:13b	Matthew 27:5a
I took the thirty pieces of silver, and threw them to the potter, in the house of Yahweh.	He threw down the pieces of silver in the sanctuary, and departed.

No.36 Price Given for Potter's Field

Prophecy	"Fulfillment"
Zechariah 11:13b	Matthew 27:7
I took the thirty pieces of silver, and threw them to the potter, in the house of Yahweh.	They took counsel, and bought the potter's field with them, to bury strangers in.

While these seemingly detailed correspondences may look impressive at first sight, a few preliminary considerations show that there is no prophecy and no fulfillment. We have looked at the episode of Judas' betrayal in chapter 14. Here we need to note the highlights of what we have found:

- Firstly, the whole story of the betrayal by Judas is very probably unhistorical[21] for a few reasons:

    o The betrayal makes no sense. Judas' motive is never made clear in the gospel, his "kiss" is of no use since Jesus was obviously a recognizable figure to the chief priests and the amount he was paid, 30 shekels, was certainly less than what he could probably have got being the treasurer of the twelve.

    o There is evidence of a divergent early tradition that does not include a traitor among the twelve apostles. (I Corinthians 15:5, Matthew 19:28 & Gospel of Peter 14:58-60)

- Secondly, there are divergent and contradictory accounts of what was done with the 30 pieces of silver supposedly prophesized. Matthew 27:3-5 said that Judas *threw* the money into the temple and then went away to hang himself and it was the *chief priests* who used the money to buy the potter's field. Acts 1:18-19 openly contradicts this by saying that it was *Judas himself* who bought the field where he fell and died.

- Thirdly, we note that Matthew made the mistake in attributing the prophecy to *Jeremiah* (Matthew 27:9) what can only be found in *Zechariah* (11:12-13)! And this mistake gives a very strong clue as to how Matthew constructed the whole story.

---

[21] In his book *The Case for Christ*, (p248) the journalist turned pastor, Lee Strobel, quoted a Jewish convert Louis Lapides, as saying that these could not have been constructed by Matthew due to three reasons: firstly, these were circulated during the lifetime of the people who would have been eyewitnesses; secondly, Matthew would not have allowed himself to be martyred for what he knew was a lie; and thirdly, the Jewish community would have been around to refute any false assertions by the Christians.

Typical of fundamentalist defenses, these only work if the reader is ignorant of the basic facts of biblical research. All three arguments are flawed. We have noted in chapter 10, why this defense does not work with the gospel accounts. Remember that Matthew was written circa 90 CE, or a full *six decades* after the event. How many eyewitnesses to these events would be alive then? The same could be answered of his third defense. Many of the Jews who could conceivably have some knowledge of the events would have been killed during the destruction of Jerusalem in 70 CE. As for the second argument, that "Matthew" would not have died for a lie, this only works if we know the author of the gospel is the apostle of that name. As we have argued earlier, this is certainly not the case.

- Finally, as is the case with the prophecy of Jesus' birth in Bethlehem above, we note that many of the details in the story were probably constructed from Old Testament sources.

Apart from the obvious unhistorical nature of the details of the Judas betrayal, there is one more additional point to mention. Tim Callahan pointed out in his book *Bible Prophecy* that the phrase "lifted up his heels" from Psalm 41:9 implies an action meant to *insult* and not to *assault*. In other words, it is not a prophecy about betrayal at all but a lament about being insulted by a trusted friend.[22]

To summarize - there can be no claim of prophecy fulfillment when all we have are contradictory reports which are obviously fictional.

Death by Crucifixion (Prophecy No.44)

As mentioned in chapter 14, the crucifixion of Jesus is an historical fact. The crucifixion is supposedly prophesied by the passage below from Psalms.

> Psalm 22:16
> For dogs have surrounded me.
> A company of evildoers have enclosed me.
> *They have pierced my hands and feet.*

This is certainly a sharp (pardon the pun!) correspondence with the crucifixion. Certainly older English translations, such as the King James Bible and the Revised Standard Version have left this as the main translation. Could this be *the* passage about an historical event in the life of Jesus that *was* prophesied in the Old Testament? No.

It is important to point out that the word *pierced* is *not found in the original Hebrew Bible*. This word is a *mistranslation* of the Hebrew word, *kaari*, which means "like a lion". The original mistranslation first appeared in the Latin Bible and, evidently, it was too fortuitous to be corrected.[23] As the textual issues regarding this verse is quite involved, so we will be treating this separately in section III of this excursus.

Crowd's Reaction at the Crucifixion (Prophecies No.41 and 42)

The Old Testament verses given in *Evidence* are as follows:

---

22 Callahan, *Bible Prophecy*: p117
23 Asimov, *Guide to the Bible*: p895
   Callahan, *Bible Prophecy*: p122

Prophecy No.41 Smitten and Spit Upon

Prophecy	"Fulfillment"
Isaiah 50: 6	Matthew 26:67
I gave my back to the strikers, and my cheeks to those who plucked off the hair; I didn't hide my face from shame and spitting.	Then they spit in his face and beat him with their fists, and some slapped him

Prophecy No.42 Mocked

Prophecy	"Fulfillment"
Psalm 22:7-8	Matthew 27:31
All those who see me mock me. They insult me with their lips. They shake their heads, saying, "He trusts in Yahweh; let him deliver him. Let him rescue him, since he delights in him."	When they had mocked him, they took the robe off of him, and put his clothes on him, and led him away to crucify him.

Perhaps McDowell was being a bit modest here, there is a passage in Mark which fits the prophecies above even more exactly:

Mark 15:29-32
Those who passed by blasphemed him, *wagging their heads*, and saying, "Ha! You who destroy the temple, and build it in three days, *save yourself*, and come down from the cross!" Likewise, also the chief priests mocking among themselves with the scribes said, "He saved others. He can't save himself. Let the Christ, the King of Israel, now come down from the cross, that we may see and believe him." Those who were crucified with him *insulted* him.

The correspondence about the crowd "wagging [or shaking] their head" and asking Jesus to "save himself" is an almost perfect correspondence to Psalm 22:7-8. But that is probably the reason why McDowell did *not* use this passage. It makes the *construction* of the whole episode from Old Testament episodes look too *transparent*.

D.E. Nineham had convincingly demonstrated that, the contents of the passage above show that the evangelist had no historical sources for this.[24]

- In the first place, the insults hurled by the passers-by amount to no more than a repetition of the charges brought against him by the Sanhedrin (his threat to destroy the temple and his claim of messianic status).

- In the second place, the presence of the chief priests and scribes at the scene of the crucifixion *on the first day of Passover* strains our credulity.

- And finally, many of the details reflect Old Testament passages so closely that it is improbable that this account did not stem ultimately from them. Some of the passages are given below:

---

[24] Nineham, *Saint Mark*: p425

Lamentations 2:15
All that pass by clap their hands at you. They hiss and wag their head...

Psalm 22:7
All those who see me mock me. They insult me with their lips. They shake their heads

Psalm 69:9
For the zeal of your house consumes me. The reproaches of those who reproach you have fallen on me.

Wisdom of Solomon 2:17-20
Let us see if his words are true and let us test what will happen at the end of his life, for if the righteous man is God's son, he will help him and will deliver him from the hand of his adversaries. Let us test him with insults and torture, that we may find out how gentle he is, and make trial of his forbearance. Let us condemn him to a shameful death, for according to what he says, he will be protected.

- In fact the Greek word for *reproach* or *insult* in the Septuagint version of Psalm 69:9 (*oneidizo*) is exactly the same as the one used in Mark 15:32. The exact correspondence between these Old Testament passages and Mark's account points to the fact that Mark's source was not working from the traditional eye-witness material but from a belief that the Old Testament contains predictions about Jesus' life. And since Matthew, as we know, copied from Mark, it is obvious that the source for the former is also the Old Testament (and *Mark*), not eyewitness accounts.

We do not need to stop here, other details of the crucifixion can easily be shown to be unhistorical and derived from Old Testament sources:

- **Prophecy No.54: The Drink Given to Jesus at the Cross**
  The evangelists contradict each other on what drink was given to Jesus at the cross. Mark 15:23 says it was wine mingled with *myrrh*, Matthew 27:34 says in contradiction to Mark, that it was wine mixed with *gall*. Myrrh is a sedative and would have been meant to reduce the pain. Gall, on the other hand, has a bitter taste and would have had the opposite effect from myrrh. Clearly, these contradictory accounts can't all be true. Yet all these allusions were obviously taken from Old Testament passages (see Proverbs 39:6, Psalm 69:21).

- **Prophecies No: 55 and 56: Jesus' Last Words**
  Jesus' last words given by Mark/Matthew, Luke and John all contradict on another:

  Mark 15:34,37 (Matthew 27:46,50)
  At the ninth hour Jesus cried with a loud voice, saying, "Eloi, Eloi, lama sabachthani?" which is, being interpreted, "My God, my God, why have you forsaken me?" ...Jesus cried out with a loud voice, and gave up the spirit.

Luke 23:46
Jesus, crying with a loud voice, said, "Father, into your hands I commit my spirit!" Having said this, he breathed his last.

John 19:30
When Jesus therefore had received the vinegar, he said, "It is finished." He bowed his head, and gave up his spirit

Because these three accounts contradict one another, they can't all be true. Furthermore, they all can be shown to be taken from Old Testament sources. Mark's source was the book of Psalms:

Psalm 22:1
My God, my God, why have you forsaken me?

Luke's source was another verse from the same book:

Psalm 31:5
Into your hand I commend my spirit.

John's version is in keeping with his portrayal of Jesus throughout the passion-his savior was triumphant. So just as he triumphantly carried the cross himself, he now exclaims the final accomplishment of his mission. As usual none of these accounts have any valid claims to historicity.

These passages prove that the details of the crucifixion were manufactured from whole cloth based on Old Testament sources. Why did the evangelists resort to this? Because very likely there were *no witnesses to this event*. For according to Mark 14:50 the disciples deserted him upon his arrest. As we have seen in chapter 14, *John*'s story about Jesus' mother being close to the cross is clearly fictional.

These considerations show us that no weight can be given to other details in the crucifixion such as that he was crucified between two thieves (Prophecy No.45), the darkening of the sky (Prophecy No. 60) and the dividing of his garments (Prophecy No.52). Like the examples above, these are fictional embroidery to an event which the early tradition had no eyewitness.

The Piercing of the Side (Prophecy No.59)

The prophecy and fulfillment verses are given thus:

Prophecy	"Fulfillment"
Zechariah 12:10	John 19:34
they will look to me whom they have pierced	However one of the soldiers pierced his side with a spear

The author of *John* claims to be an eyewitness to this. It is important to look at the passage in full:

John 19:31-35
Therefore the Jews, because it was the Preparation Day, so that the bodies wouldn't remain on the cross on the Sabbath (for that Sabbath was a special one), asked of Pilate that their legs might be broken, and that they might be taken away. Therefore the soldiers came, and broke the legs of the first, and of the other who was crucified with him; but when they came to Jesus, and saw that he was already dead, they didn't break his legs. However one of the soldiers pierced his side with a spear, and immediately blood and water came out. He who has seen has testified, and his testimony is true. He knows that he tells the truth, that you may believe.

John's claim notwithstanding, the whole episode looks very much like a hastily done insertion. We see that the Jews asked for the legs to be broken and the bodies to be taken down. Pilate, according to John, acquiesced to that. Yet just a few verses later (John 19:38) Joseph of Arimathea was reported to have come later and did the same thing (i.e. asked for permission to remove Jesus from the cross).[25]

The breaking of the legs and the piercing of Jesus' side with the lance clearly fulfills Old Testament prophesies, as John himself admits:

John 19:36
For these things happened, that the Scripture might be fulfilled, "A bone of him will not be broken."

The assertion that Jesus' bones were not broken, is found only in *John* and nowhere else. The other three gospels make no mention of it at all. It is important to note that Exodus 12:46 is not a messianic prophecy at all. In fact, the passage doesn't even refer to a human being but to *the Passover lamb*! That John meant Jesus to be the new paschal lamb cannot be doubted for, as we have seen in chapter 14, unlike the synoptics, he made the time of Jesus' death coincide with the slaughter of the Passover lamb. With such a heavily theological stench it is hard to credit John's passage with any veracity.

We can conclude that the whole episode of the breaking of the legs and piercing the sides was a hastily done insertion by the author of *John* to fulfill his theological purpose and has no grounding in history.

Once again we see how the fundamentalists had got it backwards. It wasn't the events in Jesus' life that fulfilled the Old Testament prophecies, *it was the Old Testament prophecies that were used to construct details in the life of Jesus!*

Burial in a Rich Man's Tomb (Prophecy No.61)

McDowell used this verse from Isaiah as the fulfillment of the prophecy that Jesus was buried in Joseph of Arimathea's tomb:

Isaiah 53:9 [Verse as given in *Evidence that Demands a Verdict*]

---

[25]   Wells, *The Historical Evidence for Jesus*: p189

"His grave was assigned to be with wicked men, Yet with a rich man in his death..."

We have noted in chapter 15 that the tradition of the burial of Jesus by Joseph of Arimathea is very probably *not* historical.

There is a further problem to this as Tim Callahan pointed out,[26] the translation for this passage varies and pivotal here is the use of "yet" by McDowell. Most modern translations use "and". The proper translation should be:

Isaiah 53:9
They made his grave with the wicked *and* with a rich man in his death

The use of the word *and* is a Hebrew poetic parallelism (much like the donkey and the foal episode [Zechariah 9:9] above which confused *Matthew*). This means that in Isaiah 53:9, the *rich man* is identical with the *wicked*. We have seen that all the gospels portray Joseph as a *good man* (Mark 15:43, Matthew 27:57, Luke 23:50-51 and John 19:38). Therefore, this prophecy could not have been about Joseph of Arimathea. This, like the case of *Matthew*'s description of Jesus' triumphal entry by riding on two donkeys simultaneously into Jerusalem, could have been misunderstood by *Mark* who first used it to construct the episode in his gospel.

Again, no prophecy, no fulfillment.

II: THE SUFFERING SERVANT

There are four "Songs of the Servant" in Deutero-Isaiah[27] (Isaiah 42:1-9, 49:1-6, 50:4-9, 52:13-53:12), normally referred to as "The Suffering Servant", that have always been taken by Christians to be prophetic references to the atoning suffering of Jesus Christ. In other words, Jesus *was* the prophesied suffering servant. An early example of such an identification is the story of the Ethiopian eunuch from the book of Acts. Here we are told that the apostle Philip was commanded by God to go to Gaza to meet with the Ethiopian – a powerful dignitary. This is how the story continues:

Acts 8:30-35
Philip ran to him [the Ethiopian eunuch], and heard him reading Isaiah the prophet, and said, "Do you understand what you are reading?" He said, "How can I, unless someone explains it to me?" He begged Philip to come up and sit with him. Now the passage of the Scripture which he was reading was this,

---

26   Callahan, *Bible Prophecy*: p122

27   Critical scholars generally separate Isaiah into 3 parts. The first part from chapters 1 through 39 is generally accepted by scholars to have been written by the prophet Isaiah around the 8th century BCE. The rest of the book is generally accepted by scholars to be later additions to Isaiah and are hence *pseudepigraphical* (i.e. forgery – see chapter 5). The segment from chapters 40 to 55 is called "Deutero-Isaiah" or second Isaiah, and from its internal content is generally dated to the past exilic period around the middle of the 6th century BCE. The last portion, "Trito-Isaiah" or third Isaiah, comprising chapters 56 to 66, is even later and dates to the last quarter of the 6th century BCE. [Soggin, *Introduction to the Old Testament*: p299]

"He was led as a sheep to the slaughter. As a lamb before his shearer is silent, so he doesn't open his mouth. In his humiliation, his judgment was taken away. Who will declare His generation? For his life is taken from the earth." [Isaiah 53:7-8]

The eunuch answered Philip, "Who is the prophet talking about? About himself, or about someone else?" Philip opened his mouth, and beginning from this Scripture, preached to him Jesus.

The passage quoted by the eunuch is from the fourth servant song in Isaiah. Philip (and obviously Luke) had no doubt that the passage referred to Jesus.[28] Apart from Luke, it is obvious that the other evangelists used passages from the servant songs to construct details of the passion and burial of Jesus. We have already seen some examples of this earlier: Isaiah 50:6 was used to construct the details of Jesus' humiliation during the crucifixion (Matthew 26:67), Isaiah 53:12 was used to concoct the story that Jesus was crucified among thieves (Mark 15:27) and Isaiah 53:9 was used to produce the story of Jesus' burial in the tomb of Joseph of Arimathea (Mark 15:42-46). Modern fundamentalists refer to fulfilled prophecies from these servant songs in the life of Jesus. Lee Strobel recounted how Louis Lapides, a Jew turned Christian fundamentalist, read portions of the fourth servant song (Isaiah 53:3-9, 12) and was immediately able to see that it referred to Jesus.[29] Josh McDowell managed to squeeze out at least eight "fulfilled prophecies" from the servant songs:[30]

Prophecy No.29 Light to the Gentiles

Prophecy	"Fulfillment"
Isaiah 49:6	Acts 13:47-48
[Y]es, he says, "It is too light a thing that you should be my servant to raise up the tribes of Jacob, and to restore the preserved of Israel: I will also give you for a light to the nations, that you may be my salvation to the end of the earth."	For so has the Lord commanded us, saying, "I have set you as a light for the Gentiles, that you should bring salvation to the uttermost parts of the earth." As the Gentiles heard this, they were glad, and glorified the word of God. As many as were appointed to eternal life believed.

Prophecy No.39 Dumb Before Accusers

Prophecy	"Fulfillment"
Isaiah 53:7	Matthew 27:12
He was oppressed, yet when he was afflicted he didn't open his mouth.	When he was accused by the chief priests and elders, he answered nothing.

Prophecy No.40 Wounded and Bruised

Prophecy	"Fulfillment"
Isaiah 53:5	Matthew 27:26
But he was pierced for our transgressions. He was crushed for our iniquities. The punishment that brought	Then he released to them Barabbas, but Jesus he flogged and delivered to be crucified.

---

[28]   Akenson, *Surpassing Wonder*: p248-249
      Soggin, *Introduction to the New Testament*: p369
[29]   Strobel, *The Case for Christ*: p239-241
[30]   McDowell, *Evidence that Demands a Verdict*: 157-166

our peace was on him; and by his
wounds we are healed

Prophecy No.41 Smitten and Spit Upon

Prophecy	"Fulfillment"
Isaiah 50: 6	Matthew 26:67
I gave my back to the strikers, and my cheeks to those who plucked off the hair; I didn't hide my face from shame and spitting.	Then they spit in his face and beat him with their fists, and some slapped him

Prophecy No.45 Crucified with Thieves

Prophecy	"Fulfillment"
Isaiah 53:12	Matthew 27:38
... because he poured out his soul to death, and was numbered with the transgressors...	Then there were two robbers crucified with him, one on his right hand and one on the left.

Prophecy No.46 Made Intercession for His Persecutors

Prophecy	"Fulfillment"
Isaiah 53:12	Luke 23:34
... yet he bore the sin of many, and made intercession for the transgressors.	Jesus said, "Father, forgive them, for they don't know what they are doing."

Prophecy No.47 Rejected by His Own People

Prophecy	"Fulfillment"
Isaiah 53:3	John 7:5, 48
He was despised, and rejected by men; a man of suffering, and acquainted with disease. He was despised as one from whom men hide their face; and we didn't respect him.	For even his brothers didn't believe in him... Have any of the rulers believed in him, or of the Pharisees?

Prophecy No.61 Buried in a Rich Man's Tomb

Prophecy	"Fulfillment"
Isaiah 53:9	Matthew 27:57-60
They made his grave with the wicked, and with a rich man in his death	When evening had come, a rich man from Arimathaea, named Joseph...asked for Jesus' body...Joseph took the body, and wrapped it in a clean linen cloth, and laid it in his own new tomb...

Impressive as these may seem at first sight, there are two basic facts about the servant songs that work *against* such a messianic interpretation.

Firstly, *nowhere in Isaiah is the suffering servant explicitly identified with the messiah.* And when the messiah is mentioned in Isaiah, it is in this passage:

Isaiah 45:1
Thus says Yahweh to *his messiah, to Cyrus...*

Most English translation translates the original Hebrew *messiah* into "anointed", thereby (inadvertently?) making the identification of Cyrus as God's messiah unclear to most readers. The original passage is clear though, Deutero-Isaiah identifies Cyrus, *not the suffering servant*, to be God's messiah![31]

If the suffering servant is not the messiah, who is he? It must be admitted at the outset that the passages are ambiguous and many interpretations have been offered by scholars. We have seen above how fundamentalists and conservatives identify him with Jesus. Other scholars have suggested that it is autobiographical; in other words, the author of Deutero-Isaiah referring to his own suffering and redemption. Yet others have suggested that it is a conflation of the various prophets from Moses to Jehoiachin who were made to pass through various trials. By far the best explanation for the term, which is also the one favored by most Jewish scholars, is that the servant is not an individual, but is actually Israel.[32] In other words, it is a collective term meaning *all of Israel*. Indeed, this is exactly how the suffering servant is identified in the second servant song:

> Isaiah 49:3
> [A]nd he [Yahweh] said to me, "*You are my servant; Israel*, in whom I will be glorified."

This collective identification of the servant as Israel is sometimes lost, or ignored, in English translations. As the historian Donald Akenson pointed out, a passage from the fourth servant song, Isaiah 53:8, is normally translated in the singular as "for the transgression of my people *was he* stricken." Yet the grammatical ambiguity in the original Hebrew allows also for a plural translation here: "for the transgression of my people *were they* stricken."[33]

Once the servant is seen as a collective term for Israel, many of the passages can be read in the proper light. The fourth servant song, the one which convinced Louis Lapides (see above) that the Old Testament prophesied about Jesus, is actually about Israel and how through its suffering, the world will be redeemed.[34]

While there is some ambiguity in the personification of the servant, the two facts above - that the suffering servant is not to be identified with the messiah [the messiah was identified as Cyrus!] and that in most contexts the term "servant" refers to Israel as a corporate entity – are enough to dismiss evangelical claims that it was Jesus who was being referred to in these passages.

---

[31] Akenson, *Surpassing Wonder*: p245
[32] Soggin, *Introduction to the New Testament*: p369
[33] Akenson, *Surpassing Wonder*: p249
[34] Akenson, *Surpassing Wonder*: p248

III: PSALM 22:16; A PROPHECY OF THE CRUCIFIXION?

Take a look at the King James Version Bible, or modern fundamentalist versions such as the New International Version and the New King James Version, under Psalm 22:16[35] and you will find the following:

> Psalm 22:16 KJV/NIV/NKJV
> For dogs have compassed me: the assembly of the wicked have inclosed me: *they pierced* my hands and my feet.

THE FUNDAMENTALIST CLAIM

Fundamentalists claim that the latter part of Psalm 22:16 "They pierced my hands and my feet" (which we shall designate as Psalm 22:16b) is a direct prophecy of the *crucifixion*; with the "piercing" referring to the nails going through Jesus' hands and feet.

Surely, the believer will assert, this is one certain example of a prophecy fulfilled: "they pierced" can only refer to the puncturing of Jesus' flesh by the nails used in the crucifixion. It is then added that this translation is supported by the various ancient versions of the Bible. The Latin translation, the Vulgate, for instance, uses the word *foderunt*, which is the third person plural perfect verb for *fodio* which means "to prick", "to sting", "to jab", "to dig" or "to prod". *Foderunt* could be reasonably translated as "they pierced" or "they have pierced". Similarly, in the ancient Greek version, the Septuagint, the word used is *oruxan* (ωρυξαν) which supposedly means "to bore through".[36]

The Hebrew Masoretic Text (MT) however, has a different word here. In order to see the picture clearly, I will provide the Hebrew [remember that Hebrew is read from right to left!] as well the transliteration and meaning below.

---

[35]   Psalm 22:16 is the normal rendering of chapter and verse for English bibles for this passage "For dogs have compassed me: the assembly of the wicked have enclosed me: they pierced my hands and my feet." However, we find different chapter and verse designations in different versions. The Hebrew Tanakh (based on the Masoretic Text) gives this as Psalm 22:17, the Septuagint has Psalm 21:17 while the Vulgate, like the Septuagint, numbers this passage as Psalm 21:17. The reason for this discrepancy lies in how the chapters and verses are divided in Psalms. The Septuagint combines chapters 9 and 10 of the Hebrew bible into chapter 9. This means that after chapter 9, the Septuagint chapter numbers will be one behind the Hebrew bible. It further combines another two chapters,114 and 115, into one (113). However, it splits the next chapter in the Hebrew bible (116) into two (114 & 115). Finally it splits chapter 147 of the Hebrew text into two (146 & 147). There are two combinations and two splits which means that both renditions of Psalms end with 150 chapters! Modern English bibles follow the Hebrew chapter numbering. The verses defer because the Hebrew bible counts the title of the psalm as the first verse whereas the English bibles do not. [Hoffman, *Psalm 22 (LXX 21) and the Crucifixion of Jesus: notations* page]

[36]   Archer, *Encyclopedia of Bible Difficulties*: p37

Hebrew	י	ר	א	כ
Alphabets	yod	resh	aleph	kaf
Transliteration	Y	R	(*)	K
Pronunciation	Kaari			

(*) = quiescent

Table C.1: Hebrew word for "Like a Lion"

Since the Hebrew text in its original biblical form is purely consonantal, the vowel points being a later scribal addition,[37] we will concentrate only on the consonantal text for our subsequent discussion. The word shown above actually consists of two words, the first letter (on the right) *kaf*, is a preposition (called an *inseparable* preposition because it is always attached to a noun) which means, in this case, "like" (as in *similar to*). The next three letters, *aleph-resh-yod*, form the noun *ari* which means "lion". The word is pronounced as *kaari* and is translated as "like (a) lion". The words "they pierced" are *not* found in the MT! In the Jewish translation of the Tanakh this is what we find:

Psalm 22:17 JPS
For dogs have compassed me; a company of evil doers have inclosed me; *like a lion* they are at my hands and my feet.

However, fundamentalists argue that this is a nonsensical reading because it lacks a verb. In the JPS translation above, the words "they are" have been added by the translators; in the MT the phrase actually reads "Like a lion my hands and my feet".

Furthermore, they claim, the words "like a lion" makes no sense within the context of the passage for "lions do no surround the feet of their victims". They assert that *kaari* is a corruption of the original Hebrew reading which should be *karu*. *Karu* is the third person plural from of the word *karah* which means "to dig". This, supposedly, means "to pierce" and should be the correct rendering here.[38] Below is how both *karah* (he digs, to dig) and *karu* (they dig) are written in Hebrew:[39]

---

37   Würthwein, *The Text of the Old Testament*: p21
38   Archer, *Encyclopedia of Bible Difficulties*: p37
39   Note that *vav* is normally transliterated as "W", however, in some case consonants such as *vav* (W) and *yod* (Y) can be read as the vowels "U" or "O" and "I". In the above case, the vav is transliterated as an "U".

כ	ר	ה
kaf	resh	he
K	R	H
karah		
"to dig"		

כ	ר	ו
kaf	resh	vav
K	R	U
karu		
"they dig"		

Table C.2: From "he digs" to "they dig"

Note that the change from "he digs" to "they dig" involves only the last letter, from a *he* of *karah* to the *vav* of *karu*.

More recently it has been claimed that one of the fragments found in the Dead Sea, at Nahal Hever, has this passage from Psalms and actually reads "They pierced" here instead of "like a lion". This claim was made by the directors of Dead Sea Scrolls Institute in their book *The Dead Sea Scrolls Bible*.[40] Since it supports their presuppositions, we find many evangelical / fundamentalist websites and books touting this as proof that their original emendation of the passage is correct.

To summarize, these are the fundamentalist claims with respect to Psalm 22:16b:

1. The reading of Psalm 22:16b found in the King James Version, "They pierced my hands and my feet", is an accurate rendition of the meaning of the original Hebrew text.
2. The discovery of a Dead Sea fragment supports the case that the original reading should be "they pierced my hands and my feet".
3. This is supported by the readings found in the various ancient versions such as the Greek Septuagint and the Latin Vulgate.
4. The reading as it is found in the Masoretic Text is corrupt because it is both grammatically incorrect and does not make sense within the context.

We will review the evidence for these claims below.

INVESTIGATING THE FUNDAMENTALIST CLAIM

We will be investigating the four claims in depth here. We will also provide an additional piece of evidence from the scriptural citations of the early Christians to show that "They pierced my hands and my feet" was never the reading available to them.

1. The Sources Behind the King James Version

Reading through some of the fundamentalist apologetic writings on the Hebrew original, one can be forgiven for assuming that the Hebrew manuscripts used by the

---

[40]   Abegg, Flint & Ulrich, *The Dead Sea Scrolls Bible*: p518-519

translators of King James Bible already had the "correct" reading of *karu*. This however was not the case.

The Hebrew exemplars available to the translators had *kaari*, i.e. like a lion. Evidence that the translators *knew* this meant like a lion can be found from these examples where the Hebrew word is found in other places in the Bible:

> Numbers 24:9
> He couched, he lay down *as a lion* [Hebrew = *kaari*], as a lioness; who shall rouse him up?

> Isaiah 38:13
> I waited patiently until morning. He breaks all my bones *like a lion* [Hebrew = *kaari*]

> Ezekiel 22:25
> There is a conspiracy of her prophets in its midst, *like a* roaring *lion* [Hebrew = *kaari*] ravening the prey

The same word, *kaari*, was present in Psalm 22:16b. Anyone with a copy of *Strong's Concordance* can verify this. Under the entry no. 738 *ari, aryeh* in its Dictionary of Hebrew Words in the Bible, the meaning is given as "lion" with the additional note that it could also mean "pierce" as a "marginal reading"! That *ari* could mean *pierce* is nonsense. This reveals that the source of the translation for the passage in Psalm 22:16b was not the Hebrew originals but the other versions (in particular the Latin translations) available to them.

It must be pointed out that despite the claim in the cover page that the 1611 King James Version was "translated out of the original tongues," it was actually more of a *revision* of an earlier English Bible, the 1602 edition of the Bishop's Bible.[41] It also made use of older *versions* of the Bible such as the various, old and new, Latin translations, as even the conservative F.F. Bruce admitted:

> The Authorized Version was formally a revision of the 1602 edition of the Bishop's Bible. But all existing English versions lay before the translators, and every available foreign version, Latin translations ancient and recent, the Targums and the Peshitta-all as aids to the elucidation of the Hebrew and Greek originals.[42]

The translators of the King James ignored the wording of the Hebrew originals and the Targums and opted instead for the Latin translations which used the word *foderunt*, meaning *pierce*.[43] Why did they do this? For the same reason why modern fundamentalist translators like the NIV and NKJV continue to do so; not because it was based on the best available evidence, but because it supports their presuppositions!

---

[41]   Metzger, *The Bible in Translation*: p76-77
[42]   Bruce, *The Books and the Parchments*: p229
[43]   Asimov, *Guide to the Bible*: p895

2. The Evidence from the Dead Sea Scrolls

The evidence adduced to by some scholars comes from a scroll found in Nahal Hever, a location about 30 km south of Qumran. The document is designated as 5/6HevPs.[44] There is another manuscript, this one from Qumran, designated 4QPs^f that has the verses from Psalm 22:14-17. However, this document is not legible precisely at this point. We are left with the manuscript from Nahal Hever.[45]

There are three important items to keep in mind. Firstly, Nahal Hever manuscripts were *not* from the same time as the Qumran scrolls. While the Qumran manuscripts did predate the first Jewish War (70 CE), the manuscripts from Nahal Hever came from a later period; between the two Jewish Wars (between 70 CE and 135 CE). It does not *predate* the Masoretic Text since evidence from biblical scrolls found in the surrounding location (at Masada-dated no later 73 CE and Wadi Murabba- dated to before 135 CE) shows that the consonantal text that eventually became the Masoretic Text was already established by then. Secondly, the reading found at Nahal Hever was not new. There were a few Hebrew manuscripts that were already known to have that reading prior to its discovery.[46] Thirdly, despite the claim by Abegg, Flint and Ulrich in the *Dead Sea Scrolls Bible*, the passage in 5/6HevPs does *not* unambiguously read "pierce".

First let us look at what is actually found in 5/6HevPs:

Hebrew	Source	Trans	Meaning
כ ר ו	-	*Karu*	"They dig"
כ א ר ו	5/6HevPs	*Kaaru*	(Unclear meaning)
כ א ר י	Masoretic Text	*Kaari*	"Like (a) lion"

Table C.3: Variant Readings in Psalm 22:16

---

[44] The designation for the documents found around the Dead Sea may look esoteric but is actually quite straightforward. The numbers and alphabets refer to the chronological order as well as the location in which the particular fragment was found and further details of the contents. Thus "4QD" means that the scroll was discovered in the *fourth* cave at *Qumran* and is entitled the *D*amascus document. More often numbers are given instead of the name of the document. Thus 4Q242 means the document is from the same location (fourth cave at Qumran) and is the *242nd* manuscript from that place. [Eisenmann & Wise, *Dead Sea Scrolls Uncovered*: p1, Wise, Abegg, & Cook, *Dead Sea Scrolls: A New Translation*: p39]

[45] Vanderkam & Flint, *The Meaning of the Dead Sea Scrolls*: p124-125

[46] Shanks (ed), *Understanding the Dead Sea Scrolls*: p145
Strawn, Psalm 22:17b: More Guessing: p447-448 n41
Tov, *Textual Criticism of the Hebrew Bible*: p28
Würthwein, *The Text of the Old Testament*: p32

The word found in 5/6HevPs is given in the middle row of the table above. Note a few things, it is *not* spelt in the same way as *karu* (they dig) given in the top row. The former has an additional *aleph* between the *kaf* (K) and the *resh* (R). While fundamentalists are quick to speculate that this is merely an alternate, "Aramaizing,"[47] spelling for the word, it is still the case that *there is no other known example in the available Hebrew literature that spells "karu" this way!*[48]

The fundamentalists claim as support *other* Hebrew words that have alternate spellings. The logic is similar to someone who would claim that since colour/color are variant spellings in worldwide English, it therefore follows that "donour" is an acceptable variant for "donor"![49] This is absurd. It must be emphasized that just because *some* words have variant spellings, it does not mean that *all* words have variant spellings.

As it stands, the word found in 5/6HevPs *has no known meaning.* Some Jewish writers have labeled this word "Semitic rubbish."[50] It is merely *speculation* that the word *kaaru* is a variant spelling of *karu*.

As we noted above, even before the discovery of 5/6HevPs, the word *kaaru*, is already found in a few Hebrew manuscripts. For a long time scholars have tried to suggest the most probable meaning for the word. Apart from suggesting that it could be an alternate spelling of a known Hebrew word, these scholars turn to languages that are closely related to Hebrew for similar sounding words. Given below is a list of some of the suggestions made over the past 80 or so years:[51]

- G.R. Driver, "Textual and Linguistic Problems in the Book of Psalms" *Harvard Theological Review* 29.3 [1936]; 503-506
  - *To hack off / to shear* from the Assyrian *karu* which has that suggested meaning.
- J.M. Roberts, "A New Root for an Old Crux, Psalm XXII 17c," *Vetus Testamentum*, 23.2 [1973]; 247-252
  - *To shrivel* from the Akkadian and Syrian *karu* (meaning "to be short").[52]
- R. Tournay, "Note sur le Psaume XXII 17," *Vetus Testamentum*, 23.1 [1973], 111-112

---

[47] The suggestion that the addition of the aleph between the kaf and resh is an "Aramaizing" spelling of the Hebrew *karah* (to dig), or the Assyrian *karu* (to lop off / to shear) is a favorite among fundamentalists. It was first suggested three quarters of a century ago by G.R. Driver ("Textual and Linguistic Problems of the Book of Psalms" *HTR* 29.3 [1936], 171-196). Driver however, did not convince even himself and eventually took the view that the closest cognate would be similar cognates in Akkadian, Arabic and Syriac, which mean "to bind". [Hoffman, *Psalm 22 (LXX 21) and the Crucifixion of Jesus*: p175]

[48] Hoffman, *Psalm 22 (LXX 21) and the Crucifixion of Jesus*: p174

[49] The English and Americans spell *donor* the same way.

[50] Outreach Judaism Website (http://www.outreachjudaism.org/like-a-lion.html accessed on April 9, 2004)

[51] Hoffman, *Psalm 22 (LXX 21) and the Crucifixion of Jesus*: p174-175

[52] Indeed the suggestion has been used in the NRSV:
Psalm 22:16b NRSV
My hands and feet have shriveled...

> o   *As to hack / slash* from the Phoenician, Ethiopic, Babylonian *aru* (the initial *kaf* being a comparative) meaning "cut branches".

- John Kaltner, "Psalm 22:17b: Second Guessing the Old Guess" *Journal of Biblical Literature* 117 [1998]; 503-506
  - o   *To bind* from the Arabic cognate *kwr* which actually means "to bind"

Using meanings from related languages is a procedure that is fraught with uncertainties. Take a modern example between two rather closely related languages: German and English. It is all nice to know that *Haus* in German means "house" in English and that *gut* means "good". But it does not necessarily follow that *all* words that sound alike mean the same thing in both languages. A couple of examples should do: *Kind* in German does not have the same meaning as the word in English (it means "child") and *also* in German means "therefore". Finding meanings through related languages can, at best, be no more than *guesses*. This is why, despite speculating for close to a century, there has been no consensus reached as to what the meaning of *kaaru* could be.

Now let us go back to the suggestion that *kaaru* is a variant spelling of *karu*. Even if we are to accept, for the sake of argument, that this is probable (which it is not!), it still does not do what the fundamentalists want it to do. For *karu*, and its root *karah*, do *not* mean "pierce". Indeed, the word is best translated as "to excavate" or "to dig". Given below are the instances of the use of the word *karah* in its various verbal forms in the Hebrew Bible:[53]

- to *dig* a pit:
  Exodus 21:33; Psalm 7:15, 57:6, 94:13, 119:85; Proverbs 26:27; Jeremiah 18:20, 18:22
- to *dig* a grave:
  Genesis 50:5; II Chronicles 16:14
- to *dig* a well:
  Genesis 26:25; Numbers 21:18
- to *dig up* evil (metaphorical use):
  Proverbs 16:27
- to *dig* one's ear
  Psalm 40:7

All the instances above show the meaning of *karah*; which is "to dig" or "to excavate". They do not have the connotation of "piercing" - as in *puncturing through* something. The last example is especially revealing. The KJV renders this passage metaphorically as "mine ears hast thou opened". The actual Hebrew is literally "ears you have dug for me". Within the context of Psalm 40:7, the meaning is clear, by *digging* his ear, the Psalmist is able to hear and understand what God wanted and did not want. If *karah* could be translated as "I pierce", this would mean that the Psalmist is *piercing his ears* to hear God more clearly!

---

[53]   Brown, Driver & Briggs, *The BDB Hebrew and English Lexicon*: p500

Furthermore, had the Psalmist wanted the passage to mean "they pierce my hands and my feet", he had quite a few good Hebrew words that do have the precise meaning of "to pierce" to choose from:

- *daqar* : to pierce or to stab through[54]
  - Zechariah 12:10 "They look at him whom they have *pierced*" (This was the verse used by John 19:34 as a prophecy fulfilled.)
  - I Samuel 31:4..."Draw your sword, and *thrust me through* with it..."
- *naqav*: to pierce, to puncture or to perforate[55]
  - II Kings 18:21 (=Isaiah 36:6) "Behold, you are relying now on Egypt, that broken reed of a staff, which will *pierce* the hand of any man who leans on it."
  - Habakkuk 3:14 "Thou didst *pierce* with thy shafts the head of his warriors..."
- *ratsa*: to pierce or to bore[56]
  - Exodus 21:6 "...and his master shall *pierce* his ear with an awl..."

Thus, *karah* is an extremely poor choice of words if the intention was to prophesy the crucifixion.

So let us summarize the "evidence" from the Dead Sea Scroll.

1. The word *kaaru*, in the form found in 5/6HevPs, has *no known meaning.*

2. The assertion that it could be an alternate spelling for *karu*, which means "they dig", is only a *guess*. There are a few other guesses, which includes "to bind" and "to shrivel".

3. Even if, for the sake of argument, we accept, the guess above, it still does not do what the fundamentalists want it to do. For *karu* means "they dig" or "they excavate" and does not carry with it any connotation of piercing through, or puncturing through, the human flesh.

4. If the psalmist had wanted to mean "pierce" in the context of Psalm 22:16, there were other words that would have fitted his requirement better: *daqar, naqav* and *ratsa*.

In other words, the "evidence" from the Dead Sea Scroll that the crucifixion was prophesied by Psalm 22:16b with the words "*They pierced* my hands and my feet" is non-existent.

Why then did the authors/editors of *The Dead Sea Scrolls Bible* claim that the true reading is "they pierce" when, as we have seen, scholars have been trying to guess at the meaning of the word for close to a century? Two of the three authors of that book Peter W. Flint and Martin G. Abegg are directors of the *Dead Sea Scrolls Institute*. If one visits the website for this institution the reasons become quite clear. Under the section entitled "We Believe" this is what we read:

---

[54] Brown, Driver & Briggs, *The BDB Hebrew and English Lexicon*: p201
      Callahan, *Secret Origins of the Bible*: p366
[55] Brown, Driver & Briggs, *The BDB Hebrew and English Lexicon*: p666
[56] Brown, Driver & Briggs, *The BDB Hebrew and English Lexicon*: p954

WE BELIEVE that Evangelical Christian scholars should play a significant role in the study of the Dead Sea Scrolls. The reason is clear: among these scrolls are found the oldest manuscripts of the Hebrew Scriptures (Old Testament), as well as various writings that shed important light on the world of Jesus, the early Church, and the New Testament. [57]

The above excerpt tells us that the Dead Sea Scrolls Institute is an *evangelical* institute. In an earlier posting of the same section (which was on-line in April 2004 but which has since been replaced by the above quoted paragraph) there was the added point that evangelicals should not "sit back and surrender" the field of Dead Sea Scrolls research to what they termed "non-evangelicals". Within this context, "non-evangelicals" can only means those scholars who do not share the *a priori* assumptions of fundamentalists, in other words, scholars who follow scientific critical historical methods! Part of this strategy of "not surrendering" the field to non-evangelicals has to be to provide *evangelical slants* to the interpretation of the scrolls. Within this context, the reason for the linguistically unlikely interpretation of *kaaru* as "they pierce", becomes clear.

3. The Textual Witness of Ancient Versions

One of the claims of fundamentalists about this passage is that the ancient versions [i.e. translations] support the reading "they pierced" at Psalm 22:16b.

There are two preliminary considerations that must be remembered before examining the readings of the ancient versions. Firstly, it should be remembered that the Hebrew Bible remains the most *direct* source for the original text. All translations are, in effect, *interpretations*. In translating, one to one correspondences of words between the languages are rare. More often there are a few or even many choices of words that can be used in the translation. The choice of which word to use depends in many cases on how the translators actually understand the passage before them. How they understand the passage depends not only on the text that lies in front of them but also on the *presuppositions* of the translators. Therefore, knowing the external influence that may affect the translation is important.

Secondly, we must know what exactly was the *vorlage*, or the copy of the text, that the translation was made from. Was it the Hebrew text or was it yet another version of the text? Some of the versions were not translated from the original Hebrew but from other versions. If this is the case, it must be remembered that this particular version does not form an independent witness to the original Hebrew text, especially if it supports the peculiar reading of the *vorlage*. It is therefore important to have some familiarity with these various renditions of the Bible before we can evaluate the claim that the ancient versions support the reading of "they pierced my hands and my feet" in Psalm 22:16.

Perhaps the most well known of the versions is the Septuagint. We have already described this version in some detail in chapter six. Here we will just note that the

---

[57]   Dead Sea Scrolls Institute Main Page
        (http://www.twu.ca/academics/graduate/biblical/dead-sea-institute.aspx accessed August
        12, 2006)

Septuagint was the Greek translation, which was started around the third century BCE and probably completed around the first century BCE. The book of Psalms was probably translated into Greek around the second or third century BCE.[58] Although initially translated by Jews for the use of other Jews who no longer understood Hebrew, the early Christians *co-opted* the Septuagint and it became *the* Holy Scripture for them. In their disputes with Jews, the Christians quoted exclusively from the Septuagint. The Jews would retort back by comparing the Septuagint with their Hebrew original and noting that the former either had faulty translations or contained interpolations made by Christians. As a result of these disputes and the generally deteriorating textual situation, the Jews ceased using the Septuagint towards the end of the first century CE.[59]

In the second century CE, Jews dissatisfied with the Septuagint began new Greek translations of their Bible. Around 130 CE, a Jewish proselyte named Aquila, produced a version that followed the Hebrew very closely. About four decades later, Symmachus who, according to which church father you choose to believe, was either a Jewish Christian (Eusebius) or a Samaritan convert to Judaism (Epiphanius), published another Greek translation which, although generally faithful to the Hebrew original, is generally considered to be in more elegant Greek than Aquila's. Around the end of the second century another Greek translation, by another Jewish proselyte, Theodotion, was produced. Unlike the Septuagint, which is still available to us in its entirety, these three second century translations are today extant only in scroll fragments, palimpsests and in quotations by the church fathers. For Psalm 22:16, we have only the translations of Aquila and Symmachus; there is no extant fragment from Theodotion's version with this passage.[60]

The *Targums* refer to Aramaic translations of the Hebrew scripture. Like the Septuagint originally, it was translated for Jews who could no longer understand the Hebrew - Aramaic having taken over as the *lingua franca* of post-exilic Palestine. Rather than a strict translation, the Targums are more accurately described as *paraphrased* interpretations of the Hebrew Bible. Written Targums were in use by the third century CE, but the oral tradition dates back to pre-Christian times.[61]

Like Aramaic, Syriac is a language closely related to Hebrew. Syriac versions of the Bible are called *Peshitta*. The Peshitta was probably produced around 200 CE. The origins of the Old Testament Peshitta is unclear and are still being debated among scholars. It is unclear if the translations were done by Jews or (Jewish?) Christians. As Bruce Metzger suggested, it is likely that some books of the Peshitta were translated by Jews while others by Christians. There is also uncertainty regarding the

---

[58]   Hoffman, *Psalm 22 (LXX 21) and the Crucifixion of Jesus*: p37

[59]   Hoffman, *Psalm 22 (LXX 21) and the Crucifixion of Jesus*: p37
    Metzger, *The Bible in Translation*: p18-19
    Würthwein, *The Text of the Old Testament*: p52-54

[60]   Hoffman, *Psalm 22 (LXX 21) and the Crucifixion of Jesus*: p37-38, 473
    Metzger, *The Bible in Translation*: p19
    Würthwein, *The Text of the Old Testament*: p55-56

[61]   Hoffman, *Psalm 22 (LXX 21) and the Crucifixion of Jesus*: p36-37
    Metzger, *The Bible in Translation*: p20-24
    Würthwein, *The Text of the Old Testament*: p55-56

vorlage used for the various sections of the Old Testament. For instance, it is likely that the Pentateuch was translated directly from a Hebrew text while Isaiah was translated by someone who had obvious familiarity with the Septuagint. For our purposes it is important to note that the Peshitta translation of Psalms is rather free, as opposed to a strict-literal, translations. Furthermore, it is quite obvious that the book of Psalms was translated by a Christian who already looked upon it as valuable proof text for the death and resurrection of Jesus. One clear example of this is in the introduction to Psalm 71. The Masoretic Text does not give a title for this, while the Septuagint attributes it only to David. The Peshitta however, has this for an introduction:[62]

> Psalm 71: [Introduction in Peshitta]
> Being spoken to/by David: when Saul was fighting the house of David, and *a prophecy about the suffering and rising of the messiah.*

This clear Christian slant means that this translation of the Psalms must be quite late and that the value the Peshitta is very limited in establishing the original text of Psalm 22:16b.

Sometime around 235 CE, the Alexandrian church father, Origen (185-254) attempted to resolve the textual difficulties surrounding the various Bible versions and the Hebrew text by publishing the *Hexapla*. It contained six columns consisting of the Hebrew text, the Hebrew text transliterated in Greek, Aquila's version, Symmachus' version, the Septuagint and Theodotion's version. There is very little that has been preserved of the Hexapla. However, in the 19th century some fragments of the Hexapla were discovered in a Cairo synagogue *Geniza.*[63] In this Geniza, the Hexapla fragments dating from the 6th century CE, actually a palimpsest,[64] contain portions from Psalm 22:15-28![65]

There is a Syriac translation of Origen's Hexapla, called the Syro-Hexapla, made around 616-617 CE. For our purposes the Syro-Hexapla contains translations in Psalms for the Septuagint, Aquila and Symmachus. While these versions do not allow us *direct* access to the Hebrew text, they allow us to check the texts of the Septuagint and in some cases to reconstruct the lost Greek texts of Aquila and Symmachus.[66]

---

[62] Hoffman, *Psalm 22 (LXX 21) and the Crucifixion of Jesus*: p39, 270-271
Metzger, *The Bible in Translation*: p26-27
Tov, *Textual Criticism of the Hebrew Bible*: p152
Würthwein, *The Text of the Old Testament*: p85-90

[63] A *Geniza* is a kind of storage room found in synagogues. It is used to keep old manuscripts that are no longer usable until such a time where they can be disposed of properly. The whole point is to keep the Holy Scriptures, which contains the holy name of God, away from the possibility of being defiled or misused. Indeed the term Geniza comes from the Aramaic which means "to hide".

[64] A palimpsest is a document which has something else written on top of previous writings.

[65] Hoffman, *Psalm 22 (LXX 21) and the Crucifixion of Jesus*: p37-38
Metzger, *The Bible in Translation*: p19
Würthwein, *The Text of the Old Testament*: p11, 57

[66] Hoffman, *Psalm 22 (LXX 21) and the Crucifixion of Jesus*: p38-39
Würthwein, *The Text of the Old Testament*: p59

Finally, we look at the Latin Versions. Most people think of the Vulgate and Jerome (342-420) when we speak today of the Latin Bible. However, there are a few facts to keep in mind. While the Vulgate, *in general*, was a translation from the Hebrew by Jerome, the section of Psalms in this version was *not* translated from the Jewish Bible. The book of Psalms in the Vulgate was translated by Jerome from the Septuagint - in other words, it is a translation of a translation! Jerome did make another translation of Psalm, this time from the original Hebrew. However, even in this case it must be kept in mind that he consulted other versions, Greek and Latin, when making this translation.

There is an older Latin version of the Bible, known, appropriately, as *Old Latin*. Unlike (most) of Jerome's Vulgate, the Old Latin is a translation of the Septuagint - it gives no *direct* evidence of the Hebrew text. We find evidence of the existence of Old Latin versions in the quotations of its text by second century church fathers such as Tertullian (c160-c225) and Cyprian (c200-258). Latin biblical texts can be found in areas where Latin was the predominant language, such as southern Gaul and North Africa, from as early as 150 CE.[67]

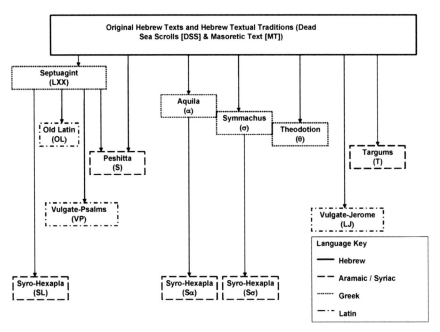

Figure C.1: The relationship between various textual versions

Figure C.1 above gives the textual relationship of the ancient versions mentioned above. The arrowed lines show the original *vorlage* used by each of the versions. The vertical distance away from the original Hebrew texts illustrate the rough chronology of the appearance of these versions. The abbreviations attached to

67   Hoffman, *Psalm 22 (LXX 21) and the Crucifixion of Jesus*: p39-40
      Metzger, *The Bible in Translation*: p29-35
      Würthwein, *The Text of the Old Testament*: p91-99

the names of the versions will be used in the tabular comparison of the readings given following this.

Having acquainted ourselves with the various ancient versions and their relationship with one another, it is now time to examine their witness to the text of Psalm 22:16b. Table C.4 below gives the readings from the Hebrew texts and the various ancient versions:

Text	Actual Reading	Translation
MT	כּאֲרִי ידי ורגלי	**Like a lion** my hands and my feet.
DSS	כּארו ידי ורגלי	**They dig** (?) my hands and my feet.
T	נכתין היך כּאריא אידי ורגלי	Biting **like a lion** my hands and my feet.
LXX	ὤρυξαν χειρας μου και ποδας μου	**They dug** my hands and my feet.
α (1)	ησχυναν χειρας μου και ποδας μου	**They disfigured** my hands and my feet.
σ	ὡς λεων χειρας μου και ποδας μου	**Like a lion** my hands and my feet.
OL	**foderunt** manus meas et pedes meos	**They dug / pricked** my hands and my feet.
VP	**foderunt** manus meas et pedes meos	**They dug / pricked** my hands and my feet.
LJ	**vinxerunt** manus meas et pedes meos	**They bound / encircled** my hands and my feet.
S	בזעו אידי ורגלי	**They hacked off / pierced** my hands and my feet.
SL	בזעו אידי ורגלי	**They hacked off / pierced** my hands and my feet.
Sα	פכדו אידי ורגלי	**They fettered** my hands and my feet.
Sσ	איך בעין למאסר אידי ורגלי	**Like seeking to bind** my hands and my feet.

Table C.4: Textual Witnesses of Psalm 22:16[68]

---

[68] The table is derived from the extensive Appendix given in Mark George Vitalis Hoffman's 1996 Yale PhD dissertation *Psalm 22 (LXX 21) and the Crucifixion of Jesus* p450-554 (Appendix A). Due to font limitation the Syriac text is transliterated into Hebrew.

We note that the Targum of Psalms and Symmachus' Greek translation gives "like a lion", supporting the Masoretic reading. The Targum adds the verb *biting* to make the sentence clearer.

For Symmachus, it is important to note that ὡς λεων (*hos leon* = "like a lion") is very likely the original reading. Some commentators, including the critical apparatus in the *Biblia Hebraica Stutgartensia* (the critical edition of the Leningrad codex of the Hebrew bible), made the erroneous assumption that the reading here should be ὡς ζητουντες δησαι (*hos zetountes desai* = "like seeking to bind"). It must be noted that this reading ("like seeking to bind") is the result of a reverse translation from the Syriac of the Syro-Hexapla back into Greek. As Mark Hoffmann demonstrated in his PhD thesis *Psalm 22 (LXX 21) and the Crucifixion of Jesus* (Yale University 1996), it clearly arose from a mistake made by the translators of the Syro-Hexapla in reading the original Greek in Origen's Hexapla.

The ancient Greek manuscripts were written in uncials (i.e. all caps) and there was no space between the words. The mistake arose when the translators of the Syro-Hexapla misread three of the Greek letters and then rephrased the incorrect reading. The table below shows this process, the reading on top is from Symmachus and the one below is what the translator of the Syro-Hexapla read by mistake:

ΩΣ**ΔΕΩΝΤΑ**ΣΧΕΙΡΑΣΜΟΥ...	ὡς λεων τας χειρας μου...	Like a lion my hands...
ΩΣ**ΔΕΟΝΤΕ**ΣΧΕΙΡΑΣΜΟΥ...	ὡς δεοντες χειρας μου...	Like binding my hands...

Table C.5: Reconstruction of mistake in the Syro-Hexapla translation

The translator of the Syro-Hexapla misread a *delta* (Δ) for a *lambda* (Λ) , an *omicron* (O) for an *omega* (Ω) and an *epsilon* (E) for an *alpha* (A). These misreadings led him to separate the words out differently than what would have been the case; and instead of ὡς λεων τας χειρας μου... (*hos leon tas cheiras mou* = "Like a lion my hands..."), the translation became ὡς δεοντες χειρας μου... (*hos deontes cheiras mou* = "Like binding my hands..."). This was then paraphrased to ὡς ζητουντες δησαι χειρας μου... (*hos zetountes desai cheiras mou* = "Like seeking to bind my hands...") - which was the reading of the Syriac in the Syro-Hexapla.[69]

The Septuagint gives the reading here as ὡρυξαν (*oruxan*) which, despite the claims of some fundamentalist apologists that it means "to bore through", is simply the third person plural past tense of ὠρυσσω (*orusso*) means "to dig". Like the Hebrew *karu*, it does not mean "pierce". The word appears 37 times in the Septuagint and in each and every case the meaning is always "to dig" (a tomb, a pit, a trench, a hole or a well). Thus a literal translation of this phrase in the Septuagint is *not* "they pierced my hands and my feet", but "they dug my hands and my feet"; something not very easily imagined![70] As Mark Hoffman remarked:

> It seems quite unlikely that the LXX translators were trying to describe the crucifixion when translating verse 17c with ὠρυσσω" (*orusso*).[71]

---

[69]   Hoffman, *Psalm 22 (LXX 21) and the Crucifixion of Jesus*: p44, 173, 466
[70]   Callahan, *Secret Origins of the Bible*: p365
[71]   Hoffman, *Psalm 22 (LXX 21) and the Crucifixion of Jesus*: p179-180

Unlikely indeed! For had the translators understood the word to mean "pierce", there was a perfectly good Greek word to use: ἐκκεντεω (*ekkenteo*), which means "to pierce". This was the word the translators of the Septuagint used to translate Zechariah 12:10 "They look at him whom they have *pierced*". Similarly John 19:34 used the exact same words to describe the prophecy fulfillment. So whatever the word in the original Hebrew may mean in Psalm 22:16b, it is extremely unlikely that *the seventy* understood it in the way Christians later understood it.[72]

The two Latin versions that were translated from the Septuagint (Old Latin and the book of Psalms in the Vulgate) remained faithful to the reading of the Septuagint. The word they used here was *foderunt* - the third person plural perfect tense for *fodio*. Now *fodio*, like ὠρυξαν (*oruxan*) in Greek, has the formal meaning of "to dig", but, unlike the Greek, it also has a looser, metaphorical, meaning of "to prick" or "to prod".[73] [We can see how the "smearing" of the less sharply applied Latin word could result in "to pierce" being eventually read here!] As an aside we see how meaningless it is for fundamentalists to appeal to the Vulgate as support for their interpretation that the original meaning of the word is *to pierce*, for the Vulgate (for Psalms) was dependent upon the Septuagint and is not an independent witness to the original text.

When we look at Jerome's translation from the Hebrew we find that the word he used was not *foderunt*, but *vinxerunt*, which means "they bound" or "they encircled". This has implications on what was in the Hebrew *vorlage* available to Jerome. While the Septuagint translation allows the possibility of both *karu* (to dig) or *kaaru* (the unclear meaning which could have been *assumed* by the translators of the Septuagint to mean the same thing - see some scholarly speculations above), Jerome's translation had to come from his interpretation of *kaaru*, for otherwise he would have simply translated *they dig*. Jerome probably interpreted *kaaru* to be based on the root *kwr*, which could mean *to be round* or *to make round*.[74]

As for Aquila's version, we have *two* different readings. According to Origen's Hexapla found at the Cairo Geniza and the church historian, Eusebius (c260-340), the Greek translation of Aquila gave the passage as *"they disfigured / shamed* my hands and feet"*. However, according to the Syro-Hexapla's translation, Aquila's version had *"they fettered* my hands and my feet"*. Since we know Jerome was familiar with Aquila's version, Jerome's use of "they bound" could be taken to mean that "they fettered" was what was written in his copy of Aquila's Greek Bible. These different readings of Aquila most probably mean, as some scholars have suggested, that Aquila had two recensions, or editions, of his translation. The first one having "they disfigured" in Psalm 22:16b and the second having "they fettered" instead. Again, it should be noted here that none of these words could have been derived from *karu*. This tells us that the word in Aquila's *vorlage* had to be *kaaru*. Aquila's first interpretation of *kaaru* was probably based on the assumption that it was rooted in words such as *nakar* or *hakar* which could mean something like "to disfigure" or "to shame". The second interpretation could be derived from an interpretation of *kaaru* similar to Jerome's guess described in the preceding paragraph.[75]

---

72   Callahan, *Secret Origins of the Bible*: p366
73   Traupman, *Latin & English Dictionary*: p183
74   Hoffman, *Psalm 22 (LXX 21) and the Crucifixion of Jesus*: p46
75   Hoffman, *Psalm 22 (LXX 21) and the Crucifixion of Jesus*: p45-46

Finally, we look at the reading in the Peshitta. Here the Syriac word used could mean "hack off" or "pierce/perforate". However, as we have noted in the section above, the translation of the book of Psalms was probably made by a Christian who already looked to it as a source of prophecy for the death and resurrection of Jesus. According to Mark Hoffman, the translators of the Peshitta were probably no more "in the know" about the meaning of the Hebrew (assuming they were translating direct from a Hebrew *vorlage*) than the translators of the Septuagint and were "simply trying to make sense of the Hebrew in the same way as the LXX". In other words, we cannot consider the Peshitta to be an independent source here for the Hebrew original.[76]

We have reviewed the whole array of textual evidence and can now pause to consider what it tells us.

1. There was no ambiguity when the word was translated (or read) as a noun - the Targums and Symmachus both translated the word as "like a lion". This means that the Hebrew text available to these translators read *kaari*, like the majority of the Masoretic manuscripts.

2. When the word was read as a verb (with the *vav* suffix), the translations started to go all over the place. We have the Septuagint saying it means "to dig", Jerome thinking it means "to surround or to bind" and Aquila initially thinking it means "to shame" before finally changing his mind and deciding that it meant "to fetter". This range of translations can only mean that the alternate reading to *kaari* was not *karu* but *kaaru*. Furthermore, by the time the versions were being translated it is obvious that the meaning of that word, if it had any meaning in the first place, was no longer known to the translators.

3. In all cases where we know of a direct translation from the Hebrew text, there is not a single version that translates the Psalm 22:16b as "They pierced my hands and my feet".

3a. Evidence from Early Christian Literature

One of the strongest arguments against the verse Psalm 22:16b being a prophecy of the crucifixion is the fact that *none of the New Testament authors made any reference to it*. This is extremely surprising if the Hebrew or the Greek of that verse was understood as "they pierce":

Paul writing circa 53 CE in Galatians 3:13 mentioned the verse from Deuteronomy 23:22-23 about the curse of one who dies "hanging on a tree". This is the only connection of the crucifixion to the Old Testament that Paul tried to make.[77]

All four gospels made allusions to Psalm 22:19 "They divide my garments among them, and for my raiment they cast lots":

---

[76] Hoffman, *Psalm 22 (LXX 21) and the Crucifixion of Jesus*: p178
[77] Hoffman, *Psalm 22 (LXX 21) and the Crucifixion of Jesus*: p182

Mark 15:24 (c70CE)
Crucifying him, they parted his garments among them, casting lots on them, what each should take.

Matthew 27:35 (c90 CE)
When they had crucified him, they divided his clothing among them, casting lots

Luke 23:33-34 (c95 CE)
When they came to the place that is called The Skull, they crucified him there...Dividing his garments among them, they cast lots.

John 19:23-24 (c90 CE)
Then the soldiers, when they had crucified Jesus, took his garments and made four parts, to every soldier a part; and also the coat. Now the coat was without seam, woven from the top throughout. Then they said to one another, "Let's not tear it, but cast lots for it to decide whose it will be," that the Scripture might be fulfilled, which says, "They parted my garments among them. For my cloak they cast lots." Therefore the soldiers did these things.

Note that John even quoted the verse from Psalms directly to draw attention to the fulfillment of the prophecy! (John 19:24). Yet, not one of the evangelists connected the crucifixion to the *piercing* of the hands and feet just two verses prior to this one in Psalms.

Furthermore, the Gospel of John even referred to *another* Old Testament prophecy, this one about the *piercing* of Jesus' side:

John 19:34,37
However one of the soldiers pierced his side with a spear... Scripture says, "They will look on him whom they pierced."

John was referring to the Zechariah 12:10. It is indeed strange that John would refer to this fulfillment but not the one in Psalm 22:16b.

Some fundamentalist apologists have tried to explain this away by hypothesizing that the evangelists and Paul knew that there were some "textual issues" regarding this phrase and thus refrained from quoting it although they fully realized its prophetic significance. This explanation meets with a quick end when we remember that Matthew 1:22-23 quoted the Septuagint reading of Isaiah 7:14 as a prophecy for the virgin birth. However, the word "virgin" is found only in the Greek Septuagint and all extant Hebrew bibles (including the ones found in the Dead Sea) have "young woman" instead. If the author of Matthew had no problems with the "textual issues" relating to *that* particular passage, it is unlikely that he would have any qualms about this one!

When we go outside the New Testament into the writings of the apostolic fathers we get the same result. None, either explicitly or implicitly, tied Psalm 22:16b to the piercing of Jesus' hands and feet. A particularly poignant example is taken from the epistle of Barnabas (c130 CE):

Barnabas 5:13
He himself willed thus to suffer, for it was necessary that He should suffer on the tree. For says he who prophesies regarding Him, "Spare my soul from the sword,

fasten my flesh with nails; for the assemblies of the wicked have risen up against me."

The passage, like the ones in the gospel is intriguing. For it is formed out of a combination of three different passages from Psalms:

Psalm 22:20
Deliver my soul from the sword...

Psalm 119:120 [Septuagint reading-Psalm 118:120]
Nail my flesh with your fear; for I am afraid of your judgments

Psalm 22:16
... A company of evildoers have enclosed me....

This is another revealing text. Barnabas was obviously looking at Psalm 22 for the fulfillment of Jesus' death and crucifixion. Indeed, he even used the very verse (Psalm 22:16) we are talking about but used the part about the Psalmist being enclosed by his enemies instead. Yet, exactly at the point where one would expect him to use "They pierced my hands and my feet", he used a passage from Psalm 119:120![78] There is really only one explanation for this: the author of the epistle of Barnabas did not read "pierce" into the Septuagint's "they dug my hands and my feet".

Let us pause here for a while and consider the evidence from early Christian literature, from the earliest extant evidence of Christian's use of the Old Testament as a source of prophecy of Jesus. There was not a single case, up to around 130 CE, of reference to the passage in Psalm 22:16b as alluding to the actual "piercing" of Jesus' hands and feet during the crucifixion.

The first Christian writer to make a direct connection of Psalm 22:16 to the piercing of the crucifixion was Justin Martyr (c100-c165). These are the two passages from his writings that made this connection:[79]

First Apology 35 (c155)
And again in other words, through another prophet, He says, "They pierced [ὤρυξαν, *oruxan*] My hands and My feet, and for My vesture they cast lots." And indeed David, the king and prophet, who uttered these things, suffered none of them; but Jesus Christ stretched forth His hands, being crucified by the Jews speaking against Him, and denying that He was the Christ. And as the prophet spoke, they tormented Him, and set Him on the judgment-seat, and said, Judge us. And the expression, "They pierced my hands and my feet," was used in reference to the nails of the cross which were fixed [παγεντων] in His hands and feet.

Dialogue with Trypho 97 (c160)
David in the twenty-first Psalm thus refers to the suffering and to the cross in a parable of mystery: "They pierced [ὤρυξαν, *oruxan*] my hands and my feet; they counted all my bones. ..." For when they crucified Him, driving in [ἐμπησσοντες, *empessontes*] the nails, they pierced His hands and feet; and those who crucified Him parted His garments among themselves, each casting lots for what he chose to have, and receiving according to the decision of the lot. And this very Psalm you

---

78 Hoffman, *Psalm 22 (LXX 21) and the Crucifixion of Jesus*: p182-183
79 Hoffman, *Psalm 22 (LXX 21) and the Crucifixion of Jesus*: p184-186

maintain does not refer to Christ; for you are in all respects blind, and do not understand that no one in your nation who has been called King or Christ has ever had his hands or feet pierced while alive, or has died in this mysterious fashion-to wit, by the cross-save this Jesus alone.

Note that unlike the writings of Paul, the evangelists and Barnabas, *explicit* reference is now made to Psalm 22:16b as referring to the *piercing* of the nails at the crucifixion of Jesus. However, even here it must be noted while he used the Septuagint word ὤρυξαν (*oruxan* = "they dug") in his citation of Psalm 22:16b, in his later explanation he used words that fit the crucifixion more closely - ἐμπησσοντες (*empessontes*) and παγεντων (*pagenton*). Both these terms are merely active and passive forms of the same root which means "to fix", "to make firm" or "to nail" something. The fact that Justin had to use this explanatory word to clarify Psalm 22:16b means that, regardless of his pretence, the term in Psalm 22:16b does not really make the prophecy clear.

After Justin we find Psalm 22:16b being increasingly used by Christians as "proof text" of the crucifixion of Jesus. We find similar confident citings of Psalm 22:16b as a direct prophecy of the method of crucifixion in the writings of later Christian writers such as Tertullian (c160-c225), Cyprian (c200-258) and Eusebius (c260-c340).[80]

Tertullian was writing in Latin and used the word found in the Old Latin version of the Bible, *foderunt*, in his citation of Psalm 22:16. *Foderunt*, as we have seen above, means "they dug" but have the "width" in meaning to include "they pricked" or "they pierced."

> Tertullian: *An Answer to the Jews* 10 (c197)
> If you shall still seek for predictions of the Lord's cross, the twenty-first Psalm will at length be able to satisfy you, containing as it does the whole passion of Christ; singing, as He does, even at so early a date, His own glory. "They dug [*foderunt*]," He says, "my hands and feet"-which is the peculiar atrocity of the cross.

Cyprian was able to devote a whole section (section 20) in his *Second Book of Testimonies Against the Jews* (248) to proving that the Old Testament prophesied that "The Jews would fasten Jesus to the cross". Eusebius in his *Proof of the Gospel* (c313) 10:8 cited Psalm 22:16b as the main prophecy that "they fastened his [Jesus] hands and feet to the cross with nails".

So the evidence from early Christian writings shows that up to the middle of the second century CE *it never occurred to Christian writers that Psalm 22:16b was an explicit reference to the nailing of the crucifixion*. It all changed with Justin Martyr sometime after 150 CE. From then onwards the citations of Psalm 22:16b as an exact prophecy of Jesus' crucifixion became more and more common.

This finding is enough for us to conclude that "they pierced" was never part of the original meaning of Psalm 22:16b. It was not present in the Hebrew Bible (regardless of whether the actual reading was *kaaru* or *kaari*) and it was not present in the Septuagint. *Certainly it was never understood as such by the earliest Christian writers - including the authors of the New Testament!*

---

[80]   Hoffman, *Psalm 22 (LXX 21) and the Crucifixion of Jesus*: p188-190

We can now indulge in a bit of speculation. Justin, as was the custom during his time, was writing in Greek and it was quite obvious from the citations above that the link in the Greek Septuagint between Psalm 22:16b and the crucifixion is linguistically tenuous; Justin had to supplement the scriptural citation with other Greek words to make the meaning clear. So what made *him* see that connection when no one before did? Why did the *paradigm shift* happen with Justin?

The most probable explanation is this: Justin had access to the relatively new Latin translation of Psalm 22:16b and that *foderunt* was used as the translation for the Greek ὤρυξαν *(oruxan)*.[81] *Foderunt* encompasses within its meaning both "to dig" and "to pierce". The shift from "dig" to "pierce", not possible in the Greek, was made possible by the Latin. We see from the quotation of Tertullian that no such linguistic problem exists when the Latin translation was used!

As we have mentioned above, Latin biblical text were already in circulation in Southern Gaul and North Africa by around 150 CE. These were areas where Latin was the dominant language and the need for a Latin translation of the Bible would have been felt most acutely. It is true that the Roman churches did not switch from Greek to Latin until the first half of the third century and Greek was still widely used there during that time. However, probably an equal number of Romans used either Greek or Latin for daily communication and the resurgence of Latin was already beginning to make headway there before this time. Furthermore, Justin, although he was not born in Rome, was very probably of Roman descent and he spent the last two to three decades of his life in Rome.[82] He would certainly have shown an interest in Latin translation of the Bible (either the whole Bible or portions of it - such as some Psalms that may be used in Christian liturgy.) Justin, being one of the pre-eminent Christian apologists, would almost certainly have had access to a copy if the translation had made its way to Rome. Furthermore, we noticed that Justin's innovative interpretation of Psalm 22:16b were made in his works that were published within a decade of 150 CE (*First Apology* c155 CE and *Dialogue* c160CE). Since the shift in meaning from "dig" to "pierce" allowed by the Latin translation would have been noticed by anyone with familiarity with the language, we would expect the first references of "piercing" to Psalm 22:16b to have happened shortly after the publication of the Latin bible. Justin's timing was exactly what one would expect.

One question naturally arises: If Justin knew of this translation why did he not make any explicit citation of the passage in Latin? The answer is simple, the Latin translation was still new and was in no way authoritative. Anyone familiar with Justin's work will know that he already had his hands full defending the authority of the relatively ancient Septuagint against his Jewish opponents.[83] One example is given below:

---

[81] To the best of the author's knowledge, nobody else has made this suggestion - of linking Justin's interpretation to the Latin translation of the Bible - before.

[82] Bruce, *The Books and the Parchments*: p63, p202-203
Ferguson, *Encyclopedia of Early Christianity*: p647-649
Metzger, *The Bible in Translation*: p30-31
Würthwein, *The Text of the Old Testament*: p91

[83] Dunn, *Jews and Christians*: p41-69

Dialogue with Trypho 68:6-8

If therefore, I shall show that this prophecy of Isaiah refers to our Christ, and not to Hezekiah, as you say, shall I not in this matter, too, compel you not to believe your teachers, *who venture to assert that the explanation which your seventy elders that were with Ptolemy the king of the Egyptians gave, is untrue in certain respects?* For some statements in the Scriptures, which appear explicitly to convict them of a foolish and vain opinion, these they venture to assert have not been so written.

Quoting from a recent *Latin* translation would not have helped his case much against his Jewish opponents! Justin probably read the Latin translation, finally "saw" that Psalm 22:16b refers to the crucifixion and tried to argue the case in his Greek writings without making direct reference to it. [By the time Tertullian was writing, around the end of the second century, the Latin translation was probably old enough to be cited without much embarrassment as to its authority.]

In conclusion, the evidence from early Christian literature tells us this:

1. Up to the year 150 CE, no Christian writer made the connection between Psalm 22:16b and the crucifixion of Jesus. The most likely explanation for this is that neither the Hebrew nor the Greek version of Psalm allows for this identification: "digging" and "piercing" do not share the same word within those languages.

2. It was only sometime after 150 CE, that the first Christian writer, Justin Martyr, made that explicit reference.
   o It is very likely that Justin got this idea from the newly translated Latin version of the Bible; where the word *foderunt* could mean both "they dug" and "they pierced."

4. The Reading of the Masoretic Text

We have settled the case above that "They pierced" was never part of the original reading of Psalm 22:16. We now look at what the original reading could be. Note that any uncertainty with what this final reading could in no way be taken to mean that the reading "they pierced" becomes more likely again, for we have eliminated that reading using considerations which are unrelated to what we will consider below.

The critical apparatus of the *Biblia Hebraica Stutgartensia* gives the following summary of the textual evidence of Hebrew manuscripts regarding the reading found in Psalm 22:16b:[84]

---

[84]   Elliger & Rudolph, *Biblia Hebraica Stutgartensia*: p1104

Hebrew	Textual Witness	Trans	Meaning
כ א ר י	Majority of manuscripts	*Kaari*	"Like (a) lion"
כ א ר ו	"A few" manuscripts	*Kaaru*	(Unclear meaning)
כ ר ו	Two manuscripts	*Karu*	"They dig"

Table C.6: Variant readings of Psalm 22:16b in the Masoretic Text

We see that the majority of the available Hebrew manuscripts support the reading of *kaari* ("like a lion"), while "a few" (defined as between three to ten manuscripts by the *BHS*) support the reading found in Nahal Hever, *kaaru* (with unclear meaning-as we have seen above) and two manuscripts supporting *karu* ("they dig"). From our analysis of the ancient versions above we can see that the first two of these three readings were in existence from around the turn of the Common Era. *Kaari* is supported by the Targums and the Greek version of Symmachus. While the proliferations of verbal meanings ("they hack", "they shame", "they disfigured", "they bound", "they dig", "they fettered" etc) can all be traced to the translators (like the modern scholars we see above!) trying to make sense of a word *kaaru* that was no longer meaningful to them. Had the original *vorlage* available to them been *karu* these would all have translated the word the same way; as "they dig". So we can say that both a study of the ancient versions and the Hebrew manuscripts support this conclusion: that in the two centuries before and after the beginning of the Common Era there were *two* variant readings in the Hebrew: *kaari* and *kaaru*.

A look at the table above also shows the probable cause of the variant: the two words differ only in the final alphabet, the *yod* of *kaari* has been changed into the *vav* of *kaaru* (or vice versa). Even someone uninitiated with the Hebrew alphabet can see how easy it is to mistake a *yod* for the slightly longer *vav*. We know that mistakes of graphical confusion like these did happen and were quite common in the ancient Hebrew manuscripts.[85]

The questions become, how do we choose between these two readings? *External criteria* - such as general reliability, numerical preponderance and age of documents - *cannot* be used for this particular case. Some scholars tend to have a bias in favor of the Masoretic Text primarily due to the fact in many cases it has shown itself to be the best witness to the text. In other words, the MT is generally more reliable than other witnesses.[86] While this is true in general, it cannot be applied to all specific instances. Similarly, like the case of the New Testament manuscripts numerical preponderance doesn't really count for much, for if 100 copies are made from a single defective manuscript, what we have are not 101 witnesses to the original text but merely 101

---

[85]   McCarter, *Textual Criticism*: p43-49
       Würthwein, *The Text of the Old Testament*: p108
[86]   Würthwein, *The Text of the Old Testament*: p115-116

faulty manuscripts! *Manuscripts should be weighed not counted!*[87] Furthermore, as we have seen above, we have evidence that the two variant readings date from very early times.

We are left basically with the internal criteria. P. Kyle McCarter, Jr. in his book *Textual Criticism: Recovering the Text of the Hebrew Bible* listed the following rules used by textual critics:[88]

1. *The more difficult reading is preferable*: in other words, ancient scribes tend to see what they *expected* to see. The more familiar reading is more often the one that is secondary. Naturally, this does not apply to obvious nonsense: "The more difficult reading is not to be preferred when it is garbage."

2. *The shorter reading is preferable*: scribes tend to expand an ancient text - this arises from their concern to preserve the text as fully as possible thus causing them to keep later glosses, duplications and explanations in the text.

3. *The reading should be appropriate for its context*

4. *Be suspicious of readings that "improve" on the text*: Readings that offer stylistic improvements, modernize, conform the text to more familiar norms and that resolve contradictions are suspect.

In other words, the rules boil down to a basic common-sensical question: "what would have changed into the other?" Since the mistake probably occurred due to the graphical confusion between the *yod* and the *vav* as the end of the word, the only rule really applicable here is rule 3. In other words, which of the two readings fit the context of the passage best?

Most discussions surrounding this verse usually start by critiquing the fact that the MT reading is missing a verb and is literally rendered as "like a lion my hands and my feet" - supposedly a meaningless phrase. Since the alternate reading "kaaru" *looks* like a verb, the *vav* suffix indicating a third person plural verbal form, the discussion then normally continues in trying to find the meaning of the root *kaar*. This, as we have seen above, have led to the proliferation of suggestions from modern scholars *and* to the varied translations in the ancient versions. There are two reasons why one should be very skeptical about *kaaru* being the original reading here:

- The possibility that *kaaru* could be *nonsense* is hardly ever discussed. Yet, given that graphical confusion is very likely the cause of the variant reading, this possibility must be taken seriously.

- The one thing about the Psalm 22 that seems to have escaped the attention of all commentators (Christian *and* Jewish) is this: *at no time were the Psalmist's enemies described as physically harming him!*[89] Note the bull,

---

87   McCarter, *Textual Criticism*: p71-72

88   McCarter, *Textual Criticism*: p72-74

89   Strawn in *Psalm 22:17b: More Guessing* p 447 who mentioned that there were three occasions of reference of physical violence towards the Psalmist by his enemies. The

the dog and the lion all are described as surrounding him (Psalm 22:12, 16), the lion is described as "opening its mouth" (Psalm 22:13) and his enemies may "stare and gloat" over him and "divide his clothes" among themselves (Psalm 22: 17-18). He asked for deliverance against the power (literally "hand") of the dog, the mouth of the lion and the horns of the bull (Psalm 22:20-21), but they are never described as actually doing anything to him (yet). If Psalm 22:16b were to describe his hands and feet being bitten, dug, hacked off, pierced, bound or fettered, this would be *the only line* in the whole of Psalm 22 where physical harm would actually be described as being inflicted on the psalmist.

When these two reasons - the possibility that *kaaru* may be meaningless and the fact that any verb which describe a physical attack on the psalmist goes against the grain of Psalm 22 - are combined, we can see that by itself - *kaaru* becomes a very unlikely alternative.

When we turn back to the MT reading, supported by the Targums and Symmachus, we find that some scholars have been too quick to dismiss the sentence as meaningless. Part of the problem comes in reading "like a lion" as the beginning a line or *stich*. However, the phrase could easily have fallen within the previous line, forming this couplet:

For dogs have compassed me.
The assembly of the wicked have encircled me like a lion.

This (suggested) couplet takes the poetic form know as "synonymous parallelism"- in both lines we have the imagery of animals (dogs/lion) and the idea of being surrounded/encircled by them. This parallelism is lost if any of the suggestions for *kaaru* were to be inserted here.[90]

---

verses he cited were: 22:12-13, 16 & 20-21 (Note Strawn was using the verse number of the Hebrew bible, so I have to minus one from there). Verse 16 is the point of the whole discussion so we will not be reviewing it here. I think Dr. Strawn is mistaken here. For verse 22:12-13 refers to the enemies of the Psalmist, metaphorically represented as bulls and lions, as surrounding him and "opening their mouth" *at* him. These are threatening gestures, no doubt - which would explain the following stanza where he describes his own fear and anxiety - but it does not presuppose any physical violence being inflicted on the Psalmist. Verse 22:20-21 is a thanksgiving stanza thanking God for saving him *from* the "power [literally "hand"] of the dog", the "mouth of the lion" and the "horns of the bull". Again, there is no indication that he actually was physically attacked for the deliverance seem to be one who rejoices after managing to *avoid* such attacks!

90 Although the second *stich* (*stich* is just a fancy term for the smallest "sentence unit" in a poetry) is longer than the first, I think this reconstruction still falls within the metrical rules of Hebrew poetry. The first line of the couple in Hebrew could contain 3 stresses if the syllable for initial *ki* ("for"), is stressed for emphasis. The second line contains four stresses. This pattern of stresses, 3/4, corresponds to the *Qinah*, or lamentation, poetic line which normally has two stichs of unequal lengths. Similarly the next couplet [My hands and my feet/I can count all my bones] has the 2/2 pattern of stresses and falls within the "normal" Hebrew poetical metrical arrangement.

What to do with "my hands and my feet"? For this we have to absorb the whole imagery of Psalm 22:11-21. [The translation below is taken from the NRSV except that I have changed the punctuation at verse 16 and have replaced the NRSV's "they shriveled" back to "like a lion".]

> Psalm 22: 11-21
> 11 Do not be far from me, *for trouble is near*
>   and there is no one to help.
>   12 Many bulls encircle me,
>   strong bulls of Bashan surround me;
>   13 they open wide their mouths at me,
>   like a ravening and roaring lion.
> 14 I am poured out like water,
>   and all my bones are out of joint;
>   my heart is like wax;
>   it is melted within my breast;
> 15 my mouth is dried up like a potsherd,
>   and my tongue sticks to my jaws;
>   you lay me in the dust of death.
>   16 For dogs are all around me;
>   a company of evildoers encircles me like a lion.
>   My hands and feet;
> 17 I can count all my bones!
>   They stare and gloat over me;
>   18 they divide my clothes among themselves,
>   and for my clothing they cast lots.
> 19 But you, O LORD, do not be far away!
>   O my help, come quickly to my aid!
>   20 Deliver my soul from the sword,
>   my life from the power of the dog!
>   21 Save me from the mouth of the lion!
>   From the horns of the wild oxen you have rescued me.

If we look at the whole passage above we find three basic themes: the Psalmist's call to God for help (Psalm 22:11 & 19), the description of the state of his anxiety (Psalm 22:14-15, 16b-17a) and the description of his enemies, metaphorically represented by three different animals -the bull/oxen, the dog and the lion. (Psalm 22:12-13, 16b-17a, 20-21). Indeed, the imagery conveyed here (Psalm 22:14-15, 16b-17a) is someone surrounded by his enemies in a state of extreme despair, suffering physical discomfort and probably dehydrated and emaciated from his trials, calling out to God for deliverance.

We can see that the imagery about *body parts* conveys an impression of his extreme despair and anxiety (Psalm 22:14-15 & 16b-17a). When the Psalmist tells us he is "being poured out like water" he means that he is being drained of vitality and energy. That his bones are "out of joint" means his limbs are tired. His heart "melting like wax" means he is troubled or fearful.[91] The next lines about his mouth and tongue

---

[91]   We find the same imagery in one of the extra-biblical scrolls as Qumran:
        1QH 4:33-34

probably refer to his thirst. That he is "laid in the dust of death" is understandable, for we have here a tired, fearful, thirsting and emaciated man.[92] After pausing to describe his enemies, he picked up the imagery of his body again in verse 16b and 17a. Raising his forearm slightly, looking at his weak limbs and emaciated body, he laments, "my hands and my feet...I can count all my bones!". Broken sentences like these convey exactly the impression the Psalmists would have wanted to convey: people in despair don't normally speak in complete sentences![93]

This is not the only example of such a rhetorical technique in Psalm 22. We can also see this in the very first verse of that Psalm. Modern translations tends to smooth out these grammatically rough sentences; the NRSV gives Psalm 22:1b as "Why are you so far from helping me, from the words of my groaning?". The Hebrew literally reads, "Far from my salvation the words of my groaning". The word is not completely intelligible in the strictly grammatical sense.[94] However, if we read the passage as "Far from my salvation...The words of my groaning", we can see that the Psalmist is saying that he is groaning about his state of being "far from salvation".

The imagery is complete - and there is no difficulty with not requiring a verb after "my hands and my feet", for it is merely a rhetorical device to describe the state of mind the psalmist was in.

Note also that Psalm 22:11-21 provides a coherent overall structure when Psalm 22:16b reads "like a lion". If we follow the description of the (metaphorical) animals that permeates this whole passage this is what the progression looks like:[95]

> A. **Bulls** Psalm 22:11
>   B. **Lion** (including mention of mouths) Psalm 22:13
>   C. **Dogs** Psalm 22:16a
>   X. **Lion** Psalm 22:16b
>   C'. **Dogs** Psalm 22:20
>   B'. **Lion** (including mention of mouth) Psalm 22:21a
> A'. **Oxen** Psalm 22:21b

Note that the progression exhibits what is normally known as a *chiastic structure*. This is merely a device use in poetry and some types of prose that crosses the terms and ideas in this manner **A - B - C - X - C'- B'- A'**. The central "lion" forms the climax to the whole section in which his ordeal or anxiety is at its greatest. After that

---

As for me shaking and trembling seize me, and all my bones are quivering;
my heart melts like wax before fire and my knees are like water pouring
down a steep place.

Here too, "heart melting like wax" refers to the state of extreme distress and fear.

[92] Hoffman, *Psalm 22 (LXX 21) and the Crucifixion of Jesus*: p158-167
Weiser, *The Psalm*: p223-224

[93] Of course we are not saying that the Psalmist was actually in a physical state of hunger, thirst and near death - but merely that this was the *imagery* he chose to describe (perhaps) his spiritual anxiety and despair.

[94] It must be noted that for this particular "broken passage" in Psalm 22:1, *all ancient versions support the reading of the Hebrew text*. [Hoffman, *Psalm 22 (LXX 21) and the Crucifixion of Jesus*: p112]

[95] Strawn, *Psalm 22:17b: More Guessing*: p447

deliverance follows quickly. A chiastic structure with a central climax fits the context of Psalm 22:11-21 very closely.

These then, are the reasons why *kaari*, "like a lion", suits the context of Psalm 22 better than *kaaru*:

1. It continues the imagery of animals (bulls, dogs and lions) as metaphors for his enemies.

2. It completes the couplet in verse 16 via synonymous parallelism.

3. It falls into the same "drift" as the rest of Psalm 22 - where the Psalmist is *threatened*, or *feels threatened*, but is never described as being physically harmed or attacked.

4. It completes the overall chiastic structure of Psalm 22:11-21.

CONCLUSIONS ON PSALM 22:16B

In our long analysis we can make the following conclusions:

- We are *certain* that there is no prophecy of the crucifixion in Psalm 22:16b. There are two alternate readings in the Hebrew text circulating in the time around the turn of the common era; the first, *kaari* ("like a lion"), obviously has no relation to any crucifixion; the second, *kaaru* may be meaningless, but even if it is meaningful, none of the meaning guessed at by the ancient independent versions (Septuagint, Jerome's Psalm, Symmachus and Aquila) or by modern scholars compels a reading of "piercing". None of the early Christian writers, right up to 150 CE, interpreted Psalm 22:16b to be a direct reference to the crucifixion.

- The reading as it stands in the Masoretic Text, "like a lion" is still the most probable reading, for it fits into the imagery of the whole of Psalm 22 better than the guesses of modern scholars or ancient translators.

CONCLUSIONS ON JESUS AND THE MESSIANIC PROPHECIES

We have seen in this excursus that the fundamentalist claim that Jesus' coming was foretold in the Old Testament is demonstrably false. While it is true that the evangelists believed this to be the case, a careful reading of the Old Testament shows that in many cases passages were taken out of context and applied to Jesus. In other cases passages from the Old Testament were used by Mark, Matthew, Luke and John to construct fictitious details about Jesus. The vague and ambiguous "Songs of the Servant" in Isaiah, were forcibly twisted to refer to Jesus when the referral was most probably to Israel as a corporate entity. Psalm 22:16 is a scribal error that was used by later Christians as a prophecy of Jesus' crucifixion.

In short, *the coming of Jesus was not foretold in the Old Testament.*

Excursus D
REPLIES TO COMMON
FUNDAMENTALIST APOLOGETICS

There comes a time for every skeptic, when he or she gets posed with rhetorical questions that are commonly seen in books by fundamentalist apologists such as *Why We Believe the Bible* by George DeHoff, *Evidence that Demands a Verdict* by Josh McDowell and *The Case for Christ* by Lee Strobel. For those who may not be acquainted with the evidence, these questions, or "challenges to skeptics" as they are sometimes called, can seem quite impressive. Actually, the questions posed are normally quite "light-weight" and are easily answered. This section answers the most common rhetorical questions posed by fundamentalists and evangelicals.

RHETORICAL QUESTIONS ON THE SPECIAL STATUS OF THE BIBLE

Q1. Doesn't the Bible's impressive continuity, despite a period of composition spanning many centuries, show that it is the word of God?

The idea of "continuity" is very vague. On the one hand, this claim is trivially true. One would *expect* some kind of continuity in the Bible just on the basis of three contingent facts:

1. The Old Testament is a collection of books from one *specific people* in the Middle East. We would expect *cultural continuity* (such as the same language [Hebrew or its derivative, Aramaic], the same adherence to holy books, i.e. The Torah etc) to be contained within the books since most cultures persist for some time through history.

2. Similarly, the New Testament is a collection of books taken from a group (although not homogeneous as we have seen above) of people who lived in the first and second centuries CE who believed that Jesus' coming is a fulfillment of the Old Testament prophecies. Finding some "continuity" in its message with the Old Testament is therefore not surprising.

3. Finally, and this must not be forgotten, the books of the Bible were collected at specific moments in history. The Old Testament for instance was collected by the inventors of Rabbinic Judaism during the years following the Jewish revolt in 70 CE. Books that did not correspond to the theological views of the rabbis were *explicitly excluded* from the canon of the Old Testament. Therefore, much of this "continuity" is not something which occurs naturally but arose out of an *active selection process* by Jewish Rabbis within a given period in history. Similarly many books were *excluded* from the New Testament because they did not conform to the

views of the church fathers that eventually won control over nascent Christianity.[1]

On the other hand, this claim of continuity is wrong. When we look at the details, we do *not* find a continuity of theologies within the covers of the Bible. There are actually many differing (in some cases diametrically opposite) theologies which can be found in the Bible. Some examples:

- In the Old Testament, for instance we find diametrically opposite views on life in Proverbs and in Ecclesiastes.[2]

- The racial tolerance preached by the book of Ruth explicitly contradicts the racist teachings of Ezra-Nehemiah. In the book of Ruth we find the non-Jewish (Moabite) heroine telling her Hebrew mother-in-law that "Your people will be my people and your God will be my God" (Ruth 1:16). The story ends with her marrying the Jew, Boaz (Ruth 4:13). In the book of Nehemiah, we are told that Nehemiah argued from the Torah that "a Moabite should not enter into the assembly of God forever" (Nehemiah 13:1). In Ezra, the eponymous priest tells the returning exiles that they "have married foreign women, to increase the guilt of Israel" (Ezra 10: 10) and that they are to cast off their wives and children (Ezra 10:11, 44).[3]

- Similarly, in the New Testament we find completely opposing views on the value of good works between the epistles of James and Paul.[4] What can be more opposite than these two verses in their positions of the importance of works compared to faith:

  Romans 3:28 [Paul]
  [A] man is justified by faith apart from the works of the law.

  James 2:24 [RSV]
  [A] man is justified by works and not by faith alone.

Recently, biblical scholar Randel Helms published a book, *The Bible Against Itself: Why the Bible Seems to Contradict Itself* (Millennium 2006), that illustrates in detail just how *not* uniform the Bible is.

The claim that the Bible has an "impressive continuity" is both trivial and wrong.

Q2. Doesn't the fact that there are more than 5,000 extant manuscripts of the New Testament (more manuscripts than any other works in history) guarantee the truth of the New Testament message?

---

[1]   See chapter 6.
[2]   We showed this in chapter 1 in the section on "Books of Poetry and Ethics".
[3]   Helms, *The Bible Against Itself*: p1-13
[4]   Painter, *Just James*: p265-269

The logic behind this question is badly flawed. *At most*, a high preponderance of manuscripts guarantees the *textual integrity* of the document but it does not provide any support whatsoever for the *factual veracity* of its contents. In other words, the preponderance of manuscripts enables us to know what the authors actually wrote in the original autographs. It does not follow from this that we have proven the contents of the manuscripts to be true. [5]

Q3. Aren't there verses in the Bible that prove the scientific accuracy of the Bible?

The few verses that fundamentalists claim to show scientific foreknowledge are vague at best. There are many more verses in the Bible that show that the biblical authors held essentially pre-scientific and grossly inaccurate views of the world around them. There are numerous errors in the physical sciences, the biological sciences and mathematics in the book. Apart from these scientific and mathematical errors, we must remember that the Bible also contains internal contradictions, numerical contradictions and failed prophecies.[6] These facts constitute further evidence for the *human*, as opposed to divine, origins of the book.

Q4. Isn't it true that archaeology has never contradicted biblical accounts and indeed confirms them?

Modern archaeology has shown that many of the myths in Genesis - the stories of Creation, Adam and Eve and Noah's Ark - were all derived, or copied, from earlier Babylonian myths.[7] Furthermore, modern archaeological discoveries have put into doubt the accounts of the Patriarchal Narratives, the Exodus and the Conquest. Even the existence of an extensive kingdom under David and Solomon has recently been called into question.[8]

Far from archaeology "proving the Bible true," there is now so much contrary evidence against the historical accuracy of the Bible that the term "biblical archaeology" has been discarded in professional archaeology! The preferred term is now Syro-Palestinian archaeology.[9] The whole paradigm of archaeology in the Near East has shifted away from thinking of the Bible as a reliable archaeological field guide to that of a collection of ancient fairy tales and legends.

---

[5]   See Chapter 6, specifically the section entitled "Overwhelming Manuscript Evidence?"

[6]   See Chapter 2.

[7]   See Chapter 3.

[8]   See Chapter 4.

[9]   Davis, *Shifting Sands*: p145

RHETORICAL QUESTIONS ON JESUS CHRIST

Q5. Wasn't the coming of Jesus so clearly foretold in the Old Testament that it is highly improbable for these prophecies to be referring to someone else?

Numbers have been quoted to support the supposed extreme improbabilities of someone else being the prophesied messiah. Lee Strobel claimed, in his book *The Case for Christ,* that the probability of someone else fulfilling the prophecies about Jesus is about one in 1 X 10^{156} - or 1 followed by 156 zeros![10]

However, a detailed examination of these so-called prophecies in the Old Testament shows that such claims are hollow. Indeed, in many cases, modern fundamentalists and evangelicals have gotten their facts upside down. It was not that the prophecies in the Old Testament were fulfilled by Jesus' life but that these passages [considered as messianic prophecies by the authors of the gospels] were *used* by them to *concoct* details about the life of Jesus - since they did not have much information about the life of Jesus.[11] Other "prophecies" such as the prophecies of the virgin birth and of the crucifixion were based on mistakes in translations. Still others are based on what modern fundamentalists *read into* the passages.[12]

Q6. Wasn't the manner of Jesus' birth proof of his divine nature?

The whole edifice of the story of the virgin birth is historically unreliable. In the two extant accounts in the gospels of Matthew and Luke, we find inconsistencies in the genealogies of Jesus, in the stories relating to Jesus' birth in Bethlehem and in the reason why Mary and Joseph settled in Nazareth. Furthermore, we find that the historical details of two events correlated with the nativity, the death of Herod and the census of Quirinius, cannot be reconciled - for *Herod died a full ten years before the census of Quirinius.* The story of Herod's slaughter of the innocents is uncorroborated by other historical documents and evidence, and is a fictional creation of Matthew. Other details of the Nativity have also been shown to be unhistorical.

And, as we have seen above, the prophecy of the virgin birth is based on a mistranslation of Isaiah. We also note that many of the details of the nativity were concocted from Old Testament passages. In some cases, Old Testament passages were *twisted* out of their original context to make them "fit" the storyline.

The virgin birth is myth, not history; fiction, not fact.[13]

---

[10]   Strobel, *The Case for Christ*: p247

[11]   For the answer to the fundamentalist stock reply that the apostles "would not have made up such stories about Jesus and would not have died for what they know to be a lie", see Q9 to Q11 below.

[12]   See Excursus C

[13]   See Chapter 11.

Q7. Wasn't the character of Jesus, as presented in the gospels, such that it is high above all human greatness?

It is hard for evangelicals to see how anyone could view Jesus with anything but the utmost awe and respect. However, it is also true that most skeptics do not see Jesus as *all that extraordinary* in terms of his teachings or his behavior.

The Jesus as portrayed in the gospels is a racist: he referred to non-Jews as "dogs" and affirmed that his teachings were meant for Jews only. The ethical lessons attributed to him were unimpressive and unoriginal. His personality was probably not much different from other peasant preachers of his era; preaching love at one moment and cursing his enemies the next. There are even passages that would make one question his intellectual prowess.[14]

Q8. Isn't it historically true that the resurrection happened - surely the existence of the empty tomb attests to that?

While most skeptics do not doubt that Jesus' earliest disciples had some kind of "resurrection experience", they do doubt that the stories of the resurrection, as told in the Gospels and Acts, are historical.

For instance there are difficulties and contradictions with the burial accounts given in the gospels. Matthew's unique story about the guards placed at the tomb completely contradicts the details given in the other gospels. The whole idea of Jesus' body being placed in a *new and unused* tomb is historically unreliable. Furthermore, there are contradictions among the gospel accounts in almost every detail in the story discovery of the empty tomb. The balance of evidence shows that there was *no empty tomb*. The empty tomb story itself was a later development, or addition, to the legend of Jesus' resurrection.

Similar to the empty tomb accounts above, the other gospels (and Paul's first epistle to the Corinthians) couldn't agree on many details of the resurrection appearances. The oldest documents, such as Paul's epistles, indicate that the resurrection was nothing more than a hallucinatory experience of the followers of Jesus. The initial appearances of Jesus were very likely hallucinatory and fleeting in nature. There are some convincing psychological explanations as to why the resurrection appearances happened to Peter and Paul.

We also note that the resurrections of gods are a very common theme in Greco-Roman paganism. Just like the case of the virgin birth, it is very likely that the details of the story of the resurrection are the result of this cultural cross breeding of myths.[15]

---

[14]   See Chapter 13.
[15]   See Chapter 13 specifically section on "The Empty Tomb"

RHETORICAL QUESTIONS ON THE "WITNESS" OF THE APOSTLES

Q9. Aren't the accounts in the gospels, *written* by the apostles (Matthew and John) or their close associates (Mark and Luke), historically reliable reports of the miracles and the life of Jesus?

There is widespread agreement among critical-historical scholars that the gospels were *not* written by Matthew, Mark, Luke and John. These names first appeared as the purported authors of the gospels only in the second century and were *guesses* made by the early church fathers. Internal evidence of the gospels themselves point to the conclusion that the Gospel of Mark was not written by Mark, companion of Peter, the Gospel of Matthew was not written by the apostle of that name, the author of Luke-Acts could not have been the companion of Paul of that name and the gospel attributed to John was not written by John, the son of Zebedee.

All four gospels were written after 70 CE, at least four decades after the death of Jesus. The latest of these, the gospels of Luke and John, were written almost a century after the crucifixion. Attempts by fundamentalists to argue for early dates of gospel composition have met with failure.

At no point do we have in the gospels the account of an eyewitness or even the friend of an eyewitness. [16]

Q10. Weren't the apostles around to ensure the accuracy of the reports regarding the life of Jesus in the gospels?

This is based on a very superficial understanding of oral tradition. Indeed, we found that even in cases where the witnesses are still alive, stories tend to take a life of their own in an unskeptical oral culture. Furthermore, as we have seen above, all the gospels were written after the calamity of the Jewish War in 70 CE. This upheaval would have killed many of the eyewitnesses, dislocated many others and dislodged the memories of most of the rest of the survivors. There are strong reasons to believe that the apostles were either no longer around or no longer in a position to counter the falsehoods in the gospels, when the documents started circulating. [17]

Q11. All the apostles died for their beliefs. Why would they give up their lives for something they know to be a lie?

There are three assumptions embedded in this question:

1. We *know* all the apostles died martyrs' deaths.

2. What the apostles *believed* about Jesus is the same essentially as what modern fundamentalists believe.

---

[16] See Chapter nine.

[17] See Chapter 10, section on "The Oral Tradition"

3.   People *will not die* for false beliefs.

All three suppositions are demonstrably false.

1.   We simply *do not know* how most of the apostles died.

With the exception of the death of James the son of Zebedee (Acts 12:2) and Judas (Matthew 27:9, Acts 1:18), no other apostolic death is recounted in the New Testament.[18] The traditional material relating to the life of the apostles is simply unreliable. Apart from the (probably) historical tradition that Peter died in Rome, *we do not know how the rest of the apostles met their end -whether it was through martyrdom, disease, accident or old age.*[19]

2.   What the original apostles believed was very likely *not the same* as that of today's conservative Christians.

It must be remembered that since the stories in the gospels were *not* written by the apostles or any of their close associates [see Q9 above] - it is unlikely that what is described therein as the teaching of Jesus actually was what the Jewish preacher taught.

    We do know that the theology in the New Testament tend to (although not always!) be in line with what was taught by the self-proclaimed apostle Paul. Yet, we have strong evidence that Paul's teachings were opposed by the apostles who knew Jesus, that he had a falling out with them at Antioch and that his last trip to Jerusalem to reconcile himself with them very probably ended in failure.[20]

    Even if it can be shown that some of the apostles died martyrs' deaths, it does not necessarily follow that they died for the same beliefs or dogmas of modern fundamentalist Christianity.

3.   People *do die* for false beliefs

All religions have their martyrs. Even some non-religious political systems - such as communism - have found people willing to die for them. The last couple of decades have given us plenty of examples. David Koresh led his Branch Davidians to fiery deaths in their final apocalyptic battle with the US Bureau of

---

[18]   There are two other deaths with which there is some historical support are the deaths of Paul and James, the brother of Jesus. Paul was not one of the twelve apostles, so his death – probably in the same general persecution that Peter died in – is of no interest. James the brother of Jesus was very probably not one of the original twelve apostles. James' death, of which probably the most reliable version is in the Antiquities of the Jews 20:9:1, was due to some internal Jewish political intrigue (he was accused of having "broken the law") which have nothing to do with the resurrection of Jesus or his faith. We know from other historical sources that James was a strong adherent of the Torah and the charge was a concocted one.

[19]   Chapter 12, section on "The Twelve Apostles"

[20]   Two good books that treat this subject in detail are Gerd Lüdemann's *Opposition to Paul in Jesus Christianity* (1989) and Hyam Maccoby's *The Mythmaker: Paul and the Invention of Christianity* (1987)

Alcohol, Tobacco and Firearms. Luc Jouret and his followers of the Solar Temple group committed suicide in Switzerland and Canada in 1994. Marshall Herff Applewhite and his followers, members of the Heaven's Gate community, willingly committed suicide; believing that they were to be picked up by aliens. The current trend of suicide bombing among Islamic militants is just another sad example of people only too willing to end their lives for their [unexamined] beliefs.

In other words, being willing to die for one's beliefs has always been the hallmark of fanatics and true believers. The willingness of these believers to die martyr's deaths provides no assurance whatsoever that what they believe is true.

A corollary to this is the general belief, as evidenced by the various apocryphal Acts of the Apostles, that the apostles who were martyred were first given a chance to recant their beliefs. This was probably based on the experiences of Christians in the early second century. We find such evidence in the exchange of letter between Pliny the Younger (63-c113). In a letter to emperor Trajan (c52-117) dated around 112 CE, Pliny explained that he first gave the accused a few chances to deny they were Christians before executing them.[21]

However, when we look at the two apostolic martyrdoms in which there is some historical evidence – that of Peter and James son of Zebedee – it is unlikely in the extreme that they were given such a chance to "witness" to their beliefs.

There is a strong early tradition that Peter died in the Neronian persecution in Rome in 64-67 CE. However, the Christians were executed not for their beliefs *per se* but for the concocted charge of being responsible for the great fire of Rome. In order to deflect accusation of being responsible for the fire, Nero used the Christian community in Rome as the scapegoat. Nero's men would not have been interested whether the Christians they executed recanted their beliefs or not. A modern analogy would be the Jewish Holocaust. The Nazis executed even those Jews who had converted to Christianity. It did not matter to them whether these people recanted their beliefs or not. If Peter did die in this general persecution, he probably would not have been given the chance to recant his beliefs. Therefore, his execution could not have been taken as someone whose death is a "witness" to the steadfastness of his belief.

As for James the son of Zebedee, again the situation is more closely related to Neronian persecution than the one of Trajan. Acts 12:2 merely mentioned that James was executed as part of Herod Agrippa's (10 BCE – 44 CE) persecution of Christians. It does not follow that he was ever given the chance to recant his beliefs.

Finally, even if they did go to their executions with their faith intact, it does not follow that they were in a position to *know* whether their beliefs were true or false. Their faith, after all, was in the form of a theology based on eschatological expectations. They could not have *known* the world would not end – since this is what they were waiting for! Even if we assume that they died testifying to their belief that Jesus was resurrected, the problem remains. The apostles

---

21   Pagels, *The Gnostic Gospels*: p94-95

certainly had "Jesus sightings" but this can be explained by modern psychology. [22] Yet such beliefs could be so deeply embedded – especially since it gave their lives meaning and prestige - that they would not have questioned the reality their experience of this even in the face of death. Such resolute convictions based on visions or hallucinations are not unique. Joan of Arc (1412-1431), the Catholic Saint, experienced celestial visions which called on her to help expel the English from France. She went to her execution fully convinced of the truth of her visions. Yet, few today would accept that God would take sides in the politics of medieval Europe. [23] Muhammad was another prominent historical figure who was prone to visions and held on to the belief in their reality throughout his life. So even if Peter and James died holding on to their resurrection experiences as "real", it does not prove therefore that there actually was a physical and tangible Jesus that rose from the dead.

---

[22]   See Chapter 13, section on "The Nature of the Appearances".

[23]   Some Catholic apologists have argued that, based on historical reports of Joan of Arc's intelligence, she was not mentally ill and that this rules out the explanation that her visions were "hallucinations". Yet, as we have seen in our analysis of the resurrection experiences of Peter and Paul, mental illness is not a precondition for such visions. According to Dr. Barry Beyerstein (PhD in Biological Psychology) intense "transcendent experiences" such as visions, which could lead to life changing conversions, "are not uncommon in ordinary, healthy individuals, many of whom imbue their experience with supernatural or religious meaning."
(http://home.comcast.net/~dchapman2146/pf_v3n3/NeuroWeird.htm accessed on August 13, 2006)

BIBLIOGRAPHY

A

Abegg, Martin, Flint, Peter & Ulrich, Eugene, *The Dead Sea Scrolls Bible*, Harper, San Francisco 1999

Akenson, Donald Harman, *Saint Saul: A Skeleton Key to the Historical Jesus*, Oxford, New York 2000

Akenson, Donald Harman, *Surpassing Wonder, The Invention of the Bible and the Talmuds*, University of Chicago, Chicago 2001

Aland, Kurt & Aland, Barbara, *The Text of the New Testament*, Eerdmans, Grand Rapids 1989

Allegro, John, *The Dead Sea Scrolls*, Penguin, London 1965

Anderson, George, *A Critical Introduction to the Old Testament*, Duckworth, London 1979

Angus, S., *The Mystery Religions*, Dover, New York 1975

Archer, Gleason L., *Encyclopedia of Bible Difficulties*, Zondervan, Grand Rapids 1982

Armstrong Karen, *The First Christian,: St Paul's Impact on Christianity*, Pan, London 1983

Armstrong, Karen, *Holy War: The Crusades and Their Impact on Today's World*, Doubleday, New York, 1991

Asimov, Isaac, *Asimov's Guide to the Bible*, Avenel, New York 1981

Asimov, Isaac, *Isaac Asimov's Book of Facts*, Wings, New York 1979

Asimov, Isaac, *X Stands For Unknown*, Grafton, London 1986

Avalos, Hector, *The End of Biblical Studies*, Prometheus, New York, 2007

B

Baigent,M. & Leigh, R., *The Dead Sea Scrolls Deception*, Summit, New York 1991

Baldwin, Matthew, *Christ in Orbit: Ancient and Contemporary Cosmologies in Biblical Interpretation*, Paper given at the Central States Society of Biblical Literature regional meeting, Kansas City, MO. 1977

Barker, Dan, *Losing Faith in Faith: From Preacher to Atheist* Freedom from Religion Foundation, Madison 1992

Barr, David L., *New Testament Story: An Introduction*, Wadsworth, Belmont 1995

Barret, David (ed), *The World Christian Encyclopedia*, Oxford University Press, Nairobi 1982

Barthel, Manfred, *What the Bible Really Says*, Wings Book, New York 1980

Bauckham, Richard, *Jesus and the Eyewitnesses: The Gospels as Eyewitness Testimony*, Eerdmans, Grand Rapids, 2006

Bauer, Walter, *A Greek-English Lexicon of the New Testament and Other Early Christian Literature*, 2nd Ed, University of Chicago Press, Chicago 1979

Becker, Adam H. & Reed, Annette Yoshiko (eds), *The Ways That Never Parted: Jews and Christians in Late Antiquity and the Early Middle Ages*, Fortress, Minneapolis 2007

Beckmann, Petr, *A History of Pi*, Dorset, New York 1971

Benet, WR, *The Readers Encyclopedia*, A & C Black, London 1987

Bentley, James, *Secrets of Mount Sinai*, Orbis, London 1985

Bernheim, Pierre-Antoine, *James, Brother of Jesus*, SCM Press, London 1997]

Bird, Michael F. & Crossley, James G., *How Did Christianity Begin? A believer and non-believer examine the evidence*, Hendrickson, Peabody 2008

Bonz, Marrianne Palmer, *The Past as Legacy: Luke-Acts and the Ancient Epic*, Fortress, Minneapolis 2000

Boyarin, Daniel, *Border Lines: The Partition of Judaeo Christianity*, University of Pennsylvania, Philadelphia 2004

Biscare Michael et. al. (ed), *The Marshall Cavendish Illustrated Encyclopedia of Plants and Animals*, Marshall Cavendish, London 1979

Bradlaugh, Charles, *Humanity's Gain From Unbelief*, Watts & Co, London 1929

Bradlaugh, C. & Besant, A., *The Freethinker's Textbook*, Freethought, London 1935

Brandon, S.G.F., *The Fall of Jerusalem and the Christian Church*, SPCK, London 1957

Brandon, S.G.F., *The Trial of Jesus of Nazareth*, Dorset, New York 1968

Brown, F., Driver, S. & Briggs, C., *The Brown-Driver-Briggs Hebrew and English Lexicon*, Hendrickson, Peabody 2003

Brown, Raymond E., *The Birth of the Messiah: A Commentary on the Infancy Narratives*, Doubleday, New York 1993

Brown, Raymond E., *An Introduction to the New Testament*, Doubleday, New York 1997

Brown, Raymond E., Fitzmyer, Joseph A. & Murphy, Roland E., *The New Jerome Biblical Commentary*, Prentice Hall, New Jersey 1999

Brownrigg, Ronald, *Who's Who in the Bible: The New Testament*, Random House, New York, 1971

Bruce, F.F., *The Books and the Parchments*, Pickering & Inglis, London 1971

Budge, E. A. Wallis, *Book of the Dead: The Hieroglyphic Transcript of the Papyrus of Ani*, Kessinger Publishing, Whitefish 2003

Bullock, A. & Woodings, R.B., *The Fontana Dictionary of Modern Thinkers* Fontana, London 1983

Bullock, A., Stallybrass & Trombley, Stephen., *The Fontana Dictionary of Modern Thought*, Fontana, London 1988

C

Cadoux, C.J., *The Life of Jesus*, Penguin, London 1948

Caird, G.B., *Saint Luke*, Penguin, London 1963

Callahan, Tim, *Bible Prophecy: Failure or fulfillment?*, Millennium Press, Altadena 1997

Callahan, Tim, *Secret Origins of the Bible*, Millenium Press, Altadena 2002

Cartlidge, David R. & Dungan, David L., *Documents for the Study of the Gospels*, Fortress Press, Minneapolis 1994

Cary, M. & Scullard, H.H., *A History of Rome*, St. Martin's, New York 1979

Chadwick, Henry, *The Early Church*, Penguin, London 1967

Chilton, Bruce & Neusner, Jacob, *The Brother of Jesus: James the Just and his Mission*, Westminster John Knox, Louisville 2001

Clements, Tad S., *Science Vs. Religion*, Prometheus, Buffalo 1990

Cline, Eric H., *From Eden to Exile: Unravelling the Mysteries of the Bible*, National Geographic, Washington DC 2007

Collingwood, R.G., *The Idea of History*, Oxford University Press, New York 2000

Comay, Joan & Brownrigg, R., *Who's Who in the Bible* (Two Volumes in One), Randon House, New York 1971

Coogan, Michael (ed), *The Oxford History of the Biblical World*, Oxford, London 1998

Cook, Michael, *The Koran: A Very Short Introduction*, Oxford, London 2000

Copan, Paul & Tacelli, Ronald K., *Jesus's Resurrection, Fact or Figment?*, Intervarsity Press, Downers Grove 2000

Crane, Frank, *The Lost Books of the Bible*, Meridian, New York 1974

Craveri, Marcello, *The Life of Jesus*, Panther, London 1969

Crossan, John Dominic, *The Historical Jesus: The Life of a Mediterranean Jewish Peasant*, HarperCollins, San Francisco 1992

Crossan, John Dominic, *Jesus: A Revolutionary Biography*, HarperCollins, San Francisco 1994

Crossan, John Dominic, *Who Killed Jesus: Exposing the Roots of Anti-Semitism in the Gospel Story of the Death of Jesus*, HarperCollins, San Francisco 1995

Culpepper, R. Alan, *John, The Son of Zebedee: The Life of a Legend*, T&T Clark, Edinburgh 2000

Cunliffe-Jones, H., *Christian Theology Since 1600*, Duckworth, London 1970

Cuppitt, D. & Armstrong, P., *Who Was Jesus?*, BBC, London 1979

D

D'Costa, Gavin, *Resurrection Reconsidered*, One World Publication, Oxford 1996

Dash, Mike, *Borderlands: The Ultimate Exploration of the Unknown*, Dell, 2000

Davidson, R. & Leaney, A.R.C., *Biblical Criticism*, Penguin, London 1970

Davis, Stephen, Kendall, Daniel, & O'Collins, Gerald, *The Resurrection*, Oxford, New York 1997

Davis, Thomas W., *Shifting Sands: The Rise and Fall of Biblical Archaeology*, Oxford, New York 2004

Dever, William G., *Who Were The Early Israelites and Where Did They Come From?*, Eerdmans, Grand Rapids 2003

Dibelius, Martin, *Studies in the Acts of the Apostles*, SCM 1956

Dodd, Charles, *The Founder of Christianity*, Fontana, London 1973

Dunn, James D.G., *Unity and Diversity in the New Testament*, Trinity Press International, Harrisburg 1990

Dunn, James D.G. (ed), *Jews and Christians: The parting of ways AD 70 to 135*, Eerdmans, Grand Rapids 1992

E

Ehrman, Bart D., *Jesus: Apocalyptic Prophet of the New Millenium*, Oxford University Press, Oxford 1999

Ehrman, Bart D., *Lost Christianities: The Battles for Scripture and the Faiths We Never Knew*, Oxford, New York 2003

Ehrman, Bart D., *The New Testament: A Historical Introduction to the Early Christian Writings*, Oxford University Press, New York 2000

Ehrman, Bart D. & Holmes, Micheal W. (ed), *The Text of the New Testament in Contemporary Research*, Eerdmans, Grand Rapids 1995

Elliger, K. (ed) & Rudolph, W. (ed), *Biblia Hebraica Stutgartensia*, Deutsche Bibelsellschaft, Stutgart 1977

Epp, Eldon J. & Fee, Gordon D., *Studies in the Theory and Method of New Testament Textual Criticism*, Eerdmans, Grand Rapids, 1993

Eusebius, *The History of the Church (AD325)*, Penguin, London 1989

Evans, Rod L.,& Berent, Irwin M., *Fundamentalism: Hazards and Heartbreaks* Open Court, La Salle Illinois 1988

F

Fenton, John, *Saint Matthew*, Penguin, London 1963

Ferguson, Everett (ed), *Encyclopedia of Early Christianity: 2nd Edition*, Garland Publishing, New York 1998

Finegan, Jack, *The Archeology of the New Testament*, Princeton University Press, Princeton 1992

Finkelstein, Israel & Silberman, Neil Aher, *The Bible Unearthed*, Free Press, New York 2001

Fogelin, Robert J., *A Defense of Hume on Miracles*, Princeton University Press, Princeton 2003

Forrell, George, *The Protestant Faith*, Prentice-Hall, Engelwood Cliffs 1960

Fox, Robin Lane, *The Unauthorized Version: Truth and Fiction in the Bible*, Penguin, London 1991

Frazer, James, *The Golden Bough*, Wordsworth, Hertfordshire 1993

Frazier, Kendrick, *Science Confronts the Paranormal*, Prometheus, Buffalo, 1986

Freed, Edwin D., *The Stories of Jesus' Birth: A Critical Introduction*, Sheffield Academic, Sheffield 2001

Freke, T. & Gandy, P., *The Jesus Mysteries*, Thorsons, London 1999

Friedman, Richard Elliot, *Who Wrote the Bible?*, HarperCollins, San Francisco 1987

Funk, Robert W., Hoover, Roy W. & The Jesus Seminar, *The Five Gospels*, Macmillan, New York 1993

Funk, Robert W. & The Jesus Seminar, *The Acts of Jesus: What Did Jesus Really Do?*, Harper, San Francisco 1998

G

Gardner, Martin, *Fads and Fallacies in the Name of Science*, Dover, New York 1957

Godfrey, Laurie (ed), *Scientists Confront Creationism*, Norton, New York 1983

Goodspeed, Edgar J., *The Twelve: The Story of Christ's Apostles*, John C. Winston, Philadephia 1957

Gordon, Cyrus H. & Rendsburg, Gary A., *The Bible and the Ancient Near East*, Norton, New York, 1997

Graham, Phyllis, *The Jesus Hoax*, Leslie Frewin, London 1974

Grant, F.C., *The Gospels: Their origin and their growth*, Faber, London 1957

Graves, Robert & Patai, Raphael, *Hebrew Myths*, Doubleday, New York 1964

Gray, John, *Near Eastern Mythology*, Hamlyn, London 1982

Guignebert, Charles, *Jesus*, University Books, New York 1956

Guirand, Felix (ed), *The Larousse Encyclopedia of Mythology*, Chancellor Press, London 1994

H

Haiven, Judith, *Faith, Hope & No Charity*, New Star, Vancouver 1984

Hall, John, *Biology*, Hodder & Stoughton, London 1974

Harrison, R.K., *Biblical Hebrew: A complete course*, Hodder & Stoughton, London 1995

Harwood, William, *Mythology's Last Gods: Yahweh and Jesus*, Promethues, Buffalo, 1992

Hedrick, Charles W., *When History and Faith Collide: Studying Jesus*, Hendrickson, Peabody 1995

Helms, Randel, *Gospel Fictions*, Prometheus, Buffalo 1988

Helms, Randel, *The Bible Against Itself*, Millennium Press, Altadena 2006

Helms, Randel, *Who Wrote the Gospels?*, Millennium Press, Altadena 1997

Hengel, *Crucifixion: In the Ancient World and the Folly of the Message of the Cross*, Fortress Press, Philadephia 1977

Hick, John, *The Metaphor of God Incarnate: Christology in a Pluralistic Age*, Westminster, John Knox, Louisville 1993

Hinnels, John, *Dictionary of Religions*, Penguin, London, 1984

Hoffman, Mark, *The World's Almanac*, Pharos, New York, 1991

Hoffman, Mark G.V., *Psalm 22 (LXX 21) and the Crucifixion of Jesus*, PhD Yale University 1996 (UMI)

Hoffman, R. Joseph, *Jesus Outside the Gospels*, Prometheus, Buffalo 1984

Hoffman, R.Joseph, *The Origins of Christianity: A Critical Introduction*, Prometheus, Buffalo 1985

Hooke, S.H., *Middle Eastern Mythology*, Penguin London 1963

Hordern, William, *A Layman's Guide to Protestant Theology*, Macmillan, New York 1968

Howell, Martha & Prevenier, Walter, *From Reliable Sources: An Introduction to Historical Methods*, Cornell University Press, New York 2001

Howell-Smith, A.D., *In Search of the Real Bible*, Watts & Co., London 1943

Hughes, Philip E., *Creative Minds in Contemporary Theology*, Eerdmans, Grand Rapids 1969

Hume, David, *An Enquiry Concerning Human Understanding*, Prometheus, Buffallo 1988

I

Ifrah, Georges, *The Universal History of Numbers: From prehistory to the invention of the computer*, John Wiley, New York 1998

J

Jackson-McCabe, Matt (ed), *Jewish Christianity Reconsidered*, Fortress, Minneapolis 2007

Jenkins, Philip, *Hidden Gospels: How the Search for Jesus Lost Its Way*, Oxford University Press, New York 2001

Jobes, Karen H. & Silva, Moisés, *Invitation to the Septuagint*, Baker Book House, Grand Rapids 2000

Johnson, Paul, *A History of Christianity*, Penguin, London 1976

Joseph, George G., *The Crest of the Peacock: Non-European Roots of Mathematics*, Penguin, London 1990

K

Kelber, Werner, H., *The Oral and the Written Gospel*, Indiana University Press, Indianapolis 1997

Keller, Werner, *The Bible As History*, Hodder & Stoughton, London 1956

Kelly, J.N.D., *Jerome: His Life, Writings and Controversies*, Christian Classics, Maryland 1975

Kendig, Frank & Hutton, Richard, *Life Spans*, Magnum, London 1981

Knight, Margaret, *Honest to Man: Christian Ethics Re-examined*, Pemberton, London 1974

Knight, Margaret (ed), *Humanist Anthology*, Pemberton, London 1961

Koester, Helmut, *Ancient Christian Gospels: Their history and development* Trinity Press, Philadelphia 1990

Koester, Helmut, *Introduction to the New Testament, Volume II: History & Literature of Early Christianity*, Walter de Gruyter, New York 2000.

Kümmel, Werner Georg, *Introduction to the New Testament* 17th edition, Abingdon, Nashville 1975

L

Laughlin, John C.H. *Archaeology and the Bible*, Routledge, New York 2000

Lemche, Niels Peter, *Prelude to Israel's Past: Background and Beginnings of Israelite History and Identity*, Hendrickson, Peabody 1998

Livingstone, Elizabeth, *The Concise Oxford Dictionary of the Christian Church*, Oxford University Press, Oxford 1977

Lofmark, Carl, *What is the Bible?*, Prometheus, Buffalo 1989

Losse, John, *A Historical Introduction to the Philosophy of Science* (3rd ed), Oxford University Press, Oxford 1993

Lüdemann, Gerd, *Heretics: The Other Side of Early Christianity*, Westminster John Knox, Louisville 1996

Lüdemann, Gerd, *Jesus: After 2000 Years*, Prometheus, New York 2001

Lüdemann, Gerd, *Opposition to Paul in Jewish Christianity*, Fortress Press, Minneapolis 1989

Lüdemann, Gerd, *Paul, Apostle to the Gentiles: Studies in Chronology*, SCM, London 1984

Lüdemann, Gerd, *The Resurrection of Jesus: History, Experience, Theology*, Fortress, Minneapolis 1994

Lüdemann, Gerd, *The Resurrection of Christ: A Historical Enquiry*, Prometheus, New York 2004

Lüdemann, Gerd, *Virgin Birth? The Real Story of Mary and Her Son Jesus*, Trinity Press, Harribisburg 1998

Lüdemann, Gerd, *What Really Happened to Jesus: A Historical Approach to the Resurrection*, Westminster John Knox, Louisville 1995

M

Maccoby, Hyam, *Judas Iscariot and the Myth of Jewish Evil*, Free Press, New York 1992

Maccoby, Hyam, *The Mythmaker: Paul and the Invention of Christianity*, Harper, San Francisco 1987

Maccoby, Hyam, *Revolution in Judea: Jesus and the Jewish Resistance*, Ocean Books, London 1973

Mack, Burton L., *The Lost Gospel: The Book of Q and Christian Origins*, Harper, San Francisco 1993

Mack, Burton L., *Who Wrote the New Testament?:The Making of the Christian Myth* HarperCollins, San Francisco 1995

MacKinnon, D.M. et.al., *Objections to Christian Beliefs*, Penguin, London 1963

Macmillan Compendium: World Religions, Macmillan, New York 1987

Marcus, Amy D., *The View From Nebo*, Little, Brown and Company, New York 2000

Marsh, John, *Saint John*, Penguin, London 1968

Martin, Ralph, *New Testament Foundations, Volume 1*, Eerdmans, Grand Rapids 1975

Mason, Steve, *Josephus and the New Testament*, Hendrickson, Massachusetts 1992

McCane, Byron R., *Roll Back the Stone: Death and Burial in the World of Jesus*, Trinity Press International, Harrisburg 2003

McCarter, P. Kyle Jr., *Textual Criticism: Recovering the Text of the Hebrew Bible*, Fortress, Philadelphia 1986

McDonald, Lee M., *The Formation of the Christian Biblical Canon*, Hendricksen, Massachusetts 1995

McDowell, Josh, *Evidence that Demands a Verdict*, Here's Life, San Bernardino 1973

McDowell, Josh, *More Than A Carpenter*, Tyndall House, Illinois 1977

McKinsey, C. Dennis, *The Encyclopedia of Biblical Errancy*, Prometheus, New York 1995

McWhirter, Norris, *Guinness Illustrated Encyclopaedia of Facts*, Bantam, New York 1981

Metzger, Bruce M., *The Bible in Translation: Ancient and English versions*, Baker Book House, Grand Rapids 2001

Metzger, Bruce M., *The Canon of the New Testament: It's Origin, Development and Significance*, Oxford New York 1987

Metzger, Bruce M., *The Text of the New Testament: Its Transmission, Corruption and Restoration* 3e, Oxford New York 1992

Metzger, Bruce, M., *A Textual Commentary on the Greek New Testament*, United Bible Societies, 1971

Metzger, Bruce M., Coogan, Michael D., *The Oxford Companion to the Bible*, Oxford, New York 1993

Micklem, Nathaniel, *Behold the Man: A Study of the Fourth Gospel*, Geoffrey Bles, London 1970

Millard, Alan, *Discoveries From the Time of Jesus*, Lion, Oxford 1990

Miller, E.L., *God and Reason*, Macmillan, New York 1972

Miller, Robert J., The Apocalyptic Jesus: A Debate, Polebridge, Santa Rosa 2001

Miller, Robert J., *Born Divine: The Births of Jesus & Other Sons of God*, Polebridge, Santa Rosa 2003

Miller, Robert, J., *The Complete Gospels*, Harper Collins, San Francisco 1992

Miller, Robert, J., *The Jesus Seminar and its Critics*, Polebridge, Santa Rosa 1999

Montgomery, John, *Damned Through the Church*, Dimension, Minneapolis 1970

Moorey, P.R.S., *A Century of Biblical Archaeology*, Westminster/John Knox, Louisville 1991

N

Neusner, Jacob, *Rabbinic Literature and the New Testament*, Trinity Press, Valley Forge 1994

Nickell, Joe, *Looking for a Miracle: Weeping icons, relics, stigmata, visions and healing cures*, Prometheus, New York 1993

Nineham, D.E., *Saint Mark*, Penguin, London 1963

Nossal, G.J.V., *Antibodies and Immunity* Penguin, London 1971

O

Olson, Steve, *Mapping Human History: Discovering the Past Through Our Genes*, Houghton Mifflin, New York 2002

Oppenheimer, Stephen, *Out Of Eden: The Peopling of the World*, Robinson, London 2004

P

Pagels, Elaine, *The Gnostic Gospels*, Penguin, London 1979

Paine, Thomas, *The Age of Reason*, Wiley, New York 1942

Painter, John, *Just James: The Brother of Jesus in History and Tradition*, Fortress, Minneapolis 1997

Parmalee, Alice, *A Guidebook to the Bible*, English Universities Press, London 1964

Patterson, Stephen J., *The God of Jesus: The Historical Jesus & The Search for Meaning*, Trinity Press, Philadelphia 1998

Pellegrino, Charles, *Return to Sodom and Gomorrah*, Avon Books, New York 1994

Perkins, Pheme, *Peter: Apostle for the Whole Church*, Fortress, Minneapolis 2000

Pervo, Richard I., *Dating Acts: Between the Evangelists and the Apologists*, Polebridge Press, Santa Rosa 2006

Plimer, Ian, *Telling Lies for God: Reason vs. Creationism*, Random House Australia, Sydney 1994

Porter, Stanley E., *Paul in Acts*, Hendrickson, Peabody 2001

Powell, Mark Allan, *What Are They Saying About Acts?*, Paulist Press, New York 1991

Powell, Mark Allan, *The Jesus Debate*, Lion, Oxford, 1998

Price, Robert M., *Deconstructing Jesus*, Prometheus, New York 2000

Price, Robert M., *The Incredible Shrinking Son of Man: How Reliable if the Gospel Tradition?*, Prometheus, New York 2003

Price, Robert M. & Lowder, Jeffrey J. (eds), *The Empty Tomb: Jesus Beyond the Grave*, Prometheus, New York 2005

Prothero, Donald R., *Evolution: What the Fossils Say and Why it Matters*, Columbia University Press, New York 2007

R

Randi, James, *The Faith Healers*, Prometheus, Buffallo, 1989

Ranke-Heinemann, Uta, *Putting Away Childish Things*, Harper, San Francisco 1995

Renan, Ernest, *The Life of Jesus*, Watts & Co., London 1935

Rhein, Francis Bayard, *Understanding the New Testament*, Barron's, New York 1974

Ridley, Mark, *Evolution* (3rd Edition), Blackwell, Malden MA 2004

Riedel, E, Tracy, T. & Moskowitz, B., *The Book of the Bible*, Bantam, New York 1981

Roberts, J.M., *The Pelican History of the World*, Penguin, London 1983

Robertson, *The Bible and Its Background, Volume II*, Watts & Co, London 1942

Robertson, J.M., *A Short History of Christianity*, Watts & Co., London 1931

Robinson, James M. (ed), *The Nag Hammadi Library*, Harper & Row, New York 1981

Rosenbaum, Robert (ed), *The Desk Concord Encyclopedia*, Time, New York 1982

Roux, Georges, *Ancient Iraq*, Penguin, London 1980

Rubenstein, Richard E., *When Jesus Became God: The Struggle to Define Christianity during the Last Days of Rome*, Harvest Book, New York 1999

Ruse, Michael, *Darwinism Defended: A Guide to the Evolution Controversies*, Addison Wesley, Reading 1982

Russell, Bertrand, *Why I am Not a Christian*, Unwin, London 1962

S

Sandars N.K., *The Epic of Gilgamesh*, Penguin, London 1972

Sanders, E.P., *The Historical Figure of Jesus*, Penguin, London 1993

Sanders, E.P. & Davies, Margaret, *Studying the Synoptic Gospels*, SCM Press, London 1989

Sandmel, Samuel, *Judaism and Christian Beginnings*, Oxford, New York 1978

Schnell, Udo,*The History and Theology of the New Testament Writings*, Fortress, Minneapolis 1998

Schneemelcher, Wilhelm, *New Testament Apocrypha, Volume II*, Westminster John Knox, Louisville 1992

Schonfield, Hugh, *The Original New Testament*, Firethorn Press, London 1985

Schonfield, Hugh, *The Passover Plot*, Bantam, New York 1966

Schopf, J. William, *The Cradle of Life: The Discovery of Earth's Earliest Fossils*, Princeton University Press, Princeton 1999

Schwartz, Jeffrey H., *The Red Ape: Orangutans & Human Origins*, Houghton Mifflin, Boston 1987

Setzer, Claudia, *Jewish Responses to Early Christians: History and Polemics, 30-150 CE*, Fortress, Minneapolis 1994

Shanks, Hershel (ed), *Understanding the Dead Sea Scrolls*, Vintage, New York 1992

Sim, David C., *The Gospel of Matthew and Christian Judaism: The History and Social Setting of the Matthean Community*, T&T Clark, Edinburgh 1998

Skarsaune, Oskar & Hvalvik, Reidar, *Jewish Believers in Jesus*, Hendrickson, Peabody 2007

Smith, George H., *Atheism: The Case Against God*, Prometheus, Buffalo 1989

Smith, George H., *Atheism, Ayn Rand and Other Heresies*, Prometheus, Buffalo 1991

Soggin, J. Alberto, *Introduction to the Old Testament*, Westminster, Louisville *1987*

Spong, John Shelby, *Resurrection: Myth or Reality?*, Harper, San Francisco 1994

Stanfield, William, *The Science of Evolution*, Macmillan, New York 1977

Stein, Gordon (ed), *The Encyclopedia of Unbelief*, Prometheus, Buffallo 1988

Stein, Robert H., *Studying the Synoptic Gospels: Origin and Interpretation*, Baker Academic, Grand Rapids 2001

Stiebing, William H., *Out of the Desert? Archaeology and the Exodus/Conquest Narratives*, Prometheus, New York 1989

Strawn, Brent, A., "Psalm 22:17b: More Guessing" *Journal of Biblical Literature* 119/3 (2000)

Streeter, B.H., *The Primitive Church*, Macmillan, London 1929

Strobel, Lee, *The Case for Christ*, Zondervan, Grand Rapids 1998

Sturgis, Matthew, *It Ain't Necessarily So: Investigating the Truth of the Biblical Past*, Headline, London 2001

Summerscale, John, *The Penguin Encyclopedia*, Penguin, London 1965

T

Talbert, Charles H. (ed), *Perspective on Luke-Acts*, T&T Clark, Edinburgh 1978

Tattersall, Ian & Schwartz, Jeffrey, *Extinct Humans*, Westview, Boulder 2001

Thiede, Carsten, *Jesus: Life or Legend?*, Lion, Oxford 1990

Thiede, Carsten, *The Jesus Papyrus*, Weidenfeld and Nicolson, London 1996

Torrey, R.A., *Difficulties in the Bible*, Moody Press, 1907

Tov, Emmanuel, *Textual Criticsm of the Hebrew Bible: 2nd revised edition*, Fortress, Philadelphia 2001

Tyson, Joseph B., *Marcion and Luke-Acts: A Defining Struggle*, University of South Carolina Press, Columbia 2006

V

Vanderkam, James & Flint, Peter, *The Meaning of the Dead Sea Scrolls*, Harper, San Francisco 2002

Vansina, Jan, *Oral Tradition as History*, University of Wisconsin Press, Madison 1985

Vermes, Geza, *The Changing Face of Jesus*, Penguin, London 2000

Vermes, Geza, *The Authentic Gospel of Jesus*, Penguin, London 2003

Villee, Claude, *Biology*, WB Sanders, Philadelphia 1977

W

Ward, Philip, *A Dictionary of Common Fallacies I*, Oleander Press, New York 1980

Ward, Philip, *A Dictionary of Common Fallacies II*, Oleander Press, New York 1980

Warner, Marina, *Alone of All Her Sex: The Myth and the Cult of the Virgin Mary*, Picador, London 1976

Weiser, Artur, *The Psalm: A Commentary*, Westminster John Knox, Philadephia 1962

Wells, G.A., *Did Jesus Exist?*, Pemberton, London, 1986

Wells, G.A., *The Historical Evidence for Jesus*, Prometheus, Buffalo, 1988

Wells, G.A., *The Jesus Legend*, Open Court, Chicago 1997

Wells, G.A., *The Jesus Myth*, Open Court, Chicago 1999

Wells, Spencer, The Journey of Man: A Genetic Odyssey, Penguin, London 2002

White, A. D., *A History of the Warfare of Science with Theology in Christendom, Vols I & II*, Prometheus Books, Buffalo 1993

White, James R., *The King James Only Controversy*, Bethany House, Minneapolis, 1995

White, L. Michael, *From Jesus to Christianity*, HarperCollins, San Francisco 2004

Wilken, Robert, *The Myth of Christian Beginnings*, SCM, London 1979

Williams, C.S.C., *The Acts of the Apostles*, ABC Black, London 1964

Wilson, A.N., *Jesus: A Life*, Fawcett Columbine, New York 1992

Wilson, A.N., *Paul: The Mind of the Apostle*, W.W. Norton, New York 1997

Wilson, Barrie, *How Jesus Became Christian*, St. Martin's, New York 2008

Wilson, Ian, *Jesus: The Evidence*, Pan, London 1984

Wilson, Stephen G., *Related Strangers: Jews and Christians 70-170 CE*, Fortress Press, Minneapolis 1995

Wise, Michael, Abegg, Martin & Cook, Edward, *Dead Sea Scrolls: A New Translation*, Harper, San Francisco, 1996

Wistrich, Robert S., *Anti-Semitism: The Longest Hatred*, Thames Mandarin, London 1991

Wright, N.T. *The Resurrection of the Son of God*, Fortress Press, Minneapolis 2003

Würthwein, Ernst *The Text of the Old Testament*, Eerdmans, Grand Rapids 1995

Y

Yerby Frank, *Judas, My Brother*, Granada, Frogmore 1968

Z

Zaehner, R.C. (ed), *The Hutchinson Encyclopedia of Living Faiths*, Helicon, Oxford 1988

GENERAL INDEX

CPSIA information can be obtained at www.ICGtesting.com
Printed in the USA
BVOW05s1138191115

427771BV00005B/42/P